NEW TESTAMENT and CHRISTIAN APOCRYPHA

NEW TESTAMENT and CHRISTIAN APOCRYPHA

François Bovon

EDITED BY GLENN E. SNYDER

Baker Academic
a division of Baker Publishing Group
Grand Rapids, Michigan

Published in 2011 by Baker Academic
a division of Baker Publishing Group
P.O. Box 6287, Grand Rapids, MI 49516-6287
www.bakeracademic.com

Originally published in 2009 as *New Testament and Christian Apocrypha: Collected Studies II*, Wissenschaftliche Untersuchungen zum Neuen Testament 237, by Mohr Siebeck, Tübingen, Germany

Printed in the United States of America

The Library of Congress Cataloging-in-Publication Data is on file at the Library of Congress, Washington, DC.

ISBN 978-0-8010-3923-2

Table of Contents

Part III. Noncanonical Gospels and Apocryphal Acts of the Apostles

Part IV. Later Transitions

Preface

Five years after my first collection of essays published by Mohr Siebeck, *Studies in Early Christianity*, I am pleased to offer a second volume of collected papers. Ten of them appear here for the first time in English and have been translated from the French with enthusiasm by Jonathan Von Kodar and Dianne Marie Cole. My first duty and intention is to thank both of them warmly for the time, the energy, and the competence they have given me. My thanks are also due to Stephen Hebert, who scanned the English articles and put them into a common file format.

I would like also to express my gratitude to Professor Jörg Frey and Dr. Henning Ziebritzki. The first, editor of the series, and the second, Theology Editor at Mohr Siebeck, have both shown an interest in my work that not only surprised me but moved me deeply. I am also grateful to Ms. Ilse König from Mohr Siebeck, who did such a good job as copy editor.

My friend Professor Bertrand Bouvier has looked at all the Greek quotations, and his famous accuracy has found some wrong breathing marks and—what is worse—some misplaced accents. I am also grateful to him.

This book would not have seen the light without Glenn E. Snyder's collaboration. His role has been so decisive that I asked the publisher to add his name as editor to the title page. Glenn, who is currently writing a dissertation on the *Acts of Paul*, took the time to check the translations and scannings, harmonize the abbreviations, coordinate the whole matter, and prepare the indices. His kindness and his competence have produced marvelous fruits. I thank him with all my heart.

In the course of my academic career I have trodden on two fields, the New Testament and Christian apocryphal literature. It is therefore not surprising that here, as in the first volume and in my *New Testament Traditions and Apocryphal Narratives* (trans. Jane Haapiseva-Hunter; Princeton Theological Monograph Series 26; Allison Park, Pa.: Pickwick, 1995), I brought together papers devoted to these two complexes of religious literature.

I am using in the Table of Contents the term "Transitions," for I believe that there have been changes in literary form and theological thinking in the first decades of Christianity, as well as in the following centuries. But I am also convinced that these changes were not εἰς ἄλλο γένος. There were always continuity and kinship despite the changes and differences. "Transition" therefore seemed the appropriate word for evoking such transformation without break.

I did not update these essays, and I apologize for that. Dialogue with more recent research on the same topic would have forced me to add developments that I have not the energy to spend now and that the book would not have the wish to accommodate. The dates of original publication, going from 1970 to 2006, are therefore important.

Cambridge, MA, September 15, 2008   F. B.

Part I
Early Transitions

"The Good" and "the Best" in Paul's Thinking

Introduction

In recent years, the apostle Paul has often been ignored or attacked by scholars. In American scholarship the apostle has been eclipsed by Jesus. Preferring a reconstructed historical figure to literary sources, history over creed, many publishers promote innumerable books on the prophet from Nazareth, leaving his major spokesman to occupy the shady corner of omission. When he is not completely neglected,[1] Paul has fallen victim to several attacks: in a self-critical movement Christian theologians have reacted not only against the Augustinian, Lutheran, and Calvinist reception of Paul, but also against the most evident Pauline affirmations of election over works and grace over law. Other scholars reproach Paul, the Hebrew among Hebrews (Phil 3:5), for having willingly or unwillingly launched the theory of Christianity's supersession of Judaism. Among the most critical are some feminist New Testament scholars, who dislike Paul altogether because of his patriarchal attitude toward women.

For the topic of this conference,[2] the most relevant conflict over interpretation turns on the apostle's identity. While Daniel Boyarin wrote his book *A Radical Jew: Paul and the Politics of Identity*, Troels Engberg-Pedersen published a book entitled *Paul and the Stoics*. A conference organized in 2001 even suggested that the comfortable distinction between Judaism and Hellenism be questioned.

In choosing an ethical topic for my paper, I do not intend to neglect Paul's theological concerns. I share with Rudolf Bultmann that the "message of the cross" is decisive in Paul's thinking, that there is no paraenetic teaching without the kerygma. But I read the Pauline epistles with the conviction that the creed remains vain if there is no ethical embodiment, if righteousness by faith does not

---

[1] Strangely John Dominic Crossan willingly omits Paul's letters from his reconstruction of the first years of Christianity. See John Dominic Crossan, *The Birth of Christianity* (New York: HarperSanFrancisco, 1998). For a review of this book, see François Bovon, "A Critical Review of John Dominc Crossan's *The Birth of Christianity*," *HTR* 94 (2001) 369–74.

[2] St. Paul: Between Athens and Jerusalem, the 3rd International Philosophical Conference, Athens, 10–11 June 2004. See *St. Paul: Between Athens and Jerusalem: The 3rd International Philosophical Conference Proceedings, Athens, 10–11 June 2004* (ed. John Panteleimon Manoussakis; Athens: The American College of Greece, 2006). The title chosen for this conference is built on Tertullian's famous sentence: "*Quid ergo Athenis et Hierosolymis?*" (*De praescriptione haereticorum*, 7.9).

bear the fruit of the Spirit, which is love, joy, peace, etc. (Gal 5:22–23). Presented within the framework of a colloquium entitled "St. Paul between Athens and Jerusalem," and not "between Jerusalem and Athens," my paper first will focus on a central aspect of Paul's ethical thinking: in practical matters Paul offered two solutions, one called "the good" and the other called "the better," with an expressed preference for the better. I will then suggest that such an ethical theory is embedded in an old Greek philosophical tradition, and that that tradition influenced Judaism in general and Paul in particular.

Although the three main examples I present here are all taken from Paul's first epistle to the Corinthians, I will claim that such an ethical attitude is present throughout the Pauline corpus: it is present in 1 Thessalonians, the oldest Pauline letter we have, and it is still present in the epistle to the Romans, considered correctly since Günther Bornkamm's famous paper[3] to be Paul's last will or testament.

In reviewing classical interpretations of Paul's ethics, I realized that the question of the origin of Paul's ethical thinking has often been the decisive one. After he analyzed Paul's anthropological presuppositions and the roots of behavior in his doctrine of redemption, Rudolf Schnackenburg[4] demonstrated the struggles of early Christians who lived "between the times," between the first and second coming of Jesus the Messiah, underlining Paul's contribution to the construction of moral conscience. Schnackenburg's interpretation took into account the influence of both the Jewish and the Hellenistic worldviews.

In his history of the early Christian ethos, Herbert Preisker[5] traced a continuous, historical line of development from Jesus to the first Christians, and from them to Paul. According to Preisker, even if the apostle is faithful to the eschatological presence of God in human time through the christological kerygma and the outpouring of the Spirit, he is forced to adapt his radical requirements to the human condition. To live in Christ becomes a prosaic reality but, Paul insists, his conception of the ethical life is different from – and even opposed to – the legalism of the Judaizers and the euphoric freedom of the Gnostics. According to Preisker's view of Paul, the Christian is at the same time both detached from the world and superior to the world (*weltgelöst* and *weltüberlegen*). Here also Paul's ethics is perceived in a historical context, albeit more precise than in the solution proposed by Schnackenburg.

----

[3] Günther Bornkamm, "Der Römerbrief als Testament des Paulus," in *Geschichte und Glaube, zweiter Teil: Gesammelte Aufsätze, Band IV* (BEvT 53; Munich: Kaiser, 1971) 120–39.

[4] Rudolf Schnackenburg, *Die sittliche Botschaft des Neuen Testaments* (2 vols.; 2d ed.; HTKNT Supplementbände 1–2; Freiburg im Breisgau: Herder, 1986–1988).

[5] Herbert Preisker, *Das Ethos des Urchristentums* (2d ed.; Gütersloh: Bertelsmann, 1949; reprinted in Darmstadt: Wissenschaftliche Buchgesellschaft, 1968).

Rudolf Bultmann,[6] to take a third example, presents Paul's ethical conception from a theological as well as historical perspective. He presents a dialectical, and not a chronological, interpretation of the famous pair "indicative" versus "imperative," placing the doctrinal indicative of redemption in the terminology of the mystery religions and the ethical imperative of commitment in the sphere of the Jewish morality. For Bultmann, ethics is another way of saying "doctrine." To be a Christian is to become what one is.

What these scholars neglected and what the attention of subsequent researchers failed to capture was what constitutes the heart of my own investigation: the Pauline unfurling of ethical solutions. The traditional Jewish – actually it is not only Jewish – opposition between the good and the bad is presented in the text of Deut 30:15–20, where the contrast between obedience and disobedience is expressed according to the opposition of life and death: "See, I have set before you today life and prosperity, death and adversity. If you obey the commandments of the LORD your God … then you shall live … But if your heart turns away and you do not hear … you shall not live long in the land … ."

The apostle Paul offers a more complicated, more sophisticated view than this one: there is of course the decision he rejects, the sinful attitude, the path of the wicked; but for the righteous, there is first a good decision or way, followed by a second better one. In 1 Corinthians, for example, once he has reckoned the word of the cross and the knowledge of Jesus Christ – and only of Jesus Christ crucified – as the core of Christianity (1 Cor 1:18–2:5), he immediately adds that there is a superior wisdom possessed by those who are the perfect (1 Cor 2:6–16). Similarly, as soon as he prescribes a Christian attitude, he suggests a better one. Let me now present three examples of this structure of Paul's ethics, before I locate this Pauline conception in the field of ancient Greek philosophy and connect it to the apostle's vision of Christ and, as attested in the scriptures of Israel, his doctrine of God.

The Good, the Bad, and the Better

In our first example Paul considers himself to be responsible for the well-being of the Corinthian community. Hearing that when they are confronted with tensions and disagreements the Corinthian Christians bring their divergent opinions to secular, imperial courts for trial, he voices complete opposition to this solution: "When any of you has a grievance against another, do you dare to take it to the court before the unrighteous, instead of taking it before the saints?" (1 Cor 6:1).

---

[6] In addition to Rudolf Bultmann, *Theologie des Neuen Testaments* (ed. Otto Merk; 8th enlarged ed.; UTB 630; Tübingen: Mohr Siebeck, 1980), see Rudolf Bultmann, "Das Problem der Ethik bei Paulus," *ZNW* 23 (1924) 123–40; reprinted in idem, *Exegetica* (Tübingen: Mohr Siebeck, 1967) 36–54.

Pagans, Paul observes, should not solve the problems of Christians; this is the negative answer. Then, if one reads 1 Cor 6:1–11 carefully, instead of offering one unique positive solution, we discern that Paul offers two. He suggests first a kind of minimum in Christian attitude: solve your problems in the community, for example, by establishing a court of wise and independent believers. This solution should be sufficient to smooth tensions and extirpate the conflicts: "Are you incompetent to try trivial cases?" (1 Cor 6:2), he asks in his rhetorical style. But once he has advanced this good, though not perfect, solution he adds another: "In fact, even to have lawsuits against one another is already a defeat for you. Why not rather be wronged? Why not be defrauded?" (1 Cor 6:7); why not suffer; why not accept being on the losing side? This is indeed the better solution.

The second example arises out of tensions and sexual problems at Corinth. Here again, Paul feels it is his responsibility to provide guidance and advice. Entering examples of several concrete situations, he takes the risk of introducing casuistic rules: What should one do if your spouse is not a Christian? What happens to the children in such a union? What about those who are widowed or single? One thing is clear: in each instance, after rejecting the bad solution, Paul offers first a solution that is good, a solution that is in harmony with justice. But, just as love is better than equity (see 1 Cor 12:31: "And I shall show you a still more excellent way"), so also self-denial, personal sacrifice, ascetic options, love for one's enemy, and non-resistance constitute the better Christian path. In the case of sexual behavior, this perfect road is already presented in the first sentence: "Now concerning the matters about which you wrote, it is well – such is the opinion of Paul and not the Corinthians – for a man not to touch a woman" (1 Cor 7:1).

Our third example concerns alimentation, food being as basic to the human condition as sex and competition. Here again Paul offers a subtle range of comments in 1 Corinthians 8 and 10. Both passages share Paul's reflection on freedom: Christians are free and therefore they can eat everything. The ritual aspect of the mosaic regulations is abandoned; only the spiritual remains: "Hence, as to the eating of food offered to idols, we know that no idol in the world really exists, and that there is no God but one" (1 Cor 8:4). Christians, therefore, are not prohibited from eating meat offered in sacrifice to pagan gods, considered here as idols, or from buying it on the common market. This is a good solution (one finds an echo of it in two Pastoral Epistles, 1 Tim 4:3–5 and Titus 1:15).

But here again wisdom and freedom are not superior to the way of love; if one's freedom hurts a Christian companion who is weak then this is not the wisest solution. There is a better way, a solution that respects totally the opinion of brothers and sisters in Christ: "Therefore, if food is a cause of their falling, I will never eat meat, so that I may not cause one of them to fall" (1 Cor 8:13). To abstain from the pleasure of one's freedom and to abstain from it freely is the superior ethical road.

It is clear that the better solution is always connected with the well-being of the community. Personal progress does not reach the highest level of attainment if it does not contribute to the οἰκοδομή of the churches.[7] The best solution to the particular sexual problems in Corinth will bring peace to the whole community.[8]

These three cases are not exceptions in Paul's thought. They represent regular concretions in Paul's approach to ethical thinking. Our most ancient document written by the apostle, the first letter to the Thessalonians, already brings this way of thinking to the attention of new converts. In 1 Thessalonians 4, the oldest ethical treatise written by a Christian, Paul already draws a distinction between the minimal attitude that each believer should adopt, namely to walk and to please God (1 Thess 4:1), and a superior, higher commitment. This superior goal is summarized in a sentence attached to a statement about minimal obedience: "To walk and to please God" is the first step on the scale; it should bring a Christian to the second step, which Paul calls "to become more abundant," probably in kindness and love, in wisdom and perfection (1 Thess 4:1).

In another quotation from 1 Thessalonians we again find the progression from the good to the better: "And may the Lord make you increase and abound in love for one another and for all, just as we abound in love for you" (1 Thess 3:12). "Love for one another" is the correct, the good ethical attitude, the fulfillment of Johannine mutual love (John 15:12); but love "for all" – love for those who do not love you, love for those who exist outside – is the better solution, the one that fulfills Jesus' command in the Sermon on the Mount that we love our enemies (Matt 5:44//Luke 6:27).

Such a possible – and even desirable – crescendo from a good to a better solution is also readily apparent in one of Paul's last letters, the epistle to the Philippians. There, Paul says that a Christian's initial love should progress toward greater abundance (Phil 1:9). The apostle does not hesitate to use the vocabulary of "progress" (εἰς προκοπήν, Phil 1:12) to describe this movement. Even in his own personal case, Paul hesitates between two goods: to live in the flesh, which means to be alive and fulfill his pastoral duty for the Philippians, or to be with the Lord, which means to die and to be united with Christ. For Paul, to live means to suffer and imitate Christ's passion; to die means to participate in the glory of the risen Christ. To remain on earth is the better solution, because it is the most ethical solution, the most profitable for the others. It is therefore only from the standpoint of Paul's self-interest that the famous sentence in Phil 1:21, "For to me, liv-

---

[7] I express my gratitude to Helmut Koester who underlined this point in a letter of March 22, 2005: "Whatever is 'the Good' may be good for the establishment of personal morality, but whatever is 'the Best' seems to me always related to *oikodome*."

[8] On the notion of οἰκοδομή, see Pierre Bonnard, *Jésus-Christ édifiant son Église. Le concept d'édification dans le Nouveau Testament* (Cahiers théologiques de l'actualité protestante 21; Neuchâtel: Delachaux & Niestlé, 1946).

ing is Christ and dying is gain," makes sense. From the perspective of Paul's superior commitment to his communities, dying is the easy solution and to live is gain. Similarly, for the Philippians, to believe is good but to add suffering for the apostle's sake is better (Phil 1:29).

The two ethical solutions appear even at the grammatical level, where the use of comparative forms confirms the progression. It is good for Paul to see his disciple Epaphroditus recuperate from illness; but it is better to send him back to his community, revealing in this way his greater zeal (σπουδαιοτέρως, Phil 2:28). The Greek expression πολλῷ μᾶλλον, "much more," to choose another example, helps Paul express this desirable progression: "Therefore, my beloved, just as you have always obeyed, not only in my presence, but much more (πολλῷ μᾶλλον) now in my absence, work out your own salvation with fear and trembling" (Phil 2:12).[9]

To be precise, I should mention a difference between the examples drawn from 1 Corinthians and those taken from the other epistles.[10] In the Corinthian cases, Paul, after rejecting the bad solution, places before his local readers a choice: the good or the best. In his early writing to the Thessalonians he supposes that the good is not static and must lead to the best. The passages quoted from the late epistle to the Philippians confirm the early perspective of 1 Thessalonians. Actually the difference between the alternative or the progression relies on a difference of situation. Considering the bad inclination of the Corinthians, Paul invites them as a minimum to choose the good and preferably to select the best. When writing to the Thessalonians or the Philippians, the apostle is pleased to see that they already are walking accordingly to a right attitude. He can only wish for them to reach the better path, to follow the best ethical standard. Behind all the examples given in these pages there is therefore the ethical structure of the good and the better. Skillfully the apostle applies this structure according to the different circumstances to which he and his communities are confronted.

Paul's Thinking and the Philosophical Tradition

The religious tradition of Israel was determined by the opposition that exists between the pure and the impure, the sacred and the profane, the holy and the unholy. This distinction was respected at the ritual level as well as the moral. Fundamentally, the ethical structure of the good and the better does not reflect this Jewish perspective. Rather, it was the Greeks who experienced that the good of a city, or of an individual, could take several different shades or degrees: this could be the average good or the most precious one. The discovery of conflicting refer-

---

[9] Even if most of the time Paul opposes in the epistle to the Romans the good and the bad, he alludes to the structure of the good, the bad, and the better in Rom 5:1–11; 8:30; and 12:1–2.

[10] I am grateful to Glenn E. Snyder who drew my attention to this difference.

ences to several goods forced the Greeks to create a hierarchy of goods. The well-being of the Greek confederation, whose unity was manifested through language and ritual celebrations, was located above the well-being of the local city. In Sophocles' *Antigone* (lines 449–55), Antigone clearly appeals to a higher dimension than Creon's reference to the laws of city of Thebes. She appeals to the law of the laws. This same distinction appears in Plato's writings, when he distinguishes in the *Republic* degrees of justice (*Resp.* 2.367), and when he affirms that there is a truth about the gods that is higher than myth (*Resp.* 2.378).

In his *Nichomachean Ethics* (1.5.2–7) Aristotle likewise distinguishes – in a way that may almost be considered arrogant – three groups in their relationship to philosophy. The first group, the crowds, represent the bad: those who have no access to wisdom. The second group, consisting of politicians, represent the good: those who are able to reach a certain level of understanding, but not the highest; they can conceive justice but not real wisdom. The third group consists of the philosophers, who alone are equipped to enter the realm of contemplation. They enjoy not only the good but also the best.

This intellectual distinction finds its concrete application – if I am well informed – in the way teaching was organized at the Athenian Lyceum. In the morning Aristotle would deliver the esoteric, or acroamatic, teaching, to those few who were considered fit for this higher education.[11] Then early in the afternoon he would teach the men of action, bringing them the rudiments of political wisdom. This was exoteric teaching.

I will not elaborate the history of this distinction, but I will insist on its presence as a common heritage in the first century C.E. It survives in the distinction the Stoics drew between the ἁμάρτημα, the bad action, the ἀδιάφορον, the indifferent, and the κατόρθωμα, the right action. It also survives in late Stoicism when the προκόπτων, the one who improves, the one who makes progresses, is inserted between the φαῦλος, the mean, the bad person, and the τέλειος, the accomplished person, the one who is perfect. The distinction also survives in Valentinian thought, as attested by Irenaeus in his *Adversus haereses* 1.7.5 and 1.8.3. According to Irenaeus, the Valentinians distinguished three kinds of human beings: the hylic, or the material; the psychic, that is, the human; and the pneumatic, or spiritual people.

It is probable that this division between the good and the best was accepted into Judaism, which was so widely influenced by the dominant culture of the Greeks from the time of Alexander the Great. It is clear to me that Paul, a Jew but also a Greek, trained in grammar, rhetoric, and perhaps philosophy at Tarsus, used this distinction with ease and profit.

---

[11] See Jean Voilquin, "Préface," to Aristote, *Éthique de Nicomaque* (Paris: Garnier-Flammarion, 1965) 6.

The Christological Model

Paul's ethical prescriptions are not only rooted in the Jewish opposition of the good and the bad and the Greek distinction of the good and the better. They find their final relevance according to the christological model. The apostle's source of his personal attitude and of the conduct he prescribes to his converts is a person and not a code of rules or an abstract ethical structure. The person of Christ is for him a redeemer and a model. Through his death on the cross, Christ not only brought believers into the realm of freedom, but he also offered his own life as a model of ethical behavior. To be redeemed, to be in Christ, does not separate a Christian from history and society. But to be alive, to be "in the flesh" – to use the apostle's words – neither forces a Christian to compromise nor compels him to sin. The way to be in the world is to behave according to Christ. This is valid for the individual as well as for the community.

Paul does not hesitate to use the vocabulary of imitation.[12] He asks the Corinthians to be his imitators as he is an imitator of Christ (1 Cor 11:1). But there is an understanding of imitation that does not coincide with Paul's understanding of it: imitation as a human effort to reach the qualities of the model to the greatest extent possible. In such a case imitation remains a subjective activity relying on the personal responsibility and forces of the individual. It is often in such a way that the Greek philosophical tradition understood imitation. But according to its origin in the cult of Dionysos and its manifestation in the Greek theater, imitation is rooted in participation in the god. Such is Paul's understanding of imitation: it is not the external appropriation of Jesus' gestures, but first the surrender of the believer to Christ and second the display of Christian virtues practiced by this regenerated person.[13] For Paul, Jesus, who gave himself to others, is primarily the redeemer, but his way of life and of dying becomes also a model of behavior.

It is interesting to note that Paul is able to bring together the christological model and the ethical structure of the good and the better. In Jesus' life, certain aspects, his faith and his just conduct, belong to the first, namely the good; other aspects, his love of others and his death for others, belong to the later, namely the better.

Several expressions and metaphors make this christological model more visible. Just as Christ was sent into the world by God, so Christians are sent out to those who stand outside their community (Gal 1:16; Rom 10:14–15). As Christ has entered this world (Phil 2:6–8), so Christians shall pass through a door – such is the metaphor in 1 Cor 16:9 and 2 Cor 2:12 – opened by God himself. As Christ

---

[12] Paul has a preference for the substantive μιμητής (see 1 Thess 1:6; 2:14; 1 Cor 4:16; 11:1; see also Eph 5:1), but the verb μιμέομαι is present in 2 Thess 3:7, 9; see Hans Dieter Betz, *Nachfolge und Nachahmung Jesu Christi im Neuen Testament* (BHT 37; Tübingen: Mohr Siebeck, 1967).

[13] I thank here Helmut Koester who in discussing this paper with me correctly insisted on this aspect.

offered himself in a sacrifice of expiation (Rom 3:25), so Paul considers it to be his apostolic duty to fulfill a sacerdotal function – according to the metaphor in Rom 15:15–16 – in order that the nations may become a sacrifice, an offering (προσφορά), agreeable to God and sanctified by the Holy Spirit. As Christ brought light and divine glory into the world, so Christians are to be – using still another metaphor – lamps or stars (φωστῆρες) in the world: "Do all things without murmuring and arguing, so that you may be blameless and innocent, children of God without blemish in the midst of a crooked and perverse generation, in which you shine like light-giving bodies in the world" (Phil 1:14–15). As Christ achieved victory over death, so also Christians are to bring to the world the fragrance (ὀσμή), the aroma (εὐωδία) of life in Christ, to those who will be saved (2 Cor 2:14–16). Or, using the classical vocabulary of love, the word ἀγάπη and the verb ἀγαπάω, Paul urges his communities to practice hospitality, forgiveness, and reconciliation.

According to Paul's argument, it is even possible to understand the reason why Christ can be imitated: it is not because of Jesus' historical behavior but, more deeply, because of Christ's incarnation that this is possible. If a believer is able to become a Jew with the Jews and a Greek with the Greeks, this is in imitation of Christ, who abandoned his divine sphere in order to enter into the realm of humanity. The Son's priority was not to bring people to himself, but to move towards them, to reach out to them. The hymn in Philippians 2 expresses the risk Christ took in order to do this, namely, he left his divine nature and made himself empty (κενόω): "Let the same mind be in you that was in Christ Jesus, who, though he was in the form of God, did not regard equality with God as something to be exploited, but emptied himself, taking the form of a slave, being born in human likeness. And being found in human form, he humbled himself and became obedient to the point of death – even death on a cross" (Phil 2:5–8). This passage is the hermeneutical key to verses in 1 Cor 9:19–21, where Paul expresses his apostolic mission as well as a Christian's ethical commitment: "For though I am free with respect to all, I have made myself a slave to all, so that I might win more of them. To the Jews I became as a Jew, in order to win the Jews. To those under the law I became as one under the law (though I myself am not under the law), so that I might win those who are under the law. To those outside the law I became as one outside the law (though I am not free from God's law but am under Christ's law), so that I might win those outside the law." For Paul, as for any Christian, to become a Jew with the Jews or a Greek with the Greeks is an expression of love, even an acceptance of death; but even if it means a loss of life, it is not a loss of identity.

To lose one's life is a way of saving it: in giving up his secure position at the side of God the Son took a risk, but he never lost his identity as the Son. Similarly, the ethical way to reach the other, through fulfilling the law or breaking its commands, does not destroy the core of one's identity in Christ. As long as communion with God is respected and one's relationship with Christ is preserved, freedom does not become a tool, a selfish tool but remains an instrument of charity. Such was Christ's behavior when he joined himself to the human condition out of love and in the hope of redemption. The crescendo from good to better applies even to Christ, and the Christian counterpart reflects in its humanity the divine model. Life in the realm of God was of course good for the Son, but the Son chose the better, the more difficult way to fulfill his divinity, namely to cross the border and assume the human condition. This movement toward the other was not an exotic selfish experience, but a generous translocation, a way of reaching the place where human beings exist, in order to help them move to a better place.

Paul's missionary theory follows this christological model. Paul refuses to receive the revelation of the Son on the road to Damascus (Gal 1:15–16) in a passive way. He is not content simply to enjoy redemption. To that good gift he prefers the better duty: he accepts being sent, and he expects all his disciples and all the Christian communities not to keep themselves quietly in the harbor of peace; as *navis ecclesiae* they must sail bravely to reach others in their own turbulent situations.

In his inimitable pictorial style Luke the evangelist captures this choice for the better in his description of the apostle in the book of Acts. Paul could stay in Caesarea as a pastor, fulfilling the dearest wishes of the community there. But, according to Luke, he prefers instead to exchange this good solution for a better one: he will leave his fellow Christians and go to Rome, where his apostolic mission will end in martyrdom. Luke's account of this decision reads as follows:

The next day we left and came to Caesarea; and we went into the house of Philip the evangelist, one of the seven, and stayed with him … . While we were staying there for several days, a prophet named Agabus came down from Judea. He came to us and took Paul's belt, bound his own feet and hands with it, and said, "Thus says the Holy Spirit, 'This is the way the Jews in Jerusalem will bind the man who owns this belt and will hand him over to the Gentiles.'" When we heard this, we and the people there urged him not to go up to Jerusalem. Then Paul answered, "What are you doing, weeping and breaking my heart? For I am ready not only to be bound but even to die in Jerusalem for the name of the Lord Jesus." Since he would not be persuaded, we remained silent except to say, "The Lord's will be done." (Acts 21:8–14)

Scriptural Authority and the Doctrine of God

As a Jewish theologian Paul aims at the harmony between his thinking and the scriptures of Israel. But here he faces a difficulty since the Hebrew scriptures, even in their Greek translation of the Septuagint, do not witness the ethical structure of the good and the better. The interplay of biblical quotations, particularly in Galatians and in Romans, makes this particularly clear. To find an agreement between his conviction and Israel's holy books, the apostle follows a double path: he dares to use the ancient scriptures according to the new model. According to the apostle, to understand righteousness in a dynamic way leading from a good beginning to a better one through a progressive moral effort is not opposed to the divine commands of the Law. But Paul is pushing his reflection even further. He risks the following hypothesis: the scriptures of Israel, which display so vividly in an antithetic position the good and the bad, the righteous and the sinner, manifest an image of God, as personal entity, promoting the ethical structure of the good and the best. Eternal and eternally faithful to himself, the God of Israel does not need the structure of the good and the best. But facing his creation and even more, his fallen creation, he will adopt in his economy of redemption a project compatible with the Greek ethical structure.

It is Paul's conviction that the God of creation is the same as the God of redemption. Paul's use of tradition, his use – for example – of early Christian hymnic and homologetical material, as in 1 Corinthians 8, makes this clear. In this brief quotation of an early liturgical fragment, Paul considers the Father as well as the Son. The mediation of the Son is made clear by the use of the preposition διά ("through"): it is through Christ that the world was created and it is also through Christ that the creation is redeemed. The authority of the Father is underlined by the use of two other prepositions, ἐκ at the origin of everything and εἰς at the destination of everything: "Indeed, even though there may be so-called gods in heaven or on earth – as in fact there are many gods and many lords – yet for us there is one God, the Father, from whom (ἐξ οὗ) are all things and for whom (εἰς αὐτόν) we exist, and one Lord, Jesus Christ, through whom (δι' οὗ) are all things and through whom (δι' αὐτοῦ) we exist" (1 Cor 8:6).

From this fragment, as well as from other Pauline passages in which the apostle establishes a symmetry and a contrast between creation and redemption, we can say that if the creation was good – and the text of Genesis says that it was – then the redemption is better. The redemption can be called a "treasure" that is poured into the "clay jars" of human creatures (2 Cor 4:7). The harmony that exists between the creatures' prayers ("the creation itself," αὐτὴ ἡ κτίσις) and the redeemed community's requests ("we," ἡμεῖς) reveals by the same token that the God of creation has reached a kind of fulfillment through his work of redemption (Rom 8:21–22).

Rudolf Bultmann said – not without some excess – that New Testament theology is anthropology.[14] What is true in Paul's statement concerning the good and the better in God remains for the most part only implicit, being deducible from his affirmations concerning its human counterpart. In 2 Cor 3:18, for example, Paul does not hesitate to say that the believers already share in the divine glory;

---

[14] See Bultmann's statement that "Es zeigt sich also: will man von Gott reden, so muß man offenbar *von sich selbst reden*" (italics Bultmann's) in Rudolf Bultmann, "Welchen Sinn hat es, von Gott zu reden?," *TBl* 4 (1925) 129–35; reprinted in idem, *Glauben und Verstehen*, vol. 1 (3d ed.; Tübingen: Mohr Siebeck, 1958) 26–37; the quotation appears on p. 28 of the collection of essays.

but even more, they are progressively transformed from glory to glory, revealing in their own being the better part of the good creator, his wish to redeem definitively: "And all of us, with unveiled faces, seeing the glory of the Lord as though reflected in a mirror, are being transformed into the same image from one degree of glory to another; for this comes from the Lord, the Spirit."

Conclusion

By way of a conclusion, I ask one final question: What advantage does recourse to this ethical structure of the good and the best offer? As a response, I will propose that simple antithetical oppositions such as holiness and sin, the righteous and the wicked, God and Mammon, were efficient in the context of preaching, mission, and conversion. But the development of a more complex crescendo, or hierarchy of goods, made it possible for philosophers as well as the theologians to offer a wider spectrum of ethical solutions in the context of teaching and catechism. These solutions brought movement, flexibility, and freedom to what could have become a static system. It is not, after all, by chance that Paul uses the term "progress," προκοπή, in such a context; nor is it by chance that he refers to the metaphor of the way and uses the preposition εἰς, "toward," "to." On their ethical way, namely in their daily lives, Christian can ascend from glory to glory, ἀπὸ δόξης εἰς δόξαν (2 Cor 3:18). Finally it is not by chance that Paul speaks of abundance and even superabundance, for he took the risk of adding sanctification to justification, love to equity, perfection to goodness, σοφία το κήρυγμα.

Bibliography

"L'événement saint Paul: Juif, Grec, Romain, Chrétien," *Esprit* 292 (Février 2003) 64–124 (a series of articles by Stanislas Breton, Michaël Foessel, Paul Ricœur, and Jean-Claude Monod).

Barbaglio, Giuseppe. *La teologia di Paolo. Abozzi in forma epistolare.* 2d ed. Bologna: Edizioni Dehoniane, 2001.

Becker, Jürgen. *Paulus, der Apostel der Völker.* 3d ed. UTB 2014. Tübingen: Mohr Siebeck, 1998.

Boyarin, Daniel. *A Radical Jew: Paul and the Politics of Identity.* Berkeley: University of California Press, 1994.

Bultmann, Rudolf. *Theologie des Neuen Testaments.* Ed. Otto Merk. Enlarged 8th ed. UTB 630. Tübingen: Mohr Siebeck, 1980. pp. 187–353.

Cerfaux, Lucien. *Le Christ dans la théologie de saint Paul.* 2d. ed. LD 6. Paris: Cerf, 1954.

Dodd, Charles H. *Gospel and Law: The Relation of Faith and Ethics in Early Christianity.* 3d printing. Cambridge: Cambridge University Press, 1953.

Daube, David. *Appeasement or Resistance, and Other Essays on New Testament Judaism.* Berkeley: University of California Press, 1987.

Dunn, James D. G. *The Theology of Paul the Apostle.* Grand Rapids, Mich.: Eerdmans, 1998.

Engberg-Pedersen, Troels. *Paul and the Stoics.* Edinburgh: T&T Clark, 2000.

–, ed. *Paul Beyond the Judaism/Hellenism Divide.* Louisville: Westminster/John Knox, 2001.

Hurtado, Larry. *Lord Jesus Christ: Devotion to Jesus in Earliest Christianity.* Grand Rapids, Mich.: Eerdmans, 2003 (contains a rich bibliography on Pauline theological themes).

Martyn, J. Louis. *Theological Issues in the Letters of Paul.* Nashville: Abingdon, 1997.

Mitchell, Margaret M. *The Heavenly Trumpet: John Chrysostom and the Art of Pauline Interpretation.* HUT 40. Tübingen: Mohr Siebeck, 2000.

Pohlenz, Max. *Die Stoa. Geschichte einer geistigen Bewegung.* 2 vols. 4th ed. Göttingen: Vandenhoeck & Ruprecht, 1970–1972.

Preisker, Herbert. *Das Ethos des Urchristentums.* 2d ed. Gütersloh: Bertelsmann, 1949. Reprinted at Darmstadt: Wissenschaftliche Buchgesellschaft, 1968.

Robin, Léon. *La morale antique.* Nouvelle encyclopédie philosophique 17. Paris: Presses Universitaires de France, 1947.

Sampley, J. Paul, ed. *Paul in the Greco-Roman World: A Handbook.* Harrisburg, Pa.: Trinity Press International, 2003.

Sanders, E. P. *Paul and Palestinian Judaism: A Comparison of Patterns of Religion.* Minneapolis: Fortress, 1977.

Schelkle, Karl Hermann. *Paulus Lehrer der Väter. Die altkirchliche Auslegung von Römer 1–11.* Düsseldorf: Patmos, 1959.

Schnackenburg, Rudolf. *Die sittliche Botschaft des Neuen Testaments.* 2 vols. 2d ed. HTKNT Supplementbände 1–2. Freiburg im Breisgau: Herder, 1986–1988.

Senft, Christophe. *Jésus de Nazareth et Paul de Tarse.* Essais bibliques 11. Geneva: Labor et Fides, 1985.

Spicq, Ceslas. *Théologie morale du Nouveau Testament.* 2 vols. Études bibliques. Paris: Gabalda, 1965.

Stendahl, Krister. *Final Account: Paul's Letter to the Romans.* Minneapolis: Fortress, 1993.

Stowers, Stanley K. *A Rereading of Romans: Justice, Jews, and Gentiles.* New Haven, Conn.: Yale University Press, 1994.

Names and Numbers in Early Christianity

Introduction

It is my hypothesis that the early Christians used the categories of 'name' and 'number' as theological tools.[1] Often they consciously interpreted names and numbers in a symbolic way. Even their non-reflexive usage relied on implicit conceptualizations very different from our nominalist-based thinking. They presupposed that names and numbers are inextricably related.[2] Is the Jewish and Christian confession εἷς ὁ θεός not a cogent expression combining a name and a number? Like other Jewish movements, the first churches were immersed in a multi-ethnic ocean reflecting centuries of Greek epistemology and Babylonian mathematics. It is therefore simplistic to imagine early Christian thought as influenced merely by Semitic, biblical thought.[3] I suggest that early Christian reflections on names and numbers not only bear witness to a strong relationship between language and reality, but also manifest a significant difference between signifier and referent. God is the master of names and numbers, thus conferring an ontological quality to any creation.[4] As the race of humans, however, is differ-

---

[1] Presidential address, Studiorum Novi Testamenti Societas, Tel Aviv, 2000. I would like to thank my colleague and friend Gabriel Widmer who discussed the matter with me. He gave me also some bibliographic references, such as the articles "Nombre" and "Nomen (nom)," in *Les notions philosophiques. Dictionnaire* (vol. 2 of *Encyclopédie philosophique universelle*; ed. Sylvain Auroux; Paris: Presses Universitaires de France, 1990) 1755–62. I would like also to express my gratitude to Elizabeth Busky who revised my English, Anna Miller who checked numerous references for me, David Warren who read the proofs with me, and particularly to Ann Graham Brock who following the preparation of this paper revised its form and content with talent and diligence. I thank finally those auditors of my address, members of the SNTS, who gave me their reactions and comments.

[2] On the contrary, in modern times, fighting an aristocratic society and Christian personalism, Lenin proclaimed that it was time to abandon names and introduce the language of numbers; see Bastian Wielenga, *Lenins Weg zur Revolution* (Munich: Kaiser, 1971); Yann Redalié, "Conversion ou libération? Actes 16,11–40," *BCPE* 26:7 (1974) 19–31, esp. 21–22. I owe my interest in the topic of names and numbers to discussions in the 1970s with Yann Redalié.

[3] I agree here with James Barr, *The Semantics of Biblical Language* (London: Oxford University Press, 1961).

[4] Irenaeus, *Adv. haer.* 2.25.1, insists on this theocentrism: it is God who is the master of names and numbers. In *Adv. haer.* 1.15.5, the bishop of Lyons criticizes Mark the Magician for imprisoning God in human names and numbers.

ent from the race of the gods, to speak with Pindar,[5] so names and numbers are also human expressions. Accordingly a total equality between language and reality cannot be reached and remains an illusion.

Not everyone may be convinced of the importance of names and numbers in early Christianity, particularly of speculations as to their various meanings.[6] Many ancient authors, both Jews and Christians, tried to inquire concerning the name of "God" with a will both to know and to communicate a religious knowledge. Certain that the real name of the divinity eludes human perception, they believed that God had revealed his sacred names, such as "Lord" or "Sabaoth," to humans.[7] For example, some manuscripts of *3 Enoch* contain an impressive list of divine names.[8] A similar interest led several ancient authors to communicate the names of angels,[9] of the fallen angels or watchers,[10] of Satan,[11] of demons,[12] of Jesus,[13] and of his disciples.[14] Those who wished to establish such enumerations were interested not only in names but also in numbers: for instance, how many angels, how many names?[15] The numerous instances of a census in the book of

---

[5] Pindar, *Nemean Ode* 6.1. I thank Ellen Aitken who helped me to find this reference.

[6] On names see Hans Bietenhard, "ὄνομα κτλ.," *TWNT* 5:242–83; A. Heubeck, "Personennamen, A. Griechische," *Lexikon der alten Welt* (ed. Carl Andresen et al.; Zurich: Artemis, 1965) 2267–68; W. Krenkel, "Namengebung," ibid., 2056; Lazlo Vanyó, "Nom," *Dictionnaire encyclopédique du christianisme ancien* (ed. Angelo Di Berardino; trans. François Vial; 2 vols.; Paris: Cerf, 1990) 2:1759–61; on numbers see Oskar Rühle, "ἀριθμέω, ἀριθμός," *TWNT* 1:461–64; Peter Friesenhahn, *Hellenistische Wortzahlmystik im Neuen Testament* (Leipzig: Teubner, 1935); Jören Friberg, "Numbers and Counting," *ABD* 4 (1992) 1139–46.

[7] See the *Prayer of Jacob*, difficult to date (1st–4th cent. C.E.); James H. Charlesworth, "Prayer of Jacob," in *OTP* 2:715–23. See also the riddle on the name of God in *Sibylline Oracles* 1.137–46.

[8] *3 Enoch* 48B; *Quaest. Barth.* 4.23. One knows the interest of Islam for the 99 names of Allah. For this idea see Arthur Jeffery, ed., *A Reader on Islam: Passages from Standard Arabic Writings Illustrative of the Beliefs and Practices of Muslims* (The Hague, Netherlands: Mouton and Co., 1962) 553–55.

[9] *2 Enoch* 40; *3 Enoch* 17.

[10] On the fallen angels, see *1 Enoch* 6.7; 69.2–14. Strangely, Kasb'el, the chief executor of the oath, has a number and a name (*1 Enoch* 69.13–14). On the watchers, associated with the angels in passages like *1 Enoch* 21.10, particularly with those in Gen 6:1–8 that were sent from heaven, see *1 Enoch* (1.4–5; 10.9; 12; 15) as well as *Jubilees* (4.15; 7.21; 8.3). See also *Acts Phil.* 8.11 and 11.3 for reference to these beings.

[11] *Quaest. Barth.* 4.23, 45.

[12] Mark 5:9.

[13] As for God, the real name of the mediator remains hidden; only "Jesus," as a name of this world, is revealed, according to *Ascen. Isa.* 8.7–9.5; see *Acts Thom.* 163.2.

[14] From Mary Magdalene to Peter, from Paul to James.

[15] On the symbolic value attributed to numbers by peoples of antiquity see Georges Ifrah, *Histoire universelle des chiffres. L'intelligence des hommes racontée par les nombres et le calcul* (Bouquins; 2 vols.; Paris: Laffont, 1994) passim; Friberg, "Numbers and Counting," 1143–45. Number speculation was characteristic of Pythagorism; see Adela Yarbro Collins, "Numerical Symbolism in Jewish and Early Christian Apocalyptic Literature," in *ANRW* 2.21.2 (1984) 1250–53; but Porphyry also may have written a work on numbers; see H. Kees, "Porphyrios," in *Paulys Realencyclopädie der classischen Altertumswissenschaft* (66 vols.; ed. Georg Wissowa

Numbers is an example of this phenomenon.[16] Actually the title "Numbers" (ἀριθμοί) is not the original one; it was given by the translators of the book into Greek. In the Hebrew Bible it is called "In the wilderness," according to its first word. Another example is the use of a particular number, such as 12,[17] which occurs many times: it is used for the tribes of Israel, then for the 12 apostles,[18] and later by the author of the *Book of the Resurrection according to Bartholomew* for their 12 thrones and their 12 garments.[19] The evangelist Luke is not the only one interested in marking time.[20] Mark has already eagerly mentioned the exact moment of several episodes of Jesus' passion: the sixth hour, the ninth hour, the evening, and early in the morning.[21] The theological significance of the number 40 is well known,[22] beginning with Moses[23] and continuing with Jesus' temptations[24] and appearances.[25] The number seven, so significant for the book of Genesis, still has a special role in the book of Revelation, as seen in the seven churches (Revelation 1–4), the seven letters (Revelation 2–3), the seven seals (Revelation 5–8), the seven trumpets (Revelation 8–11), the seven cups, and the seven angels (Revelation 15–17).[26] Often numbers are used as a cryptic way of referring to names and people, such as the famous 666 of the book of Revelation.[27] On the

---

et al.; Stuttgart: J. B. Metzler, 1953) 43:300. Plotinus's *Enead* 6.6 deals with numbers and Augustine knew this treatise; see Olivier du Roy, *L'intelligence de la foi en la Trinité selon saint Augustin. Genèse de sa théologie trinitaire jusqu'en 391* (Paris: Études augustiniennes, 1966) 70 n. 1. Quintilian, *Inst. or.* 1.10.35: geometry has two divisions; one is concerned with numbers, the other with figures. Now knowledge of the former is a necessity not merely to the orator, but to anyone who has had even an elementary education.

[16] The book contains also the mention of the 70 elders (Num 11:24–25), the names of the 12 explorers (Num 13:4–16), and the episode of the 12 rods (Num 17:1–11; see below n. 58). See also the Jewish reflection on the numbers of the biblical books.

[17] According to *4 Ezra* 14:10–12, time is divided into 12; it gets older because 9.5 periods have gone already.

[18] Mark 3:13–19 par.; Matt 19:28 par.

[19] *Book of the Resurrection according to Bartholomew* 21.8.

[20] See the famous synchronism in Luke 3:1; the date of Elizabeth's pregnancy in Luke 1:36; the end of Mary's visit to her cousin in Luke 1:56; the three periods of Jesus' life and those of the history of salvation.

[21] See Mark 15:25, 30, 33, 34; 15:42.

[22] Other numbers were believed to be pure and for some of them to represent plenitude, like 4, 7, 8 and 10; see Friedrich Hauck, "δέκα," *TWNT* 2:35–36; Karl Heinrich Rengstorf, "ἑπτά κτλ.," *TWNT* 2:623–31; Horst Balz, "τέσσαρες κτλ.," *TWNT* 8:127–39.

[23] Exod 34:29; Deut 9:9; *Barn.* 4.7–8; there are also the 40 days of the explorers (Num 14:34) and the 40 years of punishment in the wilderness (Num 14:33); see Origen, *Hom. Num.* 8.1.5.

[24] Matt 4:2 par.

[25] Acts 1:3.

[26] See Collins, "Numerical Symbolism in Jewish and Early Christian Apocalyptic Literature," 1221–87. *4 Ezra* 7:132–40 enumerates seven attributes of God: God is merciful, gracious, patient, bountiful, abundant in compassion, giver, and judge. The treatise *On the Origin of the World* (NHC II, 5 and XIII, 2) 101.24–102.2 names the seven androgynous names of the seven divine forces. The number seven is also important for the author of the *Poimandres* (*Corpus Hermeticum* 1) 9: God, called νοῦς, creates seven governors, probably the seven planets.

[27] Rev 13:18.

other hand, names can also encapsulate numbers, as when the name of Jesus is abbreviated to the number 888 according to the Valentinian Mark the Magician.[28]

In ancient Jewish or Christian texts, when a divine message is received and written, inherent in the narrative are concerns about the name of the revealing entity as well as the individual to whom the revelation is delivered. When a reflection on a sacred legacy or history emerges in these texts, numbers may articulate periods of time and destiny.[29] When the eyes of the wise contemplate creation, including heaven and earth and its many peoples, then measure and dimension, as expressed with numbers and names, appear to justify a theological claim or defend a religious orientation.[30] Such is the case in the Wisdom of Solomon.[31] Likewise, the establishment of a holy people as the recipients of divine revelation goes hand in hand with numbers. While the author of *4 Ezra* is preoccupied with the small number of the saved,[32] others are proud to be part of the happy few; still others apply the title "the many" to their congregation,[33] and the book of Revelation fixes the boundaries of the community at 144,000.[34]

Twenty centuries separate us from the origins of Christianity. Among the obstacles that scholars of early Christianity must overcome, the most difficult are also perhaps the most abstract. With our logic influenced by the binary system of modern technology, can we understand a mind that works according to another, probably ternary, logic?[35] Influenced by centuries of nominalist thinking, are we able to imagine another relationship between language and thought, or between names or numbers and reality?[36]

---

[28] See Irenaeus, *Adv. haer.* 1.15.2; see also, the first book of the *Sibylline Oracles*, analyzed below, pp. 31–32 (*Sib.* 1.324–31). In *Adv. haer.* 1.15.1–3, Irenaeus gives his interpretation of the name of Jesus.

[29] See Collins, "Numerical Symbolism," 1224–49; James C. VanderKam, *Calendars in the Dead Sea Scrolls: Measuring Time* (The Literature of the Dead Sea Scrolls; London/New York: Routledge, 1998).

[30] Such as monotheism. See *1 Clem* 29: "The bounds of the nations are established κατὰ ἀριθμὸν ἀγγέλων θεοῦ, according to the number of the angels of God."

[31] See Wis 11:20; C. Larcher, *Études sur le Livre de la Sagesse* (EB; Paris: Gabalda, 1969) 187, 218–21; David Winston, *The Wisdom of Solomon: A New Translation with Introduction and Commentary* (AB; Garden City, N.Y.: Doubleday, 1982) 234–35; see nn. 61 and 91 below.

[32] *4 Ezra* 7:45–61.

[33] See in the Dead Sea Scrolls for example 1QS 6.1–7.25; Joachim Jeremias, "Das Lösegeld für viele (Mark 10,45)," *Judaica* 3 (1947) 249–64; Géza Vermès, *The Complete Dead Sea Scrolls in English* (New York, N.Y.: Penguin Books, 1997) 28.

[34] Rev 7:4. Absorbed by polemics, the leader of a community can disregard another group in the following way: "And there shall be others of those who are outside our number who name themselves bishops and also deacons ... " (*Apocalypse of Peter* [NHC VII, 3] 79).

[35] See Johann Mader, *Die logische Struktur des personalen Denkens. Aus der Methode der Gotteserkenntnis bei Aurelius Augustinus* (Wien: Herder, 1965).

[36] The reader should not forget the importance and power of name and numbers in magic; see Fritz Graf, *Magic in the Ancient World* (trans. Franklin Philip; Cambridge, Mass.: Harvard University Press, 1997).

Biblical Memories

The Jewish Scriptures are clearly concerned with names and numbers. These passages of the Hebrew Bible or the Septuagint contained an authoritative teaching and a model for new speculations. The New Testament and early Christian literature likewise continued and even added to this reflection on names and numbers.

At the burning bush, Moses' request to know God's name is answered with a riddle that camouflages the divine name. In the Septuagint, the Tetragrammaton is translated with the present participle of the verb "to be," which represents a theological interpretation: ὁ ὤν, "the one being" (Exod 3:14).[37] This understanding of God[38] was continued but modified by the first Christians. In John 8:58 the evangelist makes an allusion to this episode with Moses and gives it a christological interpretation.

The numerous biblical attestations of the expression "name of God" or "Lord" witness the distance between God as a person and God as a name.[39] They confirm also the respect that is due to this hidden and yet revealed God.[40] The hallowing of God's name and the avoiding of the profaning of God's name are central to Israel's religion. Likewise the Decalogue, particularly its third command to the members of the covenant, states: "You shall not make wrongful use of the name of the Lord your God, for the Lord will not acquit anyone who misuses his name" (Exod 20:7 par.). Likewise, the first request of the Lord's prayer, "Hallowed be

---

[37] The episode is remembered by Josephus, *Ant.* 2.264, but with no insistence on the revelation of God's name.

[38] See *Celui qui est. Interprétations juives et chrétiennes d'Exode 3,14* (ed. Alain de Libera and Emilie Zum Brunn; Patrimoines. Religions du livre; Paris: Cerf, 1986). Josephus, *Ant.* 11.331, tells the story of Alexander refusing to kill the high priest of Jerusalem and showing on the contrary great interest by greeting the name of God inscribed on the golden plate of the Jewish hierarch.

[39] There is a shift in the location of the name of God: in the Hebrew Bible it dwells in the ark of the covenant (see 2 Sam 6:2; see also Exod 25:8), then in the Temple (see 1 Kings 9:3; see also 2 Sam 7:13; 1 Kings 8:10–11; Jer 7:10). In the early Christian writings it dwells in the new temple, the community (1 Cor 3:16), or the believer (1 Cor 6:19).

[40] Origen, *On Psalm* 2:2, tells us that the name of God was read as Adonai by the Hebrews and as κύριος by the Greeks; see Gustav Adolf Deissmann, *Die Hellenisierung des semitischen Monotheismus* (Leipzig: B. G. Teubner, 1903); Ralph Marcus, "Divine Names and Attributes in Hellenistic Jewish Literature," in *Proceedings of the American Academy for Jewish Research* 2 (1931–1932) 45–120; Efraim Elimelech Urbach, *The Sages: Their Concepts and Beliefs* (trans. Israel Abrahams; Jerusalem: Magnes, 1975) 97–134; Colin H. Roberts, *Manuscript, Society, and Belief in Early Christian Egypt* (London: Oxford University Press, 1979) 29 n. 2, 30; Marguerite Harl, "La langue de la Septante," in Gilles Dorival, Marguerite Harl, and Olivier Munier, *La Bible grecque des Septante. Du judaïsme au christianisme ancien* (Initiations au christianisme ancien; Paris: Cerf and C.N.R.S., 1988) 255–56; Martin Rosel, *Adonaj, Warum Gott "Herr" genannt wird?* (FAT 29; Tübingen: Mohr Siebeck, 2000).

thy name" (Matt 6:9 par.), fits perfectly into this religious framework, as does the early Christians' reverence for the "name of God" (for example, John 17:6).[41]

According to the book of Exodus, Moses, the admired leader, needed the help of his brother Aaron (Exod 4:10–17). Greek-speaking Jews, particularly Philo of Alexandria, contemplated why such help was necessary. Philo concludes that Moses represents the experience of God's presence while Aaron represents the need for words, particularly names, to express this religious experience.[42] God as a person remains transcendent; God's real name, nature, and person cannot be known,[43] but the experience of God can be known and needs to be expressed. There is, therefore, a correlation between religious reality and religious expression. The words are so important that some texts stipulate that this spiritual experience must be expressed in Hebrew, the divine language of creation, a language thought to have been forgotten after the fall but rediscovered in the time of Abraham.[44]

According to Gen 2:19–20 the importance of naming begins with creation because God entrusted Adam with the responsibility of giving names to the animals.[45] Even for us today, bestowing names is still an important matter (a name must fit and be well chosen). If the given name seems artificial or does not fit, often a nickname is chosen that does fit. In antiquity different solutions were given to the question of the link between *res* and *verbum*. Several pre-Socratic philosophers and all the sophists thought that names were given not by nature (φύσις) but by convention (θέσις). The Stoics, on the other hand, believed in an intrinsic relationship between names and reality. Their theory of the universal λόγος invited them to insist on the natural aspect of names. The Platonic tradition chose a middle way. Names are given by convention, but they are also the way, the only way, to reach reality. They are like the shadow cast by a body. From their δόξα there is for the industrious mind a way to go back to the realm they express.[46] Philo participates in this discussion by saying that Adam played a decisive

---

[41] See for example *Apocalypse of Paul* 6–12; Theodore Silverstein and Anthony Hilhorst, *Apocalypse of Paul: A New Critical Edition of Three Long Latin Versions* (Geneva: Patrick Cramer, 1997) 75–85.

[42] See Philo, *De migratione Abrahami* 76–85; *Quod deterius potiori insidiari soleat* 75–78, 126–32.

[43] Justin Martyr, *1 Apol.* 61.11: "For no one can give a name to the ineffable God: and if anyone should dare say there is one, he raves with a hopeless insanity."

[44] See *Jubilees* 12.

[45] The episode is mentioned in the book of *Jubilees* 3.2: "And Adam named all of them, each one according to its name, and whatever he called them became their names" (trans. O. S. Wintermute, in *OTP* 2:58); see also *Midrash Rabbah, Genesis (Bereshith)* 17.4; *Midrash Rabba*, I, *Genèse Rabba* (trans. Bernard Maruani and Albert Cohen-Arazi; intro. and ann. Bernard Maruani; Les Dix Paroles; Paris: Verdier, 1987) 200–1. Adam knows the names of the animals while the angels ignore them.

[46] See Plato, *Cratylus*; see also Bietenhard, "ὄνομα," 245–48. The prestige of the wise ὀνοματοθέτης, the "one who gives names," the "namer," in the Greek philosophical tradition underlines the importance of names and naming; see Plato, *Charmides* 175b v.l.; *Cratylus* 389d

role in the first act of naming. Adam was the first and the only individual to assign the names of the animals, whereas Greeks in antiquity believed that many sages of the past had participated in this act of choosing names. Use of the figure of Adam and this episode in Gen 2:19–20 by the author of Mark probably lies behind the enigmatic sentence in the story of Jesus' baptism: καὶ ἦν μετὰ θηρίων (Mark 1:13).

It is difficult to grasp the philosophical difference between the Hebrew text of Gen 2:19–20 and its Greek translation, but there is a subtle difference.[47] The Hebrew text does not insert any category between the animals and their names; in his writings on the Septuagint, however, Philo points out a difference between the genre (γένος) and the species (εἶδος).[48] What Adam did was to name the animals according to their species, but respecting the greater category of genre. Divine in origin, the genre preceded any human action and was imposed on Adam. As Philo says, one seal can produce many prints. Human limitation can destroy the prints but cannot touch the seal.[49] Behind Adam's names that we can hear or read are the abstract categories, the genres, which are in and of God.[50]

The Hebrew Bible offers numerous examples of symbolic names, including the children of the prophets Hosea (Hos 1:3–9) and Isaiah (Isa 8:3). In Hebrew scriptures even the change of a name is significant: for example, Abram becomes Abraham, Sarai becomes Sarah, and Jacob becomes Israel.[51] The first Christian authors were likewise well aware of the significance of a name. Matthew makes clear

---

v.l.; if, however, the term is not from Plato himself, it may originate from Neoplatonic circles; see Édouard Des Places, *Platon. Œuvres complètes*, XIV. *Lexique, deuxième partie* (Collection des Universités de France; Paris: Belles Lettres, 1964) 384. Proclus, *In Platonis Parmenidem*, in Proclus, *Opera inedita* (ed. Victor Cousin; Paris: Durand, 1864) 657 line 19. Iamblichus, *Life of Pythagoras* 82, recalls a sentence of one of the two Pythagorean schools: τί τὸ σοφώτατον; ἀριθμός· δεύτερον δὲ τὸ τοῖς πράγμασι τὰ ὀνόματα τιθέμενον: "What is the wisest? Number; second the establishment of names for things."

[47] See Monique Alexandre, *Le commencement du Livre, Genèse I–V. La version grecque de la Septante et sa réception* (Christianisme Antique 3; Paris: Beauchesne, 1988) 281. I thank my colleague Gary Anderson for this reference. Unfortunately the notes on these verses are not developed in *La Bible d'Alexandrie. La Genèse* (ed. Marguerite Harl; Paris: Cerf, 1986) 105.

[48] *Legum allegoriae* 2.9.

[49] *Quod deterius potiori insidiari soleat* 78. On Adam naming the animals see further Philo, *De opificio mundi* 148–50.

[50] It would be enlightening to know what the first Christians believed about naming, particularly when naming newborn believers during baptism. By calling upon them God's name and giving them new names, were they performing a sacramental action or using a ritual without ontological impact? It seems – if we can use the Pauline understanding of Eucharist (1 Cor 6:12–17; 10:14–22; 11:23–26) as an analogy – that some of them at least were convinced by the internal connection between names and reality. Adam had chosen the right names, not so much because he knew the divine genres, but because he had received the divine wisdom to know and communicate God's intention.

[51] Gen 17:5, 15 and 32:27–28. Other changes of names in the Hebrew Bible: Num 13:16 (Hoseah becomes Joshua); 2 Kings 14:7 (the city of Sela receives the name of Jokthe-el); 2 Kings 23:34 (Pharaoh Neco changes the name of the King Eliakim to Jehoiakim).

a link between Jesus' name and his providential function. He writes about Mary and her child: "She will bear a son, and you are to name him Jesus, for he will save his people from their sins" (Matt 1:21). The change of Simon's name to Peter (Matt 16:17–18)[52] continues this biblical tradition. Moreover, Philo wrote an entire treatise on the changing of names.[53] According to him, Jacob became Israel for at least two reasons, first because as an individual he "wrestled with God," and second because through this wrestling with God he became the representative for the collective people of God.

The distinction between heavenly and earthly also applies here. A heavenly Israel corresponds to the empirical Israel.[54] These ancient Babylonian and Greek beliefs that there exists a heavenly counterpart either to the earthly temple or to this world also found their way into the Christian faith.[55] Ignatius of Antioch considered the bishop to be an earthly counterpart of the heavenly Father and, likewise, presupposed that the liturgy of the Church is the human counterpart of the celestial liturgy celebrated by the angels.[56] Paul,[57] a Jewish theologian, considered to be a reformist by some and a heretic by others, dared to relate the new congregation of believers to the spiritual reality of Israel.[58]

In the case of Daniel, not just a single text but the whole book is worth mentioning because of the significant use of numbers throughout: the four kingdoms of chapter 2; the seven times of Dan 4:23, 25, 32; the "numbered, numbered, weighed, and divided" of Daniel 5:25–28; the four winds and four animals (the fourth with its ten horns) of Daniel 7; the several horns and the 2,300 evenings and mornings of Daniel 8; the 70 years and 70 weeks of years in Daniel 9; the four kings and the four directions of Daniel 11; the time, two times and half a time of

---

[52] The change from Saul to Paul in Acts 13:9 remains enigmatic because Luke mentions it but does not explain it. See Joseph A. Fitzmyer, *The Acts of the Apostles: A New Translation and Commentary* (AB 31; New York: Doubleday, 1998) 499–500.

[53] Philo, *De mutatione nominum.*

[54] See the *Prayer of Joseph*, Fragment A, a text probably of the 1st cent. c.e.; see J. Z. Smith, "Prayer of Joseph," in *OTP* 2:699–705, 712–13.

[55] See Heb 8:5 building on Exod 25:40; see also Rev 2:1, 8, 12, 18; 3:1, 7, 14.

[56] See Ign. *Magn.* 3.2; 6.1; 7.2; *Smyrn.* 8.1–2; *Eph.* 4.1–5.3; *Trall.* 7.2; *Rom.* 2.2.

[57] Gal 6:16.

[58] Names and numbers occur also on the garment of the high priest Aaron. The names of Israel's 12 tribes were engraved on the two stones, six on each, placed on the shoulder-straps of the ephod (Exod 28:10–14). The high priest therefore represented the people of Israel. But he also carried on his pectoral a gold tablet with the holy name of God. Inscribed on the gold tablet was the expression "Holy to the Lord" (Exod 28:36; ἁγίασμα κυρίου in the Septuagint). The high priest thus represented God when meeting the elect people. Josephus (*Ant.* 3.162–78), Philo (*De vita Mosis* 2.109–30) and the author of the book of Revelation (Rev 21:12, 19) are the witnesses of a careful reading of Exodus 28 in the first century c.e. Close to Exod 28:10–14 is Numbers 17, a passage in which each of the 12 tribes brings a rod with its name engraved in it. Only one, that of Aaron and the tribe of Levi, will bloom the next day and show the election of this tribe for the service of God. The episode is mentioned in *1 Clem.* 43 as a way of solving a crisis to avoid any kind of ἀκαταστασία, "disorder." This is the best way to glorify God's name, εἰς τὸ δοξασθῆναι τὸ ὄνομα τοῦ ἀληθινοῦ καὶ μόνου. See also *Protevangelium of James* 8–9.

Dan 12:7; and the 1,290 and 1,335 days of Dan 12:11–12. This list is most relevant for our purpose because the subsequent apocalyptic literature will rely on it.[59]

One final text must be mentioned in this section. It comes from the wisdom literature and participates in the apologetic dialogue between Israel and the intellectual Greek world, illustrating along with the Greek philosophers the importance of names and numbers. Different from the Greek presupposition, however, it reverses the perspective, transforming an anthropological opinion into a theological one.[60] According to the author of the Wisdom of Solomon, it is God, the Creator of the universe and Guide of Israel, who "arranged all things by measure and number and weight" (πάντα μέτρῳ καὶ ἀριθμῷ καὶ σταθμῷ διέταξας, Wis 11:20).[61] Likewise, the first Christians showed interest in creation and believed the world to be organized harmoniously.[62]

Enumerations and Meaningful Names

The kinship between signs for words and signs for numbers is embedded in the origins of writing (as long ago as in the proto-Sumerian culture of Uruk, around 3000 B.C.E.).[63] It will never be lost. Some Hebrew, Greek, and Roman numerals were and still are letters.[64] The selection of letters as signs for numbers[65] reflected with some exceptions the alphabetic order (α´ for 1, β´ for 2, γ´ for 3, and so on). To avoid confusion, a small stroke was added to the letter to show that the letter signified a number.[66] Conversely, the name of a person not only functioned as a substitute for this person, it could also designate some of his or her belongings. In certain contexts τὸ ἐμὸν ὄνομα meant "my account" or "my bank account."[67]

---

[59] For some discussion of numerology in Daniel, see Louis F. Hartman and Alexander A. Di Lella, *The Book of Daniel: A New Translation with Notes and Commentary* (AB 23; Garden City, N.Y.: Doubleday, 1978) 70, 208–17.

[60] It is my conviction that this position is also the position of the New Testament as it is that of Irenaeus (see n. 4 above).

[61] On the importance of this verse for Augustine, see n. 91 below.

[62] See Acts 14:15–17; 17:24–27; Col 1:15–17.

[63] See Friberg, "Numbers and Counting," 1140.

[64] See Ifrah, *Histoire universelle des chiffres*, 1:441–621. As we have seen earlier (n. 10 above), *1 Enoch* 69.13–14 brings close the number and the name of the fallen angel Kasb'el; in *2 Enoch* 40.3 (manuscript J, longer recension): Enoch received a complete knowledge from the Lord. He says: "For not even the angels know their numbers. But I have written down all their names." Manuscript A (shorter recension) has a text very close to the text of J.

[65] Friberg, "Numbers and Counting," 1143: "The oldest examples of the use of Hebrew alphabetic numerals may go as far back as the late 2d and the 1st centuries B.C. ... The relatively late dates of these first examples suggest that the Hebrew alphabetic numeration was introduced as a result of Greek influence."

[66] See Ifrah, *Histoire universelle des chiffres*, 1:529–38.

[67] Bientenhard, "ὄνομα," 244–45.

In glorifying God or praising God's messengers there was already in antiquity a tendency to enumerate deeds or titles with numbers.[68] A tradition behind the Gospel of John, perhaps the *Semeia* Source, attributed a numeric sequence to Jesus' several signs or miracles. Traces of it are still visible in John 2:1 (the beginning of the signs), 4:54 (second sign), and perhaps 21:14 (the third time). Such a tendency, perceptible already in the *catenae* of sayings,[69] miracles,[70] or appearances stories,[71] occurs also in the lives of some apostles. The *Acts of Thomas* as well as the *Acts of Philip* organize the large material into a certain number of consecutive acts. Although there are some discrepancies within the manuscripts concerning the enumerating, nevertheless the presence of numbers, spelled out completely or abbreviated with letters depending on the manuscripts, indicates a compositional intention to organize the apostolic memories. It also expresses a missionary zeal: the lives of the Savior or of his apostles do not lack order and sequence, and numbers become tools for a faith relying on divine providence. If the plural can sometimes be the means of human limitations or even sins, it can also help to express the solicitude of the many divine messengers and their continuous intention to save.

Proper names could be spelled out or – at least for some of them – abbreviated. I wish to mention here the famous *nomina sacra*.[72] It is certain that these abbreviations were not intended to save time or space. It is also clear that four names, Ἰησοῦς, Χριστός, κύριος, and θεός, constituted the first and most ancient group of *nomina sacra* (occurring in the first half of the second century C.E.). If the belief in the ineffability of the name of God is certainly Jewish, the system of abbreviations for "Lord" (κύριος) and "God" (θεός) seems to be Christian in origin. To sum up, the system of the *nomina sacra* corresponds to a double theological movement. First, it offers a special way of writing the divine name detaching it from the human network. Second, it relates the Son more closely to the Father by including both of them in a sphere secluded from the realm of creation.

An early text, the *Epistle of Barnabas*, of around 100 C.E., is a witness for a short form of Jesus (actually the suspension is ιη̄, which exists in the beginning beside the usual contraction ῑς̄).[73] It is certain that a theological interest lies behind this writing practice. Colin H. Roberts writes: "It seems then that there were two lines of development, the one owing something to number symbolism, the other, perhaps with an allusion to Alpha and Omega, taking the first and the last let-

---

[68] On the names and epithets of the gods in Greek religion, see André-Jean Festugière, "La Grèce, la religion," in *Histoire générale des religions*, II, *Grèce-Rome* (Paris: Quillet, 1948) 61–64; on the 12 deeds of Heracles, see Martin P. N. Nilsson, "La Grèce, la mythologie," ibid., 233–42.

[69] See Q, the *Gospel of Thomas*, or the *Gospel of Philip*.

[70] See *Epist. apost.* 4–5.

[71] See 1 Cor 15:3–11; John 20; 21; *Acts of John* 87–93.

[72] See Roberts, *Manuscript, Society, and Belief in Early Christian Egypt*, 26–48, 83–84.

[73] *Barn* 9.8.

ters."[74] One should not forget that the *nomina sacra* were always accompanied by a superlinear stroke, so that as they read, the ancient readers could see when they were approaching a sacred name.

The first Christians were torn between imitation of other Jewish movements and affirmation of their own identity: they paid a similar respect to divine names, but added to the name of God the name of their new Master, Jesus, considered to be the "Messiah" and the "Lord."[75] The fact that other, more recent christological titles, such as "Savior" or "Logos," did not become part of the system of the *nomina sacra* gives a clue to the early origin of the system that rapidly became universal among the early Churches.[76]

In the Name of Jesus

In a Jewish world marked by the name of God, to proclaim the name of Jesus was perceived as a new, dangerous, even blasphemous attitude. Nevertheless, the invocation of the name "Jesus" is characteristic of the early Christian traditions.[77] The expressions "in my name" or "in your name" in the Synoptic, both Markan and Q, traditions[78] are a narrative adaptation of the christological formula: see, for example, Mark 9:37 par.; Mark 13:6 par.; and Luke 10:17. The theocentric perspective, however, still dominates in the Synoptic Gospels and the term ὄνομα is associated more frequently with the Father than with the Son. The situation is different in the Pauline epistles where christological usage predominates. Central for our purpose is the second strophe of the hymn preserved in Phil 2:6–11: "Therefore God also highly exalted him and gave him the name that is above every name, so that at the name of Jesus every knee should bend, in heaven and on earth and under the earth … " (Phil 2:9–10). In my opinion the name given to the divine messenger at the resurrection is neither "Lord" nor "Jesus," but an ineffable name, a hidden expression of the divine condition. "Lord," "Messiah," and "Jesus" are the visible side of the Resurrected.[79] Not only does the Father possess an ineffable name, the Tetragrammaton of Exod 3:14, but so also does the Son.[80]

---

[74] Roberts, *Manuscript, Society, and Belief in Early Christian Egypt*, 37.

[75] The *Didache* shows a parallel phenomenon concerning fasting: like the Jews the Christians decided to fast twice a week, but unlike their Jewish opponents they chose Wednesday and Friday; *Did.* 8.1.

[76] If the date is certain, the place of origin is still debated. Roberts, *Manuscript, Society, and Belief in Early Christian Egypt*, 42–46 rejects Alexandria and Rome, and chooses Jerusalem for no strong reasons.

[77] "Parmi les nombreux passages du N.T. contenant le mot ὄνομα, un peu plus de cent l'emploient à propos de Jésus" (Jacques Dupont, "Nom de Jésus," *DBS* 6 [1960] 514).

[78] See also Matt 7:22 as a redactional example.

[79] See also Eph 1:20–21 (see particularly the expression ὑπὲρ … παντὸς ὀνόματος ὀνομαζο-μένου).

[80] This conception that the name "Jesus" is only the visible side of the Son's real name is

Similarly in the Epistle to the Hebrews, Jesus, the Son, God's representative and visible presence, is exalted over all creation. His name is over all other names: "Having become as much superior to angels as the name he has inherited is more excellent than theirs" (Heb 1:4). One should remember the development of angelology in this period and the bestowal of power to angels in order to understand the power of this phrase.[81] The expression "my name" is also present in the Johannine literature with a strong christological weight: see for example John 20:30–31. In the book of Revelation we find a similar consciousness of the inadequacy of any human name for Jesus Christ: "He has a name inscribed that no one knows but himself" (Rev 19:12). At the end of the second century Irenaeus adds to the existing explanations of the relationship between the name of the Father and the name of the Son.[82]

Lucien Cerfaux, Jacques Dupont, and Jean Daniélou concur in their suggestions that an early Christian theology of the "name" was a theological expression of the first community.[83] I see these hypotheses as still valid. The first Christians were confident and proud, believing in the power of Jesus' name not in a magical way but as the expression of the person himself. "But Peter said, 'I have no silver or gold, but what I have I give you; in the name of Jesus Christ of Nazareth, stand up and walk'" (Acts 3:6). This trust in the name continued in the second century in such authors as Justin Martyr (*2 Apol.* 6.6; *Dial.* 30.3; 85), Irenaeus (*Adv. haer.* 2.32.4), the scribes of New Testament manuscripts, who sometimes added the expression "in the name of the Lord Jesus Christ" to their copies (see the variant reading of D in Acts 6:8), and the authors of the apocryphal acts of the apostles.[84] For these Christians, Jesus Christ had revealed a new and salvific aspect of God's person. The prayer of the psalmist, "Save me, O God, by your name" (Ps 54:1), had been actualized in Jesus. It is therefore not surprising that etymology was

----

typical of Gnostic thought; it is a vital element in Mark the Magician, a Valentinian theologian: see Irenaeus, *Adv. haer.* 1.15.1. See also *Acts of John* 98.8–12 and 109.3–17; *Gospel of Philip* 11–13; *Gospel of Truth* 38.7–15; Éric Junod and Jean-Daniel Kaestli, eds., *Acta Iohannis* (2 vols.; CCSA 1–2; Turnhout: Brepols, 1983) 2:617–21.

[81] Asserting that Jesus' name is higher than the angels' names, *1 Clem.* 36.2 depends probably on the Epistle to the Hebrews.

[82] Irenaeus, *Adv. haer.* 4.17.6. The divine name that is glorified in the world is the name of the Son and through it the Father is glorified. Like a king after painting his son can say: it is my work because it is the portrait of my son and it is my personal work; see also *Adv. haer.* 2.32.4. *The Gospel of Philip* (NHC II, 3) 56.3–15, 62.7–17, and 63.21–24 has three developments on the names and titles of Jesus.

[83] Lucien Cerfaux, *Le Christ dans la théologie de saint Paul* (2d ed.; LD 6; Paris: Cerf, 1954) 357–59; Dupont, "Nom de Jésus," 514–41; Jean Daniélou, *Théologie du Judéo-Christianisme* (2 vols.; Paris: Desclée de Brouwer, 1958–1961) 1:199–216.

[84] See *Acts John* 83; *Acts Pet.* 16; *Acts Thom.* 33.2; *Acts Phil.* 6.20; see Sever J. Voicu's index in *Écrits apocryphes chrétiens* 1 (ed. François Bovon and Pierre Geoltrain; La Pléiade 442; Paris: Gallimard, 1997) 1747.

applied here: Jesus would carry his name properly: "He will save his people from their sins" (Matt 1:21).[85]

This theology of the "name" is most visible in the book of Acts.[86] It is also in this work that we find the strongest statement, namely that there is salvation to humanity only through the name, i.e., the person, of Jesus Christ. This is the argument that Luke, writing the story of the healing of the paralytic at the "Beautiful Gate" (Acts 3:2), places on the lips of the apostle Peter when he is confronted with the Sanhedrin: καὶ οὐκ ἔστιν ἄλλῳ οὐδενὶ ἡ σωτηρία, οὐδὲ γὰρ ὄνομά ἐστιν ἕτερον ὑπὸ τὸν οὐρανὸν τὸ δεδομένον ἐν ἀνθρώποις ἐν ᾧ δεῖ σωθῆναι ἡμᾶς ("There is salvation in no one else, for there is no other name under heaven given among mortals by which we must be saved," Acts 4:12).[87]

Christians claim to represent the true people of God, "those who in every place call on the name of our Lord Jesus Christ" (1 Cor 1:2). Joel's prophecy was quoted with joy and profit: "Then everyone who calls on the name of the Lord shall be saved ... " (Joel 2:32 [LXX 3:5]; see Rom 10:13; Acts 2:21). Preaching, prayers, creeds, and baptisms were performed "in his name."[88] The unknown or unusual expressions in Greek, τὸ ὄνομα with the preposition εἰς, ἐν, or ἐπί, refer to two parallel movements in opposite directions, a movement from the Lord Jesus Christ to the believer and a movement from the believer toward Jesus Christ and his flock.[89]

---

[85] This passage of Matthew influenced the *Protevangelium of James* 14.5–6: "But when night came a messenger of the Lord suddenly appeared to him in a dream and said: 'Don't be afraid of this girl, because the child in her is the holy spirit's doing. She will have a son and you will name him Jesus – the name means "he will save his people from their sins"'" (trans. Ronald E. Hock, *The Infancy Gospels of James and Thomas* [The Scholars Bible 2; Santa Barbara, Calif.: Polebridge Press, 1995] 57, 59). The spiritual meaning of the proper names contained in the Septuagint interested Philo, and those in the New Testament, Origen. This is the opinion of Jerome when he decided to write the *Liber interpretationis nominum Hebraicorum* (CCSL 72.57–161). It is not so sure that Jerome could really rely on one book by Philo and another one by Origen. Jerome knew often the philological etymology of a name but respected the popular, or the spiritual, one. He believed also that God had given some secret meanings to the biblical names. See Franz Wutz, *Onomastica Sacra. Untersuchungen zum Liber interpretationis nominum Hebraicorum des Hl. Hieronymus* (2 vols.; TU 41.1–2; Leipzig: Hinrichs, 1914–1915): "Meine 'Onomastica Sacra' sind als Nachschlagewerk gedacht, in welchem über die Namen aller bislang erreichbaren Listen Rechenschaft gegeben wird" (p. viii).

[86] See Dupont, "Nom de Jésus."

[87] See also the glorification of the name of Jesus Christ in the *Acts of John* (e.g., 109), the *Acts of Thomas* (e.g., 27.2–3), the *Acts of Philip* (e.g., 7.2), the *Life of Andrew* by Gregory of Tours (e.g., 3.4), and the *Doctrina Addai* (e.g., 10). In the Christian texts it is sometimes difficult to know if the name refers to God or to Christ. In the *Odes of Solomon* the many mentions of the name (e.g., 39.7–8, 13) must refer to the Lord Jesus Christ.

[88] For the prayer, see John 14:13–16 and Acts 22:16; for the preaching, see Luke 24:46–47; for the confession of faith, see Rom 10:6–13 and 3 John 17–18; for the baptism, see Matt 28:19 and 1 Cor 6:11. Even the suffering of believers happens "because of his name" or "in his name": see Mark 13:13; 1 Pet 4:13–16; Herm. *Vis.* 3.1.9–3.2.1.

[89] See Rudolf Bultmann, *Theologie des Neuen Testaments* (UTB 630; Tübingen: Mohr Siebeck, 1980) 135–41.

Holy Numbers

It is not necessary to wait until Origen's homilies on the book of Numbers[90] or Augustine's reflections on Wis 11:20 on measure, number, and weight to realize the strong impact numbers had on the Christian mind.[91] Irenaeus spent a great deal of time refuting the Valentinians, Mark and Ptolemy, and their speculations on numbers.[92] Although opposing their precise numerological elaborations, he did not object, however, to *any* use of numbers. It would be historically wrong to believe that such speculation was the endowment of the Gnostics. Similarly, as early as the book of Revelation or the *Epistle of Barnabas*, we read a symbolic interpretation of numbers and an interaction between letters and names.[93] In a text that cannot be accused of being either Gnostic or heretical, the so-called *Epistula apostolorum* (mid-second century C.E.), we discover the following: "We [Jesus' disciples after the miracle of the loaves of bread] were asking and saying: 'What meaning is there in these five loaves? They are a picture of our faith concerning the great Christianity and that is in the Father, the ruler of the entire world, and in Jesus Christ our Savior, and in the Holy Spirit, the Paraclete, and in the holy Church and in the forgiveness of sins.' "[94]

The mystical or symbolic use of numbers probably did not belong to the elementary doctrinal and ethical teaching of the first Christian communities. But as soon as a desire to deepen the faith occurred, such a development became possible, as we see in the *Epistle of Barnabas*. This writing connects biblical exegesis (of the Septuagint) with reflections on numbers. Abraham's use of circumcision falls short, claims the author, if we understand it as a seal of the covenant, because the author is aware that other nations, Syrians and Arabs, and even priests of pagan religions, practiced circumcision. Therefore – according to the author's words – a rich exegetical teaching needs to be gained from the book of Genesis. If Abraham was the first to use circumcision (Gen 17:9–14), he did so as a prophetic action inspired by the Spirit. The author adds: "And Abraham circumcised from his household 18 men and 300." The author draws attention to the fact that 18 in the

---

[90] See Origen, *Hom. Num.* 1; 4; 5.2.2–3; 7.4.4; 8.1.5; Origène, *Homélies sur les Nombres*, I, *Homélies I-X* (ed. Louis Doutreleau; SC 415; Paris: Cerf, 1996) 30–49, 98–113, 126–31, 188–89, 208–11. The following quotation manifests the importance of numbers in Origen's thought: "Tout le monde n'est pas digne d'accéder aux nombres divins, mais il y a des règles de priorité pour la désignation de ceux qui doivent être compris dans le nombre de Dieu" (Origen, *Hom. Num.* 1.1).

[91] See Augustine, *De Genesi ad litteram* 4.3.7–4.6.12; see *La Genèse au sens littéral en douze livres (I–VII)* (trans., intro., and ann. Paul Agaësse and A. Solignac; 2 vols.; Bibliothèque Augustinienne. Œuvres de saint Augustin 48–49, septième série; Paris: Desclée de Brouwer, 1970–1972) 1:288–97, 635–39.

[92] Irenaeus, *Adv. haer.* 1.14–16; 2.20–28.

[93] The apostle Paul (Gal 4:22–31) applied allegorical interpretation, a phenomenon parallel to the symbolism of numbers and the etymology of names.

[94] *Epist. apost.* 5.

Septuagint is mentioned *first*, distinct from the 300. It is intentional and providential: τὸ δεκαοκτώ, ιη′ ἔχεις ᾽ΙΗ, "Eighteen is written ΙΗ′. You have therefore Jesus." And because the cross in the form of the τ was going to bring grace, it also reads 300 (in Greek: τ′). It therefore refers to Jesus with the first two letters and the cross with the third letter. "He knows this who placed the gift of his teaching in our hearts. No one has heard a more excellent lesson from me, but I know that you are worthy."[95] This risky interpretation is not part of the first Christian preaching, nor is it part of the elementary ethical teaching, as we noticed.[96] The author of the *Epistle of Barnabas* believes in the divine origin of this teaching as well as in its implantation in us. The true meaning of Scripture *can* be known by the human mind, because there is a harmony between the external (the visible signs for 318) and the internal reality (the divine gift in us). But such a doctrine is not for anyone. Only the people of God, those who are worthy, can receive it and understand and enjoy it. Thus the role of the teacher is to bring into connection the Scripture and the reader, wherein a double link exists: on one side the christological content (ιη′), on the other the pneumatological agency ἐν πνεύματι.[97] According to the author, physical circumcision could not offer the security of salvation because it did not offer the seal of the covenant. Only the work of Christ, Jesus and his cross, could establish the true covenant.[98]

Book I of the *Sibylline Oracles* is difficult to date in its present form, but I would date it to the second or third century C.E. Even if the work can be considered a product of Christian propaganda,[99] its hexameters often contain doctrinal elements and in the example below (1.324–31) a christological teaching:

---

[95] *Barn.* 9.7–9. Part of a codex, the Yale Genesis Fragment, *Papyrus Yale* 1, dated approximately 90 C.E., contains Gen 14:5–8, 12–15 according to the Septuagint. The codex may have been of Christian origin. Interestingly the number 318 was not spelled out but written with letters (the passage is fragmentary but there is not enough space for the number to be spelled out). This unusual feature could open the door for such an interpretation as the one proposed by the author of the *Epistle of Barnabas*; see C. Bradford Welles, "The Yale Genesis Fragment," *The Yale University Library Gazette* 39:1 (1964) 1–8; C. H. Hoberts, "P. Yale 1 and the early Christian Book," in *Essays in Honor of C. Bradford Welles* (ed. R. O. Fink et al.; American Studies in Papyrology 1; New Haven/Toronto: The American Society of Papyrologists, 1966) 25–28; *Yale Papyri in the Beinecke Rare Book and Manuscript Library* 1 (ed. John E. Oates, Alan E. Samuel, and C. Bradford Welles; American Studies in Papyrology 2; New Haven/Toronto: The American Society of Papyrologists, 1967) 3–8. I am indebted to Prof. Carl Holladay for much valued advice on this fragment. See also Thomas E. Schmidt, "The Letter Tau as the Cross: Ornament and Content in Hebrews 2:14," *Bib* 76 (1995) 75–84.

[96] We have other traces of an advanced teaching in early Christianity. Ignatius of Antioch speaks of the three bright "mysteries" ignored by the Prince of this world and accomplished by God in silence (Ign. *Eph.* 19.1); *Did.* 16.6 explains the three eschatological "signs": the sign of extension, the sign of the trumpet, and the sign of the resurrection.

[97] *Barn.* 9.7–8; see Ferdinand Prostmeier, *Der Barnabasbrief übersetzt und erklärt* (Kommentar zu den Apostolischen Vätern 8; Göttingen: Vandenhoeck & Ruprecht, 1999) 352, 369–71.

[98] See also *Barn.* 4.6–8 and 14.1–7; Prostmeier, *Barnabasbrief*, 370.

[99] See Jörg-Dieter Gauger, *Sibyllinische Weissagungen. Griechisch-deutsch. Auf der Grund-

δὴ τότε καὶ μεγάλοιο θεοῦ παῖς ἀνθρώποισιν
ἥξει σαρκοφόρος θνητοῖς ὁμοιούμενος ἐν γῇ
τέσσαρα φωνήεντα φέρων, τὸ δ' ἄφωνον ἐν αὐτῷ
δισσόν· ἐγὼ δέ κέ τοι ἀριθμόν γ' ὅλον ἐξονομήνω
ὀκτὼ γὰρ μονάδας, τόσσας δεκάδας δ' ἐπὶ ταύταις
ἠδ' ἑκατοντάδας ὀκτὼ ἀπιστοκόροις ἀνθρώποις
οὔνομα δηλώσει· σὺ δ' ἐνὶ φρεσὶ σῆσι νόησον
ἀθανάτοιο θεοῦ Χριστὸν παῖδ' ὑψίστοιο·

Then indeed the son of the great God will come,
incarnate, likened to mortal men on earth,
bearing four vowels, and the consonants in him are two.
I will state explicitly the entire number for you.
For eight units, and equal number of tens in addition to these,
and eight hundreds will reveal the name
to men who are sated with faithlessness. But you, consider in your heart
Christ, the son of the most high, immortal God.[100]

This text offers two ways of reading the name Jesus: first by counting vowels and consonants (four vowels and two consonants, but what help is that?),[101] and second, by adding the numerical value of each letter. In this way you reach the number 888: ι' = 10, η' = 8, σ' = 200, ο' = 70, υ' = 400, σ' = 200. The text does not explain the value of this 888, but it was probably well understood by the initiated readers. It certainly meant a total plenitude, since the numeral 8 had been accepted by Christians as the number of the Resurrection (the first day of the week being the eighth day).[102] As mentioned above, the Valentinian Mark also considered the number 888 to be the result of multiplication from the Tetrad, the Ogdoad, and the Decad. He also believed that this 888 is Jesus' name, a name that includes all numbers, and he went further, to make a connection with the A and Ω, another expression of the totality.[103]

Such explanations may seem artificial and far-fetched, but as scholars we first need to recognize the general interest in both the semantic value of numbers and

---

lage der Ausgabe von Alfons Kurfeß neu übersetzt und herausgegeben (Tusculum; Zurich: Artemis & Winkler, 1998) 38.

[100] Trans. John J. Collins, "Sibylline Oracles," in *OTP* 1:342.

[101] See the Valentinian Mark's opinion according to Irenaeus, *Adv. haer.* 1.14.4: "For Jesus [Ἰησοῦς] indeed is a symbolical name, having six letters and being known by all who belong to those who are called. The name, however, which is among the Aeons of the Fullness has many parts, being of another form and of another type; it is known by those companions [of the Savior], whose Greatnesses [angels] are always with him" (trans. Dominic J. Unger and John J. Dillon, *St. Irenaeus of Lyons: Against the Heresies*, vol. 1, bk. 1 [Ancient Christian Writers 55; New York: Paulist, 1992] 61). See also the acrostic poem "Jesus Christ, son of God, savior, cross," in *Sibylline Oracles* 8.218–50, and Augustine's comment in *De civitate Dei* 18.23. I thank Jean-Michel Rössli for this reference as well as for others to the *Sibylline Oracles*.

[102] See *Sibylline Oracles* 7.139–40; Auguste Luneau, *L'histoire du salut chez les Pères de l'Église. La doctrine des âges du monde* (Paris: Beauchesne, 1964) 325.

[103] Irenaus, *Adv. haer.* 1.15.2.

in the numeric scope of letters among people of late antiquity.[104] Modern theological criticism of such speculations, legitimate as it may be, must come second.

Any scholarly examination of ancient texts and their number speculations should also consider the so-called *flexio digitorum*. Passing from tens to hundreds was particularly important, because counting up to 99 was executed by the left hand, while counting from 100 on up was done with the right hand. Remembering that the left side was considered a negative one, the passage to 100 was considered with pleasure. Juvenal, for example, celebrated the elder Nestor, who had had the privilege to live more than 100 years: "If we have any belief in mighty Homer, the king of Pylos [Nestor] was an example of long life second only to the crow; happy forsooth in this that he had put off death for so many generations, and so often quaffed the new-made wine, counting now his years upon his right hand."[105] It is therefore not surprising that the *Gospel of Truth* established a connection between the lost sheep and the fate of the whole flock. The shepherd not only saved the single animal but preserved or re-established the whole group: "He is the shepherd who left behind the ninety-nine sheep which were not lost. He went searching for the one that had gone astray. He rejoiced when he found it, for ninety-nine is a number that is in the left hand that holds it. But when the one is found, the entire number passes to the right [hand]. As that which lacks the one – that is, the entire right [hand] – draws what was deficient and takes it from the left hand side and brings [it] to the right, so too the number becomes one hundred. It is the sign of the one who is in their sound; it is the Father."[106] Even if the last sentence remains enigmatic, the interpretation of the parable manifests a strong ecclesiological component. It is as much the fate of the whole community that is at stake as the destiny of a single soul.

Should we dismiss this interpretation of the Lukan parable? I would hesitate, because it seems probable that the choice by Jesus or Q of 99 was not accidental in the original version and that the joy of the shepherd relied on the well-being of his flock as much as on the recovery of the lost sheep. I would also – to take another example – ascribe a symbolic value to the number of "leftover" baskets of bread in both feeding miracles. The 12 baskets of the first story direct the attention to the pastoral responsibility of a church placed under the leadership of the Twelve,

---

[104] See H. Gericke, "Zahlbegriff," *Lexikon der alten Welt* (ed. Carl Andresen et al.; Zurich: Artemis, 1965) 3297; R. Van Compernolle, "Zahlensysteme," ibid., 3298–302; K. Vogel, "Zahlenmystik," ibid., 3297–98; Antonio Quacquarelli, "Nombres, Symbolique," *Dictionnaire encyclopédique du christianisme ancien*, 2:1761–62, who writes in particular: "C'est pourquoi il faut se référer à des méthodes et à des usages différents des nôtres pour comprendre le passé" (1761).

[105] Juvenal, *Satire* 10.247–50; quoted by Ifrah, *Histoire universelle des chiffres*, 1:139.

[106] *Gospel of Truth* (NHC I, 3 and XII, 2) 31.35–32.17 (trans. Harold Attridge and George W. MacRae in *The Nag Hammadi Library in English* [ed. James M. Robinson: 3d ed.; Leiden: Brill, 1988] 46). On this passage, see Paul-Hubert Poirier, "*L'Évangile de Verité*, Éphrem le Syrien et le comput digital," *REAug* 25 (1979) 27–34. See also Irenaeus, *Adv. haer.* 2.24.6.

while the seven baskets of the second story evoke the Church of the Hellenists and its organization of seven leaders.[107] Even if we, as modern readers, do not make sense of these numbers, other examples of numeric symbolic values, such as the two swords of Luke 22:38 and the 153 fish of John 21:11, certainly must have had a special significance for the first Christian audience.

Unity and diversity, unity and duality

For the Platonic tradition, as well as other traditions, unity is the mark of perfection and the remaining numbers are the mark of deficiency.[108] The loss of unity is perceived as negative. Paul participates in this admiration of unity, as the First Epistle to the Corinthians makes clear. The multiplicity of so-called Lords, false gods or demons, is a negative sign. Meanwhile, the one God[109] with the one Lord Jesus Christ (1 Cor 8:4–6) acts as a positive sign. Unity and communion should be among the perfections of the people of God. Any kind of quarrels (ἔριδες) or divisions (σχίσματα) is painful (1 Cor 1:10–11). The apostle Paul is driven by a dream of unity.[110] Subsequently, his disciple, the author of the Epistle to the Ephesians, elaborates a theology of unity with a virulent assault against plurality.[111] The redemption in Christ is nothing less than a restoration of unity, the victory over "the two," a fight against division present in any number other than one. Christ is "our peace," "he has made both groups into one" (ὁ ποιήσας τὰ ἀμφότερα ἕν) and overcome hate. Israel and the nations are now reconciled. Christ fought victoriously so "that he might create in himself one new humanity in place

---

[107] Mark 6:43 (κλάσματα δώδεκα κοφίνων πληρώματα) and Mark 8:20 (πόσων σπυρίδων πληρώματα κλασμάτων ἤρατε; καὶ λέγουσιν· ἑπτά).

[108] See Heinrich Dörrie, "Platon," in *Der Kleine Pauly. Lexikon der Antike* (Munich: Deutscher Taschenbuch, 1979) 4:897–98. We find a short digression on the monad (ἡ μονάς) in the *Corpus Hermeticum* 4.10–11. According to the *Corpus Hermeticum* 11.9, 11, God can only be one. More than one God would be against the notion of order. The *Treatise of the Regeneration* (*Corpus Hermeneuticum* 13) 18 contains a hymn to unity and totality. Another passage of another treatise, *Corpus Hermeticum* 16.3, mentions also that God is one and all.

[109] That God is unique is also underlined by *The Tripartite Tractate* (NHC I, 5) 51.10: "The Father is a single one, like a number, for he is the first one and the one who is only himself." The unity itself is celebrated in *The Gospel of Truth* (NHC I, 3 and XII, 2) 24.28–25.20: "It is within Unity that each one will attain himself; within knowledge he will purify himself from multiplicity into Unity, consuming matter within himself like fire, and darkness by light, death by life" (25.10–19). In the *Gospel of Philip* (NHC II, 3) 63.25–30: "The lord went into the dye works of Levi. He took seventy-two different colors and threw them into the vat. He took them out all white. And he said, 'Even so has the son of man come [as] a dyer.'"

[110] See Margaret M. Mitchell, *Paul and the Rhetoric of Reconciliation: An Exegetical Investigation of the Language and Composition of 1 Corinthians* (Tübingen: Mohr Siebeck, 1991) 68–70, 202–6.

[111] One can read the chapter of William James on unity and plurality: see William James, *Pragmatism* (Cambridge, Mass.: Harvard University Press, 1975) 63–80.

of the two" (ἵνα τοὺς δύο κτίσῃ ἐν αὐτῷ εἰς ἕνα καινὸν ἄνθρωπον, Eph 2:14–15).[112] The influence of such a theology of unity is discernible, later, in the writings of Ignatius of Antioch. Christ is the "one physician" (εἷς ἰατρός ἐστιν, Ign. *Eph.* 7.2), the "one teacher" (εἷς οὖν διδάσκαλος, Ign. *Eph.* 15.1). Christians, as members of the body, and Christ, as its head, live in unity (ἕνωσις, Ign. *Trall.* 11.2). Thus the believer must be "one" and possess an undivided heart (Ign. *Trall.* 13.2). The unavoidable problem of a perceived duality in God, as Father and Son, is overcome by an insistence on their perfect unity, as in the Gospel of John (John 5:19–23; 10:30; 17:11, 21–23): Father and Son are one (ἡνωμένος ὤν, "being united," Ign. *Magn.* 7.1). The subject of unity[113] and the subsequent discounting of the perceived duality is also present in Ign. *Phld.* 3.2 and 9.1.[114]

The number two, however, is not exclusively the beginning of a disastrous plurality: it can also represent a companion to the "one."[115] Two can be the basis of harmony and concord: see the Jesus of the Synoptic tradition emphasizing the two major commands (Mark 12:28–34 par.; Luke 10:25–29); see the rule that a testimony receives its power from the presence of two witnesses (Deut 19:15; Matt 18:16; Rev 11:3); see the disciples who are sent two by two (δύο δύο, Mark 6:8); see the two sides of the coin in Paul's argument, the reconciliation in Christ and the ministry of that reconciliation, the work of Christ on one side and the apostolic witness on the other (ἡ καταλλαγή and ἡ διακονία τῆς καταλλαγῆς, 2 Cor 5:18–21);[116] see the two virtues celebrated by Ignatius in his letter to the Ephesians, "faith" and "love." The first is the beginning, the second the end: τὰ δὲ δύο ἐν ἑνότητι γενόμενα θεός ἐστιν, "when the two are joined together in unity it is God" (Ign. *Eph.* 14.2).[117]

---

[112] From the one God, from the Father (πατήρ), every family (πατριά) draws its name, Eph 3:14.

[113] This topic of unity is also important for the author of *1 Clement*, who attacks the unhealthy divisions and claims: "Or have we not one God, and one Christ, and one Spirit of grace poured out upon us? And is there not one calling in Christ?" (*1 Clem.* 46.6). It is also present in *The Shepherd* of Hermas: avoid the divisions (διχοστασίαι) because they could take life away from you (Herm. *Vis.* 3.9.9). See finally Polycarp, *Phil.* 11.1.

[114] One is reminded of the saying: "No slave can serve two masters; for a slave will either hate the one and love the other, or be devoted to the one and despise the other. You cannot serve God and wealth" (Luke 16:13 par.; *Gos. Thom.* 47); see also *Gos. Thom.* 22 (make one out of two) and 61 (one is saved, one is lost). The *Gospel of Thomas* likes to use numbers to express a religious thought: see the criticism of the three gods in *Gos. Thom.* 30 and the praise of the "solitary" (*Gos. Thom.* 75). See finally *Did.* 1.1: of the two ways, only one is good.

[115] Is this positive valuation of the number two a reminiscence of the function of the dual? "The dual is chiefly employed of two persons or things which, by nature or association, form a pair," writes Herbert Weir Smyth, *Greek Grammar* (rev. Gordon M. Messing; Cambridge, Mass.: Harvard University Press, 1984) §999.

[116] See *1 Clem.* 42: Christ from God, the apostles from Christ, both (ἀμφότερα) from God.

[117] Trans. Kirsopp Lake, *The Apostolic Fathers* (2 vols.; LCL; London: Heinemann, 1919) 1:189. In *Gos. Thom.* 11 and 22 the risk of transforming unity into duality is criticized and the goal is to transform the two into one. See in Polycarp, *Phil.* 10.1, a portion of the letter preserved only in Latin, the expression *in veritate sociati*, "joined together in the truth." See finally the

In his monograph on the early Christian creeds Oscar Cullmann makes a simple statement: it is not until the middle of the second century C.E., more precisely in Justin Martyr, that we find a confession of faith in *three* parts.[118] The New Testament period, *grosso modo* in the first century, is still marked by a Christian creed in two articles, a short one devoted to the Father (in a Jewish environment there was not much to add concerning God) and a long one on the Son (the great innovation, the *skandalon*). Actually, this 'heresy' from a Jewish point of view could build upon some marginal Jewish texts that insist on a split inside the divinity and distinguish between an external and an internal aspect in God, between the hidden God and some hypostazised divine qualities (Logos, Wisdom, Spirit. Name), or between YHWH and the "lesser YHWH."[119]

From the beginning of the Jesus movement, however, the duality of Father-Son was not a closed, homeostatic relationship. One can see it already in the archaic saying from Q: "No one knows who the Son is except the Father, or who the Father is except the Son and anyone to whom the Son chooses to reveal him" (Luke 10:22 par.). The reciprocity is not a rigid one, and the love between the two persons does not end in an exclusive narrowness, but opens to an inclusive invitation to those chosen by the Son. In the Matthean community as well as in the very different Pauline congregations the Spirit is soon added to the schema, and with the Spirit human participation is added to the divine economy: "Go therefore and make disciples of all nations, baptizing them in the name of the Father and of the Son and of the Holy Spirit" (Matt 28:19).[120] "The grace of the Lord Jesus Christ, the love of God, and the communion of the Holy Spirit be with all of you" (2 Cor 13:33).[121]

---

early Christian distinction between the first and the second Testament; François Bovon, *L'Évangile et l'apôtre. Le Christ inséparable de ses témoins* (Aubonne [Switzerland]: Moulin, 1993).

[118] Oscar Cullmann, *Les premières confessions de foi chrétiennes* (Cahiers de la Revue d'histoire et de philosophie religieuses 30; Paris: Presses Universitaires de France, 1948) 27–38; see Justin Martyr, *1 Apol.* 13.

[119] Such is the way Metatron is called in *3 Enoch* 12.5.

[120] I am aware that according to certain exegetes this Matthean formulation is considered inauthentic and an interpolation; see Erich Klostermann, *Das Matthäusevangelium* (HNT 4; Tübingen: Mohr Siebeck, 1927) 232. See however *Did.* 7.3: "Pour water three times on the head 'in the name of the Father, Son and Holy Spirit.'"

[121] See Gerhard Delling, "τρεῖς, τρίς, τρίτος," *TWNT* 8:215–25. Among texts insisting on "three," see the three Pauline theological virtues of faith, hope, and love (1 Cor 13:13); the division of the history of salvation in three periods by Luke; the three mysteries of Ignatius and the three signs of the *Didache* mentioned above at n. 96; the τρία γένη, the pagans, the Jews, and the Christians in Aristides, *Apologia* 2.1; the three virtues, faith, love, and works, mentioned in *The Apocryphon of James* (NHC I, 2) 8.12–14; the three Marys in *The Gospel of Philip* (NHC II, 3) 59.6–11; the division of history into three aeons (the first aeon is the aeon of the soul, the second is the aeon of the flesh, the third is the aeon that is to come) in *The Concept of Our Great Power* (NHC VI, 4) 38.5–48.13. See also in *Sibylline Oracles* 7.71–75, the three towers in which the mothers of God now live.

Conclusion

I would suggest in conclusion that the faith of the first Christians rejoiced in the salvific name of the Lord Jesus Christ (see Acts 4:12), but soon included the Spirit, first as a force, then as a person. With the Spirit a relationship was also established with the human community of believers. Called to preserve their memories of Jesus, to read the Scriptures of Israel, and to actualize the message in their life, these men and women, mostly Jews at the outset, realized the importance of names as a powerful and not artificial representation of an unseen reality. Trying to make sense of the creation around them, of history behind them, and of eschatology yet to come, they understood numbers to be signs, but, again, more than conventional signs, signs of a divine order and of a providential economy. Names and numbers are a gift from God that expresses an extralinguistic reality beyond what other words are capable of transmitting. This was culturally understood by early Jews and Christians. If we today fail to recognize the significance of names and numbers,[122] we neglect this extralinguistic reality and are vulnerable to losing a depth to our understanding of Scripture and deeper insights into its message.[123]

---

[122] If names and numbers are only conventional signs, if everything is prisoner of language, if there is no extralinguistic reality, then Christians are, to speak with Paul (1 Cor 15:19), the most miserable among humans.

[123] This paper is only a beginning and its author is happy to make his own the words of Origen (citation from the French translation as in n. 90 above): "Contentons-nous d'avoir seulement approché ces perspectives plutôt que de les expliquer et de les développer; pour ceux qui sont dans les meilleures dispositions ... il suffira qu'elles aient été indiquées et légèrement effleurées" (Origen, *Hom. Num.* 4.2.1).

The Ethics of the First Christians:
Between Memory and Oblivion

Introduction

It is now time for ethics.[1] *Doing* becomes a question of survival, or even salvation. Facing cynicism or resignation, it is important first to answer the question of reference: acting for what, or rather, for whom? From the answer to this question follows the possible term of doing: What is *to do* in his/her name? What is to be avoided or looked for? The glance then, through interdependence, mimesis, or critical comparison, becomes inquisitive toward the actions of other people. Finally, the ethic makes sense only in relation to the human condition, that is to say, with the inscription in time of each person's life.

It is in pursuing this quadruple inquiry that I will try to present the moral engagement of the first Christians, at the intersection of their historical ethos and their scriptural ethic. The first part, being relative to the normative reference, will shed light on a doctrinal shift that is often neglected. The second part, being closer to ethos, will examine the central question: τί ποιήσωμεν, "What shall we do?" The third will introduce the notion of the variety of situations, options, personal charisma, and various trends within early Christianity. The fourth will finally deal with the temporality that determines every life, even in its Christian bounty.

---

[1] It is with emotion that I dedicate this article to Pierre Bonnard who has rendered indispensable biblical studies, who has initiated Christians to a critical reading of Scripture and encouraged students in their exegetical research. Personally, I thank him for his constant support since my first article in the *Revue de Théologie et de Philosophie* up to the current drafting of my commentary on the Gospel of Luke. I present these pages to him all the more readily as they were intended, in first draft, publicly before an audience of the town of Lausanne, his town and mine. Beside other contributions, they were indeed presented to the Lausannois public at the Journée théologique organized by the Faculty of Theology, Thursday, May 10, 1990. The reader will find a bibliography on the ethics of the New Testament in this volume; see pp. 62–63 below.

I. Ethical Shifts

Going from the Hebrew Bible to the New Testament is certainly to make a doc-trinal shift. But it is also, from the promise to accomplishment, to run the risk of an ethical shift.

To bring out this change that the ongoing reminder of the Law obscures,[2] an observation has to be made that is as obvious as it is ignored. Considering that the Torah used to be the source and the norm of ethics as much as of life, Jesus, so utterly Jewish, referred to it very rarely when he suggested his ethics of the King-dom. Indeed, he knew the Torah since he recalled its normative value to those who wanted to hear it,[3] but to a new situation there is a new ethic. In his eyes, the irruption of the Kingdom destabilizes the power of the Law. Jesus often devel-oped his eschatological and ethical program without any reference to Scripture. The wisdom he suggests is not hostile to the commandments of Moses, but it is out of step with them. When he mentions the requirement of the Law, it is to substitute a prior and different requirement for it: that of the will of God.[4] Indeed, anyone who establishes a living relation to the past and to tradition carefully avoids simply repeating the creed or the commandments. But Jesus went further. He said something different from Moses: for instance, he said that it is important to follow him and not content oneself with obeying rules. He invites everyone to quit everything and bear everything. To be generous and sympathetic was not enough. The Spirit of God, alive again in those decisive and last moments, in-spired Jesus, who stated a moral of the Kingdom altogether in harmony with the Law and in discrepancy with it:[5] a moral that forgets and rethinks.

A similar discrepancy, also surprising, is shown on the path that leads from Jesus to the first Christians. Indeed, scholars indicate at that moment cases of re-lapse in legalism,[6] but it is especially the new shifts that are brought to light. The apostle Paul, as we know, declared an ethic of imitation.[7] But he chose this orien-tation without resorting to moral teaching of Jesus. The presence of the synoptic tradition is as discrete in the Pauline letters as the Mosaic edicts are in the sayings of Jesus. The μίμησις, "imitation," certainly does not mean the rigorous enforce-

---

[2] I am obviously influenced by my own denominational tradition, the reformed tradition.

[3] See for example Mark 10:17–22 par.; Luke 10:25–28.

[4] In connection to marriage, see Mark 10:2–12 par.

[5] See Charles H. Dodd, *Gospel and Law: The Relation of Faith and Ethics in Early Christi-anity* (Cambridge: Cambridge University Press, 1951) 64–83; Wolfgang Schrage, *Ethik des Neuen Testaments* (2d ed.; NTD Ergänzungsreihe 4; Göttingen: Vandenhoeck & Ruprecht, 1989) 45–72.

[6] See Siegfried Schulz, *Q. Die Spruchquelle der Evangelisten* (Zurich: Theologischer Verlag, 1972) 481–89; François Vouga, *Jésus et la Loi selon la tradition synoptique* (MdB; Geneva: Labor et Fides, 1988) 297–301.

[7] See Hans Dieter Betz, *Nachfolge und Nachahmung Jesu Christi im Neuen Testament* (BHT 37; Tübingen: Mohr Siebeck, 1967).

ment of the sayings of Jesus, keenly memorized, nor the faithful imitation of his gestures, but the inner-felt participation in the lot of Jesus Christ, his passion and his resurrection. The criticism of the Law that is expressed in Chapter 3 of the letter to the Philippians,[8] the attack on circumcision and the rejection of justification through works, which this criticism contains, does not necessarily result in an autonomy or anarchist pretension, but in an affective and cognitive attachment to a person, to "Jesus Christ, *my* Lord" (Phil 3:8).

What can we derive from these successive shifts? They reflect the sudden eschatological appearance of the Spirit that jeopardizes the letter, there expressing the communion with Christ, who liberates, and the presence of love, which enables everything. These shifts imply an ethical concentration, pinpointing in the Law what is most important, namely, the double commandment of love. They correspond to a new perception of observance in its variegated radicalism: to the love of one's neighbor is indeed added the love for one's enemies.[9] Finally, they express a reversal of doing and being. The Gospel observance stems from the new being that Christ has assumed, and then vivified in us. It stops being the enervating activity of the person who wants to mould himself/herself by what he/she does, facing a God conceived as judge. Therefore it is freedom, that is to say, oblivion and memory.

These shifts, new elaborations in the domain of ethics, were unavoidable and welcome because of the passing of time and the unexpected situations that would come up, and also because of the time of God that would draw to its end in offering room for free decisions. As history would have it, so would especially eschatology and pneumatology.[10]

II. The Question of Doing

Despite God's gift, forgiveness through Christ, and Spirit spreading in the hearts, Christianity has not erased the question of ethics. Because of eschatological reservation (the resurrection of the body has not yet taken place), because of the image we have of God (even if he gives, he still commands us), and because of the Christian anthropology (children of God, the believers are not reduced to child-

---

[8] See François Bovon, "L'homme nouveau et la loi chez l'apôtre Paul," in *Die Mitte des Neuen Testaments. Einheit und Vielfalt neutestamentlicher Theologie. Festschrift für Eduard Schweizer* (ed. Ulrich Luz and Hans Weder; Göttingen: Vandenhoeck & Ruprecht, 1983) 22–33.

[9] See Mark 12:28–34 par.; Matt 5:43–48 par. The *Didache* articulates the two commandments explicitly, making the love for one's enemies the actualizing interpretation of the love for one's neighbor (*Did.* 1.2–3).

[10] It is the same theme of fidelity to the normative heritage and of the eschatological and christological innovation that 1 John expresses, when it speaks about the commandment at the same time old and new (1 John 2:7–8; see 2 John 5–6); see Pierre Bonnard, *Les Épîtres johanniques* (CNT, 2d series, 13c; Geneva: Labor et Fides, 1983) 42–43.

like behavior), the question of *doing* is still being asked. The criticism of works and the assertion of a justice rooted in God do not cast to oblivion the philosophical and practical Jewish and Greek question of the τί ποιήσωμεν, "What shall we do?" This question is seen at the beginning of the Gospel, on the lips of those who were listening to John the Baptist (Luke 3:10–14) and at the beginning of the Acts of the Apostles, in the mouths of the listeners of Peter (Acts 2:37). It also comes up in several monologues that Luke puts in some parables of his own (for instance Luke 12:17: τί ποιήσω, "What will I do?," asks the rich man of the parable).[11]

At the risk of simplification, I would say that the *doing* of believers concerns especially their goods and their relations. With the help of a few examples, I will examine the solutions, often subtle, that the first Christian writings give to these problems.

1. The Goods of the World

Three biblical passages help elucidate: the assertions of Paul relating to the power of Christians over all things (1 Cor 3:21–23), those necessary criticisms of human goods (1 Cor 7:29–31), and the sayings of Jesus about the treasure in heaven (Matt 6:19–21).

A subtle and nuanced solution, because on one hand, "the earth is the Lord's, and everything in it" (1 Cor 10:26, quoting Ps 24:1): God is the creator and, thanks to Christ, took back creation. There is, therefore, in faith a possible valorization of goods, body, language, nature, work, and pleasure. God offers to believers a happy use of these real things, to begin with the bread that is broken in communion, and the wine that is poured on this occasion.[12]

On the other hand, however, Christians do not forget that Satan is still active and that there is nothing in common between Christ and Belial (2 Cor 6:15). The world is still somehow in the power of God's opponents, "princes of this world" (1 Cor 2:8), "the God of this world" (2 Cor 4:4).[13] It is waiting for the promised liberation, not yet received (Rom 8:19–21). This account stirs up mistrust inside believers who have to criticize material things of this world and regard everything as a loss (Phil 3:8), belittling and judging, refusing to conform to the world (Rom 12:2). Thus, it is the very goods that, as stated earlier, are gifts from God that may become, and often times are, the very instruments of Satan.

---

[11] See Bernhard Heininger, *Metaphorik, Erzählstruktur und szenisch-dramatische Gestaltung in den Sondergutgleichnissen bei Lukas* (NTAbh n.s. 24; Münster: Aschendorff, 1991). This author relies on the interior dialogue present in several Lukan parables and the question of "doing" to the monologues of the ancient novel and the new comedy.

[12] The film the *Feast of Babette* by Gabriel Axel is the happy expression of this evangelic rediscovery of worldly goods.

[13] The Greek words are τοῦ αἰῶνος τούτου, lit., "of this time," "of this aeon," which the *Traduction Œcuménique de la Bible* translates twice with "de ce monde," "of this world."

To live out Christian freedom means living within a faith shifting toward the kingdom, to be placed at the fork in the road – free to choose between usage and refusal, the renouncement ("I know how to live in poverty" Phil 4:12)[14] and grateful usage ("and in abundance" Phil 4:12). These decisions and attitudes that ensue do not depend only on goods; they depend also on the people called for making decisions and to the historical situations within which choices have to be made. For example, the same portion of meat may be eaten if no one is offended; but it must not be eaten if the gesture results in the fall of a weak brother (1 Cor 8:13). That which enables the person to choose is not first the knowledge of Jesus' instructions or Paul's prescriptions, even if the Torah, the Lord, and the Apostle direct the mind toward an attitude of faith, love, obedience, freedom, and hope. It is mainly a believer's judgment that is decisive,[15] a faithful person who knows he/she is accompanied by Christ and in whom dwells the Spirit. The ἐπιταγή ("order") of the Lord indicates forbidden zones (1 Cor 7:10 and 25); the γνώμη ("opinion") of the apostle in areas not re-commanded (1 Cor 7:25); the presence of the Spirit enables one to make a decision: "Those who are spiritual discern all things, and they are themselves subject to no one else's scrutiny"(1 Cor 2:15); "whether Paul or Apollos or Cephas or the world or life or death or the present or the future – all belong to you, and you belong to Christ, and Christ belongs to God" (1 Cor 3:22–23).[16]

It is in this perspective that one has to read the heart of 1 Corinthians 7, namely, 1 Cor 7:29–31, a passage that adds an eschatological dimension: "I mean, brothers and sisters, the appointed time has grown short; from now on, let even those who have wives be as though they had none, and those who mourn as though they were not mourning, and those who rejoice as though they were not rejoicing, and those who buy as though they had no possessions, and those who deal with the world as though they had no dealings with it. For the present form of this world is passing away" (NRSV). This excerpt, as is often the case with the apostle Paul, theologically deepens the standard Christian position. In its form, the Pauline text is not without parallel: 4 Esdras 16:40–45 (= 6 Esdras)[17] presents an apocalyptic perspective that is not exactly as that of Paul. For the apocalyptician, it is

---

[14] Among the texts relating to renouncement, I retain Luke 12:33–34 par.; 14:33; Gal 6:14.

[15] See κρίνω, "to judge" (1 Cor 11:13), ἀνακρίνω, "to examine" (1 Cor 2:14–15), διακρίνω, "to distinguish" (1 Cor 11:31), δοκιμάζω, "to test" (Rom 12:2). See Pierre Bonnard, "Le discernement de la volonté de Dieu dans le christianisme naissant (1960)," in *Anamnesis. Recherches sur le Nouveau Testament* (Cahiers *RTP* 3; Geneva-Lausanne-Neuchâtel: Revue de théologie et de philosophie, 1980) 43–50.

[16] On these passages, see Christophe Senft, *La première Épître de saint Paul aux Corinthiens* (2d ed.; CNT, 2d series, 7; Geneva: Labor et Fides, 1990), ad loc.

[17] "Hear my words, O my people; prepare for battle, and in the midst of the calamites be like strangers on the earth. Let him that sells be like one who will flee; let him that buys be like one who will lose; let him that does business be like one who will not make a profit; and let him that builds a house be like one who will not live in it; let him that sows be like one who will not reap; so also him that prunes the vines, like one who will not gather the grapes; them that marry, like

necessary to be prepared for the final struggle rather than attending to one's own affairs. Epictetus[18] does not ignore such a manner of speaking either; it is however an invitation to withdraw into oneself, into an ataraxic state, through indifference toward external goods that slip out of our control. For the apostle, as for the first Christians, the work of Christ has already taken place (contrary to Jewish apocalyptic) and it is the will of God and not one's own (contrary to Stoicism) that presents one this distance from earthly goods. Christians therefore live while regarding the world in sympathy, but from a distance. They are no longer obsessed by goods and other material things. They still *have*, but as no longer or not having, for they already *have* Christ, while not having him yet. They know to renounce or to be detached, for another good, a more precious one, belongs to them and another place awaits them.[19] In a simpler and more vivid way, it is exactly what Jesus asked of his disciples: "Do not store up for yourselves treasures on earth, where moth and rust consume and where thieves break in and steal; but store up for yourselves treasures in heaven, where neither moth nor rust consumes and where thieves do not break in and steal. For where your treasure is, there your heart will be also" (Matt 6:19–21, NRSV).[20]

To conclude this section: as σάρξ ("flesh") takes pleasure in the goods of the world, they are devalued; but as the eschatological πνεῦμα ("Spirit") rediscovers them, they can be appreciated.

2. Relation to others

Considering human relations, we notice that the New Testament, following in the manner of Israel distinguishing itself from the nations, separates Christians from others, without enmity but with clear-sightedness. The parables as much as the letters distinguish Christians, separating "those from within" (οἱ ἔσω) from the rest of humanity, "those from the outside" (οἱ ἔξω).[21]

Indeed, "those from within," the members of the new covenant, unlike Judaism, are no longer inside the community through birth, but through adoption, faith, baptism, and new birth. The distinction between two groups is still maintained – a binary structure of humanity, corresponding to the design of God, to

---

those who will have no children; and them that do not marry, like those that are widowed" (trans. Bruce M. Metzger, in *OTP* 1:558).

[18] Epictetus, *Discourses* 3.22.67–76; 4.7.5.

[19] See Gottfried Hierzenberger, *Weltbewertung bei Paulus nach 1 Kor 7,29–31. Eine exegetisch-kerygmatische Studie* (KBANT; Düsseldorf: Patmos-Verlag, 1967); see Senft, *La première Épître de saint Paul aux Corinthiens*, 101–3; Schrage, *Ethik des Neuen Testaments*, 125, 186.

[20] On this passage, see Pierre Bonnard, *L'Évangile selon saint Matthieu* (2d ed.; CNT, 2d series, 1; Geneva: Labor et Fides, 1982) 89–90, 430.

[21] See Mark 4:11; 1 Cor 5:12–13; 1 Thess 4:12; Matt 13:11; Luke 8:10; 1 Thess 3:12; 4:13; 5:15; 1 Cor 1:18; 6:1–11; 14:22–25; Phil 1:28; Rom 9:22–24.

his salvific universal will that started the eschatological ingathering of the Church, the first liberated zone.[22]

How do Christians consider those who are outside? For them, they are bogged down people. Everyone, Jews as well as Pagans, might have lived in communion with God, thanks to the Law for some and conscience for others.[23] But this potentiality was hushed up. Whatever they may say, those human beings do not lead an independent life. They are subject to cosmic forces that keep them enslaved (powers, thrones, and dominions).[24]

In regard to the Christian communities, "those from the outside" face a double presence, that of Christian preaching and that of the testimony of love. Despite their blindness, they cannot remain indifferent. Such is the opinion of Christians who will invite them to a personal judgment, a stand.

From the Christian point of view, let us move to the Christian gesture toward "those from the outside." The apostle Paul, as an example, feels sent toward the others. Even if the work of salvation in Jesus Christ is complete and enough, it must reach all humans and be proclaimed to them. The sending (Rom 10:15) is the pneumatic and ethical extension of the work of Christ. The movement of the Church toward the others is not an optional activity, but a work required by God, just like the death and the resurrection of Christ.

The image of the "door" illustrates this example. To our surprise, it is not applied to the Church whose door pagans would have to go through, but to the world in which the believers, sent by God, have to enter (1 Cor 16:9). Besides, this door does not open by a motion of our hand, but through the Lord himself (2 Cor 2:12). The responsibility of believers is to pass through the door.

Another image draws our attention: that of the "debt." Apostolic work brings the believer closer to the other. It is not a gesture of good will; it is a duty, the payment of a debt: "I am under obligation (ὀφειλέτης εἰμί, lit., "I am a debtor")," writes Paul, "both to Greeks and to barbarians, both to the wise and to the foolish" (Rom 1:14).

Paul is therefore struck by the idea that there is something to offer, to share. His goal is to lead all pagans to the obedience of faith (see Rom 1:5 and 15:18); to "win" them (κερδαίνω) for the Gospel (1 Cor 9:19–23); to "convince" them (πείθω) (2 Cor 5:11); to turn them toward the Lord (2 Cor 3:16); to "save a few of them surely" (1 Cor 9:22).

This is an ambitious program of action, in line with God's intention. The faith that the apostle hopes to awaken certainly does not represent an addition affixed to the personality of the other, a supplement of the soul; but it is tantamount to a transformation of the other. The function he fulfills is defined, in a daring meta-

---

[22] The election is only a temporary bias. It should not therefore lead to a feeling of superiority on behalf of the elect.

[23] See Rom 1:18–2:29.

[24] See Rom 8:38; 1 Cor 15:24; Eph 1:21; 2:2; 3:10; Col 1:16; 2:10, 15; 1 Pet 3:22.

phor by Paul, as a priestly function. He regards himself indeed as a priest of Jesus Christ (λειτουργός, "minister of a cult"; ἱερουγῶ, "fulfill priestly and sacred functions") among the nations, in order for them to become an "offering" (προσφορά) that is pleasing and sanctified by the Spirit (Rom 15:16).

Word and gesture can achieve this task. Preaching and presence in the world; such were already the tools for Jesus in the Gospels,[25] such is the double ministry in Acts (Acts 6:1–6); the binary structure of the Christian religion, *verbum* and *res.*

There are still two comparisons that are going to facilitate the understanding of this loving and active presence of Christians in the world, that of the "torch" and that of the "fragrance." In a sentence that attests some knowledge of the teaching of Jesus,[26] the apostle suggests this to the Philippians: "Do all things without murmuring and arguing, so that you may be blameless and innocent, children of God without blemish in the midst of a crooked and perverse generation, in which you shine like stars (φωστῆρες) in the world, holding fast the word of life (λόγον ζωῆς ἐπέχοντες)" (Phil 2:14–16, NRSV, modified at v. 16). It is appropriate first to note the separation between Christians and the world; then the bringing together of gesture and the word, the image of the "flaming torch" that conjures up darkness, and finally the hope to lead other lives to eternity.[27]

The second image is that of the "fragrance" – not the smell of flowers that beautifies the environment or conveys a liking, but a smell that is even more pervasive: "But thanks be to God, who in Christ always leads us in triumphal procession, and through us spreads in every place the fragrance that comes from knowing him. For we are the aroma of Christ to God among those who are being saved and among those who are perishing; to the one a fragrance from death to death, to the other a fragrance from life to life (ἐκ ζωῆς εἰς ζωήν)" (2 Cor 2:14–16).

Considering a paradox will enable us to go further in the analysis of this ethic. The faithfulness to the Gospel forbids to "please" humankind (Gal 1:10–11 and 1 Thess 2:4), for this would be to justify them in their sins – as it were, howling with the wolves. But it is not about judging them ("For what have I to do with judging (κρίνειν) those outside?," 1 Cor 5:12). They have to be loved: "And may the Lord make you increase and abound in love for one another (εἰς ἀλλήλους) and for all (καὶ εἰς πάντας), just as we abound in love for you" (1 Thess 3:12). This tie of love that unites the members of the body of Christ therefore links the believer to the non-believer as well; hence an attitude that consists in pleasing others: "Give no offense to Jews or to Greeks or to the church of God, just as I try to please every-

---

[25] Luke understood this well, as it is attested in the summary he gives on the work of Jesus at the beginning of the book of Acts of the Apostles: "In the first book, Theophilus, I wrote about all that Jesus did and taught (ποιεῖν τε καὶ διδάσκειν)" (Acts 1:1).

[26] See ὑμεῖς ἐστε τὸ φῶς τοῦ κόσμου, "You are the light of the world" (Matt 5:14).

[27] On these verses, see the fine commentary of Pierre Bonnard, *L'Épître de saint Paul aux Philippiens* (CNT 10; Neuchâtel-Paris: Delachaux & Niestlé, 1950) 51–52.

one in everything I do (καθὼς κἀγὼ πάντα πᾶσιν ἀρέσκω), not seeking my own advantage, but that of many, so that they may be saved" (1 Cor 10:32–33).[28]

So, do we have to please or not to please? The paradox is only superficial, for the Christian attitude is refusing to please in the satisfaction of the σάρξ ("flesh") of the neighbor, but accepting to please, through stewardship and love, the genuine being of the other, who is never completely hidden by evil.[29]

This attitude of believers corresponds to the very existence of Christ, that is to say, the taking on of the human condition that excludes sin – becoming Greek with the Greeks and Jewish with the Jews (1 Cor 9:19–23). Is this not what Christ did when he gave up his divine condition to fulfill that of humankind before losing his life in order for humans to retrieve it (Phil 2:5–11)?

III. Variety and Pluralism

If unity is the hallmark of the divine, plurality is a sign of humanity and not necessarily of evil. The same community or the same apostle meets various situations, for the good reason that one is not yet in the Kingdom of God. And, normally in all cases, the response to these various situations is a variety of attitudes. Thus, within the Pauline trajectory,[30] the Christian movement of origins that is best known, we meet the attitude of the apostle himself, under the aegis of the *justice* of God;[31] he must defend his apostolate and make his own apology with a tenacious resolve. In Luke, one of his disciples of the following generation, we see the atmosphere as less tense and the horizon more open. From the notion of the design of God[32] stems a missionary ethic in which persuasion through speech or dialogue is the main expression of the love of one's neighbor and faithfulness to God. Ignatius of Antioch, another disciple of the apostle, at the beginning of the second century, comes up against the new situation of persecution. Leaning on

---

[28] See Gerhard Schneider, "ἀρέσκω," "zu Gefallen sein," "gefallen," in *Exegetisches Wörterbuch zum Neuen Testament* (eds. Horst Balz and Gerhard Schneider; 3 vols.; Stuttgart: Kohlhammer, 1980–1983) 1:363–64. The same paradox is found concerning the verb πείθω, "to persuade," mentioned above. In 2 Cor 5:11, it is taken in a positive sense of successful proclamation of the Gospel; in Gal 1:10, in a negative sense of bad rhetoric.

[29] Structurally this relation to the others corresponds to that expressed by the famous ὡς μή ("as though ... not") of 1 Cor 7:29–31, analyzed above.

[30] For the Johannine trajectory, see Jean-Daniel Kaestli, Jean-Michel Poffet, and Jean Zumstein, eds., *La communauté johannique et son histoire. La trajectoire de l'évangile de Jean aux deux premiers siècles* (MdB 20; Geneva: Labor et Fides, 1990).

[31] See Pierre Bonnard, *L'Épître de saint Paul aux Galates* (2d ed.; CNT 9; Neuchâtel: Delachaux & Niestlé, 1972) 174: the index provides at this place references to the pages where the author analyzes the Pauline concept of "righteousness of God." See also idem, "La justice de Dieu et l'histoire," *ETR* 43 (1968) 61–68; reprinted in idem, *Anamnesis*, 169–76.

[32] See Luke 7:30; Acts 2:23; 4:28; 13:36; 20:27. On ἡ βουλὴ τοῦ θεοῦ, see Jacques Dupont, *Le discours de Milet, testament pastoral de saint Paul (Actes 20,18–36)* (LD 32; Paris: Cerf, 1962) 119–25, who prefers to translate this expression with "will of God," "deliberate will of God."

the will of God,[33] he meditates, alone, and then in the community, on the theme of suffering. This is the same school, the same inspiration, the memory of the same tradition, but with diverse attitudes because of social contexts, real situations, and different personalities.

As universal validity of the sole and unique Gospel does not erase differences, the apostle Paul allows and recommends variety and complementary identity of people and charisma. The fable of the body and members that Livy puts on the lips of the old Menenius Agrippa,[34] Paul applies to the believers of a same community (1 Cor 12:12–31). There is diversity of destiny, but also of gifts and responsibility. A diversity of options and attitudes: indeed it is about not disturbing the weakest brother,[35] but not enslaving one's own freedom either. The "already" of the work of Christ and the "already" of the ascribed righteousness propels each believer into the sphere of freedom, personal destiny, and chosen ethics. This emphasis, put on legitimate difference, is of course counterbalanced, because of the famous eschatological reservation, by calls to unity. Is there not the same Spirit, the same Lord, and the same God (1 Cor 12:4–6)? The result of this is the same body. The different kinds of freedom have to be combined. Because of the "not yet," that is to say, our humanity waiting for resurrection, protective rules have to be imposed. They become the pragmatic and lasting expression of mutual love. The Church Fathers will choose, in singing the harmony of the Gospels, musical images to describe the harmony between the Churches.[36]

The sound of various instruments is not always harmonious. Regarding the second century, I have spoken elsewhere[37] of the competing ethics. To simplify, I have kept in mind three and, to strike the imagination, I named them the ethic of the *crypt*, the ethic of the *way*, and the ethic of the *balcony*. That of the *crypt* is based on Paul and regards Christianity as a redemption that calls the heart and offers a new way of living. That of the *way* continues the teaching of Jesus and advocates the will; it places salvation at the end of our efforts. That of the *balcony* is a rereading of the Gospel of John that gives to understanding some distance toward the world and enables the contemplation of spiritual realities. Those ethics, so incompatible, correspond to three trends of antique Christianity: Christianity that became the Great Church, the various forms of Jewish-Christianity, and the numerous Gnostic conventicles.

We find the same variety of Christian movements in the first century. Exegetes consent today, even if they disagree on the number or on the identity of these

---

[33] See Ignatius of Antioch, *Eph.* 4.1; *Trall.* 1.1; *Rom.* 1.1; *Phld.* inscr.; *Smyrn.* 1.1; 11.1; *Pol.* 8.1.

[34] Livy, *Ab urbe condita libri* 2.32.

[35] See 1 Cor 8:13.

[36] See Ignatius of Antioch, *Eph.* 4.1. On the harmony that reigns between the Gospels, see Eusebius of Caesarea, *Hist. eccl.* 6.31.3.

[37] See below in this volume, pp. 53–56 .

groups.[38] Personally, I distinguish the mother community of Jerusalem around the Twelve; the movement of the Hellenists led by the seven who founded the community at Antioch; the family of Jesus under the leadership of James, the brother of the Lord; the circle of the beloved disciple, conveyer of the Johannine traditions; and the wandering preachers to whom we owe the collection of the sayings of Jesus (the Source of the *Logia*, Q); not to mention the obscure origins of Christianity in Galilee, in Eastern Syria, and in Egypt.

Contrary to the second century, where competition leads to the progressive rejection of the other, the first Christian century, also characterized by variety, does not yield to the ideology of the hostile brothers. If plurality is a given, the unity of the Church becomes an objective, a communal task to which each one pitches in. The New Testament is a witness to these exercises, strategies, and effort of mutual understanding, voluntary reconciliation, prayers for unity, and meetings of ecumenical goals.[39] At the core of the history of early Christianity, the Jerusalem Council (Galatians 2 and Acts 15) – against a background of deep differences in matters of doctrine and practice – comes to an agreement on the essence of belief and on the minimum of communal ethics. The work of God precedes human will; the pagans are invited to believe in Jesus Christ without necessarily becoming Jewish; the obedience to the Law consists from now on – and this concerns everyone – in welcoming one's neighbor and no longer complying with the observances for circumcision and the Sabbath. These are the summary results of this conference.

IV. Time

Everything is played in time:[40] the ethical and normative shift; the free and critical judgment before worldly goods, as well as before the establishment of human relations; the sudden appearance of diversity as much as the effort of communion. Christian doing, thinking, and saying: What shall we do or not do in time and of one's time? What shall we think, judge, or desire? Shall we live time in despair or hope, fear or serenity, shame or confidence? What shall we say, and what shall remain silenced?

---

[38] See François Vouga, *A l'aube du christianisme. Une surprenante diversité* (Aubonne: Éditions du Moulin, 1986). It is a reconstruction, among others, which corresponds only partially to mine.

[39] See François Bovon, "Israel, die Kirche und die Völker im lukanischen Doppelwerk," *TLZ* 108 (1983) 409–12; appeared in English translation in idem, *New Testament Traditions and Apocryphal Narratives* (trans. Jane Haapiseva-Hunter; Princeton Theological Monograph Series 36; Allison Park, Pa.: Pickwick Publications, 1995) 81–95, 209–13.

[40] See Paul Ricœur, *Temps et récit* (3 vols.; Paris: Seuil, 1983–1985) 1:85–129, who studies the bond that links the temporal character of existence to the activity of narration.

What the consciousness of time brings to these theological moments, to the shifting of the norm, to the critical judgment on doing, and to the comparison with the ethos of others, is a triple demand. That of living well the *moment*, first, in which everything is decided, in which everything is played out of anticipation; that of holding out in *duration*, where the engagement must be kept. And this is the great test, which was that of Israel and which became that of the first Christian communities. Standing there, where God seems no longer to interfere, where he is delayed. The ὑπομονή, "perseverance," made of memory and adaptation, faithfulness to tradition and inspired freedom, which follows πίστις, "faith," and completes it. At last, it is the awareness of the shortness of time which demands *haste*.

Is there another side than protestant tenacity, the virtue of the justified people, having received everything but possessing nothing yet?[41] Is it not sufficient to transfigure time with the orthodox, who are inhabited by the Holy Spirit?[42] Would it not be convenient to pass the time with Catholics who are reconciled with nature?[43] Do we really have to hurry up? Personally, to the "moment" of the theology of existence and to the "duration" of liberation theology, I will add another biblical component, "haste."[44] Like the characters in the Bible, Christians are in a hurry, not because they are late, but because they are ahead, because God placed them ahead of their time. They are hurried more because of God than because of time. When God intervenes, Abraham hastens (Gen 18:2, 6–7). When the angel conveys his message, Mary runs to her cousin Elizabeth (Luke 1:39). Running toward others, running away from the world (Are Christians not called the "fleers" in the letter to the Hebrews?).[45] Running mainly towards God: speaking of the Parousia, the first Christians compare this event with the arrival of an oriental prince in the city he intends to visit. In this occasion, the inhabitants – and such will be the movement of the Christians at the Parousia – ran to meet the Lord (εἰς ὑπάντησιν or εἰς ἀπάντησιν).[46] Such is the expected Christian at-

---

[41] See François Wendel, *Calvin. Sources et évolution de sa pensée religieuse* (EHPhR 41; Paris: Presses Universitaires de France, 1950) 185.

[42] See Olivier Clément, *Transfigurer le temps. Notes sur le temps à la lumière de la tradition orthodoxe* (Neuchâtel: Delachaux & Niestlé, 1959).

[43] See Alain Boureau, *La légende dorée. Le système narratif de Jacques de Voragine († 1298)* (Histoire; Paris: Cerf, 1984) 25–27.

[44] See Isabelle Chappuis-Juillard, *Le temps des rencontres. Quand Marie visite Elizabeth (Luc 1)* (Aubonne [Switzerland]: Moulin, 1991). David Daube, *The Sudden in the Scriptures* (Leiden: Brill, 1964), is interested more in suddenness of events than of haste which they could effect; but see pp. 72–75.

[45] Heb 6:18: οἱ καταφυγόντες; see Erich Grässer, *An die Hebräer. 1. Teilband (Hebr 1–6)* (EKKNT 17.1; Neukirchen-Vluyn/Zurich: Neukirchener Verlag, 1990) 382–83.

[46] See εἰς ἀπάντησιν, 1 Thess 4:17; Matt 25:6; εἰς ὑπάντησιν, Matt 25:1; Lucien Cerfaux, *Le Christ dans la théologie de saint Paul* (LD 6; Paris: Cerf, 1954) 36–37. The eschatology of Ignatius of Antioch is transformed in moving, through death, "to reach" (ἐπιτυγχάνω) God. See for example Ignatius of Antioch, *Eph.* 12.2; *Magn.* 14.1; *Trall.* 12.2; 13.3; *Rom.* 1.1–2; 2.1; 4.1; 5.3; 8.3; 9.2; *Smyrn.* 11.1; *Pol.* 2.3; 7.1; Théo Preiss, "La mystique de l'imitation du Christ et de

titude. It is not a disorganized haste, but a focused, willing, efficient, and credible activity of those who have a plan for life and want to achieve it for God and with others.[47]

l'unité chez Ignace d'Antioche," *RHPR* 18 (1938) 197–242; reprinted in idem, *La vie en Christ* (BT[N]; Neuchâtel-Paris: Delachaux & Niestlé, 1951) 7–45; Pierre Thomas Camelot, *Ignace d'Antioche. Polycarpe de Smyrne, Lettres. Martyre de Polycarpe. Texte grec, introduction, tra-duction et notes* (4th ed.; SC 10; Paris: Cerf, 1969) 34–36.

[47] As Bertrand Bouvier points out to me, there existed in Lebadea, today Livadia, in Boetia, close to the oracle of Trophonios, two sources from which the devotees would drink: the Source of Forgetfulness (Λήθη) and the Source of Memory (Μνημοσύνη). Memory and forgetfulness were significant anthropological categories in the eyes of the Greeks, as with the Jews, and later with the Christians. See Pausanias, *Description of Greece* 9.39.8 – and the Blue Guide!

Variety and Authority of the First Christian Ethics

This text has been written in the framework of the *Journées théologiques de la Compagnie des pasteurs et de la Faculté de théologie* at Geneva. It was presented on January 12, 1988. The theme of this meeting was the elaboration on today's Christian ethics, more particularly the link between the Bible and our contemporary decisions. Two current problems were addressed: that of the condition of women and that of AIDS, used as examples. In this program, a brief presentation on the ethics of the New Testament has been assigned to me. Therefore, I examined how the first Christians had structured their ethics and on a trial basis, I schematized their diverse opinions. These ideas, which have kept their oral and their adventurous character, I dedicate to Gabriel Widmer, who throughout the years was the most faithful speaker of these *Journées théologiques*. Through this modest tribute, I insist on expressing all my gratitude. Not only did he encourage me to come and teach in Geneva, but since then he has not stopped stimulating my theological thinking in the Faculty and in the Church.

Introduction

Before being able to invite you to follow my train of thought, I had to pave the way for myself. Let us consider these introductory comments that follow as a shovelling act, in order to make a path through the snow and gain access to the chalet.

The first stroke of the shovel – the magic shovel being so encumbered by the obstacle – is to discard the traditional and confessional preferences concerning biblical texts with ethical orientation. Some texts in fact have obtained throughout the centuries a normative scope, mainly the Decalogue, the Sermon on the Mount, chapter 7 of the first letter to the Corinthians. I do not wish to doubt the importance of these testimonies, but I am opposed to emphasizing them inequitably or to pompously describe them as instituting texts.[1] The interest in the reception of biblical texts in history helps us to flay these dull options and invites us

---

[1] The final misgivings of Saint Augustine in becoming a Christian have been removed by a Pauline text, which is quite marginal in my view and which, moreover, insisted upon actions and not on grace; Rom 13:13: "Let us conduct ourselves becomingly as in the day, not in reveling and drunkenness, not in debauchery and licentiousness, not in quarreling and jealousy. But put on

to display the whole biblical panorama. It is not because the tourism office imposes on us the Matterhorn view from Findeln that we should forget Liskamm or Täschhorn.

The second stroke of the shovel enables us to discard an obstacle (it is also a big rock that we remove out of the way, along with the snow). Once we have the ambition of looking at all the biblical texts and looking at them not through distorted lenses, how are we to build a New Testament ethics? The comparison of a few tables of contents shows there are not many ways of doing it.[2] There is on the one hand a chronological approach (ethic of Jesus, early Christianity, Paul, the Synoptics, John, the last witnesses; thus Wolfgang Schrage);[3] on the other hand, there is a systematic presentation that enhances a virtue, love or justice, or a theological structure (thus Jean-François Collange[4] who, going from the general to the particular, gradually tackles the foundations and the horizon, the ethical forces, the ethical forms, and finally the ethical acts).

The third stroke of the shovel brings some clarification:[5] the ethics of the New Testament does not resemble the philosophical ethics. It is more paraenetical than reflexive.[6] As in fact Heinz-Dietrich Wendland writes: "In the New Testament, there is no philosophical ethics that would be understood as a science of normative criteria, as a teaching of virtue and which could be inferred from a notion of moral reason, of thought and character, of categorical imperative or of any other notion of the same genre."[7]

The fourth stroke of the shovel – seeing the impressive number of Jewish and Greek parallels – one may wonder if the ethics of the New Testament, as a practical requirement, that is to say, as a paraenesis, is not trite; it was swept along the great moral Jewish shift of the time with its Mosaic source and tributary upstream from popular Greek philosophy. Is it enough to have a theocentric foundation in order to act differently from Seneca or to have an eschatological aim based on an achieved Christology in order to become more irreproachable than Philo or

---

the Lord Jesus Christ, and make no provision for the flesh, to gratify its desires." See Augustine of Hippo, *Confessions* 8.12.

　² See Jean-François Collange, *De Jésus à Paul. L'éthique du Nouveau Testament* (Le champ éthique 3; Geneva: Labor et Fides, 1980) 3–6.

　³ Wolfgang Schrage, *Ethik des Neuen Testaments* (NTD Ergänzungsreihe 4; Göttingen: Vandenhoeck & Ruprecht, 1982).

　⁴ Collange, *De Jésus à Paul*.

　⁵ See Heinz-Dietrich Wendland, *Éthique du Nouveau Testament* (Nouvelle Série Théologique 26; Geneva: Labor et Fides, 1972) 11–13.

　⁶ I recall my trepidation and surprise when, wanting to compare New Testament ethics to the ethics of the Stoics, I read a few years back, at the suggestion of Gabriel Widmer, the book by Léon Robin titled, *La morale antique* (Paris: Librairie Félix Alcan, 1938). My dread was explained by the philosophical difficulty of the work for a biblical scholar used to simple exhortations of the New Testament, and my surprise arose from the distance between the Bible and pagan philosophical texts.

　⁷ Wendland, *Éthique*, 11.

Hillel? The Church writers, to start with Justin and Tertullian, resolutely answered Yes to the question of specificity or the lack of specificity of the Christian ethic, by citing love for one's enemies[8] and in return clarifying the idea of "Look how much they love one another!"[9] I would also answer Yes, but I will have to prove it.

The fifth stroke of the shovel brings us closer to the goal: the New Testament does not exhaust the moral teachings of early Christianity. The canon was a selection and if we want to see the first Christians at work, no text must be neglected. *The Teaching of the Twelve Apostles* – with the doctrine of the two ways and its articulation of the (Old Testament) commandment for the love of one's neighbor over the New Testament's commandment for the love of one's enemies – is a document of extreme importance. It is the same for the moral teaching of Hermas of Rome; this prophet, a minister in soul, who opens a difficult path of ultimate forgiveness and final obligation to the faithful (rather unfaithful) in the capital – in any case, he offers an arduous morality. And we ought not to forget the author of the *Acts of Paul and Thecla* who, with his famous beatitudes, combines Jesus' message with that of Paul on moral and ascetic grounds.[10]

The sixth and final stroke of the shovel is undoubtedly the most decisive: it allows us to distinguish between text and history, requirement and practice, ethics and ethos. We should not confuse the *ethos* of *early Christianity* – what the first Christians lived, the collection organized by Paul, or the liberty granted by Peter to eat any meat – and the *ethics* of the *New Testament*, that is to say the requirement, expressed through parables or exhortations, through reflections or in scriptural citations, whose conformity to God's will seems to be far removed from human possibilities.

Please do not forget those strokes of the shovel, which I summarize as follows:

1. As ethical documents, in the New Testament there are passages other than the so-called great texts.

2. There are two different ways of writing the ethics of the New Testament: one travels down in time, and the other gathers elements in a systematic way.

3. The New Testament transmits a paraenesis more than an ethics; and if there is one, it is very different from the philosophical ethics based on reason and conscience.

4. The originality, the specificity of early Christian morality is to be defined.

5. The New Testament did not exist until the year 150. If we want to rebuild the ethics of the first Christians, we have to use all available materials (canonical and non-canonical).

---

[8] See *The Teaching of the Twelve Apostles (Didache)* 1.1–3.
[9] Tertullian, *Apology* 39.7.
[10] See Hermas, *The Shepherd*, and the *Acts of Paul and Thecla* 5–6.

6. It is important to distinguish the ethos from the ethics – what the first Christians did, from what they wanted to do.

Here is the plan of my presentation:

I. Competing Variety: around 100–150 c.e., I find a variety of competing Christian ethics, mainly three which I will call the ethics of the *crypt*, the ethics of the *way,* and the ethics of the *balcony.*

II. Imposed Uniformity: then at the end of the second century c.e., at the moment when the canon was closing and the early Church was being built, only one Christian morality had the right to survive. I will call it the morality of the *edifice,* of the Christian edifice, that is to say the Church.[11]

III. Harmonious Expansion: going back to Christian origins, I discovered at last a cohabitation of different ethics: the ethics of the *public place,* of the agora.

To conclude, I will come back to our time and recall from this pilgrimage what seems normative to me.

I. The Competing Variety (about 100–150 c.e.)

The image of Christianity, at the beginning and at the middle of the second century, is not very well known. However, one thing is certain: Christianity was looking for its own identity; it was all scattered around between the dissenting credal voices and the clashing practices. At the risk of over-simplification, I will distinguish three main aspects whose competing ethical options call for our attention.

a) The ethic of the crypt

Anyone who has visited San Clemente in Rome will not forget this underground third level, the level of the first and second century. The visitor to the Mithra sanctuary and to the Christian meeting place is struck by an atmosphere of mystery, bringing to mind the pages of Franz Cumont on Eastern religions in the Roman Empire.[12]

Based on the first Christian reflections relating to Jesus' death seen as a sacrificial atonement, marked by baptismal practice that was viewed as a participation

---

[11] A little later, monasticism developed with an ethics stricter than the morality imposed upon all believers. Tolerated, and then celebrated, this ethics is able to be called the ethics of the *cell,* the cell being that of the monk living either in a community or in isolation.

[12] Franz Cumont, *Les religions orientales dans le paganisme romain* (3d ed.; Annales du Musée Guimet, Bibliothèque de vulgarisation 24; Paris: Librairie Orientaliste Paul Geuthner, 1929).

in Christ's lot, and influenced by Paul's theology of reconciliation, Christianity, in one of its aspects, is introduced as a religion of salvation and as a rival of the mystery religions. As early as the end of the first century, Paul's communities developed this tendency, attested in the Epistle to the Ephesians and in the Epistle to Titus, which I quote:

For we ourselves were once foolish, disobedient, led astray, slaves to various passions and pleasures, passing our days in malice and envy, hated by men and hating one another; but when the goodness and loving-kindness of God our Savior appeared, he saved us, not because of deeds done by us in righteousness, but in virtue of his own mercy, by the washing of regeneration and renewal in the Holy Spirit, which he poured out upon us richly through Jesus Christ our Savior, so that we might be justified by his grace and become heirs in hope of eternal life. (Titus 3:3–7)

In this conception of Christianity, which is found in a more mystical form by Ignatius of Antioch, the predominance of redemption does not discard ethics. But, as the passage in the Epistle to Titus mentions, the ethics is not the cause of salvation; it is only the consequence: God saves us not because of the righteous works we do, nor because of our ethics, but because of his mercy. The ethics upon which these initiates of the crypt depends consequently maintains them in the sphere of salvation. It thus expresses itself in the Epistle to Titus: "The saying is sure. I desire you to insist on these things, so that those who have believed in God may be careful to apply themselves to good deeds; these are excellent and profitable for people" (Titus 3:8). Basically, it means: "To be ready for any honest work, to speak evil of no one, to avoid quarrelling, to be gentle, and to show perfect courtesy toward all people" (Titus 3:2). The Mosaic Law plays a role only in the simplified and summarized form of the Decalogue and of the commandment to love. The indwelling of the Holy Spirit in those believers makes obedience possible, which is impossible before redemption. In short, this Christianity as a religion of salvation is not indifferent to morality, but it makes its point with its persuasive doctrine of salvation.

b) The ethics of the way

If you read the most ancient pagan testimony concerning the Christians, you will find, besides a thousand prejudices, a keen admiration for the behavior of the followers of Christ. And it is true that the pride and identity of several communities of the second century are expressed in terms of ethics; this is what attracted many Greeks at that time – less the Christian doctrine than the ethics and more still, the noted ethos that one wanted to imitate.[13] For these followers, Christianity is a way, a path of wisdom, will, obedience, and moral success. Deep-rooted in the Jewish observance of the commandments of God and in their rabbinical interpre-

---

[13] André J. Festugière, "Aspects de la religion populaire grecque," *RTP*, 3d ser., 11 (1961) 30–31.

tation, this form of Christianity obeys less a Christ of faith than a Jesus of history. It encompasses the sayings of the master and tries to take them literally, in veneration for the moral teaching of Jesus that takes shape in the assembling of collections. Whether it is the *Sayings Source (Q)*, the *Sermon on the Mount*, the *Teaching of the Twelve Apostles*, or the *Gospel of Thomas*, each of these documents presupposes that salvation and life are obtained more than received, and that they are obtained by listening to and practicing of the words of Jesus. Christian faith for them is listening to the teaching and the practice of morals. It is difficult to figure out the kind and the number of such Christian communities. Some have remained very Jewish, adding to the ritual observance of the Old Testament the moral requirements of the New Testament. Others have been influenced by the Hellenistic mistrust of the body and have oriented the teachings of Jesus toward the ascetic. It was at that time that the encratite movement was born. This movement rejected sexuality and encouraged the practice of fasting. Christology, soteriology, and worship were indeed not excluded from each of these movements, but took on a singular form. Christ was venerated as master of wisdom and as a man of suffering. Salvation was positioned as the end result and not as the starting point, and the cult was to be limited to the reading of the commandments and to intercession, with the aim of faithfulness. Christianity as an ethics appears particularly clear at the start of the *Teaching of the Twelve Apostles*: "There are two ways, one of life, the other of death, and between the two ways there is a great difference. Now the way of life is this: you shall love first the God who created you, then your neighbor as yourself, and do not yourself do to another what you would not want done to you. Here is the teaching from these words: Bless those who curse you and pray for your enemies, fast for those who persecute you ... ."[14]

c) The ethics of the balcony

There is a third category of Christians from the second century. From the balcony of their knowledge, they distance themselves from the external world that they look upon with distrust. They scorn the Christians born again from the crypt, and they find the ethical effort of the voluntary Christians of the way un-called for. What they like is the Savior, the incorporeal and transcendent God, who came closer to humanity not to save the world, but to extract the elect. These *happy few* attain the divine world through contemplation. From the balcony of their wisdom, they admire Heaven or rather the Heaven of Heaven. The world, they understood, was to be avoided, as Christ took care not to do more than skim over it. Such is half of their moral. The other is to be altogether attached to the same Savior. The Johannine commandment of love is appropriate to them. One does not

---

[14] *The Teaching of the Twelve Apostles (Didache)* 1.1–3.

have to love one's neighbor as much as one needs to love one another within the conventicle, as the monogenes Savior loved them in the Upper Room. Situated within a heated house for refined intellectuals, the community attempts to avoid draughts. To distance itself from the world is to arrive at apathy and the absence of passions. What the tradition transmitted concerning renunciation is interpreted in the sense of this ataraxia. One of the representatives of this tendency, Nicolas, the spiritual master of the Nicolaites attacked by the Apocalypse, appears to have expressed an enigmatic precept: "It is necessary to abuse the flesh."[15] His disciples have analyzed the enigma with two opposite meanings, either in an ascetic sense, that is to say, everything must be renounced, or in a libertine sense, that is to say, no excess can truly reach us, all being indifferent. To read the Gnostic literature and what the Fathers tell us, the ethical ambivalence characterizes this particular form of Christianity, torn between the ascetic contempt of the body and the libertine indifference excused by Paul's idea of "all things are lawful for me" (1 Cor 6:12; 10:23), even if the discovery of the texts from Nag Hammadi leads us to believe that among the Gnostics, the libertines were, as a whole, less numerous and less determining than the austere ones.

In short, Christianity of 150 emphasized three primitive potentialities, so much so that they became incompatible: redemption justified by Paul, asceticism legitimated by Jesus, and knowledge suggested by John; one enhancing the heart, the other the will, and the third the intellect. At the risk of shattering everything into pieces, a revision had to be made. And, as you know, they were not the only ethical commitments that had to be tightened, but the whole of Christianity – doctrine, Scripture, discipline, sacrament, and ministry. It was the work of the theologians at the end of the second century whose ethical program we briefly summarize.

II. Imposed Uniformity

During this reformation, the main idea was to arrive at a unity of doctrine, of ethics, and of an ecclesiastical structure. This was achieved by reconciling the crypt and the way, while defying the balcony and by assimilating considerable pagan values.

To support and impose this uniformity, the theologians and the bishops worked out an image of the early Church that we depend on to this day. Everything was going to be based on the apostolic college in thought and in deed. To the apos-

---

[15] δεῖ παραχρῆσθαι τῇ σαρκί (cited by Clement of Alexandria, *Stromateis* 2.20.118); see Pierre Prigent, "L'hérésie asiate et l'Église confessante. De l'Apocalypse à Ignace," *VC* 31 (1977) 1–22.

tolic writings henceforth delineated, to the apostolic creed henceforth confessed, to the apostolic ministry henceforth installed, was going to be added apostolic ethics, that is to say, allegedly apostolic, since, owing to the difference in adjectives of this type, apostolic precisely means that which does not go back to the apostles themselves. To imagine what this apostolic ethics was and by which means it was extracted from Scripture, it is necessary to follow the outcome of the decree known as apostolic, transmitted by Acts 15.[16] In its primitive form, that is, Lukan, it was ritualistic and marked a decrease (not a suppression) of the Jewish ritual commands for the first converted pagans. When it was read again by the Great Church at the end of the second century, it became a moral elementary code prohibiting idolatry, murder, and fornication. And it was along this triangle that the penitential discipline and the catechetical formation of the early Church were elaborated.[17]

Regarding this formation, it is necessary to celebrate the exegetical prowess of the theologians. They succeeded in, on the one hand, summarizing the Law of Moses in the Decalogue, and made it coincide with the double commandment of love, a result that Jesus had reached at the end of a similar simplifying process. On the other hand, they will offer a hermeneutical key to the whole of the Hebrew Bible that no one wanted to either reject or to respect literally. Only one solution remained: the search for a second meaning. The dietary laws of Leviticus 11 were lifted as such, while their biblical terms remained. The latter became an allegory for human types that had to be avoided, obviously beginning with pork.

Of all the mosaic rituals, circumcision and Sabbath included, there remained only one moral order, allotted to the intelligence of the apostles kindled by the Holy Spirit and taught by Christ.[18] All this construction did not lack unity, harmony, or grandeur. It enabled Christianity to recall the necessity of love throughout the darkest and more violent centuries – a formidable law of freedom, but a law nevertheless. The New Testament itself became at once the *Gospel* that the Old Testament promised and the *New Law* whose Mosaic writings remained the Old Law. The Sermon on the Mount was consequently regarded as the perfect expression of this New Law, and to complete the triple office of Christ, the role of legislator and judge was also added.

---

[16] See Lucien Cerfaux, "Le chapitre XVe du Livre des Actes à la lumière de la littérature ancienne," in *Miscellanea Giovanni Mercati* 1 (Studi e Testi 121; Città del Vaticano: Biblioteca apostolica Vaticana, 1946) 107–26; reprinted in *Recueil Lucien Cerfaux* 2 (Gembloux: J. Duculot, 1954) 105–24.

[17] See Bernhard Poschmann, *Busse und letzte Ölung* (Handbuch der Dogmengeschichte 4.3; Freiburg im Breisgau: Herder, 1951); French translation titled, *La pénitence et l'onction des malades* (Histoire des dogmes 6.3; Paris: Cerf, 1966).

[18] Of the ethics of the way, everything was not therefore accepted. Certain aspects of the legalist observance of the Jewish Christians were eliminated; see François Bovon, *De vocatione gentium. Histoire de l'interprétation d'Act. 10,1–11,18 dans les six premiers siècles* (BGBE 8; Tübingen: Mohr Siebeck, 1967) 92–132.

It was obviously necessary to pay the price of this construction.

Jewish Christianity, whose various forms are still badly known, carried on respecting the letter of the Law and was abandoned to its fate. Only one moral observance remained. If there was to be a ritualism, it would no longer be Jewish but Christian (see the new fasting days, the observance of new festivals, etc.).

In addition, without always realizing it, some elements of pagan provenance formed part of this construction of a normative Christian ethics. Obvious in the writings of Clement of Alexandria and Tertullian, this integration is perceptible from the first Christian epistles, those of Paul or of Clement of Rome in particular. Some pagan values, such as discipline and control over passions in particular, moral baggage inherited from the Stoic philosophers of the imperial era, were welcomed into the Church without much criticism.

Lastly, for various reasons, the role of the women in the Church was strictly placed under control and voluntarily limited. The episcopate is strengthened by discarding the prophecy to which a considerable number of Christian women had taken part (not only the "insane" or the "weaklings" from Phrygia, as gently stated by the orthodox discussing the female colleagues of Montanus).[19] But the bishops, in their increasingly collegial structure, felt the threat of women not only in prophecy but elsewhere. They saw in them the source of temptation and the Achilles heel of the Church. They left for them the merit of maternity, but not without gradually linking it to the continuity of sin. Celibacy took over and all the Christian virtues were attached to the male. Safeguarded femininity was not connected to anthropology or to ethics, but to the Church: Eve, the source of all misfortunes, received the promise to crush the snake (Gen 3:15). An Eve-Church typology, afterwards Eve-Mary, was going to offer to femininity a global cover of ecclesiastical scope.[20] The body of the woman was spiritualized and inflated: it consequently lost its threatening and seductive character. It is too often forgotten that Augustine, two centuries later, before becoming a Christian, rejected the sweet creature he lived with and who had given him this poor Adeodatus for a son. Having given up his partner, he also refused Christian marriage arranged by his mother, and chose, not without hesitation, chastity as well as faith.[21] As for the image of Mary Magdalene, it gathered dust: only sectarian conventicles drew her from oblivion.[22]

---

[19] See Didymus, *Fragmenta ex expositione in Actus apostolorum* 10.10 (PG 39:1677); Hilarius of Poitiers, *Ad Constantium Augustum* 2.7 (PL 10:570); Hippolytus of Rome, *Philosophoumena* 8.19 (PG 16:3366).

[20] See Michel Planque, "Ève," in *Dictionnaire de spiritualité* 4.2 (Paris: Beauchesne, 1960) cols. 1772–88.

[21] See Augustine of Hippo, *Confessions* 6.12–15; on Adeodat, ibid., 9.6; see Henri-Irénée Marrou, in collaboration with Anne-Marie La Bonnardière, *Saint Augustin et l'augustinisme* (Maîtres spirituels 2; Paris: Seuil, 1959) 24–25 and 45 (nn.).

[22] See François Bovon, "Le privilège pascal de Marie-Madeleine," *NTS* 30 (1984) 50–62.

III. Harmonious expansion

Let us go back now to the origins, to the moral message of Jesus and the first Christians.

Regarding a Jewish ethics anxious to maintain the numerous commandments and not to create a hierarchy of the precepts, Jesus managed a series of bold reorientations, for which he will pay the ultimate price.

Let us say at once that he owes nothing to anyone. He did not support any human authority, master, or school. He said what seemed right to him and did not doubt that his teaching corresponded to the will of his God. This freedom of judgment, expression, and engagement is completely surprising for his time and his social background. What may also be extraordinary for a Jew is that he dared to criticize the tradition of the fathers, the oral tradition that was traced back, like the written Torah, to Moses himself.[23]

With his "But I say to you," he thwarts the Law of the Scripture, the inspired Scripture, and that was even more daring; not that he did it systematically, but he did it when he meant to favor one conduct (more often a moral conduct) over another (more often a ritual conduct): "Is it lawful on the sabbath to do good or to do harm, to save life or to kill?" (Mark 3:4). In this destabilization of the power of the Torah, a more threatening power in his eyes since he was manipulated by men who were sometimes unfaithful to God, Jesus did not act rashly. He recognizes through the Torah and often in the Torah, the expression of the will of God, but he establishes, with a sovereign freedom, a hierarchy of values. Thus, concerning divorce (Mark 10:2–9), he opposes two texts of Scripture, one authorizing divorce (Deut 24:1), the other supporting the insolubility of marriage (Gen 2:24), then he chooses what according to him corresponds with the most fundamental will of God. What followed is a radicalization and not a reduction of the requirement. In this quest, beyond the Scriptures, of the will of God, Jesus did not only and not primarily support the past manifestation of the God of Exodus, but especially the actual demonstration of the God of the Kingdom, a God who adapts his will to the ultimate conditions of human life. If he undermines the tradition of men through the written Law (Mark 7:6–8), he also undermines the written Law through the demand of the Kingdom. What stands out from this great sweeping stroke is a reduction to moral engagement, to the detriment of ritual regulations; a hierarchical organization enhancing the two highest commandments (biblical love for one's neighbor being radicalized by the love for one's enemies) and a creation of new obligations, for example, the request to follow Jesus, owing to the imminence of the Kingdom. At the level of the actual acts of Jesus, an expression

---

[23] See the beginning of (*Pirqe*) *Avot*, the ninth treatise of the fourth order (= part) of the Mishnah.

of this renewed ethic, there is a new glance which he has towards children, his free gestures toward women, and his benevolent openness toward strangers.

As Jesus granted only a limited value to the past expression of the will of God, the first Christians, Paul in particular, only granted a little significance to the moral teaching of Jesus; as if the reference was neither for Jesus nor for Paul of an ethical order extolled in a common morality, but of a dogmatic order, inserted in a graceful and imperative revelation. This determination through eschatology and through the present resolutely distinguishes this ethics from the Jewish ethics and definitely characterizes it as an ethics of freedom, certainly not freedom defined as autonomy, but freedom as conformity to the current will of God.

If Jesus was inspired by the imminence of the Kingdom and if he ethically traded this urgency for today, Paul, the other witness of that time, was not blind to the eschatological horizon, but was inspired by the work of Christ and the actual reality of the Resurrection. It results in communion, the reality of which (expressed in terms of righteousness, reconciliation, and peace with God) must still be protected because of expectation. The certainty of redemption goes hand in hand with the obligation of not losing the received treasure. This obligation Paul summarizes by a περιπατεῖν, a walk (the *crypt* and the *way* coexist in his ethical thought). And to remain on track, it is advisable to be in communion with the Spirit and with the suffering conformity of Christ (see Philippians 3). In concrete terms, that means to obey the will of God, the will that Paul, inspired by Jesus and not only dependent upon him, discovers today in the commandment of love, condensed from the written Law whose use led to a more guilty servitude than the freedom of belief (see Gal 5:14 and Rom 13:8–10). Paul's criticism of circumcision joined Jesus' criticism of Sabbath: compare 1 Cor 7:19 (to keep the commandments of God) and Gal 6:15 (new creation).

When it is a question of supporting the believers along their way, Paul gradually draws from the moral Law of the Hebrew Bible and from the sayings of Jesus; more often, he uses what he calls the "instructions" which "we gave you through the Lord Jesus" (1 Thess 4:2). With this inspired freedom of which I have spoken, he indeed sets up a manual for the pilgrims, travelers, and hikers. In fact, this freedom was threatened because its inspiration was in retreat concerning the teachings and practice of Jesus. If concerning the links with the State their positions became closer, in the relationships between man and woman Paul stands out more because of his personal visions than because of his deep-rooted faith in God. The latter dictates to him that "there is neither male nor female" (Gal 3:28); the former forced him to impose subordination and perhaps silence (1 Cor 11:2–16 and 14:34–35).

In conclusion to this part – and I only selected two examples of these many ethics – I am delighted by the freedom of Jesus from the Law and that of Paul towards Jesus, but I also note that freedom is risky and that it was not always fuelled by God. Nevertheless, the originality of the New Testament was to place the will of God still elsewhere than in the letter of a fixed Scripture, and the hermeneutics of this requirement still elsewhere than in the interpretation of ancient texts.

What was going to be registered as oppositions in the second century still cohabited harmoniously in the first because of the unique foundation in God: the previous offer (the indicative before the imperative) and the maintained requirement. In their harmonious varieties, the ethics of Jesus and of the first Christians formed a sturdy bridge at the junction of the existing strong Jewish and Greek ethics and not the least, at the existing immorality of men and women of the time.

Conclusion

Social ethics – including the case of AIDS – can only seldom be based upon firm texts of Scripture (Romans 13 locates the believer before the State, but not the State before another State). Social ethics would do well to reflect, as did John Rawls for justice or Ivan Boszormenyi-Nagy for loyalty,[24] on the great biblical virtues. It should do more, naturally, than call upon them. It should analyze the outlines, presuppositions, the conditions of possibilities and applications. Freedom, peace, love, and justice are there at our disposal; they are offered to our intelligence and to our faith.

Concerning individual ethics, regarding the condition of women and men for example, first I would like to feel in me the goodness of existence – to be useful, to be something, as Alexandre Vinet wrote in 1817.[25] Then, I would like to know how to resist, following the Epistle of James, doubt, deviance, and sloth, and to show this resolve required by Saint Paul.[26] This firm ground should not prevent me from exerting, even occasionally, openness to others for whom Jesus had the secret.

Time passes in my life, as that in the Church; I wish that faithfulness, patience, tenacity, and perseverance, these Lukan and Johannine virtues,[27] mark my actions. A difficult virtue, which the Pastoral Epistles and the apostolic tradition expect of the minister and of every Christian, should also solicit my care: gentleness made of transparency and simplicity.[28] More difficult still and yet with the

---

[24] See John Rawls, *A Theory of Justice* (Cambridge, Mass.: Harvard University Press, 1971; with numerous reprints and translations); and Ivan Boszormenyi-Nagy and Geraldine M. Spark, *Invisible Loyalties: Reciprocity in Intergenerational Family Therapy* (Hagerstown, Md.: Harper & Row, 1973; with numerous editions and translations).

[25] See Eugène Rambert, *Alexandre Vinet. Histoire de sa vie et de ses ouvrages* (2d ed.; Lausanne: G. Bridel, 1875) 45.

[26] See Jas 1:2–8; 3:1–13; 1 Thess 3:8; Gal 5:1; Phil 1:27–28.

[27] See Luke 8:15; 21:19; John 15:9–10; 1 John 2:3–6; Rev 1:9.

[28] See 2 Tim 2:25; Titus 3:2; Hippolytus, *The Apostolic Tradition* 3, following the edition of Bernard Botte, *La Tradition apostolique* (2d ed.; SC 11; Paris: Cerf, 1984) 46–47.

first rank of the Christian contest, the ability to suffer:[29] the sharing of the sufferings of Christ, a submission that does not mean the subordination to the strong, but supporting the weak, applying Philippians 2. Courage is missing from my list: to have the audacity to denounce evil and abuse, as did Jesus and the school of Matthew which followed (Matthew 23). To have a spirit enlightened by the Spirit of God, to live for this ἀνακαίνωσις τοῦ νοός (Rom 12:2), to judge everything spiritually as Paul expects (1 Cor 2:15). Lastly, as with the Philippians, to be joyful, towards and against everything, in spite of the perceived senselessness of death and of violent deaths, in spite of injustices and misfortunes (Phil 2:18; 3:1; 4:4). The Gospel is not an ethical solution, but it can be and it must be the normative source of our engagements, our decisions, and even of our intentions.[30]

Bibliography

Brown, Peter. "Antiquité tardive." In *De l'Empire romain à l'an mil*. Vol. 1 of *Histoire de la vie privée*. Ed. Paul Veyne. Gen. ed. Philippe Ariès and Georges Duby. Paris: Seuil, 1985. pp. 225–299.

Collange, Jean-François. *De Jésus à Paul. L'éthique du Nouveau Testament*. Le champ éthique 3. Geneva: Labor et Fides, 1980.

Dodd, Charles H. *Morale de l'Évangile. Les rapports entre la foi et la morale dans le christianisme primitive*. Paris: Seuil, 1958.

Grelot, Pierre. "L'Église et l'enseignement de la morale." *Esprit et Vie* 91 (1981) 465–76 and 481–89.

Houlden, James L. *Ethics and the New Testament*. New York: Oxford University Press, 1973.

Kertelge, Karl, ed. *Ethik im Neuen Testament*. QD 102. Freiburg im Breisgau: Herder, 1984.

Lohse, Eduard. *Theologische Ethik*. Theologische Wissenschaft 5.2. Stuttgart: W. Kohlhammer, 1988.

Merk, Otto. "Ethik im Neuen Testament. Zu Wolfgang Schrages Gesamtdarstellung." *TLZ* 112 (1987) 641–650.

Osborn, Eric. *La morale dans la pensée chrétienne primitive. Description des archétypes de la morale patristique*. Théologie Historique 68. Paris: Beauchesne, 1984.

Preisker, Herbert. *Das Ethos des Urchristentums*. 3d ed. Darmstadt: Wissenschaftliche Buchgesellschaft, 1968.

Robin, Léon. *La morale antique*. Paris: Librairie Félix Alcan, 1938.

---

[29] In his book, which has had considerable success in Germany but is practically unknown in the francophone world, a psychologist developed a thesis according to which our modern civilization will succumb: it will become incapable of supporting suffering; see Horst Eberhard Richter, *Der Gotteskomplex. Die Geburt und die Krise des Glaubens an die Allmacht des Menschen* (Reinbek bei Hamburg: Rowohlt, 1979).

[30] Éric Junod has brought to my attention suggestive pages which Peter Brown has written on Christian ethics in *Histoire de la vie privée* (see "Antiquité tardive," in *De l'Empire romain à l'an mil* [vol. 1 of *Histoire de la vie privée*; ed. Paul Veyne; gen. ed. Philippe Ariès and Georges Duby; Paris: Seuil, 1985] 225–299), in particular on the climate in which the first Church commented on this.

Sanders, Jack T. *Ethics in the New Testament: Change and Development*. Philadelphia: Fortress, 1975.

Schnackenburg, Rudolf. *Le message moral du Nouveau Testament*. 2d ed. Le Puy: Xavier Mappus, 1967.

Schrage, Wolfgang. *Ethik des Neuen Testaments*. NTD Ergänzungsreihe 4. Göttingen: Vandenhoeck & Ruprecht, 1982.

Schulz, Siegfried. *Neutestamentliche Ethik*. Zurich: Theologischer Verlag, 1987.

Spicq, Ceslas. *Théologie morale du Nouveau Testament*. 2 vols. Études Bibliques. Paris: Lecoffre, 1965.

Strecker, George. "Ziele und Ergebnisse einer neutestamentlichen Ethik." *NTS* 25 (1978) 1–15.

Vouga, François. *Jésus et la Loi selon la tradition synoptique*. MdB 17. Geneva: Labor et Fides, 1988.

Wendland, Heinz-Dietrich. *Éthique du Nouveau Testament*. Nouvelle Série Théologique 26. Geneva: Labor et Fides, 1972.

Wilder, Amos N. *Eschatology and Ethics in the Teaching of Jesus*. 2d ed. New York: Harper, 1950.

Missionary Practice and Transmission
of the Gospel in Early Christianity

The contemporary situation of the local Church, as well as for worldwide Christian organizations, is characterized by three theological options that also imply three styles of missionary work: first, the transmission of the Christian heritage to the masses, which mainstream Christianity makes with uneasiness and frugality; second, the spreading of the good news toward a message of conversion, resorting to forceful and euphoric means of communication; and third, the presence in the world of Christian cells in secular or non-Christian districts or countries where some work quietly and discretely through prayer, while others are active and sometimes biased assuming the role of liberator. Are these options and attitudes compatible? To make certain, it is advisable to look at how early Christianity assumed and conceived its missionary task in this promising interaction of concern and action. In the first section, I will examine the main features of the missionary reality of early Christianity; in the second, the theological motivation of the Christian mission; in the third, the risks, the uncertainties, and despite everything, the success of the first evangelization.

1. Missionary reality[1]

Contrary to a stereotyped image, the ancient world was not a vacant land that Providence would have prepared to receive the building of the Church. It was

---

[1] Heinzgünter Frohnes and Uwe W. Knorr, eds., *Die alte Kirche* (Kirchengeschichte als Missionsgeschichte 1; Munich: Kaiser, 1974); Michael Green, *Evangelism in the Early Church* (London: Hodder and Stoughton, 1970); Ferdinand Hahn, *Das Verständnis der Mission im Neuen Testament* (WMANT 13; Neukirchen-Vluyn: Neukirchener Verlag, 1963); Adolf von Harnack, *Die Mission und Ausbreitung des Christentums in den ersten drei Jahrhunderten* (4th ed.; Leipzig: Hinrichs, 1924); Martin Hengel, "Die Ursprünge der christlichen Mission," *NTS* 18 (1971–1972) 15–39; idem, *Zur urchristlichen Geschichtsschreibung* (Calwer Paperback; Stuttgart: Calwer Verlag, 1979) 63–105; Wolf-Henning Ollrog, *Paulus und seine Mitarbeiter. Untersuchungen zu Theorie und Praxis der paulinischen Mission* (WMANT 50; Neukirchen-Vluyn: Neukirchener Verlag, 1979); Mauro Pesce, " 'Christ did not send me to baptize, but to evangelize' (1 Cor 1:17a)," in *Paul de Tarse, apôtre de notre temps* (ed. Lorenzo De Lorenzi; Série monographique de *Benedictina*, section paulinienne, 1; Rome: Abbaye de S. Paul, 1979) 339–62; Wilhelm Schneemelcher, *Das Urchristentum* (Kohlhammer Urban-Taschenbücher 336; Stuttgart: W. Kohlhammer, 1981) 123–33.

instead a land bursting with religion. In addition to the traditional national religions, like the old Roman one Augustus tried to revitalize, there also circulated numerous contemporary ones: philosophical wisdom, which promoted self-control and religious hope regarding the impersonal forces of the cosmos and the empire; magic wisdom, which provided the initiate with incantations and rituals to hold power over beings and to influence the elements; spreading Eastern religions, such as Judaism or the Egyptian cult of Isis, that were labelled as superstitions by Roman writers. These convictions – some logical, others irrational – did not circulate only as a result of displaced merchants and soldiers, but also, according to ancient sources, this was due to the mobility of priests, philosophers, magicians, and itinerant missionaries who supported expansion.[2] From an external and formal point of view, the first Christian mission is thus hardly distinguishable from these other religious forms. It is moreover the term "superstition" that ancient authors, such as Tacitus, Suetonius, or Pliny the Younger, use when they come to speak of Christianity.[3]

Unfortunately, we know very little, equally so of the Christian mission in the first century in Palestine and in Syria, as that of the missions in the second century in Egypt or Africa.[4] What do we know in particular of the missionary activity of the Twelve, with the exception, if even that, of Peter?

It is nevertheless possible to identify the ways and means that made it possible for Christianity to spread so quickly (at the beginning of the second century of our era, Pliny the Younger[5] will say that, in his province of Pontus, although on the outer fringes of the empire, Christianity reached every strata of the population, the countryside equally as much as the city).

To our surprise, there was not just one Christian missionary practice. Since Ernst Käsemann[6] has already established ecclesial pluralism in early Christianity, we are certain that there existed a variety of missionary practices here.

---

[2] See Helmut Köster, *Einführung in das Neue Testament im Rahmen der Religionsgeschichte und Kulturgeschichte der hellenistischen und römischen Zeit* (Berlin: de Gruyter, 1980) 145–211, 235–59, 372–401.

[3] Tacitus, *Annals* 15.44, calls the Christian sect an "execrable superstition"; Suetonius, *Nero* 16, "a new and pernicious superstition"; Pliny the Younger, *Epistles* 10.96, writes in paragraph 8 about an "absurd, extravagant superstition" and adds, in paragraph 9, "It is not only the cities, but also the boroughs and the country that the contagion of this superstition has invaded." See Jacques Moreau, *Les plus anciens témoignages profanes sur Jésus* (Brusselles: Office de publicité, 1944) 37–53; Pierre de Labriolle, *La réaction païenne. Étude sur la polémique antichrétienne du Ier au VIe siècle* (Paris: L'Artisan du livre, 1948) 19–54.

[4] See Ollrog, *Paulus und seine Mitarbeiter*, 151–52; and von Harnack, *Die Mission und Ausbreitung des Christentums*, 361–62.

[5] See n. 3 above.

[6] Ernst Käsemann, "Einheit und Vielfalt in der neutestamentlichen Lehre von der Kirche," *Ökumenische Rundschau* 13 (1964) 58–63; reprinted in idem, *Exegetische Versuche und Besinnungen* (2 vols.; Göttingen: Vandenhoeck & Ruprecht, 1960–1964) 2:262–67.

Firstly, what may be called the missionary practice of Jesus continues beyond Good Friday and Easter. In a geographically limited area (undoubtedly Palestine and Syria), some disciples, fulfilling the missionary requirements of Jesus as conveyed in the traditions of Mark (Mark 6 par.) and Q (Luke 10 par.), went two by two, from place to place, carrying with them only one daily ration of bread. Depending upon the reception received from house to house, they proclaimed the imminence of God's Kingdom, the arrival of the Son of Man; initially they did not think of organizing a local community, but of offering an ultimate chance at salvation to "this perverse generation." Signs and exorcisms confirmed their message. The fervor of their requirement undoubtedly was necessary among each other. For the converted, it would be a world of compromises. The missionaries were perhaps invested with the title of apostle and thought of themselves as emissaries of Jesus. It is probably this type of missionaries who, in Corinth, according to 2 Corinthians 10–13, will enter into competition with the Pauline organization. It is certainly this type of evangelists and apostles whose existence is attested in the text of the *Didache*. Eschatology, individualism, and ethics determine this mission, which both relies on a Christology of the Son of Man, rejected and restored by God, and also creates a bond with the history of salvation, imminence in particular.[7]

The Church of the Hellenists, first in Jerusalem then at Antioch, appears to have carried out the mission differently:[8] evangelization is a communal affair; the local Church becomes an association for outward expansion, a programmed expansion, carrying this great innovation: the nations too are henceforth called. Acts 13:1–3 has preserved for us the memory of a community, that of Antioch, choosing for itself a missionary team empowered with the responsibility to go forth and proclaim that Jesus is the Son of God, that salvation may be realized only through him, to establish communities in chosen cities, and to return with reports to the home Church (in early Christian terms, to speak of the wonders achieved by God through their agency).

This mission makes use of the solid support of synagogues and the preaching possibility offered to transient rabbis. It also resorts to the use of a private home of a converted member to be used as the nucleus of a community in flux.[9]

Thanks to the history of traditions practiced on biblical texts, exegetes have managed to define in broad outline the preaching plans of these Hellenist mis-

---

[7] See Gerd Theissen, *Soziologie der Jesusbewegung* (2d ed.; Theologische Existenz heute 194; Munich: Kaiser, 1978) 14–21; Theissen does not sufficiently distinguish this type of evangelization mission performed by the Hellenists. See also Ollrog, *Paulus und seine Mitarbeiter*, 152–55.

[8] See Hengel, "Die Ursprünge der christlichen Mission," 27–30; and especially Ollrog, *Paulus und seine Mitarbeiter*, 155–57.

[9] See Peter Stuhlmacher, *Der Brief an Philemon* (2d ed.; EKKNT 18; Neukirchen-Vluyn: Neukirchener Verlag, 1981) 70–75, "Exkurs: Urchristliche Hausgemeinden."

sionaries:[10] to the Jews, Jesus is introduced as the Son of God and at the side of God the creator (thus one arrives at a creed in the two terms; see 1 Cor 8:6 for example), thanks to the scriptural arguments. The pagans are invited (see 1 Thess 1:9–10; Heb 6:2; Acts 14 and 17) to leave their idols behind and to turn to the living God (taken over from a Jewish Hellenistic missionary plan) and to await the Son of God Savior. This mission of the Hellenists is thus less eschatological and less radically ethical; on the other hand, it is more ecclesiastic and christological. It establishes a bond with space, the οἰκουμένη.

A third type is the kind that, thanks to Paul, will have success, as we know.[11] Paul, a worker for more than ten years in the mission of the Hellenists, is naturally inspired by this Antiochene practice. But the universal responsibility in which he feels invested (see Rom 15:18–24), as well as the tensions he experienced with Jewish-Christians (see the incident at Antioch, Gal 2:11–14), inclines him toward a mission that is organized in a new way.

Initially, it should be noted that for the missionaries and their upkeep, the apostle Paul did not base his practices on the Hellenists, but on the rules of the first missionaries (itinerancy, renouncement of goods, home, and marriage; a concern for the provision of their own needs), even if he knows and admits others practices (earned wages, the company of a wife).

Secondly, the community aspect of the mission according to the Hellenist practice is taken over, even if some corrective measures are added: Paul thinks of himself as a representative of Christ and not, as in Acts 13, of a community. Less apparent in the apostle, the community will nevertheless be represented in Paul's missionary work by his collaborators. Indeed, Paul himself selected fellow workers, in truth few in number: Silvanus, then Timothy. To be sure, he met and worked in cooperation with independent evangelists such as Apollos, but he was especially pressed to rely on representatives of the newly founded communities. These representatives, according to previous research, were used exclusively for the organization of the collection. The recent thesis put forward by Wolf-Henning Ollrog[12] also integrates them into the missionary task, a decision that obviously has important theological repercussions: a tightening of the bonds between mission and edification.

Above all, in a Pauline manner, the mission of the apostle is no longer radiating from one center, as was the case for the Hellenists, but advancing progressively throughout the world through the successive establishment of bridgeheads from country to country, thus creating numerous communities to call upon and from which to branch out locally, returning for support visits and instruction.

---

[10] See Jacques Dupont, "Les discours missionnaires des Actes des apôtres d'après un ouvrage récent," *RB* 69 (1962) 42; reprinted in idem, *Études sur les Actes des apôtres* (LD 45; Paris: Cerf, 1967) 138.

[11] See Ollrog, *Paulus und seine Mitarbeiter*, 157–60.

[12] See ibid., 109–61.

If the primary sources were more explicit, it would undoubtedly be possible to detect other missionary practices (one thinks about the ideal school desired by the community of Matthew or the resultant effort to dialogue with the contemporary world, thanks to the symbolism, in the Gospel of John). What is important here, is the report of missionary pluralism – pluralism in practice, organization, and formulation.

To this missionary variety in a strict sense, it is necessary to add various factors of decision and conversion. Since the word alone did not move the crowd, the gesture, equally so among the charismatic itinerants as among the Hellenists and Paul, became a sign that supported the word. This gesture could be a gesture of charity, a gesture of the renouncement, the gesture of a healer, the gesture of an exorcist, and finally a gesture of suffering. It should be noted too that this missionary expression in the gesture is not limited to the activity of the missionary as this is attested in Paul and in the New Testament; it is also seen in the community: in their mutual affection, the first Christians drew attention; and by undergoing suffering – and it is often those who remain stationary who endure scorn and aggravation – they pay for their testimony with their bodies.

2. The theological motivations of the mission

In this second part, I will examine the reasons that were strong enough to compel the first missionaries to take to the roads in their own country, and then even farther afield.[13] At the risk of over-simplifying, I distinguish four: the first is due to the entrusted mission, the second to the nature of the incipient community, the third to the analysis related to the present time, the fourth to the will of God. As we will see, these reasons reappear whatever the missionary practice is.

a) An entrusted mission

Expressed in a narrative or theological manner, the New Testament confirms this conviction of the first apostles and missionaries of being and having been *sent*. This conviction, while strong, imposed a designation for the first Christians who were in charge – a word, which from its root, expresses precisely not a stationary capacity but one of being sent: namely the title ἀπόστολος. The organization of *the sending* is at the heart of Christianity.

In addition, the tradition of the Gospel of Mark, as well as the source of the *Logia*, contains a missionary speech of Jesus.[14] And this speech – articulated on

---

[13] See von Harnack, *Die Mission und Ausbreitung des Christentums*, 111–331.

[14] See Hahn, *Das Verständnis der Mission*, 33–36; and Paul Hoffmann, *Studien zur Theologie der Logienquelle* (NTA n.s. 8; Münster: Verlag Aschendorff, 1972) 235–311.

account of the mission of the Twelve, their investiture, and the list of their names – starts with a formula of sending: "He began to send them out two by two" (Mark 6:7). He "sent them on ahead of him in pairs to every town and place where he himself intended to go. He said to them, 'The harvest is plentiful, but the laborers are few; therefore ask the Lord of the harvest to send out laborers into his harvest. Go on your way. See, I am sending you out like lambs into the midst of wolves'" (Luke 10:1–3, NRSV, taking over the source of the *Logia*; note the frequency of the verbs related to *the sending*).

This certainty of having been sent by Jesus accompanied the itinerant missionaries; it lived on in the Hellenist disciples, then even in Paul. If it could not be based on a mission entrusted before the Passion, they deduced their missionary principles from a mandate entrusted by the resurrected Christ. In fact, the Twelve also appear to have received confirmation of their missionary task at the time of the Resurrection appearances. An appearance pattern goes well beyond the narrow framework of the recognition scenes of the Resurrected, to include the reason for the sending and to thus achieve an official dimension: see Luke 24:47–48 (where the reason is strongly worked over again by Luke) and John 20:21 (where the expression is very Johannine: καθὼς ἀπέσταλκέν με ὁ πατήρ, κἀγὼ πέμπω ὑμᾶς). See Matt 28:19–20.

If the apostle Paul expresses this conviction in the narrative and retrospective mode ('Am I am not free? Am I not an apostle? Have I not seen Jesus our Lord?,' 1 Cor 9:1), he also states it in a reflexive manner: "For if I preach the gospel, that gives me no ground for boasting. For necessity is laid upon me. Woe to me if I do not preach the gospel!" (1 Cor 9:16). This spontaneous reference to the pagan topic of restrictive necessity, of the ἀνάγκη, expresses the conviction of having received a mission.[15] In that, Paul forms part of that line of first apostles and Christian missionaries who, resorting to the prophetic vocabulary of the Hebrew Bible, reinterpret it to specifically see in it a mission *ad extra*.

b) An open and dynamic community

The Israel of the old covenant was already aware of its responsibility with regard to the nations: to serve as a light and by that, a reference point and vehicle of truth.[16] But the traditions of Israel also conveyed the theme for the remainder of Israel and the requirement to separate itself from the nations. If the reformist monks of Qumran chose to safeguard the holy core of the elect, the first Christians realized the prophecy of Israel: salvation in Christ becomes "a light for rev-

---

[15] See Ernst Käsemann, "Eine paulinische Variation des 'amor fati,'" *ZTK* 96 (1959) 138–54; reprinted in idem, *Exegetische Versuche und Besinnungen*, 2:223–39.

[16] See Robert Martin-Achard, *Israël et les nations. La perspective missionnaire de l'Ancien Testament* (CahT 42; Neuchâtel: Delachaux & Niestlé, 1959).

elation to the Gentiles, and for glory to your people Israel" (φῶς εἰς ἀποκάλυψιν ἐθνῶν καὶ δόξαν λαοῦ σου Ἰσραήλ, Luke 2:32).

Christ ("I am the light of the world," John 8:12) spreads his light today, if the community becomes in its turn a base from which the missions radiate ("You are the light of the world," Matt 5:14).

The synoptic tradition and the Pauline tradition – it is interesting to note – have each taken and developed this relationship between the life of the community and missionary success. Here indeed is how, in the wake of the *Logia* source, Matthew develops this thematic: "You are the light of the world. A city built on a hill cannot be hid. No one after lighting a lamp puts it under the bushel basket, but on the lampstand, and it gives light to all in the house. In the same way, let your light shine before others, so that they may see your good works and give glory to your Father in heaven" (Matt 5:14–16, NRSV).

For Matthew and, without doubt, for the synoptic tradition, it is the task of the community that is specified here, a task that supplements the missionary action of the itinerant messengers: to the mission marked by travels is added a mission of local radiation. If the word dominates in the first case, the action obtains a priority function in the second.

This requirement, as I have said, is taken over by Paul, who transmits it to the Philippians: "Do all things without murmuring and arguing, so that you may be blameless and innocent, children of God without blemish in the midst of a crooked and perverse generation, in which you shine like stars in the world, holding fast to the word of life" (Phil 2:14–16a, NRSV, modified at 16a).

c) A diagnosis on the present state of the world

The quotation from the letter to the Philippians utilized an additional element: by the words qualifying the contemporary generation of the depraved and the perverted, the apostle not only expresses a theological conviction that he develops largely in Romans 1–3, but also takes up again the inherited stereotypical language of Jesus (the words, "a crooked and perverse generation," recalling Matt 17:17 and Luke 9:41 and, beyond Jesus, Deut 32:5 and 20).[17]

To grasp the sense of this analysis, one will have to avoid reading it from a moralizing viewpoint; it is necessary to give an eschatological interpretation: in the Jewish apocalyptic perspective of the two periods, aeons, Jesus, followed faithfully by the itinerant missionaries and then by the Hellenists and Paul, perceives the catastrophic state of the world, the expressions "deliver us from the present evil age" (Gal 1:4) and "the form of this world is passing away" (1 Cor 7:31) attesting that Paul had not lost the apocalyptic conscience of Jesus and the first Chris-

---

[17] See Victor Hasler, "γενεά,"in *Exegetisches Wörterbuch zum Neuen Testament* (eds. Horst Balz and Gerhard Schneider; 3 vols.; Stuttgart: Kohlhammer, 1980–1983) 1:579–81.

tians: the state of this world is all the more disastrous as it nears its end, nearing also the passage from one aeon to another. The more serious the prognosis, the more tangible is the hope of salvation. And, as the aeon to come is entirely in the hands of God, this aeon, certainly evil because of men and women who inhabit it, is above all dominated by Satan and his army (see Acts 10:38).

There is certainly a Christian correction to the Jewish scheme for both aeons, but it does not touch on the apocalyptic imminence but the "already" partial one of the new aeon, set up by the proclamation of the Kingdom according to Jesus, the message of the cross and resurrection for the apostles and, in particular, for Paul. Between the "already" inaugurated by Jesus and the final irruption of the last aeon, there is a space, a respite perceived in duration more or less according to the individual and circumstance – a foreseen delay not for the expectation of more and more disappointment, but for a mission more and more active.[18] Still, the New Testament is not as good a witness of the disparate hopes as it is a harbinger of a common conviction: the synoptic tradition of the apocalyptic speech in Mark 13, the Pauline topics, or Lukan composition of Acts, beginning with Acts 1 – all these testimonies indicate that between Easter and the Parousia there is enough space for the mission, i.e., for the Word and the Spirit incarnate in the living community and its missionary activity. By way of example of this certainty shared by all, I cite verse 10 of Mark 13: "The gospel must (see the ἀνάγκη of 1 Cor 9:16) first (that is to say, before the signs of the end) be preached to all nations," and the beginning of Acts: "Lord, will you at this time restore the kingdom to Israel?" (Acts 1:6), ask the disciples to the resurrected Christ, who answers them, "It is not for you to know the times or periods that the Father has set by his own authority. But you will receive power when the Holy Spirit has come upon you; and you will be my witnesses in Jerusalem, in all Judea and Samaria, and to the ends of the earth" (Acts 1:7–8). The first Christians thus understood the urgency. Their duty was to offer to humans who were bound in sin an ultimate occasion to unite with God and with the procession of the saved.

d) The will of God

Behind each of the three reasons enumerated up to now appeared the plan of God: Jesus decided to choose the Twelve, to invest them with authority and to send them. On this point, the will of the Son joins that of the Father. It is still God who places and wants to place the stage of the mission between Easter and the Parousia, as it is he, and not only Paul, who requires of the communities to be beyond reproach and to shine like torches in the world.

---

[18] In several of his works, Oscar Cullmann has insisted on this theological structure; for example, see idem, *Christ et le temps. Temps et histoire dans le christianisme primitif* (Série théologique de l'actualité protestante; Neuchâtel: Delachaux & Niestlé, 1947) 111–18.

It is a fundamental characteristic of this divine intention that the New Testament highlights, unanimous in these various traditions: this organizing God mobilizes believers and does not complete his project alone. His planning power corresponds to his deliberate impotence as director. In other words, God resorts to human mediation and chooses human hands to carry out his work. The apostles and the communities are in the real sense God's collaborators, without divine condescension, nor excessive pedagogy. It is this offer of collaboration that gives them such confidence and authority.[19]

In a manner certainly varied, the first Christian authors all express this common conviction. The itinerant evangelists, heirs to missionary intentions of Jesus, know that the irruption of the Kingdom is related to their service; Paul associates, in 2 Corinthians 5, with the reconciliation brought about by God alone, thanks to Jesus Christ, the word of the reconciliation in which he has, himself, as an apostle, the responsibility. As for John, he uses an image: he specifies that those who are sent are beings who know because they love and have been initiated. The Son had been sent because he had rested his head – such is the image – in the bosom of the Father (John 1:18); the disciples, at the school of the Johannine leader, the beloved disciple, are sent, because the beloved too had – the same image is used – rested his head on the bosom of Jesus during the last supper (John 13:23 and 25). To know the Father, it is necessary to look at the Son who showed us the Father; in Johannine perspective, to see the Son, it is necessary to be directed towards the beloved disciple who is at the origin of the traditions collected in the fourth Gospel. In all the cases, God remains hidden as long as human mediation does not work. He appears only by associating human collaborators to his intervention.

3. Deserved or ambiguous success of the Christian mission

Scholars as eminent as Adolf von Harnack, Eduard Norden, and Rudolf Bultmann have estimated that the Christian religion had become a force because of its capacity to adapt and its desire for assimilation. Harnack sees in the success of ancient Christianity the result of an advantageous syncretism;[20] Norden contends that the formula "No one knows the Son except the Father, and no one knows the Father except the Son and any one to whom the Son chooses to reveal him" (Matt 11:27) does not go up to Jesus, but takes over, in the Christian version, an Eastern formula of religious propaganda;[21] Bultmann defends the thesis of an application to Christian Christology of a non-Christian schema of the descent and ascent of

---

[19] In connection with Luke-Acts, see François Bovon, "L'importance des médiations dans le projet théologique de Luc," *NTS* 21 (1974–1975) 23–39.

[20] See von Harnack, *Die Mission und Ausbreitung des Christentums*, 324–31.

[21] Eduard Norden, *Agnostos Theos. Untersuchungen zur Formengeschichte religiöser Rede* (4th ed.; Darmstadt: Wissenschaftliche Buchgesellschaft, 1956) 277–308, esp. 303–8.

the Savior;[22] more recently, American scholars have insisted on mentioning the Christian appropriation motif of the divine man and the missionary use of the literary genre of the aretalogy in the form of our Gospels to communicate Christian ideas;[23] and many of exegetes see in the topic of pre-existence and the sending of the Son a Christian adaptation of Jewish Hellenistic speculations on Wisdom, elder daughter of God.[24] The question thus arises: To propagate the Gospel, did the Christian missionaries push this transculturation so far that from it they distorted the message itself? See the effort to return to the simple Gospel of the good God and of God the Father, as in the writings of Harnack,[25] and the program of demythologizing, as in the writings of Bultmann,[26] the last opportunity for scholars who wished to remain theologians, despite everything.

It appears undeniable to me that the New Testament writings, in their obviously attested variety, certainly borrowed categories and expressions from Judaism, from the Greeks (from Stoics in particular), and even from imperial ideology. But besides this concern for adaptation, which corresponds to an effort for intelligibility, another preoccupation is evident: adaptation to the Word of God. And what can appear, to the eyes of some, as tolerance to old mentalities, can be, to the eyes of others, reliance on the will of God. It is thus appropriate to judge case by case, by insertion of the message (in a cybernetic sense of the term) in the complete circuit of the communication, to critically evaluate this effort of contextualization by the first Christian theologians to which one will not award, under any motive, even if it was that of canonicity, a standing ovation for an inspired and pneumatically successful proclamation.

Without being able to establish this assessment, I claim that certain theologians of the apostolic age, Paul in particular, were sensitive to the problem. One indeed encounters in the apostle's letters two expressions that appear contradictory: in the epistle to the Galatians (Gal 1:10), the apostle claims not to seek to persuade men and women, nor to please them. In First Corinthians (1 Cor 10:32–33) and in Second Corinthians (2 Cor 5:11), he affirms the contrary, making his point of honor to convince and to please men and women. What is being said?

---

[22] Rudolf Bultmann, *Theologie des Neuen Testaments* (Tübingen: Mohr Siebeck, 1958) 362–66.

[23] See Charles H. Talbert, *What Is a Gospel?: The Genre of the Canonical Gospels* (Philadelphia: Fortress, 1977), esp. 12–14.

[24] See Eduard Schweizer, *Jesus Christus im vielfältigen Zeugnis des Neuen Testaments* (2d ed.; Siebenstern-Taschenbuch 126; Munich: Siebenstern, 1970) 83–87.

[25] Adolf von Harnack, *Das Wesen des Christentums* (intro. Rudolf Bultmann; Stuttgart: Ehrenfried Klotz Verlag, 1950).

[26] Rudolf Bultmann, "Neues Testament und Mythologie. Das Problem der Entmythologisierung der neutestamentlichen Verkündigung," in *Kerygma und Mythos*, I. *Ein theologisches Gespräch* (ed. Hans-Werner Bartsch; 5th ed.; Hambourg-Bergstedt: Reich, 1967) 15–48. See also Karl Jaspers and Rudolf Bultmann, *Die Frage der Entmythologisierung* (Munich: R. Piper, 1954).

The adversaries of Paul in Galatia reproach the apostle for gaining human approval by doubtful means – one can think of recourse to human authority such as that of the apostles of Jerusalem, with particular prestige of the Gospel or Pauline apostolate. Paul retorts that he does not seek to persuade human beings, nor to entice them by human means. He does not seek to further their pleasure nor finally to maintain them in their situation. Paul is thus sensitive to the dangers and excesses of concession.

If it can be said, in 1 Cor 10:32–33 and in 2 Cor 5:11, that he seeks nevertheless to please humanity, it is in another sense: here, to please men and women no longer means to make them secure in their position (what is of concern to the σάρξ), but to join them in their authentic being, which is the image and creation of God. By doing this, he is hoping to save some of them. Paul is therefore also sensitive to the requirement of the conscience. The contradiction is thus only apparent: in 1 and 2 Corinthians, the apostle speaks about evangelization, in Galatians, of fraudulent means of manipulation.

The apostle thus knows the difference between one type of pleasing from another, and one type of persuading from another; he is convinced that the message must always be reformulated anew, to remain faithful to the Word of God and yet accessible to one and all. He is convinced by it, because Jesus Christ is the great model of this success: having become a human being, he remained Son of God. Thanks to this faithfulness to his Father and this bond with humanity, he could bring about adoption and salvation.

Without accusing the apostle of alienation and blindness of the self, I must recognize that Paul was conscious of the double missionary task, which finally corresponds to the double command of love: on the one hand, not to exploit the congregation and to hold to the only Word of God incarnate in Jesus Christ; and on the other hand, not to cut themselves off from the world, men and women, and their language, but to search for them, and to reach out to them wherever they may be, and to convince them.

Conclusion

In conclusion, I will say that the quality of the organization and the missionary language adopted supported the diffusion of Christianity. But there were other causes for this success, which are due to the articulation of the word and of the action.[27] The Christian message was convincing, because it was a message inhabited by those who proclaimed it and lived communally by the evangelists and

---

[27] After having read these pages, Henry Mottu rightly invites me not to underestimate the sociological and political causes for this success. See from a Marxist viewpoint I. Lenzman, *L'origine du christianisme* (trans. Léon Piatigorski; Moscow, 1961; Russian original in 1958) 77–89.

congregations; it was a powerful message that put into question the practices and even endangered the lives of the faithful; it was an accessible message, because it has been adapted to contemporary schemas of comprehension; but it was also a new message, worthy to be believed and anchored in God, able to address the pretence of other religious currents – a message that finally, in a century when behavior was stuck between two extreme positions, alleged mastery of the self and servile submission to the law, structured the existence by uniting to a person, Jesus Christ, one living community, the Church.

I enumerated, at the beginning of this account, three contemporary interpretations of missionary duty: at the end of this paper, I do not wish to position them against one another, but to invite those who favor them to measure their goals with the missionary practice of early Christianity, which has its standard in the love of God and the love of the neighbor, its reference in the Christology of the Son of God, who became equal to men and women, its source in the saving grace of God, its effectiveness in the power of the Spirit, and its realization in the fragile and mortal body of Christians.[28]

---

[28] This article was already in composition when a collective work arrived to me, edited by Karl Kertelge, *Mission im Neuen Testament* (QD 93; Freiburg im Breisgau: Herder, 1982).

Christ in the Book of Revelation[1]

Introduction

In chapter 22 of the Book of Revelation, the visionary of Patmos describes the enigmatic splendor of the tree of life (Rev 22:2). What he says of this mysterious wealth can be applied without difficulty to the account that he gives of the appearance of Jesus Christ.[2]

---

[1] Lecture delivered in French at Lausanne, before the Faculty of Theology, at the re-opening session of the University, 26 October 1971, and in German, at Uppsala, before a New Testament Seminar at the Faculty of Theology, 7 March 1972.

[2] Principal Commentaries: Wilhelm Bousset, *Die Offenbarung Johannis* (Göttingen: Vandenhoeck & Ruprecht, 1896; 2d ed., 1906); Robert H. Charles, *A Critical and Exegetical Commentary on the Revelation of St. John: With Introduction, Notes and Indices* (Edinburgh: T&T Clark, 1920); Ernest Bernard Allo, *Saint Jean, L'Apocalypse* (Paris: Lecoffre, 1921; 4th ed., 1933); Alfred Loisy, *L'Apocalypse de Jean* (Paris: Émile Nourry, 1923); Ernst Lohmeyer, *Die Offenbarung des Johannes* (Tübingen: Mohr Siebeck, 1926; 2d ed., 1953); Charles Brütsch, *L'Apocalypse de Jésus-Christ* (Geneva: Labor et Fides, 1940; 5th ed., 1966, retitled *La Clarté de l'Apocalypse*).

Annotated Translations: *Le Nouveau Testament. Traduction nouvelle d'après les meilleurs textes avec introductions et notes* (trans. and ann. of the Apocalypse by G. Baldensperger; 4 vols.; Bible du Centenaire; Paris, 1928); Marie-Émile Boismard, *L'Apocalypse* (Bible de Jérusalem; Paris, 1950; 3d ed., 1959); *L'Apocalypse* (Traduction Œcuménique de la Bible; Paris, 1970).

Studies: Joachim Jeremias, "ἀμνός, κτλ.," in *TWNT* 1:342–45; Paul André Harlé, "Le Christ-Agneau. Essai sur la Christologie de l'Apocalypse" (unpublished dissertation, Montpellier, 1955); idem, "L'Agneau de l'Apocalypse et le Nouveau Testament," *ETR* 31 (1956) 26–35; Eugen Schmitt, "Die christologische Interpretation als das Grundlegende der Apokalypse," *Tübinger Theologische Quartalschrift* 140 (1960) 257–90; Traugott Holtz, *Die Christologie der Apokalypse des Johannes* (Berlin: Akademie-Verlag, 1962; 2d ed., with appendix, 1971); Pierre Prigent, *Apocalypse et Liturgie* (Neuchâtel: Delachaux et Niestlé, 1964); José Comblin, *Le Christ dans l'Apocalypse* (Paris: Desclée de Brouwer, 1965); Mathias Rissi, *Was ist und was geschehen soll danach. Die Zeit- und Geschichtsauffassung der Offenbarung des Johannes* (2d ed. of *Zeit und Geschichte in der Offenbarung des Johannes*; Zurich-Stuttgart: Zwingli, 1965); idem, *Die Zukunft der Welt. Eine exegetische Studie über Johannesoffenbarung 19,11–22,15* (Basel: F. Reinhardt, 1966); Akira Satake, *Die Gemeindeordnung in der Johannesapokalypse* (Neukirchen-Vluyn: Neukirchener Verlag, 1966); as for the unpublished dissertation of Ulrich Müller ("Messias und Menschensohn in jüdischen Apokalypsen und in der Offenbarung des Johannes," Heidelberg, 1966), I only know it by the critical account given by Holtz in the second edition of his work (*Die Christologie der Apokalypse des Johannes*, 244–46); Peter von der Osten-Sacken, "Christologie, Taufe, Homologie – Ein Beitrag zur Apc. Joh. i, 5 f.," *ZNW* 58 (1967) 255–66; Reinhard Deichgräber, *Gotteshymnus und Christushymnus. Untersuchungen zu Form, Sprache und Stil der frühchristlichen Hymnen* (Göttingen: Vandenhoeck & Ruprecht, 1967); Donatien

This richness appears on various levels. Several visions, first of all, suggest the grandeur of Christ. In chapter 1, we will discover the only description of the Resurrection that the New Testament contains: Jesus appears to John as the Son of Man and as High Priest.[3] In chapter 5, the seer is elevated to heaven and attends at the coronation of the Lamb, appearing slain yet standing, signifying crucifixion and resurrection.[4] Chapter 12 merges the story of Jesus into an ancestral myth and describes the birth of a child to a crowned woman, who is threatened by the dragon, and his removal from heaven.[5] Chapter 22 finally resorts to another genre and calls forth the wedding of the Lamb and its Church.[6]

The christological wealth of the Book of Revelation overflows the framework of the visions. It shows also through in the liturgical texts that punctuate the work.[7] Already in the address we meet a triune liturgical formula that culminates in a description of the redemptive work of Christ:

Grace to you and peace from him who is and who was and who is to come, and from the seven spirits who are before his throne, and from Jesus Christ, the faithful witness, the firstborn of the dead, and the ruler of kings of the earth. To him who loves us and freed us from our sins by his blood and made us to be a kingdom, priests to his God and Father, to him be glory and dominion for ever and ever. Amen. (Rev 1:4–6, NRSV slightly modified)[8]

This liturgical connection with Christ accompanies us until the last verse of the work, where doxology is transformed into an intercession: "Amen. Come, Lord Jesus! The grace of the Lord Jesus be with all" (Rev 22:20–21).[9]

Mollat, "La Cristologia dell' Apocalisse" (the title "Cristologia del Nuovo Testamento," on page 47, must be an error), *L'Apocalisse* (Brescia, 1967) 47–68; Klaus-Peter Jörns, *Das hymnische Evangelium. Untersuchungen zu Aufbau, Funktion und Herkunft der hymnischen Stücke in der Johannesoffenbarung* (Gütersloh: G. Mohn, 1971).

Status quaestionis: André Feuillet, *L'Apocalypse. État de la question* (Paris-Bruges: Desclée de Brouwer, 1963), with detailed bibliography.

[3] See Holtz, *Die Christologie der Apokalypse*, 109–28, 251–52; Mollat, "La Cristologia dell' Apocalisse," 48–53. It starts with the clothing of the Son of Man where one may ascertain a sacerdotal function to this. The sociologist Marshall McLuhan (*Pour comprendre les média. Les prolongements technologiques de l'homme* [French translation; Paris, 1968; English original 1964]) shows that clothing can be a means of communication, a language. See n. 79 below.

[4] See Jeremias, "ἀμνός, κτλ."; Harlé, "Le Christ-Agneau," passim; Holtz, *Die Christologie der Apokalypse*, 27–54, 248–49; Prigent, *Apocalypse et Liturgie*, 69–76; Jörns, *Das hymnische Evangelium*, 44–76.

[5] See Pierre Prigent, *Apocalypse 12. Histoire de l'exégèse* (Tübingen: Mohr Siebeck, 1959); Holtz, *Die Christologie der Apokalypse*, 89–109, 251; Feuillet, *L'Apocalypse*, 91–98.

[6] See Joachim Jeremias, "νύμφη, κτλ.," in *TWNT* 4:1092–99; Holtz, *Die Christologie der Apokalypse*, 186–91; Richard A. Batey, *New Testament Nuptial Imagery* (Leiden: Brill, 1971).

[7] For delimitation and definition of the literary liturgical genres of the Apocalypse, see Jörns, *Das hymnische Evangelium*; see also Deichgräber, *Gotteshymnus und Christushymnus*, 44–59.

[8] In addition to the commentaries, see Holtz, *Die Christologie der Apokalypse*, 55–71, 249–50; and von der Osten-Sacken, "Christologie, Taufe, Homologie."

[9] See Brütsch, *L'Apocalypse de Jésus-Christ*, 392–94.

The christological abundance finally bursts forth on a third level: titles and figures. There is initially the prevalence, unique in the New Testament, of the title the Lamb (ἀρνίον), to designate Christ victorious over death, leader of his people, Master of the universe and associated with God.[10] Next there is the discrete presence of traditional titles: Son of God, Lord, Son of the man (or, more exactly, Son of Man, without the definite article preceding the noun as in the Old Testament), and Christ, understood in an archaic or archaizing manner as the Messiah of the ancient prophesies.[11] There is finally a multitude of expressions, often to be found only in Revelation: the prince of the kings of the earth,[12] the first-born of the dead,[13] Lord of lords, King of kings,[14] The Word of God,[15] the true one,[16] the holy one,[17] the faithful,[18] the Amen,[19] the root of David,[20] the bright morning star,[21] the one who searches minds and hearts,[22] the one who has the key of David,[23] the one who holds the seven stars in his right hand,[24] the first and the last,[25] the Alpha and the Omega,[26] the beginning and the end,[27] the ἀρχή of God's creation,[28] and especially the living one[29] and the faithful witness.[30]

[10] Here I summarize the results of Harlé, "Le Christ-Agneau." See Jeremias, "ἀμνός, κτλ."; and Holtz, *Die Christologie der Apokalypse*, 39–47, 248–49.

[11] A good analysis is in Holtz, *Die Christologie der Apokalypse*, 5–26, 246–47. See Comblin, *Le Christ dans l'Apocalypse*, passim.

[12] Rev 1:5; see Comblin, *Le Christ dans l'Apocalypse*, 94ff.

[13] Rev 1:5; Holtz, *Die Christologie der Apokalypse*, 57–58.

[14] Rev 17:14; 19:16; see Holtz, *Die Christologie der Apokalypse*, 154–56; and Comblin, *Le Christ dans l'Apocalypse*, 94ff.

[15] Rev 19:13; see Comblin, *Le Christ dans l'Apocalypse*, 80–91.

[16] Rev 3:7; 19:11; see Rev 3:14; Holtz, *Die Christologie der Apokalypse*, 141–42.

[17] Rev 3:7; see Holtz, *Die Christologie der Apokalypse*, 140–41.

[18] Rev 3:14; 19:11.

[19] Rev 3:14; see Holtz, *Die Christologie der Apokalypse*, 142.

[20] Rev 5:5; 22:16; see Holtz, *Die Christologie der Apokalypse*, 151–52, 253.

[21] Rev 22:16; see Holtz, *Die Christologie der Apokalypse*, 156–59.

[22] Rev 2:23; see Comblin, *Le Christ dans l'Apocalypse*, 128ff.

[23] Rev 3:7; see Comblin, *Le Christ dans l'Apocalypse*, 74.

[24] Rev 2:1; see Rev 3:1.

[25] Rev 1:17; 2:8; 22:13; see Holtz, *Die Christologie der Apokalypse*, 148–54, 253.

[26] Rev 22:13; see Holtz, *Die Christologie der Apokalypse*, 148–54, 253.

[27] Rev 22:13; see Holtz, *Die Christologie der Apokalypse*, 148–54, 253.

[28] Rev 3:14; see Holtz, *Die Christologie der Apokalypse*, 143–47.

[29] Rev 1:18; see Comblin, *Le Christ dans l'Apocalypse*, 195ff.

[30] Rev 1:5; 3:14; see Holtz, *Die Christologie der Apokalypse*, 55–57; and especially Comblin, *Le Christ dans l'Apocalypse*, 132–67.

Status quaestionis

This abundance, which accompanies many enigmas,[31] has for a longtime dampened the zeal of the exegetes. Following Wilhelm Bousset,[32] they all acknowledged the expansion and the diversity of this Christology. No one, however, dared to expose the major components. It was not until the 1960s that we see the appearance of two books, one after the other and independent from one another, that covers our subject in all its breadth.

The first is the work of the German exegete Traugott Holtz.[33] Although it is clear in the detail of the analyses of the texts and titles, it is less convincing in the presentation of the main lines of the Christology of the Book of Revelation. For him, everything is played out on Holy Friday and Easter: the Christology of the Apocalypse is a Christology of the now victorious paschal lamb. This Christ reigns triumphant over his Church. Satan, hurled down to earth, can only marshal his last forces in a conflict already lost. The final battle hardly deserves to be described. Little light is shed on the connections that link Christ to the nations by the prophet of Patmos. According to Holtz, the Lamb puts all his attention on his betrothed, the Church. God alone judges the people.

This christocentric interpretation – which is more Barthian than Bultmannian – classifies the facts of the case according to temporal categories: the past, present, and future work of Christ. To our surprise, the view of Holtz on the Book of Revelation says little of the future. From a critical point of view, one can wonder initially whether this reference to time makes it possible to give an account of all the christological elements in Revelation, whether the future of Christ regarding the nations does not disappear entirely,[34] and finally, whether the present and future functions of the risen Christ as revealer and as witness are not clearly underestimated.

Whoever is familiar with current New Testament studies is not surprised to find a very different concept in the work of Joseph Comblin.[35] For the French exegete, the Christ of the Book of Revelation is on many points the same as the

---

[31] Why does John give preference to the title "Lamb"? What is the real power of the Lamb in the present? May one speak about the anticipated arrival of the Son of Man in his communities?

[32] Bousset, *Die Offenbarung Johannis*, 140, as quoted by Holtz, *Die Christologie der Apokalypse*, 2. According to Bousset, it is only a matter of a disorganized abundance of traditional elements.

[33] Holtz, *Die Christologie der Apokalypse*; Comblin (*Le Christ dans l'Apocalypse*) could take note of Holtz's book before the printing of his manuscript. He gives an account in the appendix (pp. 237–40) of his own work.

[34] In his analysis of Rev 19:11ff., Holtz (*Die Christologie der Apokalypse*, 166–81) wrongly limits the intervention of the Son of Man at the time of his return to the Christian community.

[35] Comblin, *Le Christ dans l'Apocalypse*. In the appendix of the second edition of his book (*Die Christologie der Apokalypse*, 241–44), Holtz gives an opinion regarding the work of Comblin. Some of his criticisms are in step with mine.

Christ of the primitive Christian tradition: Christ died for us and was resurrected in glory. But, in Comblin's opinion, the visionary of Patmos is not satisfied to repeat the tradition: he develops an original Christology – a reflective and doctrinal conception of Christ. To do so, John resorts to the Hebrew Bible and the Messianic models that it contains: the Son of Man, the Messiah, and Wisdom personified. Under the influence of his faith and the visions that he received, he undertakes a more profound rereading of these things given in the Hebrew Bible. In what manner does he do this?

According to Comblin, all becomes clear if one highlights the dominating influence of Deutero-Isaiah, the figure of the servant and the idea of a divine trial against nations in particular. The Lamb of the Book of Revelation represents the servant of Isaiah, suffering then glorified. However, the function of the servant is one of saving and witnessing – saving Israel and illuminating and judging the nations. According to Comblin, this is exactly what makes the Christ of the Book of Revelation: he saves, loves, and leads his community. In addition, he testifies in front of, or rather against, the nations in the eschatological trial that God conducts against them.

From there, Comblin introduces to the figure of the servant two other christological components that he discovers: the Son of Man of Daniel, and the Messiah of the prophets. This insertion of the Messiah and Son of Man into the category of the servant, who subsumes them, has as a consequence a transformation of these two titles and these two functions. The Son of Man is no longer attached to heaven as he was in the Hebrew Bible: he comes to earth as a witness for the prosecution. The Messiah, for his part, is not localized any longer on earth, in Israel, as it is hoped for in the Hebrew Bible. He ascends to God, accompanied by the community whose life he had redeemed.

Such would be the originality of this very elaborate and perceptive Christology.[36] In my opinion, Comblin overstates the role of Isaiah 40–55 and makes too much of the servant of Isaiah.[37] Indeed, John never attributes this title to Jesus-Christ. Moreover, the distribution of the christological data into two groups, the Son of Man and the Messiah, often forces the direction of the texts. The theme of the appearance, to take only one example, may apply to the Messiah as well as to the Son of Man, and so one does not see why Comblin connects it exclusively to

---

[36] Among the christological innovations transmitted by the visions, Comblin discovers before all certain ecclesiologic truths, which is not surprising for a Catholic author: "What is happening in the interval? Now it is here that the Church is intervening, whose revelation Saint John has received in the mystery of his testimony" (*Le Christ dans l'Apocalypse*, 234). The "mystery" of Rev 1:20 certainly relates to the Church, but in its relation to the risen Lord whose author is teaching how to know the vigilant and active presence.

[37] The following articles better illustrate the various scriptural influences: Jules Cambier, "Les images de l'Ancien Testament dans l'Apocalypse de saint Jean," *NRTh* 77 (1955) 113–22; Albert Vanhoye, "L'utilisation du livre d'Ezéchiel dans l'Apocalypse," *Bib* 43 (1962) 436–76.

the Son of Man. Finally, one may doubt that John the prophet and the apocalyptician wanted to build a Christology as systematic as that one.

Christ in Contact

In the pages that follow, I would like to propose a less doctrinal classification and
a more natural use of the data from the Book of Revelation. This classification is
drawn neither from the beginning of time, as Holtz states, nor from the Hebrew
Bible models, as Comblin would have us believe. I propose to establish it from the
bonds that are established between the characters. Indeed, like any person, the
Christ of the Apocalypse manifests and reinforces his identity in the relations he
maintains with beings and matter. He is not and cannot be without others.[38] At
the end of the paper, I will insist on two privileged modes for these relations: that
which concerns the Church, where Christ is defined as the revealer; and that
which concerns the nations, when he is seen as a witness.

Christ and His Church

As John is a member of the Church, the Christ whom he describes to us is first of
all the one who is in contact with the Christian community. The categories of
presence, gift, union, authority, and imitation allow for detailing these relations.

Christ appears initially to his Church by his living presence. One will note that
in Rev 1:18, "I died, and behold I am alive for evermore," the stress is on the
present life of the Risen One.[39] In the same way, the initial formula I quoted, the
present affection ("he who loves us") precedes the reference to the grounding act
of the past ("who freed us from our sins by his blood," Rev 1:5).[40] This presence
and this life, which explain the anticipated arrivals of the Son of Man into his
communities (Rev 3:20),[41] determine all the relationships of Christ to the others.
They allow anamnesis and prolepsis.

He who lives, the Risen Christ, is none other than Jesus of Nazareth. John
stresses this continuity by the attachment he places to the proper name of Jesus.[42]
For him, Jesus is characterized by the gift that he made of his life. He is the Lamb
who offered his blood so that the redeemed may – according to the fearful image

---

[38] I am happy to find myself here in agreement with Mollat; I took note of his contribution
only after the editing of this article. The professor from Rome insists on the relations which link
Christ to his Church (see Mollat, "La Cristologia dell' Apocalisse").

[39] On this formula, see Holtz, *Die Christologie der Apokalypse*, 80–88.

[40] See n. 8 above.

[41] See Comblin, *Le Christ dans l'Apocalypse*, 61–65.

[42] Holtz (*Die Christologie der Apokalypse*, 22–25) analyzes the name Jesus and discovers
other connotations there than I do.

– wash their robes and make them white (Rev 7:14).[43] It is necessary to underscore the relational nature of this oblative act: this gesture only makes sense if the community accepts it and proclaims it.

This gift is also found at the conclusion of the story. The Son of Man promises eschatological possessions to the faithful believers. For the end, he reserves for them, as is shown in every conclusion of the seven letters, the tree of life, the hidden manna, the white pebble, the crown of life, and the morning star.[44] In a word, he will make for them a gift of life.[45]

These past gifts and those to come are already alive to the rhythm of affection that is established between the Lamb and his Church. When this love and liturgical communion become intense presence and reciprocal oblation, they must be expressed in marital terms. John resorts then to the bridal vocabulary.[46] The Jewish novel of *Joseph and Aseneth*[47] and the Gnostic *Gospel of Philip*[48] confirm for us the theological and eschatological range of this category of marital union.

For the moment, however, the Church still marches on towards the kingdom. The marriage is not consummated yet. So, to keep his community on the path to life, Christ resorts to the authority that his Paschal victory confers on him. The love of the resurrected is an exclusive and demanding love. The identical literary structure of the seven letters shows this: after having affirmed his knowledge[49] and having posed a diagnosis,[50] Christ requires a decision that must allow the return to God of the fallen who are repentant.[51] Thus the Son of Man takes on a pedagogical function that Wisdom in the Hebrew Bible filled.[52] Like Wisdom, he is able to announce that he will return for retribution.[53] Like her, he can say: "Those whom I love, I reprove and chasten" (Rev 3:19). This pedagogical Christ, however, does not maintain his authority in a despotic way. It is in love and dialogue that he exerts his power.

Lastly, the road that the Church follows currently crosses the desert. Two of its representatives, the two witnesses of the Resurrected, are persecuted.[54] They

---

[43] Holtz (*Die Christologie der Apokalypse*, 36–109) insists rightly on the work of Jesus Christ.

[44] See Rev 2:7, 10, 17, 28; 3:5, 12, 21.

[45] Comblin (*Le Christ dans l'Apocalypse*, 207ff.) is right to stress the importance of the gift of the life that Christ will make to his Church.

[46] See the bibliography cited above in n. 6.

[47] See Marc Philonenko, *Joseph et Aséneth. Introduction, texte critique, traduction et notes* (Leiden: Brill, 1968).

[48] See Jacques Ménard, *L'Évangile selon Philippe* (Paris: Letouzey & Ané, 1967).

[49] "I know … ," Rev 2:2, for example.

[50] "You are enduring … . But I have this against you, that you have abandoned the love you had at first," Rev 2:3–4, for example.

[51] "Repent and do the works you did at first," Rev 2:5, for example.

[52] This point was clarified by Comblin, *Le Christ dans l'Apocalypse*, 120ff.

[53] "If not, I will come to you and remove your lampstand from its place," Rev 2:5, for example.

[54] There are a variety of interpretations which have been raised in chapter 11. The reader will

walk in the steps of their master and share his fate. By suffering, they advance towards glory. Chapter 11, which recounts the fate of these two witnesses, invites us to associate the identical fate of the companions to the corresponding couple described above. From the destiny of the witnesses, we understand better the life and death of the true witness. The concept of imitation makes it possible for faith to move in two directions: from Christ to the Church, but also from the Church and its ethics to Christ and to his truth.

Christ and the World

The relationships that are established between Christ and the nations are more difficult to define. In a curious way, during the penultimate stage, the fate of the impious nations until the parousia does not appear directly determined by the interventions of the Risen Christ. Misfortunes that occur on earth come from God.[55] It is also to God that the twenty-four elders address this extraordinary prayer: "We give you thanks, Lord God Almighty, who are and who were, for you have taken your great power and begun to reign" (Rev 11:17, NRSV); the destroying angels carry out on earth sentences of the divine judgment.

Analysis of the title "witness" (μάρτυς)[56] prevents from underestimating – as Holtz does[57] – the present activity of Christ regarding the pagan nations, because the "witness" in the Book of Revelation is not the martyr. It is not by his death that Christ brings testimony, but by his word. Suffering is only the consequence of a testimony that resounds beyond death. The Resurrected witness remains before the world and God during the trial between humans and their creator. As the true witness, he now announces to the nations the exclusivity of faith. As he himself states, under no circumstances would he tolerate competition: "The words of the holy one, the true one, who has the key of David, who opens and no one shall shut, who shuts and no one opens" (Rev 3:7). As witness for the prosecution, he presents to God the charges against the humans that he detains.

A similar ambiguity (Christ is at the same time inactive and active with regard to the nations) characterizes the ultimate period of history. For, to take again the

---

find a summary in the commentary of Brütsch, *L'Apocalypse de Jésus-*Christ, 183ff. See also Satake, *Die Gemeindeordnung in der Johannesapokalypse*, 119–33.

[55] Contra Jörns (*Das hymnische Evangelium*, 42–43), who insists on the inactivity of God according to the Apocalypse: "Die konsequente Vermeidung von Anthropomorphismen führt nun zu der Eigentümlichkeit der Apc., dass Gott weder handelnd noch redend (bis auf 21:5–8, …) auftritt" (ibid., 42). Rev 17:14 announces, undoubtedly, the last conflict of the Lamb (see Rev 19:11ff.).

[56] It is interesting to read the chapter "Witness" in the monograph of Comblin, *Le Christ dans l'Apocalypse*, 132–67. See Satake, *Die Gemeindeordnung in der Johannesapokalypse*, 113–19.

[57] See Holtz, *Die Christologie der Apokalypse*, 137–64, who underscores however the lordly presence of the Resurrected one in the world.

image in chapter 14, it is an angel of God who is harvesting.[58] In chapter 18, Baby-
lon falls without the intervention of Christ. In 20:11–15, it is still God who judges
and punishes each one according to his deeds. The Lamb appears to reserve all his
care for his fiancée who is being prepared for the wedding.

The vision of chapter 19, however, describes in a symbolic manner a Christ
singularly active regarding the nations. Identified as the Word of God, the Resurrected One is presented at the parousia as an adversary to any opposition to God.
Mounted on a white horse, he comes to judge and make the war at the head of an
angelic army. From his mouth comes a sword with which to strike down the nations. On his cape and on his thigh, he has the following name inscribed: "King
of kings and Lord of lords" (Rev 19:16).[59]

This tension between the inactivity and activity of Christ corresponds with
another tension, which is throughout the book, between the imminence and the
delay of the parousia. Indeed, few New Testament writings stress so forcefully the
imminence of the end: ὁ γὰρ καιρὸς ἐγγύς, "For, the time is near," we read in the
first chapter (Rev 1:3); ναί, ἔρχομαι ταχύ, "Surely, I am coming soon," we read at
the end of the book (Rev 22:20). Few biblical books evoke the delay of the parousia with, if I may say so, such impatience. Even the souls of those who had been
slain for the witness they had borne are anxious under the altar and cry out with
a loud voice, "O Sovereign Lord, holy and true, how long before you will judge
and avenge our blood on those who dwell upon the earth?" (Rev 6:10).

The relation of Christ to the world thus remains unclear. Can we know why?
Because John does not have the doctrines set forth on this subject. Himself a
Christian, he deals with it as he sees Christ dealing with the nations. However,
what he notes are the indirect and ambiguous bonds, while communion between
the Lamb and his Church remains immediate and obvious. These relationships
will be clarified only with the arrival of the Son of Man, when "every eye will see
him, every one who pierced him" (Rev 1:7). Christ is therefore the Master of history, the Lamb alone able to open the book with seven seals,[60] the prince of the
earthly kings, the King of kings and Lord of lords. But for the moment, only a
third, the believer, may confess this power and these bonds in an act of faith that
is expressed liturgically.

------

[58] When it is said, in the same chapter, that the Son of Man reaps, it must concern the eschatological gathering of the Church rather than an indictment made against the world.

[59] On this pericope, see Holtz (*Die Christologie der Apokalypse*, 166–81), though I dismiss
the limitation of Christ's intervention to the church; and Mollat ("La Cristologia dell' Apocalisse," 64–66), who, following Rissi (*Zukunft*, 11–28), restricts verses 11–13 also to the Church,
though verses 14–16, in his opinion, were well-aimed at the nations. My interpretation concurs
with that of Brütsch, *L'Apocalypse de Jésus*-Christ, 308ff.

[60] In spite of Prigent (*Apocalypse et Liturgie*, 69–73), the "book" seems to me to symbolize
the intention of God for the future of the world and the Church rather than the Hebrew Bible
and its messianic prophecies.

Christ, God, and the Spirit

The bonds that link Christ with God and the Spirit would justify lengthy developments. I can simply note that John, in a bold manner, attributes to the Lamb the majority of the titles and privileges of God: just as God, Christ is the Lord,[61] the Holy One,[62] the Alpha and Omega.[63] Instead of saying, as in the remainder of the New Testament, that he is seated at the right hand of God, the visionary of Patmos dares to proclaim that he sits with God on the same celestial throne.[64] With God, finally, he becomes the Temple of the new Jerusalem.[65]

The identification with God is not complete however. Each person keeps his own identity. God remains the Lord God,[66] the Almighty,[67] the Father,[68] while Jesus remains his Son.[69] In the final vision, the glory of God replaces the sunshine, while the Lamb is used as the lamp, thus replacing the moon.[70]

In the initial address to his work, John brings Christ closer to the seven Spirits, who undoubtedly symbolize the fullness of the Spirit of God.[71] However the πνεῦμα, the Spirit, does not apparently achieve as high a rank as the Son in the celestial hierarchy. Contrary to the Lamb, the Spirit must be satisfied with a place in front of the throne of God, beside the Church. Present on earth, to gather Israel, it joins its voice with that of the Church: "The Spirit and the Bride say, 'Come!'" (Rev 22:17). However, rather than a creature sent down on behalf of Christ, the Spirit appears to even unite the Lamb to his Church. For if the voice of the Spirit can accompany that of the Church, it happens also that it is united with the word of the Son of Man. Thus each letter, dictated by the Risen Christ, concludes by these words: "He who has an ear, let him hear what the Spirit says to the Churches" (Rev 2:7, 11, 17, 29; 3:6, 13, 22).

---

[61] Rev 11:8; 14:13; 22:20–21.

[62] Rev 3:7.

[63] Rev 22:13.

[64] Rev 3:21; 7:17; 22:1, 3.

[65] Rev 21:22.

[66] Rev 1:8; 4:8; 11:17; 15:3; 16:7; 18:8; 19:6; 21:22; 22:5, 6. See Rev 4:11.

[67] It could be that, against the usual translations, it is necessary to translate παντοκράτωρ by "the one who holds all" (*omnitenens*) rather than by "all-powerful" (*omnipotens*). κρατέω was, indeed, a verb used by the Stoics and other philosophers to describe the activity of the divinity who controls and sustains the universe. As for τὰ πάντα, it is a current expression in the New Testament that means the whole of creation. See Hildebrecht Hommel, *Schöpfer und Erhalter. Studien zum Problem Christentum und Antike* (Berlin: Lettner, 1956) 81ff. Hommel critiques the work of Wilhelm Michaelis, "κράτος, κτλ.," in *TWNT* 3:913f.

[68] Rev 1:6; 2:28; 3:5, 21; 14:1. On the relations between the Father and the Son, see Comblin, *Le Christ dans l'Apocalypse*, 191–94.

[69] Rev 2:18; see Holtz, *Die Christologie der Apokalypse*, 20–22.

[70] Rev 21:23.

[71] See Eduard Schweizer, "πνεῦμα, κτλ.," *TWNT* 6:447–49 (bibliography); and Satake, *Die Gemeindeordnung in der Johannesapokalypse*, 74–81.

Christ the Revealer

I have kept until the end an aspect of the relation between Christ and his Church: the function of the Son as Revealer. Called the Word of God,[72] the Lamb offers to his Church a revelation, an ἀποκάλυψις. ἀποκάλυψις is even the first word of the book, which, all at the same time, apocalypse and prophecy reveals what is above and what follows. "The revelation of Jesus Christ, which God gave him to show to his servants what must soon take place; and he made it known by sending his angel to his servant John, who bore witness to the word of God and to the testimony of Jesus Christ, even to all that he saw" (Rev 1:1–2). Before reaching the recipients, this revelation of Christ on behalf of God passes through various intermediaries: angel, visionary, reader. Christ, in addition, takes the necessary precautions, so that the message that may be altered through the successive mediums is retransmitted accurately.

The same assertions and the same precautions are found at the end of the book, which makes it possible for the author to complete his work with an *inclusio* (see Rev 22:6, 16). The Christ of the Book of Revelation thus fulfills the function of Revealer to his Church. He is at the source of the entire system of communication.

Chapters 1 and 22 clearly indicate what the Son of Man reveals to his Church: "What must soon take place," ἃ δεῖ γενέσθαι ἐν τάχει (Rev 1:1 and 22:6). In the interpretation of these words, it is necessary to avoid two mistakes. The first would be of radically separating this new revelation on the future from the past revelation on Christ. The Book of Revelation would then become a program for the final days. It is necessary to object to this interpretation: it is not said "what will happen" but "what must take place soon." The "what *must*" is important. It refers to a known cause, the work of Christ, whose new revelation only describes the repercussions.[73] In spite of the variety of images and figures, which must occur, it is the arrival of the Son of Man in glory, the coming therefore of one who is already known by name, because he has come already.[74] Verse 7 of the first chapter lends weight to this program: "Behold, he is coming with the clouds, and every eye will see him, every one who pierced him" (Rev 1:7). The destruction of the hostile forces is only the consequence of this coming. The Book of Revelation, therefore, does not describe calamities caused by the left hand of God who remains unaware of his right hand.

The second error would be to confuse the two revelations and to insist exclusively on the first coming of Christ, as if the faithful, with eyes fixed on the cross, could deduce a similar outcome by themselves. If indeed there is for John only one

---

[72] Rev 19:13.

[73] Holtz (*Die Christologie der Apokalypse*, passim) insists on this theological aspect.

[74] A whole chapter in the book of Comblin (*Le Christ dans l'Apocalypse*, 48ff.) is devoted to the topic of the coming of the Son of Man.

foundational act, the cross and resurrection, the meaning of this event remains inexhaustible: God must therefore continue his revelation. The prophets are still necessary to tell from the past and the future the new impact of God's intervention for today.[75] The history of the Church and the nations serves as a commentary on the works of Christ whose universality is thus underscored.

By dictating this commentary – any true commentary is a new work – Christ therefore speaks of himself. In a sense, he repeats what we already knew of him: the wedding of the Church and the fading of the nations echo the parable of the vine and vinedresser.[76] But, in another sense, Christ gives us a new revelation. The historical situation that indeed has changed needs to be seen in a new christological light. Moreover, the Revealer, Christ, refuses to lose the status of subject in the transmission of a revelation in which he agrees to be the object.[77] The Church never definitely grasps Christ, who unceasingly remains to be discovered.

Just as a text is at once closed and open, the Christ of the Book of Revelation is at once hidden and known. Limited by his cross, he is unlimited by his future. At Golgotha he ends his work, yet fulfillment remains with him. What he must achieve appears at once small and decisive: small, because Easter has provided the movement; decisive, because he must pass from invisible to visible ("every eye will see him, every one who pierced him," Rev 1:7). Contrary to various streams of early Christianity, John the prophet resolutely turns the Christ of faith towards the future.[78]

Let us note finally that our knowledge of Jesus Christ took shape by reading the Book of Revelation for other reasons still. The Canadian sociologist Marshall McLuhan claimed in a polemical way that, in our civilization, the medium is the message.[79] This bold proposal contains a truth however, because as something passes, a kind of message is transmitted by a medium of chosen communication, independently from what is spoken of or shown, regardless of message content.[80] These modern observations are useful to us at this stage of our research. The me-

---

[75] See Satake, *Die Gemeindeordnung in der Johannesapokalypse*, 47–74; and David Hill, "Prophecy and Prophets in the Revelation of Saint John," *NTS* 18:4 (1972) 401–18.

[76] John 15:1ff.

[77] Several commentators noticed that the genitive Ἰησοῦ Χριστοῦ (Rev 1:1) is at the same time subjective and objective: revelation of Jesus Christ on Jesus Christ. See Mollat, "La Cristologia dell' Apocalisse," 47.

[78] See from our time, a similar effort: Jürgen Moltmann, *Theologie der Hoffnung. Untersuchungen zur Begründung und zu den Konsequenzen einer christlichen Eschatologie* (Munich: Kaiser, 1964). See Henry Mottu, "L'espérance chrétienne dans la pensée de Jürgen Moltmann," *RTP*, 3d ser., 16 (1967) 242–58.

[79] McLuhan, *Pour comprendre les média*, 23–38. See Charles D. Maire, "McLuhan et l'Evangélisation," *Ichthus* 1 (1970) 4–12; and G. Blanchard, "Les hypothèses de McLuhan," *RRef* 83 (1970) 3–8. MacLuhan thinks that this thesis is verifiable first of all in the modern era.

[80] The semantic distinction between the media and the message is not without analogy. Louis T. Hjelmslev made the distinction between the form of an expression and the substance of an expression, on the one hand, and the shape of the contents and the substance of the contents, on the other.

dia used by Christ are indeed revealing: the Christ of the Book of Revelation enters into communication with believers through visions, oracles, and by a certain presence. This variety of media strikes the believer in several ways: through sight, aurally (let us not forget that John maintains that his book is read before an assembly; see Rev 1:3), and even through taste and touch (let us think of the promise: "I will come in to him and eat with him, and he with me," Rev 3:20). This diversity of media may reflect the concern Christ has for reaching humanity in its totality. One could find confirmation of this in the expansion of a work that, like a firework, does not quite follow the linear logic of the civilization of the book.[81] The impossibility for modern exegetes to find a coherent plan to the Book of Revelation would consequently no longer be a misfortune, but an acknowledged revelation that tackles the intellectual conception of faith and transforms our life as much as our spirit.

Sociologists also study the degree of passivity or participation in which mass media involve the spectator or listener.[82] It seems to me that the Christ of the Book of Revelation voluntarily chose mysterious visions and enigmatic words. With this performative communication, Christ attracts the attention of the spectator and listener and causes the collaboration of believing at a level of approval and interpretation. He appears as a supporter of the dialogue.

It is possible finally to make one last christological deduction from the presence of innumerable intermediaries, sought by Christ, who are placed between his word and our perception. In my opinion, these shifts reveal the love of a Christ who, in the manner of God of the Hebrew Scripture, wants to provide for us without destroying us. Such graciousness appears applicable to current events when one speaks about technology aggressing humanity, where humans are overrun by unscrupulous information.

To conclude this paragraph, I wonder – by apologizing to historians – if I would be untrue to Melanchthon by modifying his formula of the *Loci communes* of 1521:[83] *Hoc est Christum cognoscere, media eius cognoscere.* To know Christ, it is not only to know his *beneficia*, but also the means of communication that he uses.

---

[81] See Marshall McLuhan, *La Galaxie Gutenberg* (Montreal: HMH, 1967; English original 1962).

[82] See the distinction between mass media that is *cool* and one that is *hot*.

[83] Philippe Melanchthon, *Loci communes rerum theologicarum seu Hypotyposes theologicae,* 1521; in *Melanchthons Werke* (ed. Hans Engelland et al.; 7 vols.; Gütersloh: Bertelsmann, 1952) 2.1:7: *Nam ex his proprie Christus cognoscitur, siquidem hoc est Christum cognoscere beneficia eius cognoscere, non, quod isti docent, eius naturas, modos incarnationis contueri.*

The Political Christ

The revelation made by John has a political dimension. More explicitly than anywhere else in the New Testament, the Christ of the Book of Revelation displays political claims, not only for the future but also for the present. It involves his communities confronting the human world, a world that does not hide callousness.

Readers of the Book of Revelation see it carrying a virulent attack against political messianism. Supported by a religious ideology, political power can alienate humanity.[84] In the final scene, Christ expects the reversal of the oppression and the liberation of men and women.[85] Water, trees, rocks,[86] natural surroundings, city and home, cultural setting,[87] all free from their negative connotation, are now promised to those who accept Christ. The Risen Christ mentioned in the Book of Revelation thus does not take refuge in the hereafter, which would let the forces of evil have free reign on earth.

If the aim of Christ is clear, the means of establishing it are also clear: they are summed up by the Word. The Lamb as witness proclaims the Word of God to the world and proclaims to God what he censures in human beings. But this Word, as opposed to our words, is effective. It is action. The scene of the horseman (Rev 19:11ff.), sword in mouth, makes the point.

Effective, because this Word is authentic. It does not disregard its reference to God who gives him its power and its truth. Genuine, it sheds light on the instruments of tyranny. It sees fairly, describes well, and censures mercilessly. It is a sharpened word, a sharp sword. Its effectiveness is due to its truth more than with its truthfulness. Thanks to it, the oppressive power emerges from the shade in its bestial horror, and the community of witnesses emerges in his desire for love.

Word, which has weight, acts with purpose; such is the intervention present in Christ, such are the means put into effect.

In the historical context where our book fits, the critique of power appears easy when the persecution by Domitian is considered.[88] Less evident, on the other hand, is the backup solution that is presented. The alternative offered to the imperial policy is a Christian community, true counter-model, where human and non-bestial relations are established, where love replaces oppression and prayer replaces idolatry. The relentless witness, the pitiless censure finally allows only one violence, which he has done to himself. His commitment is total. He has taken it upon himself throughout his whole existence, which he does not hesitate to offer in the service rendered to truth – truth that does not tolerate any compromise.

---

[84] See Rev 13:1–18.
[85] See Rev 20:4–6; 21:6–7.
[86] See Rev 7:17; 21:6; 2:7, 17.
[87] See Rev 21:2, 10ff.; 3:12.
[88] See *L'Apocalypse* (Traduction Œcuménique de la Bible; Paris, 1970) 16f.

The fate of the true witness leads to death. Not that he proves to be the champion of a theology of the hereafter or a masochist for ethics. On the contrary, he affirms the creation of God and practices an ethics of life. But to establish and convey this life, he must fight with his word and undergo apparent defeats.

Thus it is explained, in this dialectic of political aim and nonviolent means, the title that dominates the Christology of the Apocalypse: the Lamb. Not the soft lamb of the pious iconographic kind,[89] but the triumphant Lamb, virile, upright, carrying on his side the mark of his death, a death which has spoken, which has proclaimed and communicated our life.

---

[89] See Louis Réau, *Iconographie de la Bible. Nouveau Testament* (vol. 2.2 of *Iconographie de l'Art chrétien*; Paris: Presses universitaires de France, 1957) 693–94, 700–1, 717, who indicates the principal iconographic representations of the Lamb of the Apocalypse in Christian art.

John's Self-Presentation in Rev 1:9–10

This paper will not be a historical inquiry into John's personality; nor will it be a philological analysis of the author's style.[1] In line with the tradition of French literary criticism,[2] I would like to observe what Philippe Lejeune calls the "autobiographical pact," namely, the implicit agreement which an author or narrator makes with his or her readers about his or her identity.[3] There exists a sort of contract governing the manner in which the reader should read the text put forth by a narrator and the commitments that the author has decided to take.[4] Avoiding scholarly jargon and theoretical abstractions, I will focus on how the narrator speaks in the first person singular, "I," that is, how John defines himself in Rev 1:9–10.

In everyday life, people express themselves with varying degrees of self-consciousness. The presentation of the "I" in Rev 1:9–10 is highly self-conscious: "I, John, your brother, who shares with you in Jesus the persecution and the kingdom and the patient endurance, was on the island called Patmos because of the word of God and the testimony of Jesus. I was in the Spirit on the Lord's day, and

---

[1] I have written a different, shorter paper, focused on issues that are theological rather than literary; François Bovon, "Jean se présente (Apocalypse 1,9 en particulier)," in *1900th Anniversary of St. John's Apokalypse: Proceedings of the International and Interdisciplinary Symposium (Athens–Patmos, 17–26 September 1995)* (Athens: Holy Monastery of Saint John the Theologian in Patmos, 1999) 373–82.

[2] See for example Roland Barthes, "Introduction à l'analyse structurale des récits," *Communications* 8 (1966) 1–27; Gérard Genette, *Figures III* (Poétique; Paris: Seuil, 1972); idem, *Palimpsestes. La littérature au second degré* (Poétique; Paris: Seuil, 1982). There are pertinent remarks on the construction of the author in Umberto Eco (with Richard Rorty, Jonathan Culler, and Christine Brook-Rose), *Interpretation and Overinterpretation* (ed. Stefan Collini; Cambridge: Cambridge University Press, 1992), even if Eco's attention is oriented toward the text and the reader.

[3] Philippe Lejeune, *Le pacte autobiographique* (Points, Essais, 326; new aug. ed.; Paris: Seuil, 1996). On p. 8 he writes: "Dans 'Le pacte autobiographique', je montre que ce genre se définit moins par les éléments formels qu'il intègre, que par le 'contrat de lecture', et qu'une poétique historique se devrait donc d'étudier l'évolution du système des contrats de lecture et de leur fonction intégrante." In this new edition the page numbering of the first edition, published by the same publisher in 1975 in the Collection Poétique, is preserved. New are a postscript and two bibliographies. See also Algirdas J. Greimas and Joseph Courtés, *Sémiotique. Dictionnaire raisonné de la théorie du langage* (2 vols.; Langue, Linguistique, Communications; Paris: Hachette, 1979–86) 1:242.

[4] See "True Confessions: A Special Issue," *New York Times Magazine*, 12 May 1996, sec. 6. In this issue the current literary interest in autobiographical writings is underlined.

I heard behind me a loud voice like a trumpet." This presentation and other casual uses of the everyday "I" display a striking contrast in their degree of self-awareness. In many early Christian texts, the narrator is so discreet that she or he never appears explicitly; an example is the Gospel according to Matthew.[5] In other texts, though, the ἐγώ is omnipresent – in the Pauline epistles, for example.[6] The degree of self-presentation in the Book of Revelation falls somewhere between those two extremes. What is the narrator's strategy for constructing an image of himself, and how does this self-presentation fit within his overall literary program?[7]

Cicero often uses "I" in his Letters.[8] So does Augustine in his Confessions.[9] Unlike either of them, John avoids drawing his own portrait as it might have been drawn in ancient autobiography.[10] The reader receives no information about the narrator's past, youth, or education. Nor does the narrator project his own future; neither his name nor his person is presented in the future tense (in contrast, there is a future for the second ἐγώ of the text – the speaking Jesus, who promises to come soon). The narrator is a person of the present and a person of a recent and narrowly defined past, a witness to his own visions ("I saw") and to divine voices ("I heard").[11]

---

[5] See Matt 4:24 (Syria may be the author's homeland); Matt 9:9 and 10:3 (the author is interested in Matthew, one of the Twelve); also Ulrich Luz, *Das Evangelium nach Matthäus* (EKKNT 1.1; Zurich: Benziger; Neukirchen-Vluyn: Neukirchener Verlag, 1989) 73–77, 181 n. 16.

[6] See Hans Dieter Betz, *Der Apostel Paulus und die sokratische Tradition* (BHT 45; Tübingen: Mohr Siebeck, 1972), esp. 118–37; Hans Dieter Betz, *Galatians: A Commentary on Paul's Letter to the Churches in Galatia* (Hermeneia; Philadelphia: Fortress, 1979) 1. Dieter Georgi, *The Opponents of Paul in Second Corinthians* (Philadelphia: Fortress, 1986), is important for the self-understanding, self-designation, and self-consciousness of Paul's opponents in Corinth according to the Second Epistle to the Corinthians; on Paul's own self-awareness, see ibid., 315–19.

[7] One can consider Rev 1:1–3 as a literary opening in which the author's intention is clear: to offer a divine revelation through the indispensable agencies of Jesus Christ, an angel, John himself, and the lector; see François Bovon, "Le Christ de l'Apocalypse," *RTP*, 3d ser., 22 (1972) 75–76; reprinted in idem, *Révélations et écritures. Nouveau Testament et littérature apocryphe chrétienne. Recueil d'articles* (MdB 26; Geneva: Labor et Fides, 1993) 124–25. For translation, see pp. 86–87 above in this volume.

[8] See Cicero, *Letters to Atticus* (trans. E. O. Winstedt; 3 vols.; LCL; London: Heinemann, 1912–1918); Cicero, *Letters to His Friends* (trans. W. Glynn Williams; 3 vols.; LCL; London: Heinemann, 1927–1929).

[9] See Pierre Courcelle, *Recherches sur les "Confessions" de saint Augustin* (new ed.; Paris: de Boccard, 1968); idem, *Les Confessions de saint Augustin dans la tradition littéraire. Antécédents et postérité* (Paris: Études augustiniennes, 1963).

[10] On ancient biography and autobiography, see Georg Misch, *Geschichte der Autobiographie*, I. *Das Altertum* (Bern: Francke, 1949); Arnaldo Momigliano, *The Development of Greek Biography* (exp. ed.; Cambridge, Mass.: Harvard University Press, 1993).

[11] In an attempt to relate exegesis and linguistics, I have been interested by *Reflective Language: Reported Speech and Metapragmatics* (ed. John A. Lucy; Cambridge: Cambridge University Press, 1993). The contributors examine "the nature and significance of the reflexive aspect of natural language" (p. 1).

According to Lejeune's typology of autobiographical texts, two major categories can be distinguished. The first narrative, called "autodiégétique" or "homodiégétique" of high degree by Genette, followed by Lejeune,[12] is the simplest autobiographical narrative; in it the "I" is the hero of the narrative. The second, a variation, is "homodiégétique" but of low degree. This second type of narrative interests us most here. It is the type of narrative in which the "I" is present but is not the central figure of the plot.[13] In it, the function of the "I" is to bring the narrative closer to the reader, or to give witness to the truth, or to manifest the nature of the narrative. This is exactly what happens in the Book of Revelation. Chapter after chapter, John repeats monotonously "and I saw" (καὶ εἶδον, e.g., in Rev 5:1) or "and I heard" (καὶ ἤκουσα, e.g., in Rev 7:4).[14] In contrast to Luke, who is interested in the witness of historical events, John is attentive to pneumatic testimony and to prophetic vision and hearing.[15] He says several times that he was taken "by the Spirit" or "in the Spirit of Jesus," a conventional way of articulating a religious or ecstatic experience.

The function of the first person singular is to convey to readers the narrator's role as an indispensable link between the divine realm and the human one,[16] so what we have in the Book of Revelation is a divinely directed plot made visible or readable to us by John's mediation. It is carefully orchestrated theater, but it is impossible to understand without a storyteller who is also from time to time a commentator.[17] To use another metaphor, the Book of Revelation is like a computer with two windows open: one for the visions and auditions, and one for John and his comments, with little contact between them. John does not enter the realm of "what shall come soon," and he does not receive the power to manipulate it. Two striking exceptions actually confirm the rule, when John, like a spectator called by a magician to assist, enters into the vision.[18] If John appears in the vision of Rev 10:8–11, he does so not as an actor to change the path of history but to

---

[12] See Genette, *Figures III*, 253; Lejeune, *Pacte autobiographique*, 15.

[13] See Genette, *Figures III*, 252–53; Lejeune, *Pacte autobiographique*, 16.

[14] See Rev 4:1; 5:11; 6:1, 5, 7–8; 8:13; 9:16–17; 14:1–2, 13–14; 21:1–3; 22:8, passages in which the verbs of hearing and seeing appear closely related.

[15] See François Bovon, *New Testament Traditions and Apocryphal Narratives* (trans. Jane Haapiseva-Hunter; Princeton Theological Monograph Series 36; Allison Park, Pa.: Pickwick, 1995) 56–57.

[16] This is already evident in the Hebrew Scriptures; see Ernest J. Revell, *The Designation of the Individual: Expressive Usage in Biblical Narrative* (CBET 14; Kampen: Kok Pharos, 1996).

[17] John's activity is well presented by George B. Caird, *A Commentary on the Revelation of St. John the Divine* (NBTC; London: Black, 1966) 289–301. We may take Rev 17:9–10 as an example of John's exegetical style: "This calls for a mind that has wisdom: the seven heads are seven mountains on which the woman is seated; also, they are seven kings, of whom five have fallen, one is living, and the other has not yet come; and when he comes, he must remain only a little while." Rev 6:1–17 may serve as an example of John's storytelling style.

[18] There is a possible third exception: Rev 5:4–5; the visionary's tears and the comfort offered him by the elders illustrate his participation in the story.

"eat" the book, namely, to interiorize and understand the visions.[19] Likewise, in Rev 11:1–2, the purpose of the action proposed to him is not to modify the divine program but to measure the dimensions of the temple and so, probably, to obtain a greater knowledge that he will later communicate as a witness.[20]

The five human senses and their interrelations are depicted in the literature of antiquity.[21] Origen, for example, gives an allegorical interpretation of the apocalyptic family quarrels mentioned in Luke 13:52–53 ("From now on five in one household will be divided, three against two and two against three").[22] He understands this struggle as a tension in the life of Christians who, through their eyes and ears, are close to God. Of the five senses, sight and hearing are the two most likely to accept God's reality, while the other three are reluctant and are opposed to the first two. Therefore, we are not surprised that sight and hearing are precisely the two senses which, according to John, are used for God's purpose.

John's spontaneous "I," present throughout the Book of Revelation, must be legitimized as a witness and identified as a singular person.[23] This is established in Revelation 1, and the identification is accomplished through the onomastic code: "I" receives a name.[24] Our narrator is not an anonymous figure, and his having a

---

[19]   See Pierre Prigent, *L'Apocalypse de Saint Jean* (CNT 2.14; rev. and exp. ed.; Geneva: Labor et Fides, 2000) 257–58; David Frankfurter, "The Magic of Writing and the Writing of Magic: The Power of the Word in Egyptian and Greek Tradition," *Helios* 21 (1994) 189–221. I thank my colleague Karen King for this reference.

[20]   See André Feuillet, "Essai d'interprétation du chapitre XI de l'Apocalypse," *NTS* 4 (1957–1958) 183–200; reprinted in André Feuillet, *Études johanniques* (Museum Lessianum, section biblique 4; Bruges: Desclée de Brouwer, 1962) 246–71; Charles Homer Gilblin, "Revelation 11.1–13: Its Form, Function, and Contextual Integration," *NTS* 30 (1984) 433–59; Michael Bachmann, "Himmlisch. Der 'Tempel Gottes' von Apk 11.1," *NTS* 40 (1994) 474–80. Often the measuring of the temple is understood as a measure of protection; see Gilblin, "Revelation 11.1–13," 455 n. 15.

[21]   See Michel Serres, *Les cinq sens* (Philosophie des corps mêlés 1; Paris: Grasset, 1985).

[22]   Origen, *Homilies on Luke* frag. 81; see Origène, *Homélies sur s. Luc* (ed. Henri Crouzel, François Fournier, and Pierre Périchon; SC 87; Paris: Cerf, 1962) 536–39.

[23]   On passages in the first person singular and their function, see Luke 1:3; Acts 1:1; 11:28 (variant reading); 16:10–17; 20:5–15; 21:1–18; 27:1–28:16 (Jacques Dupont, *Les sources du livre des Actes. État de la question* [Bruges: Desclée de Brouwer, 1960] 73–107; François Bovon, *Das Evangelium nach Lukas* [3 vols. so far; EKKNT 3.1–3; Zurich: Benziger; Neukirchen-Vluyn: Neukirchener Verlag, 1989–2001] 1:37); *Protevangelium Jacobi* 18.2–19.1 (Harm R. Smid, *Protevangelium Jacobi: A Commentary* [Apocrypha Novi Testamenti; Assen: Van Gorcum, 1965] 176–78); *Acta Andreae* 65 (11) (Laura Nasrallah, "'She Became What the Words Signified': The Greek *Acts of Andrew*'s Construction of the Reader-Disciple," in *The Apocryphal Acts of the Apostles: Harvard Divinity School Studies* [ed. François Bovon, Ann Graham Brock, and Christopher R. Matthews; Harvard University Center for the Study of World Religions: Religions of the World; Cambridge, Mass.: Harvard University Press, 1999] 233–58, esp. 250–58). On the anonymous *Liber ad Gregoriam*, see Kate Cooper, *The Virgin and the Bride: Idealized Womanhood in Late Antiquity* (Cambridge, Mass.: Harvard University Press, 1996) 129.

[24]   On the importance of names, see Roland Barthes, "The Struggle with the Angel: Textual Analysis of Genesis 32:23–33," in *Structural Analysis and Biblical Exegesis* (ed. Roland Barthes, et al.; Princeton Theological Monograph Series 3; Pittsburgh: Pickwick, 1974) 29–30; Greimas and Courtés, *Sémiotique*, 1:261.

name is decisive (remember that Paul's opponents usually do not receive a name; they are scornfully called τινές, "some people").[25] It is worth noting that after a name has been given, it is not repeated. John's name is vital in chapter 1 but is absent in the rest of the book, even in dialogues with the angel, where a vocative would be welcome. But the name John appears as a literary *inclusio* in the last lines of the book, to reassure the readers of the narrator's function: "I, John, am the one who heard and saw these things" (Rev 22:8).[26] Here, use of the name John is more significant for the identification of the narrator than for the etymology of the name. John does not care to avoid confusion by distinguishing himself from all the other Johns, particularly the ones with decisive early Christian roles like John the Baptist, John the son of Zebedee, and John Mark.[27] John's identity is structured by several portrayals of himself, not by distinctions from others.

Let us follow the formation of John from the very beginning of the Book of Revelation. The first three verses create an extraordinary sequence of communication: a divine manifestation, here called a "revelation" (ἀποκάλυψις), comes from God and reaches the readers, or the hearers, through three intermediaries: Jesus Christ, John, and the *lector*.[28] Although lector is a minister in the ancient church, in Rev 1:3 ὁ ἀναγινώσκων is probably not yet a title.[29] John is connected first with Christ, by the title "servant" (ὁ δοῦλος αὐτοῦ), and later in the chapter he will be related to his fellow brothers and sisters.

When we sign a letter which we have written, something strange occurs. After writing in the first person through the body of the letter, suddenly we put our name at the bottom of the page. At the very end of the letter the "I" becomes a personal name. Thus, in each letter we switch surprisingly from the first to the third person or to a mixture of both, because of the necessary task of legitimizing the "I" with our personal name.[30] This hesitation between the first and the third person occurs for the same reason in Revelation 1. In the prologue, which also fills the function of title of the book, the name John is used appropriately with a verb in the third person (Rev 1:1). Later, in the opening letter to the seven churches (Rev 1:4), the name John clarifies the identity of the bearer of the subsequent greetings, and the first person ("we," the first person plural, Rev 1:5–6) is then

---

[25] See Rom 3:8; 1 Cor 4:18; 15:12; 2 Cor 3:1; 10:2; Gal 1:7; Phil 1:15; also, Pierre Bonnard, *L'épître de saint Paul aux Galates* (2d ed.; CNT 9; Neuchâtel: Delachaux et Niestlé, 1972) 24 n. 1.

[26] See Charles Brütsch, *La clarté de l'Apocalypse* (5th ed.; Geneva: Labor et Fides, 1966) 386.

[27] See Raymond E. Brown, *The Gospel according to John* (2 vols.; AB 29–29A; Garden City, N.Y.: Doubleday, 1966) 1:LXXXVII–XCII; Helmut Koester, *History and Literature of Early Christianity* (vol. 2 of *Introduction to the New Testament*; 2d ed.; New York/Berlin: de Gruyter, 2000) 6–7, 75–78, 91, 97, 112, 203–4, 255.

[28] See n. 7 above.

[29] On the ministry of lectors, see Henri Leclercq, "Lecteur," in *DACL* 8:2241–69.

[30] I would like to know whether any studies exist on the phenomenology of signing a document.

appropriate. Thus, the first two occurrences of the name John are very close to one another but in syntactically different clauses.

The third occurrence is not far from these two, and it is the most decisive one. It is in v. 9, and it is emphasized by a strong ἐγώ. While John in 1:1 is connected with God and Christ, in 1:9 his relationship to his fellow Christians is underlined. He refuses a hierarchical clerical order and states his communion with them. He is not their father but their brother.[31] The word was used throughout the churches, but it was not yet banal. One has to remember both the Hebrew emphasis on brotherhood, in which the ideal life was "to remain together" (ישׁב יחד) and the Greek appreciation of brothers and sisters. In Sophocles' *Antigone* 891–928, for example, Antigone says that a woman can have another husband, even other children, but is incapable of replacing her deceased brothers.[32] This affective and effective union is underlined by a second expression, the redundant συγκοινωνός (literally, the "one who shares in common with"). In Greek, a κοινωνός is someone sharing political power, economic responsibility, agricultural goods, or, in a religious association, communal interests.[33] What John is passionate to share with his brothers is particularly impressive. In 1:9, he expresses first the θλῖψις, the "tribulation" and "persecution," the suffering, that he experienced ("I was on the island called Patmos because of the word of God and the testimony of Jesus").[34] Then, he expresses the enigmatic βασιλεία, meaning not only the apocalyptic kingdom of God but also the kingly power in which Christians already partake after Christ's death for them, according to the very clear opening statement that Christ "made us to be a kingdom" (1:6).[35] Finally, he expresses the ὑπομονή that is not simply "patience," with a note of passivity, but is active nonviolent resistance – "endurance" and "perseverance," but with a subversively anti-Roman element.[36]

---

[31] On this equality among the first Christians, see Ernst Troeltsch, *Gesammelte Schriften*, I. *Die Soziallehren der christlichen Kirchen und Gruppen* (Tübingen: Mohr Siebeck, 1912) 60–69.

[32] See François Bovon, "The Parable of the Prodigal Son, Luke 15:11–32," in *Exegesis and Exercises in Reading* (*Genesis 22 and Luke 15*) (ed. François Bovon and Grégoire Rouiller; Princeton Theological Monograph Series 21; Pittsburgh: Pickwick, 1978) 51–53, 66.

[33] On κοινωνός and συγκοινωνός, see Friedrich Hauck, "κοινός, κτλ.," in *TWNT* 3:789–810.

[34] On θλῖψις, see Jacob Kremer, "θλῖψις, etc.," in *EWNT* 2:375–79.

[35] On βασιλεία in the Book of Revelation, see Prigent, *L'Apocalypse de saint Jean*, 90, 96. On the eschatology of the Book of Revelation, see Elisabeth Schüssler Fiorenza, *The Book of Revelation: Justice and Judgment* (2d ed.; Minneapolis: Fortress, 1998) 35–67; this is illustrated by the phylactery on the icon of Saint Athanasios the Athonite at the gate to the monastery of Megisti Lavra on Mount Athos, which bears the inscription Ἀδελφοί, κοπιάσωμεν μικρὸν χρόνον, ἵνα βασιλεύσωμεν εἰς αἰῶνας ("Brothers, let us be in pain for a little while, so that we can reign for ever").

[36] On ὑπομονή, see Walter Radl, "ὑπομονή, etc.," in *EWNT* 3:969–71; Brütsch, *Clarté de l'Apocalypse*, 33. On the ethics of resistance, see Elisabeth Schüssler Fiorenza, *Revelation: Vision of a Just World* (Proclamation Commentaries; Minneapolis: Fortress, 1991) 129–31.

Such is John's conscious definition of himself to his audience in Rev 1:9–10. It is limited to two biographical elements: his concrete situation as a prisoner for religious opinion, and his ecstatic experience as a prophet (note the identical verbal form ἐγενόμην in v. 9 and v. 10).[37] He keeps company with Christians, but his responsibility as a prophet is also to Jesus Christ and to God. Therefore, we are not surprised to discover beside John's ἐγώ an *alter ego*, another ἐγώ, that of the divinity in the verse immediately preceding (1:8): ἐγώ εἰμι τὸ ἄλφα καὶ τὸ ὦ. The vicinity of the two "I"s will recur at the end of the book, reinforcing the *inclusio* mentioned above: to the first "I" at the end of the book, κἀγὼ Ἰωάννης (22:8), corresponds the second, ἐγὼ Ἰησοῦς (22:16).[38]

We can understand the art of John, the visionary of Patmos. On the one hand, he inscribes his life inside a religious community sharing with him a similar kingly privilege and a similar condition as servant. On the other, he emphasizes his personal destiny as a unique destiny separate from the community's. When John defines himself, he draws the picture of a prophet, an instrument of the divine manifestation and voice of the risen Christ. His highest ambition is to create and communicate the images of witness to the divine mysteries that he narrates and of brother to his Christian companions.

---

[37] On the prophets in the Book of Revelation, see Akira Satake, *Die Gemeindeordnung in der Johannesapokalypse* (WMANT 21; Neukirchen-Vluyn: Neukirchener Verlag, 1966) 47–86; Schüssler Fiorenza, *Book of Revelation*, 133–56.

[38] On Rev 22:16, see Prigent, *L'Apocalypse de saint Jean*, 496–97.

Part II
The Gospel of Luke
and the Book of the Acts of the Apostles

Tracing the Trajectory of Luke 13:22–30 back to Q:
A Study in Lukan Redaction[*]

I. Introduction

Luke 13:22–30 provides a good example of the way Luke reads, uses, and interprets Q. As the summary in verse 22 and the new episode with an indication of time in verse 31 demonstrate, we have here a well-defined pericope. The literary unit of Luke 13:22–30 falls within the larger context of the Lukan travel narrative. Since 9:51, Jesus has left Galilee and is on his way to Jerusalem (occupied more with teaching and preaching than with doing miracles). Two theological tendencies of the travel narrative should be mentioned: the spiritual and ethical training of Jesus' disciples on the one hand, and a deepening in understanding Jesus' own destiny on the other.

Chapter 13 opens with a powerful call to conversion, a call to μετάνοια: Jesus urges conversion in view of imminent judgment (13:1–5); he expresses divine hope for conversion (13:6–9); next he performs an example of liberation (13:10–17); and then without much transition, he gives a parabolic teaching on the kingdom (13:18–21). Human responsibility on one side and divine action on the other are therefore placed clearly before the eyes of Luke's readers. Luke 13:22 is a summary which recalls 9:51 and confirms Jesus' travel activity (καὶ διεπορεύετο), his ongoing ministry (κατὰ πόλεις καὶ κώμας διδάσκων), and his final destination (Ἰεροσόλυμα). The pericope that follows our text develops the christological emphasis, transmits an unveiled prophecy of Jesus' death and a lament on Jerusalem and her error (13:31–35).

---

[*] I am pleased to offer these pages to James M. Robinson. I admire this old friend for his many gifts. Trained in systematic theology, he became a leading expert in New Testament theology and is fascinated now by manuscripts and critical editions. He knows also well how to combine scholarship and friendship, care for texts and care for persons. I would like also to warmly thank David H. Warren, a doctoral student at Harvard, now a doctor and colleague, who helped me in his learned and generous way to present an adequate expression of my thoughts and a correct system of references to books and articles. For more details on this passage and more bibliography, see my commentary, *Das Evangelium nach Lukas* (4 vols.; EKKNT 3.1–4; Zurich: Benziger; Neukirchen-Vluyn: Neukirchener Verlag, 1989–2009) 2:425–42. See also H. Folkers, "Wissen wir noch nicht, 'was aus der Bibel zu lernen ist'?," in *Bruch und Kontinuität. Jüdisches Denken in der europäischen Geistesgeschichte* (ed. Eveline Goodman-Thau and Michael Daxner; Berlin: Akademie Verlag, 1995) 71–91.

Following now, as precisely as possible, the sequence of the verses 13:23–30, we discover an unusual structure, namely an extraordinary apothegm, the first part of which is very short, whereas the second is extensive. A single question (v. 23) – the first part – gives the Lukan Jesus the opportunity for a very long answer (vv. 24–30) – the second part. As we know from other passages (e.g., 11:27–28), a question or an outburst from a bystander can be the starting point for the expected, decisive sentence of the Master. Therefore, the starting point of an apothegm does not need to be an event or an historical situation.

To this question, Jesus now gives his answer: (1) It consists first of an imperative followed immediately by an infinitive in verse 24a: "Strive to enter through the narrow door." (2) This command then receives an explanation or a justification in verse 24b–c: "For many, I tell you, will try to enter and will not be able." In one sense, the apothegm could stop here, and this would be correct and more in accord with the genre. (3) As if his answer were not clear enough, the Lukan Jesus goes on to explain why "they" will "not be able" "to enter." The explanation takes a narrative tone. Verses 25–27 tell the story not of the "narrow" door but of the "closed" door; more precisely, they transmit a dialogue between "you" and the "owner of the house," who appears here in Luke for the first time. Comparing this section with verse 24, we discover two new elements: the closed door and the οἰκοδεσπότης. This dialogue is made up of two phases: (a) a first request (v. 25b) followed by a first rebuke (v. 25c), and (b) a second request followed here again by a second rebuke (vv. 26–27). The second "round" is more developed than the first: the "you" tries to argue with the master by insisting on common memories (v. 26), but the "master" underscores his second refusal (v. 27a) with a biblical sentence of rejection (v. 27b).

The text goes on without specifying if we are still inside the dialogue between "you" and the "owner of the house" or back into the dialogue between "Jesus" and the questioning listener of verse 23. The ambiguity is probably intentional, as is the bi-directional "you" – the "you" of the story in vv. 25–27 facing the οἰκοδεσπότης is not distinguished from the "you" in v. 24 who questioned Jesus in v. 23.

Verses 28–29 remain in the future tense (the whole text is future oriented and relates an initial imperative of expectation to a sequence of future events). These two verses depict the two logical endings of the previous stories: outside and inside the "house" – the tears outside, the joyful feast inside. The appended verse 30 summarizes the consequence of the outcome that is described in verses 28–29. The outsiders and insiders are now called "last" and "first." And there is a new element, a reversal: the "outsiders" have become "insiders," and vice versa.

II. Luke's Sources in 13:22–30

Luke has used his sources carefully to craft a coherent story:

1. Verse 22 is full of Lukan vocabulary and categories. It is redactional.

2. Verse 23 is without parallel in Matthew. The question posed by someone from Jesus' audience may have been dropped out by the first evangelist who did not wish Jesus to be interrupted during his Sermon on the Mount. But on the other hand, even if the question of the number of the saved was a traditional question in Judaism, the vocabulary and the phraseology of verse 23 is strictly Lukan.[1] I consider it also as redactional.[2]

3. It is interesting to note the existence of a parallel in Matthew for each of the four following small units in Luke 13: vv. 24, 25–27, 28–29, and 30. Also noteworthy is the fact that the Matthean parallels do not form a literary unit as they do in Luke but are scattered in several places. Yet it is intriguing that the Matthean parallels – despite their dispersion – follow the same order as the Lukan.

Luke 13:24	//	Matt 7:13–14
Luke 13:25–27	//	Matt 7:22–23
Luke 13:28–29	//	Matt 8:11–12
Luke 13:30	//	Matt 20:16

From this correspondence, one can probably conclude that (a) these logia all come from Q, (b) they come in this order in Q, and (c) at least the first three were quoted in close proximity to one another in Q.[3]

---

[1] One should also observe (as Julius Wellhausen did long ago in *Das Evangelium Lucae*, [Berlin: Georg Reimer, 1904] 74) that the question posed in v. 23 is intended as a direct antithesis to the seemingly universal salvation depicted in the parables of the mustard seed and of the yeast (note esp. v. 21, ἕως οὗ ἐζυμώθη ὅλον) in 13:18–21. Luke does not want his readers to be lulled into thinking that everyone will be saved.

[2] See Siegfried Schulz (*Q. Die Spruchquelle der Evangelisten* [Zurich: Theologischer Verlag, 1972] 310); Paul Hoffmann ("Πάντες ἐργάται ἀδικίας. Redaktion und Tradition in Lc 13,22–30," *ZNW* 58 [1967] 188–214, esp. 193–94 n. 16), where one finds a good summary of scholars both pro and con; and John S. Kloppenborg (*The Formation of Q: Trajectories in Ancient Wisdom Collections* [Philadelphia: Fortress, 1987] 223 n. 213), who provides a good list of the Lukanisms that he finds in v. 23.

[3] Though admitting that these logia were already found in Q, Hoffmann ("Πάντες ἐργάται ἀδικίας," 192 n. 14, 206) views their order as purely redactional, apparently still following the lead of Rudolf Bultmann (*The History of the Synoptic Tradition* [trans. John Marsh; Oxford: Blackwell, 1963] 130), who believed that Luke composed his eschatological discourse in 13:22–30 "from all sorts of pieces" (German: "aus allerlei Stücken"). But Kloppenborg (*Formation*, 223, 234–37) has argued that Luke 13:24–30 belonged to a much larger block of material that was originally contiguous in Q (13:24–30, 34–35; 14:16–24, 26–27; 17:33 [N.B., displaced by Luke]; 13:34–35), which Luke has separated by inserting "a few items" from his *Sondergut*, and more recently Alan Kirk has sought to confirm this hypothesis in *The Composition of the Sayings Source: Genre, Synchrony, and Wisdom Redaction in Q* (NovTSup 91; Leiden: Brill, 1998) 241–55.

But if Matthew did not hesitate to consider each of these logia independently, this means that he did not see them as a thematic and a literary unit – and with good reason. For in the redaction of Q, they represented a sequence of autonomous logia and did not constitute an integral literary and thematic unit. Consequently, everything which helps to create cohesion between these words can be declared Lukan and redactional (an important methodological point). This is true, in my opinion, of the simplification and rewriting of the logion on the "narrow door." Q, followed by Matthew, wanted to give to the audience or the readers a double picture with two opposite destinies (according to the Jewish doctrine of the two ways). Luke, on the contrary, is building up the first part of a story: he needs only one door, the narrow one, and his interest lies in who is inside. And because this "inside" is inside a house (or a palace with a large dining room for a banquet; v. 29), he prefers θύρα (the door of a house) to πύλη (the gate of a town, the Q word preserved by Matthew).[4] As another expression of Luke's intent to tell a story, we note the literary change of the verb: it is no longer the apparently neutral "enter," but the emotive "strive to enter" (with the so called "ἀγών-motif").

4. In order to build his "story," Luke must transform the next logion of Q. The source of the logia possessed here an independent dramatic short unit: those who are sure that they will be accepted by God discover that actually they are rejected. The theme is also characteristic of Luke, but the evangelist needs a transition. He remembers a short episode of a parable, where people at a "door" (θύρα, which serves as a catchword) were strictly rebuked despite their recriminations and insistence that they were indeed "from the house" (see Matt 25:10–12). Luke uses this episode like the missing piece of a *marquetry*. The door was "narrow," implying that there was competition. But now the contest is over. The door is "closed": it is too late for any change. Luke, therefore, has combined two traditions: (a) the dialogue of the parable in Matt 25:11–12 (which becomes in the third Gospel: " 'Lord, open to us.' Then in reply he will say to you: 'I do not know where you come from'"; Luke 13:25) and (b) the logion of Q in Matt 7:22–23 (which becomes in the third Gospel: "Then you will begin to say, 'We ate and drank in front of you, and you taught in our streets.' But he will say, 'I do not know where you come from; go away from me, all you evildoers!' "; Luke 13:26–27). This double rebuke, which is caused by the accumulation of two sources, creates a dramatic effect of irreversible damnation.

---

[4] David H. Warren reminds me that the concepts of a θύρα and of a πύλη are not so dissociated in Semitic-influenced thought, for both were expressed by the same Aramaic word, תרעא (see the Peshitta, which has the same Syriac word in Matt 7:13–14 and Luke 13:24–25). This observation explains why Luke can also use both terms, θύρα and πύλη, to describe the temple gate called "Beautiful" in Acts 3:2 and 10 (again the same word in Syriac; this confusion can even occur in Hellenistic Greek writers like Plutarch [*Cato Minor* 65.1], though "rarely"; *LSJ*, *s.v.* θύρα I.1).

2 Clement 4.5 is the witness of a similar but distinct rewriting of Jesus' rebuke developed through the oral tradition. Instead of a story, like Luke's rewriting, the preacher quotes an ethical criticism, a kind of condemnation oracle: "For this reason, if you do these things, the Lord said, 'If you be gathered together with me in my bosom, and do not my commandments, I will cast you out, and will say to you, Depart from me, I do not know whence you are, you workers of iniquity.'"

5. By comparing the Lukan and the Matthean wording of the argument advanced by "you" to enter the house, we have to conclude that Matthew christianized the prosaic arguments of Q preserved in Luke. The phrase "eating and drinking in front of you" (which does not mean "with you" despite its rendering as such in many translations) and the simple "teaching" of Jesus give the impression of being archaic. According to Luke, these people have been spectators (this explains their responsibility and hence their condemnation). Matthew, on the contrary, develops an explicit christological reference ("in your name," three times) and specifies explicit Christian behaviors (prophecy, exorcism, and miracles). According to Matthew, these people have been not only actors, but hypocritical actors. They merit their condemnation.

The definitive sentence of the Master (v. 27b) is very similar in Matthew and Luke if we consider the content, but very different if we look at the wording. In both Gospels the allusion to Ps 6:9 is evident. I cannot determine from them what the wording in Q was.

6. In verse 28 Luke adapts an observation that must have already been present in the source of the *logia*.[5] But here diverging from Q, Luke's attention concentrates first on the rebuked people. On the contrary, as Matthew has preserved Q, the newly elected and beloved come first under the light in the first Gospel. Luke has changed this and taken first what was second in the Q sentence, namely the lamentation of the condemned. Thus far in Luke (diverging from Q and Matthew), these condemned people addressed as "you" have been the only figures on the stage. Now at the end of his passage, however, Luke makes the decision to bring in also the "last" who will be the first: those who will come from the four corners of the earth, namely the Christians, primarily the Gentiles. But one should be attentive to Luke's wording. Once he decides to expand the horizon, he expands it in two cumulative directions: (a) Who will be and who will not be in the "kingdom of God"? (Luke, following Q, departs from metaphorical speech and here adopts explicit language.) First, the patriarchs and the prophets, namely God's righteous people of the first covenant, will be inside. But second, "you" – it is difficult not to think of the Jewish audience – will be cast outside. And third, people coming from the four cardinal points of the earth, namely the Christians,

---

[5] Matthew Black (*An Aramaic Approach to the Gospels and Acts* [3d ed., with an appendix on "The Son of Man" by Géza Vermès; Oxford: Clarendon, 1967] 82, 92) sees in this verse the unmistakable traces of an original Aramaic circumstantial clause that had been translated into Greek, and so concludes that it had to have come from an Aramaic source.

particularly the Gentiles, will be welcome inside. (b) Compared with Matthew, Luke mentions the four regions, Matthew only east and west. As east and west were the most important for the Jews, we may infer that Luke has modified Q adding the north and the south, insisting – as we expected from him – on the universality of the successful mission and divine call. But the most impressive element is the historical sequence: first, the patriarchs and prophets are inside; second, those addressed as "you" are outside; and third, those from the whole world are inside.

7. The logion on the last and the first was a floating logion. This saying has been quoted in the triple traditions (Mark 10:31 par.) as well as in Q. Here we have the Q version. The proper Matthean parallel to Luke 13:30 is not Matt 19:30 (as indicated in Aland's *Synopsis*)[6] but Matt 20:16. The absence of πολλοί and the presence of the relative pronoun οἵ are remarkable. The grammatical expression for the Christians, particularly the Gentiles (the last who become first), takes the initial position. The Jewish people come in second place (first becoming last). The triple tradition, on the contrary, looks first at the destiny of the Jewish people and second at the future of the Christians, particularly the Gentiles. It uses πολλοί ("many"), which was absent in Q.

It is possible that the logion had already been attached here in Q. A clue to this is found in the *Gospel of Thomas* 4, where the Greek fragment *P. Oxy.* 654 relates the logion with ὁ τόπος τῆς ζωῆς ("the place of life"), namely the kingdom. Here also in Luke, and as I believe already in Q, this junction was made.

III. Interpretation

In this third part of my presentation, I focus on the theological interpretation of Q by Luke. My objective is to show that through a few changes and adaptations Luke has obtained a drastically new and more systematic understanding.

From originally independent words, collected by Q, Luke makes an original composition: he creates an ongoing story that begins with a question on the number of those who will be saved (v. 23) and ends with an answer on the origin and identity of those who are to be saved (vv. 29–30). This Jewish question – which in apocalyptic literature had received an answer like "there will be drastic cuts in the people of Israel" – receives here a Christian answer which adds those saved from outside the community of Israel to the total number of the elect and – as an antithetical and polemical corollary – takes others away from the inside.

---

[6] Kurt Aland, *Synopsis Quattuor Evangeliorum locis parallelis evangeliorum apocryphorum et patrum adhibitis* (11th ed.; Stuttgart: Deutsche Bibelstiftung, 1980) 297.

The result of Luke's composition is a parabolic narrative, a kind of allegory. Those who are called by God would do well to hasten to the door, to the narrow door of the kingdom (v. 24), since this door is not only narrow but is soon to be locked. The οἰκοδεσπότης – Luke is sure of this – is the resurrected Lord (note the double meaning of ἐγερθῇ; v. 25): he will soon close this door for good. Those who in the past had known him and spoken to him will be surprised to be found outside at this very moment. Instead of striving correctly to come in, they have scorned and condemned the Master. With the clean conscience of children, of heirs, they knock in the expectation of entering without any problem. Here is the tragic element of the story. Confident that they are known and loved, they quickly discover that they are ignored and rebuked.

But the narrative does not stop here. Through the addition of sources, Luke, like a good storyteller, maintains the suspense awhile longer. The surprised knockers at the door enter into a phase of negotiation. "All right," they say in substance, "we are not or are no longer the sons or daughters we were certain to be. But you, Master, cannot deny that we have been present during your ministry; therefore, we merit some consideration." For the logic of his story – different from that of Matthew's – Luke depicts these people in a pre-Christian status: they do not pretend to have accepted Jesus' message. They refuse nevertheless to admit that they have been against him. But the rule "whoever is not with me is against me" (Luke 11:23) holds here: "I do not know where you come from; go away from me, all you evildoers" (v. 27)! The Master repeats his inexorable judgment (v. 25) and confirms it with a quotation or an allusion to the Scriptures. Luke the Christian theologian is sure, and he does not hesitate to proclaim to his Jewish adversaries (see Acts 28:25–28), that now the Scriptures are on the side of the Christians and that they condemn a large part of Israel as being a "stiff-necked people, uncircumcised in heart and ears" (Acts 7:51).

It is true that there exist "many" who wish to enter (v. 24b), but at the end (v. 24c) they are unable to do so (καὶ οὐκ ἰσχύσουσιν). They receive therefore a double "No" (vv. 25 and 27). Then, after their unsuccessful negotiation and attempt to manipulate the Master, comes the phase of depression and sadness: ἐκεῖ ἔσται ὁ κλαυθμὸς καὶ ὁ βρυγμὸς τῶν ὀδόντων (v. 28a). Israel is divided, and the division respects the chronology of the history of salvation: Israel of the past, represented by the patriarchs Abraham, Isaac, and Jacob, and all the prophets (note the totality in this first "half'") are inside. But "you" (ὑμᾶς δέ), the second, the contemporaneous "half," are not only rebuked outside but must submit to an apocalyptic torture: You will see (ὅταν ὄψησθε) the blessed half enjoying the delights of the kingdom (v. 28b).

According to the Lukan perspective of the history of salvation, the story is not finished. There is still space inside (see Luke 14:22). Some will come to occupy the empty seats (the future ἥξουσιν can designate the future compared with the past of Jesus' ministry, namely the period of the church, or the expected parousia of the Lord). In any case, the mention of the four cardinal directions is a clear allusion to the foreign nations, to the Gentiles already accepted into the church (after Acts 10) and soon to be welcomed into the kingdom.

I will not dwell on the several forms taken by the logion on the first and the last.[7] Let me just say that the Lukan version of the logion is more nuanced than its direct parallel in Matt 20:16 (the Q tradition) and its indirect parallel in Mark 10:31 and Matt 19:30 (the triple tradition). Not all the last,[8] but some of them – perhaps many of them, i.e., many Christians, particularly Gentiles – will be first, i.e., they will be accepted by God and his Christ in the kingdom. And symmetrically, some – perhaps many – members of Israel will be last. If this interpretation is correct, Luke has been able to summarize in a few verses the whole mystery of salvation history as he sees it. In so doing he has produced a vignette of his whole double work. To use a term taken from heraldry and employed by some literary critics, we have here a "mise en abîme" (the "abîme" is the heart of the shield).[9] This means that Luke 13:22–30 is an internal mirror of the whole work and a condensation of the Lukan understanding of the history of salvation and damnation.[10]

But Luke is not satisfied with an historical allegory. Understood objectively, it could create a triumphalist happiness for the Christians and imprison a large part of the Jews in their condemnation. Because he is not only a historical theologian but also an author with a concern for the church, pastoral care, and ethical sense, he insists here also on human decision, human responsibility, and human will to obey God. His readers would be mistaken if they were just to rejoice in the assurance of being on the right side, on the side of the winners. History can repeat itself. Some did not recognize Jesus when he spoke to them and walked among them. The same danger also exists today for Christians if they do not strive with the right ἀγών to enter through the narrow door. In the end they might knock from the outside and also hear the condemning sentence: "I do not know where you come from." The historical "you" of Jesus' audience can become the existential "you" of Luke's readers. The imperative ἀγωνίζεσθε has a double function: it serves as a reminder of a past failure and as a calling for people confronted with a

---

[7] See further discussion in my commentary, *Das Evangelium nach Lukas*, 2:429–30.

[8] Note that Luke says εἰσὶν ἔσχατοι οἳ ἔσονται πρῶτοι = "there are (some) last ones who will be first."

[9] On this literary concept, see Lucien Dällenbach, *Le récit spéculaire. Contribution à l'étude de la mise in abîme* (Genève, thèse 213; Paris: Seuil, 1977), later republished that same year by Le Seuil in its series, La collection Poétique, with a new subtitle: *"Essai sur la mise en abyme"* (now available in English as *The Mirror in the Text* [trans. Jeremy Whiteley with Emma Hughes; Chicago: University of Chicago Press, 1989]).

[10] See Franz Mussner, "Das 'Gleichnis' vom gestrengen Mahlherrn. Ein Beitrag zum Redaktionsverfahren und zur Theologie des Lukas," *TTZ* 65 (1956) 129–43; reprinted in idem, *Praesentia salutis. Gesammelte Studien zu Fragen und Themen des Neuen Testaments* (KBANT; Düsseldorf: Patmos-Verlag, 1967) 113–24.

potential danger. The question of who is saved, or how many are to be saved, has not been answered by Jesus or by Luke with a positive "you," "all of you," but rather with a threatening imperative: "Strive to enter."[11]

IV. Conclusion

It is my understanding of Luke's appropriation of Q that he likes to leave open a large range of interpretations and that he prefers to add and combine meanings instead of rigidly adopting one inflexible and monolithic one. I prefer not to choose between a reading in terms of the history of salvation and another one in terms of individual responsibility (e.g., Franz Mussner against Paul Hoffmann or Paul Hoffmann against Franz Mussner).

Patristic exegesis encourages us not to play one meaning against the other, for ancient Christian authors were sensitive readers of Luke's intentions. In his commentary on the third Gospel, for example, the Venerable Bede[12] gives a possible double interpretation of verse 26 ("you will start to say: we have eaten ... "). He first sees in this verse an allusion to the Jews, Jesus' contemporaries, who have heard his words and lived with him. But he goes on saying that the "you" concerns "us" also when we do not understand properly, when we do not "eat" the Scriptures correctly. A similarly double meaning reappears in Bede's understanding of verse 30.[13] It may well be, he says, that the Gentiles now have taken the place of the Jews, but this verse may equally well announce our tragic reversal, the reward or punishment of our deeds in the kingdom of God. If Bede is right, as I believe him to be, then Luke is not a historian of God's salvation according to a triumphalistic positivism of the revelation but according to the mystery of human and divine interrelations in love, hope, faith, and fidelity, or in abandon, weakness, and falling away.

---

[11] Hoffmann has insisted on the ethical and personal meaning for our verses in "Πάντες ἐργά-ται ἀδικίας," 196–97.

[12] Bede, *In Lucae evangelium expositio* IV.1637–60; see Bede, *In Lucae evangelium expositio, In Marci evangelium expositio* (ed. David Hurst; CCSL 120; Turnhout: Brepols, 1960) 272.

[13] Ibid., IV.1670–79 (p. 273).

Tradition and Redaction in Acts 10:1–11:18[1]

All exegetes today accept the dominant place that the story of the Roman centurion occupies in the book of Acts.[2] By its breadth, its repetitions, and its central

[1] Aside from the five volumes edited by Frederick J. Foakes-Jackson and Kirsopp Lake, *The Acts of the Apostles* (5 vols.; *The Beginnings of Christianity, Part I*; London: Macmillan, 1920–1933), and apart from the commentaries, in particular those of Ernst Haenchen, *Die Apostelge-schichte* (6th ed.; KEK 3; Göttingen: Vandenhoeck & Ruprecht, 1968), Charles S. C. Williams, *A Commentary on the Acts of the Apostles* (2nd ed.; BNTC/HNTC; London: Black; New York: Harper, 1964), and Hans Conzelmann, *Die Apostelgeschichte* (HNT 7; Tübingen: Mohr Siebeck, 1963), it is necessary to note the following bibliography: Werner Bieder, "Zum Problem Religion-christlicher Glaube," *TZ* 15:6 (1959) 435–45, esp. 435–37. Johannes Bihler, *Die Stepha-nusgeschichte im Zusammenhang der Apostelgeschichte* (Munich: M. Hueber, 1963), esp. 178–85. François Bovon, *De vocatione gentium. Histoire de l'interprétation d'Act. 10,1–11,18 dans les six premiers siècles* (BGBE 8; Tübingen: Mohr Siebeck, 1967). Martin Dibelius, "Stilkri-tisches zur Apostelgeschichte," in *Eucharistērion. Studien zur Religion und Literatur des Alten und Neuen Testaments. Festschrift für Hermann Gunkel zum 60. Geburtstage* (ed. Emil Balla et al.; 2 vols. in 1; Göttingen: Vandenhoeck & Ruprecht, 1923); reprinted in idem, *Aufsätze zur Apostelgeschichte* (4th ed.; Göttingen: Vandenhoeck & Ruprecht, 1961) 9–28; my citations are according to the reprint (= "Stilkritisches"). Idem, "Die Bekehrung des Cornelius," in *Coniec-tanea Neotestamentica 11. Zum 60. Geburtstag von Anton Fridrichsen* (Lund: Gleerup, 1947); reprinted in *Aufsätze zur Apostelgeschichte*, 96–107; my citations are according to the reprint (= "Cornelius"). Xavier Ducros, "Le Nouveau Testament et la description des faits mystiques," *Bib* 40 (1959) 928–34. Michel Dujarier, *Le parrainage des adultes aux trois premiers siècles. Re-cherche historique sur l'évolution des garanties et des étapes catéchuménales avant 313* (Parole et mission; Paris: Cerf, 1962) 136–46 and 391–93. Jacques Dupont, *Les Problèmes du Livre des Actes d'après les travaux récents* (ALBO 11; Louvain: Publications Universitaires de Louvain, 1950); reprinted in *Études sur les Actes des apôtres* (LD 45; Paris: Cerf, 1967); my citations are according to the reprint (= *Problèmes*). Idem, "Le salut des Gentils et la signification théologique du livre des Actes," *NTS* 6 (1960) 132–55; reprinted in *Études sur les Actes des apôtres*; my cita-tions are according to the reprint (= "Salut"). Helmut Flender, *Heil und Geschichte in der Theo-logie des Lukas* (BEvT 41; 2d printing; Munich: Kaiser, 1968) 20–21. Maurice Goguel, *Le livre des Actes* (vol. 3 of *Introduction au Nouveau Testament*; Paris: Ernest Leroux, 1922) 216–18. Idem, "Le récit d'Actes 15, l'histoire de Corneille et l'incident d'Antioche," *RHPR* 3 (1923) 138–44. Ernst Haenchen, "Judentum und Christentum in der Apostelgeschichte," *ZNW* 54 (1963) 155–87; reprinted in idem, *Die Bibel und Wir* (vol. 2 of *Gesammelte Aufsätze*; Tübingen: Mohr Siebeck, 1968) 338–74; my citations are according to the reprint. Ferdinand Hahn, *Das Verständnis der Mission im Neuen Testament* (WMANT 13; Neukirchen-Vluyn: Neukirchener Verlag, 1963) 39ff. and 111ff. Jacob Jervell, "Das gespaltene Israel und die Heidenvölker. Zur Motivierung der Heidenmission in der Apostelgeschichte," *ST* 19 (1965) 68–96. Rudolf Liech-tenhan, *Die urchristliche Mission. Voraussetzungen, Motive und Methoden* (ATANT 9; Zurich: Zwingli, 1946). Philippe H. Menoud, "Le plan des Actes des apôtres," *NTS* 1 (1954) 44–51. J. C. O'Neill, *The Theology of Acts in Its Historical Setting* (London: S.P.C.K., 1961). J. R. Porter, "The 'Apostolic Decree' and Paul's Second Visit to Jerusalem," *JTS* 47 (1946) 169–74. P. L.

position, our text testifies to the interest that Luke carries to this decisive stage of the history of salvation. But which stage is the question and what, in the eyes of Luke, is the real significance of the event? For the majority of scholars, Luke conceives the conversion of Cornelius, or better, the integration of the centurion to the Church,[3] as the solemn dedication of the accession of the Gentiles to salvation. Thus the matter of Cornelius could not be an innocuous episode. It represents for Luke an event whose repercussions are considerable and whose impact is without limits. By admitting this pagan into the community, Peter opens the doors of the Church to all the Gentiles. In doing so, Luke denies that the baptism of the Ethiopic Eunuch (Acts 8) is the first account of the conversion of a Gentile,[4] just as he will relegate to obscurity the important mission to the Greeks, organized from Antioch by Christian Cyprians and Cyrenians.[5] Finally, when the whole Church must define its attitude concerning the Gentiles, it is the example of Cornelius the centurion whom Peter and James will argue about. These two addresses in chapter 15, definitely redactional, are significant, because they reveal to us the direction Luke gives in Acts 10:1–11:18. It concerns indeed the call of the Gentiles to the Gospel: "You know that in the early days God made a choice among you, that I should be the one through whom the Gentiles would hear the message of the good news and become believers. And God, who knows the human heart, testified to them by giving them the Holy Spirit, just as he did to us."[6] The allusion to the adventure of Cornelius is obvious. As it had been stated by Frederic H. Chase

---

Schoonheim, "De centurio Cornelius," *NedTT* 18 (1963) 453–75. J. Sint, "Schlachten und Opfern. Zu Apg. 10, 13; 11, 7," *ZKT* 78 (1956) 194–205. Étienne Trocmé, *Le livre des Actes et l'histoire* (Paris: Presses Universitaires de France, 1957) 169–74. Willem C. van Unnik, "De achtergrond en betekenis van Handelingen 10:4 en 35," *NedTT* 3 (1948–1949) 260–83 and 336–54. Hans Heinrich Wendt, "Der Kern der Cornelius-Erzählung, Act. 10, 1–11, 18," *ZTK* 1 (1891) 230–54. Alfred Wikenhauser, "Doppelträume," *Bib* 29 (1948) 100–11. Ulrich Wilckens, "Kerygma und Evangelium bei Lukas (Beobachtungen zu Act. 10, 34–43)," *ZNW* 49 (1958) 223–37. Idem, *Die Missionsreden der Apostelgeschichte. Form- und traditionsgeschichtliche Untersuchungen* (WMANT 5; Neukirchen-Vluyn: Neukirchener Verlag, 1961). The reader may also supplement this bibliography by referencing the work of A. J. and Mary Bedford Mattill, *A Classified Bibliography of Literature on the Acts of the Apostles* (NTTS 7; Leiden: Brill, 1966) 393–97.

 [2] See for example Trocmé, *Le livre des Actes et l'histoire*, 170; Dupont, *Problèmes*, 75; "Salut," 409–12; and Haenchen, "Judentum und Christentum," 351–54.

 [3] Cornelius in fact, by all accounts in the Lukan redaction, is already turned towards God. He does not have to convert, but to move towards God.

 [4] See Haenchen, *Die Apostelgeschichte*, 263–65.

 [5] This mission, consisting of Christian Cyprians and Cyrenians who were driven out of Jerusalem, is recounted in only six verses (the clue to the fragmented story may be gleaned from Acts 8:4 and once again in Acts 11:ff.). The story of Cornelius (Acts 10:1–11:18) follows two brief but different accounts, the cure of Aeneas (Acts 9:32–35) and the resurrection of Tabitha (Acts 9:36–43). These anecdotes resemble our text because in these three cases Peter plays a role in the foreground.

 [6] Acts 15:7–8. See allusion to the story of Cornelius in James' discourse in Acts 15:14.

and Bernhard Weiss, Luke understands this adventure as the Pentecost of the Gentiles.[7]

Patristic and modern interpretations show, however, that this expression of Christian universalism does not exhaust the meaning of our account. Certain insinuations or assertions of the author orient our gaze in another direction. The author indeed seems at times to tackle another problem: not the admission of pagans but Christian ethics (What may I eat? With whom should I associate?)[8]. Did Luke want to give a double sense to this pericope, or are the two themes of purity and the call to the Gentiles related to one another to such an extent that Luke, by approaching one, could not ignore the other? Or again, is the presence of these two themes side by side a symptom of the sources or of the underlying traditions?

In the pages that follow, after a brief *status quaestionis*, I would like to clarify the import that the author gives to the event. I will then attempt to extract the traditional material that Luke may have had at his disposal. Finally, I will discuss the historical development of the facts, at least the kind that one is able to infer with some certainty from such an investigation. This method, which I consider a good one, is to proceed from the known to the unknown – from the text as we have it before us to the traditions, and from the traditions to the facts.[9]

For a long time, during the nineteenth century, the only result the exegete expected from an investigation of our text was certainty of the historical order. Scholars who discussed our pericope looked only for connections with historical reality: Did the story of Cornelius happen as Luke claims? Does the direction that Luke gives to the event correspond to the facts? The answers naturally varied according to personal inclinations and to the sources that one believed to discover in these chapters.[10] Indeed, the very act of researching sources responds more to a historical requirement than a literary one. To find a source was to approach historical fact rather than to take a new look at the work of the writer.[11]

The careful application of *Formgeschichte* to the book of Acts was going to modify this perspective, the criticism being historical before it became also literary. Martin Dibelius, already by 1923 and then even more thoroughly in 1947,

---

[7] Frederic H. Chase, *The Credibility of the Acts of the Apostles* (The Huslean Lectures, 1900–1901; London: Macmillan, 1902) 79; Bernhard Weiss, *Das Neue Testament nach D* (vol. 1 of *Martin Luthers berichtigter Übersetzung*; 2d. ed.; Leipzig: Hinrichs, 1907) 489.

[8] See Dupont, *Problèmes*, 77–78; "Salut," 411–12.

[9] There is a necessary give and take, when one needs to understand the editorial effort and to delimit traditions. The intention of the redactor is specified when the traditions are known and these traditions become apparent when the editorial scope has been established.

[10] In his commentary (*Die Apostelgeschichte*), Haenchen indicates some of these major exegetical options of the past.

[11] The pages of Wendt and Goguel cited in n. 1 above are instructive in this respect. On the problem of sources, see the remarkable work of Jacques Dupont, *Les sources du livre des Actes. État de la question* (Bruges: Desclée de Brouwer, 1960).

discovered behind Acts 10:1–11:18 a legend that recounts the marvelous conversion of the Roman centurion. Recovered and reworked by Luke, this legend takes on, according to Dibelius, a new significance. In context of the whole work, it no longer represents the conversion of one "God-fearer," but the first admission of a pagan, the opening *heilsgeschichtlich* of the Church door to the nations. By adding foreign elements, in particular the vision of Peter, it also meets an ethical need of Christians in their preoccupation with purity.[12] In 1946, roughly at the same time, in a brief but suggestive article devoted to the apostolic decree and the second voyage of Paul to Jerusalem, J. R. Porter discovered two distinct centers of interest in our text – one that he places in the account of the tradition: that of commensality and observances; the other, which he declares redactional: the admission of the Gentiles.[13]

For several reasons, *Formgeschichte* was not applied systematically to Acts and no one in a serious manner critiqued the hypothesis of Dibelius: indeed, partisans of this method, Dibelius foremost, thought that the method could not apply as such to Acts, because the mode of the transmission of the accounts diverged largely from that of the synoptic tradition. The vehicle that transports the accounts is not the inspiration of the preaching (kerygma), as in the Synoptics, but the simple pleasure of telling.[14] Moreover, contrary to the first three Gospels, which by their parallel elements facilitate form criticism, we find that Acts has only a few points of comparison. Lastly, *Formgeschichte* had not yet made its full presence felt in the study of Acts when a new method was introduced.

Indeed, to the study of the literary genres were added, since 1950, investigations concerning redaction itself. The interest that one consequently lent to the editorial work of the author equally affected the analysis of the various underlying traditions. In this respect, the commentary of Ernst Haenchen is significant. The German exegete at this point mistrusted sources, as he refused to accept any perceptible traditional intermediary between the historical fact and the final redaction. Even the vision of Peter is in his opinion a Lukan composition.[15] This position, no doubt excessive, was criticized by Ulrich Wilckens, Ferdinand Hahn, and Hans Conzelmann who, more or less, came back to the solution of Dibelius.[16] What we therefore had here was a limited undertaking. Nobody, to my knowledge, has since taken up the problem as a whole.[17]

---

[12] Dibelius, "Cornelius," 96–107.

[13] Porter, "The 'Apostolic Decree'"; according to this author, the involvement of the redactor is much less than what Dibelius thinks.

[14] On this subject see the article of Jacob Jervell, who is opposed to this view: "Zur Frage der Traditionsgrundlage der Apostelgeschichte," *ST* 16 (1962) 25–41.

[15] Haenchen, *Die Apostelgeschichte*, 306–7.

[16] Wilckens, *Missionsreden*, 63; Hahn, *Verständnis der Mission*, 41; and Conzelmann, *Die Apostelgeschichte*, 61–62.

[17] To my knowledge, the articles that have appeared between 1950 and 1970 concerning our pericope all deal with specifics: on the religious status of Cornelius and a first attempt at Chris-

1. Redaction

Acts 10:1–11:18 can be divided into seven sections. This division, suggested by Hans H. Wendt and taken up again by Ernst Haenchen and Frederick F. Bruce,[18] is confirmed by patristic interpretation. In fact, early Christian interpreters stop less in the history of Cornelius as a whole than in one of his episodes, and the episodes in which they are interested correspond to the sections named by moderns.

From the first scene (Acts 10:1–8), which tells of the appearance of an angel to Cornelius, the first miracle, Luke implies that the mission to the Gentiles responds to the will of God, and it took an order from him to be carried out. The pagans whom God loves and calls are not just any pagans but are men and women, such as Cornelius, dedicated to Jewish monotheism and righteous morals. The admission of pagans into the Church does not mean, in the eyes of Luke, the suppression of any entry condition, but the replacement of Jewish ritual requirements, which appear to him to be privileges that are outdated by the moral requirements and religion applicable to all.[19]

A second miracle, the vision of Peter, occurs during the second scene (Acts 10:9–16): God continues with the execution of his plan. He reveals to the apostle that all the nations are equally pure in his eyes and that the Church may recruit its followers from there henceforth. By his refusal and hesitations, the first missionary to the Gentiles announces on the one hand the continuity of the Synagogue and the Church,[20] and on the other hand places the initiative of this intervention in the hands of God.

---

tian universalism (van Unnik); on the ecstasy of Peter (Ducros); and on the divine order given to Peter (Sint). Only the article by Schoonheim ("De centurio Cornelius") considers the whole history. However, owing to a deficient methodology that he applies (he goes from text to history without warning!), it is not of great use. Dupont has given his opinion on several occasions, in the two articles cited, as well as in the notes of the Jerusalem Bible: this exegete recognizes two centers of interest in the pericope, and he is tempted to explain them by the existence of two sources. Dupont notes precisely that Luke's interest turns to the problem of admitting Gentiles. Alfred Wikenhauser (*Die Apostelgeschichte* [3d ed.; RNT 5; Regensburg: F. Pustet, 1956] 125) and Kirsopp Lake and Henry J. Cadbury (in Foakes-Jackson and Lake, *Beginnings of Christianity* I, 4:112) also recognized this double play.

[18] Hans Heinrich Wendt, *Handbuch über die Apostelgeschichte* (5th ed.; KEK 3; Göttingen: Vandenhoeck & Ruprecht, 1880) 229–49; Haenchen, *Die Apostelgeschichte*, 302–5; Frederick F. Bruce, *The Acts of the Apostles* (2d ed.; London: Tyndale, 1952) 214–34.

[19] In his work (*Le parrainage des adultes*, 136–46 and 391–93), Dujarier believes to have discovered in the structure and composition of Acts 10, the procedure and the ritual of the catechumen and of baptism between the years 70–80 c.e.

[20] A point that Irenaeus has insisted upon in keeping with the story of Cornelius (*Adv. haer.* 3.12.7). Wikenhauser ("Doppelträume") paid attention to the parallel revelations in the book of Acts, in particular to the visions of Cornelius and Peter. He found many parallels between them in secular literature.

The third scene (Acts 10:17–23a) shows that the first two miracles were planned by God and realized for the salvation of the pagans. A third celestial intervention – of the Holy Spirit – encourages Peter to go to the centurion: God continues his work.

The fourth scene (Acts 10:23b–33) marks a necessary transition to a new development of the story, a beneficial lull before the gust of wind of the Holy Spirit. By a closer look at the style (increase in the use of συν-,[21] offering the same plan to both Peter and Cornelius), Luke brings the characters closer. The fifth scene (Acts 10:34–43) presents the contents of the Word, a word intended henceforth for all men and women of good will. This word is the preaching of *totus Christus*: a historical Jesus and Christ of faith.

The import of this sermon is immediate and powerful, as demonstrated in the sixth scene (Acts 10:44–48). The Holy Spirit descends upon the hearers. The fourth miracle, the bestowal of divine strength, more so than prior divine interventions, witnesses that the election of the Gentiles is the work of God. We are at the peak of the account. The Christians present, especially Peter, must accept the will of God and his intervention: Cornelius and his people are baptized without formality, because they were placed by God in the same plan, exactly as the Christians of Jewish origin.[22]

In Acts 10:1–11:18 Luke therefore proclaims that the election of the Gentiles, willed by God, was imposed despite the resistance of humans. He takes care to specify that the divine call does not go to just any pagan, but to those who, being well-disposed, are already worshiping and practicing virtue.[23] He finally underscores that the first evangelization of pagans was not the work of an independent or anonymous Christian, but of the principal apostle, Peter; and that the apostolic Church, the mother community of Jerusalem, learned of this revelation and gave its accord to this initiative. Such then, in brief, is the direction that Luke gives to the events that he recounts in our pericope.

This interpretation of the whole requires some accuracies of detail, for I am relying on several verses, in my opinion redactional (for example, vv. 2, 4, 28, 34

---

[21] Father Edgar Haulotte brought my attention to this characteristic.

[22] See the four comparisons: "even on the Gentiles" (Acts 10:45), "just as we" (Acts 10:47), "the Gentiles also" (Acts 11:1), to which we may add Peter's statement, "just as he did to us" (Acts 15:8).

[23] Eduard Schweizer signals the importance this category play in the eyes of Luke. It is to these people who do not conceal their sympathy to the Jewish cause that Luke undoubtedly intends his Gospel and the book of Acts. See Schweizer, "Zu den Reden der Apostelgeschichte," *TZ* 13 (1957) 11; reprinted in *Neotestamentica. Deutsche und englische Aufsätze, 1951–1963* (Zurich: Zwingli, 1963) 427–28. Haenchen criticizes the synergism of Luke that appears in this idea of the call: "Gott und Mensch," in *Gesammelte Aufsätze* 1:11. Certainly the theology of Luke is unaware of the rigorous opposition of Paul between salvation by faith and salvation by works (see the poor summary of the Pauline thought in Acts 13:38–39). Luke is all the same aware of God's previous action when he states that "God has granted repentance unto life" (Acts 11:18). Moreover, Acts 10 concerns reward and not merit.

and 35), that certain critics consider to be traditional. In addition, I did not take into account such and such verse, redactional in the eyes of some exegetes, but traditional in my understanding.

In an article noted above, Willem C. van Unnik sees in vv. 4 and 35 of Acts 10 the expression of a Christian theology that is very ancient, prior to Paul: in his opinion, the spiritual description of Cornelius (v. 4) and the new requirement stated by Peter (v. 35) reveal a stage of intermediate Christianity between the primitive Jewish-Christians and the Pauline pagan-Christians.[24] There is not yet, according to him, a well-developed Church of Jews and pagans, but an extended Israel that includes Jews and pagans, where God, renouncing circumcision and ritual requirements, incorporates those who have demonstrated faith and virtue into the people of the covenant. Heaven, which up to that point was closed to the prayers and good works of the pagans, is now open to these virtuous men and women. God treats Cornelius as if he were a Jew.

The hypothesis of van Unnik is conceivable only at the level of tradition, because all the intention of Luke is summarized in the following affirmation: it is no longer necessary to be Jewish in order to become a Christian. The gift of the Spirit was given to the Jews as well as to the Gentiles. Now, an analysis of the vocabulary and style show that vv. 4 and 35 are clearly Lukan; and, typical of Luke, they are inspired by the Septuagint.[25] An additional clue to their redactional nature: the affinity between the centurions of Capernaum and of Caesarea, as Luke describes them, is so great that one of the authors of the Pseudo-Clementines apparently confused the two.[26] The spiritual state of Cornelius, as it appears in Acts 10, and the favorable divine reaction that it causes, does not therefore indicate a pre-Pauline solution to the problem of universality, but this popular form of Christianity, from the end of the first century and beginning of the second, which assimilated poorly the teaching of Paul and opened the way to synergism.[27]

Before van Unnik and for different reasons, Otto Bauernfeind had been interested in v. 35 of Acts 10. If he readily admits the redactional character of Peter's speech for the most part,[28] this exegete considers vv. 34–35 authentic. These vers-

---

[24] Van Unnik, "De achtergrond"; Dupont, *Problèmes*, 79–80, gives a good summary in French of this article.

[25] Van Unnik ("De achtergrond") demonstrates this himself. See also Conzelmann, *Die Apostelgeschichte*, 63.

[26] *Ps.-Clem. Hom.* 20.13 (see GCS 42; ed. B. Rehm and J. Irmscher; p. 276).

[27] See Ernst Haenchen, "The Book of Acts as Source Material for the History of Early Christianity," in *Studies in Luke-Acts: Essays Presented in Honor of Paul Schubert* (ed. Leander E. Keck and J. Louis Martyn; Nashville: Abingdon, 1966) 266. The original German to this article has just appeared under the title "Die Apostelgeschichte als Quelle für die christliche Frühgeschichte," in idem, *Die Bibel und Wir*, 322.

[28] The words in Acts 11:15 ἐν δὲ τῷ ἄρξασθαί με λαλεῖν do not leave room for a long speech.

es would be a "polemical slogan" of the apostle, which would have survived until Luke.[29] Nothing proves, first of all, that the words of the apostles were transmitted as the logia of the Lord. Acts 11:15, moreover, indicates rather that the whole discourse is an addition.[30] Lastly, the form of these verses, like their contents, is Lukan.

Of the three theses that Jacob Jervell presents in his recent article,[31] only the third one is of interest to us here. One can summarize it as follows: the participation of Gentiles in salvation is solemnly marked from the very start of the book of Acts. There one is not concerned with a new truth that would have been essential at the time of the conversion of Cornelius after the hardening of the Jews. Indeed, preaching to the Jews already included the participation of the Gentiles in salvation. Acts 3:22–26 proves that Peter already knew that the pagans were called at the time. In this case, Acts 10 cannot tell "die grundsätzliche Entscheidung für die Teilnahme der Heiden am Heil" ("the fundamental decision in favor of the participation of the Gentiles in salvation").[32] The intention of Luke in Acts 10:1–11:18 is rather to specify the conditions established for the Gentiles for their admission into the Church: "Hier geht es um die Frage, auf welche Weise und zur welcher Zeit erhalten die Heiden Anteil an den Verheissungen Israels?" ("Here the question is how and when the Gentiles receive their part in the promises given to Israel").[33] Acts 10:1–11:18 therefore makes a ruling on the problem of ritual law. The new truth that the account brings is not the salvation of the Gentiles, but freedom from the Law. If van Unnik and Bauernfeind considered some verses traditional that are in my opinion redactional, Jervell, it seems to me, commits the opposite error: because he does not distinguish sufficiently between tradition and redaction, he attributes to the final author intentions that obviously were not his but belonged to the tradition. As we will see, the Lukan interpretation of the vision of Peter found in vv. 28 and 35 deals with universalism and not freedom from the Law. Acts 11:18, definitely a redactional verse, contains this declaration: "Then to the Gentiles also God has granted repentance unto life!" – to the pagans who did not yet have it, while the Jews already had it. Jervell shifts the emphasis of this verse and reorients it when he interprets: God has given to the pagans in their capacity as pagans, that is to say liberated from the Law, repentance that leads to life.[34] In my opinion, the emphasis is related to the word καί: "to the Gentiles *also.*"

---

[29] Otto Bauernfeind, *Die Apostelgeschichte* (THKNT 5; Leipzig: A. Deichert, 1939) 142.

[30] With Haenchen ("Judentum und Christentum," 354), it should be said contra Wilckens ("Kerygma," 223f.) that in vv. 34–35 the discourse fits very well to the actual situation of Cornelius. These verses generalize the case of the Centurion and affirm Christian universalism, as Luke understood it.

[31] Jervell, "Das gespaltene Israel."

[32] Ibid., 92.

[33] Ibid., 92.

[34] Ibid., 94.

My interpretation of the redaction, which joins with that of Haenchen, Dupont, Conzelmann, and J. C. O'Neill,[35] may be summarized as follows: Acts 10:1–11:18 is a strong gauge of the book of the Acts; it is the turning point where the Church, which was a Jewish sect, now opens itself to the pagan world and prepares its conquest to the ends of the earth. In Acts 10:1–11:18, we see the green light for the evangelization of the pagans, which God gives to the Church through the intermediary of the apostle Peter.

2. Traditions

If exegetes today acknowledge that the hand of Luke looms large in the story of Cornelius, making it an expression of one of his major convictions, and if they therefore rightly assess value to the redactional effort of the author, they are far from agreeing, however, as to the nature and quantity of the materials Luke may have used – his sources or, perhaps better, traditions. It is without doubt that Dibelius pushed research the furthest in this sense, and it is for this reason that we must start from him to advance the debate.[36]

The personal legend. For Dibelius, tradition delivered to Luke the account of the conversion of a Roman centurion, Cornelius, whose story can be classified in the literary genre of the personal legend. This legend of conversion did not have any general import. It simply contained the marvelous event that the centurion had experienced. Cornelius thus occupied the center, while now it is instead Peter who holds the center of the scene. Dibelius researched the elements of this legend behind the Lukan composition. He separated as foreign to the original story the discussion on Jerusalem (Acts 11:1–18), which deals with another subject; the christological sermon (Acts 10:34–43), as he finds that Acts 11:15 has been added by Luke according to his preferred method of speech insertion; the vision of Peter (Acts 10:9–16), which doubles unnecessarily the teaching of the Spirit (Acts 10:19–20); and the interlude in vv. 27–29a, which refers to the vision. Then Dibelius cut again through Luke's text to keep only the following elements: the legend tells initially the vision of Cornelius, then the command of the Spirit to Peter, the arrival of Peter at the home of Cornelius, the beginning of the apostle's sermon that glossolalia, a visible sign of the presence of the Spirit, brings to an immediate end. The baptism of Cornelius is then administered with no other condition.

---

[35] Haenchen, *Die Apostelgeschichte* (3d ed.; 1959), 302–5; Dupont, "Salut," 409–12; Conzelmann, *Die Apostelgeschichte*, 61–62 and 83; O'Neill, *Theology of Acts*, 100–1.

[36] Dibelius, "Cornelius," 96–107.

The argument of Dibelius is accepted by Trocmé, Wilckens, Hahn, and Conzelmann.[37] It is rejected by Haenchen for not very conclusive reasons, which were subsequently reduced to nought by Wilckens.[38] For my part, I also believe that behind Acts 10 is hidden a legend of conversion.

Just as Dibelius, Wilfred L. Knox had the intuition, rightly so, that such a history had to have circulated in Caesarea itself, and that it was, in the eyes of the Christians of that city, the account of the founding of their community.[39]

The etiological legend. A certain number of confusions prevented Dibelius from going further: (a) He accounted to the Lukan redaction the vision of Peter, while at the same time supposing its traditional character.[40] (b) He did not sufficiently distinguish the redaction from the tradition in Acts 11.[41] (c) He presupposed that the difficulty of commensality was able to pose itself for the Christians only after the admission of pagans into the Church.[42] Studying the prehistory of the vision of Peter and of the dispute in Jerusalem will allow us to extract a second tradition.

The vision of Peter (Acts 10:9–16), by itself and apart from the context, indicates, in my opinion, only one possible meaning. By this strange appearance, God orders Peter, and through him all Christians, to pass over the dietary prescriptions of the Law (Leviticus 11) and to no longer distinguish pure animals from impure. The vision, because it comes from on high, from God, inaugurates a new stage in the divine economy. The dietary commands of the Law lose their value henceforth. The vision avoids, however, falling into the dualism of a good God who supplants the legislative God of the ancient covenant: just as Jesus, concerning divorce (Mark 10 par.), passes over the Mosaic commandment while resorting to the order of creation, in the same way here the heavenly voice abolishes the legal prescriptions with an allusion to the first times. The list of animals in v. 12 indeed recalls the first chapter of Genesis and, even more, the animals that must enter the ark (Gen 6:20, according to LXX). The text insists intentionally on the presence of *all* the animals of creation; emphasis is on the word πάντα.

By proposing this interpretation, I am joining Bauernfeind and Trocmé and, beyond them, the school of Alexandria, which, to our surprise, from Clement to Cyril understood this vision in the literal sense. Others, to the contrary, such as

---

[37] Trocmé, *Le livre des Actes et l'histoire*, 173–74; Wilckens, "Kerygma," 223f.; Hahn, *Verständnis der Mission*, 41; Conzelmann, *Die Apostelgeschichte*, 62.

[38] Haenchen, *Die Apostelgeschichte* (3d ed.; 1959), 305–6; Wilckens, *Missionsreden*, 63 n. 1.

[39] Dibelius, "Cornelius," 105–107; Wilfred L. Knox, *The Acts of the Apostles* (Cambridge: Cambridge University Press, 1948) 31ff. Knox is more precise than Dibelius on this point.

[40] "Wahrscheinlich gehört aber auch Act. 10, 9–16 zu der Bearbeitung des Lukas" (Dibelius, "Cornelius," 98). Further to the contrary: "Sie wäre dann ein wirkliches Erlebnis des Petrus" (ibid., 99).

[41] Dibelius, "Cornelius," 96.

[42] "Aus der späteren Zeit, da der Konflikt über die Speisenfrage brennend war" (Dibelius, "Cornelius," 99).

Haenchen and Hahn, who themselves could rely on a patristic interpretation that goes from Tertullian to Augustine, affirm that the vision has nothing to do with the dietary laws and that it should be understood in a figurative sense.[43] This divergence of opinion comes from the fact that these latter exegetes interpret vv. 9–16 of Acts 10 not for themselves, but in the Lukan perspective. It is certain, as my analysis of the redaction has shown, that vv. 28 and 34–35 (see κἀμοὶ ὁ θεὸς ἔδειξεν, v. 28, and ἐπ᾽ ἀληθείας καταλαμβάνομαι, v. 34) place, from the vision of Peter, all men and women on the same plan and affirm a Christian universalism. But that is only the Lukan interpretation of a text that was aimed quite specifically at both pure and impure animals (see the mention of Peter's hunger and his negative reaction).[44] Verse 28, in particular, is to the vision what the explanation of the Parable of the Sower (Mark 4:13–20) is to its parable (Mark 4:3–9), a secondary interpretation. Origen notes with precision: "Does not the apostle Peter [in Acts 10:28b] seem to you to have transposed onto humanity [what is said about] all these quadrupeds, reptiles, and birds with great clarity?"[45] If we place Luke instead of Peter in Origen's sentence, the true relationship between tradition and redaction becomes clear: for the tradition, the vision solves a ritual problem and adopts a new food ethics, an ethics of freedom (note that in v. 14, the grammatically neuter πᾶν κοινὸν καὶ ἀκάθαρτον indicates food); but for the redaction, the vision affirms the purification of all humans and their perfect equality before God (note in v. 28b the grammatically masculine μηδένα κοινὸν ἢ ἀκάθαρτον, emphasized by the grammatically superfluous word ἄνθρωπον). The tradition gave a literal sense to the vision, the redaction a figurative sense.

In my opinion, this second tradition was not limited only to the vision of Peter: it continued with an account of the negative reaction of the Jerusalemite community before the new ethic of freedom was advocated by Peter. We find an echo of this in Acts 11:1–18. And three arguments militate in favor of this thesis.

a) Luke does not like to acknowledge that the apostolic age was rife with disputes. A comparison between Galatians 2 and Acts 15, for example, reveals his concern to minimize the tensions and conflicts. Luke therefore did not invent the Jerusalem conflict, as some authors would have it.[46] The account of the quarrel

---

[43] For the literal sense, see Bauernfeind, *Die Apostelgeschichte*, 145; Trocmé, *Le livre des Actes et l'histoire*, 172–73. For the figurative sense, Haenchen, *Die Apostelgeschichte* (3d ed.; 1959), 307; Hahn, *Verständnis der Mission*, 41–42. According to Haenchen, the vision cannot have a relationship with the dietary laws, because, after having received the order from God, Peter could very well have hastened upon a pure animal. As Dibelius notes ("Cornelius," 98 n. 2), to argue in this manner reveals a rational mind pushing the image too far. Moreover, how is it that one must understand the command "kill and eat" given to Peter, without falling into the allegory of Augustine (the Church must kill the Gentiles for their sins and incorporate them for a better life, *Comm. Ps.* 3:7; 13:4; etc.), an allegory that Calvin has already pointed out as arbitrary (see *Act. Apost. comm.* ad loc.)?

[44] See Dibelius, "Cornelius," 98–99.

[45] *Hom. Lev.* 7:4.

[46] Haenchen, *Die Apostelgeschichte* (3d ed.; 1959), 299–300; Conzelmann, *Die Apostelge-*

predates Luke, but it certainly was not formed as an isolated tradition. Neither did it follow the legend of Cornelius, which did not contain any question of principle and which, following the rules of its literary genre, concluded with the baptism of the centurion.[47] On the other hand, it could very well have served as a conclusion to the vision of Peter, as we will see.

b) What was at stake in the dispute is not the issue indicated in the redaction. We have noted that the issue of this quarrel was, for Luke, the adoption of the principle of the election of the pagans (see Acts 11:1 and 18). However, as certain scholars have seen well,[48] this is not the only issue brought up in the meeting at Jerusalem. Such is not even the explicit objection that was formulated against Peter: Acts 11:3 indicates that "those of the circumcision" reproached the apostle for being among the pagans and for having eaten with them, thus violating the dietary commands and the purity rules. All of this leads one to believe that the tension in Acts 11:1–18 between these two centers of interest, the admission of pagans and the purity of Christians, is explained not by the interweaving of two sources,[49] but through the Lukan rereading of an earlier tradition.

Verse 3 of Acts 11 has preserved the objection formulated against Peter such as it would appear in the tradition. Here the Jerusalem community turns its gaze inward: it is looking to protect the purity of the eschatological people and avoid impurity that is propagated by the assimilation of the impure food and by contact with the pagans. But for Luke, the gaze of the community is turned towards the pagans: the Church admits, in the final reckoning, the order of God and welcomes within itself the converted pagans.

Peter's defense as it appears in Acts 11 reflects also, in its beginning, the early tradition recovered by Luke. As opposed to Acts 10, where the misfortunes of Cornelius play a greater part than the ecstasy of Peter, here it is the vision of the apostle that serves as the principal argument (Acts 11:5–10). One may thus imagine that in the tradition, Peter, attacked for his new kind of life, defended himself by recounting his ecstatic vision. The community would therefore yield before this divine revelation. But Luke takes up the tradition and inflects its meaning, as is shown in vv. 1 and 11–18, in a clearly redactional manner.

c) There is a third argument in favor of combining Peter's vision with the quarrel in Jerusalem: during his ecstasy, Peter reacts negatively (Acts 10:14). There is nothing surprising about this, as the Jerusalem community that he addresses is also against the suppression of the dietary observances.

---

schichte, 66–67; and before them, Alfred Loisy, *Les Actes des apôtres* (Paris: E. Nourry, 1920) 453ff. Wendt ("Der Kern der Cornelius-Erzählung") and Goguel (*Le livre des Actes*) have felt strongly that there must be a tradition behind Acts 11.

[47] See Dibelius, "Cornelius," 100.

[48] See Trocmé, *Le livre des Actes et l'histoire*, 171.

[49] This is the opinion of Trocmé (*Le livre des Actes et l'histoire*, 171–72) and Dupont (*Problèmes*, 77–78).

Therefore, examination of the texts in Acts 10:1–11:18 leads one to distinguish the problem of the purity of the Christians and that of the admission of the pagans. It prompts us to attribute the first problem to tradition, and the second to redaction. As the first is approached only in connection with the vision of Peter and the dispute in Jerusalem, it is likely that these two episodes (Peter's vision and the meeting in Jerusalem) formed two parts of the one and the same tradition.

It is even possible to define the literary genre of this tradition. It was to be a question of an etiologic legend aligned with the person and authority of Peter. During the early centuries, when the dietary freedom of Christians was attacked, believers often took refuge in the authority of Peter and the divine "revelation" (Acts 10:9–16) with which he had been graced. Against the attacks of vegetarian heretics, of Jews, and of Arabs who deprived themselves of pork, Christians often justified their practices with the vision of Peter and the divine commandment "Kill and eat." In this regard, the violent reaction of the Emperor Julian is significant: "Why are you not pure in your kind of life like the Jews, why do you believe more in Peter ... ?"[50] It is probable that before the Lukan redaction, Peter's vision had already allowed the Church to modify its position and to defend its new freedom. If the first Christians rejected the legal distinction between pure and impure animals, if they no longer feared contact with pagans, then it was the case that, according to them, God had made this decision and had communicated his will to the apostle Peter through a revelation.

This etiologic legend began with an apocalypse.[51] The first part of the account, the statement on the vision, belongs indeed to the apocalypse genre and is similar to Revelation 4 in particular, where the visionary John sees an open door in the heavens and hears a voice that commands him "Come up here" before making him a promise ("I will show you what must take place after this"). The ecstasy of Peter corresponds to the rapture of John.[52] The difference between the two texts is as follows: the revelation in Revelation 4 remains within the apocalyptic genre (its extraction allows knowledge of the future), while the revelation of Acts 10 serves ethics and etiology (the ecstasy commands a new moral attitude and makes it possible to justify it).

We must remember that the revelation is made to the apostle Peter. As Dibelius demonstrated,[53] the New Testament contains not only legends devoted to Jesus, but also legends where Peter is central. A comparison of our Petrine legend with the confession of Peter is essential. There too we have an etiological legend con-

---

[50] The text that came down to us is in Cyril of Alexandria's *Contra Iulianum* 9; it is fragment 314 from the Karl Johannes Neumann edition (Teubner, 1880).

[51] This is already the term that Irenaeus gives to the vision of Peter in *Adv. haer.* 3.12.7. Several early Christian authors, as well as Julian, qualify the same term.

[52] Rev 4:1–2. Hans Bietenhard (*Die himmlische Welt im Urchristentum und Spätjudentum* [Tübingen: Mohr Siebeck, 1951] 248) brings closer these two texts. See also Mark 1:9–11.

[53] Martin Dibelius, *Die Formgeschichte des Evangeliums* (3d ed.; ed. Günther Bornkamm; app. Gerhard Iber; Tübingen: Mohr Siebeck, 1959) 112–13.

nected to Peter: that text explains why Christians, following Peter, profess in Jesus the Messiah and the Son of God. It is because Peter was the first to profess in this manner, not by his own volition, but through God's influence: "Blessed are you, Simon son of Jonah! For flesh and blood has not revealed this to you, but my Father in heaven" (Matt 16:17). Therefore the novelty of Christian profession cannot be doubted since it comes from God. We recognize the same truth – this same kind of reasoning – in Acts 10:9–16, where recourse to a heavenly revelation justifies a new direction of thought and practice. The human reaction of Peter (Acts 10:14) and of the Church (Acts 11:3) also appears in Matthew 16 in the sudden refusal of Peter: "God forbid it, Lord! This must never happen to you!" (Matt 16:22). And the reprimand of Jesus, "Get behind me, Satan!" (Matt 16:23), finds its counterpart in Acts 10 in the repetition of the divine order: "What God has cleansed, you must not call common" (Acts 10:15).[54]

Before examining whether Luke recovers a third tradition in our pericope, it is necessary to present a final detail. Dupont, who rightly insists on two centers of interest in our text, argues that v. 28b is attached to the theme of ritual purity.[55] Trocmé goes in the same direction and considers this verse traditional.[56] I have explained above why I believe this verse is redactional: it indicates precisely the shift in meaning that Luke brings about from the tradition. Therefore the verse still *appears* to refer to the theme of ritual purity. But, in fact, it is halfway between the definite theme of the tradition (purity of the Christians) and that of the redaction (call of the Gentiles). It is here that the analysis of our pericope is so difficult: we have verses where the tradition is expressed without marked redactional correction (thus the Peter-God dialogue in Acts 10:13–15); we have other verses where the redaction, free from the tradition, has a free way (thus Acts 11:1 and 18); and finally others, where the redaction interprets the tradition so that it becomes more acceptable (thus Acts 10:28b).

The christological discourse. Wilckens and Dupont have indicated with precision and clarity the current state of study of the christological speeches in Acts.[57]

---

[54] I consider Matt 16:13–23, like Mark 8:27–33, as a literary unity. At the level of the tradition, the profession of Peter was undoubtedly also related to the rejection of Peter by Jesus, as shown by Oscar Cullmann (*Saint Pierre. Disciple, apôtre, martyr* [Paris: Delachaux & Niestlé, 1952] 154–66) and Erich Dinkler ("Petrusbekenntnis und Satanswort. Das Problem der Messianität Jesu," in idem, ed., *Zeit und Geschichte. Dankesgabe an Rudolf Bultmann zum 80. Geburtstag* [Tübingen: Mohr Siebeck, 1964]; reprinted in idem, *Signum Crucis. Aufsätze zum Neuen Testament und zur christlichen Archäologie* [Tübingen: Mohr Siebeck, 1967] 283–312). Do verses 17–19 in Matthew 16 come from another tradition, as these two scholars think?

[55] Dupont, "Salut," 411 (a few years before [*Problèms*, 78], Dupont made of this verse a redactional joint between the two themes taken up in Acts 10:1–11:18).

[56] Trocmé, *Le livre des Actes et l'histoire*, 173 (despite everything, he discovers a certain redactional alteration in this verse).

[57] Wilckens, *Missionsreden*, 1–31; Dupont, "Les discours missionnaires des Actes des apôtres d'après un ouvrage récent," *RB* 69 (1962) 37ff.; reprinted in *Études sur les Actes des apôtres*, 134–37. For a fuller bibliography, see Carlo Ghidelli, "Bibliografia Biblica Petrina," *ScC* 96

After the consensus of exegetes who, building on the works of Dibelius and Charles H. Dodd, regard as traditional the plan of these sermons, came the opinion that is undoubtedly the most widespread: in spite of appearances, all the speeches of Acts are Luke's own work in form and in substance. Following Philippe Vielhauer, Conzelmann, Christopher F. Evans, and Haenchen,[58] Wilckens endeavors to show that: limiting his investigation to the missionary speeches of chapters 2–13, he first analyzed the structure of these sermons, then he studied the context in which they are inscribed, before bringing his attention to their contents. The result is clear in his eyes. These sermons, and that of Acts 10 in particular, are entirely redactional. They do not represent an early kerygma, but the theology of Luke.[59]

The results of Wilckens, supplemented by those of Evans, appear unassailable to me when it concerns vv. 34–35, of which I have already noted the redactional nature, and of vv. 39–43, which recount the end of Jesus' life, his ministry in Jerusalem, his death, resurrection, and his appearances to the witnesses his life. In these verses, the hand of Luke is perceptible at every instant. But the question is more delicate for vv. 36–38, where one finds grammatical blunders.[60] Evans does not even bother with the difficulty, while the explanations of Wilckens remain embarrassments.

In light of this impasse, it is not surprising that many exegetes have maintained the traditional character of vv. 36–38 and, by extension, of the discourse as a whole: "The Greek is certainly not Luke's free composition; if it were, it would be much clearer."[61] The theory of a poorly translated Aramaic original goes back to Charles C. Torrey. It was revisited once again by Dodd, Knox, and Bruce.[62] Here is the translation of the text as restored by Torrey: "As for the word which the Lord of All sent to the children of Israel, proclaiming good tidings of peace through Jesus Christ: ye know that which took place in all Judea, starting in

---

(1968) 91* (nos. 775–89). Certain interpretations that I do not report are presented and critiqued by Dupont in an article on Peter's speeches in Acts; see Jacques Dupont, *Nouvelles études sur les Actes des apôtres* (LD 118; Paris: Le Cerf, 1984) 58–111.

[58] Philippe Vielhauer, "Zum 'Paulinismus' der Apostelgeschichte," *EvT* 10 (1950–1951) 1–15; reprinted in idem, *Aufsätze zum Neuen Testament* (TB 31; Munich: Kaiser, 1965) 9–27; Hans Conzelmann, *Die Mitte der Zeit. Studien zur Theologie des Lukas* (3d ed.; Tübingen: Mohr Siebeck, 1960); Christopher F. Evans, "The Kerygma," *JTS* 7 (1956) 25–41; Haenchen, *Die Apostelgeschichte.*

[59] Wilckens, *Missionsreden,* 96–99.

[60] Verse 36: Upon which verb does τὸν λόγον depend if one does not take the relative ὄν for a dittography? What is the subject of ἀπέστειλεν? To what does the participle εὐαγγελιζόμενος refer? Verse 37: What is the sense of ῥῆμα? To what must the nominative ἀρξάμενος be related? Verse 38: Why is Ἰησοῦν in the accusative?

[61] Bruce, *Acts of the Apostles,* 231.

[62] Charles C. Torrey, *The Composition and Date of Acts* (Cambridge, Mass.: Harvard University Press, 1916) 27 and 35–36; Charles H. Dodd, *The Apostolic Preaching and Its Developments* (London: Hoddern & Stoughton, 1944; reprinted in 1963) 27–29; Knox, *Acts of the Apostles,* 31; Bruce, *Acts of the Apostles,* 224–25.

Galilee after the baptism which John preached: that God anointed Jesus … ." The
τὸν λόγον may be explained by a hanging construction, frequent in Aramaic; the
subject of ἀπέστειλεν would be "the Lord of all," which would designate God;
εὐαγγελιζόμενος would refer to this subject; ῥῆμα would translate the Aramaic
pitgama (= event); ἀρξάμενος would agree with this word "event" in the original
and should have been rendered by a neuter. If Luke translates it as masculine, it is
to underscore that this departure was made by a man, Jesus.[63]

This reconstruction certainly offers a self-contained text, but one must ask:
why would Luke have been mistaken in the translation of only these verses in the
speech? Why does not Torrey find other Semitisms in the rest of the sermon?[64]
Moreover, is it not surprising that this author is offering us the alleged original
text? Does it not astonish that God evangelizes and that the anointing of Jesus is
so abruptly mentioned? Does not the grammatical value of Ἰησοῦν (v. 38) remain
unexplained? Torrey, in addition, did not notice that a good portion of vv. 36–38
comes from the Septuagint. The influence of scriptural argumentation in these
verses has curiously escaped many exegetes, with the exception of Dupont.[65]
Luke does not have a structure of speech that is so rigid that he cannot invert the
parts. It was noted that the mention of the prophets in v. 43 was accompanied by
no quotation. In my opinion, it is not that the references to the Hebrew Bible are
non-existent, but Luke, for variation, has placed them here at the beginning. The
expression τὸν λόγον ἀπέστειλεν, despite Dupont, undoubtedly comes from the
Ps 107:20 (106:20 LXX), while εὐαγγελιζόμενος εἰρήνην is drawn either from Isa
52:7 or from Nah 2:1.[66]

The christological speech of Acts 10 is thus averred to be redactional from beginning to end. Even if the sermon appears to be of Lukan origin, it is necessary
to dispute the validity of the inferences drawn by Wilckens. According to him,
this speech is not based on any former tradition because it is penned by Luke.[67] It
seems to me that this goes against common sense. It goes against Luke himself,
who, in the prologue of his Gospel (Luke 1:1–4), claims to have made investigations; it also goes against the famous passage of Thucydides that has often been

---

[63] Torrey, *Composition and Date*, 27 and 35–36.

[64] In his book (*The Semitisms of Acts* [Oxford: Clarendon, 1965]), Max E. Wilcox treats Peter's speech to Cornelius in various parts. He is hardly favorable to the hypothesis of Torrey or
to the Aramaic reconstruction that the latter gives to v. 36 (ibid., 151–53). He discovered only
one Semitism in this sermon (v. 38a, according to the corrector of D, to which he gives preference; see ibid., 116–18). Otherwise, he finds in this speech only the hand of Luke, the influence
of the Septuagint (on v. 39b, see ibid., 34–35; on v. 40, see ibid., 64–65), and the presence of
certain traditional kerygmatic elements, not necessarily written in Aramaic (on vv. 40–42, see
ibid., 168–69).

[65] Jacques Dupont, "L'utilisation apologétique de l'Ancien Testament dans les discours des
Actes," *ETL* 29 (1953); reprinted in *Études sur les Actes des apôtres*, 256, 262, 271, and 277.

[66] As for the participle ἀρξάμενος, it remains a grammatical mystery. Wilcox (*Semitisms of
Acts*, 149–50) sees there a Lukanism rather than an error in translation.

[67] Wilckens, "Kerygma," 230.

misused[68] (all the same, Luke would not have deprived himself of the evangelic tradition on purpose). And finally, it goes against the text itself, where many ideas are simply Christian, long before being Lukan. The expression κριτὴς ζώντων καὶ νεκρῶν (v. 42) is found, in its verbal form, in 2 Tim 4:1. ἀναστῆναι (v. 41) is seldom used by Luke, and yet it is used by a good majority of Christians.[69] It could even be that the summary of the ministry of Jesus resembles as much the plan of the Gospel of Mark as that of Luke,[70] and that it was not necessarily later than the pre-Pauline formula of 1 Corinthians 15.[71] B. Schaller and Leonhard Goppelt have pointed out that one could not compare the plan of the missionary sermons in Acts to 1 Cor 15:3–5 without further remark. The literary genres are indeed different: 1 Cor 15:3–5, the "gospel" received and transmitted by Paul, is a profession of faith; Acts 10:36–43 has the structure of a sermon addressed to Jews, proselytes, and "God-fearers."[72] The format of the speeches in Acts, because it is different from that of 1 Corinthians 15, is thus not by necessity secondary.

In conclusion, I think that this sermon has, more or less, the same structure as the other missionary sermons from the beginning of the book, and that if the kerygma has developed to this point, it is because Luke wanted to stress the importance of the entry of the first Gentile into the Church. As for the problem of the tradition, it can be solved in a paradoxical way: the discourse is redactional, but because it is from Luke and because it is kerygmatic, it contains many traditional elements and perhaps even a traditional structure.

---

[68] Thucydides, *History of the Peloponnesian War* 1.22. See Martin Dibelius, *Die Reden der Apostelgeschichte und die antike Geschichtsschreibung. Aufsätze zur Apostelgeschichte* (4th ed.; Heidelberg: C. Winter, 1961) 122–23.

[69] See Herbert Braun, "Zur Terminologie der Acta von der Auferstehung Jesu," *TLZ* 77 (1952) col. 533; reprinted in idem, *Gesammelte Studien zum Neuen Testament und seiner Umwelt* (Tübingen: Mohr Siebeck, 1962) 173.

[70] With Dodd (*Apostolic Preaching*, 46ff.), and contrary to the opinion of Wilckens ("Kerygma") who sees in our speech a summary of the Gospel of Luke. While being, according to Wilckens, a Gospel in miniature, Acts 10:34–43 would be different from the other missionary sermons. One would find neither scriptural proof there, nor a call to conversion. Moreover "you know" from v. 37 would indicate a sermon at a Christian community and not a sermon to the pagans. It is necessary to answer: (a) the scriptural proof is in vv. 36–38, and v. 43 contains an indirect call to repentance; (b) if there is not a proclamation of God the creator here, it is not that Cornelius is already Christian; he is a God-fearer who already knows the God of the covenant; (c) vv. 44–45 distinguish Cornelius and his fellow "Gentiles" from the Jewish-Christians present ("from among the circumcised"). It is upon these pagans that the Holy Spirit fell, to the surprise of the Jewish-Christians present. As Luke makes clear, the Holy Spirit "fell on all who heard the word"; it is obvious that the sermon is indeed a missionary sermon with the usual outline, and not an edifying homily that would summarize the Gospel.

[71] With Leonhard Goppelt, "Das Osterkerygma heute," in *Diskussion um Kreuz und Auferstehung* (ed. Bertold Klappert; Wuppertal: Aussaat Verlag, 1967) 212–14.

[72] See B. Schaller in a review of Wilckens' book (*Missionsreden*): *ZRGG* 14 (1962) 291; see also Goppelt, "Das Osterkerygma heute," 212–14.

In short, Luke thus appears to have had at his disposal three distinct traditions: (a) the story of the conversion of the Roman centurion, (b) an etiologic legend, and (c) a Christian kerygmatic tradition intended for the Jews.

3. History

After having defined the redactional intention of Luke and having delineated certain early traditions, it is necessary to attempt, in a third difficult stage, to move back from the traditions to history.

Concerning the legends and their historicity, Bultmann posits a methodological skepticism:

If at the same time I naturally do not deny that historical happenings may underlie legends, I mean that "unhistorical" applies to the idea of legend negatively in the sense that legends not only "have no special interest in history" (Dibelius) but that they are not, in the modern scientific sense, historical accounts at all.[73]

Would it thus be useless to determine the historical reality that could be hidden behind a legend, because a legend does not seek to render an account of a historical event, but wishes to make known an edifying person or a religious phenomenon? Evidently not, because none of the documents from early Christianity is "in the modern scientific sense, historical." The task of the historian – and no longer of the exegete – consists precisely in knowing to read and evaluate sources with various tendencies: kerygmatic, apologetic, legendary, etc. From there, he or she must sift through the historical facts that are at the origin of the traditions and accounts,[74] indicating more or less the degree of probability for each.

The conversion of Cornelius appeared incredible to many historians. At the redactional level, it may very well be so, because Peter commends, gives, and defends an evangelization of pagans that is difficult to conceive prior to Paul. Does Gal 2:6 not limit the remainder of Peter's missionary activity to the world of the circumcised? If we start from the tradition related to Cornelius, our judgment would be very positive. Indeed the conversion of the Roman centurion is not incredible, for he already was no longer entirely a pagan. His conduct had even brought him considerably close to Judaism.[75] The admission of Cornelius into the Church should not have caused a discussion of principle or a hostile reaction. A crisis and a thorough discussion of the problem will emerge perhaps when, be-

---

[73] Rudolf Bultmann, *The History of the Synoptic Tradition* (trans. John Marsh; rev. ed.; Oxford: Blackwell, 1963; reprinted in Peabody, Mass.: Hendrickson, 1994) 244–45 n. 1.

[74] See Oscar Cullmann, "Wandlungen in der neueren Forschungsgeschichte des Urchristentums, zugleich ein Beitrag zum Problem: Theologie und Geschichtswissenschaft," in *Discordia Concors. Festgabe für Edgar Bonjour* (Stuttgart: Helbing & Lichtenhahn, 1968) 51–61.

[75] On this point see, in addition to the commentaries, the article by Schoonheim ("De centurio Cornelius").

coming more systematic, the evangelization of the pagans introduces a great number of Gentiles to the Church, frightening perhaps the Jewish-Christians of Jerusalem by their sheer size and provoking a legalistic reaction.

The second tradition, formed from Peter's vision and from the dispute in Jerusalem, may also reflect a historical event. The account of the conflict at Antioch (Gal 2:11–14) is of interest to us because it signals a liberal attitude, albeit temporary, by Peter. It teaches us, in effect, that before the arrival of the James party, the apostle Peter had chosen an ethics of freedom and shared, without so much as a second thought, table fellowship with the pagans.[76] He considered as *dépassée* the distinction between pure and impure animals, between meat consecrated to God or to idols, between men and women who were ritually pure and impure. Nothing prevents the belief that a vision of the kind recounted in Acts 10:9–16 was at the origin of this attitude. Nothing prevents one either from admitting that, after reservations in the beginning, the Church in Jerusalem did accept this point of view. Later, when the influence of James would grow, legalism then regained ground. With the arrival of the party of James in Antioch, Peter takes fright, and this time yields to the Jerusalemite pressure that will lead, as we know, to Paul's anger (Gal 2:11).[77]

In conclusion, I dare state that the Lukan rereading of earlier traditions remains exemplary. For, there is a message in this effort of Luke, to interpret freely and faithfully the transmitted heritage, in the theological and ecclesiastical perspective of one's own time.

---

[76] See the unambiguous words μετὰ τῶν ἐθνῶν συνήσθιεν (Gal 2:12) and εἰ σὺ Ἰουδαῖος ὑπάρχων ἐθνικῶς καὶ οὐχὶ Ἰουδαϊκῶς ζῆς (Gal 2:14).

[77] I forsake discussing the historical reconstructions of Wendt, Goguel ("Actes 15"), Liechtenhan, Porter, etc. Personally, I think that the vision of Peter and the argument in Jerusalem took place before the Jerusalem meeting (the quarrels in Acts 11 and 15 have different objectives and they should not be identified). As for the conversion of Cornelius, it had to occur also before this date, during a journey of Peter's. On the worthiness of Acts as a source for historiography of early Christianity, see especially Alfred Wikenhauser, *Die Apostelgeschichte und ihr Geschichtswert* (Münster: Aschendorf, 1921); Martin Dibelius, "Die Apostelgeschichte als Geschichtsquelle," in *Aufsätze zur Apostelgeschichte*, 91–95; Haenchen, "The Book of Acts as Source Material."

Moses in Luke-Acts[*]

In rabbinic times the question was raised to know whether or not, during the Messianic era, the works of Moses would be remembered. Since the departure from Egypt signaled a pattern for final delivery, the rabbis feared that this last redemption would eclipse the first Exodus and make it fade from memory. They answered Ben Zoma, who brought up the subject: "That is not to say that one will no longer mention the Exodus of Egypt, but that the delivery from enslavement to other kingdoms will be foremost while the Exodus of Egypt will be secondary."[1]

The work of Luke – it is understood that the third Gospel and the Acts of the Apostles were written by a single author of undoubtedly pagan origin, in the years 80–90 C.E. – chooses a solution that corresponds to the answer of the rabbis. It grants, indeed, the pride of place to that which it regards as the catalyst of the Messianic era, Jesus of Nazareth, Christ and the Lord, and recounts his life and those of his disciples. But, in spite of this Messianic enlightenment, eschatological to a certain extent, the history of the people of Israel, in particular that of Moses and his generation, does not fade into oblivion. According to the rabbinical formula, it is relegated to a secondary position: "The law and the prophets were in effect until John [the Baptist] came; since then the good news of the kingdom of God is proclaimed, and everyone tries to enter it by force" (Luke 16:16).

I. Moses and the Law

As in contemporary Judaism and Christianity, Luke initially perceives Moses as the mediator and the writer of the Law. According to Acts 7:38a, Moses was in company of an angel and ancestors, that is, *between* them.[2] "And he received (ἐδέξατο) living oracles to give (δοῦναι) to us" (Acts 7:38b). The leper cured by

---

[*] This article is dedicated to Franz J. Leenhardt on the occasion of his 75th birthday.

[1] *Berakhot* 12b, quoted by Renée Bloch, "Quelques aspects de la figure de Moïse dans la tradition rabbinique," in *Moïse, l'homme de l'Alliance. Cahiers Sioniens* 8 (1954) 93–167 (211–85), at 160. The text is translated a little differently by Joseph Bonsirven, *Textes rabbiniques des deux premiers siècles pour servir à l'intelligence du Nouveau Testament* (Rome: Pontifical Biblical Institute, 1955), at 112 (no. 473).

[2] "He is the one who was in the congregation in the wilderness with the angel who spoke to him at Mount Sinai, and with our ancestors" (Acts 7:38a).

Jesus must be presented to the priest, *as Moses commanded* (Luke 5:14, which is taken up from Mark 1:44, referring to the ritual in Leviticus 14). The rich man in the parable, who complains of seeing the poor Lazarus resting in Abraham's bosom, endures a rejection beyond the grave. It is too late to inform his brothers: even if someone should rise from the dead (allusion to the resurrection of Jesus?), it would not be sufficient to convince them. So that they may behave better and avoid torments, Abraham explains in the parable of Jesus specific to Luke: "They have Moses and the prophets; they should listen to them" (Luke 16:29).

The double commandment of love appears already in the Law, and Luke does not doubt that it is sufficient for achieving eternal life. To the scribe who cites this, the Lukan Jesus replies: "You have given the right answer; do this, and you will live" (Luke 10:28). The parable of the Good Samaritan then illustrates to the lawyer who his neighbor is or rather to whom he proves to be a neighbor. The episode of Martha and Mary, which immediately follows this commentary on the second commandment, explains to the reader the meaning of the first, that is, the love of God. From a Lukan editorial perspective, it is necessary to hear the Word of the Lord at whose feet Mary is seated.[3]

Even more, Luke, in the wake of the synoptic tradition, considers insufficient obedience – perhaps it would be to better say a certain obedience – to the Decalogue. The rich ruler, eager to receive eternal life as his share, calmly affirms to have observed from his youth the commandments relating to adultery, murder, theft, false witness, and honoring his parents that Jesus quotes by way of example. Jesus then invites him to do one more thing (and not another): to sell all that he owns and to follow him, not in order to acquire or deserve eternal life, but, as the Lukan text states further on, "for the sake of the kingdom of God" (Luke 18:29), which has already approached and has reached the rich ruler in the person and proclamation of Jesus.

According to a suggestive manner of expression, Moses is at this point associated with the legal document, whose incarnation he becomes: the Law is Moses. Thus, in the speech that Luke attributes to James, brother of the Lord, at the Jerusalem Conference, we read – for the sake of the Christian Jews called not to abandon the Law – this astonishing sentence: "For in every city, for generations past, Moses has had those who proclaim him, for he has been read aloud every sabbath in the synagogues" (Acts 15:21). This public reading is not a repetition of a dead letter but an expression of the living work and, to a certain extent, the person of Moses.

The texts mentioned thus far, with the exception of the latter, relate to the time of Jesus. They originate from the Gospel and not from Acts. What exactly becomes of the Law of Moses during the contemporary era, the time of the Church,

---

³ See François Bovon, "Aimer Dieu (Luc 10,38–42)," *Les Échos de Saint-Maurice* n.s. 1 (1971) 33–36.

and the Spirit? We are able to indicate what appears to us to be the *pragmatic* answer of Luke. This comes through the debates at the Jerusalem Conference, whose task, as we know, was to decide if converted pagans ought to be circumcised according to the law of Moses (Acts 15): respecting the full letter of the Law for Jewish-Christians, and respecting both a ritual minimum (observance of the apostolic decree, but no circumcision) and a moral maximum for the pagan-Christians, Peter says, "Now therefore why are you putting God to the test by placing on the neck of the disciples a yoke that neither our ancestors nor we have been able to bear?" (Acts 15:10).[4]

It does not fit directly into our subject to study the theoretical underlying solution that Luke chooses. Let me simply say that the current exegetes are divided on this subject. According to some, such as J. C. O'Neill in his theology of the Acts of Apostles,[5] the movement of the book represents the Church, which is detaching itself slowly but inexorably from Judaism, Law, and Temple. The evidence is in the three notices in which Paul announces his turning away from reticent Jewish listeners to devote himself to pagans (Acts 13:46; 18:6; 28:28). Along the same line, Traugott Holtz[6] went as far as to claim that Luke had at his disposal the scrolls of Isaiah, the minor prophets, and Psalms, but that he never had before his eyes a text of the Pentateuch with which to regulate the scriptural testimonies, few that there were, which the tradition transmitted to him. The personal interest of Luke towards Moses would therefore be reduced to almost nothing. In my opinion, this thesis is unlikely and one can doubt that such a Christian milieu, taking exclusive support from the prophetic texts, existed in the first century (the scenario is much different in the second century, when one encounters Christian documents that are unaware of or reject the Law, indeed the entire Hebrew Bible).

According to other scholars, such as Jacob Jervell in his book *Luke and the People of God*,[7] Luke on the contrary has a keen sympathy for Judaism and its institutions: refusing the idea of a new covenant, to respect the old one, the evangelist regards the Church not as the true or the new Israel, disqualifying the historical Israel, but as the people reconciled with God, restored in their rights and duties by the Messiah, in short, a converted Israel. The Jews who become the followers of Jesus the Messiah constitute a single and unique people of God. They are the descendents of Abraham and heirs to the promises. The pagans can form part of the people of God only while adhering to this Israel. The proof is in the

---

[4] The image of the yoke as applied to the Law is encountered in Judaism (see Paul Billerbeck, in Hermann L. Strack and Paul Billerbeck, *Kommentar zum Neuen Testament aus Talmud und Midrasch* [6 vols. in 7; Munich: Beck, 1922–1961] 1:608ff. and 912). It has regularly a positive connotation.

[5] J. C. O'Neill, *The Theology of Acts in Its Historical Setting* (2d ed.; London: S.P.C.K., 1970) 54–93.

[6] See the special bibliography below.

[7] See Jacob Jervell, *Luke and the People of God: A New Look at Luke-Acts* (Minneapolis: Augsburg, 1972) 41ff.

regular attendance of the first Christian community at the Temple and in its fidelity to the Law; in the Judeophile portrait of Paul (compared to the historical Paul of the epistles), who circumcises Timothy, carries out supererogatory rites such as vows, and denies vigorously to have transgressed the Law or to have attacked the Temple; and finally, in the figure of James, vigilant defender of the *Torah*. If O'Neill underestimates the attachment of Luke to the Law and to the Jewish heritage, Jervell neglects the fracture brought about in the history of the Judaism by the revelation of Jesus, agent of the Spirit of God.

Only an extensive study, of Acts 15 in particular, would enable us to define the function – perhaps more ecclesiological than soteriological – that Luke allots to Law. The evangelist approves the risk taken by the Church to give up the obligation of circumcision and attests the presence of the spread of the Messianic Spirit on the community. He therefore considers that the present situation, desired by God, obliterates the ritual normativity of the Law.

II. Moses as Prophet

Identified with his literary creation, the Law, Moses encourages and imposes ethical fidelity, obedience. This *normative* aspect is however not the principal feature of the figure of Moses that Luke traces and highlights. The redactional originality lies in the resolutely *prophetic* character that the evangelist lends to Moses. Two texts that conclude the Gospel, and whose redactional nature is generally accepted by scholars, expose this in an irrefutable manner. The first appears in the account of the disciples of Emmaus: Jesus is indignant at the slowness of heart of Cleopas and his friend to believe. So Luke summarizes the purpose of the Resurrection: "Then beginning with *Moses* and all the prophets, he interpreted to them the things about himself in all the scriptures" (Luke 24:27). Such a summary is also found in the final appearance of the living Christ, the appearance to the Eleven. After having eaten a piece of broiled fish, the resurrected Jesus addressed his disciples: "Then he said to them, 'These are my words that I spoke to you while I was still with you – that everything written about me *in the law of Moses*, the prophets, and the psalms must be fulfilled.' Then he opened their minds to understanding the scriptures" (Luke 24:44–45). Therefore, what matters more in the eyes of the evangelist is not that the Law is a norm, but that the Law is a promise now fulfilled "in the last days," as he will say in connection to the prophecy of Joel realized at the Pentecost (Acts 2:17).

It follows from this interpretation that Christ and the Christians who are with him are less *scrutinizers of Torah* – as the Pharisees or the Essenes – than *charismatics*: the presence of the Spirit in them and their participation in suffering achieve the promises contained in the Law and verify the prophetic character of Moses.

One can debate the meaning that must be granted to Moses in the account of the transfiguration that the synoptic tradition, mainly Mark, relates. But from the redactional point of view of Luke, doubt is no longer allowed: Moses does not represent, or no longer represents, the Law that would balance and complement Elijah, the representative of Prophecy. Elijah and Moses incarnate both the intention and salvific promise of God. Indeed, Luke adds some words that direct the account in this prophetic sense. After having revisited the account of Mark, according to which two men were at the side of the transfigured Christ and were in discussion with him, namely Moses and Elijah, Luke makes it clear that they spoke about his ἔξοδος, his "exit" or "departure," "which he was about to accomplish at Jerusalem" (Luke 9:31). Thus both Moses and Elijah play here a prophetic role. They announce the departure of Jesus, that is to say, his death. The passion of Jesus therefore proceeds according to Scripture. Better yet, it *is* the only possible outcome, because it is the only one desired by the God of the Law and of the Prophets.

This idea according to which the Hebrew Bible, in particular the Pentateuch, proclaims a suffering Messiah, a χριστὸς παθητός (Acts 26:22–23), is missing in both Mark and Matthew. It is rare in Paul. From where does Luke draw this conviction? Does he follow a Jerusalemite Christian tradition?[8] It is difficult to say.

The dispute that places Jesus in opposition to the Sadducees, taken up again by Luke from the triple tradition, deserves attention here, because it exploits a hermeneutical quarrel on the significance of the work of Moses. The Sadducees tackle the problem of resurrection. They attempt to solve this by negating the idea through resorting to the Law understood as the immutable *norm*: "Teacher, Moses wrote for us ..." (Luke 20:28). Jesus counters by also referring to the Pentateuch, but to part of the Pentateuch that includes the *promise*. The argument is subtle, paradoxical, but convincing: "But that the dead are raised, even Moses showed, in the passage about the bush, where he calls Lord[9] the God of Abraham and the God of Isaac and the God of Jacob. God is not the God of the dead, but of the living; for all are living by him [or, another translation, for him]" (Luke 20:37–38). God is the God of the dead, one believes initially, since Abraham, Isaac, and Jacob are no longer alive when Moses hears the divine voice. Such however is not the sense of the text: resurrection is demonstrated by the fact that Moses has called Lord the God of Abraham, Isaac, and Jacob. He recognized in his day the God of yesterday. He has acknowledged as living the God of the former promise. The path to life, the true life of the resurrection, is in him and by

---

[8] Ernst Haenchen (*Die Apostelgeschichte* [6th ed.; Göttingen: Vandenhoeck & Ruprecht, 1968] 613 n. 4) is of the opinion that Luke does not transmit here a Jewish tradition of the suffering Messiah.

[9] The translations consulted make κύριον the subject and τὸν θεὸν κτλ., the complement. In my opinion, the lack of article in front of κύριον and the parallel of Acts 2:36 speak in favor of my translation and the interpretation that results from this.

him. Therefore the words πάντες γὰρ αὐτῷ ζῶσιν (Luke 20:38b) are appropriate. This interpretation is confirmed by the doctrine of two aeons to which Jesus appealed: the value of the Law is limited to this aeon; man-woman differences will disappear in the Kingdom; the rules of widowhood contained in the Law will no longer be valid. In short, the Sadducees relied on the Law as Scripture, while Jesus understood the Law to be *Word* and *Promise*: significantly, Luke lends these words to Sadducees, "Moses wrote (ἔγραψεν)" (Luke 20:28), while he has Jesus say, Moses "calls (λέγει)" (Luke 20:37).

This oral and prophetic side of Torah becomes prevalent in Acts: Moses has received and transmitted to the people "living oracles" (ὃς ἐδέξατο λόγια ζῶντα δοῦναι ἡμῖν, Acts 7:38b).

Following the cure of the paralytic at the temple by the Beautiful Gate, Peter proclaims the christological kerygma, that is to say, the message of the death and the resurrection of Jesus. After a call to conversion, he advances a series of scriptural testimonies that confirm the truth and give direction to these events. Acts 3:18 introduces the following biblical citation: "In this way God fulfilled what he had foretold through all the prophets, that his Messiah [Christ] would suffer." Verses 22ff. quote some of these proclamations: "Moses [understood here as a prophet; see v. 18] said (εἶπεν), 'The Lord your God will raise up for you from your own people a prophet like me. You must listen to whatever he tells you' … . And all the prophets, as many as have spoken, from Samuel and those after him, also predicted these days" (Acts 3:22, 24). This quotation from the Pentateuch, whose form diverges from the Septuagint, is Deut 18:15, 18–19 on the prophet who will be similar to Moses, one of the rare prophetic passages of the Pentateuch. It is a text that drew attention, indeed, also of the Samaritans, whose limitation of the canon to the Pentateuch forced them to seek in Moses an announcement of their Messiah-Prophet,[10] as did the Essenes of Qumran. This appears in a fragment from Cave 4 (4Q175 = 4QTest 5–7), undoubtedly concerning the prophet preceding the arrival of the two Messiahs.

In the same form that differs from the Septuagint, the prophecy of Deuteronomy is found in chapter 7 of Acts in the speech of Stephen to the Council (Acts 7:37). It establishes a typological relationship between Moses and the eschatological prophet identified with Jesus. On this note, we enter into the third part, devoted to typology.

III. Moses as Model for Christ

Did Luke use in an implicit way the figure of Moses and the events from the Exodus as models and paradigms making it possible to describe the ministry of Jesus

---

[10] Joachim Jeremias, "Μωϋσῆς," in *TWNT* 4:852–878, at 863.

and the foundation of the Church? This question is disputed and caution is essential. Let me propose three likely hypotheses, rejecting two others.

1. Thesis of Félix Gils, Richard F. Zehnle, and Paul S. Minear[11]

Without stating it explicitly, the Gospel of Luke introduces Jesus as a prophet, as the prophet like Moses of Deuteronomy 18. A person accustomed to reading the Torah, who reads the words and deeds of Jesus, could not miss the implicit parallels.

2. Thesis of Roger Le Déaut, Bent Noack, and Jean Potin[12]

The end of the Gospel and the beginning of Acts, mainly the account of the Pentecost, are explained only in light of the *Targums* of Exodus 19–20, and thus in light of the Sinai covenant that the Jewish festival of Pentecost conceived as a present reality (the historicization of the agrarian festival was – despite many – already done at the time). Ephesians 4, and then Christian iconography, confirms this typological bond between the Sinai and the Ascension-Pentecost grouping.

3. Personal Hypothesis

The Gospel of Luke is understood (see Luke 9:51) as a vast ἀνάλημψις that allows for quite a full distribution of the Word and the Spirit. The Lukan work brings into reality eschatological prophecy, particularly that of Isaiah 2, which speaks about a general ascension towards Mount Zion, from where the Word and Spirit spread in all directions (this prophecy of Isaiah is itself based on the Sinai tradition).[13]

I dismiss two hypotheses: a) that of Jindrich Mánek,[14] who conceives the voyage of Jesus from Galilee into Judea as a new Exodus (Jesus involving his disciples in his wake, like Moses leading the people through the desert); and b) that of Christopher F. Evans and John Bligh,[15] who interpret the gospel regulations as a Christian or new Deuteronomy.

---

[11] See the special bibliography below.

[12] See the special bibliography below.

[13] Esther Starobinski-Safran, to whom I express my gratitude, informs me that Raschi interprets Isa 2:2 in the following manner: at the end of time, the mountain of Zion will be stronger than the Sinai, Carmel, and Tabor mountains where miracles occurred. Rabbi David Kimchi (1160–1235) as well as Gaon de Vilna (1720–1797) give a spiritual interpretation of Isaiah 2: the victory of the mountain of Zion represents the ousting of idolatry that flourished on the hills, consequently beaten.

[14] See the special bibliography below.

[15] See the special bibliography below.

We arrive now at the principal question: Is there an explicit typology? In addition to the prophecy of Deuteronomy 18 quoted in Acts 3:22, it is the speech of Stephen (Acts 7) that will occupy us now, because it gives a great deal of attention to the figure of Moses.[16]

The literary context is known: Stephen, the charismatic *leader* of the group of Hellenists, whose destiny will be like those of Moses and Jesus, is attacked by a group of Jews of the Diaspora who, according to the evangelist, are not able to stand up to him. These men then bribe witnesses who falsely recount Stephen's blasphemies against Moses and against God (Acts 6:11). These accusations are presented before the Sanhedrin, to where the scene shifts, and are detailed: Stephen is then accused to have reported that Jesus would destroy the Temple and would change the customs (τὰ ἔθη) that Moses delivered (Acts 6:14). For his defense, Stephen launches into a lengthy aggressive speech (Acts 7:2–53), in fact the longest speech in Acts, which recalls the constant opposition of the people to the salvific intention of God. To underscore that the existing events reiterate a constant relationship between God and his messengers on the one hand, and the "stiffed-necked" people on the other, Luke discreetly lends to Stephen some features of Moses. Stephen, filled with grace and power, worked wonders and signs among the people (Acts 6:8). When the Sanhedrin observed him, his face was resplendent like that of an angel (Acts 6:15). Is this not similar to the account of Moses when he came down from Mount Sinai and presented himself before the people (Exod 34:29–35)?

Instead of repelling the attacks that are leveled against him, Stephen paints a vast fresco of the history of Israel, from which the bond between the accused and the destiny of newly-formed Christianity, obscure at first, slowly appears – indirectly to be sure, but certain nonetheless.

Neglecting the history of the origins of the world, the first part (vv. 2–16) begins with the call to Abraham, understood as an apparition (ὤφθη, v. 2). The account of the life of the patriarchs contains a prophecy concerning of the sojourn in Egypt, of the suffering of the people for four hundred years, of the judgment of God against the oppressors, of the "departure" – this is the term – that will follow, and of the worship which will be rendered "in this place" (Acts 7:6–7). No detail is given on this judgment of God, nor on the method of this "departure," which is not called liberation. Thus the first part of Stephen's speech is completed by the account of the fate of Joseph. Here is the translation of the second part, vv. 17–44 (NRSV), relating to Moses:

---

[16] See, in the bibliography below, comments by E. Haenchen and H. Conzelmann, as well as the studies of J. Bihler, J. J. Kilgallen, M. H. Scharlemann, and G. Stemberger, whose bibliographical items make it possible to supplement this list.

17 "But as the time drew near for the fulfillment of the promise that God had made to Abraham, our people in Egypt increased and multiplied 18 until another king who had not known Joseph ruled over Egypt. 19 He dealt craftily with our race and forced our ancestors to abandon their infants so that they would die. 20 At this time Moses was born, and he was beautiful before God. For three months he was brought up in his father's house; 21 and when he was abandoned, Pharaoh's daughter adopted him and brought him up as her own son. 22 So Moses was instructed in all the wisdom of the Egyptians and was powerful in his words and deeds.

23 "When he was forty years old, it came into his heart to visit his relatives, the Israelites. 24 When he saw one of them being wronged, he defended the oppressed man and avenged him by striking down the Egyptian. 25 He supposed that his kinsfolk would understand that God through him was rescuing them, but they did not understand. 26 The next day he came to some of them as they were quarreling and tried to reconcile them, saying, 'Men, you are brothers; why do you wrong each other?' 27 But the man who was wronging his neighbor pushed Moses aside, saying, 'Who made you a ruler and a judge over us? 28 Do you want to kill me as you killed the Egyptian yesterday?' 29 When he heard this, Moses fled and became a resident alien in the land of Midian. There he became the father of two sons.

30 "Now when forty years had passed, an angel appeared to him in the wilderness of Mount Sinai, in the flame of a burning bush. 31 When Moses saw it, he was amazed at the sight; and as he approached to look, there came the voice of the Lord: 32 'I am the God of your ancestors, the God of Abraham, Isaac, and Jacob.' Moses began to tremble and did not dare to look. 33 Then the Lord said to him, 'Take off the sandals from your feet, for the place where you are standing is holy ground. 34 I have surely seen the mistreatment of my people who are in Egypt and have heard their groaning, and I have come down to rescue them. Come now, I will send you to Egypt.'

35 "It was this Moses whom they rejected when they said, 'Who made you a ruler and a judge?' and whom God now sent as both ruler and liberator through the angel who appeared to him in the bush. 36 He led them out, having performed wonders and signs in Egypt, at the Red Sea, and in the wilderness for forty years. 37 This is the Moses who said to the Israelites, 'God will raise up a prophet for you from your own people as he raised me up.' 38 He is the one who was in the congregation in the wilderness with the angel who spoke to him at Mount Sinai, and with our ancestors; and he received living oracles to give to us. 39 Our ancestors were unwilling to obey him; instead, they pushed him aside, and in their hearts they turned back to Egypt, 40 saying to Aaron, 'Make gods for us who will lead the way for us; as for this Moses who led us out from the land of Egypt, we do not know what has happened to him.' 41 At that time they made a calf, offered a sacrifice to the idol, and reveled in the works of their hands. 42 But God turned away from them and handed them over to worship the host of heaven, as it is written in the book of the prophets:

> 'Did you offer to me slain victims and sacrifices
> forty years in the wilderness, O house of Israel?
> 43 No; you took along the tent of Moloch,
> and the star of your god Rephan,
> the images that you made to worship;
> so I will remove you beyond Babylon.'

44 "Our ancestors had the tent of testimony in the wilderness, as God directed when he spoke to Moses, ordering him to make it according to the pattern he had seen."

The speech that follows (vv. 45–50) evokes the entry of the ark into the country of Canaan under the leadership of Joshua. In one sentence, one passes from the time of David, who finds grace in the eyes of God and Luke, and then to Solomon whom the text reproaches for having built the Temple instead of being satisfied with the ark. It is helpful to read the conclusion of the speech (vv. 51–53, NRSV):

51 "You stiff-necked people, uncircumcised in heart and ears, you are forever opposing the Holy Spirit, just as your ancestors used to do. 52 Which of the prophets did your ancestors not persecute? They killed those who foretold the coming of the Righteous One, and now you have become his betrayers and murderers. 53 You are the ones that received the law as ordained by angels, and yet you have not kept it."

Then, Stephen dies as a martyr, killed by stoning without a trial. Jesus appears to him in the form of the Son of Man. Luke, who takes care to stress the resemblance between Moses and Stephen, parallels the death of the Protomartyr, as the orthodox Greeks refer to him, and that of Jesus: "Lord Jesus, receive my spirit" (Acts 7:59) picking up from Luke 23:46, with "Lord, do not hold this sin against them" (Acts 7:60), answering Luke 23:34.

Three different positions were taken concerning the origin of this passage:

a) According to Martin H. Scharlemann,[17] the speech is an exact mirror of Stephen's thought, a singular saint, he says, whose theology is unique in early Christianity. This original product of the primitive Church was subject to Samaritan influences still significant in the text.

b) Hans Conzelmann, Oscar Cullmann, and many others[18] consider these as being based probably on a written tradition, as Luke does not compose his text freely. But, far from being an original, Stephen fits into the current Hellenist milieu. This movement, according to Cullmann, had dealings with the community at Qumran, hostile to the present Temple, and even with what he calls the Johannine circle; from where the famous triangulation of John-Hellenists-Qumran is proposed.

c) For my part, without wishing to deny the contribution of the underlying tradition, I pay attention, with Johannes Bihler,[19] to the editorial direction and the redactional value of the text. Written finally by Luke, this speech is appropriate for the theological concern of the evangelist and falls under the general perspective of a Lukan work. I therefore prefer a "literary" glance to a "genetic" analysis.

The speech emerges in Luke's proposal at the precise moment where the opposition regarding the Christian community reaches the intensity that it had had

---

[17] See the special bibliography below.

[18] See the special bibliography below (for H. Conzelmann, see the commentary on Acts).

[19] "Die Rede ist eine Komposition des Lukas," concludes Johannes Bihler (*Die Stephanusgeschichte im Zusammenhang der Apostelgeschichte* [Munich: M. Hueber, 1963] 86).

against Jesus. The persecution strikes Stephen, and with him the Hellenist wing and finally the entire Church, as it had with Jesus. Throughout the speech, the author endeavors to show that in the manner of the fate of Jesus, evoked briefly towards the end, the opposition against Stephen replays the repeated resistance of the people of Israel to God and his legitimate messengers, in particular Moses.

For Luke, the destiny of the Hellenists is not a matter of misfortune; those who believed in Christ knew to draw conclusions from their universal faith, first by envisaging, then by organizing the geographical expansion, and finally by implementing an outward mission to the nations. They went into Antioch and there addressed the Greeks, according to chapter 11.

Luke will further compose a second historical retrospective, which he will attribute to Paul at Antioch of Pisidia (Acts 13). There, anxious to avoid repetitions, the evangelist will direct attention toward another period of sacred history, from Judges to David while passing through Saul. The brief mention of the Exodus that opens this second speech deserves to be quoted, because it helps us to understand the lengthy evocation of Moses in chapter 7: "You Israelites, and others who fear God, listen. The God of this people Israel chose our ancestors and made the people great during their stay in the land of Egypt, and with uplifted arm he led them out of it. For about forty years he put up with them in the wilderness. After he had destroyed seven nations in the land of Canaan, he gave them their land as an inheritance for about four hundred fifty years" (Acts 13:17–20). The perspective here is theocentric and soteriological: Moses' mediation is passed over in silence, as well as the hardening of the people. The text insists on God's attention and God's salvific intervention,[20] as in chapter 7 never tiring to stress the reservations, hesitations, and refusal of the people regarding the generous intention of God.

In chapter 13, God raised *a king*, David (v. 21), from whom Jesus is the descendant: here we find ourselves in the midst of a royal Messianic context. In chapter 7, God is also at work, but he intervenes especially by sending *prophets*. Systematically, these prophets are not listened to. Moreover, they are rejected.

Let us examine the text closer:

a) The portrait of Moses

A series of features are not drawn from the Bible, but from Jewish interpretation, i.e., comments that were made about the text in Luke's time:
  – The beauty of the child Moses (v. 20).
  – His instruction in all the wisdom of the Egyptians (v. 22).
  – Moses aged forty when he flees to Midian (v. 23).
  – The forty-year duration of this stay (v. 23).

---

[20] See the various verbs that express this generous activity of God, mainly the two uses of the verb "to give" (v. 20 and v. 21).

– The mediation of an angel (v. 38) in the theophany at Sinai (the Hebrew Bible mentions an angel only in connection with the burning bush).

– The intermediary of angels (in the plural), at the time the Law is transmitted (vv. 38 and 53).

It would be tempting to connect these rather anecdotal features to Samaritan theology. But it would be quite hypothetical, because almost all these details are found scattered in the rabbinic tradition (the angel in the Sinai),[21] in Hellenistic Judaism (physical beauty and Egyptian education of Moses, in Philo's work), in early Christianity (mediation of the angels, in Paul, Gal 3:19).[22]

b) *The figure of Moses according to the movement of the text*

The life of Moses is part of the history of salvation punctuated by *promises* and fulfillments:[23]

– It represents initially the realization of the promise made to Abraham: "And after that, they shall come out," God announced to the patriarch (v. 7).

– It is also a period of pronouncements of a later, ultimate benefit: "This is the Moses who said to the Israelites, 'God will raise up a prophet for you from your own people as he raised me up'" (v. 37).

– Moses' prophetic function is highlighted, while that of lawgiver passes to the background. Moses has the charisma of a prophet, in speech and deed (v. 22): ἦν δὲ δυνατὸς ἐν λόγοις καὶ ἔργοις αὐτοῦ (thus is established a close connection between Moses, Jesus, Stephen, and the Christians: they are people marked by the Spirit of God who do not depend first and foremost upon the written Law).

– Moses has a mission to fulfill. He wants to visit his brothers (v. 23). This theological theme of the visitation appears elsewhere in Luke, in connection with Jesus, in the same strong and positive sense.[24] The author immediately expands the perspective: the helpful intervention of Moses, in the case of the isolated Israelites who are oppressed by the Egyptians, becomes the model for global intervention by Moses on behalf of all oppressed Israelites – from which is the important v. 25, whose Lukan character is evident: "He supposed that his brothers understood that God was giving them deliverance by his hand, but they did not understand." Three points deserve attention: *theocentrism* (God is the one who

---

[21] This concept, present already in the Septuagint (Deut 33:2), frequently appears in rabbinic literature. See Billerbeck in Strack and Billerbeck, *Kommentar zum Neuen Testament*, 3:554ff.

[22] See Günter Stemberger, "Die Stephanusrede (Apg 7) und die jüdische Tradition," in *Jesus in der Verkündigung der Kirche* (ed. Albert Fuchs; Freistadt, Austria: Plöchl, 1976) 154–74, at 165–70.

[23] Even if it takes as a starting point calculations established by the rabbis, the division of the life of Moses into three forty-year periods corresponds to the Lukan concern of marking the stages of the history of salvation.

[24] See Luke 19:44: ὁ καιρὸς τῆς ἐπισκοπῆς σου.

sends forth his messengers), human mediation (Moses: διὰ χειρὸς αὐτοῦ), and salvific aim (δίδωσιν σωτηρίαν).

– Moses is at once a misunderstood and rejected prophet, whom the very hardened "did not understand" (οἱ δὲ οὐ συνῆκαν) from v. 25. One finds this opposition in v. 27, "Who made you a ruler and a judge over us?" (see the following, v. 28). This sentence is drawn here from a particular case, a little further on in the text: the refusal of two Israelites, fighting, to reconcile, and it becomes the general formulation that attests the radical criticism of Moses' leadership: "It was this Moses whom they rejected when they said, 'Who made you a ruler and a judge?' and whom God now sent as both ruler and liberator through the angel who appeared to him in the bush" (v. 35).

– Rejected, Moses is nevertheless a prophet *chosen by God*: an angel appeared to him and the voice of the Lord spoke to him in the bush (see vv. 30–34, 35b). At Sinai, the angel spoke to him (see v. 38).

– Moses did more than a prophet. He was established as *ruler* and *deliverer* by God. Luke applies to Moses the christological *Kontrastschema*, which one knows from the missionary sermons of Peter (Acts 3:13f. and 5:31, for example).

Paradoxically, Luke, who insists on the failure of Moses, must also speak about the success and power of the one who had been protected by the Egyptian princess. The departure from Egypt, willed by God, occurred. But the people left Egypt almost against their liking. As it is stated in v. 39, Israel quickly disobeyed the Law: their hearts returned to Egypt's idols; the episode of the golden calf that finishes the account summarizes the attitude of the people. Verse 53 takes up again this thesis, "You are the ones that received the law as ordained by angels, and yet you have not kept it" – whence "You stiff-necked people, uncircumcised in heart and ears" (σκληροτράχηλοι καὶ ἀπερίτμητοι καρδίαις καὶ τοῖς ὠσίν, v. 51). This expression, biblical then rabbinic, which usually indicates Israel in the desert, becomes under Luke's pen a description of the people of God to each generation.

Luke therefore generalizes once more. This religious rather than moral hardening of the desert generation is a constant element in the history of Israel. One finds it at the time of Solomon, at the time of Stephen, especially at the time of Jesus the just when his *coming* (ἔλευσις, a theological term, as that of the visitation) caused anger and hostility. For the evangelist, it is a matter of an opposition to the Holy Spirit (v. 51), both then and now. Note the comparison in v. 51: "As your fathers did, so do you" (ὡς οἱ πατέρες ὑμῶν καὶ ὑμεῖς). A typology of negative figures exists, as there is one of positive figures.

– Nothing is said about Moses' reluctance, nor his unbelief; nor further on about the wanderings through the desert, about the various stops, and especially about the death of the prophet; nor about the covenant in Sinai (the only covenant mentioned is that of circumcision, Acts 7:7; see Acts 3:25). Everything revolves around the rejection of Moses by the people – Moses, the messenger of God for the salvation of the people.

Moses truly liberated the people from Egypt. He achieved this exodus, desired and promised by God. He was the ruler and deliverer. The parallel between Moses and Jesus has established itself: despite the reluctance of the people who provoked the crucifixion of Jesus, God founded the salvation for Israel and the nations through Jesus the liberator and the ἀρχηγός, the prophet and the Lord, whom Moses had announced ("a prophet like me"), a suffering righteous one and a triumphant prophet.

We understand, consequently, that Luke opted for a discreet but certain presence of Moses in his work. Like the rabbis, he thinks that during the Messianic era one must remember Moses with gratitude, because the friend of God announced through his prophecies and his fate the arrival and destiny of the last prophet. This one, Jesus, Luke identifies with the Messiah. For the evangelist who unravels history to his theological intention, what there is to be said today is not a reminder of the Law, however venerable it may be, but the good news of the Kingdom of God.

Conclusion

In distinction to numerous contemporary Jewish authors, Luke does not write to defend, introduce, or explain the deeds of the person of Moses, but to proclaim and indicate something *other* and someone *other*: the Kingdom of God and the Lord Jesus Christ (Acts 28:31). In contrast, he does not secure his Christian position through antitheses. His double work does not contain any criticism of the Law and is distinguished there from the epistles of Paul and the Gospel of John. It does not follow either that Luke is unaware of or wants to be unaware of Moses and the Law, as certain Christian writings of the second century will be. The evangelist does not try theologically to solve the problem raised by the relations between the old and new covenant, between Moses and Jesus. In particular, he does not resort to a spatial plan – undoubtedly of Greek origin – which contrasts shade and reality, depth and height, as is found in the epistles to the Colossians (Col 2:16–17) and to the Hebrews (Heb 10:1). The Lukan perspective is chronological and slightly typological. Moses and the Law still hold for him a place of unquestionable importance, but limited by the agenda of the history of salvation and the plan of the promises and their fulfillment.

If the Law keeps a *normative* value that is difficult to specify, it especially takes a *prophetic* connotation that it shares with the texts of the Psalms and the Prophets. More than a written rule, it becomes a word full of promises. Moses who received it from God by the intermediary of an angel (Acts 7:38) takes on mainly the outline of a prophet. Various texts attest to it: the account of transfiguration

(Luke 9:28–36), the speeches of the risen Christ at Easter (Luke 24:25–27 and 44–48), and a sermon of the apostle Peter (Acts 3:22–24).

An attentive reading detects finally a discreet typology between Moses and Jesus. In places implicit, this paralleling of the figures becomes obvious in some passages, mainly in the speech of Stephen (Acts 7:17–44).

Moses in the New Testament: Biblical References

"The law of Moses": Luke 2:22; 24:44; John 7:23; Acts 13:38; 15:5; 28:23; 1 Cor 9:9; Heb 10:28

Regulations of the Law: Mark 1:44 par.; Mark 7:10 par.; Mark 10:3ff. par.; Mark 10:18ff. par.; 12:28–34; etc.

Law transmitted by the intermediary of angels: Acts 7:38, 53; Gal 3:19

Critique of the Law: Matt 5:21ff.; Rom 7:1–12; 8:3; Galatians 2–4; etc.

Moses identified with the Law: Acts 6:11; 15:21; 21:21; 2 Cor 3:15

The seat of Moses: Matt 23:2

Moses at the time of the transfiguration: Mark 9:4–5 par.

Moses, prophet, announces: Jesus: Luke 24:27, 44f.; John 1:45; 5:46; Acts 3:22f.; Acts 7:37; 26:22f.; 28:33; The resurrection of the dead: Mark 12:26 par.; The mission to the pagans: Rom 10:19; The election: Rom 9:15

Moses servant of God rejected or suffering: Acts 7:17–44; Heb 11:23–29

Moses, the eschatological accuser: John 5:45

Contrast Moses (Law) – Christ (grace and truth): John 1:17

Moses, a type for Christ: Acts 3:22f.; 7:17–44; Heb 11:26; Red Sea and desert - baptism and Christian life: 1 Cor 10:1–5; ministry of Moses – apostolic ministry: 2 Corinthians 3; birth of Moses – birth of Jesus: Matthew 1–2; faithfulness of Moses and Jesus in God's house: Heb 3:1–6; two covenants: Heb 9:15ff.; sufferings of Moses and Jesus: Heb 11:24–26 and Heb 2:8–18; hymn of Moses and of the lamb: Rev 15:3; the serpent: John 3:14; the manna: John 6:30ff.

Legendary names of the magicians of Egypt, Jannes and Jambres: 2 Tim 3:8

Allusion to the apocryphal account of the argument between the Archangel Michael and the devil on the subject of Moses' body: Jude 9

General Bibliography: *Moses in the New Testament*

Allen, Edgar L. "Jesus and Moses in the New Testament." *ExpTim* 67 (1955–1956) 104–6.

Bloch, Renée. "Quelques aspects de la figure de Moïse dans la tradition rabbinique." In *Moïse, l'homme de l'Alliance. Cahiers Sioniens* 8 (1954) 93–167 (211–85).

Chavasse, Claude. *The Servant and the Prophet: The Central Position of Moses in the New Testament.* Lemybrien: 1972. (It remains inaccessible to me.)

Démann, P. "Moïse et la Loi dans la pensée de saint Paul." In *Moïse, l'homme de l'Alliance. Cahiers Sioniens* 8 (1954) 189–242 (307–60).

Gager, John G. *Moses in Greco-Roman Paganism.* Nashville: Abingdon Press, 1972.

Jaubert, Annie. *Approches de l'Évangile de Jean.* Paris: Seuil, 1976.

–. *La notion d'alliance dans le judaïsme aux abords de l'ère chrétienne.* Paris: Seuil, 1963.

Jeremias, Joachim. "Μωϋσῆς." In *TWNT* 4:852–878. (See detailed bibliography.)

Meeks, Wayne A. *The Prophet-King: Moses Traditions and the Johannine Christology.* Leiden: Brill, 1967.

Pancaro, Severino. *The Law in the Fourth Gospel: The Torah and the Gospel, Moses and Jesus, Judaism and Christianity according to John.* Leiden: Brill, 1975.

Schulz, Siegfried. "Die Decke des Moses. Untersuchungen zu einer vorpaulinischen Überlieferung in 2. Kor. 3,7–18." *ZNW* 49 (1958) 1–30.

Teeple, Howard M. *The Mosaic Eschatological Prophet.* Philadelphia: Society of Biblical Literature Press, 1957.

Vermès, Géza. "La figure de Moïse au tournant des deux Testaments." In *Moïse, l'homme de l'Alliance. Cahiers Sioniens* 8 (1954) 63–92 (181–210).

Special Bibliography:
Moses in Luke-Acts

Bihler, Johannes. *Die Stephanusgeschichte im Zusammenhang der Apostelgeschichte.* Munich: M. Hueber, 1963.

Bligh, John. *Christian Deuteronomy (Luke 9–18).* Langley: St. Paul Publications, 1970.

Cabié, Robert. *La Pentecôte. L'évolution de la Cinquantaine pascale au cours des cinq premiers siècles.* Tournai: Desclée, 1965.

Conzelmann, Hans. *Die Apostelgeschichte.* Tübingen: Mohr Siebeck, 1963.

–. *Die Mitte der Zeit. Studien zur Theologie des Lukas.* 3d ed. Tübingen: Mohr Siebeck, 1960. pp. 146–56.

Cullmann, Oscar. *Der johanneische Kreis.* Tübingen: Mohr Siebeck, 1975.

Le Déaut, Roger. "Pentecôte et tradition juive." *Spiritus. Cahiers de spiritualité missionnaire* 7 (1961) 127–44. Reprinted in *Assemblées du Seigneur*, 1st ser., 51 (1963) 22–38.

Descamps, Albert. "Moïse dans les Évangiles et dans la tradition apostolique." In *Moïse, l'homme de l'Alliance. Cahiers Sioniens* 8 (1954) 171–187 (289–305).

Dupont, Jacques. "L'utilisation apologétique de l'Ancien Testament dans les discours des Actes." *ETL* 29 (1953) 289–329. Reprinted in idem, *Études sur les Actes des apôtres.* Paris: Cerf, 1967. pp. 245–82.

Evans, Christopher F. "The Central Section of St. Luke's Gospel." In *Studies in the Gospels: Essays in Memory of Robert Henry Lightfoot.* Ed. Dennis E. Nineham. Oxford: Blackwell, 1955. pp. 37–53.

Gils, Félix. *Jésus prophète d'après les Évangiles synoptiques.* Louvain: Publications Universitaires, 1957. pp. 28–29, 30–42.

Haenchen, Ernst. *Die Apostelgeschichte.* 6th ed. Göttingen: Vandenhoeck & Ruprecht, 1968.

Holtz, Traugott. *Untersuchungen über die alttestamentlichen Zitate bei Lukas.* Berlin: Akademie-Verlag, 1968.

Jervell, Jacob. "The Law in Luke-Acts." *HTR* 64 (1971) 21–36. Reprinted in idem, *Luke and the People of God: A New Look at Luke-Acts.* Minneapolis: Augsburg, 1972. pp. 133–51.

Kilgallen, John J. *The Stephen Speech: A Literary and Redactional Study of Acts 7:2–53.* Rome: Biblical Institute Press, 1976. (Arrived too late for me to comment on it.)

Kretschmar, Georg. "Himmelfahrt und Pfingsten." *ZKG* 56 (1954) 209–53.

Mánek, Jindrich. "The New Exodus in the Books of Luke." *NovT* 2 (1968) 8–23.

Minear, Paul S. *To Heal and to Reveal. The Prophetic Vocation According to Luke.* New York: Seabury Press, 1976. pp. 102–21.

Noack, Bent. "The Day of Pentecost in Jubilees, Qumran and Acts." *ASTI* 1 (1962) 73–95.

O'Neill, J. C. *The Theology of Acts in Its Historical Setting.* 2d ed. London: S.P.C.K., 1970.

Potin, Jean. *La fête juive de la Pentecôte.* 2 vols. Paris: Cerf, 1971.

Scharlemann, Martin H. *Stephen: A Singular Saint.* Rome: Pontifical Biblical Institute, 1968.

Stemberger, Günter. "Die Stephanusrede (Apg 7) und die jüdische Tradition." In *Jesus in der Verkündigung der Kirche.* Ed. Albert Fuchs. Freistadt, Austria: Plöchl, 1976. pp. 154–74.

Zehnle, Richard F. *Peter's Pentecost Discourse: Tradition and Lukan Reinterpretation in Peter's Speeches of Acts 2 and 3.* Nashville: Abingdon Press, 1971.

The Death of Jesus in Luke-Acts

Introduction

Olivette Genest has examined *Le discours du Nouveau Testament sur la mort de Jésus. Épîtres et Apocalypse.*[1] I now suggest reading again the Gospel of Luke and the book of the Acts of the Apostles in the same perspective of a "discourse … on the death of Jesus" in paying homage to the learned and amiable friend. In the first part, I will listen to the voice of the first Christians, that of Luke in particular, as it resounds in the book of Acts. In the second part, I will re-read the account of the Passion according to the evangelist Luke. In the third part, I will pay attention to the sayings of Jesus relative to his tragic fate, as the third Gospel conveyed them. What will be heard will not be the voice of Jesus, but that which is attributed to Jesus by the evangelist, a voice initially different to that of the historical Jesus, and finally different to the voice of Luke himself. In the fourth part, I will articulate the assertions relative to the death and to the life of Jesus according to the concept Luke developed on salvation. In the conclusion, I will undertake to tie it all together.[2]

The Book of the Acts of the Apostles

At the beginning of his second book, Luke summed up his first book and provided us with a key of the reading (Acts 1:1). He did not mention the death, but only the life of Jesus and what filled it up, the "to do" and "to teach," concretely the acts and the teachings of the master: ποιεῖν τε καὶ διδάσκειν. Only what Jesus accomplished and proclaimed in his living is accounted for. Without sparing his sorrow, Luke recounts in the Gospel the ministry of Jesus, his life in Galilee, his miracles accomplished around lake Gennesareth, the teaching of the master,

---

[1] Olivette Genest, *Le discours du Nouveau Testament sur la mort de Jésus. Épîtres et Apocalypse* (Sainte-Foy: Les Presses de l'Université Laval et Corporation Canadienne des Sciences Religieuses, 1995).

[2] This study is a continuation of the work in my article "Le salut dans les écrits de Luc. Essai," *RTP*, 3d ser., 23 (1973) 296–307; reprinted in François Bovon, *L'œuvre de Luc. Études d'exégèse et de théologie* (LD 130; Paris: Cerf, 1987) 165–79. See also Isak J. Du Plessis, "The Saving Significance of Jesus and His Death on the Cross in Luke's Gospel – Focusing on Luke 22:19b–20," *Neot* 28 (1994) 523–40.

the selection of disciples, several acts in the service of a religious cause, salvation through life and not, to this point, redemption through death.

This does not mean that the death of Jesus is absent. On the contrary, all the discourses of Acts, proclaimed by the apostles, refer to this fatal outcome, but they do not attribute it to Jesus himself nor to God. They do not refer it to nature either, but to human malice alone (Acts 2:23; 4:10; 5:30; 7:52). Nothing or almost nothing indicates here that it can have a salvific value. Few clues even make it an exemplary death, at most the ultimate prayer of Stephen who, molding himself into the model of Jesus, prays to the Father to forgive the sin of his executors (Acts 7:60). What the apostolic message repeats over and over again is what the German exegetes call the *Kontrastschema*:[3] humans killed him, but God resurrected him. Even if it was placed in his hands or placed dangerously at the mercy of his opponents, the life of Jesus remains a human affair, starting with women and ending with men, all of flesh and blood. The fate of Jesus, according to the Acts of the Apostles, corresponds to that of the heroes of the historiography of antiquity. It is the fate of a human being that ends logically in death.[4]

This observation surprises everyone all the more since the other end of the life of Jesus, his birth, was described at the beginning of the Gospel with an altogether different tone. The message of Gabriel to young Mary (Luke 1:28–37), the choir of angels (Luke 2:14), as well as the hymn of Zachariah (Luke 1:68–79) and the oracles of Simeon (Luke 2:28–35), proclaim protection and even divine intervention in favor of the new-born child. The Lukan Jesus, contrary to ordinary mortals, was conceived not by a carnal father but by the Holy Spirit. He therefore shares in one sense the divine condition.[5]

On the contrary, like everyone else, he does not escape death, indeed a violent one. When it concerned the establishment of a witness system to attest to Christian truth, Luke did not link it to the death, but uniquely to the resurrection. He dares to say that witnesses need to be relied on for the resurrection of Jesus (see Acts 1:22; 2:32; 3:15). There is no need to recall the crucifixion of Jesus, because no one doubts this obvious fact. From the beginning Jesus may have had the right to divine support, through the presence of the Holy Spirit; but the end comes to him, as for any human being, in agony to the point of giving up his last breath.[6]

---

[3] See Jürgen Roloff, *Neues Testament* (Neukirchener Arbeitsbücher; Neukirchen-Vluyn: Neukirchener Verlag, 1977) 185–86.

[4] See Gregory E. Sterling, "*Mors philosophi*: The Death of Jesus in Luke," *HTR* 94 (2001) 384–402, whose conclusions I do not accept fully.

[5] Bibliography on the Lukan birth narratives (Luke 1:5–2:52) in François Bovon, *Luke 1: A Commentary on the Gospel of Luke 1:1–9:50* (trans. Christine M. Thomas; Hermeneia; Minneapolis: Fortress, 2002) 26–28.

[6] On the passion and the death of Jesus in Luke-Acts in particular, see Raymond E. Brown, *The Death of the Messiah: From Gethsemane to the Grave* (2 vols.; ABRL; New York: Doubleday, 1994).

The assertion of the human destiny and condition of Jesus does not, however, exhaust the Lukan discourse. From the point of view of the evangelist, the radical historicity of the life of Jesus, and especially his death, does not constitute the final word. The apostles, whose testimony he enjoyed recalling, trust themselves to add a decisive precision to this observation of Jesus' humanity. There is, as they repeatedly say, behind the entire humanity of Jesus – that which he took on as well as that which he underwent – a connection, indeed subtle, that links him to the divine world. Directly absent from history, the God of Luke is interested in what is happening in this world. God's attention is first demonstrated at an inaccessible level to human beings, that of foreknowledge and even predestination. What happened to Jesus, this human fate, unfair as it was, did not escape from the divine intelligence: "This man, handed over to you according to the definite plan of God, you crucified and killed by the hands of those outside the law," states the apostle Peter on the day of Pentecost (Acts 2:23). This paradoxical convergence between human criminal activity and beneficial divine providence reappears forcefully in the first prayers of the Christians that Luke quotes or imagines: "For in this city, in fact, both Herod and Pontius Pilate, with the Gentiles and the peoples of Israel, gathered together against your holy servant Jesus, whom you anointed, to do whatever your hand and your plan had predestined to take place" (Acts 4:27–28).

There is a second, indirect way of asserting this divine plan: in articulating the intentions of Jesus toward Scripture. His crucifixion in particular achieves the enigmatic prophecy of the rejected stone: "This is 'the stone that was rejected by you, the builders; it has become the cornerstone'" (Acts 4:11, referring to Ps 118:22). More clearly, it is God, according to the first Christians, who inspired David with the words of the psalm: "The kings of the earth took their stand, and the rulers have gathered together against the Lord and against his Messiah" (Ps 2:2 according to Act 4:26). Even more apparent, the evangelist Philip provides the Ethiopian eunuch with a christological interpretation, the only acceptable interpretation, of the prophecy of the suffering servant found in Isaiah (Acts 8:32–35, which quotes and comments on Isa 53:7–8 according to the Septuagint). Acts 10:38 perfectly sums up this Lukan understanding of Jesus' life: "… how God anointed Jesus of Nazareth with the Holy Spirit and with power; how he went about doing good and healing all who were oppressed by the devil, for God was with him." Christologically, Luke is located far from Paul. He does not develop a Christology of the humility of the incarnate Son (see Phil 2:6–11), but a Christology of the man Jesus, prophet, wise man, and martyr, whom God finally justifies in raising him from the dead and exalting him at his right hand, making him Messiah and Lord (see Acts 2:36).

The Account of the Passion

Up to the half-way point on the account of the Passion,[7] Luke casts Jesus as the master of the rest of his life.[8] This man decided to enter the city of Jerusalem on his own initiative (Luke 19:28–40); then he freely organized what was to become his last Passover (Luke 22:7–13); for the last time he conversed with his disciples around a table and gave his farewell speech (Luke 22:14–46). The wind shifted when, on the Mount of Olives, he crossed the last temptation and faced those who had come to arrest him. Then, he proclaimed a decisive sentence addressing his opponents: "But this is your hour, and the power of darkness" (Luke 22:53). From then on, from the grammatical subject of the verbs and an actor responsible for his actions, Jesus became the object of derision and the direct object of the verbs dominated by his adversaries. Everything continues being played out on a human level, but it is no longer Jesus who is in control; the local authorities and the Roman governor impose their will.

To underscore the intensity of the tragedy, Luke builds space in a contrasting manner. As long as Jesus acted as he pleased, he had a welcoming place; for instance, the house where he celebrated the last supper (Luke 22:7–13). As soon as he lost control of the situation, he was forced into inhospitable buildings – the house of the great priest (Luke 22:54), the public hall of the Sanhedrin (Luke 22:66), and the tribunal of Pilate (Luke 23:1). The contrast between light and darkness, day and night, fills an analogous function. The day fell when Jesus was facing his opponents who came to arrest him, and the night prevailed when the time came for the enemies and the power of darkness had set in (Luke 22:53). Luke also suggested the late hour in signaling the sleepiness of his disciples (Luke 22:45) and the fire lit in the courtyard (Luke 22:56). On Good Friday, the day may have been present, but darkness will shroud the earth (Luke 23:44).

At the stake of adversary forces, Jesus is therefore a human actor, as his disciples and adversaries are also human. But in the Gospel, as in the Acts of the Apostles, human actions are discretely linked to the divine will. The prophecies of Jesus – inspired by this divine spirit that shaped him from the bosom of his mother and empowered him at his baptism – link the human level, the *bruta facta* of the story, to the domain of God. Jesus, the Jesus of Luke, knows that if "the one who betrays me is with me, and his hand is on the table," it is that "the Son of Man is going as it has been determined" (Luke 22:21–22). The readers become aware of this twofold level of the factual and sacred story in listening to the final statement

---

[7] See the *status quaestionis* established by Jay M. Harrington, *The Lukan Passion Narrative: The Markan Material in Luke 22:54–23:25: An Historical Survey: 1891–1997* (NTTS 30; Leiden: Brill, 2000).

[8] These pages are based on my article, "Le récit lucanien de la passion de Jésus (Lc 22–23)," in *The Synoptic Gospels: Source Criticism and the New Literary Criticism* (ed. Camille Focant; BETL 110; Leuven: Leuven University Press, 1993) 393–423.

of Jesus before his exit from the upper room and his arrest: "For I tell you, this scripture must be fulfilled in me, 'And he was counted among the lawless'; and indeed what is written about me is being fulfilled" (Luke 22:37, quoting Isa 53:12). They find confirmation in the dramatic prayer of Jesus on the Mount of Olives, "Yet, not my will but yours be done" (Luke 22:42). According to the evangelist, this unjust human story corresponds to God's design and is used to advance the cause of the Gospel.[9]

It is interesting to note that Luke resorts to four literary models to describe the death of people. There is the death of a persecutor according to a model that Lactantius will cherish: Herod Agrippa died for having caused the death of James, son of Zebedee (Acts 12:20–22). There is the death of the unworthy man, the one who received all the gifts to remain faithful to God, but who finally came to nought, foreshadowing the oncoming lot of the *lapsi* of the Great Church: Judas, the disciple and one of the twelve, suffered a divine punishment (Acts 1:16–20). There is the happy death of the repentant. Even if the repentance occurs *in extremis*, it maintains all its value: the good thief receives on the cross this promise from God: "Truly I tell you, today you will be with me in Paradise" (Luke 23:43). There is finally a noble death, that which crowns a life of goodness and virtue, the hero's death, the death of the patient wise man and especially that of the martyr: that of Stephen (Acts 6:8–7:60) and of course that of Jesus. Here, the value of life and the dignity of death correspond to and reinforce each other (Luke 22–23).

The Declarations of Jesus

In a certain veiled manner, the Lukan Christ evokes his death from the beginning of his ministry in Galilee. Thus, following Mark, Luke made Jesus say, concerning fasting, that "the days will come when the bridegroom will be taken away from them, and then they will fast in those days" (Luke 5:35). Later, the master will compare his ultimate fate to a "baptism," resorting to an image that undoubtedly evokes the fatal descent into death (Luke 12:50). At the Last Supper, the broken bread corresponds to "my body, which is given for you" (Luke 22:19), and "this cup that is poured out for you is the new covenant in my blood" (Luke 22:20). In the account of the Mount of Olives, Luke's equivalent of Gethsemane

---

[9] It is not different from some assertions relative to the death of Jesus that the evangelist advances himself or that he attributes to those speaking with Jesus: Simeon foresees negative reactions to Jesus and announces suffering to the mother of Jesus (Luke 2:34–35); the inhabitants of Nazareth think of killing him from the very start of his ministry (Luke 4:29); at the cure of the man with the withered hand, the scribes and the Pharisees, filled with fury, wonder what they can plot against Jesus (Luke 6:11); further, it is again the scribes and Pharisees who plot against the Nazarene (Luke 11:53–54). In 9:51, Luke uses the enigmatic term ἀνάλημψις, "rise," "taking up," which suggests the climb to Jerusalem, the crucifixion, and/or the Ascension.

in Mark and Matthew, Jesus alludes to his death thanks to the image of the "cup" (Luke 22:42).

Furthermore, Luke did not hesitate to mention the prophecies of the Passion he received from Mark. In Luke 9:22, Jesus responds to Peter's confession by a prophecy on the tragic fate of the Son of Man (see Mark 8:31). Luke 9:44–45 and 18:31–34 correspond to the second and third pronouncements of the Passion in Mark 9:30–32 and 10:32–34. In a part of the Passion narrative that he takes from his special material or from Mark, Luke conveys this ultimate pronouncement of the Passion, associated with the announcement of Judas' treason: "For the Son of Man is going as it has been determined, but woe to that one by whom he is betrayed" (Luke 22:22). Luke the evangelist even knew a prophecy which the other synoptics ignored (Luke 13:31–33): in response to the threat of Herod Antipas, mentioned by the Pharisees, Jesus describes his career with the metaphor of three days that correspond to three periods, the third one of which had to take place in Jerusalem, "because it is impossible for a prophet to be killed outside of Jerusalem." Then everything will be over.[10]

The more the text on the Gospel advances, the clearer the allusions become. In the parable of the Vineyard and the Tenants, where the tenants kill the son of the owner (Luke 20:9–16), Luke respects the account he inherits from Mark. In an episode that has an undoubtedly allegorical range, the master, whose servants have been spurned until now, makes this fatal decision: "What shall I do? I will send my beloved son; they will respect him" (Luke 20:13). But the wine growers do not respect the son of the owner; they kill him. In the dialogue related to the two swords, Luke's own, as we have seen, Jesus says: "For I tell you, this scripture must be fulfilled in me, 'And he was counted among the lawless'; and indeed what is written about me is being fulfilled" (Luke 22:37).

There is a convergence between the apostolic speeches of Acts and the words of Jesus. Both are formulated by Luke, but, in the manner of an actor, the evangelist knows how to withdraw in order to make a place for those he interprets. One may say of him what Louis Jouvet said about the actor who comes onto the stage: he is not the character he is playing; he is not the person he is himself; he is something else he does not know.

In short, the destiny and the ministry of Jesus unfold on earth in a network of wills and powers in conflict. Despite the human dimension of this fate, however, God, in the perspective of the evangelist, threads his way through. He does not do it in a grandiose manner – as was the case in the most ancient accounts of Exodus, when God does miracles and opens the Red Sea – but this happens, following a more recent Hebraic historiography, in an indirect and veiled manner.

---

[10] On these verses, see François Bovon, *L'Évangile selon saint Luc (9,51–14,35)* (CNT 3b; Geneva: Labor et Fides, 1996) 392–409.

The Death of Jesus and the Salvation of Humans Beings

Luke does not employ the paradox. He does not say with Paul that power is accomplished in weakness (see 2 Cor 12:9). The death of Jesus, his defeat, does not represent the victory of God. Rather, his view of the world represents a humanism. What the man from Nazareth brings as beneficial, he offers through his teachings and his acts of authority. Jesus is the living one, filled with divine wisdom, a powerful prophet, a servant of the humble, and a judge of the oppressors. This concept is strong from the beginning of the Gospel to the end of Acts.

Even if the accepted death corresponds to his course of action, it is not made less of a tragic lesson, an expression of the limitations imposed on mortals, a refusal of the fantasy of omnipotence – it is a heroic reality indeed, but a dramatic defeat nonetheless. The mocking spectators to the agony of Jesus and the bad thief are not wrong in their irony: though a miracle worker he may have been, Jesus cannot respond to the cruel invitation to save his life (Luke 23:35–39). Now, he stumbles over the inescapable limits of his own life, his own death. What Luke insists in putting forward in the twenty-four chapters of the Gospel is therefore not a theology of the cross, but a hymn to a life devoted to God. If Luke wants to remember Jesus, it is a living Jesus. When Simeon rejoiced after having seen salvation, he was holding up in his arms an infant full of life (Luke 2:30). When Jesus underscored the privilege of his contemporaries, he was contemplating more than what prophets and kings were able to see, and what there is to see is not the work of death but the acts of the living (Luke 10:24). If there is more, at last, than Solomon and Jonah, there is a man, Jesus, who is living and active; he is, in a word, alive (Luke 11:31–32). This is so true that Luke has no other verb than the verb "to live" to describe the resurrected Christ, "Why do you look for the living among the dead?" (Luke 24:5). And further, "Moreover, some women of our group astounded us. They were at the tomb early this morning, and when they did not find his body there, they came back and told us that they had indeed seen a vision of angels who said that he was alive" (Luke 24:22–23).

Luke thus describes in the Gospel a human journey and grasps this life with a view to what I called humanism. Despite all this, this humanism is not atheistic: it does not locate the heroic death at the pinnacle of an absurd hierarchy of values. The destiny of Jesus corresponds – as we saw earlier concerning the kerygma of the Acts of the Apostles, the sayings of Jesus, and the redactional affirmations of the Gospel – to the salvific plan of God. Expressed in a proleptic manner in the prophetic books (and for Luke, the Law itself is prophetic), the plan of God, his βουλή (Luke 7:30; Acts 2:23; 4:28; 13:36) and his εὐδοκία (Luke 2:14; 10:21), are actually demonstrated, at the time of Jesus, in three manners: (a) God inseminates his πνεῦμα into Mary's bosom during the miraculous conception and covers the new Messiah with his Holy Spirit on the day of his baptism (Luke 1:35; 3:22); (b) God releases the reins to Satan and temporarily gives him the authority to torment Jesus (Luke 4:1–13; 22:28), shake the apostles (Luke 22:31), and interfere with Jesus' opponents (Luke 22:3); (c) God at last puts an end to the end of Jesus' life by bringing him back to life (Luke 24). This salvific activity of God carries on in the Church through the power that the Holy Spirit confers upon the declaration of the great deeds of God accomplished through Jesus the Messiah (see Acts 4:8–12; 10:34–45; 11:15–18). All this is understandable, but it does not explain why salvation is associated more with the life of Jesus than his death.

It is first important to remember that Luke likes the category of salvation and enjoys using its vocabulary.[11] He uses the verb "to save" (σῴζειν) more than thirty times, "salvation" (σωτηρία) ten times, σωτήριον, another word for "salvation," three times, and the title Savior (σωτήρ) three times as well. Two passages enable us to understand the importance that the Gospel attributes to this vocabulary. In presenting the Baptist, Luke makes the quotation from Isaiah 40 longer than the one he borrows from Mark, and the aim of this elongation is to arrive at the famous term of "salvation." Once he has achieved it and integrated it, the evangelist can interrupt the quotation: "The voice of one crying out in the wilderness: 'Prepare the way of the Lord, make his paths straight. Every valley shall be filled, and every mountain and hill shall be made low, and the crooked shall be made straight, and the rough ways made smooth; and all flesh shall see the salvation of God" (Luke 3:4–6, quoting Isa 40:3–5) At the beginning of the book of the Acts (Acts 2:14–21), during Pentecost, Luke lets Peter speak and he quotes the prophet Joel (Joel 3:1–5). There again Luke continues the quotation beyond what is necessary in order to arrive at the vocabulary that is dear to his heart; "Then everyone who calls on the name of the Lord shall be saved" (Acts 2:21). While everything revolves around Jesus in the Lukan writing, at the same time it is concerned with human salvation.

Let us say then that Luke does not let salvation depend on the death of Jesus alone from an atonement or sacrificial perspective. There are indeed a few traces of this thought in traditional phrases, like the sayings of the Last Supper ("This is my body, which is given for you" and "This cup that is poured out for you is the new covenant in my blood," Luke 22:19–20) and in a discourse of Acts ("Be the shepherds of the Church of God which he acquired by his own blood" or, another translation, "with the blood of his own [Son]," Acts 20:28). But these phrases, which are indeed accepted by the evangelist, do not represent the heart of Lukan thought. It is rather the whole life of Jesus – from his conception to his resurrection – that is representative of the offering of salvation; in fact it is not an imposed salvation, not a salvation only in its objectivity, not a salvation thanks to the victim who substitutes himself to those who offer him; but rather it is a salvation as a relational reality. The share of human beings must correspond to the

---

[11] See Bovon, "Le salut dans les écrits de Luc. Essai"; Du Plessis, "The Saving Significance of Jesus."

share of God. The activity of those who do repent and believe must be the counterpart of the work performed by Jesus (according to Luke, salvation imposes and does not nullify the question of "What then shall we do?," Luke 3:10–14; Acts 2:37). Such as the fiancé of the Song of Songs, the objective salvation, achieved by God, which calls for subjective salvation to be achieved in the life of the believers, similar in this to the fiancée of the biblical poem. Anselm is not enough; Abelard has to be associated with it. It is not about synergy, as the one successively condemned by Augustine of Hippo and the council of Orange. It is more about a connivance of love, as the Greek or Russian Orthodox theologians enjoy describing. A master of ethics rather than dogmatic theology, a pastor attentive to his long-time parishioners rather than missionary flattered by fleeting conversions, Luke expects a lasting commitment from the new Christians. Does he not add a "daily" to the sentence on the taking up of the cross? (Luke 9:23). Does he not care about the future of Christianity? Does he not place on the lips of Jesus this distressing question: "And yet, when the Son of Man comes, will he find faith on earth?" (Luke 18:8b).

Conclusion

It is not wrong to say that Luke viewed his work as the counterpart of the Hebrew Scriptures, more precisely the Septuagint. The diptych proves to be in fact a triptych, since the Christian mission succeeds the time of Jesus. The three books – Septuagint, the Gospel, and the Acts of the Apostles – follow one another. The time of one is not the time of the other one. The promise is carried out in two successive periods and represents already an offer of salvation. It would thus be erroneous to consider the death of Jesus while disregarding this Lukan construction of the story of salvation, that is to say, apart from the categories of time, history, and eschatology.

Even if he venerated Paul, Luke did not take from him, and perhaps he did not understand the apostle's theological acuteness either.[12] His conception of the death of Jesus did not come from the Apostle to the Gentiles, but it is attached to the Christian inheritance that the evangelist probably received from the Hellenist movement finally set up in Antioch (see Acts 11:19–26). This inheritance owes much to Hellenistic Judaism, its conception of Providence and martyrdom.[13]

---

[12] One recalls the famous article of Philip Vielhauer, "Zum 'Paulinismus' der Apostelgeschichte," *EvT* 10 (1950–1951) 1–15; reprinted in idem, *Aufsätze zum Neuen Testament* (TB 31; Munich: Kaiser, 1965) 9–27.

[13] See Daniel Boyarin, *Dying for God: Martyrdom and the Making of Christianity and Judaism* (Figurae; Stanford: Stanford University Press, 1999).

God is active, but his action is often indirect and often mediated.[14] The messengers of God share the human condition. They are the champions of the moral law received from God through Moses, what Luke calls "the words of life" (Acts 7:38).[15] The people of God often balk, but they know how to react freely to the call of the voice of the prophets. They also happen to harden (see the role of Isa 6:9–10, the last biblical quotation of the book of Acts, Acts 28:26–28).[16] If human freedom coexists with divine predestination, this means that salvation is not opposed to creation in a dualistic sense. The goods of this world, to begin with life, are pleasing to God who wanted them as such. Even if the Christian commitment, so radical in Luke, apparently imposes unbearable separations (see the sayings on the renouncement of family that goes as far as adding spouse to the list, Luke 14:26), the Kingdom of God does not promise food exclusively from heaven, but the establishment of a divine and real power on this earth, a redistribution of the material and spiritual wealth, as well as the final return of justice and peace. On Easter Day, the Resurrected eats fish taken from the Lake Gennesareth, much to the docetics' great displeasure in the second century.[17]

This Jewish and Christian perspective also takes over Greek philosophical values, such as the presentation of Jesus who faces death with the courage of a condemned philosopher.[18] But resorting to Greek tradition is limited, and the work of Luke remains a narrative, and the suffering Jesus does not escape anxiety.

More important than this Greek inheritance is the influence of the historical Jesus and the Christian kerygma. A sympathizer of Judaism, Luke became a member of the Christian sect. He certainly sacrificed his material comforts, and maybe a part of his intellectual ease, on the altar of his new convictions. This may have happened without any ostentatious uproar and without any violent break. Be that as it may, Luke decided to follow only one master. With zeal, he offers his strength to the new cause. He recognizes in Jesus an exemplary life, a master of wisdom, an apocalyptic prophet (whatever views new partisans may have on the historical Jesus, one does not exclude the other), and even a Lord and Savior. He refers especially to the Christology of the initial days – that which, on the basis of

---

[14] On the mediations in Luke, see my article "L'importance des médiations dans le projet théologique de Luc," *NTS* 21 (1974–1975) 23–39; reprinted in idem, *L'œuvre de Luc*, 181–203.

[15] See my article "La Loi dans l'œuvre de Luc," in *La Loi dans l'un et l'autre Testament* (ed. Camille Focant; LD 168; Paris: Cerf, 1997) 206–25.

[16] See my article " 'Schön hat der heilige Geist durch den Propheten Jesaja zu euren Vätern gesprochen' (Apg 28,25)," *ZNW* 75 (1984) 226–32; more recently, Volker A. Lehnert, *Die Provokation Israels. Die paradoxe Funktion von Jes 6,9–10 bei Markus und Lukas. Ein Textpragmatischer Versuch im Kontekt gegenwärtiger Rezeptionsästhetik und Lesetheorie* (Neukirchener Theologische Dissertationen und Habilitationen 25; Neukirchen-Vluyn: Neukirchener Verlag, 1999).

[17] On this subject see Antonio Orbe, *Cristologia Gnóstica. Introducción a la soteriologia de los siglos II y III* (2 vols.; BAC 385; Madrid: La Editorial Católica, 1976) 2:516–517; and Bovon, "Le récit lucanien de la passion," 419.

[18] See Sterling, "*Mors philosophi.*"

the existence and fate of Jesus the man, asserts that the resurrection, the work of God, conferred onto Jesus the Messianic prerogatives and a Lordly exaltation to the right hand side of God. This Christology may be neither more ancient nor more recent than that of Paul; it is simply different. It hardly considers preexistence and does not speculate on the incarnation. It will quickly be exceeded and will survive only as one erratic block.

If Luke depends on the Hellenist Christians, these may have inherited from the Jerusalem community the concept of the man Jesus, loved by God, and finally established as Messiah. In Luke's eyes, Jesus is a κύριος, "a Lord," whom he prefers over Augustus or his successors (Luke 2:11; Acts 2:36). He is also a σωτήρ, "a Savior," whom the evangelist locates well above the healing gods that abound in the agoras (Luke 2:11; Acts 5:31; 13:23). Expressed in a more modest way, he is the physician that everyone needs. That all too often escapes the readers of Luke. The ministry in Galilee, the first part of the life of Jesus, is not only that of a prophet and sage; Jesus is also a physician who cures bodies and restores lives made uncertain by disease (see the numerous cures and the mentioning of the term ἰατρός, "physician," in Luke 4:23; 5:31). He is also the exorcist who chases away demons and restores normalcy and reason (see Luke 8:26–33). He is all this because he is above all the Messiah of Israel (Luke 2:11; 9:20; Acts 2:36; 3:20; 10:36–41).

Luke is ready to put into writing the message of this preacher the sermon of Nazareth, which regards him in God's favor (Luke 4:16–21); the beatitudes and the Sermon on the Plain, which present his fundamental teaching (Luke 6:20–49); and the many sayings and multiple parables that he has from his special material and which he adapts to his audience (see for example, Luke 10:30–37; 15:1–32; 16:19–31; 18:1–8). He insists in recalling the controversies that Jesus was involved in against the scribes and Pharisees in Galilee (Luke 5:17–6:11) or against other scribes and Pharisees, and especially against the Sadducees and the priests in Jerusalem (Luke 19:29–20:47). He looks forward to recounting the acts of power that this prophet achieved in the name of God, cures, exorcisms, and natural wonders. He is not afraid to tell the story of the passion of Jesus as much as that of the resurrection, a resurrection that does not correct but confirms the destiny of the man Jesus through a renewal of life and an entrance into glory (Luke 24:5 and 26). Consequently, believers are triply armed: by the memory of Jesus' life, the testimony of the ἀνάστασις, "resurrection," and the recollection of the cross. They have in their ears the "words" received in Church (Luke 1:4) and, before their eyes, the pages of two new books that, from a Jewish point of view, have to be declared as heretical, but from a Christian point of view announce the good news of the ultimate intervention of God. To Luke it seemed like a good idea (Luke 1:3) to add these two books to the inspired Septuagint.[19] And for the Christians re-

---

[19] On the problem of the inspiration of the Septuagint, which worries more the catholic than the protestant scholars, see Pierre Benoit, "La Septante est-elle inspirée?," in *Vom Wort des*

sponsible for the canon, for numerous scribes, such as the one who reproduced our most ancient manuscript, the Bodmer Papyrus XIV–XV ($\mathfrak{P}^{75}$), for readers and new converts, Luke did indeed do well in maintaining his program – a literary program, a historical program, in a sense where the ancients conceived history, a theological, and especially a pastoral program.

Lebens. Festschrift für Max Meinertz (ed. Nicholas Alder; Münster: Aschendorff, 1951) 41–49; reprinted in idem, *Exégèse et Théologie* (4 vols.; Paris, Cerf, 1961–1983) 1:3–12.

Part III
Noncanonical Gospels
and Apocryphal Acts of the Apostles

Sayings Specific to Luke in the *Gospel of Thomas*

Introduction

It is as a visitor that I am speaking today. Yesterday, I commented on the Lukan pericope of Jesus on the Mount of Olives (Luke 22:39–46), and the day before yesterday I followed a path through the alleyways of the apocryphal Acts of the Apostles. Yet, the visitor that I am is also a neighbor, and an inquisitive neighbor. In fact, I have always been intrigued and intimidated by the *Gospel of Thomas*.[1] I have read, in the past, the Habilitationsschrift of Wolfgang Schrage[2] and more recently, I took note of the position of John H. Sieber.[3] Do we, as Schrage, have to consider the *Gospel of Thomas* as a Gnostic re-reading of the canonical Gospels, or do we have to see in it, as Sieber does, a composition that is based on independent traditions?[4] I also know, having read April D. De Conick and Thomas Zöckler,[5] that the current trend is to interpret the *Gospel of Thomas* on its own terms, independent of the question of its sources. However, the question still remains:[6] What is the connection between the sayings of the canonical Gospels and the sayings of the *Gospel of Thomas*?

---

[1] See the remarkable survey by Francis T. Fallon and Ron Cameron, "The *Gospel of Thomas*: A Forschungsbericht and Analysis," in *ANRW* 2.25.6 (1988) 4195–251. An invaluable bibliography is contained in the two volumes of David M. Scholer: *Nag Hammadi Bibliography 1948–1969* (NHS 1; Leiden: Brill, 1971); and *Nag Hammadi Bibliography 1970–1994* (NHS 32; Leiden: Brill, 1997). Here I note that the title "The Gospel according to Thomas" is more precise, but for simplicity of reference I will use the more common designation.

[2] Wolfgang Schrage, *Das Verhältnis des Thomas-Evangeliums zur synoptischen Tradition und zu den koptischen Evangelienübersetzungen. Zugleich ein Beitrag zur gnostischen Synoptikerdeutung* (BZNW 29; Berlin: Töpelmann, 1964).

[3] John H. Sieber, "A Redactional Analysis of the Synoptic Gospels with Regard to the Question of the Sources of the Gospel according to Thomas" (Ph.D. diss., Claremont Graduate School, 1966); idem, "The *Gospel of Thomas* and the New Testament," in *Gospel Origins and Christian Beginnings: In Honor of James M. Robinson* (ed. James E. Goehring et al.; Sonoma, Calif.: Polebridge, 1990) 64–73.

[4] This was already the opinion of Gilles Quispel, "Some Remarks on the *Gospel of Thomas*," *NTS* 5 (1958–1959) 276–90; it is also that of Tim Schramm, *Der Markus-Stoff bei Lukas* (SNTSMS 14; Cambridge: Cambridge University Press, 1971) 9–21.

[5] April D. De Conick, *Seek to See Him: Ascent and Vision Mysticism in the Gospel of Thomas* (VC Supplements 33; Leiden: Brill, 1996); and Thomas Zöckler, *Jesu Lehren im Thomasevangelium* (Nag Hammadi and Manichean Studies 47; Leiden: Brill, 1999).

[6] See Zöckler, *Jesu Lehren im Thomasevangelium*, 2–3.

Classification and Procedure

In order to compare the canonical and the non-canonical gospels, several paths
are open to scholars. In the manner of *Redaktionsgeschichte* followers, Allen D.
Callahan[7] tried to decipher a principle of organization applicable to the *Gospel of
Thomas*. Other scholars, such as Stephen J. Patterson,[8] compared the sayings
among themselves, speaking of their relationship in terms of twins, brothers and
sisters, and cousins. Angus John Brockhurst Higgins[9] divided up the sayings of
the *Gospel of Thomas*, according to whether they had a Gnostic character or not.
Many scholars placed sayings side by side, in a synoptic view – the *Gospel of Thomas* and the so-called Source of the *logia* ("Q," for the German "Quelle"). Ron
Cameron and other critics were attentive to the parallels between the *Gospel of
Thomas* and Gospel of Matthew, as well as the parallels between Mark and Thomas. Heinz Schürmann,[10] Tim Schramm,[11] and Boudewijn Dehandschutter[12]
examined the parallels between the *Gospel of Thomas* and the Gospel of Luke. I
would like to walk along their steps.

I will examine the *logia* of the *Gospel of Thomas* that have an equivalent in the
Gospel of Luke and only in this Gospel, that is, the passages that have no parallels
in the Gospels according to Matthew and Mark. Those sayings of Jesus are few in
number: *Gos. Thom.* 3//Luke 17:20–21 (the Kingdom within you); *Gos. Thom.*
10//Luke 12:49 (to cast fire upon the earth); *Gos. Thom.* 61//Luke 17:34 (two in
one bed); *Gos. Thom.* 63//Luke 12:16–21 (parable of the rich fool); *Gos. Thom.*
72//Luke 12:13–14 (inheritance to share among brothers); *Gos. Thom.* 79//Luke
11:27–28 (blessed is the womb that bore you); *Gos. Thom.* 95//Luke 6:34–35a
(lend, expecting nothing in return). Since what is specific to Luke is sometimes

---

[7] Allen Dwight Callahan, " 'No Rhyme or Reason': The Hidden Logia of the *Gospel of Thomas*," *HTR* 90 (1997) 411–426. Callahan thinks that it is less the sense than formal factors which
have supported the sequences in the *Gospel of Thomas*.

[8] Stephen J. Patterson, *The Gospel of Thomas and Jesus* (Foundations and Facets: Reference
Series; Sonoma, Calif.: Polebridge Press, 1993) 17–93.

[9] Angus John Brockhurst Higgins, "Non-Gnostic Sayings in the *Gospel of Thomas*," *NovT*
4 (1960) 292–306.

[10] Heinz Schürmann, "Das Thomasevangelium und das lukanische Sondergut," *BZ* n.s. 7
(1963) 236–60; reprinted in idem, *Traditionsgeschichtliche Untersuchungen zu den synoptischen
Evangelien. Beiträge* (KBANT; Düsseldorf: Patmos, 1968) 228–47. Schürmann concludes that
Thomas does not use a source earlier than the canonical writings, from which Luke's special
source also would have drawn. Thomas resorts to Luke in several *logia*. He examines *Gos.
Thom.* 31, 47, 79, 72, 63, 103, 10, 16, 75, 64, 69, 88, 3, 113, 51, 78, 79 in their relationships to their
Lukan equivalents.

[11] Schramm, *Der Markus-Stoff bei Lukas*, 9–21.

[12] Boudewijn Dehandschutter, "L'Évangile selon Thomas. Témoin d'une tradition prélu-
canienne?," in *L'Évangile de Luc – The Gospel of Luke* (rev. and aug. ed. of *L'Évangile de Luc.
Problèmes littéraires et théologiques*; BETL 32; Leuven: Leuven University Press, 1989) 197–
207. Contra Schramm, this author concludes that Thomas depends on Luke and does not use a
source which also may have served the author of Luke's special material.

linked to what is common to Matthew and Luke, namely the Source of the *logia*, I will keep in mind the parallel passages between the *Gospel of Thomas* and Q – and at the same time I will be attentive to the redactional particularities of Luke. My comparison will not be confined to the current state of the sayings in one or the other Gospel; it will respect the principles of *Formgeschichte* in trying to add a diachronic dimension to the synchronic parallel setting.

<h2 align="center">Gos. Thom. 3//Luke 17:20–21</h2>

Gos. Thom. 3[13] first undergoes the influence of Deuteronomy (Deut 30:11–14),[14] a biblical passage, the impact of which is also felt in Bar 3:29–30 and Rom 10:6–10. It then moves closer to Luke, and only Luke, in arguing that the Kingdom is "within you."

Formgeschichtlich it plays, according to an orientation Henri-Charles Puech found in ancient philosophy,[15] with the opposition between the interior and exterior. This connection to philosophy is also found, of course, in the second part of the *logion* that is related to knowledge, more particularly to the knowledge of oneself. As for *logion* 113 of the same *Gospel of Thomas*, it is linked to Luke 17:21, 23 and Matt 24:23 (it is here, and there), but especially to Luke 17:20: "It will not come by waiting for it" is the equivalent of οὐκ ... μετὰ παρατηρήσεως, "not in an

---

[13] *Gos. Thom.*, *Logion* 3: "Jesus said: If those who lead you say to you, 'See, the kingdom is in the sky,' then the birds of the sky will precede you. If they say to you, 'It is in the sea,' then the fish will precede you. Rather, the kingdom is inside of you, and it is outside of you. When you come to know yourselves, then you will become known, and you will realize that it is you who are the sons of the living father. But if you will not know yourselves, you dwell in poverty and it is you who are that poverty." Here I am using Thomas O. Lambdin's translation published in *The Nag Hammadi Library* (ed. James M. Robinson; 3d, rev. ed.; New York: Harper-SanFrancisco, 1990) 126–38; in the French original of this article, I was giving the translation of Henri-Charles Puech, *En quête de la gnose*, II, *Sur l'Évangile selon Thomas* (Bibliothèque des sciences humaines; Paris: Gallimard, 1978). *Logion* 113: "His disciples said to him, 'When will the kingdom come?' <Jesus said,> 'It will not come by waiting for it. It will not be a matter of saying "here it is" or "there it is." Rather, the kingdom of the father is spread out upon the earth, and men do not see it.'" On *Logion* 3, see Sieber, "Redactional Analysis," 223–26; Puech, *En quête de la gnose*, 2:105–6 and 269–79; Margaretha Lelyveld, *Les logia de la vie dans l'Évangile selon Thomas. A la recherche d'une tradition et d'une rédaction* (NHS 34; Leiden: Brill, 1987) 113–31; Michael Fieger, *Das Thomasevangelium. Einleitung, Kommentar und Systematik* (NTAbh n.s. 22; Münster: Aschendorff, 1991) 23–28; Richard Valantasis, *The Gospel of Thomas* (New Testament Readings; London: Routledge, 1997) 58–59; Zöckler, *Jesu Lehren im Thomasevangelium*, 164–80; Jacobus Liebenberg, *The Language of the Kingdom and Jesus: Parable, Aphorism, and Metaphor in the Sayings Material Common to the Synoptic Tradition and the Gospel of Thomas* (BZNW 102; Berlin: de Gruyter, 2001) 486–94.

[14] Thomas Francis Glasson, "The *Gospel of Thomas*, Saying 3, and Deuteronomy XXX.11–14," *ExpTim* 78 (1966–1967) 151–52.

[15] Puech, *En quête de la gnose*, 2:269–76.

observable way."[16] If we note that *Gos. Thom.* 3 contains a parallel to the redactional introduction to Luke 17:20 ("To the question of the Pharisees who asked him … "), we need to conclude that *Gos. Thom.* 3 is based on the Gospel of Luke, which the author adapts and updates: Thomas skilfully substitutes "those who lead you" in place of Luke's Pharisees, who are no longer for Thomas people you discuss and polemic with face to face. The adaptation also touches the expression "The Kingdom of God." As we know, the writer of the *Gospel of Thomas* does not call "God" the Father whom he worships.[17] It is therefore logical that he should only talk here of the "Kingdom"[18] and not, as does Luke, of the "Kingdom of God." However, Thomas shares with the Gospel of Luke the opinion – this is the main point for the two authors – that this Kingdom is already present. In *logion* 3 of *Gos. Thom.*, it is inside and outside; in *logion* 113, it is spread upon the earth, but men and women do not pay attention to it.[19] Modern critics have here the chance to have the Greek version of *Gos. Thom.* 3 in the *Papyrus Oxyrhynchus* 654. This original of *Gos. Thom.* 3, which is moreover only partly preserved, confirms the dependence of the *Gospel of Thomas* with respect to Luke 17.[20]

Gos. Thom. 10//Luke 12:49

The Lukan saying "I came to cast fire upon the earth" has no equivalent in the other canonical Gospels. There exists, indeed, a maxim that resembles this one in Q (Luke 12:51//Matt 10:34: "Do you think that I have come to give peace on earth?"), but neither the image nor the formulation are alike. *Gos. Thom.* 10[21] is

---

[16] The translations of the Gospel of Luke are mine.

[17] See Puech, *En quête de la gnose*, 2:245–46.

[18] On this expression, see Karen King, "Kingdom in the *Gospel of Thomas*," FF: *Forum* 3 (1987) 48–97.

[19] See also *Logion* 51: "His disciples said to him, 'When will the repose of the dead come about, and when will the new world come?' He said to them, 'What you look forward to has already come, but you do not recognize it.'"

[20] The reader may consult the Greek text either in the volume published by Bentley Layton, *Nag Hammadi Codex II, 2–7 together with XIII, 2*, Brit. Lib. Orient. 4926(1), and P. Oxy. 1, 654, 655 …* (2 vols.; NHS 20–21; Leiden: Brill, 1989) 1:95–128, in a presentation by Harold Attridge; or in a book by Dieter Lührmann in collaboration with Egbert Schlarb, *Fragmente apokryph gewordener Evangelien in griechischer und lateinischer Sprache* (Marburger Theologische Studien 59; Marburg: Elwert, 2000) 115.

[21] *Gos. Thom.* 10: "Jesus said, 'I have cast fire upon the world, and see, I am guarding it until it blazes.'" See Sieber, "Redactional Analysis," 113–18; Michael Mees, *Ausserkanonische Parallelstellen zu den Herrenworten und ihre Bedeutung* (Quaderni di Vetera Christianorum 10; Bari: Istituto di letteratura cristiana antica, 1975) 151–57; Claus-Peter März, " 'Feuer auf die Erde zu werfen, bin ich gekommen … ,'" in *A cause de l'Évangile. Mélanges Jacques Dupont* (Paris: Cerf; Ottignies: Abbaye de Saint-André, 1985) 479–511; Lelyveld, *Les logia de la vie dans l'Évangile selon Thomas*, 65–68; Fieger, *Das Thomasevangelium*, 55–58; Marvin Meyer, *The Gospel of Thomas: The Hidden Sayings of Jesus* (New York: HarperSanFrancisco, 1992) 73,

therefore the only true counterpart of Luke 12:49. Not only is the sentence formed in the same manner in the two cases, but it also resorts to the same metaphor of "fire." It contains, at last, a final commentary difficult to translate in both cases, equally so in the Greek of Luke as in the Coptic of Thomas. Concerning the Coptic,[22] one may understand this last clause either as "I am guarding it until it [the world] is set on fire" or as "I am guarding it [the fire], just starting, until it really blazes." These hesitations correspond to the hesitation of Lukan exegetes who wonder whether, in Luke, Jesus rejoices over the fact that the fire has been already lit or if he vividly wishes that the fire should blaze. I feel that the uncertainty of text of Thomas reflects the embarrassment of a translator who is not sure about the meaning to give to the sentence he is translating. Anyway, the *logion* of the *Gospel of Thomas* compared to the Lukan text does not demonstrate any development. From the point of view of literary genres, both sayings are located at the same evolutionary level. The Greek text of Thomas must have corresponded to that of Luke, who contented himself in taking over a saying from his special material.

Three general observations to conclude this comparison: Puech wondered – and I do not know if he is right – whether it would not be preferable to slightly amend the Coptic text and manage to arrive at a better parallel with Luke 12:49 in reading "I have come to throw a fire … ."[23] The argument in favor of this hypothesis: the expression, "I have come," followed by the preposition є- and a verb in the infinitive, is found in the *Gospel of Thomas* (*Gos. Thom.* 16, the counterpart of Luke 12:51). Secondly, it is odd to see Thomas using the Greek word ⲕⲟⲥⲙⲟⲥ, "universe," where the parallel of Luke carries the word γῆ, "earth." Thirdly, it should not be forgotten that *Gos. Thom.* 82 (next to me, next to the fire) is a maxim unknown in the Synoptic Gospels but quoted as an *agraphon* by the Christian writers of antiquity.[24] *Gos. Thom.* 10 must therefore depend on Luke or, more likely, on Luke's special material.

---

who presents an interesting parallel, *Pistis Sophia* 141; Patterson, *The Gospel of Thomas and Jesus*, 23–24.

[22] *Gos. Thom.* 10: ⲁⲩⲱ ⲉⲓⲥϩⲏⲏⲧⲉ ϯⲁⲣⲉϩ ⲉⲣⲟϥ ϣⲁⲛⲧⲉϥϫⲉⲣⲟ. See Kurt Aland, *Synopsis Quattuor Evangeliorum locis parallelis evangeliorum apocryphorum et patrum adhibitis* (15th ed.; Stuttgart: Deutsche Biblegesellschaft, 2001) 522.

[23] Puech, *En quête de la gnose*, 2:12 n. 3.

[24] Origen, *Hom. Jer.* 20.3 (PG 13:532; this homily is numbered *Hom. Jer.* 3.3 in the critical edition Origenes, *Homilien zu Samuel I, zum Hohelied und zu den Propheten, Kommentar zum Hohelied in Rufins und Hieronymus' Übersetzungen* [ed. Willem A. Baehrens; vol. 8 of *Origenes Werke*; GCS 33; Leipzig: Hinrichs, 1925] 312–13; it has the number L I [III] in the work Origène, *Homélies sur Jérémie* [ed., intro., and ann. Pierre Nautin; trans. Pierre Husson and Pierre Nautin; SC 238; Paris: Cerf, 1977] 324–25); Origen, *Hom. Jos.* 4.3 (PG 12:845; Origenes, *Homilien zum Hexateuch in Rufins Übersetzung. Zweiter Teil. Die Homilien zu Numeri, Josua und Judices* [vol. 7 of *Origenes Werke*; GCS 30; Leipzig: Hinrichs, 1921] 311; Origène, *Homélies sur Josué* [Latin text, intro., trans., and ann. Annie Jaubert; SC 71; Paris: Cerf, 1960] 154–57); Didymus, *Exp. Psalm.* 88.8 (PG 39:1488–1489), where we have the Greek text of the saying; see Puech, *En quête de la gnose*, 2:264.

Gos. Thom. 61//Luke 17:34

Luke 17:34 states, "I tell you, in that night there will be two in one bed; one will be taken and the other left." Matt 24:40 is not an exact parallel: the question does not concern a bed, but fields and a grinding stone or a mill. *Gos. Thom.* 61, on the other hand, is surprisingly close to Luke: "Jesus said, 'Two will rest on a bed; the one will die, the other will live.'"[25] One may hesitate concerning the function of the bed. In Luke, as in Thomas, it may be about a conjugal bed, or again a family bed, or even a couch designated for welcoming guests to a meal.[26] The idea of unavoidable selection is the same here and there, yet verbs are different: "take" and "leave" on the one hand, "die" and "live" on the other. From a *formgeschicht-lich* point of view, the *Gospel of Thomas* does not appear more developed here than the Gospel of Luke. However, the context of the apocalyptic hint "on that night" is absent in Thomas. The Lukan maxim appears inscribed in a biblical tradition that removes the ambiguity from the verbs "take" and "leave." It is then logical to conclude that the formulation of Luke is original and that the author of the *Gospel of Thomas*, in suppressing the apocalyptic framework, has been forced to specify the meaning of "take" and "leave," by substituting for them, without equivocating, the verbs "die" and "live." Thomas must therefore depend here on Luke himself or, behind Luke, on Q. Here, the third evangelist has better preserved this source than Matthew did.

Gos. Thom. 63//Luke 12:16–21

Scholars manage to come to a very different conclusion when they compare the parable of the rich man in the Gospels according to Luke and Thomas. The version of Thomas is almost twice as short.[27] It only contains one sentence that the

---

[25] See Sieber, "Redactional Analysis," 134–36, 227–29; Lelyveld, *Les logia de la vie dans l'Évangile selon Thomas*, 56–60, 64–65; Patterson, *The Gospel of Thomas and Jesus*, 46–47; Fieger, *Das Thomasevangelium*, 176–80.

[26] I prefer the solution of a family rather than a marital bed because the two people are put in the masculine in Luke; see François Bovon, *L'Évangile selon saint Luc* (CNT 3a–c; 3 vols. so far; Geneva: Labor et Fides, 1991–2001) 3:157–58; Valantasis, *The Gospel of Thomas*, 138–39.

[27] *Gos. Thom.* 63: "Jesus said, There was a rich man who had much money. He said, 'I shall put my money to use so that I may sow, reap, plant, and fill my storehouse with produce, with the result that I shall lack nothing.' Such were his intentions, but that same night he died. Let him who has hears hear.'" On this version of the parable, see James Neville Birdsall, "Luke XII.16ff. and the *Gospel of Thomas*," *JTS* 13 (1962) 332–36, who is interested in the words "He who has ears, listen!"; Sieber, "Redactional Analysis," 215–18; Puech, *En quête de la gnose*, 2:31, 37; Fieger, *Das Thomasevangelium*, 182–83, who understands the parable of Thomas as a negative exemplary story and thinks that the text of Thomas is a free adaptation of the text of Luke; Patterson, *The Gospel of Thomas and Jesus*, 47–48; Valantasis, *The Gospel of Thomas*, 141–42.

rich man says to himself. On the contrary, Luke, or his source, the special material, resorts with pleasure and profit to inner dialogue. This unfolds in three steps. (a) The rich man asks the question, common in Luke-Acts, τί ποιήσω; "What shall I do?" (b) He quickly finds an answer to it that turns out to be more complex than the one in the *Gospel of Thomas*. Here, in Luke, it is about pulling down old barns and building even larger ones. In Thomas, it is simply about increasing production. (c) The rich man, according to Luke, adds an invitation, addressing his soul, conforming to the classic mould of the saying "eat, drink, and be merry." We often find this invitation to pleasure in Greece, Israel, Egypt, and in Assyria, even, it is said, on the tomb of Sardanapalus.[28] The voice of God Himself, absent from the *Gospel of Thomas*, interrupts the inner dialogue: "But God said to him, 'Fool! This very night, your soul is claimed.'" The conclusions also vary between the two Gospels. Luke carries on – it is rather God who continues talking – by asking: "So, what you have been preparing, whose will it be?" Thomas concludes soberly: "Such were his intentions, but that same night he died." Luke, who sufficiently suggested this issue, does not need to explain it explicitly. Coming to this point of the story, the two evangelists feel the need to draw a moral lesson from this sad story. If the *Gospel of Thomas* resorts to its all-purpose exhortation ("Let him who has ears, hear!"), the Gospel of Luke concludes in a more subtle way by shifting from material to spiritual goods: "So it happens to the one who lays up treasures for himself and is not rich toward God."

It is obvious in that case that, from a *formgeschichtlich* viewpoint, the version of Luke is secondary to that of Thomas. As it is unlikely that Thomas takes the version of Luke to simplify it drastically, it is more plausible that Thomas is independent from Luke and is using an archaic tradition. Luke and, undoubtedly before him, this great writer who is the author of the special material knew the same tradition, but did not hesitate to transform it by dressing it up in elegant rhetoric.[29] The version of Luke is to that of Thomas what the work of Symeon Metaphrastes is to the modest work of early Christian authors – that is to say, the work of a sophisticated writer before that of a popular story-teller.

---

[28] See Bovon, *L'Évangile selon saint Luc*, 2:255.
[29] See Tjitze Baarda, "Lk 12:13–14: Text and Transmission from Marcion to Augustine," in *Christianity, Judaism, and Other Greco-Roman Cults. Festschrift Morton Smith* (SJLA 12.1; Leiden: Brill, 1975) 107–62; Bernhard Heininger, *Metaphorik. Erzählstruktur und szenisch-dramatische Gestaltung in den Sondergleichnissen bei Lukas* (NTA n.s. 24; Münster: Aschendorff, 1991) 107–21; Patterson, *The Gospel of Thomas and Jesus*, 54–56; Bovon, *L'Évangile selon saint Luc*, 2:246.

Gos. Thom. 72//Luke 12:13–14

In these two parallel sayings, we find the solution again that had imposed itself for the saying on the fire or for that which is related to the two people who share the same bed.[30] The texts are parallel and neither is more or less developed than the other.[31] In the two Gospels, it is about a brief dialogue, introduced by a simple narrative utterance (that of Luke is slightly more precise, because it signals that the person is from the crowd). It is not easy to know why on the one hand Thomas speaks of several brothers and why on the other Luke speaks of one alone. The request is almost identical: one concerns "inheritance" (Luke), the other "my father's possessions" (*Gos. Thom.*). Are these not practically the same thing? When we know, however, that Thomas willingly calls "Father" the God whom he worships, one may think here of a redactional adaptation from an original text that Luke preserved better ("inheritance"). The refusal of Jesus is expressed here and there in the form of a rhetorical question. Even if the text of Luke is here uncertain, I suggest reading the double title "judge or divider," but I think that the term "judge" is an editorial addition (when he writes his Gospel, Luke often gives to his readers the meaning of a difficult term or expression of his source in adding a well-known expression). Therefore, I suggest that Luke and Thomas are at the same level: they know the same brief apophthegm and reproduce it without many changes. Their main contribution – I have not mentioned it until now – is to shed a particular light on the episode. Thomas adds to the question a significant redundancy: "He turned to his disciples and said to them: 'I am not a divider, am I?'" With this addition, he underscores the christological significance ("I") of the dialogue. As for Luke, he immediately moves on, inviting his readers to avoid avarice (Luke 12:15). Consequently, he extracts from the episode a moral sense. It may be that Thomas depends on an oral or loose apophthegm, but it is more probable that he, like the third evangelist, might have had knowledge of the special material of Luke.

Gos. Thom. 79//Luke 11:27–28

As in the previous case, a great affinity brings together the dialogue on happiness in Luke and in Thomas.[32] The starting situation is identical: From the crowd, a

---

[30] *Gos. Thom.* 72: "[A man said] to him, 'Tell my brothers to divide my father's possessions with me.' He said to him, 'O man, who has made me a divider?' He turned to his disciples and said to them, 'I am not a divider, am I?'"

[31] On the version of Thomas, see Sieber, "Redactional Analysis," 215–18; Fieger, *Das Thomasevangelium*, 203–5.

[32] *Gos. Thom.* 79: "A woman from the crowd said to him, 'Blessed are the womb which bore you and the breasts which nourished you.' He said to [her], 'Blessed are those who have heard the word of the Father and have truly kept it. For there will be days when you (pl.) will say,

woman pronounces a beatitude. Very similar is also Jesus' riposte, which the exegete hesitates, each time, to take for a rebuff or for a climax.[33] Two differences make one think that the author of Thomas modified the traditional sayings of Jesus: he prefers, as one may expect, the expression "word of the Father" to that of "word of God." He also specifies that obedience must be observed "truly." What follows in this exchange introduces us to the manner in which the author had composed. By association, he thinks of another beatitude of Jesus that also conjures up procreation and breastfeeding (Luke 23:29, a saying stemming from the special material of Luke). He does not hesitate to place it here, maintaining the future validity that the tradition accords to it ("For there will be days when ... "), since it contains a negation ("Blessed are the womb which *has not* conceived and the breasts which *have not* given milk").[34] If we compare this last sentence to its Lukan counterpart, we notice that Luke 23:29 provides us with three examples (the women who are sterile, those who are not pregnant, and those who do not breastfeed). It is likely that Thomas as well may have known the three examples, but that he may have reduced them to two, to make them counterpart to the pronouncement story that only presents two. By shortening it this way, he therefore does not want to simply avoid a repetition, for a woman who does not conceive is not necessarily sterile. To conclude, one cannot say that Thomas undergoes here influence by the written version of Luke. He knew the episode and the additional sentence, either in an oral form or instead in the form they took, one and the other, within the special material of Luke.

Gos. Thom. 95//Luke 6:34–35a

The last passage I am presenting is a little peculiar, because Luke's text is in a literary unit whose origin is not the special material but the Source of the *logia* (i.e., the literary unit dealing with the love for one's enemies). Within this unit whose origin is not the special material, Luke added, as he often did, a supplementary case that really corresponds to the contemporary situation of his community. As some Christians of his time did not lack money, "to love one's enemies" was not practiced, as Q imagined, only on the model of prayer or non-resistance; it also materialized with the good use of money. Inspired, Luke added the example of the non-interest loan and even of the gift. I am certain that Luke 6:34–35a, which has no parallel in Matthew (much less in Mark or John), is a redactional commentary

---

Blessed are the womb which has not conceived and the breasts which have not given milk.'" See Fieger, *Das Thomasevangelium*, 218–21; Valantasis, *The Gospel of Thomas*, 158–59.

[33] See Bovon, *L'Évangile selon saint Luc*, 2:170.

[34] See also the parallel in the triple tradition: Luke 21:23//Mark 13:17//Matt 24:19; another evaluation of the relations between the two parts of *Gos. Thom.* 79 is in Patterson, *The Gospel of Thomas and Jesus*, 59–60.

by Luke.[35] How, then, are we to explain the presence of the same sentence in the
Gospel of Thomas (*Gos. Thom.* 95)?[36] I cannot agree with the hypothesis of Patterson, who wonders whether Luke did not draw from the *Gospel of Thomas*,[37]
nor can I agree to that of Gilles Quispel, who suggests the existence of a variant
of Luke 6:34–35a, an independent variant, that is also known by a quotation in
the Pseudo-Clementines (*Recognitiones* 6.13.5: *Homiliae* 11.32.1).[38] On the contrary, respecting the difference between redaction and tradition, I believe that the
author of *Gos. Thom.* 95 had knowledge of the final redaction of the Gospel of
Luke.

Theological and Religious Orientations

Until now, I have said next to nothing about the theological and religious orientations of the two documents. The comparisons that I have done lead me to make
note of the following elements:

a) Even if he was interested in the inheritance of Israel, Luke was not Jewish and
often unconsciously showed the distance that separated him from Judaism. The
phenomenon of distance continues in the *Gospel of Thomas*: if the Pharisees are
still in opposition to Jesus in the quarrel over the Kingdom (Luke 17:20–21), it is
to "those who lead you" that the Jesus of Thomas opposed (*Gos. Thom.* 3).[39]

b) Compared to Jesus and his first disciples, who all hailed from the Galilean
country and from the shores of Lake Tiberias, Luke appeared as a city man. The
movement towards the city here also has been continued in Thomas. The parable
of the guests to the banquet only casts merchants and business people (*Gos. Thom.*
64//Luke 14:16–24//Matt 22:1–10).

c) Luke did not deny the original apocalyptic message, but he balanced it out of
his own concern for death, what one may refer to as his individual eschatology.[40]
There again, the movement carries on in Thomas: it is no longer during the apocalyptic night that one is taken and the other is left (Luke 17:34), but it is at any
time that one may die and the other may continue to live (*Gos. Thom.* 61).

---

[35] See Bovon, *L'Évangile selon saint Luc*, 1:300–21, esp. 305, 309, 311.

[36] *Gos. Thom.* 95: "[Jesus said], 'If you have money, do not lend it at interest, but give [it] to
one from whom you will not get it back.'" On this *logion* in Thomas, see Fieger, *Das Thomasevangelium*, 243–44.

[37] Patterson, *The Gospel of Thomas and Jesus*, 79–80.

[38] Gilles Quispel, "L'*Évangile de Thomas* et les Clémentines," in idem, *Gnostic Studies*, II
(Uitgaven van het Nederlands Historisch-Archaeologisch Instituut te İstanbul 34.2; Istanbul:
Nederlands Historisch-Archaeologisch Instituut te İstanbul, 1975) 17–29.

[39] The author of the *Gospel of Thomas* is not always so strict. He mentions the Pharisees in
logion 39.

[40] See Jacques Dupont, "L'eschatologie individuelle dans l'œuvre de Luc," in idem, *Études sur
les évangiles synoptiques* (presented by Frans Neirynck; 2 vols.; BETL 70A–B; Leuven: Leuven
University Press, 1985) 2:1066–75.

d) Money plays a bigger role in the city than in the countryside. Both Luke and Thomas know the dangers of money. Both state that those who are poor are blessed (Luke 6:20//*Gos. Thom.* 54) because, in their eyes, it is spiritual wealth that is the final goal (Luke 12:21 and *Gos. Thom.* 81). This spiritual wealth is only attained through the practice of renouncement and through material poverty (Luke 12:33; 14:33; *Gos. Thom.* 54; 76; 95).[41]

e) For both authors Jesus is the master of wisdom, but if Luke develops his Christology in the narrative parts of his Gospel, when he recalls the heroic deeds of Jesus, especially his passion and death, Thomas, who limits himself to the words of Jesus, must present it within the sayings (for example, *Gos. Thom.* 13; 28; 30; 37; 38; 61; 65; 72; 77; 82; 90; 91).[42] Luke uses Jesus' teaching less as a christological overture than as an ethical prescription (for example, compare Luke 12:13–15 to *Gos. Thom.* 72).

f) Luke and Thomas play with language. Thomas, it is true, ignores the allegorical exegesis of the parables of Jesus (see for example the parable of the Sower in *Gos. Thom.* 9 compared to Mark 4:1–20//Matt 13:1–23//Luke 8:4–15), but he does not refuse – on the contrary – to let words and sentences shift from the literal to the figurative meaning. In fact, he does not need to explain this second meaning, since he only needs to speak about a fisherman or a treasure for informed readers to know that it is about something other than a fisherman or a treasure. It is in this way that the words of Jesus the Living One are words filled with a secret (*Gos. Thom.* prologue) whose reader is invited to find the key of interpretation (*Gos. Thom.* 1). The words in their external appearance contain a hidden meaning that we need to bring to light (*Gos. Thom.* 5). It is certainly this structure of the secret and of the meaningful that enables the author to utter sometimes senseless words, as saying that a lion can become a man (*Gos. Thom.* 7) or that a man who knows his mother and father is called son of a prostitute (*Gos. Thom.* 105) or finally that many people are around a well, but that there is nobody in the well (*Gos. Thom.* 74).

---

[41] In his commentary, Jacques-É. Ménard (*L'Évangile selon Thomas* [NHS 5; Leiden: Brill, 1975]) is sensitive to the spiritual range of this opposition between poverty and the richness.

[42] On the Christology of the *Gospel of Thomas*, see Bertil Gärtner, *The Theology of the Gospel of Thomas* (trans. Eric J. Sharpe; London: Collins, 1961) 118–58.

Conclusion

It is obvious that the *Gospel of Thomas* shares many sayings with the double tradition (Q or the Source of *logia*)[43] and with the triple tradition (Mark and his acolytes).[44] The parallels with sayings that are specific to Luke are less numerous, which is surprising when we recall the high proportion of words that the Lukan special material contains. To take only two examples, the Good Samaritan and the Prodigal Son accounts are both absent from the *Gospel of Thomas*. Yet, as we saw, the result is not null, because several sayings of the *Gospel of Thomas* have their counterpart only in Luke.

The comparison I have made has led to four complementary results:

1. It happens that Thomas (*Gos. Thom.* 63) did not depend on Luke, but used old traditions that were circulating as *logia* or *agrapha*. In those cases, Thomas and Luke acted similarly, but independently of one another. Sometimes, it is Luke, or the author of the special material before him, who developed more this or that saying (as in the parable of the wealthy man, Luke 12:16–21//*Gos. Thom.* 63).

2. At other places, the *Gospel of Thomas* probably draws from the special material of Luke and not from the Gospel of Luke itself. This is the case for the sayings on fire (*Gos. Thom.* 10//Luke 12:49), on inheritance (*Gos. Thom.* 72//Luke 12:13–14), and on the best beatitude (*Gos. Thom.* 79//Luke 11:27–28).

3. In the example of the bed where the selection is made (*Gos. Thom.* 61//Luke 17:34), the *Gospel of Thomas* seems to follow the Source of the *logia* (Q).

4. There are at least two cases of dependence regarding Luke himself. These are the *logia* that are the most reworked in the *Gospel of Thomas*, including the saying on the presence of the Kingdom and its reflection on self-knowledge (*Gos. Thom.* 3//Luke 17:20–21, 23), as well as the ban on lending with interest (*Gos. Thom.* 95// Luke 6:34–35a).

Given the general orientation and final redaction of the *Gospel of Thomas*, which I locate in the second century, I do not imagine that Luke the evangelist may have based his work on this noncanonical Gospel even in its Greek version. It is the author of Thomas who, himself, drew on Luke, but also on the special material of the evangelist Luke and on ancient oral traditions.

To sum up, analysis of the sayings of Jesus, as preserved in the Gospels according to Luke and according to Thomas, and comparison between the two channels

---

[43] On this subject see Jens Schröter, *Erinnerung an Jesu Worte. Studien zur Rezeption der Logienüberlieferung in Markus, Q und Thomas* (WMANT 76; Neukirchen-Vluyn: Neukirchener Verlag, 1997).

[44] On this subject see Liebenberg, *The Language of the Kingdom and Jesus.*

that have served to carry them to this day, reveal the unknowns as well as the logic of an oral and written transmission, the respect of each for the words of Jesus and the freedom with which the writers fulfilled their task.[45]

[45] As a supplement to the materials above, here is a list of other works consulted for the preparation of this article: Hans-Werner Bartsch, "Das Thomas-Evangelium und die synoptischen Evangelien. Zu G. Quispels Bemerkungen zum Thomas-Evangelium," *NTS* 6 (1959–1960) 249–61; Ron Cameron, "Parable and interpretation in the *Gospel of Thomas*," FF: *Forum* 2 (1986) 5–39; idem, "Thomas, Gospel of," in *ABD* 6 (1992) 535–40; Oscar Cullmann, "Das Thomasevangelium und die Frage nach dem Alter der in ihm enthaltenen Tradition," *TLZ* 85 (1960) 321–34; reprinted in idem, *Vorträge und Aufsätze* (ed. Karlfried Fröhlich; Tübingen: Mohr Siebeck; Zurich: Zwingli, 1966) 566–88; Claudio Gianotto, "Évangile selon Thomas," in *Écrits apocryphes chrétiens* 1 (ed. François Bovon and Pierre Geoltrain; La Pléiade 442; Paris: Gallimard, 1997) 23–53; Helmut Koester, "Q and His Relatives," in *Gospel Origins and Christian Beginnings in Honor of James M. Robinson* (ed. James E. Goehring et al.; Sonoma, Calif.: Polebridge, 1990) 49–63; idem, "Three Thomas Parables, " in *The New Testament and Gnosis: Essays in Honour of Robert McL. Wilson* (ed. Alastair H. B. Logan and Alexander J. M. Wedderburn; Edinburgh: T&T Clark, 1983) 195–203; Raymond Kuntzmann and Jean-Daniel Dubois, *Nag Hammadi, Évangile selon Thomas, textes gnostiques aux origines du christianisme* (*CaE* Supp 58; Paris: Cerf, 1987); Bentley Layton, *The Gnostic Scriptures: A New Translation with Annotations and Introductions* (ABRL; New York: Doubleday, 1987); Georges W. MacRae, "The *Gospel of Thomas* – Logia Iesou?," *CBQ* 22 (1960) 56–71; Jacques-É. Ménard, "La Sagesse et le *logion* 3 de l'*Évangile selon Thomas*," in *Studia Patristica* 10 (ed. Frank L. Cross; TUGAL 107; Berlin: Akademie-Verlag, 1970) 137–40; Stephen J. Patterson and James M. Robinson, *The Fifth Gospel: The* Gospel of Thomas *Comes of Age* (with a new English translation by Hans-Gebhardt Bethge et al.; Harrisburg, Pa.: Trinity Press International, 1998); Gilles Quispel, "Some remarks on the *Gospel of Thomas*," *NTS* 5 (1958–1959) 276–90; Jesse Sell, "Johannine Traditions in Logion 61 of the *Gospel of Thomas*," *PRSt* 7 (1980) 24–37; Philip Sellew, "The *Gospel of Thomas*: Prospects for Future Research," in *The Nag Hammadi Library after Fifty Years: Proceedings of the 1995 Society of Biblical Literature Commemoration* (ed. John D. Turner and Anne McGuire; Nag Hammadi and Manichaean Studies 44; Leiden: Brill, 1997) 328–46; Risto Uro, ed., *Thomas at the Crossroads: Essays on the Gospel of Thomas* (Studies of the New Testament and Its World; Edinburgh: T&T Clark, 1998); Christopher Tuckett, "Thomas and the Synoptics," *NovT* 30 (1988) 132–57; Robert McL.Wilson, *Studies in the Gospel of Thomas* (London: Mowbray, 1960).

Fragment Oxyrhynchus 840, Fragment of a Lost Gospel, Witness of an Early Christian Controversy over Purity

I. Introduction

In his *Unbekannte Jesusworte* Joachim Jeremias writes about *Fragment Oxyrhynchus* 840: "Diese Perle evangelischer Erzählerkunst hat bis heute nicht die Beachtung gefunden, die sie verdient" ("Up until now, this pearl of Gospel narrative has not received the appreciation it deserves").[1] Fifty years later I still concur with Jeremias's judgment. Despite regular mention, this fragment remains relatively unknown. Yet there remains much unnoticed significance to this document: the intensity of the dialogue between Jesus and the priest, the relevance of the purity controversy, and the literary quality of the whole passage. *Fragment Oxyrhynchus* 840 would be deemed even more significant if it were properly interpreted. The folio is conventionally interpreted in the framework of first-century C.E. Judaism and is regarded as valuable in the quest for the historical Jesus. In my opinion, although *Fragment Oxyrhynchus* 840 may well speak about Jesus and his criticism of a Jewish priest, it actually fits better into ancient Christian controversies about the validity of water baptism. As we know, any material referring to Jesus' life is at the same time a window into the author's Christian community. Our fragment – this will be my hypothesis – reflects a Christian setting in the second or the third century.

The philological and historical problems that have been discussed since the discovery of the fragment find a more plausible solution as soon as we no longer visualize the scene in Jerusalem during Jesus' life. Every term and category fits better into the framework of ancient Christianity. The dialogue becomes clearer if we cease to hear Jesus and a Pharisee and hear instead two Christian groups engaged in a controversy. It is in the second and third centuries that the necessity of water baptism was discussed, that the symbolism of changing clothes was developed, and that the spiritual vision of holy vessels became the goal of a religious experience.

---

[1] Joachim Jeremias, *Unbekannte Jesusworte* (ATANT 16; Zurich: Zwingli, 1948) 38.

The Text

This fragment is a leaf of parchment; therefore, even if it has been published among the *Oxyrhynchus Papyri* it is not actually a papyrus.[2] It was found at Oxyrhynchos[3] in 1905 and published in 1908 by Bernard P. Grenfell and Arthur S. Hunt.[4] Although the leaf of parchment can be dated to the fourth or fifth century c.e., the date of the text itself is still uncertain. It could be of the second century.[5] Lines 1–7 contain the end of a moral speech of the Savior; lines 7–45 contain the dispute between the Savior and a Jewish chief priest.

Textual, Philological, and Historical Aspects

The following questions were vehemently debated in 1908, the year of the publication of the fragment, and remain unanswered to this day.[6] Is it not strange that the priest is at the same time a Pharisee? Has the author forgotten that the major-

---

[2] Gerd Theissen and Annette Merz are among the few modern scholars to realize that evidence (*Der historische Jesus. Ein Lehrbuch* [Göttingen: Vandenhoeck & Ruprecht, 1996] 62). The fragment should no longer be called *Papyrus Oxyrhynchus* 840.

[3] Today El Bahnasa, about 125 miles south of Cairo.

[4] Bernard P. Grenfell and Arthur S. Hunt, *The Oxyrhynchus Papyri* V (London/Oxford: Oxford University Press, 1908) no. 840. The two editors give a rich introduction, a diplomatic edition, a critical edition, a translation, and valuable notes. Their introduction mentions the name of Emil Schürer, from whom they received suggestions for the interpretation of the fragment. Because of the importance of their discovery, Grenfell and Hunt also published the fragment independently the same year: Bernard P. Grenfell and Arthur S. Hunt, *Fragment of an Uncanonical Gospel from Oxyrhynchus*, published for the Egypt Exploration Fund by Henry Frowde (London/New York/Toronto: Oxford University Press, 1908). Another edition was published in 1908 by Henry Barclay Swete, *Zwei Neue Evangelienfragmente herausgegeben und erklärt* (KlT 31; Bonn: A. Marcus und E. Weber, 1908) 3–9. This work was reprinted without change in the same collection and by the same publisher in 1924. On other editions, see nn. 10, 16, 18, and 20 below.

[5] The very small format of the fragment (8.8 x 7.4 cm) suggests that it was an amulet. Despite its tiny dimensions the text is very readable and well preserved (recto 23 lines, verso 22 lines). According to the editors, Bernard P. Grenfell and Arthur S. Hunt (*Oxyrhynchus Papyri* V, 1), the scribe used "red ink to outline and bring into greater prominence the dots of punctuation (in the middle position), initial letters of sentences, strokes of abbreviation, and even accents."

[6] The fragmentary character of the text makes the correct understanding of the first seven lines (the end of a polemical speech by Jesus) difficult. In the following lines, 8–45, the text is easier to read, even if some of the lines are damaged at the beginning or end, making reconstruction problematic. The name of the priest, Levi (line 10), is probable but not certain. Depending on the reconstitution of the text, in lines 43–44 the waters are either "waters of eternal life" (Grenfell and Hunt) or "living waters of the Holy Spirit" (Lagrange, as an alternative) or "living and pure waters" (Bertrand). "From" where are these waters coming? The text breaks down after the preposition. With Grenfell and Hunt, we may guess "from heaven" or "from the Father"; with Swete, "from the Father out of Heaven." There are other minor divergences between the editions. The best way to catch them is to look at the critical apparatus of Bonaccorsi's edition. But as Bonaccorsi does not integrate Lagrange's edition, I mention the two places where the French scholar differs from the first editors, Grenfell and Hunt: in line 1, Lagrange reads with Swete προαδικῆσαι and translates "provoquer injustement"; in lines 39–40, he proposes

ity of the Jerusalem priests were Sadduceans and that no high priest of that time was called Levi? How do we understand the presence of an extremely rare word, ἀγνευτήριον, "place of purification," a place that is not easy to locate within the area of the temple of Jerusalem? How do we explain the presence of ἡ λίμνη τοῦ Δαυείδ, "the pool of David," which no Jewish source ever mentions?[7] Is it not surprising that the priest, after his personal purification, puts on "white and pure clothes" and takes for granted that even laypeople should wear white clothes, when neither the books of the Torah nor Jewish literature makes this requirement clear? Is not the presence of "pigs" in Israel enigmatic, and is not the whole scenario difficult to imagine? Finally, how are we to interpret this surprising contemplation of holy vessels, which does not seem to have been a part of regular Jewish ritual?

II. History of Interpretation

Initial Enthusiasm

In the year of its publication a century ago, many major scholars in the field of New Testament and Christian origins expressed passionate interest in the new fragment. Each of them has given a presentation, often a translation, sometimes an edition, always with notes and comments. Writing for the readers of the *Preussische Jahrbücher*, Adolf von Harnack was convinced that, issued from a Jewish-Christian community, the fragment brought forth some original material about Jesus.[8] He wrote: "Es liegt eine Kraft und ein Feuer in der Erzählung, die nicht aus Fabelei oder Nacherfindung stammen" ("There is a power and a fire in the story which do not originate from fable or later invention").[9]

Marie-Joseph Lagrange gave a revised edition, a French translation, and an extensive interpretation of the new fragment to the readers of the *Revue biblique* without omitting any philological aspect. His balanced conclusion dismissed any historical authenticity, but accepted the value of the document for ancient Christian history: "Quoi qu'il en soit, si notre fragment n'a aucun titre à figurer parmi les témoignages authentiques de la vie de Jésus, on voit qu'il ne le cède en intérêt à aucun des *logia* que l'Égypte a déjà fournis" ("Let it be as it stands, if our fragment has no right to have a place among the authentic testimonies of Jesus' life, we real-

---

ἔνδοθεν δὲ ἐκεί[νων πεπλ]ήρωται and translates "mais leur intérieur est plein de … ." The references to these editors and translators are found in nn. 4, 10, 16, and 23 below.

    [7] See n. 28 below.

    [8] Adolf von Harnack, "Ein neues Evangelienbruchstück," *Preussische Jahrbücher* 131 (1908) 201–10; reprinted in idem, *Aus Wissenschaft und Leben* (2 vols.; Giessen: Töpelmann, 1911) 2:237–50.

    [9] Harnack, *Aus Wissenschaft und Leben*, 2:250.

ize that it shares the same value as all the *logia* that Egypt provided so far").[10] Finally, Edgar J. Goodspeed in *The Biblical World*, observing that the author seems to be ignorant "of the real conditions at Jerusalem," tried to relate the fragment to several apocryphal Gospels, particularly the *Gospel of the Hebrews*: "On the whole, the episode seems to be a later elaboration, in a somewhat rhetorical spirit, of teachings found in Matt 15:1–20, and Mark 7:1–23."[11] What a contrast between the scholarly competence and passion of these first reactions and the neglect and indifference into which the fragment has fallen since then!

The historical accuracy of the Jewish ritual of purification and the issue of the authenticity of the dialogue were at the core of the early discussions. The voices of Lagrange and Goodspeed, who advocated for an understanding in the framework of Christianity, were ignored. The very fact that the editors, Grenfell and Hunt, asked Emil Schürer's help shows where their interests lay: in the possible witness to first-century Jerusalem and to the historical Jesus. When Schürer's input dismissed the historical authenticity of the fragment,[12] the editors, following his advice, in a sense prepared the funeral of the fragment. It lost interest in their eyes and in the eyes of many after them. Otto Bardenhewer, in his *Geschichte der altkirchlichen Literatur*, summarizes this line of interpretation by calling the fragment an incredible creation.[13]

Several scholars, however, reacted against this pessimistic view by trying to demonstrate the reliability of the text: there was a place of purification inside the temple; there was a possible location for the pool of David; the change of clothes was a natural and logical requirement after purification; laypeople had to comply with the same rigorous ritual procedure as the priest in order to enter the temple; there really was a risk of the water being polluted by coming through an aqueduct; and the display of holy vessels was a partial expression of Jewish piety (the access to the viewing of these vessels by pagans was particularly shocking for Jewish sensibilities). Jewish scholars were involved from the beginning in this controversy, and most of them with care and caution did not easily disregard *Fragment Oxyrhynchus* 840. Particularly influential was an erudite article by Adolf Büchler in the *Jewish Quarterly Review*, also published in 1908.[14] Con-

---

[10] Marie-Joesph Lagrange, "Nouveau fragment non canonique relatif à l'Évangile," *RB* n.s. 5 (1908) 538–53, at 553.

[11] Edgar J. Goodspeed, "The New Gospel Fragment from Oxyrhynchus," *The Biblical World* n.s. 31 (1908) 142–46, at 145.

[12] See Emil Schürer's review of *Fragment of an Uncanonical Gospel from Oxyrhynchus* in *TLZ* 32 (1908) 170–72. In col. 172 n. 1, Schürer mentions three other book reviews: one by Adolf von Harnack (referenced in n. 8 above); one by Adolf Jülicher in *Die Christliche Welt*, 1908, no. 8; and one by Hans Lietzmann in the *Beilage zur Münchener Allgemeinen Zeitung*, 1908, no. 31 (26 February). I have not seen these last two.

[13] Otto Bardenhewer, *Geschichte der altchristlichen Literatur* (5 vols.; 2d ed.; Freiburg im Breisgau: Herder, 1913–1932) 1:512.

[14] Adolf Büchler, "The New 'Fragment of an Uncanonical Gospel,'" *JQR* 20 (1908) 330–46.

trary to Schürer and the editors Grenfell and Hunt, Büchler was convinced "that the writer of this Gospel was accurately informed on all these matters, and that tradition fully confirms the details which sound so incredible."[15]

An unanswered question lingers: What is the literary origin of the fragment? Of which book was it a part? The answers given by the first scholars are still the ones advanced today.[16] Actually, they reflect more indecision than knowledge because the brevity of the fragment precludes any precise answer. Von Harnack suggested with hesitation its extraction from the *Gospel of the Hebrews* or the *Gospel of the Egyptians* (because of the Egyptian origin of the fragment); Lagrange, the *Gospel of the Hebrews* (because in both texts water is not an efficient means for purification); Hans Waitz, the *Gospel of the Nazarenes* (because the same expression "the prostitutes and flute-girls" is found in both texts); Montague Rhodes James, perhaps the *Gospel of Peter* or the *Gospel of the Egyptians*, but surely not the *Gospel of the Hebrews*; and Erwin Preuschen, a source for the Gospel of John.[17] Such a large spectrum of answers reflects the disappointing reality that the scholars here are replacing one speculative hypothesis with another.[18]

---

[15] Ibid., 331. By quoting other rabbinic texts, Arthur Marmorstein brought new arguments to this opinion ("Einige Bemerkungen zum Evangelienfragment in Oxyrhynchus Papyri, vol. V. n. 840, 1907," *ZNW* 15 [1914] 336–38). On more recent discussions on Jewish ritual baths, see n. 28 below.

[16] See Antonio de Santos Otero, *Los Evangelios apócrifos* (2d ed.; BAC 148; Madrid: La Editorial Catolica, 1963) 79–80.

[17] von Harnack, *Aus Wissenschaft und Leben*, 2:244–47; Lagrange, "Nouveau Fragment non Canonique relatif à l'Évangile," 552–53; Hans Waitz, "Das Matthäusevangelium der Nazaräer (Nazaräerevangelium)," in *Neutestamentliche Apokryphen* (ed. Edgar Hennecke; 2d ed.; Tübingen: Mohr Siebeck, 1924) 18–19 and 31; Eduard Riggenbach, "Das Wort Jesu im Gespräch mit dem pharisäischen Hohenpriester nach dem Oxyrhynchus Fragment V Nr. 840," *ZNW* 25 (1926) 140–44 (esp. p. 140 opposes this view); Montague Rhodes James, *The Apocryphal New Testament* (Oxford: Clarendon, 1924; reprinted in 1969) 30; Erwin Preuschen, "Das neue Evangelienfragment von Oxyrhynchos," *ZNW* 9 (1908) 11.

[18] Still in the same year, Erwin Preuschen, Abraham Sulzbach, and Ludwig Blau added detailed comments in *ZNW*; see Preuschen, "Das neue Evangelienfragment von Oxyrhynchos," 1–11; Abraham Sulzbach, "Zum Oxyrhynchus-Fragment (Aus einem Brief an den Herausgeber [Erwin Preuschen])," *ZNW* 9 (1908) 175–76; Ludwig Blau, "Das neue Evangelienfragment von Oxyrhynchos buch- und zaubergeschichtlich betrachtet nebst sonstigen Bemerkungen," ibid., 204–15. Blau insists on the magic character of the book from which the fragment is part, using particularly an argument that has to be corrected. The editors had used the expressions recto and verso in an unfortunate manner. By recto they meant the hair side and by verso the flesh side of the folio. In their edition the verso comes first and the recto second. Building on this misunderstanding, Preuschen followed by Blau believed that the book had been written from the back to the front. This was of course not the case. Blau makes a case of this supposed order to determine the amulet nature of the book from which the fragment comes. But he has other, better arguments for his view. Preuschen, editor of the periodical, rectifies this mistake in a remark attached to a footnote of Blau's article (207 n. 1). The mistake of Preuschen is visible in his article in *ZNW* 9 (1908) 2. Theodor Zahn expressed his views at that time under the title "Neue Bruchstücke nichtkanonischer Evangelien," *NKZ* 19 (1908) 371–86, as well as Johannes Marinus Simon Baljon under the title "Een nieuw evangelie-fragment" *ThSt* 26 (1908) 210–19. Baljon reproduces the Greek text of Grenfell and Hunt in the beginning of his article.

The Subsequent Oblivion

Interest in the document, however, diminished rapidly and dramatically after it had been initially explored. It was reedited[19] in the *Patrologia Orientalis* by Charles Wessely, by Giuseppe Bonaccorsi, and by Aurelio de Santos Otero.[20] It became part of the apocryphal Christian literature, alongside other fragments of lost Gospels. It was translated and introduced in the several collections edited, respectively, by Edgar Hennecke then by Wilhelm Schneemelcher,[21] by James,[22] by Mario Erbetta and Luigi Moraldi each with an introduction and an Italian translation, by Wilhelm Schneemelcher in the fifth edition of the *Neutestamentliche Apokryphen*, by Keith Elliott in the new James, and recently by Daniel A. Bertrand in the first volume of *Écrits apocryphes chrétiens*.[23] These translations, introductions, and notes, as useful as they are, do not reflect new scholarly insights, nor do they reflect any substantial intellectual investment in the fragment.[24]

---

[19] As mentioned in n. 4, in 1924 a second edition of the *Zwei neue Evangelienfragmente* by Henry Barclay Swete was published.

[20] Charles Wessely, *Les plus anciens monuments du christianisme écrits sur papyrus*, 2 (PO 18.3; Paris: Firmin-Didot, 1924) 488–90; Giuseppe Bonaccorsi, *Vangeli Apocrifi*, 1 (Florence: Fiorentina, 1948) 37–39; de Santos Otero, *Los Evangelios apócrifos*, 78–82.

[21] See n. 17 above. In later editions the responsible scholar has been Joachim Jeremias; see Edgar Hennecke, *Neutestamentliche Apokryphen in deutscher Übersetzung* (3d ed. by Wilhelm Schneemelcher; 2 vols.; Tübingen: Mohr Siebeck, 1959–1964) 1:57–58; finally by Joachim Jeremias and Wilhelm Schneemelcher; see *Neutestamentliche Apokryphen in deutscher Übersetzung* (5th ed. of the collection established by Edgar Hennecke; 2 vols.; Tübingen: Mohr Siebeck, 1987–1989) 1:81–82. These last two editions have been translated by Robert McL. Wilson and published in coedition by James Clarke (Cambridge, England) and Westminster/John Knox (Louisville, Ky.) in 1963–1965 and 1991–1992 respectively.

[22] James, *Apocryphal New Testament*, 29–30. James makes an illuminating reference to the Septuagint text of 1 (LXX 3) Kings 22:38: "They washed (*Ahab's*) chariot at the fountain of Samaria, and the *swine and the dogs* licked up the blood, and the *harlots washed themselves* in the blood, according to the word of the Lord which he spake."

[23] Mario Erbetta, *Gli Apocrifi del Nuovo Testamento* (4 vols.; Turin: Marietti, 1966–1981) 1:105–6; Luigi Moraldi, *Apocrifi del Nuovo Testamento* (2 vols.; Classici delle Religione, 5th section; Turin: UTET, 1971) 1:422–23, 430–31, 436–38; J. Keith Elliott, *The Apocryphal New Testament: A Collection of Apocryphal Christian Literature in an English Translation* (Oxford: Clarendon, 1993) 31–34; Daniel A. Bertrand, "Fragments évangéliques," in *Écrits apocryphes chrétiens*, I (ed. François Bovon and Pierre Geoltrain; La Pléiade 442; Paris: Gallimard, 1997) 407–10. There is another French translation by F. Amiot in *La Bible apocryphe. Évangiles apocryphes* (ed. Daniel-Rops; Textes pour l'histoire sacrée; Paris: Cerf and Fayard, 1952) 45.

[24] Other English translations: Edward J. Jenkinson, *The Unwritten Sayings of Jesus* (London: Epworth, 1925) 112–16; Robert M. Grant in collaboration with David Noel Freedman, *The Secret Sayings of Jesus* (Garden City, N.Y.: Doubleday, 1960) 52–54 (there is no translation of the first seven lines); Ron Cameron, *The Other Gospels: Non-Canonical Gospel Texts* (Philadelphia: Westminster, 1982) 53–54; *The Complete Gospels: Annotated Scholars Version* (ed. Robert J. Miller; Sonoma, Calif.: Polebridge, 1992) 412–15. This translation contains a mistake: the waters [line 32] are said to be "stagnant," while according to the Greek text they are, on the contrary, "'running" (τοῖς χεομένοις ὕ[δ]ασι[ν]). Unfortunately, this mistake has been introduced into Robert W. Funk, *New Gospel Parallels* 1.2: *Mark* (rev. ed.; Sonoma, Calif.: Po-

Occasional Interest

For many years, Joachim Jeremias[25] was almost the only voice[26] – a voice preaching in the wilderness – trying to raise interest for this fragment. Interested, as we know, in the *ipsissima verba Jesu*, he was convinced that the Jewish *realia* of the fragment were accurate and that the story reflected a historical controversy in Jesus' life.

No new scholarly contributions occurred for almost fifty years. On one side there was silence, ignorance, or indifference; on the other was the same question of historicity in the life of Jesus. Daniel R. Schwartz contributed one of the few articles published on this fragment in the last thirty years, adding new material on the holy vessels.[27] He believed that the attitude of the priest reflected a historical tendency of the Pharisaic movement, namely, to democratize the ritual by extending to laypeople privileges previously granted priests. He also gave evidence for an exhibition of the holy vessels during the Jewish festivals. One of the expectations of the Jewish pilgrims may have been to contemplate these sacred objects, a privilege no longer restricted to the sacerdotal guild. Purification, however, was necessary to enjoy this prerogative. One detail prevented Schwartz from accepting the historicity of the entire episode: the main figure was simultaneously both a priest and a Pharisee. If I understand Schwartz correctly, he would conclude that the tradition behind this story reflected a criticism by Jesus, here in agreement with the Pharisees, against a priestly privilege. As it stands now, however, the story reflects a Christian polemic against the Pharisees. It must be added that this fragment has been regularly mentioned in the recent discussion about Jewish ritual baths, the *miqvaot*.[28]

---

lebridge, 1990) 123 and 185; and into *The Acts of Jesus: The Search for the Authentic Deeds of Jesus* (ed. Robert W. Funk and the Jesus Seminar; San Francisco: HarperSanFrancisco, 1998) 209, a translation that omits the lines 1–7.

[25] Joachim Jeremias, "Der Zusammenstoss Jesu mit dem pharisäischen Oberpriester auf dem Tempelplatz. Zu Pap. Ox. V, 840," in *Coniectanea Neotestamentica XI in honorem Antonii Fridrichsen* (ed. Seminarium Neotestamenticum Upsaliense; Lund: Gleerup; Kopenhagen: Munksgaard, 1947) 97–108; Jeremias, *Unbekannte Jesusworte*, 37–45; *Neutestamentliche Apokryphen*, 3d ed., 1:57–58.

[26] Between the discovery and Jeremias, see Riggenbach, "'Das Wort Jesu im Gespräch mit dem pharisäischen Hohenpriester nach dem Oxyrhynchus Fragment V Nr. 840"; and Roderic Dunkerley, "The Oxyrhynchus Gospel Fragments," *HTR* 23 (1930) 19–37, esp. 30–35. This last author remains interested in the possible historicity of the episode and in the delineation of two agrapha of Jesus embedded in the fragment.

[27] Daniel R. Schwartz, "Viewing the Holy Utensils (P. Ox. V,840)," *NTS* 32 (1986) 153–59.

[28] See Saul Lieberman, "Notes" (in Hebrew), *P'raqim: Yearbook of the Schocken Institute for Jewish Research of the Jewish Theological Seminary of America* 1 (1967–1968) 97–98; Ronny Reich, "Mishnah, Sheqalim 8:2 and the Archaeological Evidence," in *Jerusalem in the Second Temple Period: Abraham Schalit Memorial Volume* (ed. A'haron Oppenheimer, Uriel Rappaport, and Menahem Stern; Jerusalem: Yad Yzhak Ben Zvi-Ministry of Defence, 1980) XIV (English summary), 225–56 (Hebrew); Shmuel Safrai, *Die Wallfahrt im Zeitalter des Zweiten Tempels* (trans. from Hebrew by Dafna Mach; Forschungen zum jüdisch-christlichen Dialog 3;

More than the second quest, the so-called third quest for the historical Jesus shows interest in the noncanonical materials. Within this body of research, I was expecting special attention for the Oxyrhynchus leaf of parchment, but I was disappointed.[29] *The Complete Gospels* includes the fragment with a translation by Robert Funk and judicious notes by Philip Sellew.[30] If the fragment is not mentioned in *The Five Gospels*, it is presented, partly translated, and dismissed as a historical document concerning the historical Jesus in *The Acts of Jesus*.[31] John Dominic Crossan mentions it only *en passant*, placing it in his second stratum (60–80 C.E.).[32] In the recent books and articles I have seen on the apocryphal material considered useful for the historical Jesus, I find only an awareness of the fragment, but no new insights.[33]

Recently, in a short article published in the *Expository Times*, David Tripp proposed an unusual reading of the fragment.[34] Instead of checking once more for "the fragment's accuracy in details about the Jerusalem Temple,"[35] he suggested, without bringing convincing argumentation, that the parchment leaf reflects an

---

Neukirchen-Vluyn: Neukirchener Verlag, 1981) 176–79; Hanan Eshel, "A Note on 'Miqvaot' at Sepphoris," in *Archaeology and the Galilee: Texts and Contexts* in *the Graeco-Roman and Byzantine Periods* (ed. Douglas R. Edwards and C. Thomas McCollough; Atlanta: Scholars Press, 1997) 131–33. I thank Hanan Eshel for some of these bibliographical references and for discussing the matter with me.

[29] On the need to reintroduce apocryphal material in the question of the historical Jesus, see my article "Le Jésus historique à travers les recherches récentes," *Cahier Évangile et Liberté* 118 (April 1993) III–IV.

[30] *Complete Gospels*, 412–15.

[31] *The Five Gospels: The Search for the Authentic Words of Jesus*, A New Translation and Commentary by Robert W. Funk, Roy W. Hoover, and the Jesus Seminar (San Francisco: HarperSanFrancisco, 1993); *Acts of Jesus*, 208–9, 212. Without warning, the translation omits the lines 1–7 and contains the mistake mentioned above in n. 24. The fragment is also briefly presented and quoted in its entirety by Robert W. Funk in *New Gospel Parallels* (2 vols.; Philadelphia: Fortress, 1985) 1:XIX and 2:19 (in parallel to John 2:13–25); idem, *New Gospel Parallels* 1.2: *Mark*, XI, 123 (in parallel to Mark 7:1–13), and 185 (in parallel to Mark 11:28–33). The translation contains the same mistake as mentioned above in n. 24.

[32] John Dominic Crossan just notes: "This fragmented account of a debate between Jesus and a Pharisaic chief priest is formally more developed than the debates in the *Egerton Gospel* or Mark 7, so it may be dated tentatively around the eighties (Cameron 1982:53)" (*The Historical Jesus: The Life of a Mediterranean Jewish Peasant* [San Francisco: HarperSanFrancisco, 1992] 430).

[33] See James H. Charlesworth and Craig A. Evans, "Jesus in the Agrapha and Apocryphal Gospels," in *Studying the Historical Jesus: Evaluations of the State of Current Research* (ed. Bruce Chilton and Craig A. Evans; NTTS 19; Leiden: Brill, 1994) 485, 487, and 492; Otfried Hofius, "Unknown Sayings of Jesus," in *The Gospel and the Gospels* (ed. Peter Stuhlmacher; Grand Rapids: Eerdmans, 1991) 351–52 and 358. Craig A. Evans does not mention the *Fragment Oxyrhynchus* 840 (*Noncanonical Writings and New Testament Interpretation* [Peabody, Mass.: Hendrickson, 1992]).

[34] David Tripp, "Meanings of the Foot-Washing: John 13 and Oxyrhynchus Papyrus 840," *ExpTim* 103 (1992) 237–39.

[35] Ibid., 238.

inner-Christian polemic.[36] According to Tripp, the author of the fragment opposed mainstream Christians "as being too close to Judaism in their acceptance of material sacraments."[37]

III. Interpretation of the Text

The acephalous beginning of the text (lines 1–7) constitutes the end of an indictment. As I do not know who at this point may have been the Savior's opponents, I will not try to analyze this outburst.[38] I prefer to concentrate on the rest of the fragment, what can be considered, according to criteria of form criticism, a literary unit, namely, the polemical dialogue between the priest and the Savior (lines 7–45):

2.1 καὶ παραλαβὼν αὐτοὺς | εἰσήγαγεν εἰς αὐτο το ἁγνευτήριον και | περιεπάτει ἐν τῷ ἱερῷ. 2.2 καὶ προσε[λ]|10 θὼν Φαρισαῖός τις ἀρχιερεὺς Λευ[εὶς] | τὸ ὄνομα συνέτυχεν αὐτοῖς και ε[ἶπε]ν | τῷ σω(τῆ)ρι· τίς ἐπέτρεψέν σοι πατ[εῖν] | τοῦτο το ἁγνευτήριον καὶ ἰδεῖν [ταῦ]τα τὰ ἅγια σκεύη μήτε λουσα[μ]έν[ῳ] μ[ή] | 15 τε μὴν τῶν μαθητῶν σου τοὺς π[όδας βα]|πτισθέντων; 2.3 ἀλλα μεμολυ[μμένος] | ἐπάτησας τοῦτο το ἱερόν, τ[όπον ὄν]|τα καθαρόν, ὃν οὐδεὶς ἄ[λλος εἰ μὴ] | λουσάμενος καὶ ἀλλά[ξας τὰ ἐνδύ]|20 ματα πατεῖ, οὐδὲ ὁ[ρᾶν τολμᾷ ταῦτα] | τὰ ἅγια σκεύη.
2.4 και σ[ταθεὶς εὐθὺς ὁ σωτὴρ] | σ[ὺν τ]οῖς μαθηταῖ[ς αὐτοῦ ἀπεκρίθη·] ‖ σὺ οὖν ἐνταῦθα ὢν ἐν τῷ ἱερῷ καθα|ρεύει; 2.5 λέγει αὐτῷ ἐκεῖνος· καθαρεύω· ἐλουσά|25 μην γὰρ ἐν τῇ λίμνῃ τοῦ Δ(αυεὶ)δ και δι' ἐτέ|ρας κλίμακος κατελθὼν δι' ἑτέρας | ἀ[ν]ῆλθον, 2.6 καὶ λευκὰ ἐνδύματα ἐνε|δυσάμην καὶ καθαρά, καὶ τότε ἦλθο(ν) | καὶ προσέβλεψα τούτοις τοῖς ἁγίοις | 30 σκεύεσιν.
2.7 ὁ σω(τὴ)ρ πρὸς αὐτὸν ἀπο||[κρι]θεὶς εἶπεν· οὐαί, τυφλοὶ μὴ ὁρῶ(ν)|τ[ε]ς· σὺ ἐλούσω τούτοις τοῖς χεομένοις | ὕ[δ]ασι(ν), ἐν οἷς κύνες καὶ χοῖροι βέβλην|[ται] νυκτὸς καὶ ἡμέρας, 2.8 και νιψάμε|35 [ν]ος τὸ ἐκτὸς δέρμα ἐσμήξω, ὅπερ| [κα]ὶ αἱ πόρναι καὶ α[ἱ] αὐλητρίδες μυρί|[ζ]ου[σαι κ]αὶ λούουσιν καὶ σμήχουσι | [καὶ κ]αλλωπίζουσι πρὸς ἐπιθυμί|[αν τ]ῶν ἀν(θρώπ)ων, ἔνδοθεν δὲ ἐκεῖ|40[ναι πεπλ]ήρω<ν>ται σκορπίων καὶ| [πάσης ἀδι]κίας. 2.9 ἐγὼ δὲ καὶ οἱ| [μαθηταί μου,] οὓς λέγεις μὴ βεβα|[μμένους,

---

[36] Already Francis Crawford Burkitt considers that the sayings of the Savior that *Fragment Oxyrhynchus* 840 contains "are more likely to represent the ideas of some Egyptian Christians of the second or third century, than to be based upon what Jesus really said in Palestine in the first century" (*The Earliest Sources for the Life of Jesus* [2d ed.; London/Bombay/Sydney: Constable, 1922] 21–22). Roderic Dunkerly directed my attention to this book ("Oxyrhynchus Gospel Fragments," 31).

[37] Tripp, "Meanings of the Foot-Washing," 238.

[38] [...] 1.1 πρότερον προαδικῆσαι πάντα σοφί|ζεται. 1.2 ἀλλὰ προσέχετε μήπως καὶ | ὑμεῖς τὰ ὅμοια αὐτοῖς μάθητε· 1.3 οὐ γὰρ | ἐν τοῖς ζωοῖς μόνοις ἀπολαμβάνου|5σιν οἱ κακοῦργοι τῶν ἀν(θρώπ)ων ἀλλὰ [κ]αὶ | κόλασιν ὑπομένουσιν καὶ πολ[λ]ὴν | βάσανον. This is the text edited by Giuseppe Bonaccorsi, *Vangeli Apocrifi*, 36. "[...] 1.1 before committing some injustice, he devises everything | cleverly. 1.2 But be careful so that | you too do not suffer similar things as they do. 1.3 For it is not in their lives only that the evil-doers among people receive | 5 their retribution, but they will also endure chastisement and much | torment." In 1.3 (line 5 of the text, line 4 of the translation) the evildoers can be present "among the people" or active "against people."

βεβά]μμεθα ἐν ὕδασι ζω|[ῆς αἰωνίου τοῖς κα]τελθοῦσιν ἀπο [τοῦ]|45 [θεοῦ ἐκ τοῦ οὐρανοῦ. ἀλ]λα οὐαὶ [τ]οῖς [...]

2.1 And having taken them | he brought them into the place of purification | and was walking in the temple. 2.2 And having approached, | 10 a certain Pharisee, a chief priest, whose name was Levi, | joined them and said | to the Savior: Who gave you permission to enter | this place of purification and to see these | holy vessels, when you have not washed yourself, nor | 15 have your disciples surely bathed | their feet? 2.3 But you, in a defiled state, | have entered this temple, which is | a pure place that no one enters | nor dares to view these holy vessels | 20 without having first washed themselves and changed their | clothes.

2.4 And immediately the Savior stopped, | and standing with his disciples answered: || Are you then pure in your present state here | in the temple? 2.5 And he replied to him: I am pure, for I have washed | 25 myself in the pool of David, and having | descended by one staircase I came up by | another; 2.6 and I have put on white and | pure clothes, and only then did I come | and lay eyes on these holy | 30 vessels.

2.7 The Savior answered him | saying: Woe unto you, O blind ones, who do not | see! You have washed yourself in these running | waters where dogs and pigs have wallowed | night and day, 2.8 and you have cleansed | 35 and wiped the outside skin which | the prostitutes and flute-girls anoint, | which they wash, and wipe, | and make beautiful for human desire; | but inwardly these women | 40 are full of scorpions and | every wickedness. 2.9 But I and | my disciples, who you say have not | bathed, we have bathed in waters | of eternal life, which come down from | 45 the God of Heaven. But woe unto those [...][39]

---

[39] I quote here the edition of Bonaccorsi, *Vangeli apocrifi*, 36 and 38. It diverges only slightly from the first edition by Grenfell and Hunt, *Oxyrhynchus Papyri*, 6–7. As one can see, the damaged ends or beginnings of some of lines 8–45 make the reconstruction problematic. Besides a few orthographic differences, the differences between the two editions are the following: in 1.1, line 1 Grenfell and Hunt read πρὸ <τοῦ> ἀδικῆσαι, Bonaccorsi προαδικῆσαι; in 2.4, line 21 Grenfell and Hunt reconstruct στάς, Bonaccorsi σταθείς; in 2.8, lines 36–37 Grenfell and Hunt μυρίζουσιν, Bonaccorsi μυρίζουσαι; in 2.8, line 41 Grenfell and Hunt κακίας, Bonaccorsi ἀδικίας; in 2.9, lines 42–43 Grenfell and Hunt βεβαπτίσθαι, Bonaccorsi βεβαμμένοις; in 2.9, lines 44–45 Grenfell and Hunt τοῖς ἐλθοῦσιν ἀπὸ ... , Bonaccorsi τοῖς κατελθοῦσιν ἀπὸ τοῦ θεοῦ ἐκ τοῦ οὐρανοῦ. My intention has not been to give a new critical edition. If I give the Greek text it is only for the convenience of the reader. I have introduced the division of chapters and verses adopted in *Complete Gospels*. But for precise references to the Greek text, I mention also the lines of the fragment included in both the *editio princeps* and Bonaccorsi's edition. This translation is mine. I would like to thank David Warren, who helped me with this translation. The few textual problems have of course an impact on the translation. In 2.7 (lines 31–32) one can also translate "Woe unto the blind who do not see!" In 2.8 (lines 33–34) the dogs and pigs either "wallow" in the running waters or "are cast," two possible translations of βέβλην[ται]. In 2.9 (line 41) the expression "every wickedness" is far from certain. For discussion of other textual problems and their impact on translation, see n. 6 above. The references to the editors and translators are found in nn. 4, 10, 16, and 24 above. In their two editions (plate I of *Oxyrhynchus Papyri*; beside the title page of *Fragment of an Uncanonical Gospel*), Grenfell and Hunt have provided a photograph, but only of the first side (what they call the verso). Through the photographic services of the Bodleian Library, to which I am grateful, I have in my possession a photograph of both sides of the folio. The handwriting is not regular and is probably not the hand of a professional scribe. I admire the sharp eye of the first editors. What they have been able to make out of the fragment is admirable.

The Structure of the Dialogue

A single sentence is enough for the reader to visualize the situation: Jesus has entered sacred space.

The first speech then is introduced: the high priest approaches the group and addresses the Savior. His speech itself is constructed with two sentences: a question about legal permission and an accusation to support the question.

The answer of the Savior is then introduced. He is depicted as standing with his disciples, and his answer is extremely short. In fact he does not answer the question at all, but questions the priest's own purity.

The priest's reaction is immediate (here no narrative introduction is mentioned): he claims to be pure and then explains what he did to reach this state of ritual purity. His description includes four elements: bathing in the pool of David, dressing in new clothes, coming here, and contemplating the holy vessels. The priest therefore agrees to discuss Jesus' question and puts aside his own issue.

The high point of the episode is Jesus' vehement reaction to the priest's explanation. A severe denunciation opens the Savior's speech ("Woe unto you, O blind ones who do not see"). Before being interrupted by the abrupt end of the fragment, the Savior opposes two attitudes: the sinful attitude of the priests ("you" and the other "blind") and the legitimate attitude of himself and his disciples ("I" and "my disciples").

The modern reader can trace both the way in which the passage is constructed and the way its dialogue moves to a climax in the last words of the Savior. The episode can be represented graphically in this way:

Situation of the Savior and His Disciples (2.1)
    Verbal Reaction of the Priest (2.2–3)
        Short Reply of the Savior Shifting the Topic (2.4)
    Answer to the Priest (2.5–6)
        Verbal Denunciation by the Savior (2.7–9)

We can imagine a number of possible conclusions: a victorious departure of Jesus and his disciples, or a defeated withdrawal of the priest, or a cry of admiration by the crowd.

Characters, Sacred Places, and the Ritual of Purification

In order to understand the document fully, it is useful to examine characters, places, and rituals. The name of the major character, Jesus, does not appear in the text; the title Savior is the phrase used to identify him. This practice is different from the canonical Gospels and reminds us of the *Gospel of Peter*, Ignatius of Antioch, 2 Peter, and Gnostic and Manichaean texts.[40]

---

[40] *Gos. Pet.* 4.13; Ignatius, *Eph.* 1.1; *Magn.* inscr.; *Phld.* 9.2; 2 Pet 1:1, 11; 2:20; 3:18; *Dial. Sav.*

The name Levi[41] and his two epithets "chief priest" (or "high priest") and "Pharisee" serve a literary purpose. These identifiers help the narrator to construct a character who is responsible for correct ritual performances and purity regulations. The reader is therefore facing two religious leaders, the Savior and the high priest, who are representatives of their communities.[42]

The mention of "dogs and pigs" should be understood allegorically, as in 2 Pet 2:22.[43] This expression for describing pagans and sinners[44] must be considered in conjunction with the reference to "prostitutes and flute-girls" (2.8) as an allusion to human sinful presence in the world outside the community. The chief priest and the Savior both have to take this negative reality into consideration.

Scholars interested here in comparing the descriptions of the sites in the text to the actual topography of Jerusalem have met serious difficulties. While it is true that "the pool of David" may be a *miqveh* (some have been discovered in recent excavations), a specific *miqveh* with the name of David remains unknown, and the description of the pool with its two sets of stairs (one for going down and one for going up)[45] is very similar to the structure of an early Christian baptistery. It is possible that vessels from the table for the bread of the Presence were presented to believers. Jewish pilgrims could see inside the sanctuary when the curtain was removed, but they could not see the vessels which were then covered. There was only one exceptional occasion to view them, the day after the completion of the festival,[46] when the vessels were washed and cleansed.[47]

(NHC III, 5), for example; *Cologne Mani Codex* 79.21, as example. On the *Cologne Mani Codex*, see n. 104 below.

[41] The name of Jesus' opponent is not completely preserved, and what remains is not easy to read (2.2). Levi is the most probable reading. Safrai suggests that the original story was the story of a Levite and that this title was later transformed into a proper name, Levi, who received then the title of "high priest" (*Die Wallfahrt im Zeitalter des Zweiten Tempels*, 176 n. 150).

[42] No names of Jesus' followers are mentioned, but the traditional word "disciples" is present (2.4 and 2.9; this second occurrence is a reconstruction of the text).

[43] See also Matt 7:6; Rev 22:15; Ignatius, *Eph.* 7.1. On the spiritual meanings of animals, dogs and pigs in particular, see François Bovon, *De vocatione gentium. Histoire de l'interprétation d'Act. 10,1–11,18 dans les six premiers siècles* (BGBE 8; Tübingen: Mohr Siebeck, 1967) 100–2, 128–29, and passim. On the allegorical tendency of the text, see Lagrange, "Nouveau fragment non canonique relatif à l'Évangile," 549.

[44] Associated with them are the "scorpions" (2.8), whose symbolic value is well known from the readers of the Bible in antiquity (see *Complete Gospels*, 415).

[45] Two Jewish texts quoted in this connection, *Letter of Aristeas* 106 and *m. Šeqal.* 8:2, speak certainly of the circulation of pure and impure people, but do not mention explicitly two distinct stairs; see n. 28 above.

[46] See Büchler, "New 'Fragment of an Uncanonical Gospel,'" 338.

[47] *B. Yoma* 54a: see *Hebrew-English Edition of the Babylonian Talmud: Yoma* (trans. Leo Jung; ed. I. Epstein; new ed.; London/Jerusalem/New York: Soncino, 1974) 54a; *b. Ḥag.* 26a–26b: see *Hebrew-English Edition of the Babylonian Talmud: Taʿanith, Megillah, Ḥagigah* (trans. J. Rabinowitz; ed. I. Epstein; London: Soncino, 1984) 26a–26b; *b. Menaḥ.* 96b: see *The Babylonian Talmud: Seder Ḳodashim* (trans. Eli Cashdan; ed. I. Epstein; London: Soncino, 1948) 590; *y. Ḥag.* 3:8: see *The Talmud of the Land of Israel: A Preliminary Translation and Explanation,*

Rather than comparing the text with actual sites in Jerusalem, it may be more appropriate to examine how the text constructs the holy sites from a literary point of view. Twice the reader encounters references to a special holy site, namely τὸ ἁγνευτήριον. The meaning of this term is etymologically easy to recognize as "the place of purification" but more difficult to define with precision because it occurs so rarely. Searching the whole Greek literature of antiquity, Henri Estienne, Liddell-Scott-Jones, and Bauer-Aland mention only one non-Christian occurrence, in a fragment of the work of a Stoic philosopher of the first century C.E., Chaeremon.[48] Later, Gregory of Nazianzus uses the term twice.[49]

This place is related to τὸ ἱερόν, "the temple" or "the temple area." The two terms τὸ ἱερόν and τὸ ἁγνευτήριον seem to describe two close and related places, like a building and its precinct, not a building and an inner room.[50] In 2.1, Jesus enters "the place of purification" and walks into "the temple," an action that the priest confirms in 2.2. In 2.4 Jesus says that the priest who stands beside him finds

---

vol. 20 (trans. Jacob Neusner; CSHJ; Chicago/London: University of Chicago Press, 1986) 122. Some coins struck during the Bar-Kokhba revolt show the facade of the temple and the table of proposition; see Dan Barag, "The Table of the Showbread and the Facade of the Temple on Coins of the Bar-Kokhba Revolt," in *Ancient Jerusalem Revealed* (ed. Hillel Geva; [Israel]: Israel Exploration Society, 1994) 272–76. I thank Hanan Eshel for several bibliographical references.

[48] See Henri Estienne (Stephanus), *Thesaurus Graecae Linguae* (Paris: Firmin-Didot, 1831) s.v.; LSJ, s.v.; Walter Bauer, Kurt Aland, and Barbara Aland, *Griechisch-deutsches Wörterbuch zu den Schriften des Neuen Testaments und der frühchristlichen Literatur* (6th ed.; Berlin/New York: de Gruyter, 1988), s.v.; see Chaeremon, *Hist.* 4, in *Fragmenta Historicorum Graecorum* (ed. Karl Otfried Müller; 5 vols. in 6; Paris: Didot, 1849) 3:495. The fragment has been preserved by Porphyry, *De abstinentia* 4.6; it is now fragment 10 in the edition of Pieter Willem van der Horst, *Chaeremon, Egyptian Priest and Stoic Philosopher: The Fragments Collected and Translated with Explanatory Notes* (EPRO 101; Leiden: Brill, 1984) 18–19. I am quoting van der Horst's text and translation: ἢ ἁγνευτήρια τοῖς μὴ καθαρεύουσιν ἄδυτα καὶ πρὸς ἱερουργίας ἅγια κατανεμομένοις ("or with those who divided among themselves the rooms of purification and fasting which were inaccessible to those who were not pure and which were set apart for the religious services").

[49] Gregory of Nazianzus, *Or.* 4.111 (PG 35:648C), about some projects of Julian to imitate the Christian institutions; see Gregory of Nazianzus, *Discours 4–5 contre Julien* (intro., critical text, trans., and ann. Jean Bernardi; SC 309; Paris: Cerf, 1983) 266–69; Bernardi does not pay attention to this rare word; and *Carm.* 1.2.34.224 (PG 37:961A): the people are a reunion of God's worshipers, the temple is a venerable place of purification for the people (ναὸς δὲ λαοῦ σεπτὸν ἁγνευτήριον). A search in the *TLG* brought only one more occurrence to light. In the *Lexica Segueriana. Glossae rhetoricae (e cod. Coislin. 345)*, s.v. ἱστιατόρια (= ἑστιατόρια), we read that this word means "now the so-called ἁγνευτήρια, namely places to stay." See *Anecdota Graeca* 1 (ed. I. Bekker; Berlin: Nauck, 1814; reprinted in Graz: Akademische Druck- und Verlagsanstalt, 1965) 267 line 9. The work seems to be used by Photius in his *Λέξεων συναγωγή* and is therefore anterior to the ninth century C.E. It is strange that the term ἱστιατόρια is explained by the rare word ἁγνευτήρια. Strange also is the meaning given to ἁγνευτήρια as "place to stay." But if we are in the context of pilgrimage or monastic life, it is not completely surprising, even if unusual, that space reserved for the pilgrims or guests be called ἁγνευτήρια. I thank Annewies van den Hoek, who found this reference for me.

[50] On this point I agree with *Complete Gospels*, 414.

himself "here in the temple." The stop at "the place of purification" was necessary
for a lustration, a washing of the feet and hands, before entering the temple to see
the holy vessels. This ἁγνευτήριον reminds the reader of the water basin or fountain, located outside an ancient Christian basilica, often in the middle of the atri-
um preceding the church.[51] Even today the Roman Catholic tradition expects an
ablution from its baptized members before entering the church. In a Greek monastery, the water basin is now called a φιάλη, and it is possible that Gregory of
Nazianzus used the term ἁγνευτήριον to describe the place around such a water
basin or fountain.[52]

But how do we connect this ἁγνευτήριον, "place of purification," to ἡ λίμνη
τοῦ Δαυείδ, "the pool of David" (2.5)? This "pool" is distinct from both the
"place of purification" and the "temple." It is a place for total ritual immersion,
followed by a symbolic and concrete change of clothes. I contend that "the pool
of David," like the "place of purification," is connected to the ritual of mainstream Christian or Jewish-Christian communities. The descent from one side of
the pool and the ascent on the other is reminiscent of the baptismal ceremonies
described in the catechetical homilies of Ambrose of Milan or Theodore of Mopsuestia.[53] This description also fits the archaeological remains of baptisteries in
Tunisia, Greece, and Italy.[54] The author seems to face a community scrupulous
about ritual practices employing holy water. The priest under attack in our story
proclaims the necessity of both the full water baptism and the regular partial
lustration, probably of the feet and hands.

The richness of terminology concerning ritual purity cannot be a coincidence.
The verb λούομαι, "to bathe," occurs no fewer than four times (lines 14, 19, 24–25,
32),[55] βαπτίζω, "to dip," "to baptize," once or twice (lines 15–16, and perhaps
42–43),[56] βάπτω, "to dip," "to bathe," once or twice (lines 42–43),[57] νίπτω, "to
wash," "to cleanse" hands or feet, once (lines 34–35 in a profane sense), μολύνω,
"to defile," once (line 16), ἀλλάσσω τὰ ἐνδύματα, "to change clothes" (lines 19–
20) (later in 2.6 the new clothes are called λευκά, "white"[58] and καθαρά, "clean,"
"pure" [line 28]). Twice in 2.4 and 2.5 the text uses the classical verb καθαρεύω,
"to be pure," or "to be clean" (lines 23–24, 24), which in the early Christian lit-

---

[51] See H. Leclercq, "Canthare," *DACL* 2.2:1955–69.

[52] See n. 49 above.

[53] See Ambrose of Milan, *Des sacrements, Des mystères, L'explication du symbole* (ed., trans.,
and ann. Bernard Botte; 2d ed.; SC 25; Paris: Cerf, 1961); Theodore of Mopsuestia, *Les homélies
catéchétiques. Reproduction phototypique du ms. Mingana Syr. 561 (Selly Oak Colleges' Library, Birmingham)* (trans., intro., and index Raymond Tonneau with Robert Devreesse; Studi
e Testi 145; Vatican City: Biblioteca apostolica Vaticana, 1949).

[54] See Friedrich Wilhelm Deichmann, "Baptisterium," *RAC* 1:1157–67.

[55] In line 37 the active λούω, "to wash," is used in a profane sense.

[56] This second occurrence is text-critically not secure.

[57] These two occurrences are text-critically not secure.

[58] Or "bright," line 27.

erature is present only in the *Gospel of Peter*[59] (the transitive verb καθαρίζω, "to purify," is the usual verb among Christians). Other typical vocabulary: χέω, "to pour out," "to let run" (used here for the polluted waters) (line 32), σμήχω, "to wipe off," "to wipe," twice (lines 35, 37), μυρίζω, "to anoint," "to perfume," once (lines 36–37), λούω, "to wash," once (line 37),[60] and καλλωπίζω, "to make the face beautiful" (line 38) (these four last verbs apply to the gestures of the discredited women).

Besides the terminology of purity one must recognize the importance of two other semantic fields. The first concerns the movement of walking. In this context it must be understood as a solemn liturgical approach, as in the Epistle to the Hebrews.[61] The verbs πατῶ (lines 12, 17, 20)[62] and περιπατῶ (line 9) do not here describe a walk, but a religious procession within a sacred place. The second semantic field concerns the vocabulary of vision. The infinitives ἰδεῖν (line 13) and ὁρᾶν (line 20)[63] occur at a strategic point,[64] and they describe the religious contemplation of the holy vessels.

It is not clear to what the expression τὰ ἅγια σκεύη, "the holy vessels," refers. Contrary to previous scholars, I would not interpret this expression exclusively in the framework of ancient Judaism. If one also considers the text to be a window into Christian controversies, the "holy vessels" may describe early Christian liturgical utensils. Actually these very terms are used in the writings of early church authors to describe the vessels for the Eucharist, the "chalice" and the "plate."[65] Christians also gave a special meaning to the verb σκευοφορῶ, to "carry the holy vessels."[66] They coined the σκευοφυλάκιον for the "sacristy,"[67] and σκευοφύλαξ for the "sacristan,"[68] and the Council of Laodicea (canon 21) made a formal deci-

---

[59] *Gos. Pet.* 11.46 on the lips of Pilate, who declares himself to be pure of the blood of Christ.

[60] See n. 55 above.

[61] See W. Thüsing, "'Laßt uns hinzutreten … ' (Hebr 10:22)," *BZ* n.s. 9 (1965) 1–17; Erich Grässer, *An die Hebräer* (3 vols.; EKKNT 17; Zurich: Benziger; Neukirchen-Vluyn: Neukirchener Verlag, 1990–1997) 3:13–15.

[62] The first occurrence is text-critically not certain.

[63] This occurrence is text-critically not certain.

[64] The verb ὁράω, "to see," is used with the negation to describe the dramatic situation of the spiritually blind.

[65] Eusebius, *De martyribus Palestinae* 12 (see Eusebius, *Über die Märtyrer in Palästina* [ed. Eduard Schwartz; GCS 9.2; Leipzig: Hinrichs, 1908] 947); Athanasius, *Epistula ad episcopos Aegypti et Libyae* 19 (PG 25:584A); *Constitutiones apostolicae* 8.21.4 (see *Les Constitutions apostoliques*, vol. 3 [ed. Marcel Metzger; SC 336; Paris: Cerf, 1987] 222); Epiphanius, *Panarion* 68.7 (see Epiphanius, *Panarion*, vol. 2 [ed. Karl Holl; 2d ed. by Jürgen Dummer; GCS; Berlin: Akademie-Verlag, 1980] 148.6; PG 42:196C); Council of Laodicea, canon 21 (see n. 69 below). I owe these references to *PGL*, s.v.

[66] Cyril of Alexandria, *Comm. on Is.* 5.1 (PG 70:1164), s.v., in an explanation of Isa 52:11 (the biblical passage contains the following expression: οἱ φέροντες τὰ σκεύη κυρίου). Cyril gives a spiritual meaning to the verb. I owe this reference to *PGL*, s.v.

[67] Several references in *PGL*, s.v.

[68] Several references in *PGL*, s.v.

sion concerning the "vessels of the Lord."[69] Participation in the arcane discipline of the Eucharist was prohibited for the unbaptized. The church required that they leave after the liturgy of the Word and before the liturgy of the sacred meal, a rule that was applied from a very early time, even in the time of the *Didache* (9.5). The contemplation of the "holy vessels" may refer to a Jewish custom, but the author may also have a problem of Christian discipline in mind. The priest in the narrative requires a liturgically correct practice of the baptism to allow a correct performance of the Eucharist, while the Savior requests the right of every believer who is spiritually pure to enter into the community worship and to have access to the contemplation of the divine world. A purity that is only external is similar to the external beauty of a great sinner: it obscures ethical and spiritual impurity. To make this case, the author relies on the Jesus tradition of the Synoptic Gospels (see Mark 7:1–23; Matt 15:1–20; Luke 11:37–41) and mocks the opponents with the use of the literary formula of the "Woe!" known from the Sayings Source Q (see Matt 23:25–29; Luke 11:39–47).[70] To highlight the preliminary purification and the subsequent lustrations, the author appropriates a tradition embedded in the Johannine narrative of the washing of the feet (John 13:1–17).[71] To describe the ritual of purification in the so-called "pool of David," he or she has in mind the actual practice of mainstream Christianity.

What is important is not only the presence of the utensils but the religious experience of contemplating them. Evidence exists, particularly from some Christians Acts of the martyrs, that such contemplation was part of Christian religious experiences.[72]

IV. Waters and Vessels

I am tempted to see the figure of the priest as a representative or leader of the mainstream church defending ritual purity, and the figure of the Savior as the representative of a sectarian Christian group demanding ethical and spiritual purity. The vocabulary that creates a problem for the partisans of a "historical Jesus"

---

[69] See *Acta et symbola conciliorum quae saeculo quarto habita sunt* (Textus Minores 19; Leiden: Brill, 1974) 90: the ὑπηρέται (subdeacons, members of minor orders, or deacons?) are not allowed to touch the vessels of the Lord (οὐ δεῖ ... ἅπτεσθαι δεσποτικῶν σκευῶν). On the contrary in the *Constitutiones apostolicae* 8.21.4 (see n. 65 above), the subdeacons are responsible for the liturgical vessels.

[70] von Harnack, *Aus Wissenschaft und Leben*, 2:243.

[71] Tripp was right to bring these two texts together ("Meanings of the Foot-Washing"); on John 13:1–17, see Raymond E. Brown, *The Gospel According to John (XIII–XXI)* (AB 29A; Garden City, N.Y.: Doubleday, 1970) 548–72, and bibliography at 579–80.

[72] See Michel Meslin, "Vases sacrés et boissons d'éternité dans les visions des martyrs africains," in *Epektasis. Mélanges patristiques offerts au cardinal Jean Daniélou* (ed. Jacques Fontaine and Charles Kannengiesser; Paris: Beauchesne, 1972) 139–53.

approach is precisely the vocabulary that appeals to my hypothesis. The priest walks into the temple to experience the holy vessels. The priest knows how to be ritually pure, namely, to take a bath of purification and to change one's garments. The Savior does not dismiss the goal of viewing the holy utensils, but he contests the ritualistic interpretation of the purity requirement. He prefers the spiritual waters, the waters that confer eternal life. I suggest, therefore, that the fragment fits into the context of the second and third centuries, as these two centuries were periods of violent controversies over baptism.[73]

Jewish Christian Practices

In these centuries, water baptisms and various lustrations were favored traditions. Along with mainstream Christianity, which requires a water baptism,[74] Jewish Christian communities also accepted baptisms, even accentuating the veneration for lustrations and other purifications. At the turn of the second century, according to Epiphanius (*Panarion* 53.1.7),[75] Elchesai and his disciples "honor water and all but regard it as God, for they claim that it is the source of life," so much so that they offer repentant sinners a second baptism.[76] To these believers the baptism of water has been a convenient substitute for burnt sacrifices in the temple of Jerusalem.[77] According to Epiphanius, Ebion and his followers, the Ebionites, practiced several baptisms and ablutions. They also used water for exorcisms and read in their own Gospel that Jesus had come to abolish sacrifices. They referred to a book called the *Ascents of James*, from which they took their aversion to the tem-

---

[73] First-century texts such as Eph 5:26 and Heb 9:13–14 emphasize the spiritual purification brought forth by Christ over against material ritual. The Synoptic Gospels also prefer baptism of the Spirit over baptism of water (Luke 3:16 par.). They remember Jesus' criticism of external piety (Mark 7:14–23 par.; Luke 11:38–41 par.; see *Gos. Thom.* 89), and they recall a saying of Jesus about the metaphorical meaning of the verb "to baptize" (Mark 10:38–39 par.). John 4:10–14 prefers the spiritual water to the material water, and a similar metaphor is present in *Gos. Thom.* 13 and *Odes Sol.* 4.10; 11.6–8; 28.15; 30.1. In the second and the fourth of these passages the spiritual water is pleasing to drink.

[74] See André Benoit, *Le baptême chrétien au second siècle. La théologie des Pères* (EHPhR 43; Paris: Presses Universitaires de France, 1953); and my article "Baptism in the Ancient Church," *STRev* 42 (1999) 429–38.

[75] See Epiphanius, *Panarion*, vol. 2 (ed. Holl; 2d ed.) 315. I am quoting *The Panarion of Epiphanius of Salamis* (2 vols.; trans. Frank Williams; NHS 35–36; Leiden: Brill, 1987–1994) 2:71.

[76] See Hippolytus speaking of Alcibiades, *Elenchos* 9.13.3–4; see also 9.15.1–3, quotation of the *Book of the Revelations* written by Elchesai; see Hippolytus, *Refutatio omnium haeresium* (ed. Paul Wendland; Hippolytus Werke 3; GCS 26; Leipzig: Hinrichs, 1916) 251–53; Joseph Thomas, *Le mouvement baptiste en Palestine et Syrie (150 av. J.-C. – 300 ap. J.-C.)* (Gembloux: Duculot, 1935) 140–56; Luigi Cirillo, "Livre de la révélation d'Elkasaï," in *Écrits apocryphes chrétiens*, 1:829–72, with bibliography at 1:839–41.

[77] See Thomas, *Le mouvement baptiste en Palestine et Syrie*, 182; Michel Tardieu, *Le Manichéisme* (Que sais-je? 1940; Paris: Presses Universitaires de France, 1981) 11.

ple, the sacrifices, and the fire of the altar (*Panarion* 30.1.1–21.6, esp. 30.16.5–7).[78] The interest shown by the *Pseudo-Clementines*[79] in baths and lustrations is also worth mentioning at this point, as well as the Mandaeans, who may be considered the last witnesses of this development. The priest in our fragment fits perfectly into this first trajectory.

Antiritual Tendencies

But there was also the opposite movement, groups eager to minimize the symbolic import of water and even to criticize it openly, and the Savior of the fragment fits perfectly into this second trajectory. Among them the Ophites mentioned immobile waters, which they probably considered negatively, according to Irenaeus (*Adv. haer.* 1.30.1, 3).[80] Close to this group, the Naasenes, according to Hippolytus, used the category of "living water" to distinguish it from natural water (*Elenchos* 5.7.19),[81] and in their spiritual interpretation integrated the notion of temple, saying that the believer enters the "house of God" and becomes a bridegroom (ibid., 5.8.44–45).[82] They felt it was possible, based on an influence of the mysteries,[83] that after an initiation, the Naasene neophyte could receive a vision of the holy reality.[84] This seems similar to the expectation of the author of

---

[78] See Epiphanius, *Panarion*, vol. 1 (ed. Karl Holl; GCS 25; Leipzig: Hinrichs, 1915) 333–62, esp. 354–55; *The Panarion of Epiphanius of Salamis*, 1:119–37. This work has been identified by several scholars with Pseudo-Clementine *Recognitiones* 1.33–71 (or with its content); see Robert E. Van Voorst, *The Ascents of James: History and Theology of a Jewish-Christian Community* (SBLDS 112; Atlanta: Scholars Press, 1989) 44–46.

[79] Peter likes to take a bath every day, morning or evening, in the sea or in a secret place according to the *Ps.-Clem. Hom.* 9.2.5; 9.23.3; 10.1.1–2 and 26.2; 11.1.1; see Thomas, *Le mouvement baptiste in Palestine et Syrie*, 174–81.

[80] See Hans Leisegang, *La gnose* (trans. Jean Gouillard; Paris: Payot, 1951) 81–128, esp. 122.

[81] "The promise of washing (in baptism) is, they say, nothing less than the introduction into unfading enjoyment of him who in their fashion is washed in living water and anointed with unutterable anointing"; see Hippolytus, *Refutatio omnium haeresium* (ed. Wendland), 83; Kurt Rudolph, *Gnosis: The Nature and History of Gnosticism* (trans. and ed. Robert McL. Wilson; New York: HarperSanFrancisco, 1987) 227; see n. 85 below.

[82] Hippolytus, *Refutatio Omnium Haeresium* (ed. Wendland), 97.

[83] See Leisegang, *Gnose*, 90; and Rudolph, *Gnosis*, 285–86.

[84] See April D. De Conick, *Seek to See Him: Ascent and Vision Mysticism in the Gospel of Thomas* (VC Supplement 33; Leiden: Brill, 1996) 12, 26–27 (on the visionary experience in the *Gospel of Thomas*, see pp. 97–172). On a baptismal tradition, preserved particularly in the Nag Hammadi treatise *Zostrianos*, connecting the ritual with heavenly visions, see Harold W. Attridge, "On Becoming an Angel: Rival Baptismal Theologies at Colossae," in *Religious Propaganda and Missionary Competition in the New Testament World: Essays Honoring Dieter Georgi* (ed. Lukas Bornmann, Kelly Del Tredici, Angela Standhartinger; NovTSup 74; Leiden: Brill, 1994) 481–98. On early Syrian Christianity and its interest in knowing God through ecstatic vision, see April D. De Conick, " 'Blessed are Those Who Have Not Seen' (Jn 20:29): Johannine Dramatization of an Early Christian Discourse," in *The Nag Hammadi Library after Fifty Years: Proceedings of the 1995 Society of Biblical Literature Commemoration* (ed. John D. Turner and Anne McGuire; NHS 44; Leiden: Brill, 1997) 381–98.

Fragment Oxyrhynchus 840: that the believer would go through spiritual purification and experience the vision of the spiritual realm.[85]

From the Perates tradition, according to Hippolytus, three elements seem relevant to our topic: first, as their name indicates, they hope to "cross" or "pass," from the material to the spiritual realm, as the Savior of this fragment "walks" through the temple; second, the material world is identified with the negative water; and third, the nonbelievers are allegorically compared with the Egyptians of the scripture drowned in the Red Sea of ignorance (*Elenchos* 5.14–16).[86]

The Valentinians also had a nuanced understanding of water.[87] They accepted water baptism but only as an initial phase that had to be overcome by *gnosis*, understood as spiritual baptism. The "first baptism" is mentioned in the fragments *On Baptism A* and *B*, attached to the *Valentinian Exposition* and preserved in Nag Hammadi Codex XI, 2: it brings forgiveness of sin. Even if the text of the fragment is far from certain, it appears that more important is a "second baptism," representing the spiritual crossing through the waters of the Jordan from this world to the Pleroma, or Aeon. As in *Fragment Oxyrhynchus* 840, this movement is compared to a crossing from blindness to the seeing of God. It is perhaps this passage, this redemption, which is called "my mystery" in the *Exposition* itself.[88]

Interesting for our purposes here is the figure of Marcos the Valentinian, mentioned by Irenaeus (*Adv. haer.* 1.14–21). Even if the text of Irenaeus is difficult and polemical, we can ascertain that the main ritual of Marcos and his community was the "redemption," a ritual distinct from baptism, a spiritualization of both baptism and Eucharist introducing the initiate into the holy chamber. Again some elements are notable here: the critical interpretation of water ritual, the redemption understood as the other baptism announced by Christ in Luke 12:50, the importance of mysterious contemplation of the divine realm, and finally the fact that Irenaeus understood Marcos's teaching as a threat to church baptism (*Adv. haer.* 1.21.1).[89]

Other texts from the Nag Hammadi corpus contain not only positive statements regarding spiritual water or the water of life but also several explicitly po-

---

[85] According to Hippolytus (*Elenchos* 5.9.15–21), the Naasenes gave an allegorical and anthropological interpretation of the four rivers from paradise and used John 4:10 (in a shortened form) to describe the spiritual water, located above the firmament and accessible only to the spiritual believers, the so-called "elect of the living water"; see Hippolytus, *Refutatio Omnium Haeresium* (ed. Wendland), 101–2; Leisegang, *Gnose*, 100–1; Jean-Marie Sevrin, *Le dossier baptismal séthien. Études sur la sacramentaire gnostique* (Bibliothèque copte de Nag Hammadi. Section "Études" 2; Québec: Presses de l'Université Laval, 1986) 27.

[86] See Hippolytus, *Refutatio omnium haeresium* (ed. Wendland), 108–14; Leisegang, *Gnosis*, 105–6.

[87] See Rudolph, *Gnosis*, 317–25.

[88] *The Nag Hammadi Library* (ed. James M. Robinson; rev. ed.; New York; HarperSanFrancisco, 1990) 482. The fragments *On Baptism A* and *B* are translated on p. 488.

[89] On Marcos the Valentinian, see Rudolph, *Gnosis*, 243–44, 324.

lemical passages against water baptismal ritual.[90] In fact, the *Paraphrase of Shem* (NHC VII, 1) is openly hostile to water baptism:[91] "For I foretell it to those who have a heart. They will refrain from the impure baptism. And those who take heart from the light of the Spirit will not have dealings with the impure practice" (*Paraph. Shem* 38.3–9).[92] In 37.22–24 water is declared dark and nauseating. In 4.27–5.36 it is connected with sexuality and thus viewed negatively. In the *Testimony of Truth* (NHC IX, 3) the polemic against baptism aims probably not only at the *catholica* but also at the Valentinian movement.[93] The adversaries, according to the author, do not realize that through water baptism they are entering the realm of death (55.4–18)[94] and that "the baptism of truth is something else" (69.22–23). The last pages of the *Apocalypse of Adam* (NHC V, 5) confirm that pessimistic view: the water of life is said to have been polluted by the people with *epithymia*, which is considered the opposite of knowledge (83–85).[95]

Other Nag Hammadi tractates, such as the *Apocryphon of John* (NHC II, 1; III, 1; IV, 1; BG 8502,2), mention the expressions "water of life" and "light-water."[96] In the *Trimorphic Protennoia* (NHC XIII, 1) the Word brings living water (46.14–33), and true baptism is made tangible by the initiate dressing in a special garment (45.12–20).[97] True baptism is knowledge.[98] In *Zostrianos* (NHC VIII, 1), Zostrianos passes into heaven through numerous baptisms but returns to this world to establish a temple for himself. He calls others not to enter into water baptism, which would bring them into death (131.2–8).[99] In the *Tractate without Title* of the Bruce Codex, the reader meets the spiritual construction of a "place of metanoia." These references to sacred places are interesting if we accept that the author of the *Fragment Oxyrhynchus* 840 is perhaps offering an allegorical inter-

---

[90] See Sevrin, *Le dossier baptismal séthien*; and Françoise Morard, "L'Apocalypse d'Adam du Codex V de Nag Hammadi et sa polémique anti-baptismale," *RevScRel* 51 (1977) 214–33.

[91] In his introduction to the *Paraph. Shem*, Michel Roberge writes: "The baptismal rite is essentially bad because of its use of water – a primordial impure power, which in the beginning tried to detain the light of the Spirit and now tries to keep men prisoner through baptism ... . This part of the tractate contains a harsh antibaptismal polemic, probably directed against the Great Church" (*Nag Hammadi Library*, 341).

[92] Trans. Frederik Wisse in *Nag Hammadi Library*, 357.

[93] See the introduction by Birger A. Pearson in *Nag Hammadi Library*, 448–49.

[94] Trans. Søren Giversen and Birger A. Pearson in *Nag Hammadi Library*, 456.

[95] Trans. George W. MacRae in *Nag Hammadi Library*, 285–86; see Françoise Morard, *L'Apocalypse d'Adam (NH V,5), texte établi et présenté* (Bibliothèque copte de Nag Hammadi. Section "Textes" 15; Québec: Presses de l'Université Laval, 1985) 56–61 and 114–26; see also Sevrin, *Le dossier baptismal séthien*, 169–70.

[96] *Ap. John* (NHC II, 1 and IV, 1) 4.21 and 4.25–26; see *Nag Hammadi Library*, 107; Sevrin, *Le dossier baptismal séthien*, 14.

[97] Trans. John D. Turner in *Nag Hammadi Library*, 519–20.

[98] See Sevrin, *Le dossier baptismal séthien*, 77–78.

[99] Trans. John N. Sieber in *Nag Hammadi Library*, 430.

pretation of the temple. The Perates – we remember – described an allegorical interpretation of the crossing of the Red Sea.[100]

Among the adversaries of water baptism in the second century c.e., Justin the Gnostic deserves a special place. He not only rejects the catholic ritual, but in a theological statement he opposes two ontologically different kinds of water. The manner in which he does so is important for us because it is very similar to what the Savior does in our fragment. Here is the text of Justin quoted by Hippolytus (*Elenchos* 5.27.3): διακεχώρισται γάρ, φησίν, ἀνὰ μέσον ὕδατος καὶ ὕδατος, καὶ ἔστιν ὕδωρ τὸ ὑποκάτω τοῦ στερεώματος τῆς πονηρᾶς κτίσεως, ἐν ᾧ λούονται οἱ χοϊκοὶ καὶ ψυχικοὶ ἄνθρωποι, καὶ ὕδωρ ἐστὶν ὑπεράνω τοῦ στερεώματος τοῦ ἀγαθοῦ ζῶν, ἐν ᾧ λούονται οἱ πνευματικοὶ ζῶντες ἄνθρωποι ... ("A division has been established, he says, in the middle between water and water. There is the water which is below the foundation of this evil creation, in which the earthly and natural human beings are washed; and there is the living water which is above the good foundation, in which the spiritual living human beings are washed").[101] Justin believes that some, like our priest Levi, are baptized in impure waters that bring only the illusion of purification, while others, like the Savior and his disciples of the Oxyrhynchus folio, appreciate the spiritual water of life.

Not too dissimilar from the above mentioned texts is the position of the Archontics, mentioned by Epiphanius in his *Panarion* (40).[102] Though not as well known, but nevertheless still active in the fourth century, the Archontics spread out as far as Armenia, but most established themselves in Palestine. "They condemn baptism even though some of them were previously baptized. They reject participation in the (church) sacraments (mysteries) and deny their value, as extraneous and introduced in the name of the (demiurge) Sabaoth ... and when (the soul) acquires 'knowledge' (*gnosis*) and shuns the baptism of the Church and the name of Sabaoth who has given men the Law it ascends from heaven to heaven ... " (*Panarion* 40.2.6).[103]

---

[100] See text above.

[101] See Hippolytus, *Refutatio omnium haeresium* (ed. Wendland), 133. Hippolytus quotes a work by Justin the Gnostic called *The Book of Baruch*; see Leisegang, *Gnose*, 110–17; Ludwig Koenen, "From Baptism to the Gnosis of Manichaeism," in *The Rediscovery of Gnosticism: Proceedings of the International Conference on Gnosticism at Yale, New Haven, Connecticut, March 28–31, 1978* (2 vols.; ed. Bentley Layton; SHR 41; Leiden: Brill, 1980) 2:734–56, esp. 753; Sevrin, *Le dossier baptismal séthien*, 753; S. Lilla, "Justin le gnostique," in *Dictionnaire encyclopédique du christianisme ancien* (2 vols.; Paris: Cerf, 1990) 2:1386.

[102] See Epiphanius, *Panarion*, vol. 2 (ed. Holl) 80–90.

[103] See Epiphanius, *Panarion*, vol. 2 (ed. Holl) 82–83; quoted by Rudolph, *Gnosis*, 220. Rudolph mentions their asceticism (p. 257) and tells the story of the sect (p. 326). See Werner Foerster, *Die Gnosis*, 1, *Zeugnisse der Kirchenväter* (Zurich: Artemis, 1969) 378–82.

The Mani Codex

The discovery of the *Cologne Mani Codex* provided explicit evidence of Mani's growing opposition to the Jewish-Christian ritual of his youth.[104] We now know that in the wake of an initial revelatory vision, he tried to convince his early companions, probably Elkesaites, of the vanity of their water baptism. This brought him into an open dogmatic conflict that ended in his expulsion from the community. His only solution was then to establish a new religious movement. Here is a quotation of the *Cologne Mani Codex* explaining Mani's criticism of the purification ritual of his baptist opponents:

Therefore inspect yourself and find out what your purity means. For it is impossible to make your bodies entirely clean. Every day the body is set in motion and (again) stands still, because it discharges the waste of digestion. Accordingly, your rite (sc. baptism) is performed without a commandment of the Savior. Hence the purification mentioned in the Scriptures is the purification through gnosis, i.e., the separation of Light from Darkness, of Death from Life, of Living Waters from Turbid waters (τῶν ζώντων ὑδά[τω]ν ἐκ τῶν τεθαμβω[μέ]νων). You should recognize that the one is different from the other (i.e., Light from Darkness, etc.), and [you should keep] the commandments of the Savior in order that he may redeem [your] soul [too] from [ruin] and destruction. (83.20–85.1)[105]

It is also interesting to note that white garments played an important role in the Elkesaite movement, to which Mani's father attached himself and which Mani later attacked. The *Cologne Mani Codex* calls these people "baptists."[106] The Mesopotamian Theodor Bar Konai (eighth century C.E.), writing in Syriac, says that they called themselves *ḥele' ḥewāre'*, "white garments."[107] The sharp opposition between the Savior and the priest parallels particularly well the disputes between Mani and his former Elkesaite companions as described in the *Cologne Mani Codex*. We know that Mani used the Synoptic and apocryphal material related to Jesus' controversies with the Pharisees over purity. We know also that he conformed his own life as much as possible to the Savior's life,[108] an expression of his opposition to Jewish Christian practices. The terminology, the theological

---

[104] See the edition of Albert Henrichs and Ludwig Koenen, "Der Kölner Mani-Kodex (P. Colon. inv. nr. 4780) ΠΕΡΙ ΤΗΣ ΓΕΝΝΗΣ ΤΟΥ ΣΩΜΑΤΟΣ ΑΥΤΟΥ," *ZPE* 19 (1975) 1–85; *ZPE* 32 (1978) 87–199; *ZPE* 44 (1981) 201–318; *ZPE* 48 (1982) 1–59.

[105] See Henrichs and Koenen, "Der Kölner Mani-Kodex," *ZPE* (1978) 102–5.

[106] This name is confirmed by Ibn al-Nadim, the Arabic encyclopedist of the tenth century. He calls them *al-mughtasila*, "those who washed themselves"; see Tardieu, *Le Manichéisme*, 7.

[107] See Tardieu, *Le Manichéisme*, 8.

[108] Koenen writes: "To some extent, Mani's speech imitates Jesus' disputes with the Pharisees about their purificatory rites ..." ("From Baptism to the Gnosis of Manichaeism," 734). Tardieu writes: "Comme Mani enfant copie Jésus enfant, le jeune Mani disputant avec les autorités de sa communauté imite le Jésus des controverses antijudaïsantes rapportées par les Synoptiques" (*Le Manichéisme*, 15). See also Michel Tardieu, "Le procès de Jésus vu par les Manichéens," *Apocrypha* 8 (1997) 9–23; idem, "Principes de l'exégèse manichéenne du Nouveau Testament," in *Les règles de l'interprétation* (ed. Michel Tardieu; Centre d'études des religions du livre. Patrimoines, religions du Livre; Paris: Cerf, 1987) 123–46.

categories, and the atmosphere of *Fragment Oxyrhynchus* 840 are much more similar to the disputes between Mani and the Elkesaites than to the Synoptic Gospels and the Jewish texts on ritual purity.

V. Conclusion

Fragment Oxyrhynchus 840 describes a dispute between the Savior and a priest in Jerusalem. The author of the fragment is hostile to any water ritual, and he or she is probably a member of a Christian community located on the trajectory leading from certain Jesus traditions to Manichaeism through Gnostic communities. The use of the title Savior and the absence of the name Jesus suggest a location for the fragment within a Gnostic or Manichaean milieu using apocryphal traditions.[109] The opposition to water baptism, built upon a dogmatic dualism between two types of water, water of putrefaction and water of eternal life, also leads the reader to a later chronological date. The fragment attacks the sacerdotal attitude of the priest and the respect for water baptism and lustrations. Including references to liturgical clothes and holy vessels, all the elements are consistent with the life of a Jewish Christian baptist sect or with the practice of the mainstream Christian church. Also explained in this manner are ἡ λίμνη τοῦ Δαυείδ, the ritual pool, a prefiguration of the early Christian baptisteries, and the ἁγνευτήριον, a place for purification, similar to the early Christian water basin or fountain.

This fragment belongs, therefore, either in the second-century Gnostic opposition to a Jewish Christian baptist movement or to the mainstream church, or in the third-century Manichaean polemic against the Elkesaites.[110]

---

[109] I know that categories such as Gnosticism are actually being reconsidered. I know also that the different groups I have mentioned have been constructed at least in part by their adversaries. It is, however, not the goal of this paper to enter into this discussion.

[110] See now, going back to the question of the historical Jesus, Michael J. Krüger, *The Gospel of the Savior: An Analysis of P. Oxy. 840 and Its Place in the Gospel Tradition of Early Christianity* (Texts and Editions for New Testament Study 1; Leiden: Brill, 2005).

Canonical and Apocryphal Acts of the Apostles

The Acts of the apostles, depicting the ministry, travels, teaching, miracles, and passion of Jesus' disciples were written in the first centuries C.E. To date, scholarly comparison has either enhanced the value of canonical work by discrediting the apocryphal as literature of entertainment or has simply considered both canonical and apocryphal literature to be Christian novels. This paper emphasizes both differences and similarities between the canonical and apocryphal texts. Among the differences, the apostle's martyrdom story in the apocryphal acts, similar to Jesus' passion narrative in the canonical gospels, reveals the function of the apostle as mediator of a message of salvation.

Introduction

The commonly held title "Acts"[1] in many manuscripts invites a comparison of the canonical Acts of the Apostles and the apocryphal acts.[2] The narrative character[3] as well as the Christian nature of these documents confirms this invitation to

---

[1] A first version of this paper was presented to the Christian Apocrypha Group during the annual meeting of the Society of Biblical Literature in Boston, November 1999. I would like to thank Ann Graham Brock, Brent Landau and Taylor Grant Petrey, who helped me revise these pages. The reader should know that I use, for the *Acts of Paul*, the new division in chapters and paragraphs established by Willy Rordorf (see n. 19 below) and, for the *Acts of Philip*, the one established by the editors, Bertrand Bouvier, Frédéric Amsler, and myself (see n. 9 below). If not indicated otherwise, the translations of the New Testament are taken from the New Revised Standard Version and those of the apocryphal Acts from Wilhelm Schneemelcher, ed., *New Testament Apocrypha* (trans. Robert McL. Wilson; 2 vols.; Louisville: Westminster/John Knox, 1991). This paper was ready for publication when I received the following dissertation from its author: István Czachesz, *Apostolic Commission Narratives in the Canonical and Apocryphal Acts of the Apostles* (Groningen: Rijksuniversiteit Groningen, 2002). This dissertation has been published under the following title: *Commission Narratives: A Comparative Study of the Canonical and Apocryphal Acts* (Studies on Early Christian Apocrypha 8; Leuven: Peeters, 2007). I regret that I could not profit from this interesting monograph.

[2] On the term πράξεις as a book title, see Alfred Wikenhauser, *Die Apostelgeschichte und ihr Geschichtswert* (Münster: Aschendorff, 1921) 94–104; C. Maurer, "πράσσω, κτλ.," *TWNT* 6:643–45; David E. Aune, *The New Testament in Its Literary Environment* (LEC 8; Philadelphia: Westminster, 1989) 78.

[3] On the narrative character of early Christian stories, see Richard I. Pervo, "Early Christian Fiction," in *Greek Fiction: The Greek Novel in Context* (ed. J. R. Morgan and R. Stoneman; London: Routledge, 1994) 239–54.

compare. These canonical and apocryphal stories presuppose the same religious framework: the divine world, dominated by God[4] and Jesus Christ,[5] interferes with the human reality through the double agency of spiritual forces and apostolic commitment. Revelation, salvation, and judgment are the goals of these interventions.[6]

In the following paper I will make a distinction between formal and thematic elements, conscious of both the convenient but also artificial character of this distinction. I claim that through a careful reading, both formal and thematic similarities, as well as formal and thematic differences between these books come to light. After this formal (part 1) and thematic (part 2) comparison, I will raise the issue of their literary dependence (part 3). In my approach I will use form criticism as a methodological tool. I believe that this method suits the canonical as well as the apocryphal acts. Even if the final version of those texts is the editorial result of authors, I suppose that these authors, not separated from communities of faith, were eager to convey or rearrange traditional material.[7]

A caveat at the end of this introduction: until recently, scholars, still influenced by the antimanichaean polemic of the Church, considered five Acts of apostles as a closed corpus (*Acts of Andrew*, *Acts of John*, *Acts of Peter*, *Acts of Paul* and *Acts of Thomas*).[8] In so doing they committed a double mistake: they erased the dif-

---

[4] In the Syriac version of the *Acts of Thomas* 34, as in the canonical Acts 17:22–31, God is Creator and Redeemer; see also Acts 14:15–17.

[5] See *Acts of Peter* 7 (the apostle relies on Jesus Christ); 13 (Peter explains the prophetic writings and the words and deeds of the Lord Jesus Christ); 20 (Peter explains how to understand the Scriptures, particularly the Transfiguration story).

[6] This common aspect is often overlooked because of the too-easy argument that the apocryphal stories are written for the entertainment of their readers while the canonical are for serious teaching; this thesis has rightly been criticized by Richard I. Pervo, *Profit with Delight: The Literary Genre of the Acts of the Apostles* (Philadelphia: Fortress, 1987). The apocryphal acts have been compared with the Greek novel (see Pervo, "Early Christian Fiction"); the canonical Acts with epic (see Marianne P. Bonz, *The Past as Legacy: Luke-Acts and Ancient Epic* [Minneapolis: Fortress, 2000]).

[7] I know that other scholars think that the canonical and apocryphal acts, their stories and their speeches, were written with the use of little or no traditional elements; some insist on literary imitation; on these alternatives, see Éric Junod, "Créations romanesques et traditions ecclésiastiques dans les Actes apocryphes des apôtres. L'alternative fiction romanesque – vérité historique. Une impasse," in *Gli Apocrifi cristiani e cristianizzati*, XI Incontro di studiosi dell' antichità cristiana, *Augustinianum* 23 (1983) 271–85; Pervo, *Profit with Delight*; Dennis R. MacDonald, *The Acts of Andrew and the Acts of Andrew and Matthias in the City of the Cannibals* (SBLTT 33; Christian Apocrypha Series 1; Atlanta: Scholars Press, 1990); *Mimesis and Intertextuality in Antiquity and Christianity* (ed. Dennis R. MacDonald; Studies in Antiquity and Christianity; Harrisburg, Pa.: Trinity Press International, 2001).

[8] The Manichaeans are probably at the origin of this collection of five Acts. They gathered or canonized the *Acts of Andrew*, the *Acts of John*, the *Acts of Peter*, the *Acts of Paul*, and the *Acts of Thomas*. This collection has been attributed to an author called Leukios Charinos; see Knut Schäferdiek, "Die Leukios Charinos zugeschriebene manichäische Sammlung apokrypher Apostelgeschichten," in *Neutestamentliche Apokryphen* (ed. Wilhelm Schneemelcher; 5th ed.; Tübingen: Mohr Siebeck, 1987–89) 2:81–93.

ferences among these documents, and they ignored other apocryphal acts (*Acts of Philip, Martyrdom of Matthew, Acts of Timothy, Story of Simon and Theonoe,* and others).[9] In addition to these five I will choose my examples also from these other writings and try to respect the singularity of each of these documents.[10]

Formal Comparison

Let me begin with the formal elements, first the common and then the different.

Common Elements

Externally, the length of these works is comparable. Their maximum length is connected probably with external restraint: the usual length of a scroll or (better in that time) of a codex compelled the author to adjust his intellectual creativity to an external, even economic, reality.

The *Acts of Thomas*, completely preserved, is somewhat longer than the canonical Acts; the *Acts of Philip*, for which only a small portion is missing, is roughly as long as the canonical Acts.[11] For those that are not completely preserved, the majority, examples of lists and stichometry give us indications.[12] As later rewritings indicate, the apocryphal acts were sometimes considered to be too long. Therefore they were abbreviated[13] or their last section, the martyrdom,

---

[9] See the editions and translations, in particular Maximilien Bonnet, "Martyrium Matthaei," in *Acta Apostolorum Apocrypha* (ed. Richard Albert Lipsius and Maximilien Bonnet; 2 vols. in 3; Leipzig: Mendelssohn, 1891–1903; reprinted in New York: Georg Olms, 1990) 2.1:217–62; François Bovon, Bertrand Bouvier, and Frédéric Amsler, eds., *Acta Philippi. Textus* (CCSA 11; Turnhout: Brepols, 1999); Frédéric Amsler, *Acta Philippi. Commentarius* (CCSA 12; Turnhout: Brepols, 1999); Hermann Usener, ed., *Acta S. Timothei* (Bonn: Georgi, 1877); François Halkin, "La légende crétoise de saint Tite," *AnBoll* 79 (1961) 241–52 and 252–56; Françoise Morard, "La Légende copte de Simon et Théonoé," *Langues orientales anciennes. Philologie et linguistique* 4 (1993) 136–83; Françoise Morard, "Légende de Simon et Théonoé," in *Écrits apocryphes chrétiens,* I (ed. François Bovon and Pierre Geoltrain; La Pléiade 442; Paris: Gallimard, 1997) 1529–51; Richard I. Pervo, "The 'Acts of Titus': A Preliminary Translation, with an Introduction, Notes, and Appendices," in *SBLSP 1996* (Atlanta: Scholars Press, 1996) 455–82.

[10] On this point, see François Bovon and Éric Junod, "Reading the Apocryphal Acts," *Semeia* 38 (1986) 161–71. I am more familiar with certain writings than with others. Even if my references reach a large number of texts, I regret for example that I did not choose quotations from the *Acts of Andrew and Matthias* or from the *Recognitions* or the *Homilies* of the Pseudo-Clementine corpus. I hope not to have neglected any old apocryphal document from the second or third century C.E.

[11] I was not able to make an exact calculation.

[12] On these stichometries, see Wilhelm Schneemelcher, "Haupteinleitung," in Schneemelcher, *Neutestamentliche Apokryphen,* 1:30, 33–34.

[13] See the rewritings of the *Acts of Peter* and the opinion of Gregory of Tours in his *Life of Andrew*; Léon Vouaux, *Les Actes de Pierre* (Paris: Letouzey et Ané, 1922); Christine M. Thomas, *The* Acts of Peter, *Gospel Literature, and the Ancient Novel: Rewriting the Past* (Oxford:

cut off. This part was then used for liturgically commemorating the day of the feast of the apostle.[14]

Even if the level of language varies from one work to the other (the *Acts of Andrew* is written with philosophical phraseology, and the canonical Acts is influenced by the style of the Septuagint), all of them employ simple Koine Greek.[15] Their narrative style, marked by episodes in sequence, adds to this kinship.[16] The flow of the narration fits the chronological order, and special attention is given to geography.[17] As Luke has given a topographical framework to his two volumes (see the programmatic statement of the resurrected Christ in Acts 1:7–8),[18] the *Acts of Andrew*, the *Acts of John*, the *Acts of Paul*, the *Acts of Thomas*, and the *Acts of Philip* all contain precise geographical indications which are an easy way of dividing and scanning the text.[19] It is not by chance that some manuscripts give the title *Peregrinations* or *Travels* to the apocryphal acts.[20]

Oxford University Press, 2003). Jean-Marc Prieur, "La *Vie d'André* par Grégoire de Tours," in idem, *Acta Andreae* (CCSA 5–6; Turnhout: Brepols, 1989) 2:551–651.

[14] See the colophon of the manuscript of Mount Athos *Xenophontos* 32 of the *Acts of Philip*; Bovon, Bouvier, and Amsler, *Acta Philippi. Textus*, XVII.

[15] For Luke, see bibliography in the introduction to my commentary: François Bovon, *Luke 1: A Commentary on the Gospel of Luke 1:1–9:50* (trans. Christine M. Thomas; Hermeneia; Minneapolis: Fortress, 2002) 4–5; for the apocryphal acts, David H. Warren, "The Greek Language of the Apocryphal Acts of the Apostles: A Study in Style," in *The Apocryphal Acts of the Apostles: Harvard Divinity School Studies* (ed. François Bovon, Ann Graham Brock, and Christopher R. Matthews; Center for the Study of World Religions: Religions of the World; Cambridge, Mass.: Harvard University Press, 1999) 101–24; Evie Zachariades-Holmberg, "Philological Aspects of the Apocryphal Acts of the Apostles," in ibid., 125–44.

[16] The episodes can be related to a person, for example, Paul's escape through a wide basket (Acts 9:25) or the daughter of Peter (this episode, part of the lost section of the *Acts of Peter*, is preserved in the end, 128–41, of the *Kopt. Pap. Berolinensis* 8502). They can be related to a place, for example Malta, where Paul heals the first person of the island, Publius (Acts 28:7–10) or Ophioryme, the city in which Philip, Mariamne, and Bartholomew enter after a victory over the snakes (*Acts of Philip* 13). For the so-called Episodenstil, see Ernst Haenchen, *Die Apostelgeschichte* (3d ed.; Göttingen: Vandenhoeck & Ruprecht, 1961) 32–34.

[17] See Robert Henry Lightfoot, *Locality and Doctrine in the Gospels* (New York: Harper, 1937); Hans Conzelmann, *Die Mitte der Zeit. Studien zur Theologie des Lukas* (3d ed.; Tübingen: Mohr Siebeck, 1960) 12–86.

[18] See Erich Grässer, *Das Problem der Parusieverzögerung in den synoptischen Evangelien und der Apostelgeschichte* (Berlin: Töpelmann, 1957) 204–15.

[19] The *Acts of John* 58 contains the subtitle "From Laodicea to Ephesos for the second time," which received the following note by Éric Junod and Jean-Daniel Kaestli, "Actes de Jean," in *Écrits apocryphes chrétiens*, 1:1017 n. 58: "Les *Actes de Jean* devaient être divisés en sections introduites par des sous-titres signalant les déplacements de l'apôtre." Itinerary of Andrew, according to Gregory of Tours: Mermidona, Achaea, Amasia, Sinope, Nicaea, Nicomedia, Thrace, Perinthus, Philippi, Thessalonica, Philippi, Patras, Corinth, Megara, Patras; see Prieur, *Acta Andreae*, 2:564–651. Itinerary of Paul from the *Acts of Paul*: Damascus, Jerusalem, Antioch of Syria, Iconium, Antioch of Pisidia, Myra, Sidon, Tyre, Jerusalem[?], Smyrna, Ephesos, Philippi, Corinth, Italy, Rome; see Willy Rordorf, with the collaboration of Pierre Cherix and Rodolphe Kasser, "Actes de Paul," in *Écrits apocryphes chrétiens*, 1:117–24. Examples from *Acts of Philip*: "au pays de Parthes," "dans la ville d' Azot," "dans la ville de Nicatéra"; see Bovon, Bouvier, and Amsler, *Acta Philippi. Textus*.

It has been said that the canonical and the apocryphal acts belong to the same literary genre because they tell the same type of stories, mainly the ministry of the apostles.[21] Peter, John, or Philip travel, preaching the new religion,[22] and adding signs and miracles to their mission. The plot generally shows them converting a wide range of people, from a shoemaker[23] to a king,[24] establishing new communities, and facing growing opposition.[25] However, despite the number of elements that the literary genres of Luke-Acts and the apocryphal acts hold in common, they are not identical. The historiographical interest of Luke-Acts, following the line of the Septuagint and the books of Maccabees, is largely absent from the apocryphal acts; and for their part these books share several characteristics with the ancient novel,[26] but through their biographical orientation they resemble the canonical gospels. But if we descend into the detail of the several episodes, the same kind of stories also appear.

As God or Christ is believed to lead the course of history, the divine will is communicated to the apostle through visions, auditions, or dreams.[27] Here it is

---

[20] The book of Acts contains narratives inserted in a geographic sequence and precise itineraries; see Acts 13–14; 16:6–10 and 21:1–3. The wish to go to Rome (to gain prestige and official recognition), present also in Philostratus' *Life of Apollonius*, is explicit in the canonical Acts (in the case of Paul, the famous "calling to Caesar"; see Harry W. Tajra, *The Trial of St. Paul: A Juridical Exegesis of the Second Half of the Acts of the Apostles* [WUNT 2.35; Tübingen: Mohr Siebeck, 1989]; Harry W. Tajra, *The Martyrdom of St. Paul: Historical and Judicial Context, Traditions, and Legends* [WUNT 2.67; Tübingen: Mohr Siebeck, 1994]) and in the *Acts of Peter* 1 (Paul is in Rome); 4 (the crowd invites Simon Magus to come up to the capital); 5 (Peter is going to Rome to face Simon Magus); 9 (Peter is said to have come to Rome because of Simon Magus); *Acts of Paul* 13–14 (Paul at Rome).

[21] See Pervo, *Profit with Delight*.

[22] The authors of these works have a certain knowledge of the old pagan religion; see for example Acts 14:11–18 (Zeus, Hermes, and the priest of Zeus in Lystra); 17:15–22 (the numerous altars and the unknown god in Athens); *Acts of Philip* 1.1 (the widow worshipped faithfully the Greek gods – Ares, Apollo, Artemis, Zeus, Athena and even the Sun and the Moon).

[23] In the *Acts of Mark* published e cod. *Parisinus gr.* 881 in PG 115:164–69.

[24] See the final conversion of king Mazdai at the end of the *Acts of Thomas* 170.

[25] The canonical as well as the apocryphal acts present the motive of the persecution and also the motive of the persecutor's death; see Acts 12:1–5, 20–23 (Herod Agrippa I); *Acts of Andrew* 63.3 (suicide of Egeates).

[26] See n. 21 above.

[27] See Acts 9:9–11; 10:3, 17, 19; 11:5; 12:7–9; 16:9–10; 18:9–10; 22:17–18; 23:11; 27:23; *Acts of John* 18–19 (double vision); *Life of Andrew* 1.3–5 (Christ being the guide); 20 (apparition of John and Peter to Andrew announcing Andrew's passion); *Acts of Peter* 5 (Christ appears to Peter in a vision and sends him by boat to Italy); 6 (in Judaea Peter has been divinely instructed to go to Italy); 22 (providential dream of Marcellus); *Acts of Paul* 5.4 ("But an angel <of the> Lord had said to him in the night: 'Paul, <there is before thee> today a great conflict <against> thy body (?), but God, <the Father> of his Son Jesus Christ, will < ... > thee.' "). Some of the visions are premonitions of a fight, an ordeal, a suffering, a trial, or martyrdom: Acts 27:23–24; *Acts of Peter* 16. The person receiving such a vision or audition may be hesitant about the natural or supernatural character of the event as well as about its meaning (see Acts 10:9–20; 12:9–11). Some of these visions are *post mortem apostoli*, like *Acts of Paul* 14.6; *Acts of Thomas* 169; probably *Acts of Peter* 41. See particularly Johannes Lindblom, *Gesichte und Offenbarungen. Vor-*

Christ appearing to the Lukan Paul in Corinth; there he leads the apocryphal John to Ephesos.[28] Because preaching the gospel requires the meeting of an audience, the canonical acts as well as the apocryphal use the genre of providentially organized meetings. Often the device of the simultaneous double vision brings people together: Cornelius and Peter in Acts 10, John and Lycomedes in *Acts of John* 18–19.[29] The apostle first has to travel to the allotted city, and all the dangers inherent to traveling are exploited. Both the canonical Paul and the apocryphal John, for example, endure shipwrecks.[30] Other apostles calm storms that shake the ocean[31] and beat monsters threatening the travelers.[32] Any peregrination implies departure and separation. From the canonical acts to the apocryphal, one meets the genre of farewell scenes: a last meeting, a last act of worship, a last speech, a last attempt to force the apostle to stay as shepherd of the local community, last tears and good-byes.[33] All these works highlight individual conversions[34] and the establishment of churches[35] rather than the subsequent life and edification of communities.[36]

Miracles, although present in the canonical acts, abound in the apocryphal acts[37] in such proportion that the hero looks like a miracle-performing machine,

---

stellungen von göttlichen Weisungen und übernatürlichen Erscheinungen im ältesten Christentum (Acta reg. societatis humaniorum litterarum Lundensis 65; Lund: Gleerup, 1968); Patricia Cox Miller, *Dreams in Late Antiquity: Studies in the Imagination of a Culture* (Princeton: Princeton University Press, 1994); François Bovon, "Ces chrétiens qui rêvent. L'autorité du rêve dans les premiers siècles du christianisme," in *Geschichte–Tradition–Reflexion. Festschrift für Martin Hengel zum 70. Geburtstag* (ed. Hubert Cancik, Hermann Lichtenberger, and Peter Schäfer; 3 vols.; Tübingen: Mohr Siebeck, 1996) 3:631–53.

[28] Acts 18:9 and *Acts of John* 18.

[29] See Alfred Wikenhauser, "Doppelträume," *Bib* 29 (1948) 100–11.

[30] Acts 27; for John the story was narrated in a lost portion of the *Acts of John*; we have an indirect witness of the episode preserved in *Acts of Timothy*; see Hippolyte Delehaye, "Les Actes de S. Timothée," in *Mélanges d'hagiographie grecque et latine* (Subsidia hagiographica 42; Bruxelles: Société des Bollandistes, 1966) 408–15.

[31] *Acts of Philip* 3.10–15.

[32] *Acts of Philip* 9 and 11.

[33] See Acts 20:36–21:16; *Acts of John* 58–59; François Bovon, "Le Saint-Esprit, l'Église et les relations humaines selon Actes 20,36–21,16," in *Les Actes des Apôtres. Traditions, rédaction, théologie* (ed. Jacob Kremer; BETL 48; Leuven: Leuven University Press, 1977) 339–58; Éric Junod and Jean-Daniel Kaestli, *Acta Iohannis* (2 vols.; CCSA 1–2; Turnhout: Brepols, 1983) 2:431 n. 1.

[34] See for example the beautiful stories of the conversion of the Ethiopic eunuch in Acts 8:26–40 and of the captain of the boat, Theon, in the *Acts of Peter* 5–6.

[35] Before leaving a town the apostle organizes the new-born Christian community; see Acts 14:22–23; *Acts of Philip* 2.24; *Acts of Philip Martyrdom* 37. But the *Acts of Andrew*, the *Acts of John*, and the *Acts of Paul* are not interested in the establishment of a strong hierarchical ministry.

[36] See François Bovon, "Évangélisation et unité de l'Église dans la perspective de Luc," in *Unterwegs zur Einheit. Festschrift für Heinrich Stirnimann* (ed. Johannes Brantschen and Pietro Selvatico; Freiburg im Breisgau-Wien: Herder, 1980) 189–99.

[37] See for example the miraculous finding of Eubula's items which had been stolen by Simon the Magician: *Acts of Peter* 17. As in Acts 19:11–12, we read in the *Acts of John* 62 a scene of

such as in the *Life of Andrew* (a summary of the lost first part of the *Acts of Andrew*).[38] Of course these many miracles function as an invitation to believe or as a demonstration of a strong belief, but their inflation is also a sign of the increasing opposition the first Christians had to face.[39]

Like miracles, speeches also play a decisive role. This role has been appreciated in the canonical acts since the time of Martin Dibelius[40] and is now becoming more appreciated in the apocryphal acts.[41] Speeches are both an effective place to insert the creed that the author seeks to defend and a strategic opportunity to give meaning to the present situation.[42]

When the apostolic mission is successful, then women[43] and men, regardless of status, convert.[44] The assembly of new members into the Church gives a literary opportunity for describing worship, particularly the rituals of baptism and Eucharist. Thus some of the oldest descriptions of Christian gatherings are found

----

miracles performed by touching the apostle or his clothes. Absent from the canonical acts are the miracles in which the spiritual double of an apostle appears, being the apostle after death or Jesus Christ taking the shape of his apostle: see *Acts of John* 87; *Acts of Peter* 22; *Acts of Paul* 3.21; 14.6; *Acts of Thomas* 11; 57; 154 and passim; *Acts of Philip Martyrdom* 42.

[38] See David Pao, "Physical and Spiritual Restoration: The Role of Healing Miracles in the Acts of Andrew," in Bovon, *Apocryphal Acts of the Apostles*, 259–80.

[39] See Anton Fridrichsen, *Le problème du miracle dans le christianisme primitif* (EHPhR 12; Strasbourg-Paris: Librairie Istra, 1925); Paul Achtemeier, "Jesus and the Disciples as Miracle Workers in the Apocryphal New Testament," in *Aspects of Religious Propaganda in Judaism and Early Christianity* (ed. Elisabeth Schüssler Fiorenza; Notre Dame: University of Notre Dame Press, 1976) 149–86; Jean-Marie van Cangh, "Miracles évangéliques – Miracles apocryphes," in *The Four Gospels, 1992: Festschrift für Frans Neirynck* (ed. Frans Van Segbroeck et al.; 3 vols. Leuven: Peeters, 1992) 3:2277–320; François Bovon, "Miracles, magie et guérison dans les Actes apocryphes des apôtres," *JECS* 3 (1995) 245–59.

[40] Martin Dibelius, "Die Reden der Apostelgeschichte und die antike Geschichtsschreibung," in idem, *Aufsatze zur Apostelgeschichte* (ed. Heinrich Greeven; 4th ed.; Göttingen: Vandenhoeck & Ruprecht, 1961) 120–62.

[41] The content of the speeches, their insistence on the destiny of the soul, and their ascetic requirements have been studied more than their rhetorical form or strategy. Examples of speeches in the apocryphal acts: *Acts of Andrew* 47–50; *Acts of Peter* 7; *Acts of Paul* 9.5–10; *Acts of Thomas* 83–86; *Acts of Philip Martyrdom* 33. If in the canonical acts the majority of the speeches are addressed to a non-Christian audience (the exception being Paul's speech to the Christian elders of Ephesus who had come to see the apostle in Miletus: Acts 20:18–35), in the apocryphal the majority are addressed to a Christian audience, sometimes in the framework of a Christian worship with prayers and Eucharist (*Acts of Peter* 20; *Acts of John* 106–7; *Acts of Thomas* 132). See Junod and Kaestli, *Acta Iohannis*, 2:570–73; Prieur, *Acta Andreae*, 1:218–26.

[42] It is also the right moment to quote beatitudes or to create new beatitudes; see *Acts of Paul* 3.5–6; *Acts of Thomas* 94.2–6; 107.2; 113.24; *Acts of Philip* 1.3; 3.15; 5.20, 25; 8.9; 13.5; *Acts of Philip Martyrdom* 29 (135).

[43] Maximilla, for example, in the *Acts of Andrew* 1–18; 28–32; 37–42; or Chryse in the *Acts of Peter* 30.

[44] Stratocles, for example, in the *Acts of Andrew* 1–25; 42–45; or Marcellus in the *Acts of Peter* 8–10.

in the canonical[45] and apocryphal acts.[46] The success of the preaching and the establishment of a new religious community, however, sometimes create tension in the city. As a result, as the opposition increases, so do the scenes of polemic, confrontation, and lawsuits.[47]

Two last common formal aspects need to be mentioned. First, even a rapid glance at this literature makes manifest the different length of the episodes. If the majority are short and respect the characteristics of the small units established by the form critics,[48] a minority are much longer, creating a lack of balance in the total work. These longer units contain more than a single episode and consequently look like a cycle of related events.[49] The last part of the canonical acts is the long story of Paul's trial. The episodes of Andronicos and Drusiane in the *Acts of John* form a large literary unit different from a single event, such as the peripety of the portrayal of John.[50] It is probable that such cycles were originally independent oral or written traditions, which were integrated into the final composition.

Second, it is not uncommon that the same work mentions two similar stories (doublets). The double arrest of Peter and his companions followed by a trial in the beginning of Acts is well known and was disturbing for Adolf von Harnack and his generation.[51] The reader faces two very similar situations of the apostolic

---

[45] See Acts 1:14; 2:1–13, 42–47; 4:23–31; 12:12; 20:7–12; Philippe H. Menoud, "Les Actes des apôtres et l'eucharistie," *RHPR* 33 (1953) 21–36; reprinted in idem, *Jésus-Christ et la foi. Recherches néotestamentaires* (Neuchâtel: Delachaux et Niestlé, 1975) 63–75.

[46] *Acts of Paul* 3.5–6 (fraction of bread); 4.9 (34) (self-baptism of Thecla); *Acts of Thomas* 25–29; see for example Gerard Rouwhorst, "La célébration de l'eucharistie selon les Actes de Thomas," in *Omnes Circumadstantes: Contributions Towards a History of the Role of the People in the Liturgy: Festschrift for Herman Wegman* (ed. Charles Caspers and Marc Schneiders; Kampen: Kok, 1990) 51–77. The new-born Christian community not only worships together; personal, social, and affective bounds are created in the church; see *Acts of Peter* 5–6 (between Theon, Peter, Ariston, and Narcysse); *Acts of Paul* 13.1–4 (among Paul, Artemon, and Claude).

[47] See Acts 4:1–22; 5:17–42; 22:30–23:11; 24–26; *Acts of Paul* 3.15–17; *Acts of Thomas* 163.

[48] For example, Acts 9:32–35 (healing of Aeneas) and 9:36–43 (resurrection of Tabitha) for short units; 10:1–11:18 (Cornelius story) for a long unit. See Martin Dibelius, "Stilkritisches zur Apostelgeschichte," in idem, *Aufsätze zur Apostelgeschichte*, 9–28, esp. 17–28; François Bovon, "La vie des apôtres. Traditions bibliques et narrations apocryphes," in *Les Actes apocryphes des Apôtres. Christianisme et monde païen* (ed. François Bovon et al.; Publications de la Faculté de théologie de l'Université de Genève 4; Geneva: Labor et Fides, 1981) 141–60.

[49] See the following cycles: Lycomedes and Cleopatra (*Acts of John* 19–25); Drusiana and Callimachus (*Acts of John* 63–86); Andrew and the governor Virinius (*Life of Andrew* 18); Andrew and Stratocles (*Acts of Andrew* 1–12); Peter and Marcellus (*Acts of Peter* 1–14); Paul and Thecla (*Acts of Paul* 3.7–4.18 [7–43]); Thomas and Mygdonia (*Acts of Thomas* 82–169); Philip and Ireos (*Acts of Philip* 5–7).

[50] *Acts of John* 63–86 compared with *Acts of John* 26–29.

[51] See Acts 3:11–4:31 and 5:17–42; see other stories including prison scenes: Acts 12:6–17 (Peter miraculously liberated); 16:23–34 (Paul and Silas miraculously liberated); *Acts of Thomas* 153–55, 162; see Adolf von Harnack, *Die Apostelgeschichte* (Beiträge zur Einleitung in

group confronted with mythical monsters in the *Acts of Philip* (9 and 11).[52] Two fragments probably belonging to the *Acts of Peter*, the episodes of Peter's daughter and the gardener's daughter, are also strangely parallel and antithetical.[53] These doublets may be explained in the same way as the larger cycles.[54] A single early memory after a while gave birth to two similar stories, sufficiently different to be preserved by authors anxious to neglect nothing.[55]

Different Elements

The first verse of the book of Acts has a reference to "the first book" or "the first volume," namely, the gospel of Luke.[56] There is no such reference in any of the apocryphal acts. This is a first and formidable difference. All the apocryphal acts refer to Jesus Christ but none intends to be the literary counterpart and continuation of a gospel. The decisive structure of Luke-Acts with the three parts of Jesus' life and the spread of the good news of Jesus' resurrection through the apostolic polyphonic witnesses is absent from the apocryphal acts.[57] In the beginning we had gospels without acts (gospel of Mark or gospel of Matthew); now we have acts without gospels.[58] This literary evidence lies upon a religious conviction shared by the authors of apocryphal acts that, like Jesus Christ, the apostle is a mediator and a revealer. The apostle's destiny, and not only the apostle's witness, must be considered and understood.

---

das Neue Testament 3; Leipzig: Hinrichs, 1908) 131–88; Jacques Dupont, *Les sources du livre des Actes. État de la question* (Bruges: Desclée de Brouwer, 1960) 33–50.

[52] See the notes in Bovon, Bouvier, and Amsler, *Acta Philippi. Textus*, 274–99; and Amsler, *Acta Philippi. Commentarius*, 323–55.

[53] See Gérard Poupon, "Actes de Pierre," in *Écrits apocryphes chrétiens*, 1:1043–44. There may be also a doublet in the *Acts of Paul* 3.15–21 and 4.1–14 (26–39) where Thecla is confronted twice by a governor and sent to be punished in the theater; see Ann Graham Brock, *Mary Magdalene, The First Apostle: The Struggle for Authority* (HTS 51; Cambridge, Mass.: Harvard University Press, 2003) 107–8. Andrea Lorenzo Molinari, *I Never Knew the Man: The Coptic Act of Peter (Papyrus Berolinensis 8502.4): Its Independence from the Apocryphal Acts of Peter, Genre and Legendary Origins* (Québec: Presses de l'Université Laval, 2000), does not believe that the episode of Peter's daughter was originally written into the *Acts of Peter*.

[54] See in the memories of Jesus the double miracle of the loaves in the gospel of Mark (see Mark 6:35–44 and 8:1–9); see Étienne Trocmé, *L'Évangile selon saint Marc* (CNT 2; Geneva: Labor et Fides, 2000) 180–84.

[55] Unlike the canonical acts (see Acts 2:42–47; 4:32–35; 5:12–16; 6:7; 9:31) the apocryphal acts do not use frequently the genre of summaries of the Christians' activities.

[56] See Gerhard Schneider, *Die Apostelgeschichte. I. Teil. Einleitung, Kommentar zu Kap. 1,1–8,40* (Freiburg im Breisgau: Herder, 1980) 189–92; Haenchen, *Apostelgeschichte*, 105–6.

[57] On the structure of Luke-Acts, see Robert Maddox, *The Purpose of Luke-Acts* (FRLANT 126; Göttingen: Vandenhoeck & Ruprecht, 1982) 1–30.

[58] One can say however that *Acts of John* 88–105 appears to be a kind of "gospel" within the larger structure of the work; see Helmut Koester, *Introduction to the New Testament* (2 vols.; 2d ed.; New York: de Gruyter, 1995–2000) 2:202.

Instead, each of the apocryphal acts is an autonomous writing with no literary dependence either upon a written gospel or upon the Septuagint.[59] Each is the material expression of a spiritual reality, the communication of a religious message through words and deeds of a singular apostle.[60] While the canonical Acts deals first with Peter and the Twelve, then with the Hellenists, particularly Stephen and Philip, and finally with Paul, the apocryphal acts usually focus on one hero who has little if any connection with the other apostles.[61] If we meet a team, such as in the *Acts of Paul*, the *Acts of Philip*, or the *Story of Simon and Theonoe*, it is not a group among the Twelve working in different fields, but a companionship of several missionaries traveling together.[62] This may be a memory of the apostolic commitment of pairs (Mark 6:7) or of couples (Peter and his wife according to 1 Cor 9:5) and a way of recognizing the role of women in the propagation of Christianity.[63] Thecla, Mariamne, and Theonoe are not only passive listeners but become active apostolic leaders: they preach, do miracles, and take the risk of the apostolic burden.[64]

The third major formal difference between the apocryphal and the canonical acts of apostles is that in the apocryphal acts the life of each apostle finds its apex

---

[59] That affirmation does not imply that the authors were unfamiliar with traditions embedded in the Septuagint or in the gospels; see François Bovon, "Facing the Scriptures: Mimesis and Intertextuality in the *Acts of Philip*," in MacDonald, *Mimesis and Intertextuality*, 138–54.

[60] See Bovon and Junod, "Reading the Apocryphal Acts"; and my two articles: "Vie des apôtres," and "The Synoptic Gospels and the Non-Canonical Acts of the Apostles," *HTR* 81 (1988) 19–36.

[61] The presence of Paul in the *Acts of Peter* 1–4 is usually considered as an interpolation; see Gérard Poupon, "Actes de Pierre," 1042; and Gérard Poupon, "Les *Actes de Pierre* et leur remaniement," in *ANRW* 2.25.6 (1988) 4363–83. See nevertheless the "we" of the apostles in *Acts of Thomas* 61 and the allusion to the Twelve apostles and the Seventy-Two disciples in *Acts of Thomas* 6.

[62] Paul working with Thecla in the first case; Philip working with Mariamne and Bartholomew in the second; Simon working with Theonoe in the third. See also the relationship between Thomas and the Jewish flutist (*Acts of Thomas* 5–9) or later Thomas and Mygdonia (*Acts of Thomas* 82–105; 113–30).

[63] Women play a considerable role in both the canonical and the apocryphal acts, but in some of them women are passive recipients (listening, believing, and helping through their belongings: canonical Acts; *Acts of Peter*, esp. 22) while in others women portray active roles (they preach, baptize, and possess the apostolic authority: *Acts of Paul, Acts of Philip, Story of Simon and Theonoe*); see Stevan L. Davies, *The Revolt of the Widows: The Social World of the Apocryphal Acts* (New York: Winston-Seabury, 1980); Dennis R. MacDonald, "The Role of Women in the Production of the Apocryphal Acts of the Apostles," *The Iliff Review* 40 (1984) 21–38; Virginia Burrus, "Chastity as Autonomy: Women in the Stories of the Apocryphal Acts," *Semeia* 38 (1986) 101–17, with reply by Jean-Daniel Kaestli, and rejoinder, ibid., 118–35; François Bovon, "Mary Magdalene's Paschal Privilege," in idem, *New Testament Traditions and Apocryphal Narratives* (trans. Jane Haapiseva-Hunter; Princeton Theological Monograph Series 36; Allison Park: Pickwick, 1995) 147–58; Kate Cooper, *The Virgin and the Bride: Idealized Womanhood in Late Antiquity* (Cambridge, Mass.: Harvard University Press, 1996) 45–67; Brock, *Mary Magdalene*.

[64] See Beverly M. Kienzle and Pamela J. Walker, eds., *Women Preachers and Prophets through Two Millennia of Christianity* (Berkeley: University of California Press, 1998).

in martyrdom.[65] The only exception is the beloved disciple, John the theologian, who even if he does not die as a martyr, organizes his death in such way that it becomes a significant part of his life.[66] For all the others there is a pattern of increasing opposition against the success of the apostle, followed by a trial which is at the same time a personal vindication by a governor infuriated by the conversion of his wife.[67] In the endings of the *Acts of Andrew*, the *Acts of Peter*, and the *Acts of Thomas* there is a tense situation in which the apostle is ready to die for the message. This situation is logical because the core of the message is a call to choose the unseen, manifested in a preference for the afterlife and an exhortation to despise the body. This is very different from the canonical Acts, which explicitly does not end with a martyrdom story, neglecting to mention the death of either Peter or Paul, and instead confers a different function to martyrdom by locating Stephen's death at the beginning of the book.[68] If we have to compare the structure of the apocryphal acts, and particularly their ending, we should not use the canonical book of Acts, but rather the canonical gospels with their concentration on one hero, Jesus, their geographical sequence, from Galilee to Jerusalem, and their balance between miracles stories and Passion narrative.

Thematic Comparison

Common Elements

The spontaneous wish to compare the canonical with the apocryphal acts of the apostles, however, is legitimate. These works not only share formal elements but also many thematic concerns. Despite different christological views, they all place

---

[65] These martyrdom stories, concluding the apocryphal acts of the apostles, have often been separated to constitute independent texts ready to be read during the celebration of the feast of the apostle. On this surgery, see the colophon of the manuscript from Mount Athos *Xenophontos* 32, fol. 29ᵛ; in the Coptic rewriting of the apocryphal acts of the apostles a distinction has been made between *Peregrinations* and *Martyrdom*; see Francoise Morard, "Notes sur le recueil copte des Actes apocryphes des apôtres," *RTP* 113 (1981) 403–13; and the manuscript tradition of the apocryphal acts of the apostles, for example the *Passion of Peter* in the manuscripts of Patmos and Athos or the *Passion of Paul* (see Maximilien Bonnet, "Martyrium Pauli," in Lipsius-Bonnet, *Acta apostolorum apocrypha*, 1:104–17; Richard A. Lipsius, "Martyrium Petri," in Lipsius-Bonnet, *Acta apostolorum apocrypha*, 1:78–103).

[66] *Acts of John* 106–14 (the *Metastasis* of John); see the edition of the three Greek versions of this last part of the *Acts of John* by Junod and Kaestli, *Acta Iohannis*, 1:30–63; 2:564–80.

[67] See for example the conversions of Stratocles, brother of the governor Aegeates, and Maximilla, the wife of the governor, and then the indignation of the governor in the *Acts of Andrew* 1–65.

[68] Walter Radl, *Paulus und Jesus im lukanischen Doppelwerk. Untersuchungen zu Parallelmotiven im Lukasevangelium und in der Apostelgeschichte* (Bern: Lang, 1975) insists exclusively on the parallel between Jesus and Paul, neglecting the parallels between Jesus and Stephen and between Peter and Paul.

Jesus Christ behind the powerful apostles. No miracle is performed in the name of the apostle, but always in the name of Jesus Christ.[69] Respecting the original structure of Christianity with its two poles, Christ and the apostle, or reconciliation and the service of reconciliation, the canonical as well as the apocryphal acts[70] lay emphasis on the spreading of the good news (however it is defined) through human agency.[71]

Behind both Christ and the apostle,[72] these writings presuppose and make explicit the divine will regarding the providential economy of salvation and judgment. Peter in the canonical Acts says: "You that are Israelites, listen to what I have to say: Jesus of Nazareth, a man attested to you by God with deeds of power, wonders, and signs that God did through him among you, as you yourselves according to the definite plan and foreknowledge of God ..." (Acts 2:22–23). Compare this to the *Acts of Peter*: "But as they mourned and fasted, God was already preparing Peter for what was to come ... ."[73]

I believe Hans Conzelmann was right when he spoke of Jesus Christ being for Luke the middle of history ("Mitte der Zeit"), because the evangelist presupposes the Septuagint as the first book, the first stage in history of salvation, and considers the gospel, the proclamation of the Kingdom of God, as the central portion of the divine program.[74] According to Luke, the Acts of the Apostles describes the time of the Church, the spreading of the good news, and the third part of the history of salvation. Such a construction of time (Israel-Christ-Church) is not foreign to the apocryphal acts, even if their relationship to the past of Israel may be less articulated and their valorization of the present higher than in Luke.[75] All of them underline a revelation inscribed in time and made manifest by the apostolic message. As an example, I mention the three donkeys of the *Acts of Thomas*.[76] While Thomas was preaching, he saw a wild donkey coming to him. Asked to reveal its identity, the animal says: "I am of the family who served Balaam the

---

[69] See for example Philip's prayers during his fight against the monster, *Acts of Philip* 11.3–4.

[70] See for example *Acts of John* 98; 112; François Bovon, *L'Évangile et l'apôtre* (Aubonne [Switzerland]: Moulin, 1993) 7–32.

[71] See François Bovon, "L'importance des médiations dans le projet théologique de Luc," *NTS* 21 (1974) 23–39.

[72] *Acts of Thomas* 42 presents an original portrayal of the apostle, different from the one of the canonical acts: an apostle is a person who gives life to the soul and heals the body.

[73] *Acts of Peter* 5. See also *Acts of John* 18: "And when they departed very early in the morning and some four miles of their journey were already accomplished, a voice came from heaven in the hearing of us all, saying 'John, you shall give glory to your Lord in Ephesus, (glory) of which you shall know, both you and all your brothers that are with you and some of those in that place who shall believe through you.' Then John joyfully considered with himself what was to happen at Ephesus, saying 'Lord, behold I go according to thy will. Thy will be done.'"

[74] See Conzelmann, *Die Mitte der Zeit*, 158–92.

[75] This construction of time is less visible in the *Acts of Andrew* and the *Acts of John*.

[76] This is an aspect not mentioned by Paul-Hubert Poirier and Yves Tissot, "Actes de Thomas," in *Écrits apocryphes chrétiens*, 1:1367.

prophet and your Lord rode over my race" (*Acts of Thomas* 40). According to the author, in each stage of the history of salvation a donkey played a significant role. The two first stages are known from the Old and the New Testament: the first donkey wiser than Balaam (Num 22:21–35) and the second donkey of Palm Sunday (Luke 19:30–36). The third stage, the time of the Church, is manifested by the apocryphal writing itself: the third donkey who presents itself to Thomas and speaks with a human voice praises God, congratulates the apostle, announces the conversion of the Indians, and offers his back for the comfort of the disciple of Christ.[77]

Even if we may discuss the exact content of the Christian message according to Luke, one thing is evident: the Kingdom of God should not be confused with any earthly, political, or economic reality.[78] The divine realm is not inside nature, city, or mind but transcends all of them. A similar interest for the heavenly realm is evident throughout the apocryphal acts. Actually these texts were written to invite their readers to overcome their human life, or better yet, to shift from a human to a divine condition, from body to soul, from mortal existence to eternal life.[79] To facilitate such a transfer, the preaching plays the first role with its threat and promise. But like the New Testament, particularly in Luke-Acts, the strength of the preaching is enhanced by miraculous signs.[80] Consistently, healings and exorcisms are connected with the begetting of faith in the heart of the auditors in the *Acts of Peter* and the *Life of Andrew*.[81] Visions, dreams, and divine voices are also introduced.[82] They also have a providential relevance, but a different, complementary function: they are supposed to lead the apostle to the right way or to give meaning to a supernatural event (like the vision of the eagle in the *Acts of Philip*).[83]

---

[77] See *Acts of Thomas* 39.

[78] On the kingdom of God in Luke-Acts, see François Bovon, *Luke the Theologian: Fifty Five Years of Research (1950–2005)* (2d rev. ed.; Waco, Tex.: Baylor University Press, 2006) 1–85.

[79] See particularly the last speeches and prayers of the apostles in the *Acts of Thomas* 142–48.

[80] On the miracles that help to make penitence, to convert, to believe, and that bring the believer to real spiritual life according to the apocryphal acts, see Pao, "Physical and Spiritual Restoration: The Role of Healing Miracles in the Acts of Andrew"; van Cangh, "Miracles," 3:2277–320; Bovon, "Miracles," 245–59.

[81] See for example *Acts of Peter* 11 (Marcellus believes more strongly after the miracle he was able to perform); 17 (Eubola will recuperate miraculously the items stolen by Simon, and because of that many will believe); 26 (even tempted, the God of miracles will resuscitate the young servant); 32 (God shows his grace and power through a miracle, the miraculous fall of Simon Magus flying over Rome). Healing of the blind has a spiritual meaning: it represents symbolically the opening of the eyes of faith; see Luke 18:35–43; Acts 26:17–18; *Acts of John* 113 (blind two years, John learned through this disability to open the eyes of his spirit).

[82] See n. 27 above.

[83] *Acts of Philip* 3.5–9. Other miraculous actions are the irradiation of the face or the transfiguration of the body: see the transfiguration of Jesus (Luke 9:28–36), the shining face of Ste-

In Luke-Acts the spreading of the gospel with its cosmic perspective also has a polemical dimension.[84] If God is behind the salvific economy, Satan, his agents, demons, magicians,[85] or false apostles[86] also exist.[87] They throw all their forces into the eschatological battle to prevent the success of Christ or the apostles.[88] The various authors of the apocryphal acts share the same worldview.[89]

Once a woman,[90] such as Tertia the queen,[91] or a man, such as the young man resurrected by Thomas, has decided to accept the message of the apostle,[92] she or he has not only to be firm in her or his faith,[93] but also has to manifest the implications of the gospel in her or his existence. The canonical acts as well as the apocryphal open an ethical path. The virtues celebrated may differ; perseverance is

---

phen (Acts 6:15), the transfiguration of Philip (*Acts of Philip* 5.22–23), and the transformation of Mariamne (*Acts of Philip Martyrdom* 20).

[84] Often the forces of good, represented by the apostle, confront the forces of evil, represented by a demon or a monster. The deed of the apostle consists in a transfer of power from the incarnation of evil to the reality of good; see *Acts of Thomas* 44–46 and 76.

[85] The apocryphal apostle is often accused of being a magician (see for example *Acts of Peter* 4 [Paul accused of being a magician]; *Acts of Philip* 6.1), but the authors do not hesitate to use the same weapon and to accuse the enemies of the apostles of being themselves magicians (see for example Acts 8:6–25; 13:4–12; 19:13–20; *Acts of Peter* 5).

[86] In the *Acts of Thomas* 79 the wild donkey prophesies, announcing the uprising of false apostles and prophets.

[87] The enemies of the apostles are often pictured with evil qualities. For such demonization, see in the canonical Acts 8:20–23 (Simon Magus); 13:10 (Elymas); 20:29–30 (prophecy of future adversaries); 23 (negative picture of the Jewish leaders). For examples from the apocryphal acts, see *Acts of John* 63, where Callimachus is called "an emissary of Satan"; *Acts of Peter* 15–16 and 28, where Simon Magus is presented as a son of Satan.

[88] On the devil in Luke-Acts, see Conzelmann, *Die Mitte der Zeit* 9, 22–23, 73–74; Jacques Dupont, *Les tentations de Jésus au désert* (StudNeot 4; Bruges: Desclée de Brouwer, 1968).

[89] See for example *Acts of Thomas* 32; 44–45; 75.2; *Acts of Philip* 11.3; Erik Peterson, "Die Begegnung mit dem Ungeheuer. Hermas, visio 4," *VC* 8 (1954) 52–71; reprinted in idem, *Frühkirche, Judentum und Gnosis. Studien und Untersuchungen* (Darmstadt: Wissenschaftliche Buchgesellschaft, 1982) 285–309. Like the canonical Acts (see Acts 5:1–11), the apocryphal acts mention some cases of divine punishment (*Acts of Philip* 6.10–12) and inspired malediction (see *Acts of Peter* 8).

[90] On the role of women in the apocryphal acts of the apostles, see nn. 63 and 64 above.

[91] The author of Luke-Acts is pleased by the interest of upper class people in Christianity; see Acts 13:50; 17:12; 19:31; 25–26. The same is true of most of the authors of the apocryphal acts; see *Acts of Peter* 3 (Dionysus and Balbus are knights of noble descent and Demetrius is a governor); *Acts of Andrew* 1–65 (Stratocles is the brother of the governor; Maximilla, the wife of the governor, and Aegeates himself is the governor); similar situation in the *Acts of Philip* 15.1–*Martyrdom* 42 (Nikanora is the wife of the governor Tyrannognophos). See Shelly Matthews, *First Converts: Rich Pagan Women and the Rhetoric of Mission in Early Judaism and Christianity* (Stanford: Stanford University Press, 2001).

[92] *Acts of Thomas* 134–37 concerning Tertia, and 30–38 concerning the young man.

[93] *Acts of Thomas* 15: the fiancé who renounces consummating his marriage says that he has the boldness to confess the new God, an attitude similar to that of Peter at Pentecost in the canonical Acts 2:29 (εἰπεῖν μετὰ παρρησίας).

relevant in one case,[94] asceticism in another;[95] but in all cases the ethical component is highly present and constitutes a common element.

An important common reality is not covered by the distinctions of form and content: this is the atmosphere of the stories. By telling stories, canonical and apocryphal acts create an atmosphere of fear and joy, tension and release, expectation and fulfillment, neglect for the visible world and spiritual attention toward the invisible values and the divine realm. Such an atmosphere, induced by the plot and the tone of the narration, is not peculiar to our literature; it is also characteristic of the ancient novels and the oldest lives of the saints.[96]

Different Elements

Inside this common atmosphere, however, there is a major distinction: while the canonical Acts insist on the objective side of redemption by telling the external, historical ways of redemption,[97] the apocryphal are more interested in the subjective appropriation of salvation by way of transforming the soul of the individual. This is particularly evident by comparing the canonical Acts to the *Acts of Thomas*. The content of the missionary speeches in the Lukan Acts is historical and christological: it deals with the history of Israel or the destiny of Jesus, particularly his resurrection.[98] The third part of these speeches does not omit the requirement of conversion, but conversion is defined as adherence to the message.[99]

---

[94] See the verb καρτερέω, "to be steadfast," in Acts 1:14; 2:42, 46; 6:4; 8:13; and the term ὑπομονή, "perseverance," Luke 8:15 and 21:19; Bovon, *Luke 1*, 311.

[95] For the *Acts of Peter* the best you can wish for someone is to hope she or he will quit sexual relations and all the bonds to this world, to even abandon this life itself. Peter's daughter is an example of the renunciation of sex (fragment preserved in the *Kopt. Pap. Berolinensis* 8502); the daughter of the gardener an example of the abandonment of life (fragment preserved in the *Epistle of the Pseudo-Titus*) and Rufina a counterexample (*Acts of Peter ?*) Not all the apocryphal acts are encratic; and even the same work, being perhaps a patchwork, can have parts that have a more ascetic requirement than others. On the whole, the criticism of sexuality being moderate (praise of virginity) or strict (prohibition of marriage) is widespread. One finds it in the beatitudes of the *Acts of Paul*, the speeches of the *Acts of Thomas*, or the episodes of some of the *Acts of Philip*. Asceticism is not only a moral issue; it is also a spiritual one: there is redemption through "purity" in the *Acts of Thomas* 99.3 and 101.2; the ascetical attitude gives one contact with God, a vision of God, or a conversation with God: see *Acts of Thomas* 85.1; 126; *Acts of Philip* 1.3; 5.5.

[96] In this paper I will not compare the different apocryphal acts of the apostles among themselves. This has been an ongoing and legitimate preoccupation of Dennis R. MacDonald; see his "Which Came First? Intertextual Relationships among the Apocryphal Acts of the Apostles," *Semeia* 80 (1997) 11–41.

[97] See Bovon, *Luke the Theologian*, 273–304.

[98] See for example the speech of Stephen (Acts 7:2–53) and the speech of Peter at the Pentecost (Acts 2:14–36).

[99] See Acts 2:38; 3:19; 17:30–31; Dibelius, "Reden der Apostelgeschichte," 120–62, esp. 142–43; Ulrich Wilckens, *Die Missionsreden der Apostelgeschichte. Form- und traditionsgeschichtliche Untersuchungen* (WMANT 5; Neukirchen-Vluyn: Neukirchener Verlag, 1961); Jacques

The lengthy and numerous speeches in the *Acts of Thomas* have a very different content and function: they are designed to urge the audience members to change their lives. Christology is only marginal, and the core conveys an imperious command to substitute the spiritual values for the mundane, and to concentrate on the soul and no longer on the body.[100] This trend is less dictated by the Christian tradition than by the philosophical schools of the time.[101] This attention to individual destiny gives to the apocryphal acts sophistication in the domain of the spiritual life ignored by the canonical acts. In the *Acts of John*, for example, we read a reflection on the movement of the soul, the way to reach calmness and purity, and how to avoid discouragement.[102]

In the domain of Christology two differences appear.[103] The first, well known, concerns the problem of docetism. The apparent absence of suffering is not a sufficient criterion to speak of docetism, because the domination of passions, including suffering, is part of the philosophical heroization of Christ and his disciples. But one can speak of docetism when the spiritual cross of light, as opposed to the material cross of wood, becomes the location of redemption.[104] Striking also is the emphasis on the divine, heavenly, resurrected, glorious Christ often considered as being God, the new God, Father as well as Son.[105]

Dupont, "Les discours missionnaires des Actes des apôtres, d'après un ouvrage récent," *RB* 69 (1962) 37–60.

[100] See *Acts of Thomas* 12; 28; 36; 37; 58; 66; 83–86; 88; 94; 119; 143; 159. The numerous prayers of the apostle confirm the content of the speeches. Conversion is a moral issue in a spiritual context, marked by dualism, no longer a christological one: *Acts of Thomas* 34–36. See the presence of Christ in the process according to *Acts of Thomas* 58. The perishable life is opposed to the eternal one in *Acts of Thomas* 78.3; 88.1–3; 117; 124.2–4; 127.3; 130.1; 135.2.

[101] For the philosophical interest for the soul, unique interest of the wise, see Gregory Riley, *Resurrection Reconsidered: Thomas and John in Controversy* (Minneapolis: Fortress, 1995) 26–58.

[102] *Acts of John* 63–65; see also *Acts of John* 23–24: the impassibility of the soul is useful to the realization of a miracle; *Acts of John* 26–29: purified, the soul can reach the Lord; redemption is the transformation of the soul according to *Acts of John* 112 and *Acts of Thomas* 28; a risk of falling back exists for the purified soul, *Acts of John* 107.

[103] There are great differences concerning Christology among the apocryphal acts themselves and between the apocryphal and the canonical acts. The *Acts of Thomas*, for example, have a conscious and developed Christology; see *Acts of Thomas* 10 (in a prayer); 45 (Christ has hidden his divine nature); 72 (a hymn to Jesus Christ lists his present salvific activity); 80 (surprise that the God Jesus became a man [in Luke-Acts that would be the surprise that the man Jesus is the Son of God]).

[104] *Acts of John* 94–102; this part of the work, along with chapter 109, has probably been interpolated into the *Acts of John*; see Junod and Kaestli, *Acta Iohannis*, 1:72–75, 99; 2:581–677; and idem, "Actes de Jean," in *Écrits apocryphes chrétiens*, 1:979–81. The chapters on the polymorphic Christ in *Acts of John* 87–93, which probably have another origin than chapters 94–102 and the rest of the *Acts of John*, as well as *Acts of Peter* 20 (Peter's homily on the Transfiguration story), also present a docetic form of Christology.

[105] Christ is called Father in *Acts of Andrew* 63.2; *Acts of John* 77; 94; 98; 109; 112; *Acts of Peter* 39; *Acts of Thomas* 97; 143; *Acts of Philip* 1.3; 3.7; 8.5; 14.5; *Acts of Philip Martyrdom* 26; 38.

For my purposes, the competition between Christ and the apostles in the preaching of the new message and the constitution of the new community is more interesting. The absence of a narrative gospel as a first part of a diptych is a clue for the marginalization of Christology in the apocryphal acts. Andrew or Thomas is now the providential agent while Christ is far away in heaven on the side of God and does not function any more as the mediator.[106] However, his present role is not totally eliminated: he may appear in a vision or a dream.[107] This weakening of Christology can be exemplified in the *Acts of Thomas* where in a discussion with Vizan, the son of the king Mazdai, Thomas explains that he (not Jesus Christ) is related to God in the spiritual realm, in the same way as Vizan, the son of the king, is related to his father in the material world.[108] The author is nevertheless conscious of the christological problem such a parallel brings: he lets Thomas say at this point that he is the "servant of Jesus Christ," and later – like John the Baptist in the fourth gospel (John 1:20) – that "I am not Jesus, but a servant of Jesus. I am not Christ, but a minister of Christ."[109]

The Lukan work fulfills a double function. On the one hand, it maintains memories of the sacred origin (of course not without many changes and biases); on the other, it solves problems posed by the present situation of the Christian communities. The gospel of Luke and the canonical Acts of the Apostles not only tell the story of Jesus and his disciples, but also open a window to the ecclesiastical situation as seen by the author. The apocryphal acts fulfill similar goals: they preserve ancient traditions about the apostles, anecdotes or longer stories embedded in small units or longer cycles, and they reflect the situation of their churches in the second and third centuries. The famous triangle (conversion of a lady infuriates the husband who attacks the apostle) reflects a sociological reality of the Christian mission (see Justin Martyr, *Second Apology*). The ethical teaching with its emphasis on sexual purity finds an adequate place in the puzzle of late antiquity. The opposition against the pagan cults fits the polemic of Christianity against the old Greek or Roman religions. These illustrate the ecclesiastical realities of the time, as also seen in the trend to apostolic authority, the organization of ministry, and the practice of sacraments.

Large discrepancies exist between the two corpora, and the scholar has to use the adjective "new" for the apocryphal acts because, coming later, these writings

---

[106] In the canonical Luke-Acts, Jesus Christ is the physician or doctor (for the term in the context of Jesus' activity see Luke 4:23; 5:31; 8:43; for Jesus' medical achievement, see Luke 4:38–40; 8:40–56; 18:35–43, and the other healing stories); in the *Acts of Philip* 4.4–5; 13.4; 14.1–4; *Acts of Philip Martyrdom* 13–15; and in *Acts of Thomas* 95.2, it is now the apostle who takes over this role or represents the heavenly physician.

[107] See François Bovon, "The Child and the Beast: Fighting Violence in Ancient Christianity," *HTR* 92 (1999) 369–92, esp. 387–88; reprinted in this volume, pp. 223–45 below.

[108] *Acts of Thomas* 139.2; 160.1.

[109] Ibid.

manifest situations and solutions which are more recent.[110] Compared with the simple baptism and sharing of bread in the canonical acts, a more developed liturgy appears in the apocryphal acts.[111] The strong presence of the unction with oil, for example, is well-known in the Syriac version of the *Acts of Thomas* as the preliminary rite to baptism.[112]

Compared with the canonical conversions, the apocryphal conversions receive ascetic colors. The interruption of a wedding and the renunciation of marital life become proofs of a Christian commitment.[113]

Compared with modest divine protection given to the imprisoned apostles in the canonical acts, the destruction of temples (*Acts of John* 37–47 or *Acts of Paul* 6.1–6) or the construction of church buildings (*Acts of Philip* 2.24; 7.2–3; 11.6–8) are triumphal signs of considerable success.

Compared with the apostles presented in the canonical acts as witnesses rather than miracle-workers, the apostles in the apocryphal acts are promoted to the status of heroes and saviors.[114] This transformation explains why their physical portraits suddenly become important. In the *Acts of Paul*, in the *Martyrdom of*

---

[110] I mention here other new elements present in the apocryphal acts and not yet present in the canonical acts: speeches to the cross (*Acts of Andrew* 54.2–3; *Acts of Peter* 37–39); many hymns and early Christian poetry (*Acts of John* 94–96); prayers addressed not only to God but also to Christ (*Acts of Thomas* 10 and 72); a reflection on the Trinity (*Acts of Thomas* 70); malediction of the enemies (*Acts of Peter* 14); the role of holy water in particular to purify houses (*Acts of Peter* 19) and to exorcize demons (*Acts of Philip* 9.2–3); and animals that speak are not uncommon: see *Acts of Peter* 9–12; *Acts of Thomas* 39 (donkey); *Acts of Philip* 8.17–18; see also n. 123 below.

[111] *Acts of Paul* 3.5, 25; 8.21 (fraction of the bread, normally with water); *Acts of Peter* 20 (Christian worship with reading of a passage of the gospel, the Transfiguration story, and a sermon on the biblical text); *Acts of John* 94–96 (hymn and dance); 46 (Christian worship with homily, Eucharist, and laying on of hands); 106–10 (sermon and Eucharist on Sunday); 115 (sign of the cross); *Acts of Thomas* 27; 49–50; 120–21 (unction with oil, baptism, and Eucharist); 156–58 (baptism preceded normally by unction with oil, Eucharist); *Acts of Philip* 1.18; 2.24; 3.19; 4.6 (baptisms); 11.9–10 (Eucharist); 12.9 (sprinkling with water); 14.9 (men baptized by Philip; women baptized by Mariamne); for allusions to ritual in the *Acts of Andrew*, see François Bovon, "The Words of Life in the Acts of the Apostle Andrew," *HTR* 87 (1994) 139–54, esp. 148.

[112] See Sebastian Brock, *Holy Spirit in the Syrian Baptismal Tradition* (The Syrian Churches Series 9; Bronx, N.Y.: Fordham University, 1979); Caroline Johnson, "Ritual Epicleses in the Greek *Acts of Thomas*," in Bovon, *Apocryphal Acts of the Apostles*, 172–204.

[113] *Acts of Thomas* 4–16; see Han J. W. Drijvers, "Thomasakten," in Schneemelcher, *Neutestamentliche Apokryphen*, 2:304–10. Procreation is discredited in particular in *Acts of Thomas* 12.

[114] See the three articles on the apocryphal acts of the apostles: Gérard Poupon, "L'accusation de magie dans les Actes apocryphes," in *Actes apocryphes des apôtres*, 71–94; Françoise Morard, "Souffrance et martyre dans les Actes apocryphes," in ibid., 95–108; Jean-Marc Prieur, "La figure de l'apôtre dans les Actes apocryphes d'André," in ibid., 121–140. See also their counterpart concerning the canonical Acts of the Apostles: Jacques Dupont, "L'apôtre comme intermédiaire du salut dans les Actes des Apôtres," *RTP* 112 (1980) 342–58; Bernard Trémel, "A propos d'Ac 20:7–12. Puissance du thaumaturge ou du témoin?," ibid., 359–70; Jean Zumstein, "L'apôtre comme martyr dans les Actes de Luc," ibid., 371–90.

Mark, and possibly in a lost part of the *Acts of Peter*, the authors, for example, do not resist the temptation to give a description of the physical appearance of the apostle.[115] Even in the *Acts of John*, John's portrait is commissioned by an admirer, Lycomedes. When John contemplates the work, and then sees his reflection in a mirror for the first time, he dismisses the likeness of himself and urges Lycomedes to focus on a "spiritual" portrait.[116]

Compared with the apocalyptic expectation of the second coming and judgment, a new type of eschatology is visible: fate after death now becomes the eschatological deadline (actually Luke is already going in this direction even if he respects the traditional apocalyptic schema).[117] This individualization of eschatology, its disconnection from world history, and its link to personal destiny[118] offer the possibility of new narratives such as tours and descriptions of Hell and Paradise.[119] Often spiritual life is the substitute for eschatological existence, and new virtues replace the old eschatological ones. While Luke has a special interest in ὑπομονή,[120] the *Acts of Thomas* presents a teaching of the apostle consisting of three different virtues: holiness, asceticism, and humility (*Acts of Thomas* 85–86).[121]

Compared with the early Christian doctrine of redemption (in Luke-Acts there is already a clear enlargement from a particularistic to a universalistic perspective),[122] the apocryphal acts, or some of them, are not satisfied with a salvation limited to the humans; they open cosmic windows and do not hesitate to connect redemption to the animal world. For example, a lion is baptized by Paul, and both a leopard and the kid of a goat are welcome – not without limitations – by Philip.[123]

---

[115] See *Acts of Paul* 3.3; *Martyrdom of Mark* (according to *Vaticanus graecus* 866); for Peter in his presentation in Nikephoros Callistes Xanthopoulos, *Historia ecclesiastica*, 2.39; Christopher R. Matthews, "Nicephorus Callistus' Physical Description of Peter: An Original Component of the *Acts of Peter?*," *Apocrypha* 7 (1996) 135–45.

[116] See *Acts of John* 26–29; Junod and Kaestli, *Acta Iohannis*, 2:446–56.

[117] See Jacques Dupont, "L'après-mort dans l'œuvre de Luc," *RTL* 3 (1972) 3–21; reprinted in idem, *Nouvelles études sur les Actes des apôtres* (LD 118; Paris: Cerf, 1984) 358–79.

[118] Death is considered dangerous travel for the soul (*Acts of John* 114); one who is dead, Gad, King Gundaphorus' brother, can still convert (*Acts of Thomas* 21–27), something impossible according to Luke 16:19–31.

[119] See the *Acts of Thomas* 55 and the *Acts of Philip* 1.4–14. The *Apocalypse of Peter* is at the verge: its original redaction keeps an apocalyptic description of the judgment (see the Ethiopic version); its revision transforms this apocalyptic communal event into an individual fate detached from the last days (see the Greek version); see also the *Apocalypse of Paul*.

[120] See Lucien Cerfaux, "Fructifiez en supportant (l'épreuve), à propos de Luc 8,15," *RB* 64 (1957) 481–91; reprinted in idem, *Recueil* (3 vols.; Gembloux: Duculot, 1954–62) 3:111–22.

[121] Paul, as we know, mentions three major virtues: faith, hope, and love, and gives love the first place (1 Cor 13:13; see Gal 5:22).

[122] See Bovon, *Luke the Theologian*, 273–328; 364–86.

[123] See *Acts of Paul* 9.7–26; *Acts of Philip* 8.16–*Martyrdom* 40; Christopher Matthews, "Articulate Animals: A Multivalent Motif in the Apocryphal Acts of the Apostles," in Bovon, *Apocryphal Acts of the Apostles*, 205–32. According to *Acts of Thomas* 70.3 and *Acts of Philip* 8,

Even concerning the demonic world, the authors introduce new developments. In order to defeat the enemy, the apostle requests a genealogy of evil from the demon,[124] and the negative forces are compelled to reveal their true nature and by so doing bring about their own defeat.[125]

From the evolution of penitence we know that the problem of sin after baptism preoccupied the Christians of antiquity. The main cause of anxiety was the permanence of time and its temptations. To solve the problem the first generations of Christians adopted several solutions, both ethical (a call to the will) and/or spiritual (the request of the Holy Spirit). The epistle to the Hebrews maintained the strict rule of the prohibition of sin after baptism, while the *Shepherd* of Hermas gave a last indulgence.[126] In Luke-Acts, contemporaneous with the epistle to the Hebrews, the problem does not appear explicitly. The schema is simple and attention driven to initial conversion and not to later penitence – the preaching of the gospel invites the Jew to add the knowledge of the Son to the knowledge of God, and the pagan to turn from idols to the living God. In both cases the first conversion is the proof of a Christian commitment; what happens later is just a question of perseverance.[127] In the apocryphal acts such a simple solution is no longer possible. The *Acts of John*, for example, shows extensively how faith is threatened by time and duration. In it, Drusiane is a Christian already, but the sinful love that a young man devotes to her disturbs her so much that she gets sick and depressed. Feeling responsible for what happens she asks the Lord for delivery and prefers to die. In a sermon, John explains that faith is like a sailing vessel that carries the sailor in which one is only out of danger at the end of the journey upon safe arrival at the harbor. The soul will be criticized if after a good beginning it does not persevere till the end.[128]

---

the divine mercy reaches even the world of the animals (*pace* Paul in 1 Cor 9:9). Note the providential role of animals also in *Acts of Thomas* 73; 78; 79.

[124] The *Acts of John* 84 considers seriously the reality of evil in the soul and in the world.

[125] *Acts of Thomas* 33; 44–45; 75.2; *Acts of Philip* 11.3.

[126] See Hebrews 6:4–6; Hermas, *Shepherd*; see Heinrich Karpp, ed. and trans., *Die Busse. Quellen zur Entstehung des altkirchlichen Busswesens* (Traditio Christiana 1; Zurich: EVZ-Verlag, 1969); Pierre-Marie Gy, "Penance and Reconciliation," in *The Church at Prayer: An Introduction to the Liturgy* (ed. Aimé Georges Martimort; trans. Matthew J. O'Connell; 4 vols.; Collegeville: Liturgical Press, 1988) 3:101–16. The case of Marcellus, a Christian who succumbs to the magical power of Simon and then repents (*Acts of Peter* 10), is a visualization of a real problem of the time of the author. What do we do in the Church with the Christians who sin and repent, particularly with the *lapsi*, those who could not resist the persecution? See Gérard Poupon, "Remaniement," in *ANRW* 2.25.6 (1988) 4363–83.

[127] See for the Jewish audience, Acts 2:14–41; for the pagan audience, Acts 17:16–34; Bovon, *Luke the Theologian*, 305–28.

[128] *Acts of John* 64–69; see also 107 and 112.

Literary Relationship

Do we find in the apocryphal acts of the apostles explicit references to Luke-Acts? This is a much debated question, as we know from the divergent opinions concerning the *Acts of Paul* being a conscious continuation of the canonical acts.[129] Entering this problem, I would suggest a panoply of possible connections between the two corpora.[130] It is clear that the apocryphal acts are built upon the Christian message and that their authors are not ignorant of early Christian traditions, particularly related to Jesus.[131]

But when they use a sentence of Jesus, they often quote it so liberally that it is difficult to ascertain which gospel is quoted.[132] They may have an oral teaching in mind, like the author of the *Acts of Thomas* quoting the Lord's prayer at the beginning of a speech, or the author of the *Acts of John* citing the sentence, "Ask, and it will be given you" (Luke 11:9).[133] An interpretation is added to this quotation: that Christians are free to ask for miracles. In a context where the value of miracles was disputed, the saying of the Lord served as a legitimization of thaumaturgic activity.[134] It is also interesting to note that the most quoted sayings of Jesus are those issued from Q. From Luke-Acts in any case, it is more the gospel than the Acts which is used, and inside the synoptic tradition more Q than Mark.[135]

---

[129] See Richard Bauckham, "The *Acts of Paul*: Replacement of Acts or Sequel to Acts?," *Semeia* 80 (1997) 159–68; Richard Pervo, "Egging on the Chickens: A Cowardly Response to Dennis MacDonald and Then Some," ibid., 43–56; Willy Rordorf, "Paul's Conversion in the Canonical Acts and in the *Acts of Paul*," ibid., 137–44 (trans. Peter W. Dunn).

[130] On the notions of quotation, imitation, allusion, amputation, see Bovon, "The Synoptic Gospels and the Noncanonical Acts of the Apostles"; and idem, "How Well the Holy Spirit Spoke through the Prophet Isaiah to Your Ancestors! (Acts 28:25)," in Bovon, *New Testament Traditions and Apocryphal Narratives*, 43–50, 195–96.

[131] See Bovon, "Facing the Scriptures."

[132] See Edouard Massaux, *Influence de l'Évangile de saint Matthieu sur la littérature chrétienne avant saint Irénée* (Leuven: Leuven University Press, 1950); and Helmut Koester, *Synoptische Überlieferung bei den apostolischen Vätern* (TUGAL 65; Berlin: Akademie-Verlag, 1957).

[133] *Acts of Thomas* 144; *Acts of John* 22.

[134] It is well known that Paul and John did not consider signs without hesitation and criticism; see 2 Corinthians 12 and John 2:23–25; 4:48; Fridrichsen, *Problème du miracle dans le christianisme primitif*; and recently Riley, *Resurrection Reconsidered*.

[135] Besides the quotations and allusions to Luke-Acts mentioned in the main text of this paper, here are some others which can be found in the apocryphal acts: *Acts of Thomas* 79 (allusion to the stages of Jesus' life, particularly when he was twelve; but the reference to Jesus' teacher is a reference to an apocryphal story preserved among others in the *Infancy Gospel according to Pseudo-Thomas* 6–7; 14; 15); 107 (Thomas is pleased to see in his life the realization of Jesus' beatitudes); *Acts of Paul* 3.5–6 (sequence of encratite beatitudes including some from the canonical gospels, quoted more from Matt 5:1–12 than from Luke 6:20–22); *Acts of John* 81 (allusion to the Sermon on the Mount or in the Plain, Matt 5:38–47 and Luke 6:27–35: do not return evil for evil); 95 (allusion to Luke 7:32//Matt 11:17: to play the flute and to lament); *Acts of Thomas* 7 (Greek text) (allusion to the Twelve and to the Seventy-Two disciples of Luke 9:1–6 and 10:1); *Acts of Peter* 40 (quotation of the Lord's saying, "Let the dead bury their own dead,"

Besides the quotations, one must consider the allusions (I am conscious of the difficulty of distinguishing between these two terms). In the *Acts of Philip*, for example, there are explicit allusions to the transfiguration story[136] and to the Sermon on the Plain (refusal to return evil for evil).

Different from quotation and allusion, imitation is another kind of literary technique. It is evident to me that the scene of Patroclus in the martyrdom of Paul relies on the canonical acts. In it, the young man, patterned after Eutyches, is seated at the window. Dozing off during Paul's sermon, he falls to the ground and dies. In both texts, Paul is present to take care of the young man and to resuscitate him.[137] The second of the *Acts of Philip* was originally an independent legend, and also stands as a rewriting of Paul's stay in Athens and his dispute with the philosophers.[138]

Another sort of intertextuality appears in the *Acts of Thomas*. The author appears proud to show that New Testament teachings, sayings of Jesus, or arguments of Paul found their realization in the time of the Church. The parable of the pounds can be applied to Thomas the good servant who with one pound has earned ten pounds (Luke 19:16; *Acts of Thomas* 146). In another case, Paul's argu-

---

Luke 9:60//Matt 11:17, understood as a prohibition of embalming); *Acts of Thomas* 53 (quotation of Luke 11:9//Matt 7:7: "Ask, and it will be given you"; in the main text of this paper I refer to a quotation of the same verse in the *Acts of John* 22); 28 (quotation of Matt 6:34, "So do not worry about tomorrow," then of Luke 12:24 combined with Matt 6:26, on the sorrows; finally of Matt 6:30, God takes care of you); *Acts of Peter* 35 (the apocryphal Peter goes into himself; implicit allusion to the prodigal son, Luke 15:17); 6 (there is something more dreadful than the millstone mentioned by the Lord, Luke 17:2; it is eternal damnation); *Acts of Thomas* 61 (in a prayer Thomas affirms that he and the other disciples left everything behind them, an allusion to Luke 18:28–30//Mark 10:28–31//Matt 19:27–30); 39 (allusion to the donkey of Palm Sunday, Luke 19:28–40//Mark 11:1–10//Matt 21:1–9//John 12:12–16); 69–70 (Luke 19:31//Mark 11:3//Matt 21:3: "The Lord needs it" in the context of the donkeys); 80 (reminder of Jesus' promise, Luke 22:30//Matt 19:28, to seat at his right and at his left in the Kingdom of God). For the references to the Gospel of Luke and the canonical Acts of the Apostles in the *Acts of Philip*, see my paper "Facing the Scriptures"; reprinted in this volume, pp. 272–84 below. Harvest is not so plenty in the case of references in the apocryphal acts to the canonical Acts: *Acts of Peter* 23 (in a speech to Simon, Peter reminds him what happened to them once in Palestine; is it a reference to Acts 8:9–25 or to the first lost part of the *Acts of Peter*? In any case there are two major differences with the canonical Acts: the first encounter took place in Jerusalem and not in Samaria, and Peter was accompanied by Paul, not John); *Acts of Thomas* 83 (all humans are equal before God; an allusion to Acts 10:34–35?); 84 (implicit reference to the Decalogue and, because of the three major sins, to the moral version of the apostolic decree, Acts 15:29?); *Acts of Paul* 3.15–17 and 9.12–14 (suit against Paul similar to Acts 24–26). In the main text of this paper the cycle in Ephesus (*Acts of Paul* 9) and the episode of the sleeping Patrocles (*Acts of Paul* 14.1) are compared to Acts 19 and 20:7–12.

136 *Acts of Philip* 5.22–23; during her martyrdom, Mariamne is transfigured but there is no reference to Jesus' Transfiguration; see *Acts of Philip Martyrdom* 20.

137 *Acts of Paul* 14.1; see Acts 20:7–12; see for another opinion Willy Rordorf, "In welchem Verhältnis stehen die apokryphen Paulusakten zur kanonischen Apostelgeschichte und zu den Pastoralbriefen?," in idem, *Lex orandi – Lex credendi* (Paradosis 36; Fribourg: Universitätsverlag, 1993) 458–61.

138 See Amsler, *Acta Philippi. Commentarius*, 85–125.

ment that the hypocrite coming to the table of the Lord will be punished (1 Cor 11:29–34) receives its fulfillment in the case of the young murderer of the *Acts of Thomas* 51.

Besides quotation, allusion, and imitation, there is yet another option. Some cases in which similarities exist between the canonical and the apocryphal acts should not be explained by literary dependence, but by a common dependence upon oral tradition. The most impressive cases, also the most difficult, are the cycles of episodes taking place in Ephesos as we find them in the canonical acts (Acts 19–20), the Pauline epistles (1 Cor 15:32), and the *Acts of Paul* (9.1–28).[139] Common to these are the references to the Pentecost, the meeting with the wild beasts, the silversmiths, the theater, the prison, and the liberation from prison. But the whole organization of the stories is so different that the use here of the canonical acts by the author of the *Acts of Paul* seems out of question.

The final option coincides with what Gérard Genette calls the "hypertext," namely when the author of an apocryphal text wishes to give a continuation to the canonical acts.[140] Such a case is difficult to prove. For the earlier apocryphal acts I would prefer to speak of either the competition with the canonical acts or the ignorance of them. The *Acts of Peter* or the *Acts of Paul* either ignore the canonical acts or offer an alternative story. The later ones, on the other hand, cannot dismiss the existence of the canonical book and prefer to offer a supplement to the hungry readers. The third of the *Acts of Philip* can be considered as a complement to the story of Philip and the Samaritans in Acts 8.[141] While the canonical text describes Philip the evangelist as converting the Samaritan crowd, who then receive the gift of the Holy Spirit from the apostles Peter and John, the *Acts of Philip* introduces the same apostles Peter and John, but this time their purpose is to give Philip what he is still missing to become a real and full apostle.

The authors of the apocryphal acts can choose many ways to deal with the early Christian traditions they have received. Often using the theological category of fulfillment, they consider that Jesus' promises found a realization in the time of the Church and that the apostles obeyed Jesus' commands successfully. It becomes clear therefore that the apocryphal acts prefer to establish links with the canonical gospels rather than with the canonical acts, and with Jesus' teaching

---

[139] See Charles K. Barrett, *A Commentary on the First Epistle to the Corinthians* (New York: Harper & Row, 1968) 365–66; and Helmut Koester, "Ephesos in Early Christian Literature," in *Ephesos: Metropolis of Asia* (ed. Helmut Koester; Valley Forge, Pa.: Trinity Press International, 1995) 119–40.

[140] See Gérard Genette, *Palimpsestes. La littérature au second degré* (Paris: Seuil, 1982) 11–14; idem, *Seuils* (Paris: Seuil, 1987).

[141] See the new edition of the manuscript of Mount Athos *Xenophontos* 32 by Bovon, Bouvier, and Amsler, *Acta Philippi. Textus*, 76–113; and the explanations by Amsler, *Acta Philippi. Commentarius*, 129–38; Christopher Matthews, "Peter and Philip Upside Down: Perspectives on the Relation of the Acts of Philip to the Acts of Peter," in *SBLSP 1996* (Atlanta: Scholars Press, 1996) 23–34.

rather than with Jesus' deeds. The authors of the apocryphal acts, however, do not seem to feel any need to be literal in the quotations because the content is more important than the form.

Conclusion

The canonical acts and the apocryphal acts can be compared because they share some essential elements of Christianity. In the past such comparisons have been done for apologetic or polemical reasons. Apologetically, they have been used to prove that the canonical acts are an eloquent and orthodox Christian teaching while the apocryphal are a legendary and heretical literature for entertainment.[142] Polemically, they have been compared to prove that historically or theologically the canonical acts are not "better" than the apocryphal acts. Today we should try to avoid such traps and remain on the level of the history of literature and religious thought.

By following this path we can apply – with profit and delight – the methods of form criticism, composition criticism, and history of Christian thought. Form criticism helps us to find, define, and understand the small literary units; composition criticism helps us to observe and analyze the larger cycles and the whole books; history of Christian thought helps us to articulate the religious positions of these writings and to discover the socio-ecclesiastical problems the authors and their communities were facing.

The validity of comparison, however, has been questioned recently.[143] I defend the right, even the necessity, of comparison in order to understand texts. In fulfilling the task of comparing one would like to know the historical framework of ancient Christianity or Christianities to give meaning to the differences and similarities. This framework remains hidden as long as texts are not read and compared. Of course, like in cybernetics, error and truth, knowledge and ignorance do not appear in chronological order, but react on each other in a dialectical way. We could express the hypothesis that Luke-Acts was written at the end of the first century C.E. at the junction of Jewish historiography influenced by the Septuagint and profane Greek historiography; that the *Acts of Andrew* was composed in the second century C.E. in an atmosphere of philosophical dialogue and spiritual metaphysics; that the *Acts of Thomas*, which proclaims the redemption of the

---

[142] Contrary to this assertion, see Pervo, *Profit with Delight*.

[143] See particularly Jonathan Z. Smith, *Drudgery Divine: On the Comparison of Early Christianities and the Religions of Late Antiquity* (Chicago Studies in the History of Judaism; Chicago: University of Chicago Press, 1990); in defense of comparison see Kimberley C. Patton, "Juggling Torches: Why We Still Need Comparative Religion," in *A Magic Still Dwells: Comparative Religion in the Postmodern Age* (ed. Kimberley C. Patton and Benjamin C. Ray; Berkeley: University of California Press, 2000) 153–71.

soul from the body, fits into the historical situation of Christianity of third-century Syria. The comparison is forced upon us by the common title πρᾶξεις, "Acts," and by the more cultural categories of canonical and apocryphal. Scholars cannot avoid comparison.

There is certainly a risk, mentioned at the beginning of this paper,[144] that the differences among the apocryphal texts themselves may be smoothed out by the simple opposition between canonical and apocryphal. It has been my constant effort in this paper to keep away from such confusion. Careful readers see strong divergences in Christology (docetism can be present in certain passages of the *Acts of John*, incarnation underlined in the *Acts of Philip*) or in the realm of asceticism (marriage can be banned all together in some parts of the *Acts of Thomas* in favor of encratism and purity; marriage can be accepted if combined with strict morality in other apocryphal Acts). Those differences do not prevent authors of such different worldviews from calling upon the same literary genre. Different writers and different communities shared similar needs.

Such a large range of readings therefore helps us to understand better the first centuries of Christianity; but it leads us also to respect the differences between both the various texts and the early Christian communities. Inside a general common framework the canonical and the apocryphal acts have their idiosyncrasies: the canonical Acts brings the message of the resurrection of the crucified Jesus, the history of the first messengers of the gospel, and a confirmation of the gospel of Luke.[145] The *Acts of Peter* develops a propaganda of Christian faith through miracles and seems at home in the Roman Church of the end of the second century C.E.; written around the same time, the *Acts of Paul*, even if it became rapidly suspicious to mainstream Christianity, was very much at home in the Pauline missionary school; it defends a subversive attitude toward political authorities and a claim for female ministry;[146] the *Acts of John* calls for a veneration of the beloved disciple; and the *Acts of Philip* praises the missionary of Bethsaida, his sister Mariamne, and his companion Bartholomew.[147] From these literary distinctions we can try to recreate the historical situation, the setting of their authors, and the sociological location of their communities and first readers. This cannot be done here on a large scale. What can be said without hesitation is that there are a variety of religious experiences that lay behind these different texts. There is a common flow of ancient Christian faith but there are also a great

---

[144] See n. 10 above.

[145] See Willem C. van Unnik, "The 'Book of Acts' – The Confirmation of the Gospel," *NovT* 4 (1960) 26–59; reprinted in idem, *Sparsa Collecta: The Collected Essays of W. C. van Unnik* (3 vols.; NovTSup 29–31; Leiden: Brill, 1973) 1:340–73.

[146] See Ann Graham Brock, "Political Authority and Cultural Accommodation: Social Diversity in the *Acts of Paul* and the *Acts of Peter*," in Bovon, *Apocryphal Acts of the Apostles*, 145–70.

[147] It might be interesting to investigate the proposography of the canonical acts and the apocryphal acts.

number of fields watered by this large river. The *Acts of Andrew* and the *Acts of Peter* both tell the story of an apostle's life and death. Nevertheless the texts compared are different in their function as well as in their historical setting. By comparing the differences among similar documents one sees life arise, the life of Christians in Syria, in Rome, or in Egypt.

Among all these stories about the apostles one double book was chosen by the mainstream Christian communities, Luke-Acts. The canonization of Acts remains an obscure phenomenon for modern scholars. But the historians of Christianity can say with some confidence that this selection was not realized to gain an historical proof of the Christian origins. The canon represents more the tradition of some churches and the collection of books used for worship by dominant communities. Such liturgical reading was declared legitimate more for doctrinal than historical reasons. Nevertheless, the wish to keep a memory of the origins was also present, and modern scholars share this ancient view adding only a new emphasis: the requirement to read both the canonical and noncanonical texts in order to gain greater access to the beginnings of Christianity.

The Child and the Beast:
Fighting Violence in Ancient Christianity*

*Gerade in der Mitte der Religion droht
faszinierend blutige Gewalt.*[1]

Introduction

Popular nature programs, such as the cable-television program *Wild Discovery*, are both appealing and frightening because they confront the audience with acts of pure violence that follow the natural law of the jungle and the harsh imperative of nature's food chain. Viewers are enthralled watching the leopard catch its prey: such is the power of violence.

A contrasting theme to that of the violence in nature is presented in the successful Walt Disney movie *Beauty and the Beast*, based on the fairy tale written in the eighteenth century by Jeanne-Marie Leprince de Beaumont. In the movie, the beast is slowly tamed by the beauty. At a precise moment, he overcomes his natural cruelty and opens his paw, which is now filled with grain, and delights in the birds who come to feed on it. The message is clear: such is the power of love.[2]

In today's world the reality of violence surrounds us: the presence of violence[3] in our cities; the rapes and massacres that occur in unstable countries, such as the

---

* This essay was originally presented as a faculty research lecture at the Harvard Divinity School, 9 April 1998. For permission to reproduce figs. 1 and 2, the author gratefully acknowledges: (1) Thomas F. Mathews, *The Clash of the Gods* (1993) and Princeton University Press; (2) Antonio Ferrua, *The Unknown Catacomb: A Unique Discovery of Early Christian Art* (1990) and Geddes & Grosset, Ltd.

[1] Walter Burkert, *Homo Necans: The Anthropology of Ancient Greek Sacrificial Ritual and Myth* (Berkeley: University of California Press, 1983) 2: "Blood and violence lurk fascinatingly at the very heart of religion."

[2] One can speak of the "double bind" present in our society: just vindication trying to fight violence, and pure love trying to overcome inequity, what Gil Bailie (*Violence Unveiled: Humanity at the Crossroads* [New York: Crossroad, 1997] 19) calls our double allegiance to John Wayne and Mother Theresa.

[3] On the violence, see Georges Sorel, *Réflexions sur la violence* (Paris: Librairie de "Pages libres," 1908; reprinted in Paris: Slatkine France, 1981); Hans Windisch, *Der messianische Krieg und das Urchristentum* (Tübingen: Mohr Siebeck, 1909); Konrad Lorenz, *Das sogenannte Böse. Zur Naturgeschichte der Aggression* (3d. ed.; Vienna: Borotha Schoeler, 1964); Walter Benjamin, *Zur Kritik der Gewalt und andere Aufsätze* (Frankfurt: Suhrkamp, 1965); Marvin E. Wolfgang,

1981 atrocity in El Mozote, El Salvador, with the little girl singing hymns before her death; the economic oppression revealed by class analysis; the emergence of totalitarianism between the two world wars, with the mythological description of the dictators as Minotaur in depictions by Picasso or Dürrenmatt; the discovery of institutional violence by students on the barricades in 1968; the resurgence of the persecution of Christians in several parts of this world; and the postcolonial insight that biblical scholarship is not an innocent paradigm. In the face of all this violence, both physical and metaphorical, how can we escape a cynical resignation or a naïve utopianism?[4]

This article attempts to unveil the ethical behavior of some early Christians and to examine their religious faith in a cosmic redemption. With a high degree of realism these early Christians knew that evil and violence were universal, present in every society, in the church, and in the soul. The triumph of violence seemed inescapable. But they also knew that zones of peace could be established, that models of nonretaliation could be created, and that victory over demonic bestiality could be hoped for, not only through the victory of the cross (which can become a doctrinal abstraction) but also through the power of human love.

In the first part of this article I show that the metaphor of the beast appears in early Christian apocryphal texts as an embodiment of the power of evil and that, according to cosmic redemption, violence (symbolized by the beast) can be overcome. In the second part I argue that the love of one's enemies, as narrated in the

<hr>

ed., *Patterns of Violence: The Annals of the American Academy of Political and Social Science* 364 (Philadelphia: American Academy of Political and Social Science, 1966); Paul Blanquart et al., *A la recherche d'une théologie de la violence* (Paris: Cerf, 1968); Anthony Storr, *Human Aggression* (New York: Atheneum, 1968); Erik Erikson, *Gandhi's Truth on the Origins of Militant Violence* (New York: Norton, 1969; reprinted in New York: Norton, 1993); Hannah Arendt, *On Violence* (New York: Harcourt, Brace & World, 1970); Martin Hengel, *Gewalt und Gewaltlosigkeit. Zur "politischen Theologie" in neutestamentlicher Zeit* (Calwer Hefte 118; Stuttgart: Calwer, 1971); Burkert, *Homo Necans*; René Girard, *La violence et le sacré* (Paris: Grasset, 1972); Erich Fromm, *The Anatomy of Human Destructiveness* (New York: Reinhardt and Winston, 1973); Michel Serres, *Rome, le livre des fondations* (Paris: Grasset, 1983); Heinz-Horst Schrey and Manfred Moser, "Gewalt/Gewaltlosigkeit," in *TRE* 13 (Berlin: de Gruyter, 1984) 168–84; Robert G. Hamerton-Kelly, ed., *Violent Origins: Walter Burkert, René Girard, and Jonathan Z. Smith on Ritual Killing and Cultural Formation* (Stanford, Calif.: Stanford University Press, 1987); Robert G. Hamerton-Kelly, *Sacred Violence: Paul's Hermeneutic of the Cross* (Minneapolis: Fortress, 1992); Renzo Petraglio, *Obiezione di coscienza. Il Nuovo Testamento provoca chi lo legge* (2d ed.; Etica Teologica Oggi 1; Bologna: Edizioni Dehoniane Bologna, 1992); "Violence and Religion," in *The HarperCollins Dictionary of Religion* (ed. Jonathan Z. Smith; New York: HarperCollins, 1995) 1120–23; Calvert Watkins, *How to Kill a Dragon: Aspects of Indo-European Poetics* (New York: Oxford University Press, 1995); Bailie, *Violence Unveiled.*

[4] Is not bloody vindication the regular final solution, from the time of Homer (*Iliad* 6.57–60) and the Hebrew Bible (Ps 5:5–6)? See William Klassen, *Love of Enemies: The Way to Peace* (OBT 15; Philadelphia: Fortress, 1984) 13; François Bovon, *Das Evangelium nach Lukas* (3 vols. so far; EKKNT 3.1–3; Neukirchen-Vluyn: Neukirchener Verlag; Zurich: Benzinger, 1989–2001) 1:312–14.

Gospel of Luke, is closely related to this reconciliation. In the third segment I suggest that in various Christian circles children functioned as a symbol for all those people who accepted this liberating message. And, finally, I suggest that children received the message because Christ himself never lost his symbolic identity as a child.

It would be wrong to believe that the early Christians were the first to unveil violence (remember the Greek tragedy *Medea*),[5] the first to refuse blind vindication (witness the Pythagorean tradition),[6] or the first to share apocalyptic hope for universal reconciliation (read Josephus).[7] But at a time when theology was still very much connected with the use of metaphor and narration, the early Christian images of the child and the beast, as they appear in the canonical Gospel of Luke and in the apocryphal acts of the apostles, still can be instructive for our time and can remain relevant from a theological perspective.

It is my opinion that in recent discussions regarding violence and religion, scholars have focused excessively on the relation of violence to sacrifice, as is apparent in the works of René Girard and Walter Burkert, and in their dialogue with Jonathan Z. Smith.[8] My interest is in the theological dimension of violence as perceived by the early Christians and in their ethical direction to fight against it.

Fighting Violence in the *Acts of the Apostle Philip*

One of the happiest events in the life of a scholar is the moment of discovery.[9] I will never forget the afternoon in the Monastery of Xenophontos on Mount

---

[5] The nurse fears what her mistress Medea will do: "For late I saw her glare, as glares a bull, | On these, as 'twere for mischief; nor her wrath, | I know, shall cease, until its lightning strike. | To foes may she work ill, and not to friends!" (*Medea* 92–95 [trans. Arthur S. Way; LCL; Cambridge, Mass.: Harvard University Press, 1980] 291). See Girard, *La violence et le sacré*, 23–30.

[6] See the discussion later in this article at "Love of Enemies in the Gospel of Luke," and Isidore Lévy, *La légende de Pythagore. De Grèce en Palestine* (Bibliothèque de l'École des Hautes Études, Sciences historiques et philologiques 250; Paris: Champion, 1927) 221–23.

[7] Josephus, *Ap.* 2.213: "So thorough a lesson has he [the legislator] given us in gentleness and humanity that he does not overlook even the brute beasts, authorizing their use only in accordance with the Law, and forbidding all other employment of them. Creatures which take refuge in our houses like suppliants we are forbidden to kill. He would not suffer us to take the parent birds with their young, and bade us even in an enemy's country to spare and not to kill the beasts employed in labour. Thus, in every particular, he had an eye to mercy, using the laws I have mentioned to enforce the lesson, and drawing up for transgressors other penal laws admitting of no excuse" (trans. H. St. J. Thackeray; LCL; New York: G. P. Putnam's Sons, 1926, p. 379).

[8] See Burkert, *Homo Necans*; Girard, *La violence et le sacré*; Hammerton-Kelly, *Violent Origins*; Smith, "Violence and Religion," 1120–23; Bailie, *Violence Unveiled*. Thus Burkert, "*Homo religiosus* acts and attains self awareness as *homo necans*" (*Homo Necans*, 3). Typical are the following sentences of Girard: "C'est la communauté entière que le sacrifice protège de sa propre violence" (*La violence et le sacré*, 22), "le sacrifice est une violence sans risque de vengeance" (ibid., 29), or "c'est la violence qui constitue le cœur véritable et l'âme secrète du sacré" (ibid., 52).

[9] See François Bovon, Bertrand Bouvier, and Frédéric Amsler, *Acta Philippi. Textus* (CCSA

Athos when Bertrand Bouvier, Éric Junod, and I discovered a strange story of the apostle Philip in a neglected ancient Greek manuscript. This story, which has now become the twelfth of Philip's Acts, tells how two animals – one wild (a leopard), and one domestic (a goat kid) – were attracted to the apostle, adhered to the Christian message, felt their animal instincts being transformed by the apostolic presence, began to speak like human beings,[10] and, finally, complained of Philip's hesitation regarding their baptism and their admittance to communion.[11]

What is exciting in this story of the *Acts of Philip* is the content of the dialogue and the theological argument brought forth by the two animals.[12] These animals' point is that, for divine reconciliation in Christ to be complete, it must extend to more than humanity.[13] They believe that divine reconciliation embraces the whole of creation: "God," says the converted leopard, "cares for every nature, even for

11; Turnhout: Brepols, 1999); and Frédéric Amsler, *Acta Philippi. Commentarius* (CCSA 12; Turnhout: Brepols, 1999). French translation in *Actes de l'apôtre Philippe* (intro. and ann. Frédéric Amsler; trans. François Bovon, Bertrand Bouvier, and Frédéric Amsler; Apocryphes 8; Turnhout: Brepols, 1996); and iidem, "Actes de Philippe," in *Écrits apocryphes chrétiens,* I (ed. François Bovon and Pierre Geoltrain; La Pléiade 442; Paris: Gallimard, 1997) 1178–1320.

[10] See Christopher R. Matthews, "Articulate Animals: A Multivalent Motif in the Apocryphal Acts of the Apostles," in *The Apocryphal Acts of the Apostles: Harvard Divinity School Studies* (ed. François Bovon, Ann Graham Brock, and Christopher R. Matthews; Center for the Study of World Religions: Religions of the World; Cambridge, Mass.: Harvard University Press, 1999) 205–32.

[11] Remember the classical story of Androcles (or Androclus) and the lion, and its adaptation in the *Acts of Paul*: the lion with the needle in its paw is healed by the wise man. Later the lion remembers its benefactor and does not kill him in the arena. On the story of Androcles, see Aulus Gellius, *Noctes Atticae* 5.14; Dennis R. MacDonald, *The Legend and the Apostle: The Battle for Paul in Story and Canon* (Philadelphia: Westminster Press, 1983) 21–23. (I thank Christopher R. Matthews for the previous reference.) On the conversion and baptism of the lion in *Acts Paul* 9.7–26 (for §§ 7–14 and part of §§ 22–23 following the Coptic Papyrus Bodmer 41, pp. 1–8, and for §§ 15–26 following the Greek Papyrus of Hamburg, pp. 1–5), see Willy Rordorf, with the collaboration of Pierre Cherix and Rodolphe Kasser, "Actes de Paul," in *Écrits apocryphes chrétiens,* 1:1151–60; Matthews, "Articulate Animals," 206–11. As known from the paintings in the Roman catacombs, the memory of Daniel among the lions was well preserved among the early Christians. Remember also the speaking animals of the biblical Balaam story (Num 22:21–35) and of the apocryphal *Acts Thom.* 70.1–5.

[12] On the animal in antiquity, see *Das Tier in der Antike. 400 Werke ägyptischer, griechischer, etruskischer und römischer Kunst aus privatem und öffentlichem Besitz* (Zurich: Archäologisches Institut der Universität Zürich, 1974); Philippe Borgeaud, Yves Christe, and Ivanka Urio, eds., *L'animal, l'homme, le dieu dans le Proche-Orient ancien. Actes du colloque de Cartigny 1991* (Centre d'étude du Proche-Orient ancien, Université de Genève. Les Cahiers du CEPOA 2; Leuven: Peeters, 1985).

[13] On the human level, see the reaction of Isaac the Syrian: "An elder once asked, 'What is a compassionate heart?' He replied: 'It is a heart on fire for the whole of creation, for humanity, for the birds, for the animals, for demons and for all that exists … . This is why he constantly offers up prayer full of tears, even for the irrational animals and for the enemies of truth, even for those who harm him, so that they may be protected and find mercy'" (*The Heart of Compassion: Daily Readings with St. Isaac of Syria,* [ed. Arthur M. Allchin; trans. Sebastian Brock; London: Darton, Longman, and Todd, 1989] 29). I thank my colleague Kimberley Patton for this reference.

that of the wild beasts, because of his great pity" (*Acts Phil.* 12.5).[14] The apostle himself becomes convinced by their argument and answers: "It is now evident: God has visited the universe through his Christ, including in his project not only the human beings, but also the beasts and every animal species. Who is able to tell his loving providence, which he reveals always to us?" (*Acts Phil.* 12.6).[15]

The author's rhetorical choice of the leopard and the kid of a goat in the *Acts of Philip* parallels the text of the Hebrew Bible.[16] In a prophetic oracle of Isaiah, the paradisiac description of universal peace is drawn by using a leopard and a kid – both of which are present peacefully beside one another (Isa 11:6).[17] This biblical prophecy was particularly appealing to the Christians of antiquity, as it is to modern theologians (for example, Andrew Linzey).[18] Two different interpretations of the leopard and kid have been common among Christians drawn to this oracle.

In the first interpretation, an allegorical one, the different animals represent the different types of Christians. The church, through Christ's redemption, is the place where these evil (animal) tendencies of revenge can be overcome and where a real reconciliation among human beings can be achieved.[19]

The second interpretation can be considered millenarianist or apocalyptic. According to this vision, the animals must be taken literally. Their reconciliation is a cosmic one that will be reached in the Kingdom of God in the last days. If the dimensions of redemption are broader in this second case, its implementation is, nevertheless, still expected on earth. In other words, today one still observes how violence prevails among animals and among humans.[20]

---

[14] This phrase is the translation of the manuscript from Mount Athos, *Xenophontos* 32, as published by Bovon, Bouvier, and Amsler, *Acta Philippi. Textus*, 305.

[15] This excerpt is the translation of the manuscript of Mount Athos, *Xenophontos* 32, as published in Bovon, Bouvier, and Amsler, *Acta Philippi. Textus* 305. See n. 7 above for Josephus, *Ap.* 2.213; and notice also the interest of Philo, *Hypothetica* (*Apologia pro Iudaeis*) 7.6–9 for the Golden Rule and respect for animals. Both Josephus and Philo seem to be influenced by the Pythagorian tradition; see Lévy, *La légende de Pythagore*, 223; Isidore Lévy, *Recherches esséniennes et pythagoriciennes* (Centre de recherches d'histoire et de philologie de la IVe Section de l'École Pratiques des Hautes Études, III, Hautes Études du monde gréco-romain, 1; Geneva: Droz; Paris: Minard, 1965) 54–56.

[16] Amsler proposes to understand the leopard and the kid in the *Acts of Philip* as animals devoted to the goddess Cybele. But he does not deny the interpretation along the lines of Isaiah's prophecy, arguing that the text can be read at several levels; see Frédéric Amsler, "Les *Actes de Philippe*. Aperçu d'une compétition religieuse en Phrygie," in *Le mystère apocryphe. Introduction à une littérature méconnue* (ed. Jean-Daniel Kaestli and Daniel Marguerat; Essais Bibliques 26; Geneva: Labor et Fides, 1995) 125–40; idem, "The Apostle Philip, the Viper, the Leopard and the Kid: The Masked Actors of a Religious Conflict in Hierapolis of Phrygia (*Acts of Philip* VIII–XV and *Martyrdom*)," in *SBLSP 1996* (Atlanta: Scholars Press, 1996) 432–37.

[17] On the animal in the Jewish life, culture, and religion, see Elijah Judah, *Animal Life in Jewish Tradition: Attitudes and Relationships* (New York: KTAV, 1984).

[18] Andrew Linzey, *Animal Theology* (London: SCM, 1994).

[19] One is reminded of the famous *Physiologus*; see *Der Physiologus* (trans. Otto Seel; Lebendige Antike; Zurich: Artemis, 1960).

[20] If we can count Irenaeus among the western Church Fathers, the following three Christian

But the *Acts of Philip* affords a third interpretation: when the Gospel is preached, when the apostolic presence is visible, when the heart is transformed, an anticipation of the Kingdom, a limited but real one, can be observed. The leopard and the kid have their place as animals, reconciled and redeemed, in the Christian community.[21]

That the author of this tale has a theological agenda is confirmed by reading the entire text. The two other relevant passages belong to the well-known genre of exorcism, but, as we also find in the *Shepherd of Hermas*,[22] they tell the story of a victory over a great dragon, and not merely the story of an exorcism of a small, personal demon. The beast is described in dreadful terms, and the entirety of apostolic power, enforced by Christ's authority, is needed to overcome him. The confrontation is a mythological way of describing the tension in this world between the divine and the demonic.[23] The confrontation is as utopian as a theological program, yet it is as realistic as the State of the Union address. As soon as the dragon of the *Acts of Philip* is defeated, he admits that "Henceforth, we confess that we have been reduced to nothing. For the one who has been crucified for our misfortune has dried out our primeval nature" (*Acts Phil.* 11.2).[24] He then confesses to be the incarnation of evil,[25] which has descended from the first generation to the present one.[26]

----

authors of the western part of the Roman Empire are favorable to the literal understanding of Isa 11:6–8: Irenaeus of Lyon, *Adversus haereses* 5.33.4 (see Eusebius of Caesarea, *Historia ecclesiastica* 3.39.1 and 11–13); *Demonstratio praedicationis apostolicae* 61; Tertullian, *Adversus Hermogenem* 11.3; Lactantius, *Divinae institutiones* 7.24.

[21] In the finale of the book, the animals have to stay in the building of the church until their death (*Acts of Philip Martyrdom* 40 [146]). Because of an ancient miracle, a cock and hen are preserved alive in the church of Santo Domingo de la Cazada in Spain; see C.-M. Molas, "Dominique de la Calzada," in *Dictionnaire d'histoire et de géographie ecclésiastiques* 14 (Paris: Letouzé et Ané, 1960) 609–10.

[22] *Shepherd of Hermas* 22–24 (*Vis.* 4); see Erik Peterson, "Die Begegnung mit dem Ungeheuer," *VC* 8 (1954) 52–71; reprinted in idem, *Frühkirche, Judentum und Gnosis. Studien und Untersuchungen* (Darmstadt: Wissenschaftliche Buchgesellschaft, 1982) 285–309.

[23] The same tension is visible in the story of Jesus' temptation, particularly in a Markan peculiarity, the presence of the wild beasts (Mark 1:13).

[24] This quotation is the translation of the manuscript from Mount Athos, *Xenophontos* 32, as published in Bovon, Bouvier, and Amsler, *Acta Philippi. Textus*, 285. One should not forget Jesus' saying in Luke: "See, I have given you authority to tread on snakes and scorpions, and over all the power of the enemy; nothing will hurt you" (Luke 10:19); see Bovon, *Das Evangelium nach Lukas*, 2:49, 56–58; and in the not original ending of the second Gospel, Mark 16:17–18.

[25] See Herbert Haag, *Teufelsglaube* (Tübingen: Katzmann, 1974); Thomas M. Provatakis, Ὁ Διάβολος εἰς τὴν βυζαντινὴν τέχνην. Συμβολὴ εἰς τὴν ἔρευναν τῆς ὀρθοδόξου ζωγραφικῆς καὶ γλυπτικῆς (Thessaloniki-Oraiokastron: Ergostasion graphikon technon A. Rekou, 1980); Bernard Teyssèdre, *Naissance du Diable. De Babylone aux grottes de la mer Morte* (Paris: Albin Michel, 1985); idem, *Le Diable et l'Enfer au temps de Jésus* (Paris: Albin Michel, 1985); Richard P. Greenfield, *Traditions of Belief in Late Byzantine Demonology* (Amsterdam: Hakkert, 1988); Elaine Pagels, *The Origin of Satan* (New York: Random House, 1995); Luther Link, *The Devil: Archfiend in Art from the Sixth to the Sixteenth Century* (New York: Harry N. Abrams, 1996); Bernard McGinn, *Antichrist: Two Thousand Years of the Human Fascination with Evil*

Later the story presents a contrasting situation. No longer are there wild beasts that are tamed[27] nor a dragon that is made innocuous, but instead a tragic event occurs: the apostle himself succumbs to the desire for vindication. Crucified upside down, Philip cannot refrain from cursing his enemies, and he therefore falls back into the realm of violence. Appearing to his agonizing disciple, Jesus answers Philip's recrimination. Jesus does not give a theological response, but an ethical one, as if the author, reflecting on the tension that the early Christians had to endure, were a step short of doctrinal explanation. Jesus says, "O Philip, because you moved away from my command by the sole fact that you did not fulfill my command, which is not to retaliate evil by evil, you will be retained prisoner in the eternal realm for forty days before you will reach your final destination."[28]

These legends are more than a source of entertainment; they express the fears, hopes, and creeds of a movement in early Christianity. These followers of Jesus Christ were realistic enough to understand the potential threat of political authority in the *Acts of Philip* (the governor is named "Tyrannognophos," which loosely means "dictator of darkness"), as well as the risk of falling back into the rule of violent retribution. But they were also wise enough to defend the utopian conviction that God (through Christ) was reconciling not only the human heart but also the whole of creation, casting out the rule of violence and overcoming the law of the jungle.

What is so poignant in the *Acts of Philip*, through the use of metaphors and the themes of taming violence (or victory over evil powers), is also visible elsewhere

---

(New York: HarperSanFrancisco, 1996). I thank Nick Constas for the information concerning Richard P. Greenfield and Thomas M. Provatakis.

[26] See also *Acts Phil.* 9.1–5 (102–6) for another victory over a dragon; see also the expression ἡ ἐνέργεια τοῦ ἀγρίου θηρίου, "the power of the wild beast" that Clement of Alexandria uses (*Stromateis* 4.9.74.4) by quoting freely from the already mentioned passage of the *Shepherd of Hermas* 23.5 (*Vis.* 4.2.5).

[27] Within the ascetic tradition, Athanasius of Alexandria (*The Life of Antony* 15; PG 26:865) and John Moschos (*The Spiritual Meadow* [Pratum Spirituale][intro., trans., and ann. John Wortley; Cistercian Studies Series 139; Kalamazoo, Mich.: Cistercian Publications, 1992] 5, 13, 39–40, 45–46, 102, 130–31) show how interested the first monks – in this case, in Egypt and Palestine – were in the animal world. We read several stories telling how dangerous crocodiles could become innocuous by Antony's prayer and sign of the cross, how the aggression of a lion could be defeated by the prayer of a holy man, and how the threat of a snake could be dispelled by the piety of another father. For these monks, the wild beasts live under the rule of the jungle, like the human sinners, until they are reached by God's grace, transmitted by the mediation of the apostle or of the holy man. In the *Life of Antony* 9–10 the demons take the shape of wild beasts and they are tamed by the virtue of the saint in the presence of Christ; see PG 26:855–62; *Vita de Antonio* (Latin critical text and Italian comments by Gerhardus J. M. Bartelink; Italian trans. Pietro Citti and Salvatore Lilla; Vite dei Santi 1; Milano: Mondador, 1974) 26–31, 38–41.

[28] *Acts Phil. Mart.* 31 according to the manuscript from Mount Athos, *Xenophontos* 32, as published in Bovon, Bouvier, and Amsler, *Acta Philippi. Textus*, 395, 397; see *Acts Phil. Mart.* 25–33 (131–39); see Bouvier, Bovon, and Amsler, "Actes de Philippe," in *Écrits apocryphes chrétiens*, 1:1308–13.

in early Christian literature. Even in theological propositions without metaphor, what is shown in the *Acts of Philip* by the conversion of animals can be expressed with the notion of redemption of the whole world. The Gospel of John in its most famous verse says: "For God so loved the world that he gave his only Son, so that everyone who believes in him may not perish but may have eternal life" (John 3:16). Contrary to Rudolf Bultmann's opinion in his commentary on John, the term "world" (κόσμος) should not be restricted to the human world; it embraces all creation, including the animals.[29]

Love of Enemies in the Gospel of Luke

What we have seen in the *Acts of Philip* is that wild beasts can be transformed by divine mercy in its cosmic redemption. What we see in the Gospel of Luke is the way that this transformation is related to the love of one's enemies, facilitated by Jesus' intervention. That is, what remains unclear in the *Acts of Philip* – the way in which divine mercy reaches the human world, transforms creation, and makes possible the love of one's enemies[30] – can be explained in the Gospel of Luke.[31]

As Luke develops a theology of the relationship between the divine realm and the human world, he divides the soteriological responsibility symmetrically between Christ's share and that which belongs to humanity. To understand Christ's fulfillment of this task would require a reading not only of the passion narrative, but of the whole of Jesus' ministry. Diverging from Paul's theology, Luke does not limit reconciliation to the cross, but instead relates it to the entire messianic activity of Jesus. Using the categories of divine "visiting" and messianic "healing," the evangelist signifies divine initiative in a process that humans would be unable to work through on their own. The "pathetic Christ" (an expression taken from Acts 26:23) "was counted [himself] among the unjust" (Luke 22:37) to allow the unjust to reach the procession of the just. Jesus' death is first an act of violence, a crime. But, following a Greek line of vision, it is also for Luke the true seal of a life that has refused retaliation and overwhelming violence.

---

[29] See Rudolf Bultmann, *The Gospel of John: A Commentary* (trans. G. R. Beasley-Murray; Philadelphia: Westminster, 1971) 38.

[30] The enemy may represent not only external hostile forces, but also interior destructive reaction; see Hanna Hyams, "Shame: The Enemy Within," *Transactional Analysis Journal* 24 (1994) 255–64. I would like to thank Edna Pressler for her advice on modern psychological literature.

[31] See also Matt 5:43–48; Rom 12:4; 1 Pet 2:11–17; *Did.* 1.3–5; Luise Schottroff, "Gewaltverzicht und Feindesliebe in der urchristlichen Jesustradition, Mt 5:38–48; Lk 6:27–36," in *Jesus Christus in Historie und Theologie. Festschrift für Hans Conzelmann zum 60. Geburtstag* (Tübingen: Mohr Siebeck, 1975) 160–97; Klassen, *Love of Enemies*; Schrey, "Gewalt/Gewaltlosigkeit," 168–70; Bovon, *Das Evangelium nach Lukas*, 1:306–28.

Luke places a special emphasis on human responsibility in developing a personal conception of μετάνοια, which means "repentance" and "conversion." (I, however, read μετάνοια to mean also and primarily a new way of acting and of constructing reality.) Throughout his entire ministry Jesus offered, in the name of God, as Luke puts it, the "gift of μετάνοια" – "the gift of conversion," a tool to embrace and to practice (though not without the help of the Holy Spirit) the love of one's enemies.[32]

It is fascinating to discern how the great traditions of Israel and Greece were ambivalent about ideals of heroic victory and the death of the powerful hero (David or Achilles)[33] or the peaceful suffering of the wise (Jeremiah or Socrates).[34] In the service of the first ideal, retaliation serves as an expression of the honor of the social group, that is, vengeance in defense of a certain image of justice. In the service of the second, nonretaliation is an expression of the superiority of values over facts, of the spirit over the flesh, of God over the passions.

Sometimes, as in the Book of Proverbs, a compromise between these two positions was attempted: "If your enemies are hungry, give them bread to eat; and if they are thirsty, give them water to drink; for you will heap coals of fire on their heads, and the Lord will reward you" (Prov 25:21–22).[35] This position, which tried to apply the love command by also respecting the principle of justice, does not eliminate an ultimate conclusion of violence.[36] This conclusion, which was later adopted by the apostle Paul in Romans 12:19–21, remains visible in the Sistine Chapel (the vindictive Christ coming in his wrath to judge the living and the dead) and, we might say, is still visible in every act of capital punishment today.

In his Sermon on the Plain, Luke places love of one's enemies at the core of his master's teaching. As just noted, the Hebrew tradition, too, was concerned about the fate of the enemy, particularly for the defeated, the one who is, for example, dependent on the victorious Israelite.

---

[32] See Acts 5:31 and 11:18.

[33] On David, see Samuel Amsler, *David, roi et Messie. La tradition davidique dans l'Ancien Testament* (Cahiers théologiques 45; Neuchâtel: Delachaux et Niestlé, 1963); Kenneth E. Pomykala, *The Davidic Dynasty Tradition in Early Judaism: Its History and Significance for Messianism* (SBLEJ 7; Atlanta: Scholars Press, 1995). On Achilles, see Monique Roussel, *Biographie légendaire d'Achille* (Amsterdam: Hakkert, 1991).

[34] See Henry Mottu, *Les "confessions" de Jérémie, une protestation contre la souffrance* (MdB; Geneva: Labor et Fides, 1985); Hans Dieter Betz, *Der Apostel Paulus und die sokratische Tradition* (BHT 45; Tübingen: Mohr Siebeck, 1972). Bailie, *Violence Unveiled*, 17–20, discovers a similar tension in the contemporaneous world: see n. 2 above.

[35] See David L. Dungan, "Jesus and Violence," in *Jesus, the Gospels and the Church: Essays in Honor of William R. Farmer* (ed. E. P. Sanders; Macon, Ga.: Mercer University Press, 1987) 135–62, esp. 141–44.

[36] See Krister Stendahl, "Hate, Non-retaliation, and Love: 1QS X, 17–20 and Rom. 12:19–21," *HTR* 55 (1962) 343–55.

In Greek and Latin literature, relationship to one's enemies had also been the topic of political and philosophical reflection.[37] Two typical situations attracted the attention of teachers and thinkers: First, for any person holding a public office (the prince, general, consul, emperor) Seneca[38] and other philosophers proposed the notion of true humanity. This notion went hand in hand with the notion of civilization and pride, in opposition to barbarianism. Philanthropy became a sign of culture. The one who inflicted a defeat on the battlefield should have a modest triumph, showing mercy over his defeated enemies. Second, for the philosopher, a doctrine for breaking the chain of violence was developed. Like Socrates, the true wise teacher may be misunderstood, even despised and hated. Yet, he or she should show what a true philosopher is by refusing the easy way of retaliating an eye for an eye, hate for hate. Even if the result will be defeat and personal suffering, one will have broken the chain of violence. And this act is the real success, the only one that counts.[39]

What gives Jesus' teaching in the Sermon on the Plain real power is not only its high ethics, but also the balance between the example required and the example given. Jesus' requirements were convincing because his own deeds – including his death – were a powerful model.[40] Without the passion narrative, the beginning of the Gospel is reduced to the level of pious, wishful thinking. Jesus' crucifixion ratifies, as it were, the moral path he preached.

As we can see from the Book of Acts, Jesus' attitude, when confronted with suffering and death, became emblematic, even paradigmatic for his followers: Luke describes the first Christian martyr, Stephen, with the traits of an agonizing Jesus. Following in Jesus' footsteps, Stephen, the Christian Hellenist, knew (according to Luke) how to forgive his persecutors: "While they were stoning Stephen, he prayed, 'Lord Jesus, receive my spirit.' Then he knelt down and cried out in a loud voice, 'Lord, do not hold this sin against them.' When he had said this, he died" (Acts 7:59–60).[41]

Many ancient martyrdom accounts tell how Christians followed Stephen's example and refused to curse their persecutors. Such an attitude of benediction even as malediction is being inflicted was, of course, anything but natural. Nevertheless, nonretaliation was not completely foreign to a Jewish or Greek audience. The

---

[37] See Klassen, *Love of Enemies*, 12–26; Bovon, *Das Evangelium nach Lukas*, 1:314.

[38] Seneca, *De otio* 1.4; *De beneficiis* 4.26.1; *De ira* 2.31–34; see Schottroff, "Gewaltverzicht und Feindesliebe in der urchristlichen Jesustradition," 197–221.

[39] There was a third case. To the slave there is also a philosophical piece of advice: you may suffer from unjust masters, but – and what is so difficult for us to read today – you should not try to defend your cause: it is better for you to develop a spirit of resignation and an attitude of stoic self-control.

[40] See Gregory J. Riley, "Words and Deeds: Jesus as Teacher and Jesus as Pattern of Life," *HTR* 90 (1997) 427–36.

[41] According to Dungan, Luke is influenced by the Pythagorean traditions ("Jesus and Violence," 153–60).

Jews had their own encounters with the imperialist power of their Syrian neighbors, and they had their own martyrs. Likewise, the Greeks knew of the Pythagorean wisdom[42] of sharing among friends, of avoiding bloody sacrifices,[43] of keeping a vegetarian diet, and, most importantly, of refusing any blind retaliation.[44] Even the Roman world, despite its idealized view of heroic patriotism, was not oblivious to moral efforts for peace and some form of refusal of violence. For example, at the time of the events recounted in the New Testament, the Stoic philosopher Musonius Rufus, under the influence of Socrates, advocated the refusal of self-defense.[45]

In the Christian camp, beside the early hagiographic monuments and the literary production of Justin Martyr,[46] the *Acts of John* is worthy of comment. In a famous scene, the beloved apostle explains the following philosophy to Callimachus, who was urging Drusiana to refuse pity to the unfortunate and sinful Fortunatus:

My son, we have not learned to return evil for evil. For God also, though we have done much ill and nothing well towards him, has given us not retribution but repentance; and although we knew not his name, he did not forsake but had mercy on us; and though we

---

[42] See Lévy, *La légende de Pythagore*; idem, *Recherches esséniennes et pythagoriciennes*; see also James Redfield, "The Politics of Immortality," in *Orphisme et Orphée. En l'honneur de Jean Rudhardt* (ed. Philippe Borgeaud; Recherches et rencontres. Publications de la Faculté des lettres de Genève 3; Geneva: Droz, 1991) 103–7 and esp. 108–11; Juri G. Vinogradov, "Zur sachlichen und geschichtlichen Deutung der Orphiker-Plättchen von Olbia," in *Orphisme et Orphée*, 77–86; and the classic, Ferdinand Christian Baur, *Apollonius von Tyana und Christus oder das Verhältnis des Pythagoreismus zum Christentum* (Tübingen: L. F. Fues, 1832; reprinted with a slightly different title Hildesheim: Olms, 1966).

[43] Zarathustra is one of the first to have criticized bloody sacrifices: he casts a malediction on those who, by killing the victim, destroy the life of the animal (see *Yasna* 32.8, 12, 14; it is not clear if Zarathustra was condemning all bloody sacrifice); see Arthur Henry Bleek, *Avesta: The Religious Books of the Parsees: From Professor Spiegel's German Translation of the Original Manuscripts* (3 vols. in 1; Hertford: Stephen Austin for Muncherjee Hormusjee Cama, 1864) 90–91; Jacques Duchesne-Guillemin, *Zoroastre. Étude critique avec une traduction commentée des Gâthâ* (Les dieux et les hommes 2; Paris: Maisonneuve, 1948) 251–57; and Helmut Humbach and Pallan Ichaporia, *The Heritage of Zarathustra: A New Translation of His Gathas* (Heidelberg: Winter, 1994) 40–43; Burkert, *Homo Necans*, 7.

[44] According to Diogenes Laertius, a book was attributed to Pythagoras, called *The Scopiades*, which advised not harming anybody. See Diogenes Laertius, *De clarorum philosophorum vitis* 8.8. On the difficulty of Diogenes' text concerning the beginning of Pythagoras' book, see the critical apparatus of Armand Delatte, *La vie de Pythagore de Diogène Laërce. Édition critique avec introduction et commentaire* (Académie royale de Belgique, Classe des Lettres et des Sciences morales et politiques, deuxième série, 17; Bruxelles: Lamertin, 1922) 109. Unfortunately Delatte does not deal with this textual problem in his commentary, 165–66. The title, *The Scopiades*, is not well attested in the textual tradition; see the apparatus of the critical edition by Herbert S. Long, *Diogenis Laertii vitae philosophorum* (2 vols.; Oxford: Clarendon, 1964) 2:396.

[45] See Musonius translated by Cora E. Lutz, *Musonius Rufus, "The Roman Socrates"* (Yale Classical Studies 10; New Haven, Conn.: Yale University Press, 1947) 33–145; Klassen, *Love of Enemies*, 22–23.

[46] See n. 51 below.

blasphemed, he did not punish but pitied us; and though we disbelieved, he bore no grudge; and though we persecuted his brethren, he made no (such) return; and though we ventured many abominable and terrible deeds, he did not repel us, but moved us to repentance and restraint of wickedness and so called us to himself, as (he has called) you too, my son Callimachus, and without insisting on your former misdeeds he has made you his servant to serve his mercy.[47]

The argument is clear: even if equity is not respected,[48] morality is preserved because love and mercy are the highest values.[49] And the Christian ethic is rooted in God himself who preferred to forgive rather than to establish a strict retribution.[50] Life is possible when the rule of violent retaliation is broken by love.[51]

Metaphor of the Child

One might suppose that immense energy would be required to incorporate and actualize Jesus' teachings regarding loving one's enemies and nonretaliation. This does not appear to be the case, however. Searching for names, titles, or images to describe such a disciple, the evangelist Luke prefers the metaphor of the child.[52]

---

[47] *Acts John* 81; translation by Knut Schäferdiek in *New Testament Apocrypha* (ed. Wilhelm Schneemelcher; rev. ed.; 2 vols.; Louisville: Westminster/John Knox, 1991–1992) 2:199.

[48] Dungan, "Jesus and Violence," 135–37, insists too much on the risk of inequity in the application of nonretaliation.

[49] For me, modern equivalents are the "I-Thou" relationship, "healing through meeting" (both are Martin Buber's expressions), or non-possessive love (Carl Rodgers); see Maurice Friedman, "Reflections on the Buber-Rogers Dialogue," *Journal of Humanistic Psychology* 34: *Special Issue on Dialogue* (1994) 46–65.

[50] See the Babylonian Talmud, *Berakhot* 7a: "Said R. Zutra bar Tobiah said Rab, 'May it be my will that my mercy overcome my anger, and that my mercy prevail over my attributes, so that I may treat my children in accord with the trait of mercy and in their regard go beyond the strict measure of the law'" (*The Talmud of Babylonia: An Academic Commentary*, I, *Bavli Tractate Berakhot* [trans. by Jacob Neusner; South Florida Academic Commentary Series 24; Atlanta: Scholars Press, 1996] 33–34). I thank Kimberley Patton for this reference.

[51] In the first centuries C.E. the command to love one's enemies was a decisive part of the Christian identity; Justin Martyr, for example, considers this command as a new teaching (*1 Apol.* 15.9–10). In the next chapter, Justin likes to say that the Christians are violent people transformed into mild ones (*1 Apol.* 16.1–11). Later he declares that the Gospel breaks the chains of violent relationships (*1 Apol.* 37.8). See also *Barn.* 3.3: "But to us he says: 'Behold, this is the fast which I have chosen, says the Lord. Loose every bond of injustice, untie the knots of forcibly extracted agreements'" (*The Apostolic Fathers: A New Translation and Commentary*, vol. 3: *Barnabas and the Didache* [trans. Robert A. Kraft; New York: Nelson, 1965] 86).

[52] On the child in antiquity, see Simon Légasse, *Jésus et l'enfant. "Enfants", "petits" et "simples" dans la tradition synoptique* (Études bibliques; Paris: Gabalda, 1969) 276–87; Hans Ruedi Weber, *Jesus and the Children: Biblical Resources for Study and Preaching* (Geneva: World Council of Churches, 1979) 65–76; John Boswell, *The Kindness of Strangers: The Abandonment of Children in Western Europe from Late Antiquity to the Renaissance* (Chicago: University of Chicago Press, 1998) 1–266; Keith R. Bradley, *Discovering the Roman Family: Studies in Roman Social History* (New York/Oxford: Oxford University Press, 1991); Lloyd deMause, "The Evolution of Childhood," in *The History of Childhood* (ed. Lloyd deMause; New York: Psy-

Following one of his sources, the famous Q document, Luke preserves the following saying of Jesus: "I thank you, Father, Lord of heaven and earth, because you have hidden these things from the wise and the intelligent and have revealed them to the infants;[53] yes, Father, for such was your gracious will" (Luke 10:21). The term νήπιος is contrasted here with the respectable, powerful, wise, and intelligent. The word may have kept some of its etymology, which is identical with our English "infant." According to the Latin etymology, it means "the one who cannot speak," the one without a voice.

On three other occasions Luke elaborates the notion of child, each time adding nuance or color to the picture. In Luke 9, following the Gospel of Mark, the evangelist contrasts the future destiny of the Son of Man, marked by betrayal, suffering, and death, with the excessive ambition of some of his disciples:

An argument arose among them as to which one of them was the greatest. But Jesus, aware of their inner thoughts, took a little child and put it by his side, and said to them: "Whoever welcomes this child in my name welcomes me, and whoever welcomes me welcomes the one who sent me; for the least among all of you is the greatest." (Luke 9:46–48)

The term for child used here is παιδίον. It is the diminutive of ὁ or ἡ παῖς, the "boy" or the "girl." It is no longer the "baby" who cannot speak or walk, but the "little child" who likes to play and who is still dependent on his or her parents. The term παιδί is still in use today in modern Greek, particularly when designating one's own children (παιδιά). As often in his Gospel, Luke implements a reversal of values: the least considered in society suddenly becomes the metaphor for the blessed one. If a person is to understand the true greatness of the human condition, he or she has to consider not the strongest person, but the smallest child. We shall see that the biblical text does not valorize the innocence or purity of the child, but rather the hidden human reality within her or him. By welcoming a child one welcomes Christ.

In Luke 18, Jesus and his disciples are traveling to Jerusalem. The euphoric success of the Galilean period is over and Jesus, aware of his imminent suffering, begins to teach his disciples, both men and women, how to take over after his

---

chohistory Press, 1974; reprinted Northvale, N.J.: Aronson, 1995) 1–73; Richard B. Lyman, Jr., "Barbarism and Religion: Late Roman and Early Medieval Childhood," in deMause, *The History of Childhood*, 75–100; Michel Manson, "The Emergence of the Small Child at Rome (Third Century B.C.–First Century)," *History of Education* 12 (1983) 149–59; Jean-Pierre Néraudau, *Être enfant à Rome* (Paris: Belles Lettres, 1984); Beryl Rawson, ed., *The Family in Ancient Rome: New Perspectives* (Ithaca, N.Y.: Cornell University Press, 1986); Thomas Wiedemann, *Adults and Children in the Roman Empire* (New Haven, Conn.: Yale University Press, 1989); Beryl Rawson, ed., *Marriage, Divorce, and Children in Ancient Rome* (Canberra: Humanities Research Center; Oxford: Clarendon, 1996).

[53] The following New Testament passages use the term νήπιος: Matt 11:25, the exact parallel to Luke 10:21; Matt 21:16; Rom 2:20; 1 Cor 3:1; 13:11; Gal 4:1,3; Eph 4:14; 1 Thess 2:7 (variant reading); Heb 5:13; the verb νηπιάζω, "to be a babe," "to be like a child" occurs once in 1 Cor 14:20.

death. This essential teaching is relevant for our purposes because on each occasion the Lukan Jesus underlines an ethic that contradicts the rules of this world. When one needs possessions, he urges sharing goods and accepting poverty. If one desires power and honor, he recommends limitation and humility. When the disciples wish to protect him from the presence of children, he reacts strongly.

Beside παιδίον, "small child," yet another term, βρέφος, is used here. βρέφος means the babe in the womb, the newborn, the one who still suckles his or her mother. It is the term Luke used, beside παιδίον, for Jesus himself in the Christmas story (Luke 2:12, 16). Each of these Greek terms brings a nuance to the metaphor of the child and helps us to understand it: βρέφος implies new life; νήπιος implies voiceless character; and παιδίον implies the first games and activities of the child.

In a vehement tone Jesus urges his disciples to "let the little children come to me" (ἄφετε τὰ παιδία ἔρχεσθαι πρός με) and not to "stop them" (μὴ κωλύετε αὐτά). "For it is to such as these that the kingdom of God belongs" (Luke 18:15–16). In few words and with simple language, a clear message is delivered. The expression "to come to me" is also used at the end of the Sermon on the Plain as the quintessence of Christian existence (Luke 6:46). This same verb κωλύω, "to prevent," "to stop," also occurs in the Book of Acts (Acts 8:36) in a passage in which the apostles express their willingness to incorporate the neglected one into the church and to baptize even a foreigner like the Ethiopian eunuch. According to Luke, the kingdom of God is open to children and to those who comply with this metaphor, because his God opens the door to such people.

As if to complete the picture, Luke adds a saying that in the oral tradition was not attached to any story: a floating saying. In this *logion* the evangelist uses the same metaphor of the child (again the word παιδίον), but it tends in yet another direction: "Truly I tell you, whoever does not receive the kingdom of God as a little child will never enter it" (Luke 18:17). This saying tells how a human being can be accepted by God and transformed into a new being, thus recovering the essence of the child.

In these three passages the Gospel of Luke teaches adults to recover their childhood and to give priority to the children in their thoughts. It does so by emphasizing the following: God welcomes human beings as Jesus welcomes the little children (Luke 18:15–16); God welcomes human beings who accept the challenge to go back to their childhood (Luke 18:17); and those who receive children, receive at the same time Christ himself (Luke 9:48).

The topic of becoming a child is of interest to all branches of early Christianity: it is present in the Gospel of John, as Nicodemus is urged to be born again (John 3:3–7); in the First Epistle of Peter, when the image of newborn children is used for the new converts (1 Pet 1:3, 23; 2:2); and in the baptismal tradition of the first Christian centuries, which considers the newly baptized as small children.[54]

---

[54] The concepts of baptism as a new birth and the newly baptized as newborn children appear

More broadly, the metaphor of the child as it appears in Luke also finds resonance in other Gospels, in Matthew as well as in *Thomas*. In the *Gospel of Thomas*, for example, the metaphor of the child serves as a representation of the believer in this world: "Jesus said: 'The man old in days will not hesitate to ask a small child seven days old about the place of life[55] and he[56] will live'" (*Gos. Thom.* 4).[57] Later on:

Mary said to Jesus, "Whom are your disciples like?" He said, "They are like children who have settled in a field which is not theirs. When the owners of the field come, they will say, Let us have back our field. They (will) undress in their presence in order to let them have back their field and to give it back to them." (*Gos. Thom.* 21)[58]

This is an enigmatic saying, but it clearly indicates the precarious situation of Christians in this world. A new element is also present here: the absence of shame in the children, something that does not correspond exactly to their innocence but rather to their lack of hypocrisy and pretense.[59]

We know today that the topic of the innocence of children,[60] which was widespread in antiquity,[61] is naïve and full of illusions. We also realize now that children are far from being asexual beings. Yet, if we can no longer concur with some ancient views, we can recognize also that, aside from a certain naïveté, antiquity was not unanimous in its view of children. On the contrary, the ancients do offer some wisdom regarding children. Particularly in their philosophical and religious perspectives, the views of the ancients were not always precritical. The Romans knew that a father not only had to procreate a child, but also to accept it (of course he could also abandon his child upon its birth).[62] They may have instituted the

---

in many texts: *1 Clement* 9.4; *Shepherd of Hermas* 93.1–4 (*Sim.* 9.16.1–4); Justin, *1 Apol.* 61.3–5, 10; Irenaeus, *Adversus haereses* 1.21.1; 3.17.1; 5.15.3; Irenaeus, *Demonstratio praedicationis apostolicae* 3.7; Tertullian, *Bapt.* 1; Theodore of Mopsuestia, *Catechetical Homily* 14; Ambrose of Milan, *De sacramentis* 3.1–3; see Adolf von Harnack, *Die Terminologie der Wiedergeburt und verwandter Erlebnisse in der ältesten Kirche* (TU 42.3; Leipzig: Hinrichs, 1918) 97–143; Pierre Th. Camelot, *Spiritualité du baptême* (Lex Orandi 30; Paris: Cerf, 1960).

[55] The "place of life" is another expression for the eternal life.

[56] I interpret this "he" to refer to the "man old in days."

[57] This text is the translation of Thomas O. Lambdin in *The Nag Hammadi Library* (ed. James M. Robinson; 3d ed.; New York: HarperSanFrancisco, 1990) 126; see also Howard C. Kee, "'Becoming a Child' in the Gospel of Thomas," *JBL* 82 (1963) 307–14; Michael Fieger, *Das Thomasevangelium. Einleitung, Kommentar und Systematik* (NTAbh n.s. 22; Münster: Aschendorff, 1991) 30–32, 96–98; April D. De Conick, *Seek to See Him: Ascent and Vision Mysticism in the Gospel of Thomas* (VC Supplements 33; Leiden: Brill, 1996) 145–46.

[58] Translation of Lambdin in Robinson, *The Nag Hammadi Library*, 121.

[59] This situation resembles the situation in Eden before the fall.

[60] See the witness of Christian epitaphs gathered by Légasse, *Jésus et l'enfant*, 272–73.

[61] Augustine is an exception by not accepting this view. See Augustine, *Confessions* 1.7.11 (CCSL 27:6); Augustine, *Enarrationes in Psalmos* 44.1; 46.2 (CCSL 38:494; 530); see Légasse, *Jésus et l'enfant*, 272.

[62] Two interesting analyses of family life appear in deMause, "The Evolution of Childhood," 6–39, and Bradley, *Discovering the Roman Family*, 177–204.

practice of wet nurses and nannies not necessarily to absolve themselves of responsibility, but perhaps to express their care more concretely.[63] They also knew, as did Quintilian,[64] how to express profound sadness at the loss of their children, even though they could be very harsh with them as well, just as the Spartans were. The Jews, like the Greeks and Romans, may have been ignorant of the physiological constitution and biological evolution of children and therefore described them not as autonomous beings but as part of a social and religious group. Nevertheless, they loved and cared for them, showing in particular the determination to teach them the Passover story as their story.[65] The Greeks may have expressed their disdain for these little creatures, but they had the wisdom to detect in children a special relation to the gods.[66]

What the Christian message added to these positive elements, in turn, spread throughout the ancient world: over against the prevalent violence and omnipresent tendency toward domination is the testimony of a utopian vision through Jesus, of a hope according to which, in the divine realm, another rule prevails – one devoid of violence, retribution, and dominance. To explain this utopian vision and make it manifest, the Christian messengers chose the child as the emblematic figure. They did so because children have no articulate voice, no reasonable argument, because their freedom is circumscribed by boundaries of dependence, because their fragility is evident, because children can dream and play while the adults calculate and conduct wars. The child became the cherished metaphor for another civilization, for another world, for the presence of God.[67]

---

[63] See Bradley, *Discovering the Roman Family*, 13–36, esp. 28–29.

[64] See the preface of Book 6 of Quintilian's *Institutio oratoria*, in which he mentions the death of his two sons and his wife; see also the condolences of Marcus Aurelius at the occasion of Fronto's grandson's death, and Fronto's answer to the Emperor, his pupil, *On the Loss of His Grandson* (*De nepote amisso* I–II), in *The Correspondence of Marcus Cornelius Fronto* (ed. and trans. Charles R. Haines; 2 vols.; LCL; New York: Putnam, 1919–20) 2:220–33. One finds a different attitude by Cicero, *Tusculanae disputationes* 1.93. I owe these references to Bradley, *Discovering the Roman Family*, 28–29.

[65] See Exod 13:8; *m. Pesah.* 10.4–5. See also the comments of Eduard Baneth in *Mischnaiot. Die sechs Ordnungen der Mischna. Hebräischer Text mit Punktuation, deutscher Übersetzung und Erklärung* (3d ed.; 6 vols.; Basel: Victor Goldschmidt, 1968) 2:241–53; see also Theodor Herz Gaster, *Passover: Its History and Traditions* (New York: Henry Schuman, 1949) 58–62; David J. Wolpe, *Teaching Your Children about God: A Modern Jewish Approach* (New York: Holt, 1993); Chaim Pearl, "Children," in *The Oxford Dictionary of the Jewish Religion* (Oxford: Oxford University Press, 1997) 156.

[66] Légasse, *Jésus et l'enfant*, 278: "Dès l'époque d'Euripide on avait accordé à la candeur de l'enfant un pouvoir spécial sur les dieux" ("From the time of Euripides, a special power over the gods had been given to the ingenuousness of children"). As witness for this thesis, the French scholar quotes Euripides, *Iphi. Taur.* 1270–83.

[67] See the *Shepherd of Hermas* 106.1 (*Sim.* 9.29.1); 101.1–4 (*Sim.* 9.29.1–4); Clement of Alexandria, *Paed.* 1.5–6.

Jesus as a Child Victorious Over the Beast

Luke is interested in both the growth and the various ages of his hero, Jesus. But I contend that even though he ages physically, Jesus, according to Luke, never loses his relationship to his childhood. A comparison of Luke with Paul may help to clarify this distinction. Paul, despite his belief in the reality of the resurrection, emphasizes the preeminence of the cross. In the First Epistle to the Corinthians he maintains against his opponents: "For I decided to know nothing among you except Jesus Christ, and him crucified" (1 Cor 2:2). I suggest that Luke would say something similar: "For I decided to know nothing among you except Jesus Christ, and Jesus Christ as a child." It may sound strange, but it is possible that when using the titles "Son" or "Son of God," beside the glory and the power attached to them, Luke intended a reminiscence of Jesus' childhood. In that case, Luke would once more articulate this belief by means of the motif of imitation. As Jesus, the Son of God, remains the child, so his disciples are also children.

It is usually argued by scholars that the interest in Jesus' birth marks a development in the christological thinking of the church. After an initial period of reflection on the cross and resurrection, the first Christians, influenced less by the apocalyptic "end" and more by the Greek philosophy of the "beginning," developed the story about Jesus' beginnings.[68]

It can also be true, however, that the complexity of the birth narrative was elaborated to convey another theological thought, namely, that the powerful Messiah, the omnipotent resurrected Son of God, remained what he was in the beginning, that is, a child. When the old prophet Simeon declares that the Lord can dismiss him in peace, for his "eyes have seen the salvation," salvation is here present in the figure of a child. In the Book of Acts a clue supports my thesis: at key places in christological speeches and liturgical fragments, Luke confers upon his Lord an unusual title: παῖς, which in Greek means "child" or "young servant" (see Acts 3:26 and 4:27), as "boy" in English and "garçon" in French. I must acknowledge that these occurrences belong to archaic material and can be explained as traces of an old Semitic Christology,[69] but we can imagine that Luke, by "recycling" them, wanted to communicate an allusion to a Christology of the child.[70]

---

[68] See François Bovon, "De Jésus de Nazareth au Christ Pantocrator," *Cahier Biblique* 25 of *Foi et Vie* 75 (1986) 87–96.

[69] See François Bovon, *Luke the Theologian: Fifty-Five Years of Research (1950–2005)* (2d rev. ed.; Waco, Tex.: Baylor University Press, 2006) 206–8.

[70] It is possible also to look at the title πρωτότοκος, "firstborn," used in Luke 2:7; Rom 8:29; Col 1:15, 18; Heb 1:6; and Rev 1:5, from the same perspective. Similar to other scholars, a recent exegete does not mention the possibility of the child character of Christ as firstborn (Hugolinus Langkammer, "'Πρωτότοκος', *prototokos* erstgeboren, Erstgeborener," in *Exegetisches Wörterbuch zum Neuen Testament* [ed. Horst Balz and Gerhard Schneider; 3 vols.; Stuttgart: Kohlhammer, 1980–83] 3:458–62).

What remains a hypothesis in the canonical works of Luke becomes evident in many apocryphal stories. It is a *topos* in the various apocryphal acts of the apostles. The resurrected one, when wishing to appear to his disciple in a dream or a vision, manifests himself as a child, a beautiful and kind child, and sometimes also as a young man.[71] See the allusion to the *Acts of Andrew* in Evodius of Uzala: "There it is also written that when Maximilla and Iphidamia went away together to hear the apostle Andrew, a handsome little boy, whom Lucius would have us understand either as God or at least as an angel, handed them over to the apostle Andrew."[72] The literary reference recalls *Acts Andr.* 32.2: "And when she [Maximilla] came to the gate of the prison she found a small comely boy standing, the gates being open, and he said to them: 'Go in, both of you, to the apostle of our Lord, who has long been expecting you.'"[73] Likewise, references to Jesus as the child appear in the *Acts of John*: "The Lord appeared to me in the tomb like John and as a young man" (*Acts John* 87);[74] "And my brother [when he heard] this said: 'John, what does he want, this child on the shore who called us?'" (*Acts John* 88);[75] and finally, "And when he came to the place, at John's command the doors came open, and [we saw] by the grace of Drusiana a handsome young man who was smiling" (*Acts John* 73).[76]

Similar references appear in the *Acts of Peter*:

Now as I fasted for three days and prayed that this crime should come to light, I saw in a vision Italicus and Antulus, whom I had instructed in the name of the Lord, and a boy who was naked and wearing a loincloth,[77] who gave me a wheaten loaf and said to me, "Peter, hold out for two days and you shall see the wonderful works of God." (*Acts Pet.* 17)[78]

Likewise, in the *Acts of Paul*:

And as Paul thus testified (or adjured God), there came in a youth very comely in grace and loosed Paul's bonds, the youth smiling as he did so. And straightway he departed. But because of the vision which was granted to Paul, and the eminent sign relating to his fetters,

---

[71] See Erik Peterson, "Einige Bemerkungen zum Hamburger Papyrus-Fragment der *Acta Pauli*," *VC* 3 (1949) 142–62; reprinted in idem, *Frühkirche, Judentum und Gnosis*, 183–208, esp. 191–97 and 206–7 n. 88 of the collection of essays; Éric Junod and Jean-Daniel Kaestli, *Acta Iohannis* (2 vols.; CCSA 1–2; Turnhout: Brepols, 1983) 2:479–80; Antonio Orbe, *Cristología gnóstica. Introducción a la soteriología de los siglos II y III* (2 vols.; BAC 384–385; Madrid: La Editorial Catolica, 1976) does not pay much attention to the appearances of the resurrected Jesus Christ in the form of a child.

[72] Evodius of Uzala, *De fide contra Manichaeos* 38 (CSEL 25.2; Vienna: Tempsky, 1892) 968–69. Translation by Jean-Marc Prieur in Schneemelcher, *New Testament Apocrypha*, 2:103.

[73] Translation by Gregor Hahn in Schneemelcher, *New Testament Apocrypha*, 2:144.

[74] Translation by Knut Schäferdiek in Schneemelcher, *New Testament Apocrypha*, 2:179.

[75] Ibid., 2:180.

[76] Ibid., 2:196.

[77] I am following Gérard Poupon's conjecture (read *cinctum* instead of *vinctum*); see Gérard Poupon, "Actes de l'apôtre Pierre et de Simon," in *Écrits apocryphes chrétiens* 1:1080 n. F.

[78] Original translation by Wilhelm Schneemelcher in Schneemelcher, *New Testament Apocrypha*, 2:300; translation slightly revised by the present author.

his grief over the fight with the beasts departed, and rejoicing he leaped as if in paradise. (*Acts Paul* 9.19)[79]

In the *Acts of Thomas*: "And when they had been sealed there appeared to them a young man carrying a blazing torch, so that the very lamps were darkened at the onset of its light. And going out he vanished from their sight" (*Acts Thom.* 27.3).[80] In the *Acts of Philip*, Aristarchos, the adversary of the apostle, admits: "I saw a child coming down from heaven and going to you in order to command you to heal me. And now I am looking around me to see where he is. Here he is, who appears again to me going up to heaven!" (*Acts Phil.* 6.12 [76]).[81] Philip then explains: "The beautiful child that you saw, this is Jesus, the one who never abandons us. You, yourself, believe also in him, so that you live for ever" (*Acts Phil.* 6.12 [76]).

I also would like to add another domain where this evidence applies. In a recent book entitled *The Clash of Gods: A Reinterpretation of Early Christian Art*,[82] Thomas F. Mathews has challenged the traditional view that holds that the first early Christian images of Christ were determined by Roman imperial ideology. His criticism may be right, but instead of insisting on Jesus the magician or the feminine Jesus, I strongly suggest that these images express the view that the resurrected one is still the young boy, the firstborn of the dead, the divine, smiling, and generous child (see the first depictions of the Good Shepherd, the first examples of Jesus' entrance into Jerusalem, some miracle scenes, or the first representations of the triumphant Christ). More explicitly than Luke himself, the first Christian artists, like the authors of the various apocryphal acts, believe in Jesus as the child of God (figs. 1 and 2, next page).

Such a childish or juvenile appearance of Jesus Christ is far from limited to the apocryphal literature or early Christian art. It is also present in some of the visions that the martyrs had during their prison stays or during the night preceding their executions. Even some Christian authors mention this outlook of the resurrected.[83]

Such is the case for Clement of Alexandria, probably the best witness for a Christology of the child. In the first book of the *Pedagogue*, with a rare sense for theological inquiry and spiritual progress, the Alexandrian author examines var-

---

[79] Translation by Wilhelm Schneemelcher in Schneemelcher, *New Testament Apocrypha*, 2:252.

[80] Translation by Han J. W. Drijvers in Schneemelcher, *New Testament Apocrypha*, 2:350.

[81] This is the translation of the manuscript from Mount Athos, *Xenophontos* 32, as published by Bovon, Bouvier, and Amsler, *Acta Philippi. Textus*, 195, 197.

[82] Thomas F. Matthews, *The Clash of Gods: A Reinterpretation of Early Christian Art* (Princeton, N.J.: Princeton University Press, 1993).

[83] See for example *Passio Montani et Lucii* 7.3 (*Ausgewählte Märtyrerakten* [4th ed.; SAQ n.s. 3; Tübingen: Mohr Siebeck, 1965] 75); *Acta Dorotheae et Theophili* 11 (*Acta Santorum*; Antwerp: Meursius, 1658) 1:774; Jacqueline Amat, *Songes et visions. L'au-delà dans la littérature latine tardive* (Paris: Études augustiniennes, 1985) 141, 257–60.

Figure 1: Statuette of Seated Christ, 4th century, Rome, Museo Nazionale delle Terme.

Figure 2: The Feeding of the Four Thousand, Rome, Catacomb of the Via Latina.

ious terms used to describe Christians. He quotes the several that we have mentioned: his favorite terms are "children," "little children," or even "babies." Then he compares the Christian initiation to the instruction of children (hence, the title of his work, *Pedagogue*). Finally, he reaches exactly the point I want to emphasize: if we are the children of God, it is because Jesus the Son of God is and remains the child, the living and resurrected child. Clement writes:

And in defence of the point to be established, I shall adduce another consideration of the greatest weight. The Spirit calls the Lord himself a child, thus prophesying by Esaias: "Lo, to us a child has been born, to us a son has been given, on whose own shoulder the government shall be; and His name has been called the Angel of the great Counsel." Who, then, is this infant child? He according to whose image we are made little children ... . O the great God! O the perfect child! The Son in the Father, and the Father in the Son. And how shall not the discipline of this child be perfect, which extends to all, leading as a schoolmaster us as children, who are His little ones? ... To this child additional testimony is born by John, "the greatest prophet among those born of women": "Behold the Lamb of God!" For since Scripture calls the infant children lambs, it has also called Him – God the Word – who became man for our sakes, and who wished in all points to be made like to us – "the Lamb of God" – Him, namely, that is the Son of God, the child of the Father.[84]

If such a Christology of the child is indeed present in early Christianity we can connect it first with the biblical metaphor of the Christians as children and the command for the love of enemies.[85] Beside the objective soteriology, according to which Jesus saves humanity by pure grace and without its collaboration, is the subjective soteriology, according to which Jesus leads us to salvation through his example. This second aspect, strongly present in Luke and in Clement of Alexandria, implies the concept of imitation. If the first type of soteriology suggests a redemption despite us, or even without us, the second implies our agreement and participation. As you know, the Sermon in the Plain communicates the saying "Be merciful, just as your Father is merciful" (Luke 6:36).[86]

---

[84] Clement, *Paed.* 1.5.24; translation by William Wilson in *The Writings of Clement of Alexandria* (Ante-Nicene Christian Library 4; Edinburgh: T&T Clark, 1867) 129–30.

[85] See the titles conferred to the Christians by Clement of Alexandria, *The Rich Man's Salvation* 31, in a passage analyzed with sagacity by Ann Graham Brock, "The Significance of φιλέω and φίλος in the Tradition of Jesus Sayings and in the Early Christian Communities," *HTR* 90 (1997) 395. Here is the translation of the passage by Clement: "Those He calls children and young children and babes and friends; also little ones here, in comparison with their future greatness above" (*The Exhortation to the Greeks, the Rich Man's Salvation, and the Fragment of an Address Entitled to the Newly Baptized* [trans. G.W. Butterworth; LCL; Cambridge, Mass.: Harvard University Press, 1953] 334; translation slightly revised).

[86] Following this conception of Christ's example we can say: "Be a child as Jesus is!" Beautiful in your behavior, refusing any wish of retaliation, and gentle as he was, loving your enemies even in a time of persecution. In its criticism of the natural family bonds *Gos. Thom.* 105 suggests a new type of relationship, a new way of being children of God: "Jesus said: 'He who knows the father and the mother will be called the son of a harlot'" (translation by Lambdin in Robinson, *The Nag Hammadi Library*, 137).

Second, we must relate the Christology of the child to the patristic conception of the beast, to the incarnation of evil in the form of a monster or a dragon. According to many early Christians, it was not only during his human life, but also on the cross, and particularly in his *descensus ad inferos* and his resurrection that Jesus overcame the power of the beast. Defeated in heaven, the beast will also later disappear on earth. However, today it is still present, throwing its last energy into a battle that is lost in advance. Nevertheless, this fight brings with it much harm and suffering. It is this last battle, in which Christians are engaged, that the communion between the Child and the children is decisive.[87]

Conclusion

Many early Christian texts use the metaphor of the beast to articulate negative forces in a visible way. The beast is a frightening reality that becomes concrete in the several scourges that can fall upon humanity: persecutions, famines, diseases, and wars.

Despite this inescapable threat, Christian hope remains that the creation does not escape the control of God. Through his Son, God beseeches the beast and offers divine reconciliation to the entire world. Even the rule of violence and the law of the jungle will finally be broken. Concretely, this reconciliation means that even the wild animals of this world will be tamed by the divine Word. By forsaking their aggressive nature, they will share with re-created humanity in the messianic peace. Already in their time, some ancient Christian writers wrote that the cosmic dimension of redemption becomes visible in the miraculous conversion of various animals, as if life in Paradise had begun.

Encompassing humanity, divine reconciliation establishes believers as newborn creatures. The image of the children of God, embedded in the metaphorical world of early Christianity, is an adequate image for those believers who are deprived of knowledge, power, and experience, yet accepted by God and therefore find their identity in this "non-having," their essence in a sort of "non-being." In this Christian paradigm, children – despite their weakness – finally know better than adults, and receive confidence and authority, whereas the adults remain insecure and anxious. But – and this is the surprise – these children can be strong and confident *only* if they accept and consider Jesus Christ, the powerful Lord, as a child, the newborn of the cradle and the firstborn of the resurrection.

---

[87] It is probably not by chance that Jesus' birth in the Gospel of Matthew provokes such a violent reaction from the prince of this world, Herod, familiar of the Beast. But it is neither a coincidence that a text like the *Ascension of Isaiah*, a Christian story and vision, describes the destiny of Christ, called the "Beloved one," as the descent of a child through the seven heavens in a secret manner, and then his ascension is recognized and applauded.

Let us conclude with a quotation by Leo the Great, the Roman pope from the middle of the fifth century:

Christ loves childhood, which he first assumed in both his soul and body. Christ loves childhood, teacher of humility, rule of innocence, model of gentleness. Christ loves childhood, toward which he directs the conduct of the adults, toward which he brings back those who are older; and turns to his own example those he raises to the eternal kingdom.

Amat Christus infantiam, quam primum et animo suscepit et corpore. Amat Christus infantiam, humilitatis magistram, innocentiae regulam, mansuetudinis formam. Amat Christus infantiam, ad quam maiorum dirigit mores, ad quam senum reducit aetates; et eos ad suum inclinat exemplum, quos ad regnum sublimat aeternum.[88]

---

[88] Leo the Great, *Sermo* 18(XXXVII).3 (PL 54:258–59); also Léon le Grand, *Sermons*, 1 (intro. Jean Leclercq; trans. and ann. René Dolle; 2d ed. SC 22; Paris: Cerf, 1964) 280–81.

Women Priestesses in the Apocryphal *Acts of Philip*

In honor of Elisabeth Schüssler Fiorenza and her significant contribution to the study of women's participation in the life of early Christian churches, I would like to draw attention to a new witness from late antiquity that argues for the existence of women in priestly ministry. The witness is part of the *Acts of Philip* attested in a neglected manuscript from Mount Athos, *Xenophontos* 32.[1]

Mentioned among the rejected books by the so-called *Decretum Gelasianum*, the *Acts of Philip* does not seem to have been very popular in antiquity, although it was not ignored in the Byzantine world.[2] Until recently, this noncanonical work was known for the most part only through *Vaticanus graecus* 824, discovered by Maximilien Bonnet at the end of the nineteenth century.[3] There is evidence in this manuscript of a tendency to censure the heretical nature of the original and to eradicate most of the elements concerning women's ministry. The end of the *Acts of Philip*, a section known as the *Martyrdom*, is better preserved; it is known in three recensions through several Greek manuscripts because the text was used regularly in the Byzantine Church on the feast of Saint Philip, which was celebrated on 14 November.[4] Constantin von Tischendorf was the first to publish two forms of the *Martyrdom* in the middle of the nineteenth century.[5] With different degrees of intensity, all three recensions show traces of orthodox rewriting. The discovery of *Xenophontos* 32 gives us access to several acts that were at one time

---

[1] See François Bovon, Bertrand Bouvier, and Frédéric Amsler, eds., *Acta Philippi. Textus* (CCSA 11; Turnhout: Brepols, 1999); Frédéric Amsler, *Acta Philippi. Commentarius* (CCSA 12; Turnhout: Brepols, 1999).

[2] See Wilhelm Schneemelcher, "General Introducion," in *New Testament Apocrypha* (ed. Wilhelm Schneemelcher; trans. Robert McL. Wilson; Louisville: Westminster/John Knox, 1991) 1:28–40.

[3] Maximilien Bonnet, "Acta Philippi," in *Acta apostolorum apocrypha* (ed. Richard Albert Lipsius and Maximilien Bonnet; 2 vols. in 3; Leipzig: Mendelssohn, 1891–1903; reprinted in Darmstadt: Wissenschaftliche Buchgesellschaft, 1959) 2.1:vii–xv, 1–90.

[4] Ibid., 41–90; Bovon, Bouvier, and Amsler, *Acta Philippi. Textus*, 342–431; Joseph Flamion, "Les trois recensions grecques du Martyre de l'apôtre Philippe," in *Mélanges d'histoire offerts à Charles Mœller* (Université de Louvain: Recueil de travaux publiés par les membres des conférences d'histoire et de philologie 40; Louvain/Paris: Bureau du Recueil, 1914) 1:215–25.

[5] Constantin von Tischendorf, *Acta apostolorum apocrypha* (Leipzig: Avenarius & Mendelssohn, 1851; reprinted in Hildesheim: Olms, 1990) 75–104; see also idem, *Apocalypses apocryphae Mosis, Esdrae, Pauli, Iohannes, item Mariae dormitio, additis evangeliorum et actuum apocryphorum supplementis* (Leipzig: Mendelssohn, 1866; reprinted in Hildesheim: Olms, 1966) 141–56.

completely lost: the end of act 11 and complete versions of acts 12–15.[6] A comparison with *Vaticanus* 824 reveals that *Xenophontos* 32 has a second merit: it preserves a version of acts 1–9 in its more original, less-revised form.[7]

This essay focuses primarily on *Acts of Philip* 1, which takes place in Galilee, the point of departure for Philip's missionary journey. In the acts that follow, the evangelist travels alone to and through several countries, including Greece, Parthia, and Palestine. *Acts of Philip* 8 and following take place in Asia Minor, particularly in Phrygia. This second part narrates the story of a single, linear missionary journey that ends in Ophiorymos, which is identified with Hierapolis of Phrygia. On this particular journey Philip is accompanied by two companions, his sister Mariamne and his fellow apostle Bartholomew. According to the last part of the work, the *Martyrdom*, it is in Ophiorymos that Philip dies.[8] It is also in Hierapolis of Phrygia that, according to witnesses dated as early as the second century c.e., Philip's tomb was located. Veneration of Philip seems to have been particularly intense in this part of the ancient world. As a location for the writing of the *Acts of Philip*, then, Asia Minor seems probable, even certain.

Although scholars suggest that the work was written in the fourth or fifth century c.e.,[9] it is extremely difficult to assign a date to this work. Parts of the *Acts of Philip* may be earlier than the fourth century. Some prayers and stories, for example, go back to the third if not the second century c.e. Indeed the work is the result of a literary process that merged at least two cycles of stories, one related to Philip the evangelist of the canonical Acts (*Acts of Philip* 3–7) and the other related to the apostle Philip found in the Gospels and in the lists of Jesus' disciples (*Acts of Philip* 8–*Martyrdom*). In the final version of the work, these two figures constitute a single apostolic figure. Frédéric Amsler and Christopher Matthews demonstrate that *Acts of Philip* 2 is a later orthodox compilation,[10] and I am in agreement here. Amsler also suggests that *Acts of Philip* 1 was first an independent story.[11] In my opinion this may have been true in a preliterate stage, when the act

---

[6] The work is preserved in the form of numbered acts. Unfortunately, the loss of several folios still deprives us of act 10 and the beginning of act 11; see François Bovon, "Les Actes de Philippe," in *ANRW* 2.25.6 (1988) 4472.

[7] For *Acts of Philip* 8, we rely on a manuscript from Athens: *Atheniensis* 346. See the description of these manuscripts in Bovon, Bouvier, and Amsler, *Acta Philippi. Textus*, xiii–xxx.

[8] While Amsler (*Acta Philippi. Commentarius*, 521–24) identifies Ophiorymos with Hierapolis, I suggest ("Les Actes de Philippe," 4521) that Ophiorymos may have been the city of the martyrdom and Hierapolis the city of the tomb, basing my judgment on the *Translation of Philip's Remains*. See Montague Rhodes James, "Supplement to the Acts of Philip," in *Apocrypha anecdota* (ed. M. R. James; Texts and Studies 2.3; Cambridge: Cambridge University Press, 1893; reprinted in Nendeln, Liechtenstein: Kravis, 1967) 158–63.

[9] See Amsler, *Acta Philippi. Commentarius*, 437–39.

[10] See Christopher R. Matthews, *Philip, Apostle and Evangelist: Configurations of a Tradition* (NovTSup 105; Leiden: Brill, 2002) 186–89; Amsler, *Acta Philippi. Commentarius*, 85–127.

[11] Amsler, *Acta Philippi. Commentarius*, 25–83.

was an oral story, but it shares so much in common with the second half (*Acts of Philip* 8–*Martyrdom*) that I have decided to consider these sections together.

The first part of this essay considers act 1, which includes several interesting lists of Christian ministers who were members of the author's marginalized community. The second part treats the apostolic role of Mariamne and connects her role and example with the women ministers found in *Acts of Philip* 1.

The Christian Priestesses in *Acts of Philip* 1

Xenophontos 32, the most ancient version of *Acts of Philip* 1, presents the story of a young man who is the only son of a widow and who is miraculously resurrected by the apostle Philip at his mother's request. Differing from *Vaticanus* 824, this longer version includes a description of a tour of Hell that the young man made during his short stay in the underworld, which he relates to the apostle at the instant of his resurrection (*Acts of Philip* 1.4–17).[12] Among the many punishments that confront his soul is the chastisement that people receive because they mistreated the leaders and the ascetics of another church. These leaders and ascetics are presented in three groups, divided according to gender. The result is three categories of two: priests and priestesses, deacons and deaconesses, eunuchs and virgins. This strange situation in the underworld most likely reflects a quarrel among competing Christian groups in this world. Those who are punished in Hell are probably members of the majority church who while alive on earth abused their social standing and power to persecute members and ministers of the author's minority Christian community.

The writer's point of view is the one attested by the young hero and is recognized as legitimate by the apostle Philip as he listens to the narration of the tour of Hell.[13] This point of view accords well with the perspective of a minority Christian community that can be called an ascetic community. For in the same act the apostle Philip sings the merits of ἁγνεία, a term difficult to translate but undeniably of an ascetic venue, meaning "purity, encratism, abstinence, continence." The type of asceticism to which the apostle, the mother, and her son adhere is more than an ethical obedience. In an explanatory sermon on the merits

---

[12] On the narrative of this tour of Hell, see Richard N. Slater, "An Inquiry into the Relationship between Community and Text: The Apocryphal *Acts of Philip* 1 and the Encratites of Asia Minor," in *The Apocryphal Acts of the Apostles: Harvard Divinity School Studies* (ed. François Bovon, Ann Graham Brock, and Christopher R. Matthews; Center for the Study of World Religions: Religions of the World; Cambridge, Mass.: Harvard University Press, 1999) 281–306. See also Amsler, *Acta Philippi. Commentarius*, 50–70.

[13] On the genre of the tour of Hell, see Albrecht Dietrich, Νέκυια. *Beiträge zur Erklärung der neuentdeckten Petrusapokalypse* (Leipzig: Teubner, 1893); Martha Himmelfarb, *Tours of Hell: An Apocalyptic Form of Jewish and Christian Literature* (Philadelphia: University of Pennsylvania Press, 1983).

and virtues of ἀγνεία Philip says that through ἀγνεία God communicates with the Christian (αὐτῇ τῇ ἀγνεία ὁ θεὸς ὁμιλεῖ, *Acts of Philip* 1.3).[14] Later in the work the reader discovers a similar saying: through ἀγνεία the believer can see God (ἡ ἀγνεία ὁρᾷ τὸν θεόν, *Acts of Philip* 4.1;[15] the influence of the Matthean beatitude ["Blessed are the pure in heart, for they will see God," Matt 5:8] is evident here, if only implicit). Asceticism is more than a moral attitude; it is a religious practice that draws the devotees closer to God, bringing them into intense communion with the deity.

The people who are punished, however, belong to an ecclesiastical organization that is less ascetic in nature. They correspond to the majority church, the mainstream of Christianity. They have probably used their political power to marginalize the ascetic community. Such a situation is not unfamiliar to fourth-century sources and is consistent with the struggle that the Great Church of the fourth century waged against ascetic minorities. Basil of Caesarea and Amphilochius of Iconium are typical examples, as we can see from Basil's letters and Amphilochius's fragment on the Apocrypha.[16] Such tension may have arisen only in the fourth century. We know very little about encratism in the third century C.E., but criticism that the majority church addresses against Montanism in the second century sounds very similar: appropriation of the Spirit, excessive ascetic practices, and women in leadership positions are among the usual accusations made against them. I would even suggest that the social and religious reality of such a group is not a late development of the Constantinian period, but represents on the contrary – not without alterations, of course – an archaic witness of an early Christian reality, like the anomalous block of stone that a receding glacier leaves behind in the middle of a meadow or on the beach beside a lake.

The depiction of punishments for those who mistreat ascetic leaders continues as the young hero exits through the door of Hell. There he sees a man and a woman being attacked and eaten by the famous dog Cerberus. Taken by pity he tries to rescue the two people but the archangel Michael, his *angelus interpres*, urges him not to do so:

---

[14] In Bovon, Bouvier, and Amsler, *Acta Philippi. Textus*, 8–9, we translated: "C'est précisément en compagnie des purs que Dieu se complaît."

[15] In ibid., 117, we translated: "La pureté voit Dieu."

[16] See Basil the Great, *Epistulae* 188 and 199, in Saint Basile, *Lettres* (ed. and trans. Yves Courtonne; 3 vols.; Paris: Les Belles Lettres, 1957–1966) 2:120–31, 154–64; and Amphilochius of Iconium, *Contra Haereticos*, in *Amphilochii Iconiensis Opera* (ed. Cornelius Datema; CCSG 3; Turnhout: Brepols, 1978) 181–214; see Frédéric Amsler, "Amphiloque d'Iconium, Contre les hérétiques encratites et apotactites. Traduction française," in *Poussières de christianisme et de judaïsme antiques. Mélanges Jean-Daniel Kaestli et Éric Junod* (eds. Albert Frey and Rémi Gounelle; Publications de l'Institut romand des sciences bibliques 5; Prahins [Switzerland]: Zèbre, 2007) 7–40. Amsler expresses his gratitude to Bertrand Bouvier who helped him for the translation.

Leave it as it is because they also have pronounced blasphemy against priests [πρεσβυτέρους], priestesses [πρεσβύτιδας], eunuchs [εὐνούχους], deacons [διακόνους], deaconesses [διακονίσσας], virgins [παρθένους] accusing them wrongly of impudicity and adultery. Once they had done their misdeed, they met me, Michael, as well as Raphael and Uriel, and we gave them as food to this dog till the great day of judgment. (*Acts of Philip* 1.12)

At this point the young man is convinced of the couple's guilt and ceases his rescue attempt.

Several details in this episode are noteworthy. First, the man and the woman being punished are not identified as Christian ministers. Because of the phrase "they also," they are among those who participated, along with others previously mentioned, in these attacks and slanders. Second, the location of the couple in custody is surprising: they are close to the gate protected by Cerberus. Initially, the reader hesitates to consider them inside Hell, but the next paragraph makes it probable that they are still inside the gate. This vagueness may suggest that the author considers them somewhat less guilty than the other sinners, who are strictly confined to the interior of Hell. Third, there is a different order within the three groups of Christian leaders and ascetics who suffered vexation and persecution on earth. Because we have only one manuscript of the story, this anomaly is difficult to explain. However, the separation of the eunuchs from the virgins is probably accidental. This pair is mentioned in other passages in *Acts of Philip* 1, and at those times the sequence is coherent: the eunuchs and virgins form a group just as the deacons and deaconesses and the priests and the priestesses do.

It is well known that in antiquity many ascetic male Christians wanted to interpret literally Jesus' remark about the eunuchs and the kingdom.[17] Origen is not the only case in point here. The reaction of shock on the part of many bishops at the end of the second century C.E. and the first half of the third bears witness to the fact that not only a few Montanists but also many male Christians from the up-and-coming Great Church, particularly in Egypt (but not only in Egypt), wanted to eradicate the physical desire of the flesh and thus condemned sexuality and even marriage. That the females also felt a strong drift toward virginity is well attested. Even if we cannot be certain about the way in which the future *catholica* organized the young and older virgins – both female and male – who wished to remain in celibacy, we do know that such ascetic Christians were highly venerated among the churches, particularly in minority Christian communities (sects or heresies in the traditional ecclesiastical historiography). It is not improbable that these young contempters of the flesh tried to participate in a kind of community life, creating an early form of monasticism. The risk they took was in refusing to separate the young women from the young men. The calumny of "impudicity and adultery," therefore, as attested in our text, was all too easy to level against them. The text does not imply that these two groups of ascetics were liv-

---

[17] See Ulrich Luz, *Das Evangelium nach Matthäus* (EKKNT 1; 4 vols.; Zürich: Benzinger; Neukirchen-Vluyn: Neukirchener Verlag, 1985–2002) 3:88–89, 103–12.

ing apart from the local community; rather, they seem to have participated in the same common worship. Their precise ministerial status, however, remains uncertain.

We know from patristic and epigraphic evidence studied by A. Lambert, Georges Blond, Frédéric Amsler, and Richard N. Slater[18] that some ascetic and encratite communities of the fourth century c.e. did not distinguish secular life from monastic life. These witnesses also suggest that the organization of ministries within minority communities, including the Apostolics and Apotactics in fourth-century Asia Minor, was not so different from the organization found in the Great Church. We are not surprised, therefore, to find in the minority church of the author the classical distinction between priests and deacons. There is, nevertheless, a major difference: in the Great Church of that time, the diaconate was still mixed, including deacons and deaconesses, but women were excluded from priesthood. The Council of Laodicea, Canon 11, is clear here: "About the fact that in the Church the so-called priestesses or female presidents should not be appointed" (περὶ τοῦ μὴ δεῖν τὰς λεγομένας πρεσβύτιδας ἤτοι προκαθημένας ἐν ἐκκλησίᾳ καθίστασθαι). In the minority communities, as attested by the *Acts of Philip*, πρεσβύτιδες rule beside πρεσβύτεροι. Priesthood was accessible to both sexes. Although Bertrand Bouvier and I published this new text in 1989[19] and Amsler presented the case in his Geneva dissertation published in 1999,[20] notice of this important witness has escaped the attention of recent studies on the role of women in ministry in antiquity.[21]

Several other passages in *Acts of Philip* 1 mention ministers and ascetics in the minority community. In 1.6, for instance, the young man visits in Hell a damned man who has been thrown into an infernal pit because he struck and slandered ἐπισκόπους ... καὶ πρεσβυτέρους (bishops ... and priests). Then, in 1.7–8, he meets a young man, damned to lying on a bed of embers because he could not control his tongue when he was alive; he respected neither his parents nor the

---

[18] See A. Lambert, "Apotactites et apotaxamènes," in *DACL* 1.2:2604–26; Georges Blond, "L'hérésie encratite vers la fin du quatrième siècle," *Recherches de science religieuse* 32 (1944) 157–210; Amsler, *Acta Philippi. Commentarius*, 469–520; Slater, "Inquiry into the Relationship between Community and Text."

[19] Bertrand Bouvier and François Bovon, "Actes de Philippe, I, d'après un manuscrit inédit," in *Œcumenica et Patristica. Festschrift für Wilhelm Schneemelcher zum 75. Geburtstag* (ed. Damaskinos Papandreou, Wolfgang A. Bienert, and Knut Schäferdiek; Stuttgart: Kohlhammer; Geneva: Metropolie der Schweiz, 1989) 367–94, esp. 393–94.

[20] See Amsler, *Acta Philippi. Commentarius*, 81–82.

[21] The witness is absent from Karen Torjesen, *When Women Were Priests: Women's Leadership in the Early Church and the Scandal of Their Subordination in the Rise of Christianity* (San Francisco: HarperSanFrancisco, 1993); and from Ute E. Eisen, *Amtsträgerinnen im frühen Christentum. Epigraphische und literarische Studien* (Forschungen zur Kirchen- und Dogmengeschichte 61; Göttingen: Vandenhoeck & Ruprecht, 1996). Following my remarks, Eisen added mention of it in the English translation of her work; see Ute E. Eisen, *Women Officeholders in Early Christianity: Epigraphical and Literary Studies* (trans. Linda Maloney; Collegeville, Minn.: Liturgical Press, 2000) 136 n. 24a.

πρεσβυτέρους (priests), and he insulted a παρθένος (virgin) by saying that she was not a virgin. Distressed by the extent of the punishment, the young traveler asks his guiding angel to lead him to τοὺς εὐνούχους καὶ τὰς παρθένους (the eunuchs and the virgins). He wishes to intercede with these elect on behalf of the damned so cruelly tortured. But once again the archangel Michael replies harshly, explaining that the young man will not obtain any softening of the punishment from the eunuchs and virgins (οὔτε εὐνούχους οὔτε παρθένους).

Later, in 1.10, the young man visits a bold, drunk man who is being punished by burning charcoal placed on his head. This damned man also tells him his story: the cause of his punishment, his sin, was that while drunk he could not resist criticizing bishops, priests, eunuchs, and virgins (κατὰ ἐπισκόπων καὶ πρεσβυτέρων καὶ εὐνούχων καὶ παρθένων). Again the young man would like to help, and he inquires as to the whereabouts of the virgins (αἱ παρθένοι). In response, he is told that unless he returns to the world of the living and is baptized he will not receive permission to see any eunuch or virgin (οὔτε εὐνοῦχον οὔτε παρθένον). Finally, near the end of his speech, the young man says (1.12, quoted above) that at the moment of leaving Hell he saw a man and a woman being continually beaten by the guardian dog Cerberus at the gate of the underworld. Holding their liver in their hands, they implore the visitor for mercy. Having been moved slightly toward pity, the young man is once again rebuked by the archangel Michael, who tells him: "Leave it as it is, because they also have pronounced blasphemy against priests, priestesses, eunuchs, deacons, deaconesses, virgins, accusing them wrongly of impudicity and adultery."[22]

Until this point the young man in Hell has visited only people who were not recognized as leaders of the majority church. Instead, they seem to be laypeople – we can imagine the population of Asia probably being largely Christianized by this time – who attacked the ascetic community because they considered it a sect or heresy. Just after he passes through the gate on his way back to earth, however, the young man sees an altar, and hypocrite ministers are celebrating at it (1.13). They seem not to be dead, and their negative actions are told in the present tense. The narrative is therefore skillful: it gives the impression of still being located in the underworld, but at the same time, it is present and reflects an actual situation in which priests and church leaders, divided among themselves, abuse their power. The next paragraph, representing the end of the young man's travel report, is more apocalyptic: it describes a beautiful throne and the trial of the guilty celebrants at the same altar mentioned in the previous paragraph. The judgment integrates the same criticisms made against the laypeople in the remainder of the tour of hell: the grievances against them are drunkenness, slander, hypocrisy, and wrath. The eschatological judge, visible only through a thunderbolt and a voice,

---

[22] See the remarkable analysis of the tour of Hell by Amsler, *Acta Philippi. Commentarius*, 24–83.

quotes the Scriptures to condemn the wicked celebrants: they are called οἱ λει-τουργοὶ τοῦ θυσιαστηρίου (the servants of the altar).

In this essay I have translated the term πρεσβῦτις "priestess," but this is not the only possible translation. In Greek the term signifies first an aged woman, according to Liddell-Scott-Jones,[23] and a glance at Lampe's *Patristic Greek Lexicon*[24] indicates that in the Christian tradition the term was applied to senior widows and female presbyters. Lampe insists that for the masculine πρεσβύτερος "it is difficult to distinguish between this gen[eral] use of π[ρεσβύτερος], and its technical use to denote a member of a particular ministerial order."[25] In my opinion, what is true for the masculine must apply to the feminine.

To make the matter even more complex, we must be aware that Greek, in addition to the standard πρεσβῦτις, has two other feminine nouns with same root: πρεσβυτέρα and πρεσβυτερίς. The origin of the first is clear: it is an adjective in the comparative, used substantively. Its occurrence however is ambiguous: as does πρεσβῦτις, πρεσβυτέρα can mean an old woman or the head, or senior, of a women's community. The second noun, πρεσβυτερίς is probably a Christian neologism that was perhaps invented by Epiphanius; the word seems to be extremely rare. Epiphanius applies it to a female presbyter in a text written against the Collyridians, which condemns any woman whose status involves the exercise of priesthood or priestly functions: "Now it should be noted that church order required only deaconesses; it also included the name 'widows,' of whom the older were called 'eldresses,' but were never assigned the rank of 'presbytresses' or 'priestesses'" (χήρας τε ὠνόμασε καὶ τούτων τὰς ἔτι γραοτέρας πρεσβύτιδας, οὐδαμοῦ δὲ πρεσβυτερίδας ἢ ἱερίσσας προσέταξε; Epiphanius, *Panarion* 79.4).[26] Epiphanius uses here πρεσβῦτις in the general meaning of an older woman and πρεσβυτερίς in the technical meaning of a female presbyter. This distinction marks a divergence from the *Acts of Philip* and Canon 11 published by the Council of Laodicea.[27] With the Council of Laodicea, however, the bishop of Salamis reveals his hostility toward the ordination and sacerdotal functioning of women. The sect condemned by Epiphanius approves of this ministry for women, as does *Acts of Philip* 1. Epiphanius adds an interesting detail, stating that his adversaries were using Acts 21:9, among other biblical authoritative proof-texts, where mention is made of Philip's four prophesying daughters. Another apocryphal text, the *Martyrdom of Matthew*, mentions the appointment not only of a priest

---

[23] Henry George Liddell, Robert Scott, and Henry Stuart Jones, *A Greek-English Lexicon* (9th ed.; Oxford: Clarendon, 1961) 1462.

[24] G. W. H. Lampe, *A Patristic Greek Lexicon* (Oxford: Clarendon, 1961) 1130.

[25] Lampe also writes: "Accurate distinction between above sense [i.e., 'equivalent to ἐπίσκοπος, bishop'] and that of *priest* in threefold ministry is rendered difficult by long survival of inexact or untechnical terminology, by which πρεσβύτερος = *ruler in a church*."

[26] On this passage see Eisen, *Amtsträgerinnen im frühen Christentum*, 115–19.

[27] See E. J. Jonkers, ed., *Acta et symbola conciliorum quae saeculo quarto habita sunt* (Textus Minores 19; Leiden: Brill, 1974) 88.

(πρεσβύτερος), but also of a priestess (πρεσβῦτις). If Matthew established the king as a priest and the son of the king as a deacon, "then he established the wife of the king as a priestess, and the wife of the king's son as a deaconess" (καὶ τὴν γυναῖκα τοῦ βασιλέως κατέστησεν πρεσβύτιδα, καὶ τὴν γυναῖκα τοῦ υἱοῦ αὐτοῦ κατέστησεν διακόνισσαν, *Martyrium Matthaei* 28).[28] The presence of women in these ministerial roles disturbs the community so little that the author concludes that there was a great joy in the church! To this list we can add epigraphic evidence that mentions a πρεσβῦτις by the name Epictos.[29] And as I discuss below, the *Acts of Philip* 8-*Martyrdom* valorizes another of Philip's female relatives, his sister Mariamne.

Ute Eisen is correct in saying that some early Christian churches accepted the ministry of women, not only at the level of virgins, widows, and deaconesses but also at the sacerdotal level of what I call "priestesses." She is probably not specific enough when she speaks repeatedly of the "church" or the "early church."[30] We should attempt to specify the period, region, and type of Christian community. One such community is the one found in the *Acts of Philip*, which was an ascetic movement in Asia Minor during the fourth, perhaps the third century C.E. The existence of this ministerial role for women in this community is confirmed in the second part of the book, *Acts of Philip* 8–*Martyrdom*.

Mariamne as a Model of Faith and Leadership in *Acts of Philip* 8-*Martyrdom*

Mariamne is introduced as Philip's sister in *Acts of Philip* 8.2.[31] She is said to have been active during Jesus' time, probably during the last supper: she prepared the bread and the salt, thus preparing the breaking of bread while Martha was busy with many other things. Mariamne is equated with Mary in the Lukan and Johannine episodes; she is Martha's sister (Luke 10:38–42).[32] Mariamne received

---

[28] Maximilien Bonnet, "Martyrium Matthaei," in *Acta apostolorum apocrypha*, 2.1:259 lines 3–5. This is one recension of the text. The other recension, followed by the Latin translation, characterizes the two women as only deaconesses. This second recension and the Latin translation are printed below the first Greek version on the same page; ibid., lines 11–12, 28–29, 31.

[29] The inscription from Thera, Greece, is presented by Eisen, *Amststrägerinnen im frühen Christentum*, 123–25. In the same chapter, Eisen cites other inscriptions in which the evidence is less clear.

[30] Ibid., e.g., 9, 23, 26; see the critical review of the English translation by Robin M. Jensen in *JECS* 10 (2002) 135–38.

[31] See Amsler, *Acta Philippi. Commentarius*, 312–17.

[32] It may be appropriate to mention here a strange apocryphal episode preserved in the so-called *Ecclesiastical Constitution of the Apostles* 26, where Christ refuses Mary and Martha the right to celebrate the Eucharist; see Adolf von Harnack, *Die Lehre der zwölf Apostel nebst Untersuchungen zur ältesten Geschichte der Kirchenverfassung und des Kirchenrechts. Anhang. Ein übersehenes Fragment der Διδαχή in alter lateinischer Übersetzung* (Leipzig: Hinrichs, 1884)

another responsibility from the Savior: she is to carry the list of the countries to which the resurrected Jesus will send his disciples.[33] The Savior grants her a third responsibility as well: she is to accompany her brother in his apostolic ministry, and when he becomes weak and quick tempered, she is to be strong and calm. Mariamne is called upon right at the outset. When Philip hears the name of the city to which he is being sent, his courage melts at once. But Mary, who has – says the text – the body of a woman but – according to the ancient view – the spirit of a man, leads him on the right way and brings him back to the proper spiritual disposition. She does not console the weak apostle, but rather leads him to a mature understanding of his responsibilities.

Obeying a divine order, similar to *logion* 114 in the *Gospel of Thomas*, Mariamne must change her appearance: she has to cut the long summer outfit she wears and transform her appearance into that of a male.[34] She wears male clothing as she travels with her brother. But these two are not just traveling together as brother and sister. Following the two-by-two distribution commanded by Jesus in his missionary speech and respecting the grouping of the New Testament lists of the Twelve, Bartholomew is sent by the Lord also as the companion of Philip. The reader discovers, therefore, that the missionary expedition consists of a group of three people – Philip, his sister Mariamne, and his companion Bartholomew. As the text makes clear, these three together are called οἱ ἀπόστολοι (the apostles): Mariamne is an apostle as well as the other two; she also has been sent by the Savior.[35]

Mariamne's story does not differ from other early Christian traditions concerning Mary Magdalene. Actually, the name Mariamne is a Greek equivalent of Mary and not another name.[36] The connection between Mariamne and the post-resurrection sending of the apostles in the *Acts of Philip* does not differ from what the New Testament presents with respect to the role of Mary Magdalene and the

---

236; François Bovon, "Mary Magdalene's Paschal Privilege," in idem, *New Testament Traditions and Apocryphal Narratives* (trans. Jane Haapiseva-Hunter; Princeton Theological Monograph Series 36; Allison Park, Pa.: Pickwick, 1995) 234.

[33] The Greek expression for this list is ἡ ἀναγραφὴ τῶν χωρῶν.

[34] Instances of a woman's changing her clothing to that of a man in this work are not limited to Mariamne. In *Acts of Philip* 4.6 a girl named Charitini, who is healed by Philip, changes her garments and adopts a male dress. On the change of clothing, see Stephen J. Davis, "Crossed Texts, Crossed Sex: Intertextuality and Gender in Early Christian Legends of Holy Women Disguised as Men," *JECS* 10 (2002) 1–36.

[35] This is noted with perspicacity by Ann Graham Brock, *Mary Magdalene, The First Apostle: The Struggle for Authority* (HTS 51; Cambridge, Mass.: Harvard University Press, 2003) 124 n. 4, 126–27.

[36] See my two articles: "Mary Magdalene's Paschal Privilege," 228; and "Mary Magdalene in the *Acts of Philip*," in *Which Mary?: The Marys of Early Christian Tradition* (ed. F. Stanley Jones; SBL Symposium Series 19; Atlanta: Scholars Press, 2002) 75–89; reprinted in this volume, pp. 259–272 below. Against the identification of Mariamne with Mary Magdalene, see Stephen J. Shoemaker, "Rethinking the 'Gnostic Mary': Mary of Nazareth and Mary of Magdala in Early Christian Tradition," *JECS* 9 (2001) 555–95.

other women in their proclamation of the resurrection to the group of the Eleven. It is, in fact, identical with a very old tradition preserved by the Manichean Psalms, according to which Mary's courage brings the Eleven back together when they were ready to run away: she gives them back their courage.[37] This is exactly what Mariamne is doing when she cares for her cowardly brother, the apostle Philip.

Even a cursory reading of the sequence of episodes in the *Acts of Philip* reveals that at each step of the missionary journey Mariamne fulfills the duties and has the privileges of an apostle. If her preaching activity is limited even in *Xenophontos* 32, a manuscript not suspected of excessive orthodox editing, it is likely that in an earlier version of the text, which is now no longer recoverable, Mariamne must have been endowed with a full preaching load. What remains is still impressive. As soon as the apostolic group finds a location in Ophiorymos, she stays at the door of the house (actually an abandoned dispensary) and calls the passersby, inviting them to enter and hear Philip's apostolic message (*Acts of Philip Martyrdom* 3 [recension Γ]). One of the passersby is Nicanora, the governor's wife. Syrian by birth, as were Mariamne and her brother – both being born at Bethsaida – Nicanora is happy to speak Aramaic or Hebrew with Mariamne. This female apostle begins to convince her of the Christian message. In the present form of the text this development provides an invitation to learn more from Philip, but in the original it was most likely Mariamne who provided the complete apostolic preaching, and this with no male mediation. A confirmation of my hypothesis is found in the later distribution of roles: Philip will baptize the male converts, and Mariamne will baptize the women. The text is clear here. Mariamne does not just function as an adjunct for a sacrament performed by Philip her brother. She performs a sacrament as a minister.

Acts of Philip 8–*Martyrdom* also offers a description of other aspects of Mariamne's ministry.[38] She shares, for instance, in the healing ministry of Christ and his apostles (the *Acts of Philip* describes conversion as a process of healing, with numerous miraculous cures and successful exorcisms as medical symbols of salvation). What seems strange today, but did not seem strange to the evangelist Mark, is the use of saliva as a curative medication: like the saliva of the Markan Jesus, Mariamne's saliva that is dipped from her mouth by Philip's finger restores Stachys's sight (*Acts of Philip Martyrdom* 14.7).[39]

---

[37] See Charles Robert Cecil Allberry, ed., *A Manichaean Psalm-Book: Part II* (Manichaean Manuscripts in the Chester Beatty Collection 2; Stuttgart: Kohlhammer, 1938) 192; Bovon, "Mary Magdalene's Paschal Privilege," 154, 232.

[38] See Bovon, "Mary Magdalene in the *Acts of Philip*."

[39] I must add that this story shocked one reader into a drastic solution: to extract violently the rest of the story (the text breaks at the point when Philip dips his finger in his sister's mouth to anoint Stachys). We remember here also that the evangelists Matthew and Luke opposed two Markan narratives (Mark 7:31–37 and 8:22–26) that are similar to this one: they did not copy them, which is in effect also a form of censorship.

Luke, the author of the canonical Acts of the Apostles, knew of feminine relatives around Philip the evangelist: his four daughters (Acts 21:9). Several other authors in the early centuries c.e. circulated traditions about these young women concerning their gift of prophecy, a resurrection story involving both them and Philip, and mention of their tombs in Hierapolis of Phrygia.[40] One finds such short allusions particularly among Christians who practiced prophecy. The number of daughters tends to vary, possibly indicating that Luke was not the only source of information about them. Some authors even claimed to know where one or the other had been buried. The Montanists relied on them as a warranty for their own religious experiences. According to Epiphanius, quoted above, the Collyridians found in Acts 21:9 justification for their practice of allowing female presbyters.

Orthodox writers could not censure the Lukan passage since this book had become canonical for them. They tried their best, however, to adapt its meaning to their own agenda. In a controversy not over prophecy but over asceticism, Clement of Alexandria rejoiced in the fact that Philip had daughters, even as Peter had a mother-in-law.[41] For Clement this meant that both apostles were married. A similar process of adaptation occurred for the ascetic community of the *Acts of Philip*. In a period when the book of Acts was neither familiar nor canonized,[42] this community transformed the daughters into one sister.[43] By the same token, they identified this sister with Mary Magdalene and with Mary the sister of Martha. The intention of such a manipulation is evident: in so doing, these Christians had at their disposal a first-rate female apostle, living proof of the validity of women's priestly ministry and the best advocate of strict asceticism. Philip is no longer married, and he can thus become for men the paragon of continence.

Conclusion

The connection between the πρεσβύτιδες in *Acts of Philip* 1 and the figure of Mariamne in *Acts of Philip* 8–*Martyrdom* is clear. If we accept that the community of the author of the *Acts of Philip* advocates for women's ministry in the

---

[40] See Papias in Eusebius, *Hist. eccl.* 3.39.9; see also Polycrates in 3.31.2–3 and 5.24.2, and the Montanist Proclus in 3.31.4.

[41] Clement of Alexandria, in Eusebius of Caesarea, *Hist. eccl.* 3.30.1. See Amsler, *Acta Philippi. Commentarius*, 7–9.

[42] In the beginning of his first homily on the Book of Acts, John Chrysostom complains that in his time many people did not know the content of this biblical book; see John Chrysostom, *Homilies on Acts* 1.1 (PG 60:13); see my *De vocatione gentium. Histoire de l'interprétation d'Act. 10,1–11,18 dans les six premiers siècles* (BGBE 8; Tübingen: Mohr Siebeck, 1967) 7–8.

[43] Even the number four, with respect to four daughters (see Acts 21:9), is not consistent across the texts. Polycrates identifies their number as three; Papias and an anti-Montanist writer do not specify their number at all (see Eusebius, *Hist. eccl.* 3.31.2–3; 3.39.9; 5.17.3; 5.24.2).

church even at the level of priesthood, then the presence of a female apostle beside Philip, the evangelist and apostle of Phrygia (the apostle and the evangelist being one and the same person), becomes not only a possibility but a theological and ecclesiological necessity.

The community of the author lists among its members eunuchs and virgins, deacons and deaconesses, priests and priestesses. Such church order seems legitimate because in the beginning the apostles were sent out not only two by two, like Philip and Bartholomew, but also male and female side by side, like Philip and Mariamne. If the Great Church can claim that their threefold hierarchical system of bishops, priests, and deacons is biblical, then the ascetic community of Phrygia, like other marginal churches of that time, has the same right and the same authority to defend a church order that includes both men and women in priestly ministry.

Actually, the author of the *Acts of Philip* is less interested in canon law than in pastoral care and spiritual life. She or he needs an apostolic model for the present time. Models are not taken from legal documents, but from narratives. *A sa façon,* the work she or he writes or compiles, the *Acts of Philip,* fulfills this need. This literary composition gives legitimacy and courage to the marginalized, persecuted community.

The price paid is perhaps high: the distortion of apostolic memories. But who did not distort history in that time? And who is able to judge the distortion? Is the final victory granted to men, since Mariamne must wear male clothing? Perhaps so, but she is the strongest among those in her apostolic group. And her salvation is not due to her bearing children but to her practicing an ascetic life, ἀγνεία, a spiritual discipline that opens the eyes of faith to the vision of God.

Mary Magdalene in the *Acts of Philip*

1. The Name Mary

Sura 19 of the Qur'an gives Mary, Jesus' mother, the honorary epithet "sister of Aaron."[1] A few Jewish texts of late antiquity and the Middle Ages merge the Virgin Mary with Mary Magdalene.[2] Such connections were made possible and even attractive because of the similarity in names. First I would like to reflect on the several forms of the name Mary and then examine the persons of that same name.

Miriam is the Hebrew name.[3] It is applied to the sister of Aaron and Moses. The Septuagint regularly translates this name with Μαριάμ. Philo follows this usage,[4] while Josephus never uses this term and instead calls the sister of Aaron and Moses Μαριάμμη.[5] The New Testament manuscripts do not witness the name Μαριάμμη, preferring Μαριάμ or Μαρία for Jesus' mother, the woman from Magdala, and the several other Marys.[6] We have, therefore, three different spellings in Greek. The Coptic authors, translators, and scribes use the same three forms of the name known from the Greek. The Latin translators of the Bible used

---

[1] See Jaroslav Pelikan, *Mary through the Centuries* (New Haven, Conn.: Yale University Press, 1996) 72–73.

[2] See R. Travers Herford, *Christianity in Talmud and Midrash* (London: Williams & Norgate, 1903) 355, 358. I thank my colleague Jon Levenson, who helped me in this matter. One finds the same assimilation in a Coptic homily probably from the sixth century c.e.; see Pseudo-Cyril of Jerusalem, *Homily on the Dormition* (E. A. Wallis Budge, *Miscellaneous Coptic Texts in the Dialect of Upper Egypt* [London: British Museum, 1915] 630). I thank Ann Graham Brock for this information.

[3] On the Hebrew name, its origin, structure, and meaning, see Scott C. Layton, *Archaic Features of Canaanite Personal Names in the Hebrew Bible* (HSM 47; Atlanta: Scholars Press, 1990) 183–86. I thank Professor Jo Ann Hackett for this reference.

[4] See Philo of Alexandria, *Leg.* 1.76; 2.66; 2.103; *Agr.* 80–81; *Contempl.* 87.

[5] Or Μαριάμη according to manuscript evidence; see Abraham Schalit, *Namenwörterbuch zu Flavius Josephus* (suppl. 1 of *A Complete Concordance to Flavius Josephus*; Leiden: Brill, 1968), s.v. Besides the sister of Moses and Aaron, Josephus knows six different Μαριάμ(μ)η. He mentions also once a Μαρία (*B.J.* 6.201).

[6] The author of Luke-Acts uses Μαριάμ for Jesus' mother. In the only genitive use of this name he prefers Μαρίας; he calls Mary Magdalene Μαρία, and the sister of Martha Μαριάμ. But we must be careful: the textual evidence can vary from one manuscript to the other. Matthew can use Μαριάμ or Μαρία for the same person. The same is true of John.

only the name Maria when they refer to the sister of Aaron and Moses, Jesus' mother, or Jesus' friend.

I spent an afternoon in the Widener Library poring over the venerable Pape, *Wörterbuch der griechischen Eigennamen*, Bechtel, *Personennamen*, and Preisigke, *Namenbuch* (with its supplement *Onomasticon alterum papyrologicum*), the more recent *Lexicon of Greek Personal Names* according to regions (two volumes so far), Kajava's *Roman Female Praenomina* as well as Kajanto's *Onomastic Studies in the Early Christian Inscriptions of Rome and Carthage*, Jones and Whitehorne's *Register of Oxyrhynchites*, and Tcherikover and Fuks's *Corpus papyrorum judaicarum.*[7]

What I found was an intriguing thread. In Jewish inscriptions and papyri, the names Μαρία and Μαριάμ are attested in the time of the Roman Empire.[8] With variations in Greek spelling, the name Μάρεια can be applied to the Lake close to Alexandria (Lake Mareotis) and to the city on its shore. Μαρία appears also as the name of an island along the African coast of the Red Sea. Μαριαμμία (sometimes written Μαριάμμη) exists in Syria as a city known later as the metropolis of a bishop.[9] But as a name for a woman neither Μαρία nor Μαριάμ are Greek. If they are attested as such, it is in later records and under Jewish, Christian, or perhaps Latin influence. Of course Μαρία has been very popular in Greece through the present, but under Christian influence.

---

[7] Wilhelm Pape and Gustav Benseler, eds., *Wörterbuch der griechischen Eigennamen* (2 vols.; repr. of 3d ed.; Orbis litterarum; Graz: Akademische Druck- und Verlagsanstalt, 1959); Friedrich Bechtel, *Die historischen Personennamen des Griechischen bis zur Kaiserzeit* (Halle: Niemeyer, 1917); Friedrich Preisigke and Enno Littmann, *Namenbuch* (Heidelberg: Selbstverlag des Herausgebers, 1922); Daniele Foraboschi, *Onomasticon alterum papyrologicum. Supplemento al Namenbuch di F. Preisigke* (TDSA 16, Serie papirologica 2; Milan-Varese: Istituto editoriale cisalpino, 1971); Peter Marshall Fraser and Elaine Matthews, eds., *A Lexicon of Greek Personal Names* (Oxford: Clarendon, 1987–); Mika Kajava, *Roman Female Praenomina: Studies in the Nomenclature of Roman Women* (AIRF 14; Rome: Institutum romanum Finlandiae, 1995); Iiro Kajanto, *Onomastic Studies in the Early Christian Inscriptions of Rome and Carthage* (AIRF 2.1; Helsinki: Helsinki University Press, 1963); Brian W. Jones and J. E. G. Whitehorne, *Register of Oxyrhynchites 30 B.C.–A.D. 96* (ASP 25; Chico, Calif.: Scholars Press, 1983); Victor A. Tcherikover and Alexander Fuks, eds., *Corpus papyrorum judaicarum* (3 vols.; Cambridge: Harvard University Press, 1957–64); see also August Fick, *Die griechischen Personennamen nach ihrer Bildung erklärt mit den Namensystemen verwandter Sprachen verglichen und systematisch geordnet* (Göttingen: Vandenhoeck & Ruprecht, 1874); Olli Salomies, *Die römischen Vornamen. Studien zur römischen Namengebung* (Commentationes humanarum litterarum 82; Helsinki: Societas scientiarum Fennica, 1987). I would like to thank Eldon J. Epp, who gave me the titles of some of these works.

[8] The name Μαρία is present in two Jewish papyri of the beginning of the second century C.E. and one Egyptian grave inscription; see Tcherikover and Fuks, *Corpus papyrorum judaicarum*, vol. 2, nos. 223 and 227; vol. 3, no. 1535: Μαρία Ἀβιήτου, who died 31 March 116 C.E. (no. 227); Μαρία Δημᾶτος, who died 28 February 116 C.E. (no. 223); a Maria from Antinoopolis daughter of Phamsothis (inscr. 1535).

[9] See Wilhelm Enßlin, "Maria," PW 14:1712–13.

One must recall that the Greeks and the Jews had a simpler onomastic system than the Romans, in having no *praenomina* nor *cognomina*. To distinguish between two women with the same name they indicated – as you know – the name of the father or the husband.

Let us turn now to the Latin onomastic. Normally in Rome a woman was named according to her *nomen gentilicium* (name of her *gens*, *grosso modo* our last name): Cornelia for a woman from the *gens* of the Cornelii.[10] If she was of a noble family, she could keep the name of her family instead of taking the one of her husband. There was an evolution in the Latin onomastic system. While the *nomen* had been for a long time the only name for a woman, a *praenomen* and even a *cognomen* developed thereafter. The Latin Maria represents the feminine form of the *nomen gentilicium* Marius.[11] Incidentally – to complicate the matter – the name Marius existed among the Oscs, a people of South Italy (Campania),[12] conquered early by the Romans.[13] I cannot discern if the Oscs used *praenomina* and if the feminine Maria as a *praenomen* is attested among the Oscs. The Latin Maria was probably pronounced Mária because Latin cannot accept an accent on the penultimate if this syllable is short.[14] In such cases the accent goes back to the previous syllable. But in the early Roman Empire Maria was introduced as *praenomen* under Jewish influence.

Bertrand Bouvier, my co-editor of the *Acts of Philip*, reminded me of a particular piece of philological evidence. When a Greek word ends with a consonant, the consonant can only be ν, ρ, or ς. Any name ending with another consonant therefore sounds foreign or barbaric. And that would be the case of Μαριάμ. This very fact may explain the two other forms of Mary, namely, Μαρία and Μαριάμμη, chosen perhaps to erase the impression of strangeness, the foreign character of the name.[15]

In my view, to disentangle the changing usage of the name, more work must be done, and I would suggest that the following criteria be applied. First, scholars should consider the language in which the name occurs; second, they should respect the period in which the text being considered was composed; third, they should establish the geographic location of the document; fourth, researchers

---

[10] More precision would follow with the name of her father or of her husband or both.

[11] In the second century B.C.E., two sisters of C. Marius bore the name Maria: one became the wife of M. Gratidius, the other the mother of C. Lucius; in the fourth century C.E., a Maria is known as the wife of the emperor Honorius; see Ruth Albrecht, "Maria," *DNP* 7:887–90.

[12] "Peuple de langue sabellique de l'Italie ancienne, établi en Campanie, influencé par les Grecs et soumis par les Samnites, mais qui conserva sa langue jusqu'au ~ 1ᵉʳ siècle" (*Le Petit Robert 2. Dictionnaire universel des noms propres, alphabétique et analogique, illustré en couleurs* [ed. Paul Robert and Alain Rey; Paris: Le Robert, 1991], s.v.).

[13] See Salomies, *Die römischen Vornamen*, 77–78.

[14] If today we say María (accent on the *i*) in Italian, it is an exception under Greek influence of the Byzantine period. The same is true for Lucia, pronounced today Lucía.

[15] It must be added finally that Μαριάμμη was spelled sometimes Μαριάμη or Μαριάμνη, as one can see from the manuscript traditions.

should examine the class or social milieu of the author; and fifth, they should understand the prevalent intellectual or religious traditions.[16]

Why, for example, does Josephus choose the name Μαριάμμη for the sister of Moses and Aaron, and why does he *not* follow the translation chosen by the Septuagint? Is it because he desires to avoid the barbaric character of that name and perhaps follows a hellenizing Jewish tradition? Or, since all the other Μαριάμμη he mentions are Jewish princesses, does he wish to underline the aristocratic character of the sister of Aaron and Moses? The deliberate choice of Μαρία or Μαριάμμη expresses in my view an assimilation into Greek language and culture.

2. The Two Marys

If we turn now from the names to the person,[17] there is evidence that the same person may have received each of the three forms of the name. The mother of Jesus is called Μαριάμ or Μαρία in the New Testament, Μαριάμμη in three passages of the *Protevangelium of James* (according to the most ancient manuscript, P. Bod. V).[18] The assignment of names to Mary Magdalene is identical.[19] She is

---

[16] See N. C. Cohen, "The Proper Name 'Miriam' in Greek and Latin Transliteration [Hebrew with English summary]," *Les* 38 (1974) 170–80; Stephen J. Shoemaker, "Mary and the Discourse of Orthodoxy: Early Christian Identity and the Ancient Dormition Legends" (Ph.D. diss., Duke University, 1997) 170–97.

[17] As it is known from Josephus, *B.J.* 2.439; 5.170; and 7.1, Μαριάμμη was also the name of a tower in Jerusalem.

[18] See Émile de Strycker, *La forme la plus ancienne du Protévangile de Jacques* (SHG 33; Brussels: Société des Bollandistes, 1961) 315–16.

[19] In recent years the secondary literature on Mary Magdalene has grown enormously; for ancient bibliography, see François Bovon, "Le privilège pascal de Marie-Madeleine," *NTS* 30 (1984) 50–62; English translation in idem, *New Testament Traditions and Apocryphal Narratives* (trans. J. Haapiseva-Hunter; Princeton Theological Monograph Series 36; Allison Park, Pa.: Pickwick, 1994) 147–57, 228–35; for more recent works, see Renate Schmid, *Maria Magdalena in gnostischen Schriften* (Material-Edition 29; Munich: Arbeitsgemeinschaft für Religions- und Weltanschauungensfragen, 1990); J. Kevin Coyle, "Mary Magdalene in Manichaeism?," *Mus* 104 (1991) 39–55; Maddalena Scopello, "Marie-Madeleine et la tour: *Pistis et sophia*," in *Figures du Nouveau Testament chez les Pères* (CBiPa 3; Strasbourg: Centre d'analyse et de documentation patristiques, 1991) 179–96; Carla Ricci, *Maria di Magdal e le molte altre donne sul cammino di Gesù* (Naples: D'Auria, 1991); Susan Haskins, *Mary Magdalene: Myth and Metaphor* (New York: Harcourt Brace, 1993); Hannele Koivunen, *Madonna ja huora* (Helsinki: Otava, 1995) [in Finnish; based on the author's dissertation "The Woman Who Understood Completely: A Semiotic Analysis of the Mary Magdalene Myth in the Gnostic Gospel of Mary," University of Helsinki, 1994]; Antti Marjanen, The *Woman Jesus Loved: Mary Magdalene in the Nag Hammadi Library and Related Documents* (Nag Hammadi and Manichaean Studies 40; Leiden: Brill, 1996); Ingrid Maisch, *Maria Magdalena zwischen Verachtung und Verehrung. Das Bild einer Frau im Spiegel der Jahrhunderte* (Freiburg im Breisgau: Herder, 1996); Shoemaker, "Mary and the Discourse of Orthodoxy"; Frédéric Amsler, *Acta Philippi. Commentarius* (CCSA 12; Turnhout: Brepols, 1999) 312–17; Silke Petersen, "*Zerstört die Werke der*

called Μαρία ἡ Μαγδαληνή in Matt 27:56; Μαριὰμ ἡ Μαγδαληνή a few verses later in Matt 27:61; and Μαριάμμη in the *Gospel of Mary*, Hippolytus, *Haer.* 5.1.7, Origen, *Cels.* 5.62, and, in a Latin form, in Priscillian's *Apologeticum* 1.[20]

Is there a tendency in the *catholica* to call Jesus' mother Μαρία and a pattern in nonorthodox communities for referring to Jesus' friend as Μαριάμμη? Probably not. When Mary Magdalene is designated Μαρία, a reference to her hometown Magdala often clearly identifies who she is.

The figure of Μαριάμνη (spelled sometimes Μαριάμμη in one or two manuscripts,[21] particularly the oldest one, P) present in the *Acts of Philip* cannot be Jesus' mother (mentioned once or twice as Μαρία in the text: *Acts Phil.* 6.13 [V and A], *Acts Phil. Mart.* 35.6 [Γ, absent from Θ and Δ]), because if she were, Philip would be Jesus' uncle! This figure is not connected with Jesus' birth but with his ministry and resurrection. The woman, it is my contention, is Mary Magdalene. I will insist on such a presence of Mary Magdalene in the *Acts of Philip* because this evidence has been neglected and because of the new manuscripts recently discovered and edited.[22]

3. Mariamne in the *Acts of Philip*

To be clear, I am not interested here in the reconstruction of the historical figure of Mary Magdalene, but in her portrayal in literary texts, particularly in the *Acts of Philip.*[23]

3.1. The Presence of Mariamne

Mariamne is quite present in the second half of the *Acts of Philip.*[24] Philip the apostle is the leader of the small group of missionaries sent by the resurrected

---

Weiblichkeit!" Maria Magdalena, Salome und andere Jüngerinnen Jesu in christlich-gnostischen Schriften (Nag Hammadi and Manichaean Studies 48; Leiden: Brill, 1999). More bibliography in Petersen, "*Zerstört die Werke der Weiblichkeit!,*" 351–71.

[20] There are of course other Marys in the New Testament: Mary, Martha's sister (Luke 10:38–42; John 11:1–12:8), merged in the *Acts of Philip* with Mary Magdalene; Mary of James (Matt 27:56; Mark 15:40; 16:1; Luke 24:10; see Matt 28:1); Mary of Joses (Mark 15:40, 47); Mary of Clopas (John 19:25); Mary, mother of John Mark (Acts 12:12); Mary who worked hard (Rom 16:6).

[21] I am referring to the sigla used in the edition of François Bovon, Bertrand Bouvier, and Frédéric Amsler, *Acta Philippi. Textus* (CCSA 11; Turnhout: Brepols, 1999). P is the *Parisinus gr.* 881; A is Athos, *Xenophontos* 32; V is the *Vaticanus gr.* 824; G is *Atheniensis* 346; Γ, Δ, and Θ represent three different Greek recensions of the *Martyrdom of Philip*, the last part of the *Acts of Philip*.

[22] See n. 21 above for the reference to the edition.

[23] See Bovon, "Le privilège pascal," 50–62; English translation in idem, *New Testament Traditions*, 147–57, 228–35.

[24] Mariamne is absent from the first half of the *Acts of Philip* (*Acts Phil.* 1–7), which leads

Savior. Twice when the trio, Bartholomew, Mariamne, and himself, meets a formidable dragon, Philip remains calm while Mariamne is frightened (*Acts Phil.* 11.5), and he performs the victorious exorcism (*Acts Phil.* 9.1–5 and 11.6–7). After the governor's wife, Nicanora, has made the acquaintance of Mariamne, it is Philip who takes the leading position (*Acts Phil. Mart.* 11 [V]). On another occasion he celebrates the Eucharist and gives her communion, not the other way around (*Acts Phil.* 11.1 and 10). Nevertheless, as Ann Graham Brock pointed out in her dissertation,[25] Mariamne is part of the group (see *Acts Phil. Mart.* 7 [V] and 26 [V]) and carries with Philip and Bartholomew the prestigious title οἱ ἀπόστολοι (see *Acts Phil.* 8.16, 21; 13.1–2.4).

3.2. Mariamne's Healing Activity

At two occasions in this text Mariamne is connected with a healing activity. First, while the apostolic group arrives in the city of Ophiorymos, Philip, like an itinerant physician, looks for a place to exercise his art. He shares with Mariamne the satisfaction of finding an abandoned clinic or dispensary (ἰατρεῖον) and invites her discreetly to install the group in that place that will become, he says, "this spiritual dispensary" (τὸ πνευματικὸν τοῦτο ἰατρεῖον, *Acts Phil.* 13.4).

Second, in the following act, *Acts Phil.* 14, the reader meets an aged man Stachys,[26] who has suffered blindness for forty years, but a dream has brought him to the apostles. Imitating Jesus' enigmatic gesture, Philip will use saliva to cure this blindness. But different from the Markan Jesus (Mark 8:22–26), Philip does not use his own saliva but dips his finger into Mariamne's mouth and extracts *her* saliva as a curative unguent. Alas, the first readers of the *Acts of Philip* could not bear that narrative, and the end of the episode has been expurgated in the only manuscript that has preserved this story (A). Like the evangelists Matthew and Luke, who considered Mark's episode too shocking to accept, a reader has torn away the folio between folios 87 and 88.

3.3. Mariamne's Teaching Activity

Philip is the apostle entrusted with preaching the good news, but the reader encounters several episodes in which Mariamne is a powerful, charismatic speaker and not simply an audience. In the martyrdom story, the apostolic group is active

---

scholars to believe that this work is a composite one and that *Acts Phil.* 1–7 are of another origin, probably related to Philip the evangelist (see Acts 6–8).

[25] Ann Graham Brock, *Mary Magdalene, The First Apostle: The Struggle for Authority* (HTS 51; Cambridge, Mass.: Harvard University Press, 2003) 124–29.

[26] Stachys's name and story have been preserved till today in the *Synaxarion* of the Orthodox Church for the Feast of Saint Philip celebrated 14 November; see Hippolyte Delehaye, *Synaxarium ecclesiae constantinopolitanae*, 117 and 1165 (index).

in Ophiorymos. The apostles have expanded their mission: they now use the house of Stachys as a gathering place where the guests can hear the Christian message, and Mariamne is represented as being posted at the entrance of the house as a sort of hostess, inviting the public in to hear the good news.

The martyrdom story of the *Acts of Philip* is preserved in three recensions. One recension (Θ) has, in an orthodox way,[27] eradicated Mariamne's teaching role, while another (Γ),[28] more open here to another orientation, recognizes her teaching activity (*Acts Phil. Mart.* 3).[29] But even this approbation is not without limitation: the recension Γ restricts Mariamne's role to calling the visitors to enter and to listen to Philip. It is probable that in the original form of the story, Mariamne was the legitimate missionary to women while Philip was the evangelist for men. An invective formulated by future pagan opponents accuses Mariamne of following men and of deceiving women (*Acts Phil. Mart.* 19 [Γ and Δ]), which I understand to mean that Mariamne is guilty both of fraternizing with Philip and Bartholomew and of preaching the encratite private life to women.

There is a confirmation of Mariamne's preaching activity in her encounter with Nicanora, the governor's wife (*Acts Phil. Mart.* 9). Mariamne is not content to relate to Nicanora via Philip's proselytizing, but she herself begins to profess to her listener a serious doctrinal teaching. She communicates the following message to Nicanora: you have fallen away from the divine family house and succumbed to the demonic power of the snake; you are guilty of having forgotten your origins, your Father in heaven, and your spiritual Mother; if you wake up, however, you will receive illumination. Nicanora has two reasons to exult: by Mariamne's κήρυγμα she has been spiritually saved and physically cured (*Acts Phil. Mart.* 10).[30]

3.4. Mariamne's Liturgical Activity

At several occasions the *Acts of Philip* presents Mariamne sharing ministerial responsibilities in the community. She is said to have prepared the bread and the salt for the communion[31] while Martha was serving the crowds[32] (*Acts Phil.* 8.2; in

---

[27] As historians we can use these categories for the time of the Byzantine compilers and scribes.

[28] Manuscript V presents the text of recension Γ, manuscript A the text of recension Θ.

[29] The third recension Δ starts later in *Acts Phil. Mart.* 17.

[30] Manuscript V reads "the preaching of my fathers" and A "your [pl.] preaching." I suggest that the original meaning was the apostolic teaching, delivered here by Mariamne, which fits into the faith of Nicanora's ancestors, the Jewish patriarchs.

[31] Women were present and active in the community of the Therapeutae; bread and salt were also the food of the Therapeutae described by Philo of Alexandria, *Contempl.* 37 and 73; see the quotations and summary of Philo's works in Eusebius of Caesarea, *Hist. eccl.* 2.17.

[32] Is the word "crowds" an ecclesiological expression, like the "many" in the Dead Sea Scrolls (see for example 1QS 6.1–7.27) and in Mark 10:45?

this ascetical text, the wine of the communion is not mentioned).[33] At the very beginning of the Christian movement, at the time of the sending of the apostles, her actions evoke the Last Supper, and to have participated in the preparation of the Last Supper confers authority and prestige to Mariamne, of course. There is an echo of this claim and at the same time a criticism of it in one of the ancient church orders, the so-called *Ecclesiastical Constitution of the Apostles*.[34] In a short narrative the "orthodox" Jesus of the *Constitution* forbids both Mary and Martha to conduct the celebration of the Eucharist.

Similar in importance is Mariamne's baptismal activity. Twice the text affirms that Mariamne was responsible for the baptism of women, and this does not represent an exception but the rule, as the imperfect tense indicates: "Philip baptized the men and Mariamne the women" (*Acts Phil.* 14.9; see also *Acts Phil. Mart.* 2 [Θ]).[35] We know that women were active in the celebration of baptism in the orthodox communities: in some regions of the East deaconesses had the responsibility to perform an unction with oil[36] and to hold out the requisite white garments to the newly baptized women at the moment of their ascent from the water.[37] But these responsibilities were limited. The baptism itself was performed by a man, the bishop or later the priest. Such is not the case here: Mariamne carries the whole responsibility of the baptism of women.

3.5. Mariamne's Suffering

Mariamne does not escape the persecution that reaches Philip. Nicanora's husband, the governor with the terrible name of Tyrannognophos, is furious at the new ascetical, encratite lifestyle of his wife. Not without reason he accuses the Christian apostles for the changes that his wife embraces, and he imagines some magical tricks. The apostolic trio is arrested, taken under custody in a pagan temple, and then subjected to a bodily search (*Acts Phil. Mart.* 14–20). A miracle protects Mariamne from eventual shame during her humiliation: the moment the soldiers try to strip away her clothing, the form of her body is transformed. One recension reads that a discreet cloud took her away from the indiscreet eyes of her enemies [Γ]. The two other forms of the text [Θ and Δ], probably closer to the original, say that her body was transformed to a κιβωτὸς ὑελίνη, a "shrine of glass." This term κιβωτός is extremely interesting because it is the same term that the Septuagint uses for the ark of Noah (Gen 6:14–9:18) and the ark of the cove-

---

[33] The text presupposes that Mary Magdalene and Mary of Bethany are the same person.

[34] See *Ecclesiastical Constitution of the Apostles* 26; and Bovon, Bouvier, and Amsler, *Acta Philippi. Textus*, 240 n. 5.

[35] Compare Firmilian's letter to Cyprian in Cyprian, *Epistle* 75.10.

[36] See *Const. ap.* 3.16; *Didascalia apostolorum* 16.

[37] Aimé Georges Martimort, *Deaconesses: An Historical Study* (trans. K. D. Whitehead; San Francisco: Ignatius, 1986) 43–44, 52–57.

nant (Exod 25:9–21 and passim). It is also the term that the Christian liturgy applies in a typological way to the Virgin Mary, referring to her as the receptacle of God's presence.

For the author of this segment of the *Acts of Philip*, as for many Christians of late antiquity, men and women can appear in three different forms: in the dress of sinful luxury, in the modest clothing of faith, and in the glorious body of the resurrection. What happens for Mariamne is a temporary manifestation of her resurrectional status. Her suffering is therefore not an inexorable ending. During the violent aggression of the governor, she is allowed to put on her dress of light, although for just a short time, but it is time enough to realize the power and the presence of the divine glory. After this transformation from humility to glory there is a return to her human condition; as the Jesus of the canonical Gospels is finally back on earth "alone" (Mark 9:8 par.), so too Mariamne recuperates her "first type" (*Acts Phil. Mart.* 25 [Θ] and 32).

Human existence is limited in time, and death remains inexorable. The *Acts of Philip* takes this reality seriously, and without mentioning martyrdom, twice the text announces Mariamne's death. Here the author is concerned with a special form of funeral for Mariamne. An order is given by the agonizing Philip to place her coffin in the River Jordan (*Acts Phil. Mart.* 31 [A] and 36), and this is a mysterious affirmation for two reasons. First, to my knowledge there is no other text locating Mariamne's death in Palestine. The Bible, however, mentions Miriam's burial at Kadesh (Num 20:1), a place that our author may have imagined not far from the River Jordan. Second, the location of her tomb in a river is also exceptional. I know only of one other case, Alaric I, king of the Visigoths, who died at Cosenza (Italy) in 410 c.e. and was buried by his soldiers in the River Busento.

3.6. Mariamne's Manly Faith and Male Clothing

Several ancient Christian texts describe the role of Mary Magdalene during the critical days of Jesus' death and resurrection. Preserved in a Coptic and an Ethiopic version, the *Epistula apostolorum*, for example, underlines the effort of three women to convince the disciples of the reality of their Lord's resurrection.[38] Both versions of this text explicitly name Mary in this context (the Ethiopic version underlines the priority of Mary Magdalene). Building on the same tradition, the *Manichaean Psalms* praise Mary, called Marihama (last letter not clear), for having brought together the fleeing disciples like a fisherman captures fish in his net.[39] The *Acts of Philip* offers a full picture of this scene and confirms the vitality of this widespread tradition.

---

[38] *Epistula apostolorum* 10–11.

[39] Psalms of Heracleides, "There Were Ten Virgins," in *A Manichaean Psalm-Book: Part II* (ed. Charles R. C. Allberry; Manichaean Manuscripts in the Chester Beatty Collection 2; Stuttgart: Kohlhammer, 1938) 192 lines 21–22.

I first need to situate this passage of the *Acts of Philip* in the manuscript tradition. We cannot here rely on our major manuscript, *Xenophontos* 32, because the gesture of a censor has violently extracted twenty-four folios. We possess the short version of *Vaticanus* 824, but it is not so useful because its scribe also has applied a kind of censorship by avoiding much of the compromising material. The most valuable witness of a more complete version remains therefore the manuscript *Atheniensis* 346 (G).

Acts Phil. 8, the beginning of the ancient acts, depicts the comforting role of Mariamne among Jesus' disciples after the resurrection. The apostles are called together by the resurrected Savior, and Mariamne is among them (as Jesus' appearance to Mary Magdalene is part of the New Testament resurrection stories). She is said to have carried then the list of countries where the disciples will be sent, the ἀναγραφὴ τῶν χωρῶν (*Acts Phil.* 8.2 [G]), and in this way fills the function of special assistant to the Savior, a kind of chief of staff. Mariamne is also described as the sister of the apostle Philip. Because of this kinship she is asked by the Savior to take care of her brother, who is anxious at the prospect of his dangerous mission to the Greeks. She is even urged to travel with him and to defend virtue, and *Acts Phil.* 8 [G] represents Philip as weak and Mariamne as strong.

This is an ancient concept. One of the ancients, Plato, expressed his conviction that occasionally a man can be weak and a woman strong.[40] For this philosopher and many after him, the categories of male and female were not neutral: the first connoted positively, the second negatively. According to *Acts Phil.* 8 [G], Philip as a man has a female faith and attitude, and spiritually, Mariamne expresses herself like a male facing the hostile world: "And the Savior told her: 'I know that you are good and brave in your soul and blessed among women. A feminine spirit has entered Philip while the male and courageous spirit is in you'" (*Acts Phil.* 8.3 [G]). Mariamne owes these qualities to the Savior's favor, being the object of a special calling (*Acts Phil.* 8.3–4 [G]). Her duty to her faith is also immense. *Acts Phil.* 8.3 affirms that the apostolic mission and her part in it involve nothing less than "the sufferings of martyrdom and the redemption of the whole world."

Few ancient Christian texts describe so vividly what this commissioning implies. In *Acts Phil.* 8 [G] the Savior organizes Mariamne's enterprise and counts on its success. He gives her the following practical advice: "You, Mariamne, change your gown and your outward appearance. Put off all that in your form resembles a woman, in particular your summer dress [a rare word is used here: τὸ θέριστρον]. Do not let your fringe be dragged on the ground, do not twist it, but cut it; then walk together with your brother Philip to the city called Ophiorymos, which is understood as the 'promenade of the snakes'" (*Acts Phil.* 8.4 [G]).

---

[40] See Plato, *Resp.* 5.1 (453–456, esp. 455d). I thank Stanley B. Marrow, who helped me locate this passage.

A theological explanation is given for the necessity of this change. From the beginning of the world, there has been hostility – the text seems to defend an unusual position here – between Adam and Eve (and not between Eve and the Serpent). This hostility gave the Serpent the opportunity to revolt against Adam and to befriend Eve. The result was Adam being deceived by his wife. For Mariamne to lose the feminine form is to abandon Eve's appearance. It can only be beneficial. When Mariamne enters into the city, the snakes will see her transformed (*Acts Phil.* 8.4). The author explains then in an obscure paragraph that the skin of the Serpent has to be identified with its venom – a reality that polluted Eve – and that this kind of original sin was then communicated from generation to generation starting with Cain. The author concludes with a dogmatic sentence: "Therefore, Mariamne, flee away from Eve's poverty and be rich in yourself" (*Acts Phil.* 8.4 [G]).

3.7. Mariamne as Sister and Twin

The notion of sisterhood plays a double role in the plot, first as a physical sister, second as a spiritual twin. Mariamne is introduced as Philip's sister. She is later presented as the twin sister of Nicanora. Behind Mariamne there is another sister, Miriam, the sister of Aaron and Moses, called Mariamme by Josephus. Even if implicit, such a typology is present in the text. As Miriam, Philip's sister participates in the salvific exodus. As Miriam she has a ministerial responsibility. Just as Miriam leads the choir of the women while Moses sings with the men of Israel after the victorious crossing of the Red Sea,[41] so Mariamne in the *Acts of Philip* baptizes the women while her brother Philip baptizes the men. Interestingly Philo affirms that the community of the Therapeutae has taken over this distribution in their liturgy.[42]

Sisterhood is the adequate relationship for ascetic Christians, because it is a feminine companionship without the risk of sexuality. A mother is *per definitionem* the opposite of virgin. A daughter implies only the intimate intercourse of her parents.

It is possible that there were two diverging traditions in the first centuries of Christian thought regarding Philip and the women around him, one with his daughters (Clement of Alexandria, *Strom.* 3.52.5, is very pleased to infer from Acts 21:9 that Philip with his daughters was not opposed to marriage), and another with his sister (this ascetical tradition is present here in the *Acts of Philip*). As Christ of the Fourth Gospel entrusts his mother to the beloved disciple, so the Savior of the *Acts of Philip* entrusts the apostle Philip to his sister. It is not by

---

[41] See Jean Doignon, "Miryam et son tambourin dans la prédication et l'archéologie occidentale au IVᵉ siècle," in *Studia Patristica* 4 (ed. Frank L. Cross; TU 79; Berlin: Akademie-Verlag, 1961) 71–77. I thank Nick Constas for this bibliographic reference.

[42] See Philo of Alexandria, *Agr.* 80–81; *Contempl.* 87.

chance that in the church the terms *sister* and *brother* became terms for several dimensions of a nonsexual relationship between male and female Christians. Spouses in late antiquity who decided to interrupt marital relationship and live ascetically choose the terms *brother* and *sister* to explain their new relationship.

The categories sister and brother did more than eliminate the suspicion of sexual attraction. They were also a convenient metaphor for a spiritual kinship. Beyond the relationship of brother and sister, the term "twin" suggested such a deeper kinship. As an example, Judas Thomas is considered as the twin of Jesus in the *Gospel of Thomas* and the *Acts of Thomas*.[43] This is the term used in the *Acts of Philip* to represent the spiritual bondage between the elect. Inside the true community, the believers are not only "so to speak" brothers and sisters, but are "really" brothers and sisters,[44] not at the despicable level of the flesh but at the respectable level of the spirit.

Again this theory is not a Christian invention, but the appropriation of a Hellenic concept. The Greeks developed two opposite views on humanity. On one side they claim with Pindar, "different is the race of the humans, different is the race of the God"; on the other they affirm, with Plato, that the true human beings are related as members of the same spiritual family (συγγένεια).[45] Mariamne and Nicanora feel close to one another not only because they are both of Hebraic origin, speaking the same language, but because they share the same spiritual bondage; they are "twins" in the spirit of the Savior: σὺ ἀδελφή μου εἶ· μία μήτηρ ἐγέννησεν ἡμᾶς διδύμους (*Acts Phil. Mart.* 9 [Γ]).

Ann Graham Brock discusses in her dissertation the way in which certain traditions concerning Mary Magdalene have been appropriated by orthodox groups and applied to Mary the mother.[46] The portrayal of Mariamne in the *Acts of Philip* makes evident that a symmetrical appropriation took place in the other direction. Titles, metaphors, and functions applied to the mother in patristic texts appear here as characteristic of Mariamne. *Acts Phil.* 8.3 applies the highest epithet εὐλογημένη ἐν γυναιξίν (see also Jdt 13:18) to Mariamne, while Luke applies it to Mary the mother (Luke 1:42). At a critical moment, as we have seen, she is transformed into a κιβωτός, a "chest," an "ark," the place of the divine presence, a category commonly applied to the Virgin Mary.[47] She is finally the counterpart or the antitype of Eve and through her faith and courage she undoes the sin that Eve

---

[43] *Gospel of Thomas* Prologue; *Acts of Thomas* 31 and 39.

[44] On the *virgins subintroductae*, see Wolfgang Schrage, *Der erste Brief an die Korinther* (EKKNT 7; Zurich: Benziger, 1991–) 2:153, 208.

[45] Pindar, *Nem.* 6.1; Plato, *Prot.* 322a.

[46] See Brock, *Mary Magdalene, The First Apostle*, 123–42; Petersen, "*Zerstört die Werke der Weiblichkeit!*," 291–94.

[47] See for example *Questions of Bartholomew* 2.8. I thank Ann Graham Brock for this reference.

has introduced into the world (an argument that Justin Martyr and Irenaeus apply to the Virgin Mary).[48]

4. Mariamne and the Feminine Ministry

What is new in the long text of the *Xenophontos* 32, compared with the short text of the *Vaticanus graecus* 824 [V], is a long tour of Hell in *Acts Phil.* 1. A young man resurrected by Philip tells the story of his travels in the underworld. He has been guided to several places of punishment where he can ask his *angelus interpres* questions. The punishments that are described are those inflicted on orthodox Christians, mainly ecclesiastical leaders, who had criticized the encratite movement. They receive their punishment because they have slandered the ministers of the marginalized community. Lists of the different categories of ministry are mentioned. They must reflect the ecclesiastical and sociological reality of the marginal community. Three categories, each of two pairs, are prominent: the eunuchs and the virgins, the deacons and deaconesses, the priests and the priestesses (*Acts Phil.* 1.12). From this list it is clear that the encratite community that is behind *Acts Phil.* 1 vindicated women's ministry.[49] Inscriptions from Asia Minor as well as council decisions (Council of Laodicea, canons 11 and 44) also mention or presuppose the presence of women ministers in the encratite communities.[50] We have here a new and strong confirmation.

What has not been noticed so far is the connection between women's ministry attested in *Acts Phil.* 1 and the ministerial activity of Mariamne described in *Acts Phil. 8–Mart.* At least for the compiler of the two parts in the fourth century C.E., but probably earlier already for the authors of *Acts Phil.* 1 and *Acts Phil. 8–Mart.*,

---

[48] Justin Martyr, *Dial.* 100.3–4; Irenaeus, *Haer.* 3.22.3–4; see Aloïs Müller, *Ecclesia-Mater. Die Einheit Marias und der Kirche* (2d ed; Fribourg: Universitätsverlag, 1955); Amsler, *Acta Philippi. Commentarius*, 315–18. Actually Hippolytus in his *Commentary on the Song of Songs* establishes a similar contrast, this time between Eve and the women at the empty tomb on the day of Easter, particularly Mary Magdalene; see G. Nathanael Bonwetsch, *Hippolyts Kommentar zum Hohenlied* 24–25 (TU 23.2; Leipzig: Hinrichs, 1902) 60–71. See also in the *Acts of Andrew* 37(5) and 39(7) the pair Andrew-Maximilla reversing the fate of Adam and Eve.

[49] See Bertrand Bouvier and François Bovon, "Actes de Philippe, I, d'après un manuscrit inédit," in *Œcumenica et Patristica. Festschrift für Wilhelm Schneemelcher zum 75. Geburtstag* (ed. Damaskinos Papandreou, Wolfgang A. Bienert, and Knut Schäferdiek; Stuttgart: Kohlhammer; Geneva: Metropolie der Schweiz, 1989) 367–94, esp. 393–94; Bovon, Bouvier, and Amsler, *Acta Philippi. Textus*, 29; Amsler, *Acta Philippi. Commentarius*, 81–82; Ute E. Eisen, *Women Officeholders in Early Christianity: Epigraphical and Literary Studies* (trans. Linda M. Maloney; Collegeville, Minn.: Liturgical Press, 2000) 136. It escaped Karen Torjesen: see Karen Jo Torjesen, *When Women Were Priests: Women's Leadership in the Early Church and the Scandal of Their Subordination in the Rise of Christianity* (San Francisco: HarperSanFrancisco, 1993).

[50] See Amsler, *Acta Philippi. Commentarius*, 485–87; Eisen, *Women Officeholders in Early Christianity*, 116–23, 148–52.

Mariamne was not only a famous figure of the past; she was also the model and the justification for the present women's ministry. Those women who are called virgins, deaconesses, or priestesses could find an example to follow and to imitate in the figure of Mariamne. They have developed their manly faith and chosen the right type of clothing, not only a modest one, but also a masculine one. Virgins, deaconesses, and priestesses do not have the same function. The highest one, the priestess, must particularly feel a kinship with the apostle Mariamne as the priests identify themselves with the apostle Philip.

Such a daring spiritual ecclesiology combined with a dangerous Christology and an excessive ascetical life (to use the categories of the orthodox adversaries of the encratites of Asia Minor) explain why finally, despite its interest for the apostle Philip, a work like the *Acts of Philip* was rejected (its name is present on the list of the rejected books of the *Decretum gelasianum*, Gaul, sixth century c.e.). It is a miracle that nevertheless the manuscripts *Atheniensis* 346 and *Xenophontos* 32, and to a lesser extent *Vaticanus* 824, have saved these stories from a complete ship-wreck.[51]

---

[51] This paper was sent for publication when the following article was published: Stephen J. Shoemaker, "Rethinking the 'Gnostic Mary': Mary of Nazareth and Mary of Magdala in Early Christian Tradition," *JECS* 9 (2001) 555–95. I disagree with the author on several major points.

Facing the Scriptures:
Mimesis and Intertextuality in the *Acts of Philip*

Introduction

The goal of this paper is to describe the relationship that the *Acts of Philip* establishes with other texts, particularly respected and authoritative documents anterior to the *Acts of Philip*.[1] I will examine, of course, the explicit biblical quota

---

[1] On the relationship between the apocryphal acts of the apostles and other texts, see Éric Junod and Jean-Daniel Kaestli, *Acta Iohannis* (2 vols.; CCSA 1–2; Turnhout: Brepols, 1983) 2:694–700; Dennis R. MacDonald, ed., *The Apocryphal Acts of Apostles: Semeia* 38 (1986); Richard I. Pervo, *Profit with Delight: The Literary Genre of the Acts of the Apostles* (Philadelphia: Fortress, 1987); Christopher R. Matthews, "Philip and Simon, Luke and Peter: A Lukan Sequel and Its Intertextual Success," in *SBLSP 1992* (ed. Eugene H. Lovering, Jr.; Atlanta: Scholars Press, 1992) 133–46; Dennis R. MacDonald, "*The Acts of Paul* and *The Acts of Peter*: Which Came First?," in ibid., 214–24; Robert F. Stoops, "Peter, Paul, and Priority in the Apocryphal Acts," in ibid., 225–33; Richard Valantasis, "Narrative Strategies and Synoptic Quandaries: A Response to Dennis MacDonald's Reading of *Acts of Paul* and *Acts of Peter*," in ibid., 234–39; Gonzalo del Cerro, "Los Hechos apócrifos de los Apóstoles su género literario," *EstBib* 51 (1993) 207–32; James Keith Elliott, "The Apocryphal Acts," *ExpTim* 105 (1993) 71–77; F. Stanley Jones, "Principal Orientations on the Relations between the Apocryphal Acts (*Acts of Paul* and *Acts of John*; *Acts of Peter* and *Acts of John*)," in *SBLSP 1993* (ed. Eugene H. Lovering, Jr.; Atlanta: Scholars Press, 1993) 485–505; Dennis R. MacDonald, *Christianizing Homer: The Odyssey, Plato, and the* Acts of Andrew (New York: Oxford University Press, 1994); Enrico Norelli, "Avant le canonique et l'apocryphe. Aux origines des récits de la naissance de Jésus," *RTP* 126 (1994) 305–24; Julian V. Hills, "The Acts of the Apostles in the *Acts of Paul*," in *SBLSP 1994* (ed. Eugene H. Lovering, Jr.; Atlanta: Georgia, 1994) 24–54; Richard I. Pervo, "The Ancient Novel Becomes Christian," in *The Novel in the Ancient World* (ed. Gareth Schmeling; Leiden: Brill, 1996) 685–711; Johannes B. Bauer, "Schriftrezeption in den neutestamentlichen Apokryphen," in *Stimuli. Exegese und ihre Hermeneutik in Antike und Christentum. Festschrift für Ernst Dassmann* (ed. Gerog Schöllgen and Clemens Scholten; JAC, Ergänzungsband 23; Münster: Aschendorff, 1996) 43–48; and in Robert F. Stoops, Jr., ed., *The Apocryphal Acts of the Apostles in Intertextual Perspectives: Semeia* 80 (1997). Methodologically important is an article by Gary A. Anderson, "Between Biblical Commentaries and Apocryphal Narratives: The Narrativization of Biblical Exegesis in the *Life of Adam and Eve*," *Jewish Studies* 36 (1996) 31*–39*; and a review article of Marc Van Uytfanghe's dissertation by Jacques Fontaine, "Bible et hagiographie dans le royaume franc mérovingien (600–750). Une soutenance remarquée à l'Université de Gand," *AnBoll* 97 (1979) 387–96. A general bibliography on the apocryphal acts can be found in *The Apocryphal Acts of the Apostles: Harvard Divinity School Studies* (ed. François Bovon, Ann Graham Brock, and Christopher R. Matthews; Center for the Study of World Religions: Religions of the World; Cambridge, Mass.: Harvard University Press, 1999) 355–63. Still important is Eckhard Plümacher, "Apokryphe Apostelakten," in *Paulys Realencyclopädie*

tions, but I will also try to unveil the allusions and imitations, the recasting and reinterpretations of canonical and noncanonical material. Despite some polemics with pagan cults and confrontations with Jewish opponents, the text does not integrate much literary material from these two worlds, which would have been foreign to the author. I do not see in this popular composition any influence of Homer, the tragedies, Plato, nor of any Jewish text independent of a Christian appropriation.

The pioneering scholar Constantin von Tischendorf edited in 1851 and 1866 the *Martyrdom of Philip* (in two forms) and *Acts Phil.* 2.[2] Years later Maximilien Bonnet discovered *Vaticanus graecus* 824, then the only manuscript to transmit such long and new sections as *Acts Phil.* 1 and 3–9. Bonnet's 1903 edition of vol. 2.2 of the *Acta apostolorum apocrypha* has remained the standard for nearly a century.[3]

In recent years the collation and critical edition of new manuscripts have given me, and my colleagues Bertrand Bouvier and Frédéric Amsler, access to a much longer and more complete text.[4] In these manuscripts the form of the text is less censored than in *Vaticanus graecus* 824 (V).[5] Most important is the manuscript from Mount Athos, *Xenophontos* 32 (A), which offers several completely new acts (*Acts Phil.* 11 [the end], 12, 13, 14, and 15) and a less adulterated version of *Acts Phil.* 1–9.[6] The codex *Atheniensis* 346 (G) provides an original new text of *Acts Phil.* 8, including the commissioning of the apostles and the decisive role played by Mariamne, probably Mary Magdalene, considered here as Philip's sister.[7]

For this paper I am using the Greek text of the *Acts of Philip* according to the new critical edition in the *Series apocryphorum* of the *Corpus Christianorum.* I

der classischen Altertumswissenschaft (ed. Georg Wissowa et al.; Supplementband 15; Munich: Druckenmüller, 1978) cols. 11–70. A general bibliography on the *Acts of Philip* is available in François Bovon, "Les Actes de Philippe," in *ANRW* 2.25.6 (1988) 4523–27; and in Frédéric Amsler, *Acta Philippi. Commentarius* (CCSA 12; Turnhout: Brepols, 1999) ix–xxxvi.

  [2] Constantin von Tischendorf, *Acta apostolorum apocrypha* (Leipzig: Avenarius & Mendelssohn, 1851; reprinted in Hildesheim: Olms, 1990) XXXI–XL and 75–104; idem, *Apocalypses apocryphae Mosis, Esdrae, Pauli, Iohannes, item Mariae dormitio, additis evangeliorum et actuum apocryphorum supplementis* (Leipzig: Mendelssoh, 1866; reprinted in Hildesheim: Olms, 1966) 141–56.

  [3] Maximilien Bonnet, "Acta Philippi et Acta Thomae, accedunt Acta Barnabae," in *Acta apostolorum apocrypha* (ed. Richard Albert Lipsius and Maximilien Bonnet; 2 vols. in 3; Leipzig: Mendelssohn, 1891–1903; reprinted in Darmstadt: Wissenschaftliche Buchgesellschaft, 1959) 2.2:VII–XV, XXXVI–XXXVII, and 1–90; see also Pierre Batiffol, "Actus sancti Philippi apostoli. Nunc primum edidit," *AnBoll* 9 (1890) 204–49.

  [4] See Bovon, "Actes de Philippe," 4431–527; Bertrand Bouvier and François Bovon, "Actes de Philippe, I, d'après un manuscrit inédit," in *Œcumenica et Patristica. Festschrift für Wilhelm Schneemelcher zum 75. Geburtstag* (ed. Damaskinos Papandreou, Wolfgang A. Bienert, and Knut Schäferdiek; Stuttgart: Kohlhammer; Geneva: Metropolie der Schweiz, 1989) 367–94.

  [5] On this manuscript, see François Bovon, Bertrand Bouvier, and Frédéric Amsler, eds., *Acta Philippi. Textus* (CCSA 11; Turnhout: Brepols, 1999) XX–XXI.

  [6] On this manuscript, see ibid., XIII–XX.

  [7] On this manuscript, see ibid., XXVI–XXX.

mention this technicality because it is relevant to our topic. The Orthodox Church in the East and the Catholic Church in the West both condemned the *Acts of Philip* as fraudulent and apocryphal.[8] The only chance for these apocryphal stories to survive was to be hidden in a decent and respected text or to endure a radical cure of orthodoxy, which would have included a rewriting along the lines of biblical phraseology.[9] *Vaticanus graecus* 824 is such a rewriting; it presents a new formulation of *Acts Phil.* 3, the calming by Philip of the raging waters, which is here influenced by New Testament narratives (Matt 8:23–27 par.) more than is the same story present in the *Xenophontos 32.* No manuscript – not the Nag Hammadi codices nor even the Bodmer papyri – can claim to represent a secured original text.

In my opinion, the *Acts of Philip* belongs to an ascetic marginal movement of the fourth century C.E. probably located in Asia Minor, an encratite community under the criticism of the mainstream church.[10] It fits well among those attacked by the Council of Gangra (mid-fourth century C.E.) and by the Cappadocian Fathers, particularly Basil of Caesarea and Amphilochius of Iconium. What is important for our investigation is the way that the author deals with the Christian past. He or she writes from the biblical legacy but does so in a unusual way, finding inspiration in the Bible only through an unorthodox reading of it, a reading enriched by other noncanonical but authoritative texts. Just as it is unwise to read Paul's letter to the Galatians and omit the Jewish exegesis situated between the Hebrew Bible and early Christian interpretation, so it is dangerous to read the *Acts of Philip*, compare it to the Hebrew Scriptures or the New Testament, and neglect earlier Christian apocryphal literature.

---

[8] See Bovon, "Actes de Philippe," 4466–67. More generally on the condemnation of the apocryphal acts of the apostles, see Éric Junod, "Actes apocryphes et hérésie. Le jugement de Photius," in *Les actes apocryphes des apôtres. Christianisme et monde païen* (ed. François Bovon et al.; Publications de la Faculté de théologie de l'Université de Genève 4; Geneva: Labor et Fides, 1981) 11–24; and Ferdinand Piontek, *Die katholische Kirche und die haretischen Apostelge-schichten bis zum Ausgang des 6. Jahrhunderts. Ein Beitrag zur Literaturgeschichte* (Breslau: Nischkowsky, 1907).

[9] See François Bovon, "Byzantine Witnesses for the Apocryphal Acts of the Apostles," in Bovon, *Apocryphal Acts of the Apostles*, 87–98.

[10] One study remains important on the *Acts of Philip*: Richard Adelbert Lipsius, *Die apok-ryphen Apostelgeschichten und Apostellegenden. Ein Beitrag zur altchristlichen Literaturge-schichte* (2 vols. in 3, and supplement; Braunschweig: Schwetschke, 1893–1900; reprinted in Amsterdam: Philo, 1976) 2.2:1–53, and supplement 64–73; idem, "Zu den Acten des Philippus," *Jahrbücher für protestantische Theologie* 17 (1891) 459–73.

On the religious community behind the *Acts of Philip*, see Erik Peterson, "Die Häretiker der Philippus-Akten," *ZNW* 31 (1932) 172–79; idem, "Zum Messalianismus der Philippus-Akten," *Oriens christianus*, 3d ser., 7 (1932) 172; Bovon, "Actes de Philippe," 1521–23; Frédéric Amsler, "Introduction," in *Actes de l'apôtre Philippe* (intro. and ann. Frédéric Amsler; trans. François Bovon, Bertrand Bouvier, and Frédéric Amsler; Apocryphes 8; Turnhout: Brepols, 1996) 80–82; Richard N. Slater, "An Inquiry into the Relationship between Community and Text: The Apocryphal *Acts of Philip* 1 and the Encratites of Asia Minor," in Bovon, *Apocryphal Acts of the Apostles*, 281–306.

What this author produced is an enormous text, longer than the canonical Acts of the Apostles. Put under scrutiny, the work appears to be composite, because its author was not shy to incorporate older material. The first part, *Acts Phil.* 1–7, is probably a collection of independent tales by individual authors that have been combined into a patchwork with more or less success by the final author. The second part, *Acts Phil.* 8 to the end, forms a literary unit, starting like the *Acts of Thomas* with the sending of the apostle to his mission field.[11]

In this paper I limit my investigation to the second part, *Acts Phil.* 8 to the end, but it may be helpful to mention some aspects of intertextuality in the first part. *Acts of Philip* 1 is an imitation of the resurrection story of Luke 7:10–17 (son of the widow of Nain), itself a rewriting of stories concerning Elijah (1 Kings 17) and Elishah (2 Kings 4). New in the *Xenophontos* 32 version, when compared to *Vaticanus graecus* 824 and the Bible, is an impressive tour of Hell undertaken by the young man during his stay in the underworld (*Acts Phil.* 1.5–17).[12]

Acts Phil. 2 is inspired by canonical Acts 17, *Acts Phil.* 6, and probably *Acts Phil. Mart.*: Philip is in Athens and tries to convert the philosophers of the city. Significantly, the apostle does not use philosophical arguments but relies on Jesus' sayings and biblical material. It is therefore logical that in this episode, diverging from canonical Acts 17, the Greek philosophers seek the High Priest from Jerusalem hoping that he will rescue them. Strangely, the controversy between the Jewish leader and the Christian hero does not include (as will be the case in *Acts Phil.* 6) a polemic over precise Jewish biblical prophecies but, instead, contains a general theological discussion. Writing the epilogue of this tale, the author imitates a biblical narrative, the revolt of Korah, Dathan, and Abiram (Numbers 16), and mentions the split of the earth as punishment of the high priest.[13]

The influence of canonical Acts, here Acts 8, is also visible in *Acts Phil.* 3.1–3. As Philip's new converts in Acts 8:14–17 need the apostolic laying of hands by Peter and John, here Philip himself asks for apostolic support so that he, the evangelist or deacon, may carry on the task of a true apostle.[14]

In *Acts Phil.* 5.22–23, during the long description of Ireos's conversion, Philip at one point is transfigured, but when he notices that the brightness of his new

---

[11] On the history of composition of the *Acts of Philip*, see the reconstructions of Amsler, "Introduction," in Amsler, *Actes de l'apôtre Philippe*, 25–27; and Amsler, *Acta Philippi. Commentarius*, 429–39 passim, as partly distinct from Bovon, "Actes de Philippe," 4443–56 and 4521–23.

[12] On the first act, see Bouvier and Bovon, "Actes de Philippe, I, d'après un manuscrit inédit"; Slater, "Inquiry"; and Amsler, *Acta Philippi. Commentarius*, 25–83.

[13] See Christopher R. Matthews, *Philip, Apostle and Evangelist: Configurations of a Tradition* (NovTSup 105; Leiden: Brill, 2002) 156–97; and idem, "Peter and Philip Upside Down: Perspectives on the Relation of the *Acts of Philip* to the *Acts of Peter*," in *SBLSP 1996* (ed. Eugene H. Lovering, Jr.; Atlanta: Scholars Press, 1996) 28–31.

[14] On this act see the notes in Bovon, Bouvier, and Amsler, *Acta Philippi. Textus*, 77–83; and Amsler, "Introduction," in Amsler, *Actes de l'apôtre Philippe*, 37–52.

appearance becomes a threat to his admirers, he "remembers Jesus" and decides to return to his human condition (*Acts Phil.* 5.23). The reference to the New Testament episode is explicit.

In the middle of that same story of Ireos and his family (*Acts Phil.* 5–7), there is a controversy between the apostle and a Jewish scholar. The topic of the dispute is the relevance of the prophetic scriptures to the Christian faith (*Acts Phil.* 6.13[77]). Following the pattern of a battle of quotations, as found in the canonical Gospels (Matt 4:1–11 and Luke 4:1–13, the dispute during the temptation between Jesus and the Devil) and in the *Acts of Peter* 23–28[15] (the fight between the first apostle and Simon Magus), the two opponents in the Ireos context cast several biblical proofs on each side, and several points deserve attention here. First, the controversy deals explicitly with prophetic oracles of the Bible and doctrinal statements, so the commands of the mosaic law are absent from the discussion. Second, the author reaches an anti-Semitic paradox: almost all the biblical quotations are taken from the Septuagint and are spoken by the rabbi with an ostensible lack of accuracy.[16] All are imprecise or truncated. For the Christian author this is an easy and wicked way to scorn his adversary. Third, the Jewish opponent finally admits his defeat and ironically accepts as legitimate and true the Christian interpretation of the Hebrew prophets! Fourth, neither the individual biblical quotations nor their sequence corresponds to any book of *Testimonia* preserved from antiquity. This dissimilarity remains an enigma.

Apart from the controversy just mentioned (*Acts Phil.* 6.13–15[77–80]), what I have been concerned with so far is not quotations from the Bible but imitations of biblical episodes. The author had new stories to tell, developments of the Hebrew Bible and the New Testament. It was the author's conviction that God had not, with those texts, brought an end to the manifestation of a providential love toward humanity. Thus these new salvific events did not contradict the old wisdom, the old revelation. On the contrary, they were witnesses to the ongoing, divine care for the created world. Furthermore, these testimonies are embedded in a network of harmonious and coherent authoritative texts. This conception, present in the first part of the *Acts of Philip*, will be confirmed in the second.

The Presence of the Hebrew Bible in *Acts Phil.* 8 to *Acts Phil. Martyrdom*

The presence of the Bible is as irregular and surprising in the second part of the *Acts of Philip* as it was in the first. The Exodus tradition, the Sinai tradition, and the lives of the patriarchs, judges, or kings are virtually absent from the text. The God of the author is more the God of the creation than the God of law or cove-

---

¹⁵ See Matthews, "Peter and Philip Upside Down," 28–31.
¹⁶ See Amsler, *Actes de l'apôtre Philippe*, 163 n. 283 (Frédéric Amsler's note).

nant. Like a large river, divine providence shares its love toward humanity at each generation. A theological proximity with the Creator of the Hebrew Bible is evident from the following prayer:

My Lord Jesus Christ, hope and strength of all, King of glory, who created the heavens, locked the depths and condemned the enemy to stay there; you who spread out the firmament and placed in it the lights in order to make blazing your works, who disposed the air for an enjoyable usage and for the breathing of all those who need it; you who gave your sweetness to the waters in order that your creatures could live; you who rebuked the sea and provided calm to the waves, you are the Lord of all higher knowledge; the release of those who are in servitude; the Savior of the aeons. (*Acts Phil.* 12.7 [A])

The *Acts of Philip* accounts for evil with reference to the first chapters of Genesis, but it emphasizes the role of the snake, not that of Adam, in generating evil. The devil, the dragon, the viper, and the fifty snakes play a considerable role in the narrative. The hostile forces of the enemy constantly confront the apostolic trio – Philip, Mariamne, and Bartholomew – during their missionary journey. In *Acts Phil.* 3, during a sea voyage, the apostle Philip has to show his divine power in calming a storm, the symbol of negative forces. In *Acts Phil.* 9 there is an initial confrontation and a victory over a dragon. A second episode occurs in *Acts Phil.* 11. Then, in *Acts Phil.* 13, the apostles have to overcome guardian snakes at the gate of the city, which carries the symbolic name of Ophiorymos, literally the street or promenade of the snakes. At one point, the dragon explains to the apostolic group not only the origin of evil but also its transmission from generation to generation. In paragraphs that are not always clear, in a prose that tries to be theologically sophisticated, the dragon suggests a direct influence on Eve and, through their coalition, the presence of sin in human history. After Eve, the poison of the snake, like a mortal seed, contaminated Cain and influenced his will to kill Abel. Now it will be Philip's responsibility to oppose the dragon and to overcome the snakes. It will be Mariamne's duty to reverse Eve's fallibility. In his commissioning speech the Savior speaks to the sister of Philip saying:

Concerning you, Mariamne, change your clothing and your appearance: take away everything that outwardly resembles a woman, the summer dress that you wear. Do not let the fringe of your cloth hang on the ground, do not drape it but cut this out; then go on your way in the company of your brother Philip toward the city called Ophiorymos, which means the promenade of the snakes; for the inhabitants of this city worship the mother of the snakes, the viper. As you will enter the city, it is necessary that the snakes of that city see you released from the appearance of Eve, that nothing in your outlook manifests a woman, because the appearance of Eve is the woman, and it is she who embodies the feminine form. Concerning Adam, he embodies the form of the man, and you know that, from the beginning, enmity arose between Eve and Adam. It was the beginning of the rebellion of the snake against this man and of its friendship toward his wife, Eve; consequently Adam has been deceived by his wife Eve; the molting of the snake is its venom; the snake put it on through her, and through this skin the original enemy found a place to stay in Cain, son of Eve, so that he could kill Abel, his brother. Therefore you, Mariamne, escape from Eve's poverty to get rich in yourself. (*Acts Phil.* 8.4[G])

In *Acts Phil.* 11.3 one finds a confirmation of this theory on the lips of the dragon itself:

And the dragon who was among them answered: "Here is the place from where I draw my origin: the plot stirred up in Paradise; it was there that the one who now wishes to kill me through you cursed me. For then, after I withdrew from the garden with every kind of plant, I found a place to hide in Cain, because of Abel. After I put up the feminine beauty in the face of the angels, I then hurled them down from heaven. Then, having generated sons of high stature, [editor's note: here the MS includes four words that do not make sense]. After they had multiplied, they started to devour human beings like grasshoppers. After the flood had killed them off, they generated the race of the demons and snakes, when Moses' rod confounded the nature of the Egyptian wise men and magicians. We are the fifty snakes that Moses' dragon then gobbled down. From now on it is you, Philip, who is victorious over us." (*Acts Phil.* 11.3 [A])

An intriguing passage connects the Hebrew Bible and the New Testament. Actually this passage, *Acts Phil.* 8.11–12, shows that the biblical traditions of both Testaments were envisaged by the author through the glasses of apocryphal traditions not so different from the ones that can be found behind the *Second Epistle of Clement* (see particularly *2 Clem* 4.5 and 5.2–4).[17] In *Acts Phil.* 8.11–12 the major concern remains evil, its nature and reality, and how to overcome it. Among the negative forces responsible for the presence of evil on earth, the author often mentions the revolt of the fallen angels and their descent to the so-called Egregores (see *Acts Phil.* 8.11 and 11.3).[18] Noah is also mentioned as the agent chosen by God to preserve and save the human race and several species of animals from the flood. Through their number, the seven pairs of pure animals express God's forgiveness. The two pairs of impure animals manifest that God is also a righteous judge who knows how to punish with equity.[19]

After that introduction – the Risen Savior here teaches Philip at the moment of his commissioning – one finds an explicit reference to a New Testament episode remembered through an apocryphal tradition:

Therefore, your brother Peter remembered what Noah had done at the day of the punishment of the sinners, when he told me: "Do you want me to forgive my brother until seven times, in a manner similar to the one Noah forgave?" And I answered him: "I do not want you to be satisfied by following the example of Noah but to forgive seventy times seven!" Now, Philip, do not be tired of practicing the good toward those who do evil to you. (*Acts Phil.* 8.12 [C])

For the author of the *Acts of Philip*, the memory of the biblical story of Noah is preserved in the New Testament tradition, and this New Testament tradition is

---

[17] On these passages, see the remarks of Klaus Wengst, *Didache (Apostellehre), Barnabasbrief, Zweiter Klemensbrief, Schrift an Diognet* (Schriften des Urchristentums 2; Darmstadt: Wissenschaftliche Buchgesellschaft, 1984) 222–23.

[18] See the note in Bovon, Bouvier, and Amsler, *Acta Philippi. Textus*, 258–59 n. 25.

[19] See ibid., 258–59 n. 26.

preserved in an apocryphal development that establishes an explicit relation between Jesus' words and Noah's attitude.[20]

Another episode in the *Acts of Philip* is typical of the author's relationship to biblical tradition. The reader of the Bible remembers the episode of Elijah, who destroyed in heavenly fire the messengers of the wicked king Ahaziah (2 Kings 1:9–16). The Gospel of Luke makes a reference to this episode in a critical perspective: Jesus condemns the disciples who suggested the miraculous use of that heavenly fire as a weapon for retaliation against the unwilling Samaritans (Luke 9:54).[21] In the *Acts of Philip*, the apocryphal apostle not only makes the same suggestion as the New Testament disciples but, like the biblical prophet Elijah, does in fact retaliate against his enemies with violence.[22] If his expressed wish is to follow Elijah's steps (*Acts Phil. Mart.* 21[127] A: "Let us say ourselves that fire from heaven come down and consume them"), then his concrete retaliation recalls Moses' punishment of Korah, Dathan, and Abiram (Numbers 16). He orders the earth to split and gobble up his opponents (*Acts Phil. Mart.* 25[131]–28[134]).[23] But what was tolerable in the story of Moses and the rebellious Israelites is contrary, according to our author, to Jesus' teaching on nonretaliation.

The whole ending of the Martyrdom story is related to this sin of the apostle, Jesus' verbal rebuke, and future punishment (*Acts Phil. Mart.* 26[132]–33[139], 34[140], 37[143]). Jesus' teaching not to combat evil with a second evil is the decisive criterion by which Philip's attitude and action are to be judged. Strangely enough, there is no explicit quotation of the Sermon on the Mount in this context but only a general reference to what Jesus taught. We should remember that such a teaching in antiquity was not the appanage of the Christians. The venerable Pythagorean tradition proclaimed the same message on nonviolence and pled the same refusal of violent retaliation.[24]

Similarity and difference also characterize the Savior's protracted sermon at the beginning of the missions of Philip and Mariamne, when compared with the New

---

[20] I have not been able to locate that apocryphal tradition.

[21] See François Bovon, *Das Evangelium nach Lukas. 2. Teilband Lk 9,51–14,35* (EKKNT 3.2; Zurich: Benziger; Neukirchen-Vluyn: Neukirchener Verlag, 1996) 27–28.

[22] See my article, "The Child and the Beast: Fighting Violence in Ancient Christianity," *HTR* 92 (1999) 369–92; reprinted in this volume, pp. 223–45 above.

[23] The earth swallows not only his opponents but also the inhabitants of the city, worshipers of the Viper.

[24] According to Diogenes Laertius a book was attributed to Pythagoras called *The Scopiades*, which had as a beginning an advice not to harm anybody (*Lives* 8.8). On the difficulty of Diogenes' text concerning this beginning of Pythagoras' book, see the critical apparatus of Armand Delatte, *La vie de Pythagore de Diogène Laërce. Édition critique avec introduction et commentaire* (Académie royale de Belgique, Classe des lettres et des sciences morales et politiques, deuxième série, 17; Bruxelles: Lamertin, 1922) 109. Unfortunately, Delatte does not deal with this textual problem in his commentary (165–66). The title *The Scopiades* is not well attested in the textual tradition; see the apparatus of the critical edition by Herbert S. Long, *Diogenis Laertii vitae philosophorum* (2 vols.; Oxford: Clarendon, 1964) 2:396.

Testament sayings of Jesus (*Acts Phil.* 8.3–7, 9–14). His sermon offers first the advice that Mariamne remain the strong woman, as we have seen. Second, it explains to Philip and his sister that their missionary duty fits into the framework of divine providence. Third, it assures them of his ongoing care and spiritual presence at their sides, even during their confrontation with the enemy. Finally, in dialogue with Philip, the Savior conveys a short catechism on the art of nonretaliation and on the habit of forgiveness. If the literary form is similar to the biblical commissioning stories and farewell speeches, its content has only an occasional kinship with Jesus' teachings in the New Testament.

New Testament and Apocryphal Traditions Alive in the Text

The first explicit quotation appears in the Martyrdom story (*Acts Phil. Mart.* 34[140]). Hanging on his cross, Philip succumbs to the temptation to curse his enemies, as we have seen. His Lord, appearing in a heavenly vision, corrects the apostle. Finally, ashamed of his vindictive desires, Philip repents, and the reader assists at a collective delivery from the split earth (this part of the Martyrdom probably influenced the episode of *Acts Phil.* 2 mentioned above). The apostle, deeply moved, then proclaims not curses but praises. Addressing newly baptized converts from the city of Ophiorymos who surround his cross, he explains that he has come to their city not to make any sort of trade but to release them from the power of the Devil. He goes on to say that he is now crucified upside down (a motif taken over from the *Acts of Peter* 37) to fulfill Jesus' command.[25] He then quotes a saying of his Lord, not a canonical but an apocryphal saying, an *agraphon* preserved by ancient Christian writers. Actually, it is quoted by some authors of the Church and appears in the *Gospel of Thomas* 22 as well as the *Acts of Peter* 38: "I repeat here the command of Christ the Savior: 'If you do not make right the things which are left, if you do not consider as precious the things which are vile, you will not be able to enter into the kingdom of God'" (*Acts Phil. Mart.* 34[140] A).[26] For the author, as for many ancient Christian writers, the authority of Jesus' words is more important than the canonicity of the books in which they are included. That one saying comes from the Gospel of Matthew and another from an oral source, *Acts of Peter* or *Gospel of Thomas*, does not matter.

---

[25] On the relation of the *Acts of Peter* to other texts, see MacDonald, "*The Acts of Paul* and *The Acts of Peter*," 214–24; Christine M. Thomas, "Word and Deed: The *Acts of Peter* and Orality," *Apocrypha* 3 (1992) 125–64; eadem, "The 'Prehistory' of the *Acts of Peter*," in Bovon, *Apocryphal Acts of the Apostles*, 39–62; and Dennis R. MacDonald, "Which Came First? Intertextual Relationships among the Apocryphal Acts of the Apostles," *Semeia* 80 (1997) 11–41.

[26] See Jonathan Z. Smith, *Map Is Not Territory: Studies in the History of Religions* (SJLA 23; Leiden: Brill, 1978) 147–71; and Matthews, "Peter and Philip Upside Down," 31–34.

Then the apostle communicates his last will to his survivors. To his fellow apostle Bartholomew in particular he commands an ascetic life and reminds him of their Lord's teaching: " 'Everyone,' he says, 'who looks at a woman with lust in his heart has already committed adultery in his heart' " (*Acts Phil.* 36[142] A; Matt 5:28 is cited).[27] This is one of the few explicit quotations of the New Testament, and is introduced by "Teaching us, our Lord said." The quotation, however, is not precise and is followed by a kind of narrative commentary: "Therefore, our brother Peter fled every place where a woman could have been present" (*Acts Phil.* 36[142] A).[28] The speech goes on to a reminder of the apocryphal episode preserved at the end of the *Papyrus Berolinensis* 8502, which probably originated in the *Acts of Peter*, or the miraculous and providential paralysis of Peter's daughter.[29]

Another quotation offers a third type of reference. In *Acts Phil.* 9 the apostolic group faces a horrible dragon. To strengthen his companions' spirits, Philip refers to words of the Savior promising protection: "Now we need assistance from the Savior. Remember the word of Christ who sent us by saying: 'Do not fear anything, neither persecution, nor the snakes of this country, nor the dark dragon!' Let us therefore remain firm, like columns strongly established before God, and all the power of the enemy will be wiped out and his threat will fall down" (*Acts Phil.* 9.2 [V]). The saying quoted is not, as one would first expect, from the New Testament, Luke 10:19 or Mark 16:18. It is neither an *agraphon* nor a saying of the Lord taken from another apocryphal text. It probably represents an intratextual, free reference to a saying of the Savior pronounced in an earlier speech, in his commissioning speech, *Acts Phil.* 8.7 (G): "Now then, brothers, do not fear the bites of the snakes, nor their venom; because in front of you their mouth will be shut and their threat abolished. If they lift up their head, apply to them the sign of the monad; if the vipers come out and meet you, protect yourselves with the cross and at once they will bend down their heads."[30] Because the Lord is a spiritual, divine being, his words may be preserved in the Gospels but also in oral tradition

---

[27] Actually, this is the case only in the recension Θ (manuscript A is one of the witnesses of this recension) and of *Acts Phil. Mart.*; on the recensions of the *Acts of Philip*, see Joseph Flamion, "Les trois recensions grecques du Martyre de l'apôtre Philippe," *Mélanges d'histoire offerts à Charles Mœller* (Université de Louvain: Recueil de travaux publiés par les membres des conférences d'histoire et de philologie 40; Louvain/Paris: Bureaux du Recueil, 1914) 215–25.

[28] On this passage, see Ann Graham Brock, "What's in a Name: The Competition for Authority in Early Christian Texts," *SBLSP 1998* (Atlanta: Scholars Press, 1999) 1:108 n. 7. Brock refers also to Terence V. Smith, *Petrine Controversies in Early Christianity: Attitudes towards Peter in Christian Writings of the First Two Centuries* (WUNT 2.15; Tübingen: Mohr Siebeck, 1985) 107–8.

[29] This episode is analyzed by Michel Tardieu, *Écrits gnostiques. Codex de Berlin* (Sources gnostiques et manichéennes 1; Paris: Cerf, 1984) 403–10; see also Matthews, "Peter and Philip Upside Down," 28.

[30] See the notes in Bovon, Bouvier, and Amsler, *Acta Philippi. Textus*, nn. 6 and 253.

(*agrapha*), in the stream of apocryphal literature, or even in the text of the *Acts of Philip* itself.

The most interesting case is to be found on the Savior's lips earlier in the Martyrdom story, while the apostle is still disobedient, sending his opponents and all the inhabitants of Ophiorymos alive into the abyss. At this moment, the Savior appears to his apostle and speaks to him, trying to bring him back to reason, to Christian reason:

At that moment, the Savior appeared and said to Philip: "Who is the one who puts his hand to the plow, then looks back, and makes his row straight? Or who is the one who gives his lamp to others, then himself remains sitting in the darkness? Or who is the one who lives on a pile of manure and leaves his habitation to foreigners? Or who is the one who undoes his clothes, and goes naked into the hard winter? Or what enemy rejoices in the joy of the one who hates him? Or what soldier goes into the war well-armed and does not put on the vestment of victory? Or what slave, having fulfilled the service of his master, will not be invited by the latter to the meal? Or what athlete runs with ardor in a stadium and does not receive the prize, O Philip? Here, the wedding chamber is ready; blessed is the guest of the spouse, for rich is the harvest of the fields, and blessed is the worker who is able." (*Acts Phil. Mart.* 29[135] A)

These words are among the last that the Savior tells the apostle. After that, the Lord will leave him, assigning him a final punishment after death, a waiting period of forty days before entering into Paradise.

These sayings represent a strange case of intertextuality.[31] The Savior does not speak here in the usual style of the post-resurrection dialogues frequent in the Nag Hammadi codices but in a collection of sayings similar to the Q Source or the *Gospel of Thomas*. These words, however, are not to be found in the canonical gospels, in any apocryphal collection, nor in any known series of *agrapha*.[32] The closest parallel appears in the *Acts of John* 67, part of the last speech of the apostle John before his death. It is my contention that these sayings of the *Acts of Philip* are not a composition of the author of the *Acts of Philip* but a free quotation from an unknown gospel. They represent a curious occurrence of intertextuality (an

---

[31] The notion of intertextuality must be used carefully; see the advice of Matthews, "Peter and Philip Upside Down," 23–26; and Thomas R. Hatina, "Intertextuality and Historical Criticism in New Testament Studies: Is There a Relationship?," *BibInt* 7 (1999) 28–43.

[32] Although this series was known through the publications of Tischendorf (*Acta apostolorum apocrypha*, 87; and *Apocalypses apocryphae*, 147), Alfred Resch mentions only a small part of it, the beatitude about the crown and the bridegroom. Besides this reference, he cites the saying on the prohibition of retaliation (*Acts Phil. Mart.* 31 [137]), the saying on reversal of left and right (*Acts Phil. Mart.* 34 [140]), and the passage of the *Acts of Philip* quoted by Pseudo-Athanasius Sinaita, *De tribus quadragesimis*, PG 89:1396–97; see Alfred Resch, *Agrapha. Aussercanonische Evangelienfragmente* (TU 5.4; Leipzig: Hinrichs, 1889) 9–10, 79, 129, 131, 245, 254, 416–17, and 480; idem, *Agrapha. Aussercanonische Schriftfragmente* (TU n.s. 15.3–4; Leipzig: Hinrichs, 1906) 279–81. In his second edition Resch does not use Maximilien Bonnet's edition, published in 1903 (Lipsius-Bonnet, *Acta apostolorum apocrypha*, vol. 2.2).

implicit quotation or adaptation);[33] therefore, they earn a special interest from the historians of early Christianity.[34] Because all these stories belong to the same salvific plot, to the same ongoing divine fight, the author thought it appropriate to use old motives, past sermons, or ancient episodes to fill a present necessity. The process is understandable and has been followed in later centuries by hagiographers.

The quarrel between Philip and the Jew Aristarchos (*Acts Phil.* 6.9–21) borrows without hesitation from the *Acts of Peter* 23–28 (the conflict between Peter and Simon Magus).[35] It is also from the *Acts of Peter* that the author draws the episode of Peter's daughter (*Acts Phil. Mart.* 36[142]).[36] The celebration of the Eucharist (*Acts Phil.* 11.9) rewrites a hymn mentioned in the *Acts of John* 94–96, 109.[37] The commissioning of the apostle Philip (*Acts Phil.* 8.1–2) resembles the beginning of the *Acts of Thomas*.[38] The newly discovered beatitudes, pronounced by Philip (*Acts Phil.* 5.25), are similar in form to the beatitudes of the canonical gospels (Matt 5:3–12 and Luke 6:20–23) and of the *Acts of Paul* 5–6.[39] The description of the dragons (*Acts Phil.* 9.1[102] and 11.2–8) shares common traits with the Shepherd of Hermas 22.6–24.1 (*Vis.* 4.1.6–3.1), the *Acts of Thomas* 31, or the *Questions of Bartholomew* 4.13.[40] Several times (*Acts Phil.* 2.9, 17; 11.6; *Acts Phil. Mart.* 25 [recension Δ]) Philip, who is here so ready to anger, receives the nickname that the Gospel of Mark attributes to the sons of Zebbedaios, namely "son of thunder" (Mark 3:17).[41]

This relation to former texts and scriptures can even explain the very composition of the global work by amalgam and appropriation. The final author did not hesitate to bring together several traditions and texts related to Philip, merging together in this huge river the memories of Philip the evangelist, one of the Seven, and Philip the apostle, one of the Twelve.

---

[33] The resurrected Christ is quoting the historical Jesus, and that phenomenon occurs also in Luke 24:44–48 and in Acts 1:4–5.

[34] On this important passage see my article, "The Synoptic Gospels and the Noncanonical Acts of the Apostles," *HTR* 81 (1988) 30–31.

[35] On this relationship, see Matthews, "Peter and Philip Upside Down," 28–31.

[36] This has been disputed in a study by Andrea Lorenzo Molinari, *I Never Knew the Man: The Coptic Act of Peter (Papyrus Berolinensis 8502, 4): Its Independence from the Apocryphal Acts of Peter. Genre and Legendary Origins* (Bibliothèque copte de Nag Hammadi, Études 5; Québec: Presses de l'Université Laval; Louvain: Peeters, 2000).

[37] See Bovon, "Actes de Philippe," 4500–3; and the notes in Bovon, Bouvier, and Amsler, *Acta Philippi. Textus,* 296–99; and Amsler, *Acta Philippi. Commentarius,* 348–54.

[38] See Jean-Daniel Kaestli, "Les scènes d'attribution des champs de mission et de départ de l'apôtre dans les Actes apocryphes," *Les actes apocryphes des apôtres,* 249–64.

[39] See Bovon, "The Synoptic Gospels and the Noncanonical Acts," 31.

[40] See Erik Peterson, "Die Begegnung mit dem Ungeheuer. Hermas, Visio IV," *VC* 8 (1954) 52–71; reprinted in idem, *Frühkirche, Judentum und Gnosis. Studien und Untersuchungen* (Freiburg im Breisgau: Herder, 1959; reprinted in Darmstadt: Wissenschaftliche Buchgesellschaft, 1982) 285–309.

[41] See the note in Bovon, Bouvier, and Amsler, *Acta Philippi. Textus,* 290 n. 29.

Conclusion

This author does not consider his reference books or his own composition to be sacred in the sense that only a literal quotation would be admissible and any imitation prohibited. The free use of the Bible, of both Testaments, is confirmed by a similar type of reference to the tales from apostolic times. For the author, there is an ongoing process of revelation and manifestation of divine love through the centuries. The time of Adam and Eve, the time of Cain and Abel, the time of Moses in the wilderness, the construction of the Temple under Solomon, spoken of by a defeated dragon, the time of Jesus understood as the crucified, the teacher, and the commissioner – all these periods are marked by the presence of negative forces, dragons, snakes, and the viper, but at the same time by powerful divine providence and its successful agents: the prophets, the Savior, the apostles. The creative memory of this group of salvific events can still give direction to readers and believers more than any canonical or noncanonical scriptures.

Salvific events were more important for our author than were the Holy Scriptures. According to him or her, holy periods were not limited to the biblical history of redemption. God has to express love, manifest providence, and overcome the enemy's ferocity in every generation. Therefore, not only biblical quotations but also apostolic memories and apocryphal traditions are welcome and used for shaping the stories of the neglected apostle Philip.

The author and the Christian ascetic community perhaps felt neglected and marginalized.[42] The mainstream Church, the victorious Church of the Councils and bishops, could establish its identity on Peter, Paul, or John. As Encratites, who preferred vegetables to meat, water to wine for the Eucharist, and accepted as ministers women as well as men,[43] they also wanted to preserve the memory of Philip. Of course, this preservation has little in common with the task of a modern archivist; it is much more the construction of a sacred origin, an initial time that can be actualized or reiterated when faith and obedience cooperate in a polemical struggle against all the possible dragons.

---

[42] On the social and religious location of the author of the *Acts of Philip*, see the hypothesis of Amsler, "Introduction," in Amsler, *Actes de l'apôtre Philippe*, 13–86; and idem, "The Apostle Philip, the Viper, the Leopard, and the Kid: The Masked Actors of a Religious Conflict in Hierapolis of Phrygia (*Acts of Philip* VIII and *Martyrdom*)," in *SBLSP 1996* (ed. Eugene H. Lovering, Jr.; Atlanta: Scholars Press, 1996) 432–37.

[43] See *Acts Phil.* 1, 12; Bouvier and Bovon, "Actes de Philippe, I, d'après un manuscript inédit," 393–94; Bovon, Bouvier, and Amsler, *Acta Philippi. Textus*, 29.

Part IV
Later Transitions

The Reception and Use of the Gospel of Luke
in the Second Century

Several scholars have investigated the way various New Testament writings were received and used in the second century. Elaine Pagels and Jean-Michel Poffet, for instance, investigated the reception and use of the Gospel of John.[1] Andreas Lindemann and Ernst Dassmann pursued reception of the Pauline corpus, while Edouard Massaux and Wolf-Dietrich Köhler tracked the Gospel of Matthew.[2] Some scholars dared to trace the development of the synoptic tradition as a whole, while others attempted to detect the earliest traces of the book of Acts.[3] But apart from interest in Marcion, only a few scholars have investigated the reception and use of the Gospel of Luke in the second century since Edouard Zeller's work in 1848.[4]

---

[1] Elaine H. Pagels, *The Johannine Gospel in Gnostic Exegesis: Heracleon's Commentary on John* (SBLMS 17; Nashville: Abingdon, 1973); Jean-Michel Poffet, *La méthode exégétique d'Héracléon et d'Origène, commentateurs de Jn 4. Jésus, la Samaritaine et les Samaritains* (Paradosis 28; Fribourg, Switzerland: Éditions Universitaires, 1985); Jean-Daniel Kaestli, Jean-Michel Poffet, and Jean Zumstein, *La communauté johannique et son histoire. La trajectoire de l'évangile de Jean aux deux premiers siècles* (MdB 20; Geneva: Labor et Fides, 1990).

[2] On the Pauline corpus, see Andreas Lindemann, *Paulus im ältesten Christentum. Das Bild des Apostels und die Rezeption der paulinischen Theologie in der frühchristlichen Literatur bis Marcion* (BHT 58; Tübingen: Mohr Siebeck, 1979); and Ernst Dassmann, *Paulus in frühchristlicher Frömmigkeit und Kunst* (Geisteswissenschaften Vorträge/Rheinisch-Westfälische Akademie der Wissenschaften, G 256; Opladen: Westdeutscher Verlag, 1982). On the Gospel of Matthew, see Edouard Massaux, *Influence de l'Évangile de saint Matthieu sur la littérature chrétienne avant saint Irénée* (BETL 75; Leuven: Leuven University Press, 1986); and Wolf-Dietrich Köhler, *Die Rezeption des Matthäusevangeliums in der Zeit vor Irenäus* (WUNT 2.24; Tübingen: Mohr Siebeck, 1987).

[3] On the synoptic tradition, see Helmut Koester, *Synoptische Überlieferung bei den apostolischen Vätern* (TUGAL 65; Berlin: Akademie-Verlag, 1957); R. T. France and David Wenham, eds., *Gospel Perspectives* (6 vols.; Sheffield: JSOT Press, 1980–1986); Jean-Marie Sevrin, ed., *The New Testament in Early Christianity* (BETL 86; Leuven: Leuven University Press, 1989); and William L. Peterson, ed., *Gospel Traditions in the Second Century: Origins, Recensions, Text, and Transmission* (Christianity and Judaism in Antiquity 3; Notre Dame, Ind.: University of Notre Dame Press, 1989). On the book of Acts, see Ernst Haenchen, *The Acts of the Apostles: A Commentary* (Philadelphia: Westminster Press, 1971); François Bovon, *De vocatione gentium. Histoire de l'interprétation d'Act. 10,1–11,18 dans les six premiers siècles* (BGBE 8; Tübingen: Mohr Siebeck, 1967); and Werner Bieder, *Die Apostelgeschichte in der Historie. Ein Beitrag zur Auslegungsgeschichte des Missionsbuches der Kirche* (Zurich: EVZ-Verlag, 1960).

[4] Eduard Zeller, "Die älteste Überlieferung über die Schriften des Lukas," *Theologische Jahrbücher* 7 (1848) 528–72.

Zeller's work produced a number of conclusions and findings. He agreed with Ritschl's thesis that Marcion did not rewrite the Gospel of Luke but Luke's primary source. He noted the absence of any reference to the third gospel in the Apostolic Fathers and demonstrated that Justin used both the final version of the third gospel as well as Luke's major source. He further concluded that the *Epistle to Diognetus* does not contain any reference to Luke. Zeller claimed that there is evidence to support that the *Pseudo-Clementines*, like Justin, had access to Luke and his principal source. Zeller deduced from Irenaeus that the Gnostics – the Valentinians in particular – used the Gospel of Luke. He also established that the pagan philosopher Celsus, as well as the apologist Theophilus, both knew the third gospel. With regard to the book of Acts, Zeller considered that this book was unknown to Justin and is clearly attested only by Irenaeus. Finally, Zeller concluded that the final version of the Gospel of Luke was written between 130 C.E. – that is, after the time of Marcion, who did not know of it – and before Justin, who clearly uses it.

Between Zeller's paper in 1848 and today I can only mention the eight pages of John Martin Creed's introduction to his commentary on the Gospel of Luke[5] and a study I discovered after the first version of this chapter was written – Andrew Gregory's fine dissertation. Creed, who did not refer to Zeller's paper, detected evidence of the Gospel of Luke in the *Didache*, a text that was not available to Zeller; but Creed believed that the references to Luke belong to a later interpolation (*Did.* 1.3–2.1). Creed did not find any influence of the third gospel in Ignatius, Barnabas, or Hermas, but he felt there was evidence that the writer of the *Gospel of Peter* (another text that was unavailable to Zeller) was somewhat familiar with it. He detected Lukan influence in Justin, Theophilus, and the so-called Gnostics, in Basilides, who seems to know the parable of Lazarus and the rich man (Luke 16:19–31), and in Ptolemaeus and Heracleon, as they are known to us through Irenaeus and Clement of Alexandria. Creed concluded that the influence of our final version of Luke on Marcion is clear; thus he does not address Ritschl's and Zeller's hypothesis. After mentioning Tatian's use of the third gospel in his *Diatessaron*, Creed mentions the *Epistula apostolorum* (yet another text that was discovered only after Zeller's time),[6] and claims that the author of the *Epistula apostolorum* knew the four gospels.

Creed arrived at three conclusions with respect to our four canonical gospels. First, he concludes that, because they were thought to have been written by apostles, Matthew and John were the most popular gospels in the second century. Second, Creed claimed that Mark, whose material is almost completely integrated

---

[5] John M. Creed, *The Gospel according to St. Luke: The Greek Text with Introduction, Notes, and Indices* (London: Macmillan, 1930) XXV–XXXII.

[6] Creed follows Schmidt's date and location of that text: Asia Minor around the year 160 C.E.; see Carl Schmidt, *Gespräche Jesu mit seinen Jüngern nach der Auferstehung. Ein katholisch-apostolisches Sendschreiben des 2. Jahrhunderts* (TUGAL 43; Leipzig: Hinrichs, 1919).

into Matthew and Luke, dropped into the background. And third, Creed thought that because of the extent of the special material in Luke, particularly the parables, this gospel occupied an intermediate position.

Andrew Gregory's dissertation *The Reception of Luke and Acts in the Period before Irenaeus*[7] deals explicitly with my topic, as the title indicates. It contains an excellent bibliography and goes into much greater depth and detail than the present chapter. Gregory's general conclusions often agree with mine on negative results. For example, in orthodox writings it is impossible to prove the use of the Lukan redaction of Jesus sayings until Justin and Irenaeus.[8] Concerning Marcion, he writes, "Marcion is instead the first witness to the sustained self-conscious exclusive use of any single text concerning Jesus."[9] I agree also with his judgment relative to Justin Martyr, namely, that "Justin must be considered to depend on *Luke*."[10] These major agreements between us are important, and I am pleased to mention them.

There are still – even after having read Andrew Gregory's work – questions regarding Luke's Gospel that remain unanswered to this day, which leave us wondering about this gospel's destiny in the early patristic period. Which groups or communities, for example, possessed the Gospel of Luke in the second century? How was this gospel transmitted? Why are there different textual forms of this Gospel (and of Acts)? Who decided to dissociate the gospel from the book of Acts? What was the earliest interpretation of Luke's Gospel? When and by whom was it considered Holy Scripture? How early in the second century can traces of Luke's Gospel be detected? These intriguing questions demand that the investigations of Zeller, Creed, and Gregory be reopened and that historical answers be found.[11]

New research tools and methods also compel fresh inquiry. The volumes of *Biblia patristica*[12] made information about Luke's Gospel much more accessible than it had previously been. Recent critical editions of second-century Christian literature promise more reliable results than nineteenth-century scholarship could have achieved. New discoveries, such as the *Gospel of Thomas*, have opened

---

[7] See Andrew F. Gregory, *The Reception of Luke and Acts in the Period before Irenaeus: Looking for Luke in the Second Century* (WUNT 2.169; Tübingen: Mohr Siebeck, 2003).

[8] Ibid., 171–72 and 293–98.

[9] Ibid., 210.

[10] Ibid., 291.

[11] I demonstrated my interest in the history of reception of Luke's Gospel in the second century c.e. at the end of my paper "Le récit lucanien de la passion de Jésus (Lc 22–23)," in *The Synoptic Gospels: Source Criticism and the New Literary Criticism* (ed. Camille Focant; BETL 110; Leuven: Leuven University Press/Peeters, 1993) 393–423, esp. 416–20. See the English translation published in my *Studies in Early Christianity* (WUNT 161; Tübingen: Mohr Siebeck, 2003) 74–105, esp. 98–101.

[12] Jean Allenbach et al., *Biblia patristica* (7 vols.; Paris: Éditions du Centre National de la Recherche Scientifique, 1975–1991).

up new possibilities for studies. Thus it is time, as Andrew Gregory notes,[13] that this lamentable lacuna in Lukan studies be filled. How was Luke's Gospel received and used in the second century?

But before we attempt to answer this question, we must consider another. How should we proceed with our investigation? There are a number of possibilities. One could imagine, for instance, the theological problems and ecclesiastical quarrels that took place during this time period and then evaluate the role of Luke's Gospel in these discussions. For example, how might Luke 1:35 have been a response to questions about Jesus' birth?[14] Or how might Luke 24:39 have influenced developing thought about the resurrection?[15] But this path is uncertain since it risks abandoning the concrete, historical plane and embarking upon an abstract, theological one that has no solid footing. Or, one could employ socio-geographical categories and investigate the status of Luke's Gospel in Asia, Rome, or Antioch.[16] But since the original setting of so many early Christian texts is uncertain, this path has little to recommend it.

One could follow the Gospel of Luke itself and examine successively the way second-century writers understood Jesus' birth, his parables and miracles, his passion and resurrection. One might discover a significant interest in the ethical (love of enemies) and eschatological (the parousia) aspects of Jesus' teaching, with a corresponding lack of interest in his miracles. But the drawback to this procedure is that it attributes the same value to each Lukan passage.

In light of the documents now at our disposal, I shall propose another course. Namely, what was the attitude of second-century authors who were confronted with Luke's Gospel? How did they receive it? How did they make use of it? My research indicates that there were two different lines of response in the second century. Some authors adopted Luke as a source for their own gospels. For them, his writing was a ready reserve for their own retelling of stories about Jesus and his disciples. For other authors, Luke's text became an authoritative document. It became their Scripture, something to be preserved and interpreted.

Luke as a Source for New Writings

One response to Luke's Gospel was to view it merely as a source for further narration. It came as a surprise to me to discover that Luke the *historian* (the anony-

---

[13] Gregory, *Reception*, 22.

[14] See Sebastian P. Brock, "The Lost Old Syriac at Luke 1:35 and the Earliest Syriac Terms for the Incarnation," in Petersen, *Gospel Traditions in the Second Century*.

[15] See Bovon, "Le récit lucanien de la passion," 419.

[16] Apparently Polycarp was unaware of Luke's Gospel in Asia, just as *1 Clement* and Hermas suggest no knowledge of it in Rome; likewise, Ignatius of Antioch seemed to be unacquainted with Luke's Gospel.

mous author of a διήγησις, Luke 1:1) was used as a source by many anonymous authors of the second and third centuries. New storytellers read and drew from this ancient storyteller as if there had been a familiarity between them. But here one must exercise caution, for just as Luke was not the first storyteller (see Luke 1:1), the possibility that some second-century authors did not use Luke himself so much as one of his sources should not be dismissed. And what is true of the stories is all the more true of the words attributed to Jesus.

It appears that the authors of the following texts had knowledge of passages of Luke's Gospel that are unique to him and have no synoptic parallels:

(a) The *Gospel of the Ebionites* is a very old gospel harmony known only through quotations found in Epiphanius. This gospel is probably older than Tatian's *Diatessaron*, since, unlike the latter, it melds only three gospels. Knowledge of Luke's Gospel is revealed in the affirmation that John the Baptist was from priestly roots: "It was said that he [John the Baptist] was from the descent of the priest of Aaron, son of Zacharias and Elizabeth."[17]

(b) Several quotations from the *Gospel of the Nazarenes* are preserved in the works of Jerome as well as in a medieval manuscript entitled *Historia passionis Domini*. While most of these quotations are related to the Gospel of Matthew,[18] two of them reveal unmistakable knowledge of the Gospel of Luke: the Lukan episode (Luke 22:43–44) where an angel appears to comfort Jesus when, seized by anxiety in the garden, he begins to sweat clots of blood (*Hist. pass. Dom.*, fol. 32ʳ);[19] and Jesus' final words on the cross ("Father, forgive them, for they know not what they do," Luke 23:34).[20] These two passages, which are unique to Luke, seem to indicate that the author of this gospel was well aware of the Gospel of Luke.

(c) Two passages from the *Gospel of Peter* must also be considered. The first affirms that Herod was present and active during Jesus' trial (*Gos. Pet.* 1.1–2.5), which is also stated in Luke 23:6–12 and Acts 4:27–28. It is most likely in this instance that the *Gospel of Peter* does not depend directly upon the Gospel of

---

[17] This quotation is preserved by Epiphanius, *Pan.* 30.13.6. For an English translation, see *New Testament Apocrypha* (ed. Wilhelm Schneemelcher; 2 vols.; Louisville: Westminster/John Knox Press, 1991–1992) 1:169.

[18] The *Gospel of the Nazarenes* is similar to the Gospel of Matthew in that both are orthodox Judeo-Christian gospels.

[19] The Latin text is available in Kurt Aland, *Synopsis quattuor evangeliorum* (15th ed.; Stuttgart: Deutsche Bibelgesellschaft, 1996) 457. Justin Martyr (*Dial.* 103.8) also knows of this episode.

[20] Preserved by Jerome, *Epist.* 120.8; PL 116:934.

Luke but shares with it a common oral tradition.[21] The same holds true for the utterance of the good robber crucified along with Jesus (*Gos. Pet.* 4.13).[22]

(d) The fragments of Papyrus Egerton 2, the so-called "Unknown Gospel," sound very Johannine, but they also echo Luke. For example, the attempt to arrest Jesus[23] includes statements very similar to those found in John 5:39, 45–46. But the use of the term "lawyer" (νομικός) is more Lukan; the term is found seven times in Luke but only once in Matthew, and it is absent from the Gospels of Mark and John. Also, the participle στραφείς depicts a frequent gesture of Jesus that is found primarily in Luke; the gesture is found eight times in Luke, twice in Matthew, once in John, and is absent from Mark. And in the next episode, the story of the leper,[24] much of the language resembles that found in Luke 5:12–14 and 17:14. Finally, Luke is the only New Testament evangelist who uses terms such as συνοδεύω, συνεσθίω, and πανδοχεῖον.[25]

(e) In the *Gospel of Thomas* there ar at least seven verses that have parallels only in the Gospel of Luke:

Gos. Thom. 3	The kingdom of God is within you and outside you (see Luke 17:21).
Gos. Thom. 10	I have cast fire upon the world (see Luke 12:49).
Gos. Thom. 39	The Pharisees and scribes have received and hidden the keys of knowledge (see Luke 11:52).
Gos. Thom. 63	The parable of the rich man (see Luke 12:16–21).
Gos. Thom. 79	An apothegm in the form of dialogue with two beatitudes (the woman: blessed is the womb; Jesus: blessed are those who have heard the word; see Luke 11:27–28, mixed with an apocalyptical sentence known only by Luke [Luke 23:29]).
Gos. Thom. 95	Do not lend money at interest (see Luke 6:34–35).
Gos. Thom. 113	On what day does the kingdom come? The kingdom does not come so that one can expect it (see Luke 17:20–21).

There may be other parallels, but the common elements between Luke and the *Gospel of Thomas* listed above are indisputable. And even if one were to try to dismiss these parallels as being due to a common source (either oral or written tradition), there is one instance among them where the final redaction of the *Gos-*

---

[21] Pace Massaux, *Influence de l'Évangile de saint Matthieu*, 377.

[22] The good robber's rebuke (ἡμεῖς διὰ τὰ κακὰ ἃ ἐποιήσαμεν οὕτω πεπόνθαμεν, οὗτος δὲ σωτὴρ γενόμενος τῶν ἀνθρώπων τί ἠδίκησεν ὑμᾶς; see Aland, *Synopsis*, 484; see Schneemelcher, *New Testament Apocrypha*, 1:223) is similar to that found in Luke 23:41.

[23] See Papyrus Egerton 2, fol. 1ᵛ (Aland, *Synopsis*, 200, 323; see Schneemelcher, *New Testament Apocrypha*, 1:98).

[24] See Papyrus Egerton 2, fol. 1ʳ (Aland, *Synopsis*, 60; see Schneemelcher, *New Testament Apocrypha*, 1:98).

[25] Massaux, *Influence de l'Évangile de saint Matthieu*, 331–33, 339.

pel of Thomas depends on the final redaction of the Gospel of Luke: the disposition of a loan without interest (*Gos. Thom.* 95 = Luke 6:34–35; see Matt 5:42).

(f) Clement of Alexandria mentions in *Stromata* 2.45.4, 3.26.3, and 7.82.1 a noncanonical work called the *Traditions of Matthias*. In *Stromata* 4.6.35.2, he attributes the decision made by Jesus' interlocutor in the gospel ("Here, Lord, I give half of my possessions to the poor," Luke 19:8) to Zacchaeus, knowing that some claim these words came from Matthias's lips. The Savior's response to this promise was, "The Son of Man has come σήμερον [see Luke 19:10 and 13:15, "today"] to find what had been lost."[26]

(g) *Papyrus Cairensis* 10735 (sixth or seventh century, but the text may be much older) contains a very fragmentary birth narrative.[27] Here again we have either a parallel story or an instance of free usage of Luke (and Matthew): on the recto of the fragment there is the account of the flight into Egypt (see Matt 2:13) and on the verso the story where Mary receives as a sign the message of John's conception in Elizabeth's womb (see Luke 1:36).

(h) In the *Ascension of Isaiah*, an early Christian apocalypse (probably early second century), the prophet shares with Luke (and with Luke only: Luke 12:37) a special hope: in the kingdom, Christ the Lord will be a servant and will give food to the elect and blessed ones (*Ascen. Isa.* 4.16).[28] The author may have used Luke's redaction or even the parable in its original form.

(i) The *Questions of Bartholomew*, a very strange text (probably second or third century C.E.), seems to rewrite quite freely a chapter from Luke's Gospel. As a way of explaining Jesus' conception the author lets Mary herself tell the story of the annunciation:

And when they had done that, she began: "When I lived in the temple of God and received my food from the hand of an angel, one day there appeared to me one in the form of an angel; but his face was indescribable and in his hand he had neither bread nor cup, as had the angel who came to me before. And immediately the veil of the Temple was rent and there was a violent earthquake, and I fell to the earth, for I could not bear the sight of him. But he took me with his hand and raised me up. And I looked toward heaven; and there came a cloud of dew on my face and sprinkled me from head to foot, and he wiped me with his robe. Then he said to me: 'Hail, you who are highly favored, the chosen vessel.' And then he struck the right side of his garment and there came forth an exceedingly large loaf, and he placed it upon the altar of the Temple, and first ate of it himself and then gave to me

---

[26] There is also the memory of a Zacchaeus in the Pseudo-Clementines; see *Recognitiones* Preface 14; 1.20.1; 1.21.2; 1.72.3; 1.72.4; 1.73.1; 1.74.1; 2.1.2; 2.19.1; 2.19.3; 3.65.5; 3.66.3; 3.66.4; 3.66.5; 3.67.2; 3.68.1; 3.68.5; 3.74.1; 7.33.3; 9.36.5.

[27] Aland, *Synopsis*, 4, 17; see Schneemelcher, *New Testament Apocrypha*, 1:101.

[28] Schneemelcher, *New Testament Apocrypha*, 2:609.

also. And again he struck his garment, on the left side, and I looked and saw a cup full of wine. And he placed it upon the altar of the Temple, and drank from it first himself and gave it also to me. And I looked and saw that the bread did not diminish and the cup was as full as before. Then he said: 'Three years more, and I will send my word and you shall conceive my son, and through him the whole world shall be saved. But you will bring salvation to the world. Peace be with you, favored one, and my peace shall be with you forever.' And when he had said this, he vanished from my eyes and the Temple was as before." (*Quaest. Bart.* 2.15–21)[29]

(j) The *Epistula apostolorum*, a very old text, combines pseudepigraphy and apocalyptic inspiration from a catholic perspective, to combat Simon and Cerinthus. With this purpose in mind, the author quotes and rewrites quite freely the four gospels, which for him are *not yet canonical*. In a summary of Jesus' miracles the author mentions the story of the woman with a hemorrhage and quotes an utterance of Jesus that is unique to Luke: "I have noticed that strength went out of me" (Luke 8:46; *Epist. apost.* 5 [16]).[30] In another passage the author demonstrates knowledge of the birth stories, particularly the annunciation (*Epist. apost.* 14 [25]; see Luke 1:26–35).[31] Here we have a Christian keen to defend orthodox views, possessing good knowledge of the four gospels but not yet regarding them as canonical, holy writings.

(k) Similarly, the scribe who added the long ending to the Gospel of Mark also knew the Gospel of Luke, or its source. In any case, he profits from the story and uses the appearance of the resurrected Christ to the eleven in his effort to provide a conclusion to Mark's Gospel. While the sequence Mark 16:12–13, 14–15 suggests knowledge of our Gospel of Luke, the summary of the Emmaus story (Mark 16:12–13) seems to depend upon a traditional oral narrative.[32]

(l) Apparently in the second century the responsibility of the scribe could cohabit with narrative freedom. Only such a conclusion could account for the many variations within the textual tradition itself. Some scribes used their freedom in a cautious, conservative way, trying to bring Luke's Gospel closer to Matthew's.[33] The most unusual example is found in one of the genealogies: Codex Bezae

---

[29] Schneemelcher, *New Testament Apocrypha*, 1:544–45. Note that in this story there are three years between the annunciation and Jesus' birth, just as in *Prot. Jas.* 8.2 and 12.3.

[30] This story was popular in so-called Gnostic circles.

[31] Note also the allusion to Luke 16:23, the parable of Lazarus and the wicked rich man, in *Epist. apost.* 27 [38], and the allusion to Luke 24:37, 39, the resurrection scene where the disciples are encouraged to touch Jesus and verify that he is not a ghost, in *Epist. apost.* 11 [22]. There is also a passage in *Epist. apost.* 31 [42] that reveals knowledge of the book of Acts. See finally, in *Epist. apost.* 35 [46], Jesus' words about the two disciples on the road to Emmaus being slow of heart (Luke 24:25).

[32] In Mark 16:12 the two disciples are going εἰς ἀγρόν ("into the country"); in Luke 24:13 they are going εἰς κώμην ("to a village").

[33] Note the frequent occurrence of the siglum "p" in the apparatus of the Nestle-Aland edi-

(siglum "D" or 05) transforms the Lukan genealogy of Jesus into the Matthean but respects Luke's logic by beginning with Jesus and working backwards. Scribes also liked to develop novel details or episodes; Codex Bezae, for example, supplies an incident in Luke 6:4, where Jesus confronts someone working on the Sabbath day. This tendency is well known, but I would set it within the context of a broad and free movement in the second century, a movement of continual rewriting that actually originated in the first century. And in light of the way Luke used his own sources, he himself is already a witness to this tendency.

(m) A most impressive free use of Luke's Gospel appears in the *Protevangelium of James*. The author's intention was to write the life of Jesus' mother for purposes of defending her virginity.[34] In so doing, he freely integrates the birth stories from both Matthew and Luke:

And she took the pitcher and went forth to draw water, and behold, a voice said, "Hail, thou art highly favored, the Lord is with thee, blessed art thou among women." And she looked around on the right and on the left to see whence this voice came. And trembling she went to her house and put down the pitcher and took the purple and sat down on her seat and drew out (the thread). And behold an angel of the Lord (suddenly) stood before her and said, "Do not fear, Mary, for you have found grace before the Lord of all things and shall conceive his Word." When she heard this she doubted in herself and said, "Shall I conceive of the Lord, the living God, (and bear) as every woman bears?" And the angel of the Lord came and said to her, "Not so, Mary, for a power of the Lord shall overshadow you; wherefore also that holy thing which is born of you shall be called the Son of the Highest. And you shall call his name Jesus, for he shall save his people from their sins." And Mary said, "Behold, (I am) the handmaid of the Lord before him: be it to me according to your word."

And she made (ready) the purple and the scarlet and brought (them) to the priest. And the priest took (them) and blessed Mary, and said, "Mary, the Lord God has magnified your name, and you shall be blessed among all generations of the earth." And Mary rejoiced, and went to Elizabeth her kinswoman, and knocked on the door. When Elizabeth heard it she put down the scarlet, and ran to the door and opened it, (and when she saw Mary) she blessed her and said, "Whence is this to me, that the mother of my Lord should come to me? For behold, that which is in me leaped and blessed thee." But Mary forgot the mysteries which the (arch)angel Gabriel had told her, and raised a sigh toward heaven and said, "Who am I, (Lord), that all the women (generations) of the earth count me blessed?" And she remained three months with Elizabeth. Day by day her womb grew, and Mary was afraid and went into her house and hid herself from the children of Israel. And Mary was sixteen years old when all these mysterious things happened (to her). (*Prot. James* 11.1–12.3)[35]

---

tion of the New Testament: *Novum Testamentum Graece* (27th ed. Stuttgart: Deutsche Bibelgesellschaft, 1993).

[34] The oldest known title of the work is γένεσις Μαρίας found in the third-century Papyrus Bodmer V.

[35] See Schneemelcher, *New Testament Apocrypha*, 1:430–31.

(n) The author of the *Infancy Gospel of Thomas* demonstrates a similar enterprise. His intention is to tell the stories of Jesus as a boy, in order to demonstrate that the divine power was already in him at that time. Chapter 19 of this gospel is present in some of the oldest forms of the text and must be original. It retells the story of Jesus in the temple at the age of twelve (Luke 2:41–52) with an interesting expansion, a dialogue between the scribes and Mary:

But the scribes and Pharisees said, "Are you the mother of this child?" And she said, "I am." And they said to her, "Blessed are you among women, because God has blessed the fruit of your womb." (*Inf. Gos. Thom.* 19.4; see Luke 1:42)[36]

(o) An impressive free usage of gospel writing in the second century is found in the *Apocalypse of Peter*, a text preserved only in Ethiopic. Since it is more than a rewriting – indeed it constitutes a commentary on the text as well as reasoning with the text – we shall return to examine this passage in the second half of this chapter.

(p) The only Greek fragment of the *Diatessaron*[37] (found at Dura Europos) reflects knowledge of Luke 23:49–51 (of the Lukan redaction, and not only of the tradition used by Luke).

(q) *Sibylline Oracles* 8.478–80 gives a three-verse summary of the Lukan story of Jesus' birth:[38]

478   And when Bethlehem became the homeland of the Word through God's choice

479   The child, wrapped up in the crib, was presented to those who obey God,

480   Shepherds who look after cows, goats, and lambs.

While one might dismiss this instance on the basis of its late date,[39] it is nevertheless a poetic witness to the continuous narrative power that did not stop with the written form of our canonical New Testament Gospels but carried on in both oral and written traditions well into the second century and even later.

---

[36] See Schneemelcher, *New Testament Apocrypha*, 1:449.

[37] See Bruce M. Metzger, *The Canon of the New Testament: Its Origin, Development, and Significance* (Oxford: Clarendon, 1987) 115.

[38] Another text, *Odes Sol.* 19, discusses the virgin birth. See Majella Franzmann, *The Odes of Solomon: An Analysis of the Poetical Structure and Form* (NTOA 20; Göttingen: Vandenhoeck & Ruprecht, 1991) 146–52. It is clear that this ode is dependent on Matthew and Luke.

[39] The latest possible date for this part of book 8 is provided by Lactantius (ca. 260 C.E. to ca. 330 C.E.), who quotes from it extensively. But Johannes Geffcken argues for a date toward the end of the second century; see Johannes Geffcken, *Komposition und Entstehungszeit der Oracula sibyllina* (TU 23; Leipzig: Hinrichs, 1902) 44.

Luke as a Normative Text for Preservation and Comment

Irenaeus tells us that the Ebionites used only the Gospel of Matthew, the Valentinians primarily John, and Marcion an amputated version of Luke (*Adv. haer.* 3.11.7). It is not my intention here to concentrate on Marcion, except to mention that his theological mind made more use of philology than exegesis. Even if we are unsure of the extent to which his *Antitheses* attempted an exegetical analysis of Luke,[40] we can be certain that his understanding of the written gospel coincided with a rewriting, not with a scholarly commentary. In one sense Marcion's attitude toward Luke's Gospel was not so different from that of the apocryphal writers — aside from his historical and philological claims and his preference for emendation rather than interpolation. Instead of extratextual exegesis, Marcion preferred an implicit understanding, embedded in a manipulation of the text. As it stood after the restoration, after the glosses had been erased, the text was clear — according to him anyway — and did not need any commentary. Marcion was opposed to allegorical interpretation and is not the originator of New Testament exegesis. Having a special, indeed religious, respect for the Gospel of Luke is not the same as intentionally writing commentaries on it. As for Marcion, orthodox Christians may have canonized Luke's Gospel without feeling any need to give a written explanation of it. But as time went on, New Testament exegesis arose. Why?

The *Acts of Peter* provides a double clue to the answer to this question. First, the work attests — as does Justin Martyr's *First Apology* 67.3, written about the same time — to the liturgical reading of New Testament texts during Christian worship, followed by someone preaching upon the same text. Thus in *Acts Peter* 20,[41] as Peter enters the house of Marcellus, he comes upon some Christians reading the story of Jesus' transfiguration in "the gospel," and so begins to expound upon the text and explain the significance of that event. Within the context of the second century (see 2 Peter), the sermon served a polemical purpose. Liturgical necessity together with polemics kindled oral comment on the New Testament, and particularly on Luke's Gospel.

But there was another reason for the production of the first Christian exegeses, especially in written form: the divergences among the gospels. As soon as a plurality of gospels[42] was accepted, for ecumenical and ecclesiastical reasons, it became imperative to harmonize their contradictions and differences. A good part

---

[40] von Harnack believed Marcion's *Antitheses* contained much exegesis and commentary on his amputated version of Luke; see Adolf von Harnack, *Marcion. Das Evangelium vom fremden Gott. Eine Monographie zur Geschichte der Grundlegung der katholischen Kirche* (2d ed.; TUGAL 45; Leipzig: Hinrichs, 1924) 76. I remain convinced that it was more doctrinal in nature.

[41] See Schneemelcher, *New Testament Apocrypha*, 2:303–4.

[42] I believe that our four canonical gospels were accepted by several churches ca. 120 C.E.

of the five books of Papias entitled Λογίων κυριακῶν ἐξηγήσεις[43] may have been devoted to this special exegetical task.

In my commentary on the Gospel of Luke[44] I tried to follow the very rational and – at the same time – fundamentalist explanation that Julius Africanus gives for the divergent genealogies of Jesus in Matthew and Luke.[45] Julius Africanus enlists the aid of an apocryphal family story involving levirate marriage in his effort to harmonize the differences.[46] There is similar reasoning and exegesis in Irenaeus when he tries to harmonize the book of Acts with the Pauline epistles.[47] Irenaeus' conclusion is very similar to that of Julius Africanus, who claims that the gospel is true and there are no contradictions among the different texts. He further states, "So Paul's preaching and Luke's witness to the apostles are converging and more or less identical."[48] "Und die Bibel hat doch recht!"[49]

One archaic way of exegeting Luke's Gospel lay midway between the use of Luke as a source and the use of Luke as normative Scripture. According to this method, exegesis took the form of pseudepigraphical revelation whose beneficiary and witness, supposedly an apostle, provided the right interpretation of New Testament traditions. Such an exegetical path was possible in orthodox circles only as long as the gospels were not fully canonical. This phenomenon was actually a transmission of the gospel story into a hermeneutical perspective and was not yet an exegetical explanation of the gospel text. The *Didache*, the *Epistula apostolorum*, and the *Apocalypse of Peter* contain such authoritative apostolic comments on Jesus' teaching. The most impressive case is that found in the *Apocalypse of Peter*.[50]

The framework of this apocalypse is the dialogue between Jesus and his disciples on the Mount of Olives; Matt 24:3 helps create the scenario. The question that disturbs the disciples (meaning that the church during the author's time asks this question) concerns the parousia and the signs that accompany it. The Savior responds first with the short synoptic parable of a fig tree, where the first leaves announce the coming of summer.[51] After a new question from Peter, the Savior pursues this explanation with a different parable of a fig tree, known only from Luke 13:6–9. Interestingly enough, the author responds to the question with an

---

[43] Eusebius, *Hist. eccl.* 3.39.1.

[44] See François Bovon, *Luke 1: A Commentary on the Gospel of Luke 1:1–9:50* (trans. Christine M. Thomas; Hermeneia; Minneapolis: Fortress, 2002) 135.

[45] On Julius Africanus, see Eusebius, *Hist. eccl.* 1.7.1–16.

[46] Ibid., 1.7.16.

[47] Ibid., 3.13.1.

[48] Ibid., 3.14.1.

[49] "And nevertheless the Bible is right!" See Werner Keller, *Und die Bibel hat doch recht. Forscher beweisen die historische Wahrheit* (Düsseldorf: Econ-Verlag, 1955).

[50] See Richard Bauckham, "The Two Fig Tree Parables in the *Apocalypse of Peter*," *JBL* 104 (1985) 269–87.

[51] See Matt 24:32–36; Mark 13:28–29; and Luke 21:29–33.

allegorical interpretation: "Have you not understood that the fig tree is the house of Israel?" (*Apoc. Pet.* 2). The parable he quotes has a form that is parallel to the one in our canonical Luke, but there are significant differences that seem to imply that he is using the parable at its oral, pre-Lukan level.[52]

Allegorical interpretation is already present in the synoptic tradition itself. The Gospels of Mark, Matthew, and Luke are written witnesses to the application of this method to the oral form of the parables. This method is developed further in the *Apocalypse of Peter*. Later, nothing will prevent the use of allegorical interpretation in exegeting the written form of the gospel.

There is patristic evidence for such an exegesis of the parable of the Good Samaritan. One of Origen's homilies on Luke, preserved in Jerome's Latin translation, remembers the witness of a so-called "elder."[53] This man, according to Origen, gave a christological interpretation of the parable,[54] an interpretation shared by Irenaeus, whose respect for the "elders" is well known. The so-called "elders," or πρεσβύτεροι, in the second century may have carried out the first orthodox allegorical interpretation of the gospels.[55]

Another surprise in this study was the discovery that, while the Gospel of John has always been characterized as the favorite among the Gnostics, Luke the historian also attracted their attention. Nearly all the Gnostic schools had an ongoing interest in Luke's Gospel. According to the Ophites, Elizabeth and Mary represent two ways of human procreation: "Prounikos functioned through Jaldabaoth – though he was ignorant of what she was doing – and emitted two men, one from the sterile Elizabeth and the other from the Virgin Mary."[56]

If Carpocrates refused to believe in the gospel birth stories,[57] Ptolemaios tried to respect them while rejecting a strict incarnation.[58] He used a famous explanation: the psychical Christ, son of the demiurge, attested by the prophets, went through Mary "like water through a pipe."[59] The Savior, who is pneumatic, came upon him in the form of a dove at baptism.

Irenaeus gives us insight into the Gnostic exegesis of Luke's Gospel and specifies that the Gnostics applied the biblical passages to events that occurred outside

---

[52] See Schneemelcher, *New Testament Apocrypha*, 2:626.

[53] Origen, *Hom. Luc.* 34.3.

[54] See the catena attributed to Titus of Bostra in John A. Cramer, *Catenae Graecorum patrum in Novum Testamentum* (8 vols.; Oxford: Oxford University Press, 1844) 2:87–88.

[55] In any case, Irenaeus regards the elders as the oldest and best interpreters of the New Testament (*Adv. haer.* 4.26.2).

[56] Ibid., 1.30.11.

[57] Ibid., 1.25.1.

[58] See ibid., 1.7.2.

[59] See Michel Tardieu, "'Comme à travers un tuyau.' Quelques remarques sur le mythe valentinien de la chair céleste du Christ," in *Colloque international sur les textes de Nag Hammadi (Québec, 22–25 Août 1978)* (ed. Bernard Barc; Bibliothèque copte de Nag Hammadi, Études 1; Québec: Les Presses de l'Université Laval, 1981) 151–77.

the pleroma but were connected with it.[60] The daughter of Jairus was an image of Achamoth. The lost sheep is also the lost Achamoth, searched for by Christ the shepherd, while the woman looking for her lost drachma is the superior wisdom looking for ἐνθύμησις (intuition). Simeon is a figure of the demiurge, who, at the coming of the Savior, learns that he has to change his location, and so he praises the ἄβυσσος. Anna the prophetess is a figure of Achamoth.

The Gnostics considered the numbers twelve and thirty to be significant. They interpreted the story of Jesus at the age of twelve in the temple as the emission of the twelve aeons.[61] Other evidence suggests the popularity of this story in the second century.[62] According to Marcos's disciples, the episode demonstrates the way Jesus announced the unknown God. This dangerous interpretation – from an orthodox point of view – had to be refuted: Origen devoted no less than four sermons to this story.

Typical also of the double reception of Luke's Gospel in the second century is the importance attributed to the age of Jesus ("thirty years old") when he begins his ministry. This information is provided only by Luke (3:23). These thirty years are accepted not only by apocryphal writers but also became the foundation for allegorical interpretation among Gnostic theologians.[63]

Other so-called Gnostic interpretations that reflect knowledge of Luke's Gospel include the following:

(a) The Roman officer at Capernaum (Matt 8:5–13//Luke 7:1–10)[64] is understood as a figure of the demiurge, because he learns his real identity only upon meeting the Savior. The meaning of his statement on obedience and his dialogue with the Savior is that the demiurge will lead the economy of this world to the prescribed moment for the sake of the church he is responsible for and because he knows his future reward: his transfer to the place of the mother.

(b) Jesus' words on reconciliation before two people take their dispute to court (Luke 12:58–59) have been used by Gnostic allegorical interpretation to justify belief in metempsychosis.[65]

(c) Heracleon gave an interesting interpretation of Jesus' teaching on confessing one's faith (Luke 12:8–9). He attempted to show that the heart is more important than the lips and conviction more decisive than words alone. Orthodox writers

---

[60] Irenaeus, *Adv. haer.* 1.8.2.

[61] Ibid., 1.3.2.

[62] See *Inf. Gos. Thom.* 19.1–5 (Schneemelcher, *New Testament Apocrypha*, 1:448–49).

[63] See Irenaeus's discussion of Ptolemaios in *Adv. haer.* 1.1.3 and 3.1. Later, in 1.16.1, Irenaeus chides that the Gnostics interpret everything according to numbers.

[64] Ibid., 1.7.4.

[65] Ibid., 1.25.4.

accused him of giving this explanation in order to avoid any real confrontation with judges during a time of persecution.[66]

(d) Another *logion* received special attention: the so-called Johannine passage in the Synoptic tradition on mutual knowledge between the Father and the Son (see John 10:15; 17:25–26). Several writers of the second century, particularly the Gnostics, used a reading from the gospel text (Luke 10:22; Matt 11:27) that is different from our canonized version. Our text reads, "No one knows who the Son is but the Father, and who the Father is but the Son." The Gnostic reading was, "No one knows who the Father is but the Son, and who the Son is but the Father." As they read it, they were comforted in their belief that the unknown God was revealed only through the Savior.[67]

(e) The three *logia* of the call to discipleship in Luke 9:57–62 were used by Gnostics to distinguish three human races: the man who receives the reply that "foxes have their holes ... " represents material (*hylic*) humanity; the man who receives the reply to "leave the dead to bury their dead" represents spiritual (*pneumatic*) humanity; and the man who desires first to go and say goodbye to his family represents living (*psychic*) humanity.[68] But while the Lukan text surely lies behind the Gnostic interpretation, the Gnostic order differs from that which is found in our Luke, indicating that perhaps the Gnostic text of Luke had another sequence: Luke 9:57–58 (*hylic*), 61–62 (*psychic*), and 59–60 (*pneumatic*).

(f) According to Irenaeus, some Gnostics also used the story of Zacchaeus in their classification of humanity: Jesus' reply ("Make haste and come down, for today I must stay in your house," Luke 19:5) was applied to the pneumatic human being.[69]

(g) Some Gnostics could accept the passion of Jesus but they refused to read it historically. Instead, they understood it allegorically and discovered in it the fate of the one who fell under the passion.[70]

Other Gnostic references to Luke could be gathered from the Nag Hammadi library and Clement's *Excerpts from Theodotus*, but these examples are sufficient

---

[66] Clement of Alexandria, *Strom.* 4.71–73; see Annewies van den Hoek, "Clement of Alexandria on Martyrdom," *StPatr* 26 (1993) 324–41, esp. 330–31.

[67] See the long discussion by Irenaeus in *Adv. haer.* 1.20.3 and 4.6.1. It is gratifying to see that such an important second-century reading was finally included in the critical apparatus of Nestle-Aland, *Novum Testamentum Graece*, at Matt 11:27 (p. 28); it is, however, still lacking at Luke 10:22 (p. 192).

[68] Irenaeus, *Adv. haer.* 1.8.3.

[69] Ibid., 1.8.3. Irenaeus does not say more about this, and his text remains obscure.

[70] Ibid., 2.20.4.

to demonstrate the honored position that second-century Gnostics gave to the Gospel of Luke. These theologians competed against one another as to the best spiritual, allegorical interpretation of Luke's stories and Jesus' words. Surely such comments were a polemical response against orthodox readings, since Irenaeus systematically reproaches them for several exegetical deficiencies. According to him, the Gnostics brought non-canonical materials into their exegesis, twisted the meaning of biblical texts to support their own doctrines, disturbed the sequence of word order in the Scriptures, and freely transferred and transformed the words of the Lord to suit their own purposes. Irenaeus believed that when the Bible is interpreted correctly, it is a beautiful mosaic depicting a king. But the Gnostics only see an image that looks like a dog or a fox.[71]

Through their allegorical readings, these Gnostic readers compelled orthodox readers to ask themselves whether their simple harmonizing exegesis was sufficient and whether their common-sense, plain-meaning explanations could satisfy the intellectual needs of converts. As we have seen, in orthodox circles the second century was also a century of preaching on the gospel's narrative, a century of harmonizing discrepancies between the synoptic gospels, and – under the leadership of the "elders" – a century of allegorical interpretation.

Conclusion

The presence of the Gospel of Luke in the second century is irregular and surprising. The epistles from Paul's disciples and bishops do not show any trace of it. What remains from early apologetic works is silent. Justin Martyr is the first apologist who demonstrates evidence of contact with Luke's Gospel and with Lukan traditions; there is, for example, an allusion to the annunciation in the *First Apology* 33.4–5.[72] In his *Dialogue with Trypho* there are several points of contact with Lukan passages that have no synoptic parallels.[73]

For the words of Jesus, Justin seems to rely not only on our written gospels but also upon an oral tradition that is still alive. The same is probably true for *2 Clement*, as *2 Clem.* 4.5 is similar to Luke 13:27 ("Go away, you workers of injustice!"), but it is an oral version of the *logion. Second Clement* 5.2–4 is an apocry-

---

[71] Irenaeus, *Adv. haer.* 2.20.4.

[72] See also the following echoes from the synoptic tradition: "Love your enemies" (*1 Apol.* 15–16); "Give to Caesar the things that are Caesar's" (*1 Apol.* 15.17); "He who hears you hears me" (*1 Apol.* 63.3); "No one knoweth the Father, but the Son" (*1 Apol.* 63.13); "Things impossible for man are possible for God" (*1 Apol.* 19.6).

[73] For example, the statement that Elizabeth is barren (*Dial.* 84.4), that Jesus is thirty years old (*Dial.* 88.2), the annunciation to Mary (*Dial.* 100.5), and Herod at the passion (*Dial.* 102.4). In *Dial.* 105.5 Justin quotes Luke 23:46. In *Dial.* 106 his belief in the prophecy of the Scriptures is similar to that found in Luke 24:25–27. Massaux (*Influence de l'Évangile de saint Matthieu*, 556–60) mentions several other passages, in particular *Dial.* 76.6a; 81.4; 100.3; 49.3; and 53.5.

phal dialogue between Jesus and Peter that is similar to Luke 10:3 ("I am sending you out like sheep among wolves") and 12:4–5 ("Fear him who after death has power over body and soul"; the wording here differs from our Lukan text). *Second Clement* 6.1 ("No servant can serve two masters") follows the text of Luke 16:13 rather than Matthew 6:24. But most authors and apologists, especially those who were educated and orthodox, suggest no knowledge of the Gospel of Luke until the middle of the second century. None of the Pauline churches reflect any familiarity with it.

The situation was different for storytellers and visionaries, since the authors of gospel harmonies as well as the authors of pseudepigraphical revelations used Luke's Gospel.[74] Among the apocryphal acts of the apostles, the *Acts of Andrew*, the *Acts of John*, the *Acts of Peter*, and the *Acts of Paul* show no indication of contact with Luke's Gospel. Only the *Acts of Thomas*, the youngest (latest) of the five, mentions episodes or words known only from the Gospel of Luke; for example, the sending out of the 70 in Luke 10:1 and the *logion* of Jesus in Luke 9:62 ("No one who sets his hand to the plough ... ").[75]

It is possible that Marcion received the Gospel of Luke in his homeland of Pontus; in Rome he began reading Paul's epistles. Rome does not seem to know the third gospel until the middle of the century; *1 Clement* and Hermas show no knowledge of it at all. Marcion's task was to simplify the gospel into an earlier, more authentic and literal form. The Gnostics, who also knew the Gospel of Luke, dared to emphasize strongly the figurative meaning of the parables and to extend an allegorical significance to historical events. In so doing they were the antipode of Marcion.

But what place do we give the scribes who copied Luke's Gospel in the second century?[76] Is Christian-Bernard Amphoux correct in connecting their work with the first orthodox schools of theology in Asia and Egypt?[77] Confronted by various attempts to produce a harmony from the plurality of gospels, the teachers of these schools may have wished for a fixed text of Luke, since they would have rejected Gnostic allegories and Marcion's philological equations.

Thus there were two ways of receiving Luke's Gospel in the second century: either as a source for authors wishing to create new stories or as a fixed text for commentators to interpret and explain. And these two categories must be subdivided even further since preachers and theologians often used different methods of exegesis. There are even differences among theologians, since some were at-

---

[74] See Massaux, *Influence de l'Évangile de saint Matthieu*, 329.

[75] *Acts Thom.* 6.3 and 147.1.

[76] 𝔓⁴ (the same MS as 𝔓⁶⁴ and 𝔓⁶⁷) probably dates from the third century, as do 𝔓⁴⁵ and 𝔓⁶⁹. 𝔓⁷⁵ falls between 175 and 225 C.E.

[77] See Christian-Bernard Amphoux, "Les premières éditions de Luc, I," *ETL* 67 (1991) 312–27; and idem, "Les premières éditions de Luc, II. L'histoire du texte au IIᵉ siècle," *ETL* 68 (1992) 38–48, esp. 48.

tempting to reconcile the four Gospels by harmonizing their wording, while others were merely trying to draw spiritual teachings from them through allegorization. Similarly, the storytellers may have had various intentions: some were writing a gospel for their own communities – just as Matthew and Luke were attempting to do – while others who were confronted with our three synoptic gospels or with all four of our canonical Gospels felt compelled to bring them to a unity. Still others added complements to the Gospels, filling in the lacunae about the life of Jesus' mother and the childhood of Jesus.

Thus there is evidence that the orthodox reading of Luke's Gospel was established in stages. In its final outcome, such a reading meant to accept the whole Gospel and to receive it with the three others; to use the creed[78] as a normative reference point to avoid wild interpretations; to use logic, grammar,[79] and a historical method to ensure the integrity of the text and safeguard its cohabitation with the other, now canonical, Gospels; to explain obscure passages by means of clear passages (that is, not only intertextuality but also intratextuality within the normative Scriptures); and to ask the ancients for help in receiving the spiritual, apostolic meaning of Jesus' teaching. It is only then, "through the polyphony of the texts," writes Irenaeus, that "only one harmonious melody will sound in us, praising in song the God who created everything."[80]

---

[78] That is the rule of faith received at baptism; see Irenaeus, *Adv. haer.* 1.9.4.

[79] Ibid., 3.8.1; Irenaeus uses a philological argument to explain the meaning of the Semitic word "mammon."

[80] Ibid., 2.28.3.

Paul as Document and Paul as Monument[1]

Introduction

a) The aim of the essay

To recognize that between the epistles of Paul and today, there is an historical depth due to life, faith, and the interpretation of many generations.

b) General observation

In these successive readings and this uninterrupted care, there were at the same time obvious anachronisms and listening efforts; that is to say, sometimes Paul's texts were solicited and sometimes the Word of God that came out of them was brought to consciousness. Historical knowledge took away the aura of the sacred history from the history of the Church. The catholic Church claimed Paul as a person, in order to honor him of course, but also to ensure her own authority. The Protestants, for their part, became fervent advocates of the apostle Paul through anti-Catholic polemics. Several political authorities at last used Romans 13 to legitimize their power.

c) The thesis to be defended

The second century is an era of the various receptions reserved for the memory of the Apostle, a time of polychromic reception of the Pauline epistles. Enthusiastic assimilation, unintelligent reading, radicalized interpretation, polite indifference, and horrified rejection are brought together. The great Church takes two dispositions: Paul survives either in the form of a document or in the form of a monument; that is to say, either as a text or as a figure.

---

[1] The distinction between document and monument, which has resurfaced in recent years, is not new. It is dealt with, for example, in the foreword of Leopold von Ranke to his *Weltgeschichte*, to which Henri-Irénée Marrou refers in his work *De la connaissance historique* (Points, histoire 21; Paris: Seuil, 1954; reprinted in 1975) 65.

d) First, a word concerning the end of the first century

When he was alive, Paul was tolerated, accepted, admired, ignored, or criticized. The death of the apostle as a martyr, as far as we may know, forced the Pauline communities and the group of missionaries who were with him to take their responsibilities and to get organized. The New Testament left some traces of these reactions, which are the preliminaries for the ecclesiastical options of the second century. A man like Luke tried in the Acts of the Apostles to preserve the memory of Paul, that is to say, the memory of his activity as a missionary (thus the figure of the saint was shaped). However, the author of the Epistle to the Ephesians who, in my opinion, is a disciple of Paul, continues theological reflections that are Pauline in character and produces a dogmatic synthesis on the redemption of Christ and the mystery of the universal Church. Finally, the pastoral Epistles, seek to offer a Pauline infrastructure (in fact deutero-Pauline) to the communities that were shaken at the death of the Apostle. Therefore, we are assisting the continuation of the theological and pastoral work of the apostle (the Pauline work comes to be understood as a sacred text).

1. The reception of the second century

a) The admiration for the image of the apostle, for his work of evangelization and his martyrdom

This admiration is expressed in orthodox writings. The orthodoxy that is being formed is based on Peter and Paul, the two pillars that the Roman Church will soon be claiming. *1 Clement* 5.5–7: the worthy examples of our generation; Peter who undergoes martyrdom, then Paul: "Following jealousy and dispute, Paul showed the price reserved for constancy. Chained seven times, exiled, stoned, he became a herald in the East and then in the West. He was of a great renown, thanks to his faith. After he had taught justice in the entire world, he reached the limits of the West. He gave his testimony before the rulers; that's how he left the world and went on a journey of sanctity – illustrious model of faithfulness!" This interest in the persona of Paul is often accompanied by some sort of misunderstanding of the apostle's thought.

b) Forgetting Pauline thought

Among those who venerated it most, as within the communities established by other missionaries, Pauline thought falls into oblivion. The conflict on righteousness is no longer understood. Paul wanted freedom from the Law, but the apostolic Fathers and apologists presented Christian discipline as a new Law. The gospels, particularly that of Matthew, incarnated the truth of the Gospel, the good news of obedience that leads to life. We only need to read the beginning of *Didache* and its teaching of the two ways: "There are two ways: one leading to life and the other leading to death; but the difference is substantial between the two. Therefore here is the path to life: you will first love God who created you, then your neighbor as much as you love yourself, and what you do not wish to be done to you, do not do to others. Here is the teaching of these words: Bless those who curse you, pray for your enemies and fast for those who persecute you" (*Didache* 1:1–3). In the second century the theology of baptism that Paul had developed is also forgotten. It was only rediscovered in the fourth century by Cyril of Jerusalem in his *Baptismal Homilies*.

c) The radicalization of Pauline theology

In the second century, the one who best and least understood Paul was the Greek ship owner, Marcion, who worked first in the Church and after many disputes with the Church of Rome organized a very efficient international network of Marcionite communities. Only the Epistles of Paul and the Gospel of Luke were relevant to him. These Epistles and this Gospel were expurgated from all trace of Judaism (for example, Romans 9–11). For him there is an irreducible opposition between the Law and the Gospel.

The thought of Paul will also be taken up by the majority of the Gnostic movements of that period. But those receptions of Paul did not go without profound modifications: the scandal of the Cross was eliminated because of a Christ who did not assume the human condition until death. The Law of Moses is criticized, but in a radical and non-dialectical way, similar to what the apostle did. The nature of mankind no longer corresponded to the creature before God but to that of a partially divine being. Salvation meant the reconstruction of the divine integrity and no longer the liberation of mankind. Salvation would not be achieved through faith anymore, but through knowledge.

d) The rejection of Paul in strict Judeo-Christianity

The *Pseudo-Clementine Homilies* preserved a certain theology of history: God does not cease to reveal himself to humanity through the intermediary of a true prophet who is often presented in various figures. He appeared in the person of Adam, then of Moses, and finally of Jesus Christ. So also, in each generation a false prophet precedes and thwarts the mission of the real prophet. Paul was presented, in the figure of Simon Magus, as an incarnation of the false prophet.

e) The alleged continuation of the work

Without one knowing very well what the relation was between them, Pauline believers felt they were authorized to continue the literary work of the apostle. Thus emerges the *Third Epistle to the Corinthians* (polemic on the resurrection) and an *Apocalypse of Paul* (in a prophetic and mystical environment that took its inspiration from 2 Cor 12:1–3), traces of the authority which the apostle then enjoyed.

f) Orthodoxy asserts itself

As early as the middle of the second century, one may talk about the Church marked by a baptismal symbol and an episcopal ministry. This Church, established in the four corners of the Empire, fixed two forms of its veneration towards Paul: (a) Paul as *document*. The *Muratorian Canon*, for example, contains a list of the New Testament including the Pauline Epistles, and its objective was undoubtedly anti-Marcionite. Since then, the Epistles, like a jewel in a box, had been venerated, but this veneration can cause a good as well as a poor interpretation of the text. (b) Paul as *monument*. One starts to venerate the tomb of the apostle on the Ostia road in Rome. A text informs us about the veneration of this tomb being regarded as a trophy (see Eusebius of Caesarea, *History of the Church* 2.25.6–7). Since then, Peter and Paul are the two figureheads of the Roman Church (Luke had started the movement). The ecclesiastical ideology in fourth century Rome then will see that political power is based on these two apostles.

Another example of the prestige of Paul in the orthodox environment comes to us from the East. This is about the funerary inscription of Aberkios, a Christian (bishop?) of Hieropolis in Phrygia in the second century. In imaginary terms, the deceased man asserted that he had gone to Mesopotamia with the apostle Paul on his chariot; he thus expresses his attachment to the apostle's letters that he took away with him during his trip and recalled the canonicity of the Pauline epistles at the various stops he had made in those Eastern Churches.

Ignatius, bishop of Antioch at the second century, must have been the best interpreter of Paul. His letters were inspired by Paul's creed on the death and the resurrection. He understood the decisive function of the Cross of Christ. We may notice however two moves: Ignatius asked for an imitation of Christ, whereas Paul insisted on being in communion with Christ (hence the theology of martyrdom of Ignatius). In addition, he substituted for the Pauline hope in the Parousia of the Lord, a doctrine of the immediate and individual meeting of the believer with his Lord at the moment of death.

2. Two examples from late Christian Antiquity

a) *Origen, the reader of the document*

Origen was the main witness of the antique Christian exegesis of the Epistles of the apostle Paul. These Pauline documents, in his opinion, are part and parcel of the Holy Scripture. He explains them in the same manner as the rest of the Bible: that is to say, on a philosophical and allegorical level, unifying the texts in concordant harmony. He happened to divide the Scripture into three parts (the Old Testament, the Gospel, the Apostle, i.e., especially Paul) or in four parts (the Law-Prophets on the one hand, the Gospel-Apostle on the other, i.e., especially Paul). But in any event, the Apostle is canonical and is inspired.

In his effort at clarification of the Christian doctrine, Origen wrote in particular a full commentary of the Epistle to the Romans, which was preserved in fragments in Greek and transmitted in Latin in a tendentious translation. Not without emotion, the reader perceives the effort of the Alexandrian theologian in order to follow the logic of Paul. Yet some categories of his thought prevented him from grasping the argument of the Apostle. For example, for Origen, God's righteousness is first a quality, a divine virtue, and only after this, the act of the living God who justifies his people. This divine justice, he said, is expressed today through patience; in the age to come, it will be demonstrated as retribution. Sometimes he found some biblical emphasis: "If Abraham was justified by his faith when he was not yet circumcised, anybody believing in God may also be justified through faith even if he is not circumcised ... " (*Comm. Romans* 4:2; PG 14:956BC). Besides, the natural knowledge of God, free will (as opposed to ancient determinism), and individual moral responsibility are part and parcel of the doctrine of Paul according to Origen.

b) *John Chrysostom, the admirer of the monument*

If Origen, in the third century, snatched the Epistle to the Romans from the hands of the Gnostics and Marcionites, at the end of the fourth century Chrysostom celebrated the person of the apostle to the Gentiles in a series of panegyrics. In order to understand those texts, we need to say a few words on the worship and the reverence of which the apostle was the object. Tertullian teaches us that, about the year 200, a presbyter from Asia who had an excess affection for the apostle wrote the *Acts of Paul*. If this presbyter was dismissed, his work circulated for some time without being criticized. Paul appears to be accompanied by Thecla, a holy woman, a devotee of the apostle who preached and baptized. This reverence towards Paul and Thecla developed in Asia Minor. Revised, these *Acts of Paul* reached the Roman tradition centered around the tomb of the apostle. Part of it, a *Passion of Paul* circulated: it recounts the martyrdom of the apostle at the hands of the Romans. Almost everywhere, churches were built in his honor, beginning with the Basilica di San Paolo fuori le Mura (St. Paul-Outside-the-Walls) in Rome that Constantine built above a modest second century edifice. A day of celebration slowly established itself, probably first on December 28 (from the moment the East accepted Christmas on December 25, they had been looking for ways to celebrate the birthdays of the main disciples and apostles of Christ as close to Christmas as possible). Then it was fixed on June 29, in a joint celebration of Peter and Paul. It is at these occasions that the preachers indulge in elaborate encomia in honor of the martyr, of the apostle, or of the saint. It is necessary to distinguish these panegyrics from the Sunday homilies on the Epistles of the apostle. A Panegyric was a recognized literary genre common to Greek civilization: it was necessary, after an introduction, to list the origin of the hero, his formation, followed by praises of his merits. Even if Chrysostom, who was suspicious of the profane character of the panegyrics, does not totally respect this literary genre, he had to keep certain rules of the genre.

What themes did he use in the *Seven Panegyrics of Saint Paul* that he undoubtedly still pronounced at Antioch between 387 and 397? (a) the superiority of Paul over the characters in the Old Testament; (b) Paul as the supreme example of virtue (filled with the love of Christ, a model of charity); (c) the vocation of Paul and his missionary search based on the Gospel, the power of which lies in the Cross; (d) the attitude of Paul: the mortal body is not an obstacle to virtue; (e) the defense of Paul, criticized by some; he was blamed for holding different views, for example his verbal attack against the High Priest, Acts 23:3, and his attitude in regards to John Mark. Here is an extract: "Each time those who carry the standards of the emperor that are announced by the sound of the trumpet and preceded by many soldiers, make their entry into the cities, all the people come forward in order to hear the sound of the instrument and to see the standard that is held high, as well as the bravery of the one who carries it. Since Paul today also makes his entrance not into a city but into the entire universe, let us all rush forward. Actually, he also carries a standard, not that of the king of the earth but the Cross of Christ, the King of Heaven. And it is not men who walk before him, but angels, anxious to honor the emblem that is carried and to protect the one who holds it in his hand .... Undoubtedly in the temporal order those who were judged to be worthy of such an honor wear clothes and bands of gold, and their entire person resplendent. Paul, on the contrary, is wearing a chain in place of gold, and he carries the Cross: he is persecuted, he is scourged, and starving" (*Panégyrique* 7.1).

3. The West regarding the document

According to the *Confessions*, it is a verse from the Epistle to the Romans that caused the conversion of Augustine. And it would be the reading of Augustine's treatises that will lead the monk Martin Luther, of the order of Augustinians, to read again the Epistles of Paul and to rediscover in them the power of the justice of God, no longer as distributive justice, but as an active justice of God who forgives the guilty. Therefore Augustine had a deep attachment to Paul: admittedly this was not immediate, because after his conversion, the son of Monica was still thinking in philosophical terms. Once he was bishop, in particular when his friend Simplicianus questioned him, Augustine defined the justice of God no longer in a Greek sense (a human or divine quality), but in a Semitic sense, a loving movement of God. With this, the election (Romans 9–11), the unconditional grace, and the role of faith will be the preferred theological themes of Augustine, the theologian, preacher, and writer, who faced Pelagius and those who were improperly called semi-Pelagians, some monks from Hadrumetum, Marseilles, and Lerins.

However, an observation has to be made: Pelagius, the adversary of Augustine and a strong advocate of human responsibility in the work of salvation, was a perseverant and studious reader of the apostle Paul. He believed he could support his theological positions with the text from the Epistles on which that he made lengthy commentaries. Thus the same collection of Pauline letters inspired two contemporary writers, which simultaneous led them in opposite directions. Pelagius and Augustine had two different concepts of sin and human condition.

In the Middle Ages there will be an Augustinian exegesis on Paul that leads to (a) the theology of grace (more or less overshadowed during certain periods), (b) a political theology (resorting to one legitimizing interpretation of Romans 13), and (c) a theory of the interpretation that is based on Gal 4:24 ("these things are said allegorically") and which took direction from the Augustinian spiritual understanding (whose origin goes back to Philo, Tertullian, and Origen) to lead to the medieval theory of the four meanings of Scripture. Through allegory, those of the Middle Ages thought that they were being faithful to Augustine and Paul. Were they right? The Pauline text, as any biblical text, comes out of the medieval interpretation fragmented and often solicited.

It is important now to discuss the argument of Thomas Aquinas on the Epistle to the Romans and his doctrine of justification, which Catholic theologians have compared to the theology of Martin Luther and Karl Barth. We should then analyze the Epistle to the Galatians and the Epistle to the Romans, more particularly, in the theology of Luther. Luther indeed makes a fundamental distinction between the Law and the Gospel. The Law reveals sin, sometimes even encourages it to spread. The Gospel on the other hand releases humanity from sin and declares it righteous before God. Luther sought to have these theses, whose effect will be momentous, prepared faithfully based on Paul's epistles. It is Paul who, in his opinion, best thought and justified the relationship between the Law and the Gospel. Rather than dwelling on Luther and his two commentaries on Galatians, I would prefer to quote a few sentences from Calvin drawn from the argument that precedes his *Commentary on the Epistle to the Galatians*: "But although he taught them faithfully about the Gospel, there were false apostles who came in his absence, who corrupted the good seed with false and ill-intended doctrines. Indeed, they were teaching the idea that the observation of these rituals was necessary. This did not seem crucial since it did not appear to be of great importance: but Saint Paul was debating it here as a main article of Christian faith. And with good reason, for it is no small harm when the clarity of the Gospel is overshadowed, when the consciences are linked together, when any difference is removed between the Old and New Testament. He saw that with these mistakes there was an evil and pernicious opinion mixed altogether: that is to say, the merit of justice. That is the reason why he debated with such passion and effort. Yet we had been warned of what consequence is the subject he was dealing with here; let us be attentive in reading it. If we want to judge the cause according to the commentaries of Saint Hieronymus and Origen, we will be astounded to realize why Saint Paul was so bothered over a few external ceremonies. But if we look at the source itself, we may find that things are worthy of being so bitterly debated."

4. Modernity or the shattered monument

The thesis may be prior to the nineteenth century. But it is at that time that it surfaced acerbically: the treason against Jesus and true Christianity taught by the Church, to begin with the apostle Paul. This theme of the eclipsing of the truth by the Church can take political and ideological forms. People are saying that either the teaching of Jesus was betrayed by Paul (a Christian changed from a revolutionary to an upholder of the faith), or that the morals of Jesus in this lower world became a religion of redemption for the beyond. We are witnessing a sort of inversion of the Lutheran schema: Paul became for some people a symbol of a new Law that covers and conceals the Gospel.

The example of Nietzsche seems to me particularly relevant: the subtitle of his book of 1888, *The Antichrist*, is clear: "Essay on the criticism of Christianity." First argument to remember: Christianity took position for everything that was weak, low, and unbecoming. Second argument: it is necessary to blame the theologians who defended Christianity: "It is against the theological instinct that I am waging war. Everywhere I found its traces. Anyone with a theologian's blood in his body is immediately in a very dubious and a distrustful position. The pathos that results from this is called 'faith' ... what a theologian feels as true is *necessarily* false: there we almost have a criterion of truth .... What is more harmful to life is called here 'truth'" (16–17). Here is what he writes about Jesus: "I will go back. I am recounting the true history of Christianity. – Already the term 'Christianity' is a misnomer, basically there was only one Christian and that one *died* on the cross. The 'Gospel' died on the cross. What at that moment is called 'Gospel' was already the opposite of what he had lived: a '*bad* news,' a '*Dysangelium.*' It is wrong to the point of absurdity, to see in a belief, thus in the belief of redemption through Christ, the distinctive feature of the Christian: the Christian practice, a life *lived* as the man who died on the cross, only that is Christian" (60). And on Paul: "Jesus however had abolished up to the notion of 'guilt' – he denied that any flaw could separate God from mankind, he *lived* this unity between God and mankind as *his* 'good news'! ... And *not* as a privilege! – From that moment, we see introduced gradually the type of the redeemer: the doctrine of last judgement and the advent, the doctrine of death as sacrifice, the doctrine of the *resurrection* with which all the design of the 'beatitude,' the only and unique reality of the Gospel is found evaded – to the profit of a state *after* death! ... This concept, this *obscene* concept, Paul, with the famous insolence of a rabbi that distinguishes him in everything, he systematized it up to that point of saying: '*If* Christ was not resurrected from the dead, then our faith is empty.' And immediately the Gospel became the most wretched of empty promises, the *shameless* doctrine of immortality of the person ... the same Paul had the gall to teach it as a *reward*!" (64–65).

Next to Nietzsche, I would place Karl Barth and the most important modern commentary on Paul: the *Römerbrief* (1919). This book, like lightening, flashes across the peaceful sky of liberal theology. Summarizing the biblical and theological orientation of his predecessors, Barth reproached them for putting man at the core of their preoccupation. Using the Epistle to the Romans, he resolutely places there God, his Word, his revelation, and his Son Jesus Christ. That is how, thanks to Barth, a return to the Bible takes place after years of moral, philosophical, and anthropological theology.

In his famous foreword to the second edition, Barth refuses the simplicity to which the theologians then aspired. Neither the Epistle to the Romans, nor the theological situation, nor the international scene, nor man's and woman's place before God is simple. Therefore, he wrote, no pseudo-simplicity, but a search for the truth, "Lasst uns in dreissig Jahren weiterreden von der Einfachheit, heute aber von der Wahrheit!" (VII; "We will speak again of simplicity in thirty years, but today let us speak of the truth!").

Then the theologian tackles the historical-critical method of his time, not because it is scientific and critical, but because it is not enough. Therefore there is no fundamentalist reaction with Barth. In his opinion, the historical-critical method is not scientific enough, because the attribute of science is to be true to its object. Indeed, Paul spoke of God and that is what Luther and Calvin understood better than the learned commentators of the nineteenth century. In order to find what

Paul is talking about, the *Matter* (Sache), that is to say, God, it is necessary to follow step by step what is written ("was da steht") until the wall that separates the first century from the twentieth century collapses. In order to do this, we must link Paul's words with the Word of God translated into the human language.[2]

5. Bibliography

The authors mentioned or cited from the second century are as their works are presented in the first two volumes of Johannes Quasten, *Initiation aux Pères de l'Église* (trans. J. Laporte; 4 vols.; Paris: Cerf, 1955–1986).

Two works by Ernst Dassmann, *Der Stachel im Fleisch. Paulus in der frühchristlichen Literatur bis Irenäus* (Münster: Aschendorff, 1979) and Andreas Lindemann, *Paulus im ältesten Christentum. Das Bild des Apostels und die Rezeption der paulinischen Theologie in der frühchristlichen Literatur bis Marcion* (BHT 58; Tübingen: Mohr Siebeck, 1979), study the reception of Paul in the second century.

The commentary on the Epistle to the Romans of Origen in the translation of Rufinus is accessible in the Patrology of Jacques-Paul Migne, *Patrologiae cursus completus. Series Graeca* (PG 14). The Greek fragments were published by Jean Scherer, *Le commentaire d'Origène sur Romains 3,5–5,7 d'après les extraits du papyrus N° 88 748 du Musée du Caire et les fragments de la Philocalie et du Vaticanus Gr 762. Essai de reconstitution du texte et de la pensée des tomes V et VI du "Commentaire sur l'Épître aux Romains"* (Cairo: Imprimerie de l'Institut français d'archéologie orientale, 1957).

The patristic exegesis on the Epistle to the Romans was analyzed with great care by Karl Hermann Schelkle, *Paulus Lehrer der Väter. Die altkirchliche Auslegung von Römer 1-11* (Düsseldorf: Patmos, 1956).

The Panegyrics of John Chrysostom have been published and translated: Jean Chrysostome, *Panégyriques de saint Paul. Introduction, texte critique, traduction et notes* (ed. Auguste Piédagnel; SC 300; Paris: Cerf, 1982).

On Augustine and Pelagius, readers of Saint Paul, see Georges de Plinval, "Luttes pélagiennes," in *Histoire de l'Église, depuis les origines jusqu'à nos jours* 4 (ed. Augustin Fliche and Victor Martin; Paris: Bloud and Gay, 1939) 79–128.

Concerning the Middle Ages, I refer to the work of Father Henri de Lubac, *Exégèse médiévale* (2 vols. in 4; Théologie 41, 41, 42, 59; Paris: Aubier, 1959–1964); Otto H. Pesch, *Theologie der Rechtfertigung bei Martin Luther und Thomas von Aquin. Versuch eines systematischtheologischen Dialogs* (Walberger Studien der Albertus-Magnus-Akademie 4; Mainz: Matthias-Grünewald-Verlag, 1967).

Hans Küng, *La Justification (Rechtfertigung). La doctrine de Karl Barth. Réflexion catholique* (trans. H.-M. Rochais and J. Évard; Textes et études théologiques; Paris: Brouwer, 1965).

Luther has published two commentaries on the Epistle to the Galatians, a short one already in 1519 (second edition in 1523) and another more detailed in 1535, republished in 1538. René H. Esnault published a French translation of the second commentary, while following the text of 1535. This *Commentaire de l'Épître aux Galates* appeared under the title Martin Luther, *Œuvres* XV–XVI (Geneva: Labor et Fides, 1969–1972).

---

[2] With regret, I had to abandon, for lack of ability, to mention the fate of the Pauline epistles in Catholic exegesis since the sixteenth century.

Several doctoral theses from the University of Geneva have these last years carried on with the interpretation of the Epistle to the Romans of the various Reformers. Among these, see Benoit Girardin, *Analyse d'un discours théologique. Le Commentaire de Calvin à l'Épître aux Romains (Strasbourg, 1540)* (Paris: Beauchesne, 1979).

L'Antéchrist of Friedrich Nietzsche in the French translation that I quote appeared in the paperback book: Friedrich Nietzsche, *L'Antéchrist* (trans. Dominique Tassel; Paris: Éditions 10/18, 1967).

The *Römerbrief* of Karl Barth, 2d ed., Munich, 1922, has been translated into French under the title *L'Épître aux Romains* (trans. Pierre Jundt; Geneva: Labor et Fides, 1972).

See the lists of commentaries on the Epistle to the Galatians written during the twenty centuries that separate us from the time of Paul, established by Wilfrid Werbeck, at the end of the articles "Paulusbriefe," in *Die Religion in Geschichte und Gegenwart* (7 vols.; 3d ed.; Tübingen: Mohr Siebeck, 1957–1965) vol. 5, cols. 198–99, and "Galaterbrief," in ibid., vol. 2, cols. 1189–90.

Since the original publication of this article, see particularly Origen, *Der Römerbriefkommentar des Origenes. Kritische Ausgabe der Übersetzung Rufins* (ed. Caroline P. Hammond Bammel; 3 vols.; Vetus Latina, die Reste der altlateinischen Bibel. Aus der Geschichte der lateinischen Bibel; Freiburg im Breisgau: Herder, 1985–1990); and Margaret M. Mitchell, *The Heavenly Trumpet: John Chrysostom and the Art of Pauline Interpretation* (HUT 40; Louisville: Westminster/John Knox Press, 2002).

Canonical, Rejected, and Useful Books

The Greek word for "canon," a Semitic loanword, means a "straight rod," "reed," "rule," "standard," "formulation," or "rule of faith." From the first to the third centuries c.e., Christians insisted on the word's fundamental meaning – as a criterion for faith preserved in the preaching, confession, or gospel. Only in the fourth century did the term refer to a formally recognized collection of books (see Athanasius, *Decrees of the Synod of Nicea* 18 [soon after 350] and the Council of Laodicea, canon 60 [date uncertain]).

The "early church" was not a unified religious and social entity in the first century. Accounts of Jesus' ministry, passion, and resurrection were products of different groups, including the Twelve, the seven Hellenists, the Johannine community, the first Galilean Christians, the family of Jesus, and the transmitters of the sayings source (Q) and of the *Gospel of Thomas*. Each group had a view of authority and its expression in rituals, ministry, or writing. Unity prevailed, however, in the case of Holy Scripture: like fellow Jews, Christians accepted the Torah – in Hebrew or in Greek. As a prophetic and apocalyptic movement, most Christians also revered the prophets, particularly Isaiah. The Psalms, composed by the king and prophet David, enjoyed great favor. The third part of the scriptural canon was not fixed, as it still was not for contemporary Jews. Paul and the Letter of Jude cited texts later excluded from the Jewish canon (see 1 Cor 2:9; Jude 14–16). With respect to the sacred books, one of the Pastoral Epistles speaks for all: "All scripture is inspired by God and profitable for teaching, for reproof, for correction, and for training in righteousness" (2 Tim. 3:16).

Common among "Christian" movements was respect for Jesus Christ, and his name became an authority alongside Scripture. His ministry was remembered; he was present in Christians' missionary or liturgical activity. Citing Papias, Eusebius highlights the importance of oral traditions among early Christians (*Hist. Eccl.* 3.39.4). This companionship of oral and written word is not surprising, given the parallel of tractate *Avot* in the Mishnah, with its two channels of revelation, the written and the oral Torah.

As time passed, respect for the words of Jesus did not prevent new compositions: passion narratives, collections of sayings, and miracle stories, often preserved in writing (see Luke 1:1). The gospels written at the end of the first century corresponded initially to different communities, including texts that did not achieve canonical status, such as the *Gospel of Peter* (probably not only a passion narrative, but a general account of Jesus' ministry) or the *Gospel of Thomas* (a collection of Jesus' sayings; NHC II, 2).

Early Christian groups, despite tense relations, strove for unity. Matthew and Luke readily adapted texts from Mark, the sayings source (Q), and other documents. Somewhat later the *Gospel of the Ebionites* tried to harmonize the three Synoptic Gospels (Matthew, Mark, and Luke). Evidencing a strong preference for one account, Tatian, a late-second-century Syrian theologian, composed in Greek a single work developed out of the four Gospels, the so-called *Diatessaron* (lit., [one] through four). Such was its success that its Syriac form was canonical for many decades. Only in the fourth century was it replaced by the four Gospels, called the "gospel of the separated" (see Theodoret of Cyrrhus, *Compendium of Heretical Tales* 1.20). Without any official decision, the increasingly collaborative early Christian movements became the majority church in the second century and accepted the Gospels of various communities. The collection of four Gospels is presupposed by the second-century figures Papias (in Eusebius, *Hist. Eccl.* 3.39.14–17) and Hegesippus (4.22.3). Yet in 180 Irenaeus (*Adv. haer.* 3.11.8) had to legitimate the "weakness" of having four Gospels. Defenders of the fourfold canon also had to explain the contradictions between the Gospels, particularly the divergent beginnings.

The theological bipolarity of Gospel-Apostle encouraged the creation of a corpus of the major documents of the new covenant in the mid-second century, in which the four Gospels and the Pauline Epistles appear side by side. Luke's two volumes were both accepted, but Acts was detached from the Gospel of Luke to become the beginning of a companion series. To this category belong also some Catholic Epistles (e.g., 1 Peter and 1 John) and the Book of Revelation. Since then, these texts (Gospels, Epistles, Book of Acts, and Book of Revelation) were considered to be holy books and thus served as liturgical readings, reservoirs of knowledge, and arsenals of arguments.

One theologian, Marcion, dismissed oral tradition. For theological reasons, he refused the revelation preserved in the Hebrew Bible and decided to "purify" the Christian message. He resolved to build his teaching only on written texts – one Gospel (a drastically revised Luke) and a collection of Pauline letters. Marcion removed from these any trace of Jewish influence and contrasted the unknown God revealed in Jesus to the tyrannical and vengeful demiurge of the Hebrew Bible. His rejection of the Old Testament forced Christians to decide whether it should be preserved. The various authoritative texts of groups marginalized as "gnostic" also elicited a reaction. Therefore, in the second half of the second century a canon of Christian scripture emerged. Christians in various places accepted a tripartite Scripture consisting of Gospels, Epistles, and the "rest." Evidence for this development includes the Muratorian Fragment for Rome; the writings of Tertullian for North Africa; Irenaeus for Asia Minor, where he was born, and for Gaul, where he later moved; and Clement of Alexandria for Egypt.

Ultimately the readers of the books were as important as the books themselves. The four Gospels were assembled because the groups who respected individual texts were in contact and accepted the validity of other communities' texts. In that light the situation of the Johannine community becomes clear. It long comprised an independent branch of Christianity, but around 100 an internal dispute concerning Christology occurred – was Jesus a fully human person or, as divine, did he only appear to be human? The Johannine Epistles took a stand and became, with the Gospel of John, the canon of the "orthodox" wing of the Johannine community. After the schism of the Johannine community (see 1 John 2:19), the orthodox group must have joined mainstream Christian communities, taking their books along. This development explains the presence of both the Gospel of John and 1 John, an orthodox explanation of the Gospel, in the New Testament canon. That the Gospel of John was a latecomer is clear from its very position as the fourth and last of the canonical Gospels. The *Acts of John* and other Johannine documents are vestiges of the "heterodox" Johannine community.

A problem arose in the West: everybody knew that no apostle had written Hebrews, an epistle accepted from the beginning in the East. Out of respect for the East, the West finally acknowledged this epistle but claimed that Paul himself wrote it. The East believed that, if the content was Pauline, the form was due to a follower of Paul such as Luke.

A parallel problem arose in the East: after an initial period of favor (shared with the *Apocalypse of Peter*, another apocalypse mentioned in the Muratorian Fragment), the Book of Revelation was widely disregarded. Some still accepted it but allegorically eliminated its subversive orientation and never read it liturgically. Others, particularly in Alexandria, rejected the book, as well as its millennarist and Montanist appropriations.

One must distinguish a collection's birth from its formal canonization. The creation of the corpus of four Gospels or of Pauline letters was a work of second-century piety, recognizing the authority of these documents. Not yet a formal canon validated by official decision, its existence was a common opinion shared by those who considered themselves to be the orthodox church. Around 200 the reality of a New Testament, a companion volume for Christians to the First Testament, came into existence. Unity, however, long remained an abstraction, for in practice it was still a collection of several manuscripts. Even the name New Testament was slow in coming. Christian authors still used the old terms *Lord* or *Gospel* for the Gospels and *Apostle* for the Epistles.

One would have to wait until the fourth century for official decisions and authoritative lists: in the East the Thirty-Ninth Festal Epistle by Athanasius of Alexandria (367), in the West the African synods of Hippo (393) and Carthage (397 and 419). Christian communities had delineated criteria of canonicity since the second century: canonical writings must be of apostolic origin, used in the liturgy, and must conform to the truth venerated by the church. The fourth century further specified that a book must be apostolic to be part of the canonical Christian Scriptures, and if so, it is also inspired by the Holy Spirit.

Without being part of the Holy Scripture, many other texts nevertheless still possessed authority. When in the third century Origen reflected on the matter, he delineated undisputed books, rejected books, and disputed books (Eusebius, *Hist. Eccl.* 6.25). Origen deemed the third category needed (a) because some books were accepted by some and rejected by others and (b) because in addition to the canonical books, others were useful for personal devotion or theological inquiry.

In his *Against Marcion* 4.2 Tertullian chose a Latin term applied to legal documents (*instrumentum*) to define the scriptures of the literary collection of the new covenant (*instrumentum evangelicum*). In the *Passion of Perpetua and Felicitas* 1.4 the author, probably Tertullian, used the same term (*instrumentum ecclesiae*) for the acts of the two martyrs. Both types of documents, the canonical and the hagiographical, are useful "tools" for Christian believers. Two centuries later, realizing the miraculous power of relics, Augustine invited his miraculously cured parishioners to record their stories (in the so-called *libelli*; see *City of God* 22.8; *Sermons* 320–24 in *Patrologia latina* 38.1443–45). He deemed it important to have, in addition to the wonders of the New Testament, witnesses of contemporary miracles, evidencing the Spirit's continued work. There was therefore space between the canonical and the apocryphal documents for a third category: inspired narratives and hagiographies. The so-called *Protevangelium of James*, a life of Mary, was never part of the canon, but the Eastern church, considering it useful, never rejected it as apocryphal. When Eusebius of Caesarea revisited Origen's New Testament canon, he also respected this division in three categories (*Hist. Eccl.* 3.25). The Byzantine period and the Middle Ages confirmed the importance of this tripartition. Christian art amply demonstrates how deeply these useful texts enriched its iconographic program. One of innumerable expressions of this influence occurs in a group of mosaics of Monreale in Sicily that include scenes of the apostles' lives inspired by noncanonical texts. A focus on these texts, uninhibited by a canonical bias, reveals the rich details of a vital religiosity.

Bibliography

Aragione, Gabriella, Éric Junod, and Enrico Norelli, eds. *Le Canon du Nouveau Testament. Regards nouveaux sur l'histoire de sa formation.* MdB 54. Geneva: Labor et Fides, 2005.

Campenhausen, Hans von. *The Formation of the Christian Bible.* Trans. J. A. Baker. Philadelphia: Fortress, 1972.

Cohen, Shaye J. D. *From the Maccabees to the Mishnah.* 1st ed. LEC 7. Philadelphia: Westminster, 1987. pp. 174–213.

Kaestli, Jean-Daniel. "Histoire du canon du Nouveau Testament." In *Introduction au Nouveau Testament. Son histoire, son écriture, sa théologie*. Ed. Daniel Marguerat. Geneva: Labor et Fides, 2000. pp. 449–74.

McDonald, Lee M., and James A. Sanders, eds. *The Canon Debate*. Peabody, Mass.: Hendrickson Publishers, 2002.

Metzger, Bruce M. *The Canon of the New Testament: Its Origin, Development, and Significance*. Oxford: Clarendon, 1987.

Norelli, Enrico, ed. *Recueils normatifs et canons dans l'Antiquité. Perspectives nouvelles sur la formation des canons juif et chrétien dans leur contexte culturel*. Publications de l'Institut romand des sciences bibliques 3. Prahins (Switzerland): Zèbre, 2004.

Scripture as Promise and as Closure

Introduction

In the pages that follow, written in honor of a friend and an advocate of Scripture,[1] I would like to meditate on the status of the Bible, its frontiers downstream, and its bipartite structure. By way of introduction, I am going to state two obviously neglected facts.

Here is the first. The Christian Bible in one volume, largely diffused, is a modern invention, a result of the double effect of printing and of the Reformation.[2] Complete Bibles were exceptional in Antiquity and these books were intended neither for public readings nor for personal piety but were copies for reference and control. For liturgical reading, the system of lectionaries had developed rather early, as it is attested in the imposing collection of lectionaries in uncial writing, preserved in the library of the monastery of Megisti Lavra, at Mount Athos.[3] Rare complete Bibles then were used to recopy the Gospels collections, the Pauline Epistles, or the Acts of the Apostles followed by the Catholic Epistles. That one had to set up lists of biblical writings, such as the Muratorian Canon,[4] to make inventories suggests that there existed at the beginning only scrolls or partial *codices*, limited to such biblical books or such groups of writings of the same genre. The Papyrus Bodmer XIV–XV ($\mathfrak{P}^{75}$), from the beginning of the third century, contains only the Gospels of Luke and John.[5]

---

[1] Daniel Marguerat knows how to awaken or reawaken the interest of his contemporaries for the Bible. He does it with talent, through his courses, seminars, conferences, public talks, scholarly publications, and interviews on radio and television. It is with the same dedication that he participated in collective projects, such as the Vaumarcus Biblical Camp, and set up collective works, such as an introduction to the New Testament. I had the joy of collaborating with him for several years in several of these projects and I am happy to participate in the homage that is being paid to him by the publication of this collection.

[2] See Étienne Trocmé, "La naissance du Nouveau Testament," *ETR* 62 (1987) 329–34.

[3] Up to now these manuscripts from the 5th to the 9th cents. were largely neglected by specialists in textual criticism.

[4] In spite of the thesis of Albert C. Sundberg, "Muratori Canon: A Fourth Century List," *HTR* 66 (1973) 1–41, which places the origin of this document to the 4th cent. in the East, I maintain the traditional thesis following the argument of Jean-Daniel Kaestli, "La place du *Fragment de Muratori* dans l'histoire du canon. À propos de la thèse de Sundberg et Hahnemann," *CNS* 15 (1994) 609–34.

[5] Victor Martin and Rodolphe Kasser, eds., *Papyrus Bodmer XIV–XV* (2 vols; Cologny-Geneva: Bibliotheca Bodmeriana, 1961).

What is noticeable during the Patristic era corresponds to a usage attested for the Hebrew Bible during the apostolic age. In the walls and in the arks of synagogues,[6] there were several recesses in which to place scrolls of various biblical scriptures.[7] The theologians of today would do well not to think of Holy Scripture in a too abstract and dogmatic manner. If there is a biblical unity, it will be beyond the diversity of the books and elsewhere than in the artificial harmony of the letter.

Here is the second fact. From the earliest Christian origins, the disciples of Jesus were aware of a time prior to Christ and a time after Christ. The time prior to the appearance of Christ was one represented by Jewish Scripture, and the post-biblical time by the Christian message, which quickly materialized into various forms: epistles, gospels, acts of the apostles, and into an apocalypse. These pre- and post-Christ times remain connected. Often indeed did authors of the New Testament refer to the Old Testament. Without going into the problematic of citation,[8] I notice a paradox: when I quote, I refer and, out of concern to remain true to the text, I say the same thing as the original; but also when I quote, I cut and rearrange and necessarily change things; and by moving away from the quoted text, I say something different.

The paradox relating to the quotation is confirmed as far as the whole corpus is concerned. Following the project of those who had canonized it, the New Testament as a whole states the same thing as the Old Testament, but it also states something else. It states the same thing, because it expresses the constant role of God, faithful in his plan. It states something else because it claims to be the ultimate revelation of God. In the First Epistle to the Corinthians, the apostle Paul asserts that the Good news is new, since it is inscribed in a history that does not repeat itself, but it is also old because it is attested by Scripture (see the presence side by side of the word εὐαγγέλιον ["Gospel"] and the expression, itself reiterated, κατὰ τὰς γραφάς, "in accordance with the Scriptures," in 1 Cor 15:3–4). As a "reader," the New Testament does not say anything new; as an "author," it says everything new.

---

[6] Paul Billerbeck, "Ein Synagogengottesdienst in Jesu Tagen," *ZNW* 55 (1964) 143–61; L. Michael White, "Synagogue and Society in Imperial Ostia: Archaeological and Epigraphical Evidence," *HTR* 90 (1997) 23–58. This last article raised a criticism that resulted in a reply: Anders Runesson, "The Oldest Original Synagogue in the Diaspora: A Response to L. M. White," *HTR* 92 (1999) 409–33; L. Michael White, "Reading the Ostia Synagogue: A Reply to A. Runesson," ibid., 435–64.

[7] See Charles Perrot, *La lecture de la Bible dans la synagogue. Les anciennes lectures palestiniennes du Shabbat et des fêtes* (Hildesheim: Gerstenberg, 1973).

[8] See Antoine Compagnon, *La seconde main ou le travail de la citation* (Paris: Seuil, 1979); François Bovon, "Il a bien parlé à vos pères, le Saint-Esprit, par le prophète Esaïe (Actes 28,25)," in idem, *L'Œuvre de Luc* (LD 130; Paris: Cerf, 1987) 145–53.

1. The Presence of Hebrew Scripture in the New Testament

The pupil who studies classical Greek is surprised by the simplicity of New Testament Greek compared to that of Aeschylus or Thucydides. One is also smitten by the foreignness of what needs to be called a sociolect, that is to say, the language spoken by a social group, class, or subculture. Christian Greek is rooted in the Greek of the Jews of the Diaspora, which is influenced by Hebrew, a language sacred in their view. The vocabulary of the first Christian writings displays words borrowed from the Septuagint, such as ἐκκλησία ("assembly"), ("church"), or rare terms such as ἀγάπη ("attentive and unselfish love"), probably a neologism, an abuse of redundancies and pleonasms, as those in the initial eulogy found in the Letter to the Ephesians (Eph 1:3–14), various shifts in meaning, as that of διαθήκη ("testament"), in order to mean a "covenant," where one would be expecting συνθήκη. The syntax is also characteristic – an abundance of parataxis, parallelisms, and reduplications of Semitic characters. This way of speaking indeed does not constitute a distinct language, but a way to express themselves that is particular to Christians, distinct from pagan customs and Jewish practices.[9]

Apart from the biblical tone of the language, we have to mention the categories of Scriptures eagerly gathered by the first Christian writers.[10] Prayer, atonement, covenant, faith in a personal God who is nearby, the story of a chosen people – all these great categories that are not as such in the environment surrounding the Bible bring the New Testament close to the Hebrew Scriptures. If there are indeed shifts, such as the important insertion of a human death – that of the Son – in the founding sacrifice of the covenant established between God and his people, a remarkable thematic continuity yet remains.

It is the same for biblical heroes. Paul, to take only one example, thought through biblical characters and themes. Through the figure of Adam (Rom 5:12–20 and 1 Cor 15:11 19), he thought of the links between sin and grace; through that of "our father Abraham" (Rom 4:1), he makes clear the nature of faith; finally through that of Moses, he sets up by contrast, the foundations of a Christian ethic (Rom 10:5–6). Paul and the evangelists resort to these figures not in an unconscious manner, but in a deliberate one. He follows some semantic shifts, as is the case for the title of the "Son of David" in the synoptic gospels. This title does not correspond exclusively to biblical tenor; it also contains accents that we may call post-biblical. The "Son of David," was originally King Solomon; but in that

---

[9] The verb σπλαγχνίζομαι, literally "to have stirred up the bowels," "to be moved with compassion," for example, is not classical. It is attested on the other hand in the Hellenistic Jewish literature, in the *Testaments of the Twelve Patriarchs*; see Helmut Köster, "σπλάγχνον κτλ.," *TWNT* 7:548–59.

[10] See Adrian Schenker, *Versöhnung und Sühne. Wege gewaltfreier Konfliktlösung im Alten Testament. Mit einem Ausblick auf das Neue Testament* (BibB n.s. 15; Fribourg [Switzerland]: Schweizerisches Katholisches Bibelwerk, 1981).

era, Solomon did not only represent the king, he was also the custodian of wisdom, the healer, and the magician.[11]

Several biblical accounts are mentioned, summarized, or simply mentioned in the New Testament. In them we find in particular a literary genre that is also attested in Jewish literature: that of the historical survey.[12] As much in the speech of Stephen (Acts 7) as in that of Paul at Antioch of Pisidia (Acts 13), they summarize the story of Israel with a few recollections, which, in order not to be repetitive, complete one another. Luke makes a selection here and there of different facts; in the first case, the history of ancient Israel, of Abraham to Moses; in the second case, the more recent story of Moses to David. We also find, as in the Wisdom literature, some biblical examples – examples of judgment and deliverance in 2 Peter 2, examples of πίστις, of "faith," in Hebrews 11. Sometimes, the authors content themselves to hint at an event of the holy story – and only one: creation (Mark 10), Exodus (Hebrews 3–4), the adventure of Jonah (Matt 12:39). There also we witness displacements or developments: the prophets are no longer only the heralds of the Word of God, they also become martyrs (so it is in Heb 11:32–40).

As for biblical quotations, I will limit myself to recount only the most important: Gen 2:24 (man will leave his father and his mother); Gen 12:3 (all the tribes will be blessed); Gen 15:6 (Abraham is justified by faith); Deut 18:15, 18 (a prophet like Moses); 2 Sam 7:14 (lineage of David); Ps 2:7 (today the Son is begotten); Ps 8:5–7 (what is man?); Psalm 22 (the suffering of the righteous); Ps 110:1 (the Lord says to my Lord); Ps 118:22–23 (the stone rejected by the builders); Isa 6:9–10 (ears that do not hear); Isa 28:16 (the cornerstone); Isa 40:3–5 (the voice in the wilderness); Isa 52:12–53:13 (the suffering servant); Isa 53:1 (who has believed what we have heard?); Isa 61:1 (the good news to the oppressed); Jer 31:31–34 (the new covenant); Dan 7:13 (Son of Man on the clouds); Joel 3:1–5 (the Spirit of God poured on all flesh); Amos 9:11–12 (the booth of David); Hab 2:3–4 (the vision will come without fault); Zech 9:9 (your king comes to you); Mal 3:23–24 (the return of Elijah). These quotations, which are introduced according to several surprisingly stable formulae,[13] are used as a hitch to eschatology: they announce the achievement of the promises, they indicate the messianic identity of Jesus, they justify the failure of the cross, they support the credo of resurrection, and they explain the hardening of Israel and the call to the Gentiles.

Do the authors of the New Testament think of their relation to the Hebrew Scriptures? If the implicit reflection is constant, they only encounter it explicitly

---

[11] When the two blind men call Jesus for help by naming him "Son of David" (Matt 9:27), they are perhaps thinking of this aspect of Solomon, more so than of the royal identity of the monarch of Jerusalem.

[12] See Wisdom of Solomon 10–19, the book of *Jubilees*, and the *Biblical Antiquities* of Pseudo-Philo (*Liber Antiquitatum Biblicarum*).

[13] On these formulae, see below.

in two places. The first is the famous passage of the pastoral epistles relative to the inspiration of Scriptures (2 Tim 3:14–16). The second is that of the ways of introducing the scriptural quotations. The assertion of 2 Timothy depends on a Jewish doctrine already spread throughout Judaism.[14] The author does not intend to introduce anything new, but, under the constraint of the polemic, he intends to recall an obvious fact. Accepting the persecution and remaining attached to the teaching constitutes the context in which the words of the author are inscribed. It is about refusing the seduction of impostor prophets, the γόητες of v. 13, and respecting "the sacred writings," τὰ ἱερὰ γράμματα, known from childhood (v. 15). That these Scriptures represent a way of salvation (v. 15) corresponds to the convictions of Hellenistic Judaism. The moral notions of instruction, criticism, reproof, teaching, capability, and of maturity are also Hellenistic Jewish (v. 16). The author tends to make these categories Christian by adding a clause related to the "faith in Jesus Christ" (v. 15). That every biblical passage, πᾶσα γραφή,[15] should be θεόπνευστος ("inspired by God") does not mean, in my opinion, that the letters are inspired, but that the author is. This Jewish doctrine, taken up by Christians, is an apologetic doctrine, meant to outwit Greek intellectuals who were eager then for the spiritual breath.

The formulae of introduction to the quotation of Scripture bear witness to an embryonic reflection on both Testaments, mainly on the role of God and of humans in the writings of the sacred texts. In the context of healing, Matthew writes: "This was to fulfill (ἵνα πληρωθῇ) what was spoken [by God] through the intermediary (διά and not ὑπό) of the prophet Isaiah saying ..." (Matt 12:17). We will note here the double speaker, God and the prophet, the accomplishment of the saying, in life and in history, and the reality of the saying being more important than the medium of the scripture. In Matt 13:14, in a context of parables, the reader encounters another formula: καὶ ἀναπληροῦται αὐτοῖς ἡ προφητεία Ἡσαΐου ἡ λέγουσα, "thus for them was fulfilled the prophecy of Isaiah who said ... ." This is the fulfilment of a prophecy that is emphasized. In John 19:24, the same idea of fulfillment is put in relation to a written passage and not to an oral prophecy: it is the word γραφή, probably in the sense of "scriptural passage," which is used. As for the apostle Paul, he is the faithful witness of the classic formula καθὼς γέγραπται, "as it is written" (see for example Rom 15:3). Finally I note the formulae of the letter to the Hebrews (Heb 3:7) and of the book of the Acts of the Apostles (Acts 28:25) that dare to say "Therefore, as the Holy Spirit says ..." (the former) and "The Holy Spirit was right in saying ..." (the latter).

---

[14] See Hermann L. Strack and Paul Billerbeck, *Kommentar zum Neuen Testament aus Talmud und Midrasch*, IV. *Exkurse zu einzelnen Stellen des Neuen Testaments. Abhandlungen zur neutestamentlichen Theologie und Archäologie* (2 parts; Munich: Beck, 1928) 1:415–51 (p. 16 Exkurs).

[15] "All (the) Scripture" would be written as πᾶσα ἡ γραφή.

To conclude this section, I shall say this: for the authors of the New Testament, the books of the Hebrew Bible are as much oral as written words; the prophecies that it contains have their origins in God, and they are transmitted through the intermediary of human beings, the prophets above all, but also through the legislator; this conviction is expressed in terms of inspiration. At the heart of this faith, there is the connection between the promise and fulfillment, saying and reality; this connection may be regarded sometimes as inscribed in time, following the schema of the promise and the fulfilment, sometimes in thought, in placing the adequacy of the thing in its model.

2. The New Testament as Closure

Three personal recollections will explain the position I shall propose here.[16] Throughout my studies, the publication of the theology of the Old Testament by Gerhard von Rad, as well as the books of Albrecht Alt and Martin Noth, not to mention the courses of Walther Zimmerli at Göttingen, have given me the theory of "relecture" and rewriting of ancient traditions already mentioned, which were brought up to date in the freedom and faithfulness to the kerygma of origins. To this was added at Basel the influence of Oscar Cullmann who inserted these re-readings in the plan of God, in the history of salvation. The second recollection involves Friedrich Gogarten – one of the pioneers of dialectic theology – who gave in 1960–1961, at Göttingen, one of his last courses. It dealt with Luther, and I had the privilege of taking it. One of his lessons, naturally, was devoted to the relationship between the Law and the Gospel according to the reformer. I kept in mind that for Luther, the entire Old Testament is not the Law, and the entire New Testament is not the Gospel. There is the Gospel since the old covenant and there is still the Law in the new economy. The dialectic between these two greatnesses does not take place absolutely within the limits between the two visible entities that are the Old and the New Testament. The third recollection: during the editing of my doctoral thesis, I tackled the links between the Law and the Gospel in the writings of the Church Fathers. An article by Willem C. van Unnik and a few pages of Marcel Simon[17] proved to me that not all the ecclesiastic writers of Antiquity maintained the easy solution according to which the Law of the Old Tes-

---

[16] For other solutions, I mention the book of David L. Baker, *Two Testaments, One Bible: A Study of Some Modern Solutions to the Theological Problem of the Relationship between the Old and the New Testaments* (Downers Grove: InterVarsity, 1976); if the book is a little schematic, it nevertheless contains a useful summary, pp. 363–74, and a remarkable bibliography, pp. 387–535; Richard B. Hays, *Echoes of Scripture in the Letters of Paul* (New Haven, Conn.: Yale University Press, 1989); E. Earle Ellis, *The Old Testament in Early Christianity: Canon and Interpretation in the Light of Modern Research* (Tübingen: Mohr Siebeck, 1991).

[17] Willem C. van Unnik, "De beteekenis van de Mozaïsche wet voor de kerk van Christus volgens de Syrische didascalie," *Nederlandsch Archief voor Kerkgeschiedenis* 31 (1939) 65–100;

tament keeps its demand in moral matters, but stops being normative in the ritual field that has to be understood figuratively since then. Among various Christian authors, there is another solution being held, a solution that gives pride of place to the account of the Golden Calf. There is, such is the solution, a second gift of the Law (Exod 34:1–4) after the dramatic episode of Exodus 32, literally a deuteronomy. Some people assess that these new commandments represent a punishment for Israel. Others, on the contrary, being inspired by the Jewish idea of tradition following Scripture, consider that this second wave of instruction confirms the essence of the first. I would like to resort to this phenomenon of "deuteronomy," taken in this last meaning.

Inscribed in the Hebrew Scripture itself, this phenomenon is a demonstration of successive rereadings of the ancient old kerygmatic formulae. Hosea, for example, anticipates a new exodus (Hos 2:16–25), and Isaiah conjures up the future in terms of the past ("day of Madian," Isa 9:4). A new particular expression needs to be mentioned, one that is invested with authority and marked by modesty, which intends to put an end to the process itself. Taken within a tradition, an author or a school completes a work, adds a new and last part, and takes the whole to its completion, from his point of view, to its perfection.[18] This addition obviously brings something new, but its author, who claims to be the legitimate heir and the ultimate interpreter of the tradition, only wishes to come to a close. If he creates something new, it is out of respect for something old. This concluding and interpretative addition is located in general towards the end of the corpus. It is the same for Deuteronomy, at the end of the Pentateuch, and of Third Isaiah at the end of the work of the prophet. The apocalyptic literature, the Apocalypse of John in particular, also reveals that everything has been said and that there is nothing else to expect but God. Nevertheless, there is a difference between Christian literature and Jewish apocalyptic literature that was fulfilling the same function in other areas: if Christians assert the end of the revelation, they do not content themselves with the invitation to patience until that great day. They dare say that in Jesus of Nazareth, the great day has come closer and even that it is already mysteriously present.

The birth of the New Testament writings, as well as the canon of the New Testament itself, may be explained by the phenomenon of "deuteronomy." The Christian communities who canonized the gospels and letters think that God put an end to the revelation and made it known. Therefore it is necessary to bear wit-

---

Marcel Simon, *Verus Israel. Étude sur les relations entre chrétiens et juifs dans l'Empire romain (135–425)* (2d ed.; Paris: de Boccard, 1964) 111–17.

[18] See Gérard Genette, *Palimpsestes. La littérature au second degré* (Collection Poétique; Paris: Seuil, 1982).

ness to it and to think that the Old Testament is closed. Such is the first aspect to remember.[19]

The text of the Golden Calf[20] invites us to recognize a second aspect of the "deuteronomy." A second version of the Law turns out to be necessary following the toughening and relapses of the people of God. Thus many Church writers understood this, when they said that the prohibitions had been abandoned today following this secondary adaptation, and made necessary because of the infidelity of Israel. A theological intuition was being delineated behind this narrative of the phenomenon. At the same level as the Old Testament, the New Testament is justified because it vouches for the fact that God, who is always the same, made the decision to put an end to the rebellion of humans, by sending forth his Son, to offer eschatological forgiveness in the form of a sacrifice, an atonement for sins while at the same time, founding a covenant. By its very existence, the New Testament attests to the movement of God who erases sins and does it for the last time.[21]

In conclusion, the New Testament is for the Christians the "Deuteronomy" of the Old Testament, and it is so for a twofold reason. First, it is the inspired hallmark of the completion and the closure of the Old Testament. In doing so, it makes something new, but to the benefit of something old. It is then the demonstration of the ultimate attempt of God, the expression for the reparative will of the Lord of Israel who, for the last time, offers to his people – and through his people to everyone – a possibility to live in peace within the framework of the covenant.

3. The Hebrew Bible as a Promise

To these two characteristics is added a third, the encounter between promise and fulfillment, of the word that precedes and of the act that follows. This outline determines the links between the old and the new economy, but it is also written in Scripture since Genesis. Instead of looking toward Werner Georg Kümmel,[22] I will open the book of J. R. Searle, *Speech Acts*.[23] Following Austin, Searle analyses the acts of language and distinguishes three: the *utterance acts*, the *propositional*

---

[19] By adding the New Testament to the Old, Christians perhaps supported the Jewish closure of the Hebrew Bible.

[20] For the history of the interpretation of the episode, see Pier Cesare Bori, *Il vitello d'oro. Le radici della controversia antigiudaica* (Turin: Boringhieri, 1983).

[21] It is understood, from this point of view, that there is no excuse for a new relapse of the people; see Heb 6:4.

[22] Werner Georg Kümmel, *Verheissung und Erfüllung. Untersuchungen zur eschatologischen Verkündigung Jesu* (3d ed.; ATANT 6; Zurich: Zwingli, 1956).

[23] John Rogers Searle, *Speech Acts: An Essay in the Philosophy of Language* (Cambridge: Cambridge University Press, 1969).

acts, and the *illocutionary acts*. Each category is marked by an aspect of language; the first, by the words and their order; the second, shows the linguistic expression of the referent and the extra-linguistic action; the third, by the illocutionary force (the perlocutionary aspect needs to be added, that is to say, the effects of the illocutionary act). The illocutionary acts are the acts of belief, of desire, or of intention. Searle pays particular attention to one of these illocutionary acts, the promise. What he says about it from the point of view of a philosopher and a linguist helps to clarify the theological subject dealt with in this paper.

Searle speaks of the promise as a particularly complex act of speech. "How to promise: a complicated way" is one of his subtitles. In order to have a promise, he writes, several conditions have to be fulfilled. Among these conditions we have: the prior communication between the person who makes a promise and the one who receives it; the promise ought to be put into an understandable discourse; the promise should contain an act that eludes the necessary order of things; this act being really that of the man or the woman who promises; a promise has to be sincere and not one that is disingenuous; a promise is distinguished, finally, from a threat. In short, the fulfillment is nothing without the promise, neither is the promise without any prior agreement, and without the trust of the man or the woman who receives it and awaits its fulfillment.

The God of Scripture, if I may say so *cum grano salis*, has fulfilled the conditions stated by Searle. He has followed the complex path of promise. Through his covenant he has set up the essential framework. His way of speaking has found its truth in his subsequent way of doing. The promise itself is read in the Scripture, the philosophy of which only finds the reflection in contingent realities of this world, a real reflection because of the λόγος σπερματικός, the divine Word spread in the creation and accessible to the attentive intelligence of mankind.

But what did God promise and what did he fulfill? Was it only the salvation of his people or was it only the judgment of his people? His manifestation or his silence? I will say: the communication of who God is, a living God who meets human beings and makes them share his life, a communication offered to every man and woman, because of the choice of a lineage, a people, and a chosen man, his Son.

Trinitarian Conclusion

What gives unity to the Bible is the person of God

I follow in the path of Irenaeus of Lyon, summarized by his most recent translator, Adelin Rousseau: "Not two distinct Gods, a subordinate Demiurge and a transcendent Father, but only one and the same God, infinite in perfection, above whom there can be no other. It is he who, by his Word, created the universe and fashioned man from clay. It is in him that Abraham and the Patriarchs believed. It is he who gave the Law to Moses, and who spoke to the prophets. And it is again from this God, and no other God, that the Son himself came to us in order to sum up in him his own creation, triumphing over our disobedience through his obedience, spreading over us his Holy Spirit as down payment of the future resurrection of our flesh and our eternal life in God."[24] This is not the God of the philosophers, but the God of Abraham, of Isaac and of Jacob – a formula that Pascal loved so much and which I understand as follows: it is about the foremost God who made man and woman in his own image and not a secondary god that humanity made in its own image. The God of the Christians, the God of the Scriptures, is never "our" God in the sense that we create or possess an object. He is "our" God as long as we are in a relation of affection and engagement with him, and he with us. Conversely, it is the entire Scripture that makes us know this unique God and, more particularly, the New Testament that asserts the unity of this God and its conformity with the God of the Hebrew Bible. Witnessing the words of Christ and the Apostles, the Christian part of the Scriptures enhances the profound agreement of the Testaments, relentlessly restored in the face of the Marcionite threat who removed from, and the Montanists who added to, the Scriptures.

What gives the Bible its unity is the person of Christ

The thesis of the progressive revelation of God is flawed. Believing it, the unity of the Old and New Testaments would not be given at one time, since God might have progressively revealed the content of his promise. Thus, we would have advanced step by step through the conscience of Israel, then through that of the Church, from an image of a God especially local and revengeful to that of a paternal and universal God.

Nevertheless, we have to admit that God does not give himself to be known in the same manner in Israel and in the Church. To go from the Hebrew Scriptures to the Gospel is first to notice the shift from the presence of God, from the Temple or from the Law, to the person of the Son. This means to undermine the institutions of Israel and to confer upon them, as in the Epistle to the Hebrews, the theological status of shadows, but shadows that carry promises.[25]

To go from the Scriptures of Israel to the New Testament is, then, for the Christians to go from the plural to the singular, from the diversity of the interventions of God to the ultimate and unique intervention in his Son (see Heb 1:1–4). However, it would be exegetically and theologically illegitimate to oppose the obvious

---

[24] "Introduction" to Irénée de Lyon, *Contre les hérésies. Dénonciation et réfutation de la gnose au nom menteur* (Paris: Cerf, 1984) 17.

[25] See Heb 8:5 and 10:1; see also Col 2:17.

luminous fact of the New Testament against the dark ambiguity of the Old Testament. All the biblical testimonies recall the paradoxical nature of the Glory of God demonstrated in Jesus of Nazareth. Following the Synoptics, this revelation escapes the sages and holds only the attention of children.[26] According to John the Evangelist, it is about elevating the crucified man, and, according to the apostle Paul, it is about the scandal of the cross.[27]

So then, all attention is required to hear God through the entire scriptural testimony, because there is no creed that is at the disposal of the believers. Human language is of course the medium of the revelation, but it is also the shield. Every picture can turn into an icon, as every image can become an idol. If, to decipher them, there is a hermeneutic of exhibition (to contemplate the icons), there is also another one, that of scouring (to destroy the idols).

What gives the Bible its authority is the activity of the Spirit

The theory of the literal inspiration of Scriptures sins through its supernatural and mechanical character. To my mind, the letter of Scripture remains a letter; therefore it is not a letter and Spirit. God, on the other hand, did not stop working through his Spirit in the life and history of Israel and of the Christians. Paul did not only meet Christ on the road to Damascus, but he also received the long-term inhabitation of the divine πνεῦμα, the "Spirit" of God. All the authentic witnesses who speak in the Scripture had the same experience.

Similar to the writings of a human that form a concrete part his most intimate being, Scripture is closely associated to the people of God. It holds its authority not only through its salvific content, but through the spiritual relationship that, beyond the distance between the Creator and the creature, God establishes between the Spirit and the flesh, light and the obscure, the transparent divine and the opaque hearts of human beings. It is in this sense and this sense alone that one may speak about the inspiration of the Scriptures. Actually, the Bible is not the only one to have profited from the breath of God. A cloud of witnesses, who precede us, surrounds us, and will succeed us, have received, are receiving, and will receive a share of the Holy Spirit. From time immemorial, Christian Churches knew to read, beside the canonical writings, other works, whose testimonies of faith and invitations to piety – inspired in their own way – have encouraged innumerable men and women believers.

---

[26] See Luke 10:21.
[27] See John 3:14; 8:28; 12:32–34; 1 Cor 1:23, and Gal 5:11.

Publication Credits

"The Good" and "the Best" in Paul's Thinking

A first different version of this paper has been published in *St. Paul: Between Athens and Jerusalem. The 3rd International Philosophical Conference Proceedings, Athens, 10–11 of June 2004* (ed. John Panteleimon Manoussakis; Athens: The American College of Greece, 2006) 34–46.

Names and Numbers in Early Christianity

"Names and Numbers in Early Christianity," *New Testament Studies* 47 (2001) 267–88.

The Ethics of the First Christians: Between Memory and Oblivion

"L'éthique des premiers chrétiens entre la mémoire et l'oubli," in *La Mémoire et le Temps. Mélanges offerts à Pierre Bonnard* (ed. Daniel Marguerat and Jean Zumstein; Le Monde de la Bible 23; Geneva: Labor et Fides, 1991) 17–30.

Variety and Authority of the First Christian Ethics

"Variété et autorité des premières éthiques chrétiennes," in *Hommage à Gabriel-Ph. Widmer. Bulletin du Centre protestant d'études (Genève)* 40:5–6 (1988) 6–20.

Missionary Practice and Transmission of the Gospel in Early Christianity

"Pratiques missionaires et communication de l'Évangile dans le christianisme primitif," *Revue de Théologie et de Philosophie* 114 (1982) 369–81.

Christ in the Book of Revelation

"Le Christ de l'Apocalypse," *Revue de Théologie et de Philosophie*, 3d ser., 22 (1972) 65–80.

John's Self-Presentation in Rev 1:9–10

"John's Self-Presentation in Revelation 1:9–10," *The Catholic Biblical Quarterly* 62 (2000) 693–700.

Tracing the Trajectory of Luke 13:22–30 back to Q: A Study in Lukan Redaction

"Tracing the Trajectory of Luke 13, 22–30 back to Q: A Study in Lukan Redaction," in *From Quest to Q. Festschrift James M. Robinson* (ed. Jon Ma. Asgeirsson, Kristin de Troyer, and Marvin W. Meyer; Bibliotheca Ephemeridum Theologicarum Lovaniensium 146; Leuven: Leuven University Press/Peeters, 2000) 285–94.

Tradition and Redaction in Acts 10:1–11:18

"Tradition et rédaction en Actes 10, 1–11, 18," *Theologische Zeitschrift* 26 (1970) 22–45.

Moses in Luke-Acts

"La figure de Moïse dans l'œuvre de Luc," in *La figure de Moïse. Écriture et relectures* (ed. Robert Martin-Achard; Publications de la Faculté de théologie de l'Université de Genève 1; Geneva: Labor et Fides, 1978) 47–65.

The Death of Jesus in Luke-Acts

"La mort de Jésus en Luc-Actes," in *"Christ est mort pour nous." Études sémiotiques, féministes et sotériologiques en l'honneur d'Olivette Genest* (ed. Alain Gignac and Anne Fortin; Montréal: Médiaspaul, 2005) 359–74.

Sayings Specific to Luke in the *Gospel of Thomas*

"Les sentences propres à Luc dans l'*Évangile selon Thomas*," in *Colloque international. "L'Évangile selon Thomas et les textes de Nag Hammadi" (Québec, 29–31 Mai 2003)* (ed. Louis Painchaud and Paul-Hubert Poirier; Bibliothèque copte de Nag Hammadi, Études 8; Québec: Les Presses de l'Université Laval; Leuven/Paris: Peeters, 2007) 43–58.

Fragment Oxyrhynchus 840, Fragment of a Lost Gospel, Witness of an Early Christian Controversy over Purity

"*Fragment Oxyrhynchus 840*, Fragment of a Lost Gospel, Witness of an Early Christian Controversy over Purity," *Journal of Biblical Literature* 119 (2000) 705–28.

Canonical and Apocryphal Acts of Apostles

"Canonical and Apocryphal Acts of Apostles," *Journal of Early Christian Studies* 11 (2003) 165–94.

The Child and the Beast: Fighting Violence in Ancient Christianity

"The Child and the Beast: Fighting Violence in Ancient Christianity," *Harvard Theological Review* 92 (1999) 369–92.

Women Priestesses in the Apocryphal *Acts of Philip*

"Women Priestesses in the *Apocryphal Acts of Philip*," in *Walk in the Ways of Wisdom: Essays in Honor of Elisabeth Schüssler Fiorenza* (ed. Shelly Matthews, Cynthia Briggs Kittredge, and Melanie Johnson-DeBaufre; Harrisburg, Pa.: Trinity Press International, 2003) 109–21.

Mary Magdalene in the *Acts of Philip*

"Mary Magdalene in the *Acts of Philip*," in *Which Mary?: The Marys of Early Christian Tradition* (ed. F. Stanley Jones; Society of Biblical Literature Symposium Series 19; Atlanta: Scholars Press, 2002) 75–89.

Facing the Scriptures: Mimesis and Intertextuality in the *Acts of Philip*

"Facing the Scriptures: Mimesis and Intertextuality in the *Acts of Philip*," in *Mimesis and Intertextuality in Antiquity and Christianity* (ed. Dennis R. MacDonald; Studies in Antiquity and Christianity; Harrisburg, Pa.: Trinity Press International, 2001) 138–53.

The Reception and Use of the Gospel of Luke in the Second Century

"The Reception and Use of the Gospel of Luke in the Second Century," in *Reading Luke: Interpretation, Reflection, Formation* (ed. Craig G. Bartholomew, Joel B. Green, and Anthony C. Thiselton; Scripture and Hermeneutics Series 6; Bletchley, Milton Keynes: Paternoster Press; Grand Rapids, Mich.: Zondervan, 2005) 379–400.

Paul as Document and Paul as Monument

"Paul comme document et Paul comme monument," in *Chrétiens en conflit. L'Épître de Paul aux Galates. Dossier pour l'animation biblique* (ed. J. Allaz et al.; Essais bibliques 13; Geneva: Labor et Fides, 1987) 54–65.

Canonical, Rejected, and Useful Books

"Sacred Texts and Canonicity: Christianity," in *Religions of the Ancient World: A Guide* (ed. Sarah Iles Johnston; Cambridge, Mass.; Harvard University Press, 2004) 637–39.

Scripture as Promise and as Closure

"L'Écriture comme promesse et comme clôture," in *Raconter, interpréter, annoncer. Parcours de Nouveau Testament. Mélanges offerts à Daniel Marguerat pour son 60ème anniversaire* (ed. Emmanuelle Steffek and Yvan Bourquin; Le Monde de la Bible 47; Geneva: Labor et Fides, 2003) 15–26.

Illustrations

Figure 1

Statuette of Seated Christ, 4th century, Rome, Museo Nazionale delle Terme. Courtesy of Saskia Ltd., © Dr. Ron Wiedenhoeft.

Figure 2

The Feeding of the Four Thousand, Rome, Catacomb of the Via Latina. Foto Pontificia Commissione di Archeologia Sacra.

Index of Ancient Authors

1. Manuscripts

2. Greek, Latin, and Other Ancient Literature

3. Hebrew Bible (Tanakh, Old Testament)

5. Qumran Literature

6. Rabbinic Literature

7. New Testament

8. Christian Apocrypha with Nag Hammadi, Hagiography, and Related Literature

9. Patristic, Byzantine, and Medieval Literature

Index of Subjects

Ophites   191, 301
Oral traditions   59, 105, 134, 168–69, 172–
   73, 204, 217, 219, 236, 248, 281–82, 294,
   296, 298, 299, 301, 304, 318–19, 328

Paul   3–15, 46, 60, 67, 70, 71, 92, 142, 289,
   307–17
– festival day, original (28 December)   312
– festival day, with Peter (29 June)   312
– tomb of   310
Pharisees   174–75, 180, 183, 185
Philips, multiple   247–48, 284
Philip the evangelist   12, 148, 206, 219
– as developed in *Acts of Philip*   219
Philip of *Acts of Philip*, cult, etc.   200 n. 16,
   201, 204 n. 49, 206 n. 62, 210 n. 83, 219,
   225–30, 241, 246–58, 259–272, 273–85
– as combination of two Philips   247–48,
   284
– festival day (14 November)   246
– tomb of   247
– commissioning of   284
– liturgical activity   214 n. 111
– with leopard and kid   215, 225–30
– at Hierapolis of Phrygia   247, 257
– at Ophiorymos   247, 256, 264–65, 278,
   281, 283
– versus dragon, viper, fifty snakes   228–
   29, 264, 278–79, 282, 285
– quarreling with Aristarchos   284
– touring Hell with Michael   248–54, 271
– sin of   280–81
– crucifixion of upside down   281
– daughters of   257
– with sister (see Mariamne)
Philosophy, Greek   4–5, 8–9, 10, 14, 16 n. 1,
   21–22, 24, 40, 51–52, 58, 65, 85 n. 67, 147
   n. 4, 155, 163, 186, 200, 212, 218, 220, 232–
   33, 237, 239, 268, 276, 280, 290, 311, 313,
   315
– Pythagoreans, Pythagorism   17 n. 15, 22
   n. 46, 225, 228 n. 227, 232 n. 41, 233, 280
– Stoics, Stoicism   3, 9, 21, 42, 51 n. 6, 58,
   73, 85 n. 67, 186, 232 n. 39, 233
Priestesses in *Acts of Philip*   253–54, 271
Purity, Dietary Restrictions   57, 112–13,
   119–23, 174–96, 211 n. 95, 212–13, 221, 235,
   248

Rituals
– baptize, baptism   22, 28, 35, 42, 53, 64
   n. 1, 111, 114 n. 19, 115, 118, 121, 125, 143,
   149, 152, 174, 187, 189–96, 203, 204 n. 46,

   206 n. 63, 214–16, 226, 236, 252, 256, 266,
   269, 281, 301, 306 n. 78, 309–11
– Eucharist, communion   22 n. 50, 40, 150,
   185, 188–89, 192, 203–4, 214 (esp. n. 111),
   226, 254 n. 32, 264–66, 284–85, 295–96
– healing   28, 68, 148, 156, 200 n. 16, 203
   n. 38, 204 n. 48, 208 n. 72, 209, 213 n. 106,
   226 n. 11, 230, 241, 255 n. 34, 256, 264,
   326–27
– oil, unction, anointing   125, 148, 183, 188,
   191 n. 81, 214, 256 n. 39, 266
– prayer   13, 20, 27–28, 47, 55, 64, 83, 89,
   116, 147–48, 150, 169, 203 n. 41, 208 n. 69,
   209 n. 79, 212 n. 100, 212 n. 103, 214 n. 110,
   217, 226 n. 13, 229 n. 27, 232, 240, 247, 278,
   309, 325
– preaching (kerygma, sermon, speech)
   3–4, 14, 28, 30, 44, 45, 47, 66, 68–69, 71,
   101, 105, 113, 115–18, 123–27, 130, 134,
   136–43, 149, 151–52, 155–56, 175 n. 6, 180,
   184, 198 n. 7, 201–4, 206, 208–9, 211–12,
   213, 214 n. 110, 214 n. 111, 216–18, 228, 232,
   239, 245, 248–49, 252, 255–56, 264–65,
   278, 280–84, 299–300, 302, 304–5, 311–13,
   318, 321, 326, 328–29
– "redemption"   192, 211 n. 95

Saliva as curative   256, 264
Salvation in Luke-Acts   152–54
Samaritans   130, 134, 138, 140, 172, 219,
   280, 301
San Clemente (Rome)   53
San Paulo fuori le Mura (Rome)   312
Scribes   27, 130, 150 n. 9, 156–57, 175 n. 5,
   183 n. 39, 199–200, 259, 265 n. 27, 268, 294,
   296–98, 305
Scripture(s)   12–14, 285, 291–92, 300, 318–
   22, 323–33
Septuagint   12, 20, 22, 23 n. 58, 28 n. 85, 29–
   30, 116, 125, 134, 140 n. 21, 148, 154, 156,
   200–1, 206, 208, 220, 259, 262, 266, 277,
   325
Sources for Jesus   25, 38, 60, 152, 161–73,
   176 ff., 179 n. 24, 218, 276, 281–83, 291,
   318–19
– *agrapha*   165, 172, 180 n. 26, 181 n. 33,
   281–83
– Q ([Synoptic] Sayings Source)   25 n. 69,
   26, 32, 35, 38 n. 6, 47, 55, 66, 68, 69, 70,
   101–9, 162, 163, 164, 166, 169, 172, 173
   n. 45, 189, 217, 235, 283, 318, 319
– L (Luke's special material)   103–6, 151,
   156, 162 n. 12, 165, 167–69, 172, 290, 291